A BIOGRAPHICAL HISTORY OF YORK COUNTY, PENNSYLVANIA

Edited by
JOHN GIBSON

CLEARFIELD

Originally Published as
Part II of
History of York County, Pennsylvania
Edited by John Gibson
Chicago, 1886

Excerpted, Re-titled, and Reprinted
Genealogical Publishing Co., Inc.
Baltimore, 1975

Reprinted for
Clearfield Company, Inc. by
Genealogical Publishing Co., Inc.
Baltimore, Maryland
1996, 2001

Library of Congress Catalogue Card Number 75-7834
International Standard Book Number: 0-8063-0675-0

Made in the United States of America

CONTENTS

BIOGRAPHICAL SKETCHES.

	PAGE.
Carroll Township	83
Chanceford Township	89
Codorus Township	93
Conewago Township	94
Dover Township	95
Fairview Township	96
Fawn Township	100
Franklin Township	104
Hanover Borough	59
Heidelberg Township	108
Hellam Township	73
Hopewell Township	111
Jackson Township	117
Lower Chanceford Township	121
Lower Windsor Township	127
Manchester Township	131
Monaghan Township	146
Newberry Township	150
North Codorus	159
Paradise Township	160
Peach Bottom Township	161
Penn Township	59
Shrewsbury Township	169
Springfield Township	185
Spring Garden Township	187
Warrington Township	194
Washington Township	197
West Manchester Township	199
West Manheim Township	200
Windsor Township	201
Wrightsville Borough	73
York Borough	3
York Township	203

ILLUSTRATIONS—PORTRAITS.

	PAGE.
Bittenger, John W	6
Black, Chauncey F	7
Bollinger, O. J	8
Boyd, Stephen G	10
Hammond, Hervey	152
Hammond, W. S.	153
Heffener, H. W.	23
Kinard, J. W	129
Kocher, S. R.	79
Lewis, C. E.	30
Myers, E. B.	142
Noss, Herman	38
Scott, F. T.	42
Seacrist, H.	23
Seitz, N. Z.	181
Spangler, Hamilton	48
Williams, D. G.	57

BIOGRAPHICAL SKETCHES.

YORK BOROUGH.

JOHN AHL, M. D., is a native of York, born April 15, 1822, son of Peter and Mary (Stroman) Ahl, the mother a daughter of ex-Sheriff Stroman of York County, and of German descent. The father was born in Virginia and is also of German descent. Peter Ahl, subject's grandfather, was a native of Germany and came to America prior to the Revolutionary war, in which he was a surgeon. The father of our subject came to York when a young man, was a butcher, and died in 1874. Subject's mother died in 1875. Dr. Ahl was educated at the public schools and York County Academy. He began the study of medicine in 1842 under Dr. William McIlvain, of York, also attended Washington University, of Maryland, and graduated in 1845. He located immediately in York, but in 1846 moved to Dover, and after a number of years returned to York. He was married November 6, 1853, to Mrs. Elizabeth A. Cone of Baltimore County, Md., daughter of Samuel Cone. Politically he is a Democrat and was elected first coroner of York County about 1849, served two terms and was again elected in 1878, and again served two terms. Dr. Ahl is the oldest resident physician now practicing in York. He has been a Mason thirty years.

CAPT. JOHN ALBRIGHT was born in Baltimore, Md., in 1826, is a son of Christopher and Mary (Burk) Albright, and is of Hungarian origin. The father of Mr. Albright was born in Lancaster County, Penn., and his mother in the same county. In early life his father came to York County, remained a short time and then removed to Baltimore, Md. When subject was ten years of age, he, with his parents, came to York County, and here he received a common school education. His father died in 1845, and his mother in 1876. At eighteen years of age, Mr. Albright began learning the cigar-maker's trade, and as a journeyman he labored for twenty years. In 1861 he enlisted in Company K, Second Pennsylvania Volunteers, for three months and was appointed orderly-sergeant; in August of the same year, he re-enlisted in Company K, Eighty-seventh Pennsylvania Volunteers, and was commissioned first lieutenant, and as captain in October, 1861. He participated in the battles of Monocacy, Fisher's Hill and Winchester, at which last he was taken prisoner, and was an inmate of the famous Libby prison for eleven months, and a prisoner of war for twenty-one months and fifteen days. He was mustered out of the service in 1865. His marriage took place in 1845 to Miss Mary Ann Shell, a native of Wrightsville, York County, and daughter of Nancy Shell. To this union have been born three children, viz.: Arvilla, Alfred and Mary M. Mr. Albright is a member of the G. A. R. and is a Republican.

Since 1867 he has been engaged in the cigar and tobacco business.

S. A. ALEXANDER, general foreman of locomotives and car affairs for the North Central Railway at York, is a native of Philadelphia, was born August 31, 1829, a son of Andrew and Virginia (Clark) Alexander, and is of Scotch-Irish origin. His parents and grandparents were all natives of Pennsylvania. The father of Mr. Alexander was lost at sea in 1832. Our subject received a common school education at Philadelphia. In 1843 he joined the United States Navy and spent five years in that service. Since 1848 he has been engaged at his present occupation. He came to York in 1875 and here has since resided. He has invented a cross-head pusher, hydraulic jack, balanced slide valve and a rotary steam engine. He is also the author of a very popular book on the subject of running and care of locomotive engines. He was married, in 1850, to Miss Jemima James of Pottsville, Penn. To the marriage were born seven children. Mrs. Alexander died in 1866 and two years later our subject was married to Mrs. Elizabeth McAlister, of Cumberland County, Penn. One child has been born to this union. Mr. Alexander is a Mason, Republican and a member of the Episcopal Church. Mrs. Alexander is also a member of that church.

ABRAHAM K. ALLISON, baker and confectioner, was born in Codorus Township, November 7, 1829, to Adam and Magdalene (Kesler) Allison. In a family of twelve children, Mr. Allison is the eighth, and is ' of English-German origin. The paternal grandfather of our subject came to America some time in the last century, and settled in Codorus Township, York County, where he died. In this township the parents of Mr. Allison were born, his father in 1801, and his mother in 1797. They were members of the Lutheran Church for almost half a century. They were among the early settlers of Codorus Township. The father died in York in 1869, and the mother in the same place in 1874. The boyhood of Mr. Allison was spent on the farm, and there he remained until twenty-four years of age. He came to York, and, in partnership with his father, engaged in the grocery business, which he continued until 1874, when he began the baking business, and this he yet successfully continues. He also learned the milling business, in which he was interested for about four years. He was married in 1860, to Miss Louisa Lau, a native of Jackson Township, and a daughter of John and Rebecca Lau. To this marriage were born twelve children, the following of whom are living: Laura K., John A., Jacob H., Mary V., Maggie E., Anna L., Hattie R. and George W. Mr.

Allison is a Democrat, and has held offices of assessor and councilman—councilman when rebel Gen. Early took possession of York. He and his wife are prominent members of the Lutheran Church.

JACOB H. BAER, banker and financier, is a native of and a descendant from an old family of York County. He was born April 2, 1830, and is a son of Daniel and Susan (Hershey) Baer. His life was passed upon his father's farm until he was eighteen years of age, attending the schools of his neighborhood, and as an assistant upon the farm. Being ambitious for a more extended field in life, he entered the York County Academy and engaged upon a regular course. He graduated in 1853, and soon after engaged in the commission business in York, which he continued for twelve years. He then began his career as a financier and banker, starting a private bank, which he conducted two years. This enterprise was merged into the Western National Bank which he organized and of which he was president for two years. Resigning this position he again embarked in a private banking business which is recognized as one of the sound institutions of the county. In the latter enterprise he has been ably seconded by his sons Charles F. and J. Allen. Mr. Baer possesses rare attributes as a business manager, and as a citizen has the confidence and esteem of his fellow-men. He formed a matrimonial alliance in June, 1860, with Miss Mary, daughter of John and Maria Winters, of York County. They have four children: Charles F., J. Allen, Annie M. and Howard D. Mr. and Mrs. Baer are members of the Lutheran Church.

ROBERT M. BARNITZ learned the watch-making and jewelry business under F. R. Polock, of York, after which he formed a partnership with his father, Edwin A. Barnitz, who was also a watchmaker and jeweler, and who had been engaged in that business in York since 1843, and who died in 1880. Our subject continues the business under the old firm name of E. A. Barnitz & Son, it being one of the oldest establishments of the kind in the borough.

GEORGE J. BARRY, seventh of eleven children of James and Roseanna (McLaughlin) Barry, was born October 31, 1846, in York, Penn., and after receiving a common school education went to Frederick City, Md., in 1861, to clerk in a store. After six years' stay in Frederick he went to Chicago, and thence to Cincinnati, where he lived about one year; returned to Frederick after his brother's death to accept the position of book-keeper in the packing establishment of L. McMurray & Co. September 2, 1879, our subject married B.V. Carr, daughter of John and Susan Carr, of York, Penn. Three children were born of this marriage: Mary, born July 6, 1880; James Howard, born July 21, 1882; and Rose Teresa, born January 1, 1883. Our subject's father, James Barry, was born February 9, 1811, in Tullamore, Kings Co., Ireland, and came to this country in his eighteenth year. Roseanna (McLaughlin) Barry was born in Dromore, Tyrone Co., Ireland, and came to America with her parents when three years old.

THE BAYLER FAMILY. Henry Bayler was born in York, Penn., in the house in which he now resides, September 14, 1819, and is a son·of Jacob and Mary (Lanius) Bayler, and is of Swiss-German descent. His father was born in York County, Penn., in 1796, and died in 1857; his mother was born in 1796 and died in 1859. In 1846 Mr. Bayler engaged in the tanning business, which he continued until 1865, when he began the lumber business, which he carried on for some years and then retired from active life. He was married in 1841 to Sarah A. Klinefelter, a native of York County, and a representative of one of the early families, and daughter of Adam and Sarah A. Klinefelter. The marriage has been blessed with seven children, four of whom are living: Adam K., Albert, Charles A. and Sarah A. Mrs. Bayler died in 1876, a member of the Lutheran Church. Mr. Bayler is a Democrat, and cast his first presidential vote for Martin Van Buren. He is a member of the I. O. O. F. and of the Lutheran Church.

ADAM K. BAYLER, cigar manufacturer, was born March 3, 1846. His boyhood was spent in York, his native town, where he availed himself of the advantages offered by the public schools and York County Academy. In 1864 he entered the United States naval service, and was with Admiral Farragut's fleet in the passage of the forts at the entrance of Mobile Bay, and at the evacuation of Charleston, S. C. In 1865 Mr. Bayler went to China in the United States store-ship "Supply;" remained two years, and then returned to America. He made three cruises to China during his service of thirteen years in the United States Navy. In 1872 he went to Europe and China via the Suez Canal in the United States flag-ship "Tennessee," and in 1877 returned to York, where he has since remained. In 1882 he engaged in the manufacture of cigars, his factory being one of the most extensive establishments of the kind in York. He was married in 1880 to Ida M. Leader, daughter of Joseph (deceased) and Harriet Leader. Mr. Bayler is a stanch Republican, and cast his first presidential vote for Grant.

ALBERT BAYLER was born in York, Penn., September 1, 1847, and is the second of a family of seven children. He attended the public schools of York and the York Academy, and at seventeen years of age began serving a three years' apprenticeship to the machinists' trade, at the North Central Railway shops at Baltimore. Returning to York he worked for E. C. Smyser for two years, and then went to Springfield, Ohio, where he worked for one year in the Champion shops. In 1877 he went to Baltimore, and for three years was engaged in the produce business. Mr. Bayler is now engaged in the manufacture of cigars. He was married in 1875 to Kate Halbert, a native of Carlisle, Penn., born in 1854, daughter of Joseph Halbert. They have two children: Charles H. and Rose M. Mr. Bayler is a Republican, and is a member of the Masonic fraternity. He and his wife are members of the Lutheran Church.

CHARLES A. BAYLER was born March 18, 1853, and is the youngest son living born to Henry and Sarah A. (Klinefelter) Bayler. He is a wholesale dealer in lumber and cigars. He received his schooling at the public schools of York County, and at the York County Academy, and at twenty-five years of age began business for himself; but prior to this he had learned the carpenter's trade. In 1877 he engaged in the lumber business, and continued until 1882, when he began the cigar business. He was married in 1878 to Rose B. Mason, a native of Columbia. Mr. Bayler is a Republican.

C. H. BECKMEYER, general merchant, is a native of Germany, was born in 1850 and is a son of Frederick and Sophia Beckmeyer. He is the sixth in a family of nine children, and of pure German lineage. The boyhood of our subject was spent in his native country, where he attended the public schools. In 1866 he came to America and took a clerkship in a store. Remaining in New York City ten years, he came in 1876 to York and engaged in his present business. He was married in 1879 to Miss Minnie Bode, a native of York, and a daughter of William and Charlotte Bode, natives of Germany. They have three children: William, Charlotte and Edward. Mr. Beckmeyer is an enterprising citizen, and has made life a success. He and wife are members of the German Lutheran Church.

BIOGRAPHICAL SKETCHES.

GEORGE W. BELL, superintendent of Weigle's planing-mill and sash factory, was born in New York City, February 28, 1851, to George S. and Julia R. (Slawson) Bell, and is of Scotch-Irish origin. The father of Mr. Bell was born in Boston, Mass., in 1820, and his mother in Rensselaer County, N. Y., in 1824. His mother died in New York City in 1873. The paternal grandfather of our subject was Edward A. Bell, a native of Boston, Mass. His great-grandfather came from Ireland to America, and settled in Massachusetts. Mr. Bell was educated at the public schools of New York City, and subsequently learned the carpenter's trade, and studied architecture, and at this continued for some years. In 1878 he came to York and accepted the position he now occupies. He superintended the erection of the York City Market House, in 1878 and 1879, and the York Opera House in 1881 and 1882, and also designed some of the best business houses and private residences and churches in York. We would mention particularly the new St. Mary's Roman Catholic Church, just finished, and the banking house of Weiser, Son & Carl. In 1880 Mr. Bell was married to Miss Mary Kissinger, daughter of Prof. E. J. Kissinger. To this marriage were born two children: Emma D. and Mary E. Mrs. Bell died in 1883. Politically Mr. Bell is a Republican. In 1884 he was elected to represent the Ninth Ward in the borough council. In the famous flood of 1884, Mr. Bell, as one of the members of the health committee, did effective service, and also, as one of the members of the relief committee, spent much time and labor in helping all those that were in distress, and by his energy many people were helped, and their homes put in a comfortable position once more.

DR. THEODORE H. BELTZ, son of Henry E. and Julia A. Beltz, natives of Manchester, Carroll Co., Md., was born in December, 1841. His father was a physician. Dr. Beltz began his professional studies at Irving College, Manchester, Md., and graduated from that institution in March, 1861. He then went to the Medical University of Maryland, and graduated in March, 1863. On his return home he formed a copartnership with his father, Dr. Henry E. Beltz, who had practiced medicine in Manchester for more than forty years. He remained in partnership with his father three years, and then went to Jefferson, York Co., Penn., where he remained three years, and then came, in 1880, to York. He married, in December, 1874, Nettie S., daughter of George A. Shower, of Manchester, Md. They have one child—Harry S.

EDMUND C. BENDER, son of Christian and Sarah (Carl) Bender, was born in Dillsburg, York County, January 22, 1831, and at an early age moved with his parents to York. Here he attended school until the age of sixteen, when he entered the dry goods house of Rex, Brooke & Brown, of Philadelphia, and from there went to Baltimore as bookkeeper for the commission house of Lewis Frysinger & Co., of that city. While there, the firm of P. A. & S. Small, knowing him as a young man of great integrity and excellent business qualities, offered him the position of manager of their large grain depot and warehouse at York; accepting this he returned to his former home. He subsequently became manager of the lumber-yard of the same firm, and eventually, on account of his superior business tact, became a partner, under the firm name of Smalls, Bender & Co. This copartnership existed for several years, enjoying a large trade, when the firm changed to Bender & Weiser, with Gates J. Weiser as partner. In 1875 he sold his business interests in York to Weiser Bros., and together with Messrs. J. F. Steiner and Charles S. Weiser, leased a large tract of valuable, fine timber land, near Philipsburg, Center Co., Penn., and removed with his family to that town. At this place he remained for nine years, a part of which time Gates J. Weiser was a partner with him. They cut down and had sawed into building material vast quantities of lumber. While in Philipsburg his son, Edmund, showing a desire to engage in the art of printing, he purchased the *Journal* of that town, and conducted it until he removed to York. Under his proprietorship it was a live, well-edited paper. After returning to York, he engaged in the grain business with his brother Martin, under the firm name of Bender Bros., and also in the grocery business with his son, as Bender & Son. On May 15, 1856, he was married to Margaret M. Weiser, daughter of Daniel B. and Matilda Weiser, of York. They had two children: Sarah M. and Edmund C. Bender. The death of this estimable gentleman and model business man occurred on August 29, 1883. By his strict adherence to every enterprise in which he engaged, and correct habits, he accumulated a large estate. Mr. Bender early in life became a member of the Lutheran Church, and at the time of his death was secretary of the Lutheran Church Extension Society, a director of the York National Bank, a director of the Farmers' Market. As a citizen of York, he was universally esteemed and respected. His son, Edmund C. Bender, Jr., succeeds his father in the excellent stand, on the corner of West Market and Penn Streets, opposite the Farmers' Market, where he has one of the largest and most attractive grocery stores in York. He is a young man of excellent business qualities.

MARTIN BENDER, second son of Christian and Sarah (Carl) Bender, was born March 21, 1832, in York. His education was received in the public schools of his native town. After leaving school, he assisted his father for a number of years. His father, who died at an advanced age in York, was for forty years actively engaged in business, and was a worthy citizen. At the age of twenty-one Martin Bender embarked in business in York, opening a dry goods store, which he conducted for nine years. During the five years following he was associated with John F. Patton in the drug trade. He then opened a flour and feed store, and engaged in the purchase of grain, in West York, for a time, in partnership with his brother, E. C. Bender. The firm is now Bender, Bond & Co., manufacturers and dealers in flour, feed, grain, etc., in which line they are doing a large trade. Mr. Bender was united in marriage, in 1867, with Miss Emma, daughter of Samuel and Anna M. Weiser. They have had two children: Willie C. (deceased) and Helen B. Mr. Bender is a member of Zion Lutheran Church, of York, in which he has been an elder for many years, and for a long time has served very acceptably as superintendent of the infant department of the Sunday-school. He is a gentleman of exemplary character and a prosperous business man. Since writing the above, Emma, wife of Martin Bender, died, September 30, 1881. She was a consistent member of St. Paul's Lutheran Church, Rev. Dr. Gotwalt, pastor.

CHRISTIAN BENDER, a representative of an old and prosperous family, descendants of the first settlers of York County, was born in York, December 2, 1833, and is the son of George and Hannah Bender. The ancestors of the Benders emigrated from Germany, and landed in this country about the year 1740. The father of our subject was a brickmaker, and owned a yard in the vicinity of York. The son, in his younger days, while yet attending school, assisted his father. In 1875 he engaged in the coal and wood business, on East Market Street, York. As a reward for his energy and integrity he has now established a large trade, having among his patrons many of the most influential citizens of his native town. On January 7, 1855, Mr. Bender was married to Sarah, daughter of Daniel and Mary A. Craver, of York. They had five children, viz.: John C., Lavinia M., Amelia A., Irene E. and Christopher C. His first wife died in 1873. His second marriage was with Martha C. Herman. Mr. Bender and family are members of the Lutheran Church. For a number of years he has been a member of the Masonic fraternity.

PETER BENTZ (deceased) was a native of York, Penn., born November 21, 1830, son of Michael and Anna Bentz, and was of German extraction. The Bentz family came from Germany to America and settled in Pennsylvania. Subject was educated at the York public schools. By occupation he was a musician and proprietor of a music store for thirty-five years. He was one of the leading musicians and music teachers of York for many years. For a quarter of a century he was the organist at St. John's Episcopal Church. In 1861 he was married to Miss Ellen J. Griffith, a native of Baltimore, Md. To this union were born four children, viz.: W. Stewart, Harry, Mary S. and Anna. Politically Mr. Bentz was a Republican. He was a Mason and a member of St. John's Episcopal Church. He was a prominent man and highly respected citizen. His death took place in September, 1884.

E. D. BENTZEL, attorney at law. Baltzer and Philip Bentzel, emigrated from Germany to America, and arrived at Baltimore in the year 1745. Soon after their arrival, Baltzer came to what is now York County, Penn., and settled near York: he was a shoemaker by trade, reared a family of two sons and four daughters: Henry, David, Catharine Ellman, Anna Maria, Lizzie and Barbara Kump. The father was a captain in the Revolutionary war; he died when David, who was born in August, 1777, was a young man. When David was twenty-four years of age, he married Miss Elizabeth Meisenhelter, and settled upon a farm, on the Little Conewago Creek, near what is now Weigelstown. He was a successful farmer, and in 1811 erected a large distillery, manufacturing whisky which he conveyed by his teams to Baltimore, there being no railroads at the time where it was marketed. He reared a family of five sons and five daughters: Henry, Felix, David, Samuel and Daniel M., Barbara, Mary, Elizabeth, Nancy and Sarah (who died young), all of whom were married except Felix, who died young. David was born May 3, 1815. He learned the trade of milling from his uncle, George Meisenhelter, at his father's mill, on the Little Conewago, which he bought at his father's death, and where he is still living. He married Sarah, daughter of John Eisenhart, who was a carpenter and cabinet-maker; she died December 25, 1880. One of her brothers, Samuel M. Eisenhart, is now a resident of York. Six children were born to this union: Henry M., born in 1844, located in California, where he died in 1877, leaving to survive a son, Frederick; Edward D. and David E., born in 1857; Nancy, wife of Henry W. Jacobs; Kate E., wife of Peter Binder, and Leah, who died in her infancy. Our subject was born February 22, 1846, and learned the milling trade of his father, which he was forced to abandon on account of a violent illness, which crippled him in his lower limbs to such an extent, that he was compelled to use crutches. He then secured an excellent education, having the advantage of the York County Normal and the Academy. Subsequently he became a teacher, which he continued for six terms in York Borough and the county. He then entered the political field, and in 1872 was elected clerk of the courts, the duties of which position he honorably discharged for three years. Deciding upon the profession of law, he entered the office of James B. Ziegler, Esq., and in 1878 was admitted to practice, at which he has been actively engaged up to the present time. Mr. Bentzel is an uncompromising Democrat, a valued leader in politics, and a citizen of worth and progressive ideas. He was married to Ida Kate Wehrly, daughter of George Wehrly, proprietor of the Pennsylvania House, York, February 24, 1881. They have three children: Edith May, Earnie and Edward Wehrly.

JOHN W. BITTENGER, one of the leading attorneys of the York County bar, is a descendant of old Pennsylvania ancestry. His great-grandfather, Capt. Nicholas Bittenger, a native and resident of Adams County, was a soldier in the Revolutionary war. Upon his mother's side, John Wierman, also a native and citizen of Adams County, was a wealthy farmer and, for a number of years, a justice of the peace. His grandparents were Joseph Bittenger, of Adams County, and Hon. Daniel Sheffer, a native of York County, who, in early life, was a physician. He became subsequently associate judge of Adams County, and in 1836 was elected to represent Adams and Franklin Counties in congress, attained distinction and became one of the leading political factors of his time in the State. The parents of our subject were Henry and Juliann (Sheffer) Bittenger, both natives of Adams County. The father is now a resident of Hanover. The mother died in 1887, leaving three children: Mrs. George C. Barnitz of Middletown, Ohio, Mrs. Reuben Young of Hanover, and the subject of this biography.

JOHN W. BITTENGER, was born in Adams County in the year 1834. He received a good education, attending the academies of Strasburg, Penn., and Rockville, Md., supplemented by a partial course at the Pennsylvania College at Gettysburg; during the latter he was also a student of law with the late Hon. Moses McClean. He subsequently went to Rockville, Md., and finished reading in the office of W. Viers Bouic, now judge of the circuit court of that county, being admitted to the bar at Rockville, in 1856. After graduating at the law school, of Harvard College, he went to Lexington, Ky., where he entered upon the practical duties of his profession, remaining in that State three years. In 1860 Mr. Bittenger became a citizen of York, where he has since been in constant practice. His ability was soon recognized, and in 1862 he was elected district attorney, of York County, serving six years. He has also served as counsel for the county commissioners and as attorney for the borough of York. Mr. Bittenger has attained a prominent position among his fellows and was a leading candidate for the nomination for county judge in 1881, and in 1885 secured the candidacy. As a citizen he is of the progressive type, and as a politician one of the leaders of the Democracy. Mr. Bittenger is a member of the Masonic order, of the I. O. O. F. (Encampment), and the I. O. R. M., also of the York Club. In 1877 he was united in marriage with Miss Anna Brenneman, a native of York County. They have two children living: Ida May and Julia Anna, and one deceased, John H., who died at the age of seven years.

CHAUNCEY F. BLACK. The stock from which the present lieutenant-governor springs needs no introduction to Pennsylvanians. His illustrious father, Jeremiah Sullivan Black, was pre-eminently a Pennsylvanian by blood and birth, by education and public service. He unites the ruling types in the rural portions of the State—the sturdy Pennsylvania German and energetic Scotch-Irish. Born in the Glades, Somerset County, his father was of Scotch-Irish ancestry, his mother of Scotch-Irish on her father's side, as her name, Sullivan, indicates, and of Pennsylvania German descent on her mother's side. Judge Black's father, Henry Black, was a man of prominence in southern Penn-

sylvania; he served in the legislature from 1814 to 1818, was an associate judge for a term, and was a member of the National house of representatives when he died. His wife was the daughter of Chauncey Forward, who was a member of congress and a brother of Walter Forward, secretary of the treasury under Tyler. Chauncey Forward Black, who bears his mother's family name, was born in Somerset County, Penn., November, 1839. His early education was obtained at Monongalia Academy, Morgantown, W. Va., at Hiram College, in Ohio, and he finished his studies at Jefferson College, Canonsburg. When he was a pupil at Hiram the late President Garfield was a tutor there, and the acquaintance thus formed ripened into a personal friendship, which was only interrupted by the president's tragic death. Their political differences were the widest, as illustrated by the scholarly and irresistible paper, in which Mr. Black took issue with Mr. Garfield's exultant boast that the influence of Jefferson is on the wane in our political system. He was admitted to the bar of Somerset, and also of York, but never practiced much, showing early inclination toward journalism and other forms of literary work. From the time of beginning his law studies he wrote for various journals on a wide range of topics, doing a vast amount of effective political work, for which he has trained himself by study of the fathers of the republic. Jefferson found in him an appreciative but discriminating admirer, and the Hamiltonian theories encountered his early criticism and dissent. Study of the constitution and of the discussions over its adoption and construction, convinced him that they who had founded our institutions had builded wiser than they knew, formulating a system which could be practicably and profitably applied to every question that arose. Mr. Black, though a student of politics, has never failed to take a laboring oar in the practical work of campaigns. Besides the engagement of his pen for effective work in many quarters, he has been heard upon the stump year after year, and a number of the later platforms of the Democratic State conventions are accredited to his authorship. In 1879 he represented York County in the State convention, and in 1880 he was one of the delegates from that congressional district to the Cincinnati convention, voting on the first ballot for Judge Field, and on the second for Gen. Hancock. Prior to the late State convention, from the time his nomination for lieutenant-governor was first broached, the suggestion was received with popular favor, and he was chosen by a large majority on the first ballot. The selection was ratified most heartily not only by the Democratic press of Pennsylvania, but by many journals of large influence outside the State.

From his youth up Mr. Black has been a supporter of those principles which he comes to by inheritance and holds by intelligent conviction. With ready pen and eloquent tongue he has steadily maintained them for over twenty years. In all his utterances and writings they never found abler nor more fitting expression than in his successful efforts to revive the Jeffersonian societies and extend the study of Jeffersonian principles. To this patriotic task he has applied himself, not because of any retrospective tendency of his mind, nor by reason of any failure to profoundly appreciate the spirit of true progressiveness and to adapt himself and his political principles to the wonderful development of our national life. He holds that in the Jeffersonian philosophy are the germs of all political progress.

Since 1873 Mr. Black has been closely and continuously identified with the journalism of the country. He has been uninterruptedly an editorial

contributor to the New York *Sun* and other prominent journals of the country, his facile pen being devoted to no special range of subjects, and often wandering into the more graceful lines of literature, while his fulminations are vigorous and effective when hurled at political evils. The geniality and native humor of his temperament, which make him a social favorite wherever he is known, unmistakably manifest themselves in his literary work, but the sturdy Anglo-Saxon and virile thought of his editorial expression make it recognizable.

In November, 1882, he was elected lieutenant-governor of Pennsylvania. His majority in York County was one of the largest ever received by any candidate, when opposed by the opposite party. In January, 1883, he entered upon his duties as presiding officer of the senate of Pennsylvania. His dignified bearing, affable manners and courtesy have won the admiration of the senators of both parties, and of the officers, of the various departments, with whom he has had official intercourse.

In 1863 Mr. Black was married to the daughter of the late Hon. John L. Dawson, whose home was at Friendship Hill, Fayette County, the former residence of Albert Gallatin, and the present residence of Mr. Dawson's widow, which is still in the ownership of the family. Mr. Dawson represented the (then) Twenty-first District in congress with great distinction. He was in reality the father of the homestead law now in force. Of the four children at "Willow Bridges," the three boys illustrate their distinguished lineage by the names Jeremiah Sullivan, John L. Dawson and Chauncey Forward. Possessed in eminent degree of those fireside virtues which are the best qualities of public men, Mr. Black has social accomplishments which make him extremely popular with his acquaintances. Upon his nomination for lieutenant-governor he received the hearty congratulations of his neighbors and assurances of their support regardless of party, because of the warmth of feeling which his personal characteristics have awakened for him. No local interest fails to engage his sympathy, and his former friends and neighbors are accustomed to count him among those who regard their agricultural concerns with community of interest. He was one of the charter members of Springettsbury Grange. No. 79, organized in Spring Garden Township, York Co., Penn., January 4, 1874, by R. H. Thomas, State secretary. He attends the Episcopal Church.

On the left hand side of the Northern Central Railroad, about a mile southwest of York, Penn., and in the township of Spring Garden is a beautiful home, bowered among apple trees, which are thickly set on a smoothly kept lawn. Well trimmed hedges run all around this little farm; through them, here and there, grow the osage trees and towering elms, while drooping willows and whispering maples shade the enclosed grounds. The ivy grows over the stone springhouse; Virginia creepers cling to trellises and branching trees and flaunt their graceful foliage in the summer wind. Within the house which adorns "Willow Bridges," are the signs of solid comfort and refinement. Near by, an office of rustic beauty, furnished with all the facilities for literary labor, is the workshop of Chauncey F. Black.

Inheriting from a hardy race of ancestors a love of nature, he lives here in the country at the foot of Webb's Hill, over which the spacious and highly cultivated farm of his father's estate spreads itself. He breaths pure air, drinks spring water, supplies his table from his own garden, and catches inspiration from all his surroundings for the vigorous work which he has done in the promotion of a healthy and honest policy for the commonwealth.

A. R. BLAIR, M. D., was born in Strasburg, Lancaster Co., Penn., in 1826; is a son of James and Jean (Campbell) Blair, and is of Scotch-Irish origin. His father was born in Ireland in 1790, and his mother in Pennsylvania in 1795. He first came to York in 1850. He received an academic education at the schools of Maryland and southern Pennsylvania. He read medicine under Dr. Samuel Kenagy of Strasburg, Penn., and Dr. Theo. Haller of York, and also attended lectures at Jefferson Medical College, Philadelphia, from which he graduated in March, 1853. The same year (1853) he located in York and practiced until 1856, when he was elected superintendent of the public schools of York County. He resigned in 1862 and was appointed acting assistant surgeon by Gen. William A. Hammond, surgeon-general, United States Army. He remained in this service until September, 1865, and immediately resumed the practice of his profession. He is a member of the York County Medical Association, State Medical Association and American Medical Association. In 1864 he married Miss Cassandra Morris Small, daughter of the late Phillip A. and Sarah Small, of York. One child has been born to him, Philip A. The Doctor was formerly a Whig, but is now a Republican, and he and Mrs. Blair are members of the Presbyterian Church.

DR. T. A. BLAKE was born in Little Britain Township, Lancaster Co., Penn., April 30, 1846; moved to Winterstown, York County, in 1852, and remained with his father on the farm, attending school in the winter season until August, 1864, when he enlisted in the Third Pennsylvania Heavy Artillery; was discharged at Camp Hamilton, Va., June 7, 1865; came home and attended the Pleasant Grove Academy until the summer of 1868. He then took up the study of dentistry; attended the Baltimore Dental College, during the sessions of 1868 and 1869, and has been in the continuous practice of dentistry since. He was married in September, 1872, to Helen M., daughter of Ambrose and Annie (Miller) McGuinyan. They have one child—Abbie A. Dr. Blake has held the office of justice of the peace of Winterstown for eight years. He is a member of the Brotherhood and of the G. A. R.

HENRY BOLL, boot and shoe dealer, was born in York, February 13, 1848, and is a son of Jacob and Gertrude (Werkman) Boll. His parents were born in Germany and came to America in 1836 and settled in York. At twelve years of age our subject began learning the shoemaker's trade under his father. In 1867 he began as a dealer and has since continued. He now has a full line of all kinds of boots and shoes and is prepared at all times to give his customers first-class goods at the most reasonable prices. His marriage occurred August 27, 1865, to Mary A. Kahler, a native of York. They have five children: C. Bowan, Ella M., Ida Kate, William H. and Virginia Gertrude Mary. Mr. Boll was a soldier in the late war; he enlisted in 1865 and served a short time. He is an active and influential Democrat and has been assessor of the First Ward for nine consecutive years, and is secretary of the Mechanics' and Workingmen's Building and Loan Association, and Anchor Building and Loan Association of York, Penn.

OLIVER J. BOLLINGER, whose portrait appears in this work, is a well-known inventor and manufacturer of turbine water-wheels and mill machinery. He was born in Adams County, Penn., April 13, 1827, and is the only child of Matthias and Elizabeth (Eckert) Bollinger, and of German lineage. His father was a native of Carroll County, Md., born in 1801. He became a resident of York County in 1838, settling in Codorus Township, where he resided until his death, in 1879. He was a millwright by trade, and was actively engaged in that branch of industry for over forty years. Our subject's early life was passed upon a farm, receiving his education in the common schools, the White Hall Academy and the Pennsylvania Commercial Institute. His father being a millwright, at the age of eighteen he left the farm and apprenticed himself to the millwright trade, under his father, where he remained several years, acquiring a thorough knowledge of the business, and finally succeeded his father, who, retiring, left the entire control to the son. Mr. Bollinger has continued the business successfully since then, a period of forty years, and is to-day probably the oldest and best known, as he is certainly the best qualified. It is but natural to one who dates his knowledge of mills and machinery from infancy, and his attempts

BIOGRAPHICAL SKETCHES.

at mill construction from the jack-knife, the shingle and the country stream or roadside brook, where his childish ambition reveled in its fancied great accomplishment of his efforts. In 1860 he took up the manufacture of the Jonval turbine water-wheel, but an experience of several years demonstrated clearly to him that improvements were not only desirable, but necessary, and after a long period of experiments and attempts at different constructions, he, in June, 1870, patented and gave to the trade the old Bollinger turbine water-wheel, sometimes styled the "Success." Though he afterward disposed of the right and title to manufacture that wheel, it was destined for him to perfect another, styled "Bollinger's new turbine water-wheel," June 1, 1875, and to this new wheel he is devoting his time and attention, offering the same to the public with elaborate explanation by catalog and circular. To his manufacture of water-wheels he adds mill machinery, and we particularly call the attention of those interested, to his inventions of mill-stone supports and driving devices, which reflect much credit upon the inventor and give the trade articles of sterling value. In 1874 Mr. Bollinger became one of the members of the York Manufacturing Company, then just started, and took position in the firm as mechanical engineer and foreman of the shops. He remained there for two years, when, realizing the value of his new wheel, he began devoting all his time to it, and so he continues to-day.

It can be said, in brief, that the new Bollinger turbine water-wheel, patented June 1, 1875, is the result and embodiment of the inventor's valuable experience of about thirty-five years in the designing and construction of water-wheels and mill machinery, and that in this turbine, good and well-tried features have been preserved, while register gates, pivot or claptrap gates, cams, eccentrics, racks and pinions under water, worm-gears, windlasses, and all such trappy and complicated devices which have heretofore rendered turbine wheels troublesome, impracticable and worthless, have been dispensed with, and substituted by new and substantial improvements, protected by letters patent. All wheels and machinery are built under the immediate supervision of the inventor, who invites the special attention of wheel builders and wheel buyers.

Mr. Bollinger has for sixteen years been a resident of York, and has added much to its progressive business interests. He belongs to that class of men who, active and fertile in mechanical and inventive resources, have done much to give life and reality to the ideas which emanate only from men of natural inborn mechanical attributes. In 1856 he was united in marriage with Susan C. Fife, a native of York County and daughter of John and Elizabeth Fife. To this marriage were born three children. Mrs. Bollinger died in 1888, at forty-five years of age. For twenty-five years Mr. Bollinger has been a member of the Evangelical Lutheran Church. Politically he is a Republican, and has served as a member of the borough council. Affable and of a kindly nature, warm in his friendships and sincere in his attachments, he is regarded as a good citizen, alive to all matters pertaining to his city's welfare, a reliable, straightforward business and moral man.

EMANUEL W. BOWMAN, dealer in coal and wood, was born in Springfield Township, August 1, 1830, to George and Catherine (Walter) Bowman, and is of German origin. The father of Mr. Bowman was born in Chanceford Township, March 14, 1803, and his mother in North Codorus, December 27, 1807. The paternal grandfather of our subject was Philip Bowman. The father of Mr. Bowman was a farmer, whose death occurred on November 28, 1884. His mother died on March 27, 1838. When our subject was about eight years of age, he removed with his parents to Adams County, where he remained until his seventeenth year, when they removed to Carroll County, Md., where they remained a short time, and then returned to York County. In 1855 he went to Cumberland County, Upper Allen Township, where he remained until the beginning of the war, when he again returned to York County and settled in Franklin Township. He enlisted August 30, 1864, in Company I, Two Hundred and Ninth Pennsylvania Volunteers, and was honorably discharged at the close of the war. In February, 1867, he returned to York, where he has since resided. For nine years he was employed by the Northern Central Railroad Company, and for more than eight years was employed by P. A. & S. Small. In February, 1884, he began the wood and coal business, which he now continues. The marriage of Mr. Bowman occurred April 30, 1854, to Miss Margaret Myres, a native of Adams County, born June 9, 1836, daughter of Peter Myres. To this marriage has been born one child—Sarah E. Mr. Bowman is a Mason and Republican. Mr. and Mrs. Bowman are members of St. Paul's Lutheran Church.

STEPHEN GILL BOYD, the subject of this sketch, is the oldest child of John C. and Martha (Farmer) Boyd, and was born in Peach Bottom Township, this county, on the 6th day of December, 1830. On his paternal side he is descended from an old Scotch-Irish family that emigrated from the County Antrim, Ireland, in the year 1736, and his maternal grandparents emigrated from Shropshire, England, in the early part of the present century, and settled near Darlington, Hartford Co., Md. During the minority of Mr. Boyd, his summers were devoted to working on his father's farm, and his winters to attending the district school. Upon reaching his majority he repaired to York, and entered, as a student, the grammar school of the late Dr. Andrew Dinsmore, and spent his time, until he was twenty-seven years of age, mainly in teaching, obtaining academic instruction at various educational institutions, principally at White Hall Academy in Cumberland County, Penn., and at Bryansville Academy in his native township, and in managing his farm, for several years farming in summer and teaching a district school in winter. In his twenty-seventh year, Mr. Boyd, in order to obtain a more thorough education, removed with his family to Lancaster, Penn., and for a term became a student at the Millersville State Normal School, then under the management of Dr. Wickersham. From this time until 1866, he devoted his time exclusively to teaching and study, teaching in Lancaster County, Lancaster City, and in Wrightsville, in this county. In the spring of the year last referred to, at the request of Prof. S. B. Heiges, who was then county superintendent of schools of this county, he came to York and joined him in the management of a normal school, organized for the benefit of the young teachers of the county, with which school he was connected as one of its principal teachers for four years. In the fall of this year (1866) he was elected to a seat in the house of representatives, and was re-elected the ensuing year. In the spring of 1869, he was elected county superintendent of schools to succeed Mr. Heiges, and in 1871 he was elected to the presidency of the Peach Bottom Railway Company, which latter position he filled for the term of six years, and until the road was completed and put into operation from York to Delta. In the spring of 1877 Mr. Boyd, in conjunction with some of the more enterprising citizens of Hartford and Baltimore Counties, undertook the organization of a company to construct a railroad from Delta to Baltimore, and on the 21st day of January, 1884, this road was completed and opened to traffic. Mr. Boyd's conduct as a representative was characterized by a deep interest in all legislation calculated to promote the educational interests of the State and the material interests of his own county. During his first term he finally prepared and secured the passage of the bill to incorporate the York and Chanceford Turnpike Company, in which company, after its organization, he served as a director until his removal to Baltimore, in 1878. During his second term he prepared and secured the passage of the bill to incorporate the Peach Bottom Railway Company, and during this term also he took an active part in the passage of the bill giving to the non-accepting school districts of the State, their for-

feited appropriations from the State treasury, for the last ten years prior to its passage, and had the pleasure of seeing Manheim Township, in this county, accept the system during his first year as county superintendent. In his second year in the office of county superintendent he co-operated with the board of school control of the borough of York in the reorganization of the schools of the borough, favoring a comprehensive and thorough course of study, and the borough superintendency. Mr. Boyd, since his withdrawal from the management of the Maryland Central Railroad, in the autumn of 1884, has been engaged in educational work, having adopted the educational platform as a profession. In addition to his labors on the platform, he frequently appears in print as an essayist, and is the author of a work on the signification of Indian local or place names. Much of his life has been given to the study of literary and scientific subjects, and no small part of it to the promotion of the material interests of his county.

H. C. BRENNEMAN, assistant principal of the York High School, was born in Washington Township, January 14, 1858, and is a son of Jacob Brenneman, a prominent farmer of the upper end, residing near the village of Wellsville. Mr. Brenneman received the rudiments of his education in the public schools, and early in life showed an ardent thirst for knowledge, which the excellent schools of the vicinity encouraged. In them he zealously studied, and succeeded so well that in the fall of 1875, he passed creditably at the town examination, and was employed as a teacher for that winter term. The following spring he attended Union Seminary at 'New; Berlin, Union Co., Penn. Returning home he very successfully taught in the public schools of his native township for three more winter terms, and in 1878 entered the State Normal School at Millersville, where he graduated with a class of thirty-seven in the spring session of 1880. After graduating he taught one term in Adamstown, Lancaster County, and returned to the normal school again, taking a more extended course in the natural sciences and mathematics. He next taught a normal and select school in Millersburg, Dauphin County, and was afterward elected principal of the schools of that town, but before the fall term opened, was elected in 1881 to the position which he now holds. Prof. Brenneman is a young man of fine literary tastes, excellent scholarship, and thoroughly devoted to the responsibilites of his profession.

DR. C. H. BRESSLER was born in Clinton County, Penn., in February, 1821, and is a son of George and Eliza (Darneck) Bressler, the former a native of Lancaster County, and the latter of Philadelpha, Penn. Dr. Bressler was educated at the common schools of Clinton County, and subsequently attended select schools at Flemington and Mill Hall. He began the study of dentistry, in 1839, at Lancaster, under Dr. Eli Perry, and continued for three years and a half, during which time he also studied medicine under Dr. Perry, who was a graduate of the Medical University of Philadelphia. During the last year of his stay at Lancaster, Dr. Bressler studied under Dr. Washington Atlee. In 1842 he went to Philadelphia and attended a course of lectures during the winter at the Pennsylvania Medical College; in the fall following he entered the Jefferson Medical College at Philadelphia, from which institution he graduated in March, 1844. He located at Bellefonte and practiced dentistry until 1849, when he went to Lancaster and formed a partnership with Dr. Perry in the practice of dentistry. In the fall 'of 1849, he with Dr. Perry and others petitioned the legislature for a dental college; this was the first effort toward securing an institution of this kind in the State, and the following fall a charter was granted. Dr. Bressler returned to his practice at Bellefonte, where he remained until 1854, when he came to York and became the successor of Dr. James Perry. He has been twice a candidate for congress and has served as sheriff of York County. In May, 1849, he married Sarah A., daughter of Rev. John Tanner of Bellefonte, Penn. Their union has been blessed with eight children, as follows: John T., George Bowman (deceased), Emma B., Charles, Clara V., Wilber C., A. Curton, and Ella M. The Doctor and family are members of the Methodist Episcopal Church; he is a Mason, a member of the Blue Lodge and Commandery of York.

JOHN W. BUCKINGHAM, dealer in paper and paper stock, is a native of Gettysburg, Penn., and was born May 5, 1832; is a son of Ezekiel and Maria (Test) Buckingham, is the third son by his father's second marriage, and is of English descent. The father of our subject was born in Maryland about 1796. By occupation he was a coach-maker. His death occurred in Gettysburg in 1849. The mother of Mr. Buckingham was born in York about 1810. At the early age of about eleven years, the subject of this sketch was compelled to make his own way in life. He first learned the tailoring trade, and this he continued some years. His present business was established in 1860. The marriage of Mr. Buckingham occurred in 1850, to Miss Rebecca Meginley, daughter of Andrew and Catherine Meginley. To this marriage have been born eight children, five of whom are living, viz.: Maria C., William A., Henry E., R. Lizzie and Lewis E. W. Mr. Buckingham is a firm friend of education. His daughter, R. Lizzie, and son, Henry E., are graduates of the York High School, and his youngest son, Lewis E. W., is now a member of the junior class of the high school. Our subject is a Republican. His brother, Capt. H. F. T. Buckineham, was for four years a captain of a cavalry company. His death occurred in Baltimore in 1880. Mr. Buckingham is a Mason and a member of the Independent Order of Odd Fellows. He and wife are members of the Methodist Episcopal Church.

DR. J. DE BURKARTE, a distinguished physician and surgeon, was born in Philadelphia in 1831 and is the eldest son of Dr. S. and Mary De Burkarte. His father was a physician of Paris, France, and his mother a native of Berlin, Prussia. The subject of this sketch, in early life, received a good education in all of the ordinary branches, as well as a knowledge of medicine, and graduated at Harvard College in 1849, and has finally become a physician of extensive practice. During the years of 1850-51-52, he attended two full regular courses of lectures at the University of Philadelphia, and the College of Physicians and Surgeons of New York, supplemented with three regular full courses of lectures at the University of Maryland. He commenced the practice of medicine at Philadelphia, in 1853, where he remained in active practice until 1860, when he removed to Harrisburg, where he continued his practice until 1863, when he enlisted as a private in the Union Army. In 1864 he had, through valor and courage, risen in the ranks to first lieutenant. At the battle in front of Petersburg he was severely wounded, which confined him to the hospital. Upon regaining strength he accepted an appointment as surgeon and was transferred to McClelland Hospital at Philadelphia, where he served until the latter part of August, 1865, when, on account of wounds and disability, he received an honorable discharge. After a few weeks' respite he returned to Harrisburg and resumed his practice, continuing until 1868, when he removed to York, where he has since resided, engaged in active and continuous practice. Dr. De Burkarte has established a large and extensive practice in York County, and keeps abreast with the progress of the age, not only in his profession, but in general literature. As a citizen he is popular, liberal and enterprising. In 1867 he was united in marriage with Miss Mary Garverich, of Scotch ancestry. They have had born to them two children: Maurice (who was a promising young medical student and had passed his first course of lectures at the Baltimore City College, and died upon the day he was to enter upon his second course at the University of Maryland, in the seventeenth year of his age) and Harrie.

NATHAN F. BURNHAM, York, was born in the city of New York March 13, 1822, and is of English-Irish and French descent. His father was a millwright, and with him Nathan F. worked at the trade in Orange County, N. Y., until he was sixteen years old. He then commenced learning the watch-maker's business, which he was obliged to relinquish after three years on account of his health. He then went to Laurel, Md., in 1844, and engaged with Patuxent & Co. as mercantile clerk and bookkeeper. In 1856 he commenced the manufacture of French turbine water-wheels. In 1859 he sold out his Laurel interests and came to York, commenced manufacturing his own patents, and here has since resided. May 22, 1883, he founded the Drovers' & Mechanics' National Bank of York and was elected its first president, which position he still holds. In 1881, with others, he built the York Opera House at a cost of $40,000; it was opened in 1882. Mr. Burnham was married July 3, 1850, to Ann Eliza Gray, of Maryland; she died a few years later, leaving one child, Horace H., born September 16, 1851, and died January 28, 1857. Mr. Burnham's second marriage took place June 8, 1854, with Mrs. Delilah Israel, nee Jones; she bore him the following children: Ann Elmirah, born January 21, 1856, died March 6, 1861; Frank A., born August 18, 1858; William H., born September 21, 1860. Mrs. Delilah Burnham died May 1, 1881, aged forty-eight years, six months and twenty-eight days. Mr. Burnham has been constantly engaged in manufacturing and selling turbine wheels since 1856, and is the inventor and patentee of several, which are used in nearly every country in the world; among them may be mentioned the following: Improved Jouval Turbine, patented February 22, 1859; New Turbine Water Wheel, patented March 3, 1868; Improved New Turbine Wheel, patented March 9, 1871; Standard Turbine Wheel, patented March 31, 1874; Improved Standard Turbine, patented March 27, 1883. Burnham Bros., Mr. Burnham's sons, took charge of the Standard Turbine Wheel business October 1, 1881, and since then Mr. Burnham has devoted his time to the improvement of the standard turbine wheel, which, after many experiments, he has made to run on either a vertical or horizontal shaft, and to discharge a larger amount of water and get a better percentage of power from the water used. This Improved Turbine, discharging one-half more water, with full gate drawn, yields as great a percentage for the water used as the Standard; and when one-half the water is used, which each is capable of discharging at full gate, the gain is sixteen per cent over the Standard. During the past year he has had four experimental wheels tested at Holyoke, much to his satisfaction, both in manner of testing and percentage obtained. This Improved Standard Turbine is guaranteed equal to any other make of turbine in the economical use of water at either full or part drawn gate. Mr. Burnham is a Knight Templar, and is Past Master of the I. O. O. F. and Past Sachem of Red Men.

LEWIS CARL, deceased, was born in York County in 1826, to Martin and Mary Carl. He attended the public schools of York. At eighteen years of age he began the mercantile business in York, and for many years he was one of the prominent merchants of the county, and continued in business until a short time before his death, having accumulated quite a fortune. He was married September 20, 1866, to Susan Hay, a native of York and a daughter of John and Susan Hay; no children were born unto them. For many years he was a member of the Lutheran Church. He was extensively known and a much respected citizen. His death occurred October 24, 1878.

JERE CARL, banker, was born in York County, Penn., in 1829, and is a son of Martin and Mary (Deardorff) Carl, and is of Swiss-German extraction. The Carl family has for many years been identified with the interests of this county. The father of our subject died in 1855, and the mother ten years previous. Jere Carl received a common school education and afterward learned the printer's trade. He then engaged in the mercantile business, which he continued until 1853, when he was appointed book-keeper of the old York Bank, which position he held for fourteen years. He then engaged in the banking business, becoming a member of the firm of Weiser, Son & Carl, and in this business relation still continues. He was married in 1861 to Adaline A. Weiser, daughter of Charles and Anna M. Weiser, of York, Penn. Three children were born to this marriage: Charles W., born in 1864, died in 1882; and Balle. Mr. Carl has always been a supporter of the Democratic party. In 1875 he was elected chief burgess of York, and was re-elected in 1876 and 1878. Mr. and Mrs. Carl are members of St. Paul's Lutheran Church.

HENRY CASLOW, son of John Peter and Barbara (Flinchbaugh) Caslow, of York Township, was born May 14, 1810, in York Township, and is of English and German descent. He is the fourth child in a family of eight children, viz.: John, deceased; Liddie, deceased; Infant, deceased; Henry, Peter; Daniel, deceased; Leah, deceased; and Amos. Our subject was reared on a farm, and the death of his father, when our subject was a small boy, made it necessary for him to assist his mother in rearing the family. He began to learn the trade of shoemaker when fourteen years old, and continued at that trade for twenty-four years. His health required a change of occupation, and he bought the mill property on the Peach Bottom Railroad, near Ore Valley. He ran this mill about eight years, and then removed to York, where in 1850, he bought the Seven Stars Hotel on South George Street. After a stay of twenty years, he removed to his present location, corner of Queen and College Avenue, where he has since conducted a retail grocery store. In March, 1832, he married Helena Houseman of Windsor Township. Our subject's father-in-law, Christian Houseman, was a soldier in the Revolutionary war. Elenora, wife of Jacob Sechrist, is the only child of our subject. He is a member of the Lutheran Church.

EDMUND T. CHAMBERS, ticket-agent for the Pennsylvania and North Central Railways, is a native of France, born in 1846, son of John and Mary (Kennedy) Chambers. His parents were born in Ireland and immigrated to America in 1849, and settled in Baltimore, Md., where the father died in 1881. Our subject received a common school education at the public schools of Baltimore. In 1869 he came to York, Penn., and for some time was a clerk in the store of Thomas Chambers & Co, after which he accepted his present position. Mr. Chambers was married in 1871 to Amelia Bender, daughter of Henry Bender, ex-treasurer of York County. To this marriage have been born five children: John H., William E., Daisy E., James H. and George R. Mr. Chambers is a Democrat. He and his wife are members of the Roman Catholic Church.

ANDREW F. CLINCH, foreman of the boiler department at A. B. Farquhar's, is a native of Jersey City, N. J., was born in 1856, and is a son of Michael and Margaret (Ingersol) Clinch, and is of Irish extraction. His father was born in Ireland in 1811, came to America in 1847, and settled in Jersey City, and there remained eleven years, and then removed to Wilmington, Del., where the early portion of the life of our subject was spent. After receiving a common school education he learned the steam-fitter and boiler-maker trades. For nine years he was in the employ of Pusey Jones & Co., of Wilmington, Del. In 1879 he came to York, and has since been employed at his present occupation, and is one of the leading mechanics of York. In his department he has charge of fifty men. The marriage of Mr. Clinch was solemnized in 1878 to Miss Cora Litsinger, of Westminster, Md. To this union have been born three children, viz.: Florence May, George and Alice. He is a Democrat in politics.

HENRY M. CRIDER, publisher and bookseller, York, Penn., is the son of Jacob and Catherine (Mower) Crider. He was born near Chambersburg, Franklin Co., Penn., October 14, 1839. His father removed to near Newburg, in 1842, where the subject of this notice received an injury, while at school, which threatened to make him a cripple for life. In the years of suffering which followed, when he was debarred from the sports incident to childhood, he developed a fondness for books and an aptness for learning which determined his father to give him, if possible, a liberal education. A second removal of the family was made, in 1853, to Green Spring, Cumberland Co., Penn., where such opportunities for improvement as the district school afforded were eagerly embraced. At the age of sixteen, he began teaching in the rural districts of his county, attending, during the summer months, various institutions of learning, with a view of advancing his own education. In 1858 he became a student of Otterbein University, where his poems and essays in the literary and rhetorical societies attracted considerable interest and comment. In 1861 he was licensed to preach, when he returned to his native State, and for a short time was engaged in the ministry. December 24, 1861, he was married to Miss Sadie Elizabeth Kaufman, of Boiling Springs, Cumberland Co., Penn., and having resumed his former profession, he was for some years engaged in teaching in various towns and cities. In 1866 he was selected as a member of the faculty of Cottage Hill College, near York, Penn., and, in connection with his duties there, established a night school and commercial college for young men, which was liberally patronized by the best 'eitizens of York. About this time, he wrote a book of poems, entitled "Pedagogic," in which he embalmed in verse the various specimens of the district school teacher of "Ye olden time." Its unique character called forth many favorable press notices. It was extensively read before teacher's institutes, and passed through several editions. In 1866 he originated and published the photograph marriage certificate, which was subsequently modified into many varieties, and by a liberal and judicious system of advertising succeeded in introducing his certificates throughout the United States and Canada; and at this writing, 1885, nearly 2,000,000 copies have been sold. In August, 1867, he established a paper, which he edited for two years, the circulation of which, at one time, exceeded 5,000 copies. His first wife was removed by death in 1874. In 1875 he was married a second time, to Miss Amanda C. Fahs, a lady long and favorably known in York as a teacher in the public schools and the York County Academy. He is the father of one son and three daughters. The son, W. H. Crider, has reached his majority, and is now engaged in teaching in the State Normal School, at Morris, Ill.

DAVID W. CRIDER, who is familiarly known as a publisher and bookseller of York, is a son of Jacob and Catherine (Mouer) Crider. His father was a native of Lebanon County and his mother of Cumberland County, both of German ancestry. The son grew to manhood on his father's farm, in Franklin County, where he was born in 1842. He received the rudiments of his education in the public schools, subsequently attending the Cumberland County Normal School. While there he enlisted in Company E, One Hundred and Thirtieth Pennsylvania Volunteer Infantry, as a private, and served nine months. His regiment was in the Army of the Potomac, and participated in the battle of Antietam, where 196 of his regiment were killed. In this engagement he was wounded in two places, the neck and leg, and was at first officially reported dead. After his term of enlistment expired, and the country demanded more soldiers, he responded by re-enlisting, and joined the Two Hundred and Seventh Pennsylvania Volunteer Infantry, in which he remained until the close of the war. He was present at a series of battles in front of Petersburg, the battle of Chancellorsville and many minor engagements and skirmishes. He had the honor of being present at the surrender of Gen. Lee, and was at the grand review of the Union troops at Washington, D. C. In the last enlistment he was quartermaster-sergeant of his regiment, which was mustered out of service at Alexandria, Va. After returning to his home he entered Lebanon Valley College, and subsequently taught school one year in Maryland. In 1865 Mr. Crider became a member of the firm of Kephart, Crider & Bro., the members being S. L. Kephart, H. M. Crider and D. W. Crider. Mr. Kephart soon after retired from the firm, and the name became Crider & Bro. In 1876 D. W. Crider became sole proprietor, with the firm name unchanged, retaining all copyrights. The first named firms were engaged in the publishing business, and had taken out copyrights on three beautiful marriage certificates. The firm of Crider & Bro. have had issued to them thirty-three copyrights upon these certificates. Upon embarking in business alone, Mr. Crider added the general book trade. He now has twenty-eight copyrights on his marriage certificates, which are sold in all the States and Territories, Nova Scotia, Mexico, New Brunswick, Canada, Europe and nearly all over the civilized world. "The Oak and Vine" and "Cedar and Vine" have reached an immense circulation. "The Orange Blossom," copyrighted in 1882, has reached the largest sale, and his certificates of other issues, many of which are of beautiful design, have also reached a large sale. In 1879 Mr. Crider obtained a copyright on "The Song Treasury," an excellent Sunday-school, prayer and praise-meeting book. This book has attained a circulation of 63,000 copies. "Bright Gems" was copyrighted by him in 1881, and "Silvery Echoes" in 1880; the latter, for infant Sunday-schools, has reached a large sale. "Songs of Love and Praise," an excellent work for Sabbath-schools and the home circle, is also handled by him in large quantities direct from the publishers. Mr. Crider has one of the leading bookstores in southern Pennsylvania, and carries a valuable stock of books, stationery, fine Russia leather goods, and a large, attractive and well displayed line of fancy goods. which are sold at wholesale or retail. In public affairs Mr. Crider is public-spirited, and as an active business man he is well and favorably known. He takes a prominent interest in Sunday-schools, and is the president of the York County Sunday-school Union. In December, 1870, he was united in marriage with Miss Sarah Spangler, only daughter of Nathaniel Spangler, a prominent farmer and lineal descendant of the earliest settlers of York County. They have six children: Horace W., Charles E., Flora I., David N., Sadie C. and Lillie M. Mr. Crider is a member of the United Brethren Church, and his wife of the Reformed Church, of York. He was one of the originators of the Emigsville Camp Meeting Association, a liberal contributor to its support, and is now vice-president of its board of managers. He is also a trustee of Lebanon Valley College.

CAPT. MURRY S. CROSS was born in Windsor Township, York Co., Penn., March 12, 1835; is a son of Samuel Cross, and is of Scotch-Irish extraction. The Cross family has been connected with the history of York County for nearly a century. Capt. Cross was reared on a farm, in his native township, receiving a common school education in the meantime. When about twenty years of age he went to Baltimore and learned the carpenter's trade. Returning to York County, he followed his trade until Fort Sumpter was fired upon, when he enlisted for three months in the Sixteenth Pennsylvania Volunteer Infantry. After an honorable discharge, he was one of the principal men in raising Company C, in York County. He was elected first lieutenant, and December 25, 1862, was commissioned captain. He participated in many engagements, some of the more prominent of which were as follows: Winchester, Wilderness, Cold Harbor, Spottsylvania, Weldon Railroad, Oquaquen, now Winchester, and Fisher's Hill. Capt. Cross was discharged October 13, 1864. In 1868 he became the proprietor of what is now the Central Hotel. Here he continued five years. He began his present business in 1882. The marriage of our subject took place October 4, 1850, to Miss Cecelia Hartman, a native of York and daughter of Henry Hartman. Two children have been born to this union, viz.: Edward M. S. (who died in 1888 of injuries received while in the employ of the Northern Central Railway) and Harrison H. Capt. Cross is a Republican and a member of the I. O. O. F.

GEORGE DARON, justice of the peace, and ex-treasurer of York County, was born in Manchester Township, January 12, 1830, to George and Lydia (Kern) Daron. In a family of fourteen children Mr. Daron is the fourth and is of French-German stock. His father was born in Hellam Township in 1799, and died in 1857. His mother was a native of Manchester Township, born in 1804, and died in 1873. The paternal grandfather of our subject was born in Hellam Township in 1771, and his great-grandfather was born in France and came to America at fifteen years of age. Mr. Daron remained in his native township until 1850 when he went to Dover, and four years of his time was employed in teaching school and at work on the farm. In 1854 he began the hotel business and continued that until 1859, when he came to York, and here has since resided. Politically Mr. Daron is a Democrat and for many years has taken an active part in politics. In 1865 he was elected treasurer of York County and served one term. Afterward he was a clerk of the commissioners one year, and from 1877 to 1882 he held the office of deputy prothonotary. In 1882 he was elected justice of the peace. He was married November 22, 1855, to Miss Mary A. Leathery, a native of York County. Mrs. Daron died March 30, 1874, and November 20, 1876, Mr. Daron was married to Miss Malvina Crisman, a native of Blairstown, N. J. Mr. Daron is a member of the I. O. O. F.

OLIVER DEARDORFF, proprietor of the States Union Hotel, was born in Washington Township, York County, February 22, 1840, to David and Rebecca (Geise) Deardorff. He is the eldest in a family of seven children, and is of German origin. The father of Mr. Deardorff was born in Washington Township in 1808, and his mother in Paradise Township. The parents of Mr. Deardorff died in 1880. Mr. Deardorff was educated in the public schools of his native township. In 1871 he came to

York, and for four years clerked for William Kroutz in the States Union Hotel, and in 1875 became the proprietor, and in this occupation he has since continued. He is one of the successful hotel men in York. Mr. Deardorff was united in marriage December 25, 1874, to Miss Sarah Fake, a native of York County. To this marriage have been born three children, viz.: Eli, David and Oliver. Politically our subject is a Democrat, and a member of the German Reformed Church. Mrs. Deardorff is a member of the Lutheran Church. Mr. Deardorff is a thorough business man and of an enterprising spirit.

D. G. DEARDORFF, liveryman, was born in Washington Township, June 11, 1851, to David and Margaret (Giese) Deardorff, and is of German descent. The early years of Mr. Deardorff's life were spent on the farm and attending the public schools of Washington Township, at which he acquired a common school education. At seventeen years of age he began teaching school, but after having taught five terms he abandoned the profession. In 1881 he began the tanning business in his native township, which he continued until 1883, when he removed to York and engaged in his present occupation. His stable is located on Mason Alley, near the court-house. The marriage of Mr. Deardorff to Miss Sarah E. Grove was solemnized in 1871. Mrs. Deardorff is a native of York County. They have children as follows: Harvey, Kurvin, Arthur and George. Politically Mr. Deardorff is a Republican. In 1876 he was elected justice of the peace, and re-elected in 1881, and held the office until his removal to York.

L. T. DEININGER, president of the Vigilant Steam Fire Engine Company, No. 1, York, son of the late Rev. C. J. and Maria (Treat) Deininger. He was born at East Berlin, Adams County, August 24, 1847, and (with the exception of about six years of his boyhood, when he lived in the place of his birth and in Indiana County, Penn.) has always been a resident of York. His father and grandfather, both deceased, were well-known Lutheran clergymen, having been residents of York and Adams Counties, Penn., for more than fifty years. Mr. Deininger was educated at the public schools of York, the York County Academy, and the Pennsylvania College at Gettysburg. In 1867 he engaged in the book and stationery business, which he still continues. He was married, October 20, 1870, to Laura C. Small, daughter of William Small, an old and much respected citizen of the Fourth Ward, York, lately deceased. To this marriage have been born two children: Ella T. and Horace S. In 1879 Mr. Deininger became president of the "Vigilant Steam Fire Engine Company." He was made a Mason in 1872, and is a member of St. Paul's Lutheran Church.

SAMUEL DICK, merchant, son of Henry and Ellen (Plat) Dick, was born January 27, 1858, in York, Penn., and has always resided in York. He received his education at the public schools of York, and went to his trade, ornamental painter, when quite a young man. For ten years he had the responsible position of foreman in the painting department of A. B. Farquhar's Agricultural Works, which position he relinquished on account of his health, by advice of his physician. He then turned his attention to the mercantile business, in which he is now engaged on North Duke Street extended. July 3, 1880, Mr. Dick married Mary Butcher, daughter of William and Elenora (Gemmell) Butcher, of Hopewell Township. Two children have blessed this union: William and Mollie. Samuel Dick, the grandfather of our subject, was the leading carriage builder in York in his time.

HON. DANIEL DURKEE. Judge Durkee was of English descent, the family coming to America early in the eighteenth century, and settling in Windham, Conn. Here, his great-grandfather, Nathaniel Durkee, was married, August 21, 1727, and from there his son Timothy (Judge Durkee's grandfather) removed to Vermont while that State was yet a wilderness. His maternal grandfather, Elisha Rix, also went from Connecticut to Vermont about the same time, both families settling in the valley of White River. In their journey of about 200 miles, they were guided by marked trees. They settled on adjoining farms, granted by the government of New York, then claiming jurisdiction over the territory. The families were united by the marriage of Heman, the eldest son of Timothy Durkee, to Susan, daughter of Elisha Rix. Heman succeeded to the Durkee farm, and both farms have remained in possession of members of the family until recently. Situated in the township of Royalton, they adjoin South Royalton, a thriving village and railroad center. Here Daniel Durkee, the subject of this sketch, was born on August 27, 1791. His father's death occurring when he was but a boy, the years of his early manhood were spent in the home and on the farm of his mother. He married, April 8, 1813, Mary, daughter of Capt. John Wright, of Norwich, Vt. A few years after his marriage he commenced the study of law with Jacob Collamer, of Royalton (afterward United States Senator from Vermont and postmaster-general), and Judge Hutchinson, of Woodstock, Vt. He was admitted to the bar in Chelsea, Orange Co., Vt., June 12, 1818, and opened an office in Williamstown in the same county. Desirous of settling in Pennsylvania, he left Williamstown the following December, and came to Lebanon, Penn., taking an office just vacated by his brother-in-law, John Wright, Esq., who had removed to York. Some months later, illness in his family compelling Mr. Wright to return to New England, Judge Durkee came to York, where he continued to reside until his death. At that time, Lebanon was thoroughly German; so universally was that language spoken there, that there was but one family in the town with whom the Durkee family could communicate in the English tongue; while in York there was a large English element, though the German was almost universally spoken in the surrounding country. Without any knowledge of that language, he soon became a popular lawyer with the German population, and a successful practitioner. Pennsylvania thenceforth became the State of his adoption, but he was ever loyal to New England and to his native home, which continued to be the home of his mother until her death in 1852. It was his "Mecca." He never failed to go there annually (in the thirty-six years of his life in Pennsylvania), taking his family or several members of it with him in each alternate year. The New England festival "Thanksgiving" was always observed in his home, the appointment of the governor of Vermont being regarded, until in later years it became a national appointment. Judge Durkee was admitted to the bar in York County in 1820. In 1832 he was elected to the legislature. In 1833 he was appointed by Gov. Wolf judge of the district court. In 1835, the district court having been abolished, he was appointed president judge of the Nineteenth Judicial District, composed of the counties of York and Adams. He held the office for ten years, when, at the expiration of his term, he was succeeded by Judge Irwin. On the resignation of the latter in 1849, Judge Durkee was again appointed to the president judgeship, by Gov. Johnson, and held the office until 1851, when the judgeship, having been by a constitutional amendment, made elective, Judge Fisher was chosen to succeed him. He then resumed the practice of his profession, which he continued to the time of his death. He died November 23, 1854, aged sixty-three years and three months. Thus, for nearly half the entire period of his residence in Pennsylvania, Judge Durkee held the office of president judge. On the bench Judge Durkee was careful and painstaking, and showed great discrimination in separating, from the mass of less important matters, the real points involved in the cases brought before him. In his charges he was remarkably happy, and successful in presenting cases to juries, and in enabling them to perform their duties intelligently, and in preventing them from falling into errors. Of eminent sagacity, clear perceptions and sound conclusions, he enjoyed during his official career the confidence and respect of the bar, and in a great degree that of the appellate court, which reviewed his judgments. As an evidence of the esteem in which he has been held, there is subjoined an extract from the York *Gazette* of September 24, 1839, which, as published by a political opponent of Judge Durkee, is all the more valuable a tribute to his worth: "We find in the *Adams Sentinel* of a late date, a communication in which the Hon. Daniel Durkee, president judge of this judicial district, is spoken of in terms of high commendation. We feel proud of this justly merited tribute to the worth of one of our citizens; and here in York, where Judge Durkee is 'at home,' we feel sure that every word will be attested by every one who reads it. We hope that this district will not lose the services of so upright and excellent a judical officer under the operation of that provision of the new constitution, which limits the tenure of office of president judges of the courts of common pleas to ten years. Every friend of justice and morality, all who desire to see the bench occupied by a stern foe to vice and disorder, are interested in keeping the judicial ermine upon the shoulders of Judge Durkee." As a practicing lawyer, Judge Durkee always occupied a high position at the bars of York and Adams Counties. His specialty was the conducting of trials before juries. He managed his causes with great tact and judgment, and while at the bar always had a large portion of its forensic practice. Few causes of magnitude or importance were tried in which he was not one of the leading counsel. His influence with a jury, whether he addressed them from the bar or charged them from the bench, seemed almost magical. Although Judge Durkee was not indebted to the culture of the schools, he had evidently practiced self-discipline long and carefully. But it was from nature he received his best gifts—gifts, the absence of which no amount of educational facilities can supply. The characteristics of his mind were clearness and originality. Both these mental qualities, so rarely met, even singly, he possessed in a very considerable degree. They manifested themselves on the bench, at the bar, in social conversation, and even in casual remarks, in the working out of his intellectual processes, in the language he selected, and in the figures and illustrations he employed. For this reason he was always listened to with attention and interest. It was well known that there was no danger of being wearied by anything feeble or commonplace or obscure in what he said. Most frequently the products of his mind exhibited the freshness of vigorous and independent thinking, were expressed in strong, idiomatic English, which, adapting itself to the tournure of the thought, fitted close to it, and conveyed to others his ideas with all the clearness in which they existed in his own mind, were elucidated by illustrations, which were apt, striking, felicitous, and when the subject or occasion would admit, were enlivened by the scintillations of genuine wit. In his legal investigations and discussions, he always sought for the reason of the law, and endeavored to be guided by principles rather than by discordant and irreconcilable decisions. With his great powers of mind, he united great kindness of heart and an eminently sympathetic and affectionate disposition, causing him to be beloved in his neighborhood and idolized in his family. Judge Durkee had none of the arts and stooped to none of the tricks and methods of the politician. His popularity grew out of his genial and kindly disposition, and his well-known integrity. In times like these, when the judicial office is becoming yearly more the object of a scramble by unworthy aspirants, it were well if his high example had more imitators.

HENRY A. EBERT, retired merchant and a representative of one of the old families of York County, was born in West Manchester Township, December 10, 1841. He is a son of Henry and Sarah (Smyser) Ebert, the latter a daughter of Jacob Smyser, and born March 19, 1815; the former was also born in West Manchester Township, February 12, 1809, and died March 28, 1884. The paternal grandfather of Mr. Ebert was Adam Ebert, also a native of York County. The Ebert family has been identified with the history of this county for more than 100 years. Our subject was educated at the public schools and at the York County Academy. In 1864 he began the merchant tailoring business in York, and continued until 1878, when he retired from this business and began dealing in real estate. The marriage of Mr. Ebert occurred June 7, 1870, to Miss Mary L. Sheller, daughter of Dr. Sheller, of Lancaster County. They have three children, viz.: A. Laura, Ella V. and Harry Sheller. Politically Mr. Ebert is a Republican. Mr. Ebert is a member of the Lutheran Church and Mrs. Ebert is a member of the Presbyterian Church.

EDWARD EBNER, of the firm of B. Noedel & Co., York, was born in Neun Kirchen, Austria, in 1848. His parents were Franz X., and Anna (Hasslauer) Ebner, natives of the same country, and for over thirty-five years engaged in the hotel business there; they are both deceased. Edward was educated, and until 1875 engaged in the mercantile trade in his native country. Immigrating to America, he located in Philadelphia, where he remained seven years, the five last years of which he was the manager of Charles Engel's restaurant. In 1882 he came to York and became associated, as partner, with B. Noedel, and in this connection he has remained up to the present time. Mr. Ebner was married in 1882 to Mrs. Mary A. Boll, widow of Jacob W. Boll, late of York. Mrs. Ebner's maiden name was Mary A. Brasch, and she is a native of York County. They are members of St. Mary's Catholic Church.

CAPT. WILLIAM F. EICHAR, book-keeper, is a native of Mount Pleasant, Penn., born December 8, 1841, to Henry and Catherine (Lichty) Eichar. He is one of a numerous family and is of German descent. He remained in his native township until 1861, when he enlisted in Company B, Twenty-eighth Pennsylvania Volunteers, for three years. He participated in the battles of Antietam, South Mountain, Boliver Heights and many other minor engagements. He was honorably discharged in 1864, and the following year came to York, where he has since lived. Soon after his removal to York he accepted a position in the employ of A. B. Farquhar, and here continues. He is one of the most competent and exact accountants in York, and enjoys the supreme confidence of his employers. He was married in 1864 to Miss Eliza B. Welty, who bore him six children. Mrs. Eichar died in 1879, and the following year Mr. Eichar was united in marriage to Miss Maria C. Buckingham, a native of York County. One child has been born to this union. Mr. Eichar is a member of the Republican party. In 1878 he was elected assessor of the Second Ward. He is a member of the G. A. R., Sedgewick Post,

No. 37. Mr. and Mrs. Eichar are members of the Methodist Episcopal Church.

HENRY W. EISENHART, foreman of the wood department of A. B. Farquhar's, was born in Adams County, Penn., in 1839, is a son of George and Mary (Wolf) Eisenhart and is of German extraction. His parents were born in York County, his father in 1805 and his mother in 1808. His paternal grandfather was Conrad Eisenhart, a native of York County. When Henry W. was about four years of age he was by his parents removed from Adams County to Paradise Township, York County, where he obtained a common school education. In 1858 he began learning the carpenter trade, and in 1861 went to Harrisburg and there continued his trade for about one year. He then came to York and remained a short time and then went to his native county. In 1865 he returned to York, and for five years was in the employ of Shireman, Hoffeins & Co. In 1873 he accepted his present position, and is the oldest foreman now in the employ of A. B. Farquhar & Co., has charge of sixty-five men. He was married in 1863 to Miss Kate Nickey, a native of Adams County, and a daughter of John Nickey. They have one child, Albertus G. Politically Mr. Eisenhart is a Democrat, and became an Odd Fellow in 1857. Mr. and Mrs. Eisenhart are members of the Reformed Church.

C. A. EISENHART, D. D. S., was born in York County in 1844. His early life was passed as an assistant upon his father's farm until sixteen years of age, attending in the meantime the schools of his native county. Prior to his removal to Marshall, Mich., he was a teacher in the schools of West Manchester Township. A natural inclination for the profession of dentistry led him to become a student, and his close application and determined spirit enabled him to master it in all of its details. In 1860 he formed a co-partnership with Dr. Eggleston, which relationship was mutually beneficial, and the success of our subject farther advanced. Upon the dissolution of this firm Dr. Eisenhart returned to York, where he has since been in constant and continual practice. The success of Dr. Eisenhart has not been confined to the practical duties of his profession, but has extended into the field of invention. He made application for a patent upon a method for the application of electricity to supersede the use of anæsthetics in extracting and filling teeth. This invention has been wonderfully successful, and has met with a large sale among the dental profession, and has extended the fame of Dr. Eisenhart, and placed him among the leading dentists of Pennsylvania. Dr. Eisenhart is a citizen of worth and progression in all matters of public advancement. He has been a school director seven years, and president of the board of education, and interested in the Safe and Lock Works, and is president of the Park Loan & Building Association. December 5, 1872, he was united in wedlock with Miss Emma C., daughter of Charles and Catherine (Weiser) Pfahler, and a native of York County. They have four children: William S., Luther P., Jacob C. and Harry W. The family are members of the Lutheran Church, of which Dr. Eisenhart has been a teacher in the Sabbath-school for over ten years.

F. J. ELICK, proprietor of Elick's Tobacco Emporium, was born in Philadelphia in 1850, and is a son of Christopher and Margaret (Walter) Elick. The parents of Mr. Elick were born in Germany and immigrated to America, and settled in Philadelphia, where the family resided until about 1853, when they removed to York. The subject of this sketch was educated at the public schools, and afterward learned the confectioner's trade, which he continued for some time, and then served an apprenticeship at the barber's trade. In 1870 he began business for himself. In 1881 he added to his barbering business a complete line of choice tobaccos and smoker's supplies, and made a specialty of meerschaum pipes. Mr. Elick was married in 1870 to Miss Emma Hildebrand, of York County. They have two children: Laura and Mabel. Mr. Elick is a Mason and a member of the I. O. O. F.

PHILIP H. EMIG was born in Codorus Township, July 12, 1832, and is a son of Philip and Sarah (Shaffer) Emig. He is the seventh in a family of nine children, and is of German-English origin. His great-grandfather emigrated from Germany, and settled in North Codorus Township. His grandfather was Michael Emig. For more than 150 years the Emig family has been known in York County. His father was born in Codorus Township, and his mother in York. The father died in 1846, and the mother in 1879. When our subject was about ten years of age he came to York, and here has since resided. At the age of fourteen years he began learning the shoemaker's trade, which he has since continued. The marriage of Mr. Emig occurred December 16, 1852, to Miss Ellen E. Beck, a native of York, Penn. To this union have been born six children, viz.: Calvin J., Virginia M., Mary E., Harry F., Sarah Kate and Emma. Politically Mr. Emig is a Republican. He has been a Sabbath-school teacher for more than twenty-five years, and is a highly esteemed citizen.

DAVID EMMITT has for over half a century been identified with the business interests of York. He was born in York, January 27, 1819, and is a son of Jacob and Lydia (Ilgenfritz) Emmitt, of Irish and German descent. His father, who was a relative of Robert Emmitt, of Ireland, was one of the early men of York, and a soldier of the war of 1812, belonging to the "Independent Blues," a company of 200 men, of Baltimore. He was an active and respected citizen, and a resident of York until his death in 1865. The subject of this sketch received a good education, having the advantage of the schools of York and the York County Academy. He early learned the trade of carpenter, and followed that occupation from 1836 to 1849, when he embarked in the grocery business, on the corner of Beaver and Philadelphia Streets, at which he has since been successfully engaged. Mr. Emmitt is a charter member of the Mt. Zion Lodge, No. 74, I. O. O. F., and a man who has done much to develop the moral interests of his native town. He has been identified for more than thirty-five years with St. Paul's Lutheran Church, and over thirty years as a member of the church council. He has been an active member and a liberal giver for all projects of true moral worth. In 1847 he was married to Miss Mary E. Rauss, daughter of Luke and Mary L. (Beitzel) Rauss. She was born in York, July 22, 1822, and is a descendant of families that have been long identified with the history of York County.

MICHAEL H. ENGLE was born in Ridgeville, Lancaster Co., Pa., September 21, 1851, is a son of Daniel M. and Mary (Hoffman) Engel, of Swiss-German descent. His parents were born in Lancaster County. Our subject received a common school education at Millersville, Penn. In 1870 he began the tobacco business, and in 1878 came to York, and continued that business. He was married in 1874 to Miss Melvina A. Blake, a native of York County. They have three children: N. D., Mary M. and M. R. Mrs. Engle is engaged in the millinery and notion business, and at her store can be found at all times a full stock of choice goods. Mr. Engle is a Republican.

D. M. ETTINGER, civil engineer, and native of Hopewell Township, was born September 12, 1806, to Adam and Elizabeth (Miller) Ettinger. He is one of fourteen children and is of old German

BIOGRAPHICAL SKETCHES.

stock. The parents of Mr. Ettinger were both born in York County. His father died in 1877 and his mother, in 1855. His maternal grandfather was a soldier in the Revolutionary war. At an early age, D.M. Ettinger began teaching school and continued to teach for about thirty years, and was one of the most successful teachers of the day and one of the most popular York County ever had. For fourteen years he was a teacher in the York County High School. In 1853 he was employed by the Chicago & Northwestern Railway, as civil engineer. For over forty years he has been acting in the capacity of surveyor and engineer, and is unquestionably one of the most accurate civil engineers of Pennsylvania. Mr. Ettinger was married, in 1880, to Miss Lovinia Toomy, a native of York County. To this marriage were born seven children, viz.: Alvina, Martin L., Sarah, Josephine (deceased), Newton (deceased), Daniel (deceased), and Paul (deceased). Mrs. Ettinger died October 4, 1882. Mr. Ettinger was formerly a Whig but is now a thorough Republican. Although he is passing into the "sere and yellow leaf," his years sit lightly upon him.

ELIAS EYSTER, proprietor of the Eyster House, was born in Jackson Township, York Co., Penn., in 1840. His parents, Peter and Sarah E. (Spangler) Eyster were both born in York County, the father in 1811 and the mother in 1814. The Eysters are of Swiss origin, and our subject is the second in a family of five children. His paternal grandfather was a soldier in the Revolutionary war. The mother of Mr. Eyster died in 1859 and his father in 1871. Mr. Eyster worked for his father on the farm until his nineteenth year, when he began farming for himself, and this he continued until 1870, when he removed to York and began the hotel business, in what was known as the American House, but in 1877 the name was changed to that of Eyster House which it has since borne. During the years 1871 and 1872, Mr. Eyster was engaged in the iron ore business at Roth's Ore Bank. In 1880 he was engaged in the manufacture of washing machines, in partnership with Messrs. Booker and Baer. He was united in marriage in 1861 to Miss Sarah A. Stover, a native of Jackson Township. They have three children: Emma J., Elmyra E. and Peter E. Mr. Eyster is a Democrat and manifests much interest in general politics. In 1872 he was made a member of the Masonic fraternity.

ROBERT J. FISHER. A large part of the judicial history of York County, is inseparably associated with the career of Hon. Robert J. Fisher, who, for more than thirty years, presided over its courts. On the 4th day of November, 1828, when twenty-two years of age, he was admitted to practice in the several courts of York County. He had received a thorough legal education, at the Yale Law School, New Haven, Conn., and in the office of his father, a widely known and honored attorney of Harrisburg. For twenty-three years he worked diligently at the bar, attaching to himself by his integrity and ability a large clientage and a host of friends. In 1851, he was elected to the bench of the Nineteenth Judicial District, composed then of the counties of York and Adams. Being twice re-elected (1861 and 1871), he was, until 1875, the only law judge of the two counties, accomplishing a vast amount of labor, and rendering with promptness and widely recognized learning, decisions which have commanded general respect. His rulings have almost universally been upheld by the appellate tribunals, and his opinions have been quoted as an authority, in this and other States, with more frequency than those of almost any other contemporaneous *nisi prius* judge. Although an earnest Democrat, during his official career, he carefully abstained from all connection with politics. Judge Fisher possessed, in an unusual degree, the rare ability of viewing a question impartially and deciding on principle unaffected by prejudice or fear. Particularly was this characteristic strikingly illustrated in his course during the Rebellion. Now that the intense excitement and intolerant partisanship of the time have passed away, his undeviating adherence to the established principles of the common law, appears most admirable. Though a decided and uncompromising Unionist, he was, nevertheless, determined in his opposition to every unwarrantable encroachment of the military upon the civil power. When passion and fear deprived others of their judgment, he seems never to have lost his cool discretion, either in the presence of Federal soldiers or rebel invaders. On one occasion, a citizen had been illegally arrested by the military authorities at the hospital on the commons, and a writ of *habeas corpus* was taken out in his behalf. Upon its return, the prisoner was brought into court by a squad of soldiers with fixed bayonets. That show of force, however, failed to affect the action of the Court. Promptly he required the soldiers to recognize civil authority, saying that as citizens they had a right to be there, but as armed men they must withdraw. After a hearing the prisoner was released. At the time of the Confederate occupation of York, in 1863, the rebel commander sent to Judge Fisher for the keys of the court house. He replied that he did not have them, and that the commissioners were the only legal custodians of the public buildings; upon another summons being sent, however, he went with the messenger and found that the soldiers had in some way obtained admission to the prothonotary's office and were preparing to destroy the records there deposited. As the chief judicial magistrate of the county, he warmly expostulated against the destruction of these valuable evidences, the loss of which would be irremediable. The General, at first said it would be only be just retaliation for the depredations of the northern armies in the South, but after a long discussion, the judge compelled him to acknowledge the unlawfulness of all such acts of useless plunder, and persuaded him to withdraw his men. The records and valuable documents of the county were thus saved by the coolness and firmness of the venerable judge. There are several other occasions, which many citizens recall during those turbulent times, when he showed like remarkable courage, facing mobs with fearless dignity, and with unusual mildness, but at the same time unusual determination, maintaining order and insisting upon the supremacy of the civil law. Judge Fisher comes of one of the oldest and most respectable families of the State. Born in Harrisburg, May 6, 1806, he is the son of George Fisher, Esq., and Ann Shipper, daughter of Robert Strettell Jones of Burlington, N. J. He was baptized Robert Strettell Jones Fisher, but dropped the second name early in life. His maternal grandfather was a member of the New Jersey Legislature, and secretary of the Committee of Safety in 1776. His great-grandfather, Isaac Jones, was twice mayor of Philadelphia (1767 and 1768), and a member of the common council in 1764. His great-great-grandfather Fisher was one of the original company of Quakers, who came from England with William Penn, in 1682, and who laid out the city of Philadelphia. His grandfather, George Fisher, received from his father a large tract of land in Dauphin County, upon which he laid out the borough of Middletown. Judge Fisher was twice married, and in the quiet scenes of domestic life he always experienced great satisfaction. His first wife, Catharine, daughter of Horatio Gates Jameson, M. D., became the mother of eight children, and died in 1850. In 1853 he married Mary Sophia, daughter of Ebenezer Cadwell of Northbridge, Mass., who bore him two children. His eldest son, George Fisher, Esq., is a well established member of the York County bar, and his other son, Robert J. Fisher, Jr., having been for several years connected with the patent office, is now one of the three examiners-in-chief. In matters of religion, Judge Fisher has always been eminently catholic. From childhood, his associations have been largely with the Protestant Episcopal denominations, although particularly charitable toward those of different faith and order, and a frequent attendant at their services. In 1870, he became a communicant member of St. John's Church in York, has been for many years a vestryman, and was the first chancellor of the diocese of central Pennsylvania.

GEORGE FISHER, attorney at law, was born at York, Penn., on the 29th of September, 1836, and is a son of Hon. Robert J. Fisher, and his wife Catharine, who was a daughter of Horatio Gates Jameson, Sr., M. D., a distinguished surgeon and physician of Baltimore. In April, 1847, George was entered as a student at the York County Academy, then under the direction of the venerable Rev. Stephen Boyer. From 1851 to 1853, he was a student at Sherwood School, at that time a flourishing institution of learning in the vicinity of York, under the direction of Maj. Bland, who was at one time an officer in the British Army of that rank. From 1853 to 1854, he was a student at the Collegiate Institute, Northampton, Mass. In 1854 he was admitted to the class of 1859, at Yale College. In October, 1856, he removed to Iowa City, and held a position in the office of Hon. Elijah Sells, then secretary of state of Iowa. In 1857 he commenced the study of the law in York under the direction of his father, Hon. Robert J. Fisher, who was then and had been for several years, and for more than twenty years afterward, president judge of the Nineteenth Judicial District of Pennsylvania, and in 1859 he was admitted to the bar of the county of York. In 1863 he was clerk to the board of revenue commissioners of the State of Pennsylvania. Said board was abolished by act of the General Assembly approved April 12, 1864, and the powers thereof vested in the State treasurer, auditor-general, and secretary of the commonwealth. In 1869 he removed to Stroudsburg, Monroe Co., Penn., and engaged in the practice of the law. In 1872 he was a candidate for district attorney of Monroe County. There being four candidates before the people for the office, he failed of an election by forty votes. In 1873 he returned to York and resumed the practice of the law there. In 1875-76 he was a clerk of the house of representatives of Pennsylvania, and during part of the session of 1877, journal clerk. In 1871 Mr. Fisher married Mary, daughter of Robert Barry, of Baltimore, Md., and continues to reside and practice his profession in York.

JOEL E. FISHER, carpenter and builder, was born in York County, April 8, 1836, and is a son of Seth and Mary (Ratcliff) Fisher. He is one of a numerous family, and is of English extraction. His father was born in York in 1798, and his mother was born in Virginia. At seventeen years of age he began learning the carpenter's trade and this has been his life work. In 1866 he was married to Miss Christiana R. Gotwalt, daughter of Jacob Gotwalt, of York. To this marriage have been born four children, viz.: William H., Charles A., Annie C. and Mary E. He is a Republican and a member of the Lutheran Church, of which his wife is also a member. Mr. Fisher, though in the humble walks of life, is an influential and highly respected citizen.

F. F. FLINCHBAUGH is a son of F. F. and Mary (Kindig) Flinchbaugh of Hopewell Township, where our subject was born February 18, 1818, and was reared on a farm. He received a limited education, as school advantages were very poor when he was a boy. His first regular work was for the firm of P. A. & S. Small, and it is worthy of mention here that Mr. Flinchbaugh remained in the service of this firm forty-eight years, nine months and sixteen days, and as an evidence of their appreciation of his long and faithful service they presented him with an elegant gold watch. Some of the newspapers of York gave full account of the event at the time it occurred. Mr. F. was married three times. His first wife was Sarah Corpman, of York, who bore him one child, Catherine (deceased); his second wife was Mary Morthland. Five children were born to this union: Annie M. E., Emma E., Lyddie, William R. (deceased), Frederick M. (deceased). His third wife was Louisa Feiser, and to this marriage were born Frederick L., Ellsie R. and an infant boy (deceased). Mr. Flinchbaugh is a prominent member of the First United Brethren Church. He was the first member of the First United Brethren Church as well as the oldest.

S. S. FLINCHBAUGH, a native of Hopewell Township, is a son of Samuel D. and Lydia (Strayer) Flinchbaugh, and was born in 1848. The father was a farmer of Hopewell until 1868, and died in York Township, in 1876; his widow is still living. S. S. Flinchbaugh, the eighth of ten children, remained on the farm until twenty-one years old, and then for six years taught school in different localities. He next farmed a year or more, and then, in 1877, commenced the manufacture and sale of cigars in York Township; in 1878, he manufactured for six months in Dallastown, and then returned to York Township and employed five or six hands in his business. In 1881, he moved his headquarters to York Borough, and for one year was located on George Street. In 1882, he built his present factory at 126 and 128 Maple Street, where, and at his branch in York Township, he employs from thirty to forty hands. In addition to manufacturing cigars, he deals largely in leaf tobacco, and has been altogether successful in his business transactions. He was married in 1881, to Miss Alice Scratz, from Lower Windsor. Mr. and Mrs. Flinchbaugh are members of the United Brethren Church, and Mr. Flinchbaugh has served as Assessor of York Township.

SILAS H. FORRY was born in York, Penn., on September 26, 1838. He is the son of Abraham Forry, who was a prominent citizen of York, and five times elected to the office of chief burgess. He died in October, 1872, leaving to survive him Silas H. Forry and Elizebeth A. Forry, who was afterward married to Col. William L. Peiper, of Lancaster City, now deceased. The subject of this sketch passed his earlier life in the common schools and subsequently, for several years, was a pupil of the York County Academy, where he graduated at the age of eighteen. Having selected the practice of law as his profession he entered the office of V. K. Keesey, Esq., a prominent and well-known lawyer of York, under whose instructions he was qualified for admission to the bar. On May 28, 1861, having passed a creditable examination, he was admitted to the bar, and immediately thereafter commenced the practice of law in York, and has continued therein up to the present time. Being a Republican he has never held any political office in Democratic York County, although in 1866 he received the nomination, by his party, as district attorney for the county. He was one of the organizers of the Western National Bank, of York, in which he served as director for several years. He subsequently became a director in the Farmers' National Bank, of York, in which capacity he still is serving. In 1865 he was elected secretary of the York County Mutual Insurance Company, and has filled that office ever since; he is also the legal solicitor of this company. Mr. Forry was united in marriage with Miss Lucy A., daughter of William and Susan Hoke, of York

County. From this union have been born five children, three of whom are living, viz.: Mary Sue, Bessie and Lucy A. Forry. Mr. Forry has alway staken an active interest in St. Paul's Lutheran Church, of which he is a member. He has served as deacon of this church and has taken a leading part in the Sunday-school work.

DAVID P. FRANK was born in Hanover, Pennsylvania, and is a son of Peter and Elizabeth (Graybill) Frank. He received his education in the schools of Hanover; was apprenticed and learned the blacksmith trade with his father, and after becoming a proficient and skillful workman, engaged at his trade in Hanover until 1881, when he removed to York. Here he has established a blacksmith and agricultural implement repair shop, and is widely known and doing a thriving business in his line. Mr. Frank was united in marriage April 27, 1882, with Miss Emma H., daughter of Henry Myers, of York.

ALEXANDER J. FREY (deceased), was a native of York, born in 1818 to Jacob and Catherine (Hoover) Frey. He was the fifth in a family of six children, and was of German extraction. He attended the early schools of York and received a good common school education. In early life he served an apprenticeship at the hatter's trade, and subsequently began the manufacture of hats upon his own responsibility, and this he successfully continued for many years. He was for more than twenty years a director of the York National Bank. He was a man of excellent business qualifications, and one of the most successful business representatives of this section of Pennsylvania. Politically he was a Democrat until 1850, and during the latter portion of his life, he was identified with the Republican party and took a prominent part in all questions of State and national issue. He was postmaster at York during Lincoln's administration, and managed the affairs of that position successfully. The marriage of Mr. Frey was solemnized in 1845 to Miss Sophia Schall, of York, a daughter of Joseph and Mary Schall, and born in 1819. To Mr. and Mrs. Frey were born seven children, viz.: Isabel, Joseph, Emma, Mary, Benton, John and Anna. Mr. Frey died in 1882, a leading member of St. Paul's Church. Mrs. Frey is also a member of that denomination.

WILLIAM FRYSINGER, manufacturer and dealer in carpets, is a native of Hanover, York County, born in 1821 and is a son of George and Elizabeth Frysinger, also natives of the county. The father was in the iron trade and manufacturer of carriages. William learned the printer's trade which he followed only a short time in Hanover. Came to York in 1840, where he has since resided. First engaged at merchandising with John Stine until 1854. He then continued the business with John F. Stine until 1868. He then commenced the carpet trade; he commenced the manufacture in 1872, and has increased since. He sold out the retail trade in 1883, and is now devoting his entire time to manufacturing. He has in employ about 100 skilled hands, and has in all about 800 hands manufacturing rag and jute carpets. His works are the largest in the world in this line. He ships all over the United States, using 300 tons of new rags per annum and 150,000 pounds of cotton and woolen yarns; sales amounting to $150,000 per annum. Mr. Frysinger married, in 1842, Henrietta Stine, of York. They have five children: Francis, Horatio, Elizabeth, Hettie and Alice. Mr. Frysinger and wife are members of the Methodist Episcopal Church, Mr. Frysinger having been a member over forty years.

ELI F. GROVE, agent of Singer Sewing Machine Company, was born in Hopewell Township, York County, in 1852. He is the son of Henry and Mary (Strayer) Grove, natives of the county. He came to York in 1872 and engaged in the sewing machine business (Howe agency), and has been for the past nine years agent for the Singer Machine Company for York and Adams Counties. They have a branch at Gettysburg. Mr. Grove was married in 1877 to Lucy Peeling, of York. Has always done a large trade and is an enterprising young man. He has devoted his entire time to his business, and established a large trade, having eight wagons, and has sold up to the present time over 8,000 machines.

S. M. GABLE, wholesale and retail druggist, was born in Windsor Township, York County, March 21, 1847, to Valentine and Mary (Miller) Gable. Subject's father was born in Hopewell Township in 1809, and his mother the same year in Windsor Township. This family has been prominently connected with the history of York County for more than a century. The early life of our subject was spent in his native township. At eighteen years of age he began teaching school in Spring Garden Township. There he remained two years and then went to Lancaster County, and continued teaching for a number of years, and in the meantime he attended the State Normal School at Millersville. In 1872 he came to York and taught one year, and then went to New Albany, Ind., remained two years and then returned to York and in 1879 began the drug business. He has one of the choicest lines of drugs to be found in York, and his store is a credit to the town. In 1883 he graduated from the Maryland College of Pharmacy, at Baltimore. He was married Centennial year to Miss Alice Peeling, a native of York Township, and daughter of John Peeling. Mr. Gable was for many years one of the leading teachers of Pennsylvania. He still manifests great interest in the cause of education. Mr. and Mrs. Gable are members of the Methodist Episcopal Church.

I. C. GABLE, M. D., whose portrait, as one of the leading representative physicians of York, appears in this work. is a native of York County and was born in Windsor Township June 26, 1849. His ancestors, who were of German and Swiss descent, immigrated to America about the middle of the seventeenth century; his paternal grandfather was a soldier in the American Revolution and fought under Gen. Anthony Wayne in the war against the Indians. The subject of our sketch received his preliminary education in his native county and in the State Normal School at Millersville, Lancaster County. In 1867 he began teaching in the schools of Spring Garden Township, and subsequently became the principal of the schools of Port Royal, Juniata County, Penn., and Murray, Ind. On July 4, 1871, Dr. Gable began a tour through the Western States and the Indian Territory, acting a portion of the time as a newspaper correspondent. After three years' travel, visiting the leading cities and towns and gathering much useful information, he determined to return to York and engaged in the profession of medicine. With Dr. J. W. Kerr, of York, he finished a course of preliminary reading, and in September, 1875, he went to Philadelphia and under the preceptorship of Dr. Charles T. Hunter, late chemical surgeon in the University of Pennsylvania, continued his studies in that city until he was graduated from the university March 12, 1877, subsequently taking a post graduate course in his alma mater, devoting most of his time to the special study of general surgery in that institution and in the surgical dispensary of the Pennsylvania Hospital. Dr. Gable located for practice in York in November, 1877, where he has since been actively engaged and has established a most successful general practice. His special professional taste, however, apparently inclines in favor of surgery. He is a young man of untiring energy and a devoted student to his chosen profession. In person Dr. Gable is a genial gentleman and thoroughly progressive; is a member of the National State and County Medical Association, and a member of the Presbyterian Church of York.

A. F. GEESEY, ex-treasurer of York County, was born in York Township, this county, November 21, 1841, son of Jonathan and Sarah (Flinchbaugh) Geesey. He is one of a family of ten children and is of Swiss extraction. His parents were also born in York County, Penn. The father was born in 1809 and died in 1877, and the mother was born in 1807. The paternal grandfather of our subject was born in this county. The Geesey family came to York County in 1732 and made settlement about eight miles southeast of York. A. F. Geesey worked on the farm until seventeen years of age, and then in a store for two years, after which he began teaching school. In 1864 he enlisted in Company K, One Hundred and Third Pennsylvania Veterans, and served one year. Upon returning home he taught school one year and then engaged in general merchandising at Dallastown, York Co., Penn., which he continued nine years. In 1876 he came to York, Penn., where he has since resided. Mr. Geesey has always been a Democrat, and for several years has been one of the leaders of that party in York County. In 1878 he was elected treasurer of York County. In 1866 he married B. Ellen Howis, a native of this county, and they have one child, Clarence A. Mr. Geesey is a Mason. He and his wife are members of the Lutheran Church.

DANIEL L. GLATFELTER, son of Elijah and Mary (Lefever) Glatfelter, was born in York County, April ,18, 1846, was educated at the public schools, and until the age of fifteen years assisted on the home farm. He then began life on his own account, and is now one of the most successful farmers in the township. In 1881 he formed a co-partnership with John Waltz and William Miller, erected a building at York, procured the proper machinery and engaged in the manufacture of paint; he still retains his interest in this business in conjunction with his extensive farming interests. In November, 1870, Mr. Glatfelter married Miss Annie, daughter of George Pfaltzgraff.

GEORGE GRAYBILL is a native of York County, born in 1846, and son of Samuel and Christianna (Zeigler) Graybill, both natives of the county. His father was a farmer and horticulturist of West Manchester. He died August, 1882. Mother died about 1856; four children were born to them, our subject being the youngest. He was reared on a farm and nursery until fourteen years of age. He received a good education in the common schools and the York County Academy, At the age of fifteen, he commenced to learn the milling trade, at which he was employed until 1862, when he enlisted in Company A, One Hundred and Sixty-sixth Regiment,Pennsylvania Volunteer Infantry,as corporal, and was with regiment until it was mustered out July, 1863. He was a participant in the following engagements: siege of Suffolk, Carrsville, Franklin, Black Water River and several minor engagements. He then went to a military school for a few months in Philadelphia, and in August, 1864, he re-enlisted in the Two Hundredth Pennsylvania Volunteer Infantry as private, and was promoted to first sergeant, serving with this regiment until May 1865, taking part in various engagements, Petersburg, Fort Steadman, Hatches Run, Jerusalem Plank Road, Fort Hell, capture of Petersburg and the surrender of Gen. Lee. In April 18, 1865, he was commissioned second lieutenant of the Third United States colored troops, and served until November, 1865. Upon his return he went to Reading and graduated from the People's Business College. Return-

ing to York, he was engaged as a clerk, until 1870, when he engaged in the fire and life insurance business, at which he has since been engaged. He represents nine fire, two life, and one-plate glass company—all good companies representing $28,000,-000 capital. Mr. Graybill is an active business man and does large business. He has served on the town council. He has been an officer in various militia organizations and is now State treasurer and member of the executive committee of the State Volunteer Fire Association, and president of the Fireman's Union of York.

D. K. GOTWALD, M. D., is a son of Rev. L. A. Gotwald, D. D., and Mary A. (King) Gotwald, of York, and was born in Cumberland County, Penn., in 1860. He received his education in York, attending the academy and college, subsequently entering the drug store of H. C. Blair's Sons of Philadelphia, where he remained two years. Deciding upon the profession of medicine, he entered the office of Dr. Jacob Hay, remained under his instructions until he graduated from the University of Pennsylvania, receiving the first prize, in 1882. He then entered the Philadelphia Hospital, where he remained one year. In 1883 he commenced the practice of his chosen profession in York, where he is still engaged. Dr. Gotwald is a member of the York County Medical Society, and a young man of promise. He was united in marriage September 6, 1883, with Miss Julia Kurtz, daughter of William H. Kurtz of York. They have one child.

H. J. GRESLY, green-grocer and provision dealer, was born in York in 1834, son of Andrew and Rosanna (Schrum) Gresly, and is of German origin. He is the eldest in a family of eight children. His father was born in Baden, Germany, in 1801, and his mother in Wurtemburg, in 1803. The Gresly family came to America in 1832, and settled in western Pennsylvania for a time and subsequently came to York County. By occupation the father of Mr. Gresly was a butcher. He died in York. in 1882. The mother died in 1858. The subject of this biography was reared in York, and here he attended the common schools. He learned the butcher's trade with his father. In 1853 he entered the United States Navy and for three years and four months was on the United States Frigate "Savannah," on the coast of Brazil. In 1856 he came to America and in 1857 went to Decorah, Iowa, and there engaged in the butchering business, and there remained until 1859, when he returned to York. In 1862 he again joined the United States Navy, and was on the United States steamship "New Ironsides." Serving fourteen months he returned to York and engaged in his present business, which he has since continued. He has also been, and is engaged in the cattle business. The marriage of Mr. Gresly was solemnized in 1857, to Miss Anna M. Jamison, of York, Penn. To this union were born four children, as follows: David A., Bertha L., Nellie G. and R. J. Mrs. Gresly died in 1874, and in 1880 Mr. Gresly was married to Miss Mary H. Snyder, of Hanover, Penn. Politically Mr. Gresly is a Republican. In 1879 he was elected chief burgess of York and re-elected in 1882. He is the only Republican elected to this office in York since 1862. He is a member of the G. A. R., and of the Lutheran Church. He is a successful and leading citizen. Mr. Gresly had a brother killed in the Mountain Meadow massacre in Utah, in 1857, and another brother died in the famous prison at Andersonville in 1864.

JOHN K. GROSS, passenger and freight agent for the Pennsylvania and Northern Central Railways, was born in Harrisburg, Penn., in 1845, son of D. W. and Elizabeth (Kunkel) Gross and is of French-Swiss extraction. His father was born near Harrisburg, Penn., in 1810, and his mother in the

BIOGRAPHICAL SKETCHES.

same vicinity in 1822, and died in 1882. The Gross and Kunkel families have long been recognized as early settlers of this part of the Pennsylvania commonwealth. John K. Gross was educated at Franklin and Marshall College, from which he graduated with honors in 1867, and then began the study of law in Harrisburg under the guidance of John C. Kunkle, who died soon afterward. Mr. Gross then continued his studies under Judge Simonton. In 1872 he came to York and the following year was appointed agent for the Pennsylvania and Northern Central Railway Companies at this place and has since held that position. In Mr. Gross the railway companies have a most faithful and trusted employe and under his administration their business has been greatly increased at this place. Mr. Gross was married in 1874 to Annie Mesick, daughter of Rev. John F. Mesick, who for many years was pastor of the Reformed Church of Harrisburg, Penn. They have four children: Elsie K., Janet P., John M. and Margaret Perrine. Mr. Gross is a Republican and for many years has taken much interest in State and national politics and has always been an earnest Cameron advocate. He is a Mason. Mr. and Mrs. Gross are members of the Presbyterian Church.

PROF. GEORGE W. GROSS, A. M., principal of the York County Academy, was born in Jackson Township, York County, Penn., January 17, 1856, son of Israel F. and Malinda (Hantz) Gross, and is of German descent. His parents were both born in this county, the father in 1832, and the mother in 1833. Our subject, at eight years of age, removed with his parents from Jackson Township to the town of York. He was educated at the public schools of York, the York County Academy and the Pennsylvania College at Gettysburg. He graduated from the last-named institution in 1877, and the same year began the study of the law in York under the direction of Henry L. Fisher. He was admitted to the York County Bar in 1879. In 1880 he was elected principal of the York County Academy to succeed Prof. G. W. Ruby. As an educator Prof. Gross, takes rank among the most prominent in York County. He is a Republican and is a member of the Lutheran Church.

JOHN H. HAMME, son of Jonas and Catherine (Eisenhart) Hamme, was born in Dover Township, March 6, 1838. He is the fifth of ten children: Annie, Eliza, Adam, Ellen, John H., George H. (deceased), William (deceased), Amanda, Martin and Rebecca. Mr. Hamme's mother was the daughter of Dr. George H. Eisenhart, of West Manchester Township, and she still lives, at the advanced age of eighty years, in the village of Dover, York County. November, 1871, Mr. Hamme married Sarah Bentzel, and this marriage was blessed with six children: Carrie C., William (deceased), Annie V., Shuman F., Harry L. and Minnie May. Mr. Hamme's occupation has always been farming, to which he was reared. He recently leased the Motler House in York.

HANTZ BROS. (B. Franklin and Charles F. Hantz), hardware merchants of York, are sons of Jacob Hantz, who, in 1842, was elected the first Whig sheriff of York county, and are of Swiss-German ancestry. John Nicholas Hantz married Anna Barbara Burghart in the province of Starkenburg, Sponheim County, Germany, in 1737. He died in the Fatherland, date unknown, and left four children, viz.: John Andreas, Maria Catrine, Mary Margaretta and Catrina Elizabeth. On June 22,1751,the widow of John Nicholas Hantz was married to John Peter Streher, and three years later the entire family set sail from Rotterdam, Holland, for America, and located in Dover Township among the first settlers. In 1758 John Peter Streher became one of the founders of the Dover Church, and at times, during the absence of ministers, was empowered by the Lutheran synod to officiate at certain religious services. He taught the first parochial school at the Dover Church. John Andreas Hantz, who accompanied the emigrant party in 1754, became the ancester of the Hantz family in America. One of his sons, Andrew Hantz, born in Dover Township, was married to Mary Sharp. They had children as follows: John, Jacob, Philip, Daniel, Joseph, Catharine, Susan and Mary Ann. Jacob Hantz, the second son, was born 1797, married Magdalena Hershey in 1821, and the same year began keeping Hantz's Hotel in York, now known as the Motler House, which, under him, was a very popular and well-kept house of public entertainment. He continued the business at the same stand until his election as sheriff of York County, which office he filled with signal ability. Afterward engaged in the hardware business, under the firm of Hantz, Frick & Co., at the stand now occupied by his sons. He died in 1868, and his sons then succeeded him. He left three sons: Henry A., B. Frank and Charles F. Henry A. Hantz married Henrietta L. Beeler. They have three daughters, viz.: Annie M. (married to Ivan Glossbrenner), Lucy H. (married to Edward Chapin, Esq.), and Mary A. (married to Robert Stair). B. Franklin (married to Rebecca Graybill of West Manchester Township). They have three children as follows: Charles Edward, Alice and Grant.

COL. GEORGE HAY, deceased, was born in York, Penn., August 1, 1809, and was a son of John and Susan (Smyser) Hay. He was the third in a family of seven children, and of German descent. He was a representative of an old-time family of this county, and here his father and grandfather were born. By occupation Mr. Hay was a cabinetmaker and undertaker, and this work he continued until his death, which occurred May 24, 1879. The marriage of Mr. Hay took place in 1830, to Miss Susan Demuth, a native of York County, and one of six children born to her parents, who were natives of York County. To Mr. and Mrs. Hay were born five children, only one of which survives the father, viz.: Amanda. Col. Hay was a brave and true soldier in the late war, and was also a member of the I. O. O. F., and of the Lutheran Church. He was a leading and prominent man, and greatly respected citizen of York.

SAMUEL HAY, ex-deputy sheriff, son of George and Susan (Schall) Hay, of York, Penn., was born September 16, 1810, in York Borough. He attended the borough school, and also the York County Academy, and afterward learned the trade of cigar making. January 31, 1833, he married Susan Wilt, daughter of Peter and Catherine (Ernst) Wilt, of York,Penn. Two children were born to them, Sarah (deceased wife of George Gardner), and Catherine (deceased wife of Hamilton Bletcher). Our subject's grandfather came from Germany, and was one of the early settlers of York. He owned all the land on which several hundred houses are now built on Queen, King, Princess Streets, and the surrounding neighborhood. Few men are better or more favorably known throughout York County than our subject, he having been deputy sheriff over twenty years, and a better or more efficient officer never held that position.

JACOB HAY, M. D., is a native of York, and was born in 1833. His parents were Dr. Jacob and Sarah (Beard) Hay, representing two families of early settlers in York County. His grandfather, whose name was also Jacob Hay, was an emigrant from Scotland to the province of Pennsylvania, early in the colonial period, and located in York, where he became a prominent merchant and justice of the peace. George Beard, his maternal grandfather, was one of the first immigrants that settled in the present region of Spring Garden Township, on land still occupied by the Indians to whom he gave a pick and shovel to please them and make his title doubly sure. The two occupations of farming and hotel keeping, were successfully followed by him. Dr. Jacob Hay, Sr., who for fifty-five years was a prominent and influential physician and public spirited citizen of York, after receiving an elementary education in his native town, entered Princeton College, at which institution he graduated. He read medicine with Dr. John Spangler of great local fame, and completed his course by graduating at the University of Maryland. For a number of years he was president of the York Bank, and a trustee of the York County Academy. He died in York, April, 1875, and his wife died in July of the same year. Both were members of the Lutheran Church. They had eight children, as follows: Dr. John, a successful physician who died at forty-two; Mary E., now widow of the late Dr. J. A. Brown, president of the Lutheran Theological Seminary, at Gettysburg; Caroline; Lucy, widow of W. H. Davis; Dr. Jacob; William, a graduate of Pennsylvania College, and many years a prominent member of the York bar. He was a presidential elector from this district, representing the Republican party in the campaign of 1876. He died at the early age of forty-seven, after a very successful career in the practice of his chosen profession. He was a gentleman of very high repute and universally esteemed for his manly virtues and estimable character. The two youngest children were Henry and Sarah, both deceased. Dr. Jacob Hay, who is now familiarly known in York Borough and through the county as a very extensive practitioner, spent his school-boy days in the York County Academy. After reading medicine in the office of his father, he entered the medical department of the University of Maryland, where he graduated in the spring of 1854; since that time he has been in continuous practice. He is a member of the National, State and County Medical Association, and was for a time president of the last named body; is a member of the Masonic order of Knight Templars, York Commandery. For a period of twelve years Dr. Hay has been an active member of the board of school control of York, and served as president of the board for several years. In 1865 he was married to Catherine Smyser, daughter of Joseph Smyser, of York. They have four children, namely: Nellie, Lucy, Joseph and Katie. Dr. Hay and family are members of the Lutheran Church.

DAVID HECKERT is a native of York, Penn., born in 1825, is a son of Jacob and Salome (Herbach) Heckert, is of German extraction and is traced authoratively to Francis Heckert, who was born in New Bamberg, in the kingdom of Bavaria, in 1703. His father's name was Conrad Heckert, a native of the same town. Francis Heckert was married February 25, 1728, to Miss Mary Margaretha Hilda Seymering, of Wallerthum, Bavaria. To this union were born three children as follows: Magdalena, John Jacob and John Peter. This family came to America in 1737, and settled in the territory that now comprises York County. The great-grandfather of our subject was John Jacob Heckert, born in Bavaria, April 13, 1730, and his grandfather was Jacob Heckert, who, one year (1775) prior to the Revolutionary war, was bound out to Lawrence Etter, of York Township, to learn the wagon-maker's trade. He was tax collector of York during the years 1793 and 1795, and member of the house of representatives 1812–13. The father of Mr. Heckert was born in York, August 21, 1791, and died October 2, 1871. The boyhood of our subject was spent in attending the early schools of York. His first tutor was a Mrs. Willis. At seventeen he began serving an apprenticeship to the tinner and coppersmith trades, and in September, 1847, he went to Baltimore, Md., and continued his trade for some time. In 1850 he went to Independence, Mo., and there remained seven months, and then removed to Memphis, Tenn., where he continued his trade more than one year, and then returned to his native town and county. Here, in 1855, he began business, in which he has since continued, the firm being now known as Heckert & Bros. In 1884 he erected his business and residence block on Lot No. 26 East Market Street. Politically he affiliates with the Republican party. Ancestors Lutheran. List of members for the house of representatives of commonwealth of Pennsylvania for the session of 1812–13 for York County: James S. Mitchell, Adam Hendricks, Peter Storm, Jacob Heckert. Officers for same term: George Heckert, clerk; Samuel D. Franks, assistant clerk; John Benjamin, sergeant-at-arms; Henry Lechler, doorkeeper. George Hecker's residence at that time was at Lancaster City. He was a lawyer by profession, and practiced law at Lancaster bar later on in life. He was a son of Jacob Heckert, who resided in Lancaster City till late in life. He had four children—three sons and one daughter. George the eldest lived to the age of eighty-six; Catharine, eighty-four; Jacob, eighty-one; Daniel, forty-seven. Daniel Heckert was a printer by profession in the year 1811. He was in connection with Updegraff, doing business under the firm name of Heckert & Updegraff. Published a paper called the *York Expositor*, issued weekly. In 1812 he enlisted in the company which went from York to the defense of Baltimore, and marched to North Point; was in the engagement at that place; died in 1829.

HEFFENER & SEACRIST, cigar-box manufacturers of York, are extensively known as prosperous business men. This industry was started in 1872 by H. W. Heffener, on a small scale, in the rear of College Avenue, then only employing four hands. Business increasing he moved to another location, where, with better facilities, he increased the number of his employes to fifteen hands. In 1879 he associated with his present partner, H. Seacrist. In 1881 they removed to their present location on Charles Avenue, where they erected a building sixty-three feet long and thirty-two feet wide, especially adapted to their business. They have since added two new apartments, increasing their force to the extent of employing fifty workmen, and use a twenty-horse power engine, running four saws. The capacity of their establishment is 25,000 boxes weekly, which are made principally of cedar and poplar. They expend $2,000 per month for label paper and their trade is extended over Pennsylvania and Maryland. Messrs. Heffener & Seacrist are both practical workmen and superintend their business personally; the success that has attended their efforts is the result of faithful application to business and honorable methods; their business is rapidly increasing.

H. W. HEFFENER, the senior member of the firm, was born in York in 1845, and is a son of William H. and Charlotte (Reika) Heffener, natives of Germany, who settled in York the same year our subject was born. At the age of sixteen he enlisted in Company G, Ninth Pennsylvania Veteran Cavalry, and soon after his regiment was placed under Gen. Kilpatrick's command, the only Pennsylvania Cavalry in Sherman's famous march from Atlanta to the sea. He participated in all of the engagements and skirmishes of his regiment from Atlanta, Ga., to Morrisonville, N. C., where he saw Gen. Joseph E. Johnston's force surrender, and remained with Sherman's army until the close of the war. At Waynesboro, his horse was shot dead from under him. He was one of the 100 men selected to carry important dispatches from Gen. Kilpatrick to Gen.

BIOGRAPHICAL SKETCHES.

Sherman. They performed the daring act of piercing the Confederate lines, and passing through them to their general (Sherman) in command. This was considered one of the most daring acts of the war, and richly merits the admiration of all. The Ninth captured during its service some 8,000 prisoners and twenty-eight pieces of artillery, and destroyed hundreds of miles of railroad and bridges. The Ninth was known as Krider's Mounted Rangers, and did scout duty for all the prominent generals in the department of Kentucky. Mr. Heffener was one of thirty scouts under the famous "Kentucky Bill," that burnt the house of Gen. Battle, where all the guerillas had their headquarters, and were commanded by a son of the General. After being mustered out at Harrisburg, our subject returned to York and followed the trade of painting until 1868. He then became a fireman on the Northern Central Railroad, until he engaged at his present business. He is a member of the G. A. R., a member of the town council of York, vice-president of the Anchor Building Association, a director in the Protective Building Association, and a member of the Rescue Fire Company. Mr. Heffener was married to Miss Rebecca Brenner, of Adams County, in April, 1883. They have one child, George W. Heffener.

H. SEACRIST, the second member of this firm, was born in Manchester Township, in 1838. He is the son of Henry and Martha (Dailey) Seacrist; the father is a native of the county, and the mother of Maryland. Our subject was educated in the schools of the county, and at the age of nineteen learned the carpenter's trade, which he followed until 1879, when he embarked in his present business. Mr. Seacrist is an efficient business man, and gives his entire attention to its requirements. He was united in marriage, in 1858, with Miss Susan Stough, a daughter of David Stough, whose ancestors were among the first German settlers in that section of the county, immigrating about 1750. Mr. Seacrist and wife have three children: Henry C., Sarah N. and Emma J. The family are members of the Reformed Church.

J. D. HEIGES, D. D. S., son of Jacob and Elizabeth (Mumper) Heiges, was born in September, 1833. His father was a chair manufacturer and cabinet-maker of Dillsburg. J. D. Heiges assisted his father until 1854, when he began the study of dentistry under Dr. Beuny, of Mechanicsburg, Cumberland Co., Penn., with whom he remained several years; then came to York and engaged with Dr. Thomas Tyrrell, with whom he remained until the fall of 1858, when he entered the Baltimore Dental College. After attending the first sessions, he took up the practice of dentistry, and subsequently returned to the college for the sessions of 1862–63, and graduated in the fall of the last named year. He returned to York where he has since continued to practice with success. Dr. Heiges was married, in September, 1867, to Annie C., daughter of William and Mary E. (Boyer) Smith, of York. They have eight children, viz.: William S., Thomas T., John C., Philip B., Horace M., Jay Clifford, Amiee E., Robert R. Dr. Heiges is a member of St. John's Episcopal Church, in which he has been vestryman for about fourteen years.

HON. GEORGE W. HEIGES, attorney at law, was born in Dillsburg, York Co., Penn., May 18, 1842. His father, Jacob Heiges, was a prominent chair manufacturer of York County. His mother was Elizabeth Heiges, whose maiden name was Mumper. The Heiges family is of German origin. Mr. Heiges was educated at the public schools of York and at the York County Academy. He later was principal of the York Classical and Normal Institute, and again was appointed one of the principals of the local normal school and a tutor at the York County Academy. Completing the usual course of legal studies, he was admitted to the bar in 1867, and immediately began practice. In 1872 he was elected to the legislature and re-elected in 1873. He was a member of several important committees, and during his last term he was noted for the prominent action that he took on all important questions. He is a Democrat, one of the leading lawyers at the York County bar, and was elected chief burgess of York in 1885. He is a prominent

YORK BOROUGH.

Mason. He has always taken an active part in all the political movements of the county and State, and is especially interested in all matters of advancement and increase of public and educational interests. In 1877-78-79 he was attorney to the board of commissioners of York County. He was married, in 1874, to Miss Mary E. Gallagher, a native of York and a daughter of John Gallagher (deceased). He is the father of two children: Helen Days and Stewart Sprigg.

MICHAEL HEIMAN, son of John and Anna Mary (Hultzler) Heiman, was born in Bavaria, Germany, May 1, 1842. His parents immigrated to America when he was but three years old, settling in Baltimore, where they remained three years, and then removed to York County. Our subject was one of the first in the county to respond to the call of President Lincoln for volunteers, and on the 19th of April, 1861, he offered his services to protect the property of the Northern Central Railroad between York and Baltimore. April 29, 1861, he enlisted in Company G, Sixteenth Regiment Pennsylvania Volunteers, for three months' service, at the expiration of which he re-enlisted in Company B, Eighty-seventh Regiment Pennsylvania Volunteer Infantry, for three years' service. He was engaged in all the battles participated in by the Eighty-seventh Regiment until June 23, 1864, when, at the battle of Petersburg, Va., he was taken prisoner and confined in Libby prison, subsequently being removed and confined in the following prison pens in the South: Belle Island, Danville, Va., thence to Andersonville, Millen, Blackshire, and Thomasville, Ga., and then returned to Andersonville, escaping on his way, about the 23d of December, 1864, and after traveling about two weeks through the swampy land of Irwin and Isabella Counties for about seventy-five miles, was recaptured and taken back to Andersonville. He again escaped from Andersonville about April 17, 1865, and after enduring great hardships finally reached the Union lines at Macon, Ga., and from thence returned home and was discharged June 19, 1865, at Harrisburg, Penn. Time in service over four years. He was in Southern prisons from June 23, 1864, until May 2, 1865. Mr. Heiman has resided in York continually since the war, and is now engaged at shoemaking, 118 East King Street. He is a member of Post No. 37, G. A. R. October, 1867, he was united in marriage with Miss Mary Sowers, of Adams County, Penn. Five children have been born to them: John, Anna C., Henry, William and Erasmus M.

THEODORE R. HELB was born in York County, and is the son of Frederic and Rebecca (Henry) Helb, the former a native of Germany; and the latter a native of York County. His father, by trade, was a tanner, but subsequently engaged in the brewing business at Shrewsbury Station, York County. Theodore attended the common schools of York County, and subsequently went to Baltimore, Md., and took up a course of studies at the Knapp German and English Institute. After finishing his studies, he apprenticed himself to Jacob Seeger to learn the brewing business at Baltimore, Md. He finished his trade and returned to Shrewsbury, York County, and assisted his father in the brewing business. In 1878 he came to York, and erected a large, commodious brewery, and engaged in the business himself, in which he is doing a large trade. He was married January 22, 1874, to Miss Louisa, daughter of John and Margaret Rausch, of Baltimore, Md. To this union were born two children: Louis F. and Herbert T. Mr. Helb is a member of the I. O. O. F., also of the K. of P., I. O. of Heptasoph and I. O. R. M.

JOHN W. HELLER, attorney at law, is a native of Franklin, Va., born October 24, 1838, son of Rev. J. and Eliza (Fisher) Heller, and is of German origin. The father of Mr. Heller was born in Adams County, Penn., in 1806. He was a German Reformed minister for many years. His death occurred in Highland County, Ohio, in 1875. The mother of the subject was a native of Franklin County, Pa. Mr. Heller received a common school education. In 1857 he went to Fremont, Ohio, and there began his legal studies under Judge T. P. Finefrock, and was admitted to the bar at that place. For three months he was a soldier and member of the Eighth Ohio Volunteers. In 1865 he came to York, and the same year was admitted to the York County bar, and has been engaged in the active practice of his profession. In 1877 he was elected district attorney for York County, and successfully held the office one term. He is an able lawyer, and enjoys an extensive practice at the York County bar. His marriage to Miss Ella J. Engles, daughter of ex-sheriff Engles, of York County, was solemnized in 1867. To this union have been born five children, viz.: Thomas P., Sarah E., George E., John and Henry T. Mr. Heller is an earnest advocate of the principles of the Democratic party, and a prominent man.

DR. T. J. HERBERT, veterinary surgeon, York, Penn., treats all diseases of horses and cattle, and of all domestic animals.

JACOB HERMAN, a native of York County, was born June 22, 1849. His parents, Adam and Catharine Herman, were also natives of the county, and farmers of West Manchester Township. Jacob obtained his education in the public schools, and the York County Academy; in the latter institution he remained for eight years. After completing his studies, he was connected with Brillinger, Lanius & Co, lumber merchants at York, for one year. He then engaged in the nursery and seeding business with E. J. Evans, and subsequently engaged in the sewing machine trade, continuing for a period of five years. Mr. Herman next embarked in the flour, feed and grain business, and has succeeded in establishing a successful trade. He was united in marriage December 25, 1876, with Miss Dollie E., daughter of John and Elnoran Brougher, of Cumberland County, Penn. This union has been blessed with two children: Nora K. and Elve A.

W. H. HERMAN was born in York in 1851, and is a son of Rutter and Mary C. (Strickler) Herman, of German descent. The family is one of the oldest in York Borough. W. H. Herman received a good academical and high school education, and then served an apprenticeship of three years in A. B. Farquhar's machine shops. He next learned the art of printing under Hiram Young, of York, finishing at the office of the Lancaster *Inquirer*. Returning to York in 1876, he established a job-printing office, the first in the borough, and has established a fine trade. In 1880 he married Annie L. Heckert, of York. Mr. and Mrs. Herman are connected with the Presbyterian Church, of which Mr. Herman is choir-leader.

EDWARD R. HERR was born in Baltimore, Md., July 16, 1846, and is a son of John and Elizabeth (Reinicker) Herr. Mr. Herr's father, a native of Lancaster County, was born January 19, 1806, his mother was born in Baltimore, Md., about 1816. The father of our subject removed to Baltimore at an early age, and engaged in commission business, in which he continued until 1846, when he came to York and was elected president of what was then the York & Cumberland Railway. He remained in active railway life until 1860 when he retired from business. He was a member of the Methodist Episcopal Church, and one of the most popular railway men of York County. His death occurred February 3, 1876. At fifteen years of age Mr. Herr enlisted in Company I, Eighty-seventh

Pennsylvania Volunteers. He was at the battle of the Wilderness, Spottsylvania, Cold Harbor, Winchester, etc., and was taken prisoner near Bunker Hill, Va., on the retreat from Winchester to Harper's Ferry, and for a short time was in Libby prison also at Belle Isle. He was discharged at York, October 13, 1864. He was married December 20, 1881, to Miss Emma Landes, a native of York. To this marriage has been born one child, viz.: Reinicker. The maternal grandfather of our subject was George Reinicker, who was born April 31, 1785, and who died September 10, 1805. Mr. Herr is a member of the G. A. R.

GEORGE W. HESS, manufacturer of lounges, wire, hair and husk matresses, was born in York in 1848, is a son of William and Sarah (Welsh) Hess, and is of German origin. At the early age of eight years, Mr. Hess was thrown entirely upon his own resources, and for several years was employed at different occupations. Later he was given a clerkship in the store of P. A. & S. Small, where he remained in faithful service for thirteen years. In 1881 he began the mattress business and this yet continues. He was married in 1872 to Miss Emma V. Schall of York. They have two children: William and George. He is a Republican, and a member of the K. of P.

ALBERTUS HIBNER, contractor and builder, was born in York, Penn., November 15, 1833, is a son of Augustus and Margaret (Rodgers) Hibner, is of French-English descent, and is the eldest in a family of three children. His father was also a native of York, Penn., and was born in 1809; his mother was born in Freystown, in 1814. His paternal grandfather was Frederick Hibner, a native of France, who came to America with a fleet fitted out by Gen. La Fayette, and took part in the Revolutionary war. Mr. Hibner received a good common school education, and at seventeen years of age began a four years' apprenticeship at the carpenter's trade under Jacob Quichel. In 1860 he began carpentering and contracting for himself, which occupation he still continues, and is one of the successful contractors of York. The marriage of Mr. Hibner occurred in 1858, to Miss Sarah Krone, a native of York, Penn. Politically Mr. Hibner is a Democrat, and has held the office of borough surveyor, and been a member of the school board for a number of years In 1855 he was made an Odd Fellow, and is now a member of Harmonia Lodge, No. 858, and for ten years has represented this lodge in the Grand Lodge of Pennsylvania.

R. HOFFHEINS, one of the leading dealers, and formerly manufacturer of agricultural implements, is a descendent of Johann Adam Hoffheins, who with his brother, Johann Daniel, emigrated from the Upper Rhine country to America, arriving at Philadelphia. on the ship Pallas, November 25, 1763. The latter settled in Lancaster County, where he married a sister of the Rev. Wagner, of the German Reformed Church. The former began farming near Reading; about 1780 he removed to Dover Township, York County, losing in the interval all his means through the depreciation of Continental money. His son, Sebastian, who was born in Berks County, in 1767, was married to Barbara, daughter of Joseph and Mary Gochenour. She was born in 1764 and died in 1844. Sebastian was a farmer, shoemaker, and school-teacher, and a resident of Dover Township until his death in 1852. Their son, Jonas, the father of our subject, was a farmer and resided in Dover Township all his life. He died in Dover Borough in 1857. The mother of our subject was Susan, daughter of Peter and Catherine Weigel of West Manchester Township. She is still living, and a resident of York. Two brothers of Barbara Gochenour and two uncles of Catherine (Upp) Weigel were soldiers in the Revolution. Two children are descendents of Jonas and Susan Hoffheins, Samuel, a resident of Adams County, Penn., and Reuben, the subject of this biography. He was reared upon the farm in Dover Township, and until seventeen years of age was an assistant of his father. He then learned the carpenter trade, which he followed several years, embarking at the expiration of that time in business for himself by starting a shop at Dover, for the repair of agricultural implements. Possessing natural mechanical aptitude he soon extended his field of operations and began the manufacture of various farming implements with valuable patented improvements, invented by himself, among which may be named the self-raking reaper; horse hay rake and cultivator and planter, together with other articles of minor importance. In 1865 he removed to York, and under the firm name of Hoffheins, Shireman & Co., began the manufacture of reapers, mowers and agricultural implements upon a scale which the enlarged facilities of York afforded, employing at that period about sixty hands. In 1869 Mr. Hoffheins disposed of his interest in the manufacturing business and has since devoted his time to farming and the sale of agricultural implements. His headquarters are in York, where he carries a full line of all the implements necessary to agriculture. He has branch houses at East Berlin and Table Rock, Adams County, and one at Dover, all of them being under his general supervision. Mr. Hoffheins has done much to improve the machinery in this field and has several valuable patents. He has always been deeply interested in farming, and is at present vice-president of the York County Agricultural Society. Mr. Hoffheins was united in marriage in 1857, with Miss Lydia Lenhart, daughter of William Lenhart, of York Township, and a descendant of an old York County family. Two children are living: William L. and Franklin G.; both assisting their father in his business enterprises.

AMOS HOFFMAN is a dealer in clothing, gents furnishing goods, hats, caps, etc., and in connection has a complete merchant tailoring department. Mr. Hoffman is a native of Rohrerstown, Lancaster Co., Penn., was born in 1842, is a son of Frederick and Elizabeth (Huffnagle) Hoffman and is of German descent. His father was born in Lancaster County, Penn., in 1802, and his mother in 1804. His grandfather was Philip Hoffman. The great-grandfather of our subject came to America from Germany and settled in Pennsylvania. Mr. Hoffman's father died in 1880 and his mother in 1882. Our subject received a common school education. Later in life he learned the printer's trade, serving a regular apprenticeship. After continuing at this trade for several years he engaged in the merchandise business. In 1878 he came to York and has since been engaged in the clothing business which he successfully continues. In 1884 he removed to his present salesroom in York; the main department being 25x150 feet. The marriage of Mr. Hoffman occurred in 1871, to Miss Clara Malthaner, a native of Bethlehem, Penn. Mrs. Hoffman died in 1874, and in 1879 he was married to Miss Bessie Hess, of Lancaster, Penn., daughter of Thomas and Elizabeth Hess of Lebanon County, Penn. They have one child, Charles W. In 1863 Mr. Hoffman enlisted in Company K, Forty ninth Pennsylvania Volunteers. He is a Republican, a member of K. of P., Red Men Lodge, G. A. R. and I. O. O. F. Mr. and Mrs. Hoffman are members of the Reformed Church.

THOMAS HOLLAND, agent for the New York Powder Company, was born in York County, in in 1825, to Thomas and Elizabeth (Cremer) Holland and is of English extraction. By occupation, the father of Mr. Holland was a cooper; his death occurred in York about 1840. The boyhood of our subject was spent among strangers, and when very young he was thrown upon his own resources. At thirteen years of age he was bound out for six years to learn the tailor's trade, and afterward taught school for some time. He then learned the cigar trade, and in 1849 he began the cigar and tobacco business, which he continued until 1868, when he engaged in the hardware business in partnership with the firm of Thomas, Chambers & Co., which he continued until 1876, when he sold his interest to John F. Thomas, but continued as a salesman in the store until 1882, and since that time has been engaged in his present occupation. Mr. Holland was married in 1847 to Miss Rebecca Thomas. Three children were born to this union, Emma E. only survives. Mrs. Holland died in 1860, and seven years later Mr. Holland was married to Evaline Hummer, a native of Dover, York County, daughter of Michael Hummer. They had two children; Thomas H. only survives. Mr. Holland was formerly a Whig, but is now a Democrat, although in local matters he supports those who in his judgement are the best men. He is a member of the Methodist Episcopal Church and Mrs. Holland is a member of the Evangelical Association.

WILLIAM HOSE, a representative of the manufacturing interests of York, is a native of the county and was born August 20, 1828. At the age of eighteen years he commenced an apprenticeship with the firm of Horn & Mitchell, carpenters and builders, with whom he remained for three years. Having become thoroughly proficient in his trade, he engaged at car building for two years, at the expiration of which time he accepted a position as foreman with the Billmeyer & Small Car Company, remaining with that company for over thirty years. Mr. Hose then purchased the sash and door manufactory, operated by Eden & Blouser, and has rearranged it, purchasing new machinery, etc. He has established a large trade, having added planing machinery, and now has facilities for turning out all kinds of building material. He is a public spirited citizen, a member of the I. O. O. F., the I. O. R. M., and of the I. O. of Heptasoph.

JOHN H. HOSHOUR, book-keeper at A. B. Farquhar's, was born in Glen Rock, York County, is a son of J. V. and Maggie (Koller) Hoshour, and is one of four living children. His father is also a native of York County, and was born August 21, 1814; his mother was born in Shrewsberry Township, in October. 1817. His paternal grandfather was born in Heidelberg Township. His great grandfather came from Germany and settled in York County. The father of Mr. Hoshour, at the age of twenty years, began teaching school, and four years later went into the store of Small, Myers & Latimer, at Shrewsberry, where he remained two years, and then began railroading and civil engineering. In 1836 he came to Glen Rock. He has been an active and successful business man, and it was not until February, 1885, that he retired from active life. At seventeen our subject entered Pennsylvania College at Gettysburg, Penn., and continued three years; when, on account of ill health, he was compelled to abandon his studies. In 1870 he entered the employ of Fry, Herbst & Co., at Glen Rock, as book-keeper. For some years. Mr. Hoshour was engaged in the manufacturing business, at Glen Rock; selling his interest in 1879, he came to York, and has since been in the employ of A. B. Farquhar. The marriage of Mr. Hoshour occurred March 14, 1872, to Miss Alice Cramer, daughter of E. L. and Polly Cramer, of Baltimore, Md. Mrs. Hoshour was born November 2. 1854, in Codorus Township, York Co., Penn. To this union were born two children, viz.: Howard P., born November 4, 1872, and Elvin H., born April 5, 1874. Mrs. Hoshour died June 15, 1877. In April, the year following, Mr. Hoshour married Miss Lida J. Armacost, of Baltimore County, Md., born July 4, 1860. To this marriage two children have been born: Carroll M., December 16, 1878, and J. Murray, January 30, 1881 (died October 26, 1881). He is a Republican and a member of the Lutheran Church.

GEORGE W. ILGENFRITZ. for many years a prominent manufacturer and business man of this section of Pennsylvania, was born in York, in 1821, to Daniel and Elizabeth (Deitch) Ilgenfritz, and is one of eight children. The great-grandfather of our subject was a native of Germany, who came to America in 1741, and settled in Conewago Township, York Co., Penn. Subject's father was born in this county in 1790 and died in 1833. His mother was born in the same county in 1791, died in 1884. At twelve years of age our subject was thrown solely upon his own resources, and from that time he was forced to make his own way in life. First he learned the blacksmith's trade, then coach-making under Joseph Small, at which he continued to work for several years. In 1845 he began the manufacture of agricultural implements, which he continued some time, and then began the construction of railway cars, and in this line of manufacture he was extensively engaged. In 1864 he sold his establishment, but in 1866 he again engaged in business and continued some years. Mr. Ilgenfritz was married, in 1844, to Miss Isabella Emmett, a native of York County. Of eight children born three yet survive: Anna, David E. and Della. Mr. Ilgenfritz is a Mason and a member of the Lutheran Church, of which his wife is also a member.

JOHN E. ILGENFRITZ, son of Martin and Mary Ann (Plowman) Ilgenfritz, of York, Penn., was born December 16, 1833, in Shrewsberry Township. When our subject was a youth school advantages were limited, but he received a little instruction in the schools of his village, and also attended one short term in Dunkard Valley, Springfield Township. He then served a three years' apprenticeship at mill-wrighting, and as a journeyman worked at his trade ten years. He kept a restaurant eight years in Glen Rock, and then, in 1864, enlisted in the One Hundred and First Regiment Pennsylvania Volunteers, served until the close of the war and was honorably discharged at Harrisburg. After the war he began the butchering business at York, Penn. December 3, 1854, he married Rebecca Klinedinst, daughter of David and Catherine Klinedinst, of North Codorus Township. The children born to this marriage are the following, living: Margaret, Leonard, Zarvilla, David, Martin Edward, Ellsworth. Deceased: Martha J., Robert C., Charles L., John Wesley, Milliard Kemp and Minnie May. Mr. Ilgenfritz has, in connection with his butchering, a well-stocked grocery store, and has always received a good share of patronage in his line of business.

WILLIAM H. KAIN was born January 4, 1848, in West Manchester Township. At the age of sixteen he began teaching school, and at nineteen entered Pennsylvania College at Gettysburg, and graduated four years later. At the age of twenty-three he was appointed county superintendent to fill the unexpired term of Stephen G. Boyd. This occurred in 1871. He was elected in 1872, and re-elected in 1875, serving in all about seven years. In the year 1876 he prepared for the State Department a history of the progress of education in York County Mr. Kain had a keen zest for learning, and was untiring in the pursuit of knowledge. Though firm in his disposition, he was free from dogmatism and pedantry. Having a predilection for the practice of law, he was admitted to the bar in 1878, had acquired a lucrative practice, and obtained prominence in his profession, when his career was cut short by premature death on February 3, 1883. He was a man

BIOGRAPHICAL SKETCHES.

of indefatigable energy in whatever he undertook.

DR. J. B. KAIN, a son of John and Susan (May) Kain, was born in April, 1850. He attended the common schools, and assisted his father on the farm until the age of seventeen, when he taught school three winters and attended the normal school and York Academy in the summers. He then began the preparatory study of the medical profession under the instruction of Dr. C. M. Nes, of York, with whom he remained three years, then attended lectures at the Jefferson Medical College at Philadelphia, from which institution he graduated March 13, 1871. He returned to York and began practice in partnership with Dr. A. R. Prowel, of Manchester Borough, which partnership continued about two years, when it was severed by the death of Dr. Prowel. Dr. Kain continued to practice in Manchester until March, 1884; he then came to York, where he is now practicing. In April, 1869, he married Mary L., daughter of Daniel and Mary (Upp) Kauffman, of York. Their union was blessed with five children named as follows: Carrie V., C. Harry, Mamie M. (deceased), Sallie A. and John R. Dr. Kain is a member of the Lutheran Church, and a brother of Prof. W. H. Kain (deceased), who was county superintendent of the schools of York County.

EMANUEL KAUFFMAN, third of eleven children of Joseph and Susan (Sprenkle) Kauffman, was born October 26, 1831, in Spring Garden Township, and was reared on his father's farm. May 15, 1860, he married Mary M. Diehl, daughter of Daniel and Louisa (Loucks) Diehl, of Spring Garden Township. Their children are William H., Emma J., Martha A. and Daniel W. Mr. Kauffman is extensively engaged in the manufacture of brooms. His factory is at 536 West Philadelphia Street. He started in this business in 1880, and it has steadily increased. He sells to the trade in York and Lancaster Counties, and has the reputation of manufacturing the best brooms in the market.

JAMES W. KERR, M. D., is a native of Lancaster County, Penn., born September 19, 1813, the second of seven children to Rev. William and Mary (Wilson) Kerr, and is of Scotch-Irish extraction. The father of Dr. Kerr was also born in Lancaster County in 1776, and his mother was a native of Dauphin County, born in 1789. The paternal grandfather of Dr. Kerr was also a native of Lancaster County. The father of subject was a minister of the Presbyterian Church ; for nearly a quarter of a century he was the pastor of a congregation at Donegal Church, in Lancaster County. His death occurred September 22, 1821. The mother of Dr. Kerr died February 22, 1850. The subject here mentioned was reared on the farm. He attended the common schools and subsequently spent some time at West Nottingham Academy in Maryland, and then entered Jefferson College, in Washington County, Penn., from which he graduated in 1834. After his graduation he went to Harrisburg and took up the study of medicine under Dr. Roberts, and then attended medical lectures at the University of Pennsylvania, from which he graduated in 1840, and the same year came to York and began the practice of his profession, which he has without intermission, since continued. He is the oldest practitioner of medicine now in York. The marriage of Dr. Kerr occurred in 1844 to Miss Jane McIlvain, a native of York. Of three children born, only one survives the mother, viz.: Martha, now Mrs. Dr. Bacon. Mrs. Kerr died March, 1881. Dr. Kerr is a Republican and a member of the Presbyterian Church, having united with that denomination at seventeen years of age. In 1840 he was elected Sabbath-school superintendent of the Presbyterian Sabbath-school, and has since held that office. For almost half a century he has taken great interest in Sabbath-school work. He is an old and prominent physician and an earnest Christian gentleman. He is a member of York County Medical Association, the State and national Associations.

ALEXANDER KIDD, president and director of the York County Alms-house, and manufacturer of cedar ware, was born in Baltimore County, Md., September 11, 1833; is the son of John B. and Leah (Whitmire) Kidd ; is their only child, and is of English-German descent. In childhood our subject came with his mother from Baltimore County, Md., to York. At fifteen years of age he began serving an apprenticeship at the cedar cooper's trade at which he continued work until 1864, when he enlisted in Company H, Two-hundredth Pennsylvania Volunteers, served one year and was honorably discharged in 1865. In 1866 Mr. Kidd resumed his trade in the city of Baltimore, where he remained until 1875, when he returned to York and here has since resided. He was married in 1858 to Miss Caroline Shillinburg, a native of Baltimore, Md. The marriage has resulted in the birth of two children : Mary J. and John W. In politics Mr. Kidd is a Democrat. During the years 1881 and 1882 he represented the Seventh Ward in the York Council. In 1882 he was elected resident director of the York County Alms-house. During his administration some very important improvements have been made ; the most notable perhaps is the introduction of the steam-heating process into the alms-house. He is a member of the order of Red Men. Mrs. Kidd is a member of the Methodist Episcopal Church.

ELI KINDIG, farmer and dealer in horses and mules, was born in Windsor Township, January 11, 1823, son of Joseph and Salomi (Landis) Kindig, and is of Swiss-German origin. His father was born in Hellam Township, in 1787. He was one of the prominent early settlers of York County. His death took place in Windsor Township in 1857. The mother of our subject was born in Windsor Township in 1800, and died in 1888. Subject's grandfather came to York County from Lancaster County in early life. His death occurred in 1824. Subject's great-grandfather was a native of Switzerland, and immigrated to America some time in the seventeenth century. At twenty years of age Mr. Kindig began life for himself. For a number of years he carried on farming and subsequently engaged in his present vocation. He is one of the most extensive dealers in horses and mules, and for many years has been one of the most extensive farmers in York County. He was married in 1846 to Miss Lydia Flinchbaugh, daughter of Frederick and Mary Flinchbaugh. They have eight children: Benjamin, Ellen, Eli, Henry, Harrison, Joseph, Milton and Frederick. Mrs. Kindig died in 1877, and two years later our subject was married to Miss Elenora Stump, a native of York Township. Mr. Kindig now owns the old Kindig homestead. He has 400 acres of well-improved land. He is a thorough Republican in politics.

DANIEL R. KING, baker and surveyor, is a native of Manchester Township, York County, was born November 6, 1833, and is a son of Daniel and Anna (Coleman) King. His father was born in this county in 1806, and his mother in 1807. Here his grandfather King was born in 1772. His great-grandfather, Philip King, and his great-great-grandfather was Nicholas King. Our subject is one of six living children, is of German extraction, and was reared on the farm. At nineteen years of age he entered York County Academy, where he remained some time, and then began teaching school, which he continued for thirteen years. In 1867 he removed to York, and clerked in a store for several years. In 1871 he began the baking business. He is also engaged in the cracker business in Columbia, Penn.

His marriage occurred in 1856, to Miss Sarah J. Fisher, daughter of George and Catherine Fisher. Mrs. King was born in York in 1837. To this union have been born William A., Charles E. and Sadie C. Mr. King is a Democrat, and he and wife are members of the United Brethren Church.

BENJAMIN J. KING was born in Spring Garden Township, September 25, 1839, a son of Henry and Leah (Johnston) King. natives of York County, Penn. He was brought up in York, and educated at the York County Academy, and Bland's school on the Plank Road. When fifteen years old he began clerking in a drug store, which he continued two years, then clerked in a dry goods store two years, and afterward followed the trade of house painting until the breaking out of the war. April 19, 1861, he enlisted at York, Penn., in Company A, Sixteenth Pennsylvania Volunteer Infantry, and served three months. He re-enlisted on August 24, 1861, for three years, in Company E, Eighty-seventh Pennsylvania Volunteer Infantry, and was honorably discharged on account of disability, April 10, 1863. He entered the service as sergeant and came out with that rank. When he returned from the war he engaged in draying freight until April, 1883, and was transfer agent of the Peach Bottom, Pennsylvania & Northern Central Railroad for eleven years, when he sold his business to the Northern Central Railroad Transfer Company, when he began the bottling business, which he followed one year. He then sold out and purchased the Violet Hill Hotel, one-half mile south of York, and moved there July 1, 1884, and kept hotel until April 1, 1885, when on account of sickness of his wife he moved to York, Penn. Mr. King has leased his Violet Hill Hotel to Frank M. Egee for one year, with the privilege of five years. Mr. King has moved to York, and leased his bottling works to Henry Weigee for one year, with the privilege of five, and is not engaged in any business at the present time. Mr. King was married in York, Penn., April 23, 1861, to Margaret J. Ilgenfritz, daughter of Thomas Ilgenfritz. They have three children living: Harry J., Lillie and Samuel J. T. Mr. King is a member of the I. O. O. F. and Encampment. He was one of the organizers of the city market, and is a stockholder in the York Opera House.

H. B. KING. M. D., is a son of E. A. and Arabella F. (Nes) King, who were both natives of York County; his grandfather, Dr. Henry Nes, was an old and skillful practitioner of the county, and a resident until his death. He represented his county in congress several terms, and was highly honored and esteemed. The father of our subject was a prominent business man in his day Engaged in the marble business, in which he was a skillful workman and sculptor. He was also engaged in the phosphate trade and general farming and milling. A valuable farm and mill property, together with valuable real estate, located in York, descended to our subject. The father died in 1877, the mother in 1882. H. B. King, our subject, was born in York in 1860, was educated in the schools and academy at York, and early began the study of medicine under the tutelage of Dr. B. F. Spangler. He subsequently entered the Jefferson Medical College of Philadelphia, and graduated in 1883, after a three years' course, subsequently taking a post graduate course at the same institution. He is now engaged in practice in York, and is a member of the York County Medical Society.

CASPER H. KLEFFMAN, is a brother of Frederick and Gottlieb Kleffman, of Spring Garden Township, whose sketches appear elsewhere. At the breaking out of the late war, our subject enlisted in Company E. Eighty-seventh Pennsylvania Volunteer Infantry, and took part in all the marches and engagements of his regiment until taken prisoner at Carter's Woods, near Winchester, Va., June 10, 1863, after which he was confined in Libby Prison and the prison on Belle Isle until July 7, when he was paroled; he rejoined his regiment October 13, same year, was wounded at the battle of Locust Grove November 27, and was honorably discharged October 13, 1864. In June, 1878, he married Elizabeth Rabe, who has borne him one daughter, Wilhelmina C. Mr. Kleffman is now a merchant at the corner of Queen and South Streets, and is doing a prosperous trade. In religion he is a Lutheran, and is a consistent member of St. John's Church.

ELIAS KOHLER, proprietor of the Central Hotel, was born in York Township April 15, 1845, and is a son of Jacob and Anna (Sechrist) Kohler. Mr. Kohler is the eighth in a family of nine children and is of German descent. Mr. Kohler worked for his father on the farm until twenty-one years of age, when he began for himself. He went to Dallastown and engaged in the butchering business, remained there two years, then came to York and continued the same business for three years and then engaged in the livery business, which he continued three years; he then became proprietor of the Central Hotel. In 1881 Mr. Kohler invented what is known as the Kohler Improved Cattle Car, one of the best improvements of the kind ever invented. Our subject was married in 1868, to Miss Harriet Peeling, daughter of John Peeling. They have four children: Minnie A., Chauncy C., Gertrude and Erle C. Mr. Kohler is a Democrat and a member of the I. O. O. F. He has been a member of the town council and is a popular man.

HENRY KRABER, a representative of one of the old families of York County, was born in York in 1822, and is a son of John and Catherine (Graybill) Kraber, whose ancestors came to America from Germany in 1670. Their descendants have since been prominently identified with the history of York County. His grandfather, Adam Kreber (so spelled), resided in York all his life; he was a blacksmith and wagon-maker, and manufactured running gear of cannons for the Revolutionary war. He had one son and three daughters. John Kraber followed smithing and subsequently farming near Dillsburg. He died in 1859; his wife died in 1853. They were the parents of eight children: Henry, Daniel, John, Adam, Michael, William. Henry and Sarah Ann; four are now living. Our subject, Henry Kraber, was engaged in the mercantile business twenty-seven years in York. He was prominently identified with the Farmer's Mutual Insurance Company, of which he was president twenty years; also engaged in mining ore in York and Cumberland Counties, and is at present interested in mining coal in Alabama; he is also interested in the Alleghany Extract Company, and is general agent for the State for the Watertown Insurance Company; with his sons, he is engaged in dealing at wholesale in cigars and tobacco. He was married in 1847, to Miss Catherine E. Reichenbaugh, of Lancaster. They have two children living—George B. and Henry R., both in business with their father; and two deceased, George and Catherine. Mr. Kraber has been connected with the Presbyterian Church all his life.

JACOB L. KUEHN, superintendent of the York Gas Company, was born in York March 28, 1836, to John L. and Catherine (Laumaster) Kuehn. The parents of our subject were born in Germany, the birth of his father occurring in 1801 and that of his mother in 1808. In 1816 the Kuehn family came to America and settled in York County, Penn. His maternal grandfather, however, was a soldier in the Revolutionary war. Both families are old settlers of York County. Mr. Kuehn was educated at the public schools of York. At fifteen years of age he began carpentering and continued that for some years. In 1856 he was appointed superintendent of the Gas Company, and this position he has since held. In 1882 he was appointed superintendent of the York Water Company. Almost all his life Mr. Kuehn has been connected with public works. He was married in 1857 to Miss Anna C. Vogel, daughter of Francis S. Vogel. They have two children: A. Lizzie and Hattie A. Mr. Kuehn is an earnest supporter of Republicanism. Mr. and Mrs. Kuehn are members of the Presbyterian Church.

THE KURTZ FAMILY. The origin of this family in America is authoritatively traced back to Rev. Nicholas Kurtz, who immigrated to America some time in the seventeenth century, and settled in Pennsylvania. George Peter Kurtz was one of a family of twelve children born to Nicholas and Helena (Albright) Kurtz. He was born in Berks County, October 4, 1749. He was one of the early men who came to York County and one of York's pioneer merchants, and an active, enterprising and respected citizen. Here he resided until his death. His son, George Peter Kurtz, was born in York, October 17, 1799. This representative of the Kurtz family was educated for the ministry, but subsequently he learned the carpenter's trade, and chose what seemed to him a more humble sphere in life. He was married, in 1825, to Miss Eliza E. Fisher, also a native of York County, and a daughter of Dr. John and Eliza E. Fisher. The result of this union was two children. viz.: Catherine and Amelia. Mr. Kurtz died in 1886; his widow died in 1882. Another important personage of the family was Charles Kurtz, born August 30, 1791. He was married to Julia Ann Eichelberger, a native of this county. Two children were born to them: William H. and Catherine, now residing in Minneapolis, Minn. The former was born in York, in 1823, and here he has since resided. His early education was acquired at York County Academy, but his extensive knowledge of business has been acquired through his own efforts and in actual practical life. At fourteen years of age he was thrown upon his own resources, and for seven years he was employed as a clerk in a store. In 1848 he engaged in the malting business, and continued until 1872, when he became a member of the firm known as Baugher, Kurtz & Stewart, iron and brass founders, machinists, and manufacturers of turbine water-wheels. There is in connection with this establishment the Codorus Tannery, which is one of the most extensive institutions of its kind in Pennsylvania. A complete sketch of these enterprises may be found in another portion of this work. The marriage of Mr. Kurtz with Miss Mary Baugher was solemnized August 17, 1856. To this union have been born two children: Charles and Julia. Mrs. Kurtz died in 1861, and, five years later, Mr. Kurtz was married to Miss Julia A. Baugher, a sister of his former wife, and daughter of Frederick Baugher, who was one of the leading citizens of York. Mr. Kurtz is enterprising in business, liberal in all affairs of true worth and merit, and ranks as one of York County's most valued citizens. Mr. Kurtz and wife are members of the Lutheran Church.

CAPT. WILLIAM H. LANIUS, one of the leading representative business men of York County, is a descendant of Christian and Anna (Updegraff) Lanius (grandparents). The former was born at Kreutz Creek, York County, September 16, 1773; died in York, February 16, 1847. The latter was born in York, March 16, 1774, died at the same place October 9, 1830. The parents of our subject were Henry and Angeline (Miller) Lanius. The former born September 20, 1809, died June 26, 1879. The mother was born March 28, 1822, and is still living in York. Henry Lanius was a prominent business man of York and highly esteemed. He was extensively engaged in the lumber trade, and continued an active business man up to his death. In 1860 and 1861 he served as chief burgess of the borough, and was for several years a director on the school board. He was a prominent member of the Moravian Church, and at the time of his death, president of the church council. Eight children are descendants, viz.: Marcus C., Annie L., William H., Ellen A., Charles C., Sarah F., Paul and Susan H. Capt. Lanius was born at Flushing, Long Island, N. Y., November 26, 1843, and when a youth, came with his parents to York, where he received a liberal education, attending the public schools and the York County Academy. In August, 1861, he enlisted as a private in Company A Eighty-seventh Regiment, Pennsylvania Volunteer Infantry, but was soon after transferred to Company I, as first sergeant, remaining until the close of their service. He was commissioned second lieutenant, March 1, 1863; first lieutenant, November 18. 1863, and as captain, June 25, 1864. Capt. Lanius was with his regiment in all its engagements and battles, among which may be named Winchester, Mine Run, Locust Grove, Wilderness, Spottsylvania, Cold Harbor, Petersburg, Monocacy, Opequan and Fisher's Hill. He was wounded at the battle of Monocacy, July 9, and honorably discharged October 13, 1864, after over three years' faithful and active service. Capt. Lanius embarked in business in York in 1867, engaging in the lumber trade, which he has continued up to the present time. In 1871 he formed a business association with his brother, Marcus C., conducting a branch at Wrightsville until 1878, and at the present time has extensive lumber interests at Williamsport. Capt. Lanius has also been identified with various other enterprises, and ranks as one of the leaders in all measures of progress. He published in 1884 a superior map of the borough of York, and has laid out a valuable addition to the same in the Fifteenth Ward. He is the originator and president of the West End Improvement Company, described in another portion of this book. He organized the first Post of the G. A. R. in York County; is a member of York Lodge No. 266, A. F. & A. M., and a representative in the common council. Capt. Lanius has always taken an active interest in political affairs, and early in life organizing the Boys in Blue in the campaign of 1866 at the age of twenty-two years, and was made president of the organization, and remaining in that position in 1868 and 1869. In 1884 he was a delegate to the Republican National Convention at Chicago. In 1867 he was united in marriage with Miss Lucy Smyser, daughter of Michael Smyser, of York. They have three children: Mary S., Grace A. and Perry L.

ISRAEL LAUCKS, of the leading firm of Laucks & Son, dealers in dry goods and notions, was born in York County, in September, 1827, and is the son of George and Elizabeth (Smyser) Laucks. He remained at home with his father on the farm until he was twenty years of age, in the meantime attended the common schools. At the age of twenty he came to York and entered the York High School. After finishing his studies he formed a co-partnership with S. K Myers, and engaged in the boot and shoe, dry goods and notion business at York. This partnership was afterward dissolved by mutual consent, and Mr. Laucks formed a partnership with his son, George W. Laucks, December 31, 1883, under the firm style of Laucks & Son, dealers in dry goods and notions. They have a large stock and do a thriving business. Mr. Laucks was married May 4, 1854, to Imilda A., daughter of William A. and Lyda Wilt, of York. To this union were born six children, as follows: Irene E., George W., Amanda L., Grace V., Sadie M. and S. Farry. Mr. Laucks

YORK BOROUGH.

has been director of the First National Bank of York; treasurer of the Farmers' Market Company, and is president of the York Coach Company, also president of the York Safe and Lock Company. He has been an active member of the Reformed Church for more than thirty-seven years, and was elected to the office of deacon, and subsequently elder in the church of his choice.

LEHMAYER & BROTHER, dealers in clothing, hats, gents' furnishing goods, and sole agents for the celebrated Pearl Shirt. Mr. N. Lehmayer is a native of Germany, and came to America in 1847. Among the business interests of York there is none that deserves more prominent mention than the firm here mentioned. This enterprise was established in 1847, beginning with limited means and a small stock, but energy and a determined will were not lacking. For many years this firm has maintained a front rank in the clothing trade of York County. Here is kept constantly on hand a most complete and varied assortment of all kinds of clothing and gents' furnishing goods. Special attention is given to the latest styles and changes. This firm buys directly from the manufacturers, for cash and in large quantities, and is ever prepared to extend to the trade the best possible bargains. There are no advantages to be gained by the people of York and York County by going to the large cities, when this firm offers the equal in every particular. The building was enlarged in 1884, and now the principal sales department is 125x32 feet, and is steam-heated. Six assistants are employed in the establishment. Mr. Lehmayer is a striking example of the proverbial thrift of his race. Mr. Lehmayer, by his uniform courtesy, has won the respect of a large circle of friends, and is known as a most reputable man. His residence, on East Market Street, is one of the most elegant and extensive in York.

C. E. LEWIS is a descendant of Ellis Lewis, who, with John Rankin and James Bennett, removed from Chester County, about 1736, and settled in the region of York County, where afterward his son, Eli Lewis, laid out the town of Lewisberry. Dr. Webster Lewis was grandfather of C. E. Lewis. Ellis Lewis, chief justice of Pennsylvania, James Lewis, attorney at law at York, and Eli Lewis, president of the First National Bank of York, were sons of Eli. Dr. Robert Nebinger Lewis, who practiced medicine in Dover for many years, and Mary Moore, were subject's father and mother. C. E. Lewis was born in Dover, April 5, 1844. He attended the common schools until seventeen years of age, when he entered the York County Academy, then under Prof. G. W. Ruby, as principal, and D. M. Ettinger, the accomplished mathematician and surveyor, as teacher in arithmetic, algebra, geometry and other branches related thereto, and attended its sessions three years, and afterward for a short period was its assistant principal. With his brother, Rush Webster Lewis, C. E. Lewis started in York the manufacture of shoes by machinery, and this was the first business in which he was engaged. Previous to this, however, he had spent a year and a quarter in the city of Lynn, Mass., and Amesbury, Mass., where he was for some time engaged as foreman in the finishing room of the Salisbury and Amesbury mills. Subsequently he became book-keeper for James N. Buffum's lumber manufacturing establishment, at Lynn, Mass. He returned to York in June, 1866, and July following was elected a clerk in the First National Bank at York, and continued in the bank until January 1, 1871, having gained the position of teller in the meantime. It was at this time he left the bank to engage in the manufacture of shoes, in which business he was engaged eight years. In January, 1879, he was elected as cashier of the Western National Bank of York, where he is now engaged. April 26, 1869, he married Ellen Sarah, the second daughter of Joseph Smyser, of the borough of York, Penn., and has had born to him the following children: Ellis Smyser, member of St. Paul's Church, and clerk in the Western National Bank; Joseph Smyser, Mabel Rebecca, Sadie Moore, Clay Eugene, Nellie Kate, and Margie Violet, all living.

WILLIAM Y. LINK, ex-prothonotary of York County, was born in Dover Township, York County, January 14, 1838, to Benjamin and Margaret (Yesler) Link, and is of German-Scotch descent. The parents of Mr. Link were natives of York County, the father, born about 1805, died in 1839, and the mother, born in 1806, died in 1872. The grandfather Link was also a native of York County, and still resides in Dover Township. The Yesler family is an ancient one, of York County. Mr. Link was educated at the public schools of Dover Township. At ten years of age he was thrown entirely upon his own resources. He worked on the farm until he was nineteen years of age, and then learned the carpenter's trade, and continued this until 1875. In 1875 he was elected prothonotary of York County and served three years, since which time he has been working at his trade. The marriage of Mr. Link took place in 1863, to Miss Catherine Aughenbaugh, daughter of George Aughenbaugh, a native of Manchester Township. They have six children, viz.: William F., Laura J., Harry E., Bertha K., Chauncy A. and Chester G. Mr. and Mrs. Link are members of St. Paul's Lutheran Church.

HENRY LINT, second of three children of Peter and Elizabeth (Smyser) Lint, was born in West Manchester Township, July 20, 1829, where he was reared on his father's farm and lived in this township until he removed with his father to the home where he now lives. He removed to York in 1840. His maternal ancestors, the Smysers, were the pioneer settlers in West Manchester Township. Mr. Lint is a member of the Lutheran Church. (For our subject's ancestral history, see sketch of his brother, Peter Lint).

DR. L. M. LOCKMAN, son of the Rev. A. H. Lockman, of York, was born in August, 1829, at Harrisburg, Penn. He attended the common schools of York in youth, and completed a course in York Academy. He then entered the drug store of Dr. Alexander Barnitz as clerk, and remained with him two years. He then began the study of medicine with Dr. Jacob Hay, Sr., with whom he remained two years, then began a course of study with Dr. James W. Kerr, of York, with whom he remained until he graduated. He attended the Pennsylvania Medical College, of Philadelphia, and graduated in 1852. He returned to York and began the practice of his profession. He remained in York until 1858, then went to Littlestown, Penn., remained one year, and then moved to Liverpool, Manchester Township, where he remained six years. In 1869 he again returned to York, where he still continues the practice of his profession. He married, March, 1853, Maria, daughter of Dr. John F. Fischer, of York. Their union was blessed with four children, as follows: William C. (deceased), John F. (deceased), Augustus (deceased) and Harry D. The Doctor is a member of St. Luke's Lutheran Church.

ZACHARIAH K. LOUCKS is a grandson of John George Loucks, who was one of the early emigrants from Germany that settled in the beautiful region of Berks County, known as Tulpehocken, where he purchased a tract of land. About the year 1780, hearing of the fertile lands west of the Susquehanna, he immigrated to York County to continue his chosen occupation of farming, and purchased land southwest of York. May 13, 1805, he purchased the mill and farm where Z. K. Loucks now lives. George Loucks, son of John George Loucks,

BIOGRAPHICAL SKETCHES.

father of the subject of this sketch, was born August 18, 1787, and died October 29, 1849, aged sixty-two years, two months and eleven days. He followed the two occupations of miller and farmer at the Loucks' homestead. He purchased a great deal of real estate, and at his death owned the mill property. He was married to Susanna Weltzhoffer, of Hellam Township, and had three sons and four daughters. Zachariah K. Loucks, the subject of this sketch, was born March 14, 1822, on the place where he now resides. He received his education in the York County Academy, under Rev. Stephen Boyer. For a number of years was a class-mate of Prof. Kirkwood, now the famous astronomer and mathematician. He commenced business in York first as a clerk with the firm of Schriver, Loucks & Co., and afterward was a clerk for Loucks & Becker at the old Manor Furnace in Chanceford Township, where he remained one year. He then entered the store of Henry Becker in York until 1839, when he returned to his home in Spring Garden Township, and attended to the duties of the grist-mill and farm until his father's death. After this event he and his brother, Henry I., succeeded their father in business at the old homestead, where they still reside, about one mile north of York, along the line of the Northern Central Railroad. In his new and elegant mansion, built in 1881, with its large piazzas, porticoes and beautiful lawn around it, he is afforded all the comforts, conveniences and enjoyments of rural life. For many years he turned his attention closely to farming and milling. Here, on this site, was erected one of the first grist-mills west of the Susquehanna. The old two-story mill, distillery and saw-mill were destroyed by fire on April 29, 1864. The present commodious, five-story brick mill was built during the fall of 1864, at a cost of $30,000. It contains the latest improvements of milling machinery, and has a capacity of 150 barrels of flour in twenty-four hours. During the past twenty years it has been leased by P. A. & S. Small, of York. Cars are pulled by water power to the mill, over a switch from the Northern Central Railway to load flour. In connection with milling and farming, Mr. Loucks has been largely engaged in other business. At the time of the organization of the First National Bank of York, in 1863, he was elected a director. He was afterward elected vice-president, and in the year 1877 was chosen president of that institution, and now occupies that position. He was a director and general financier of the York & Peach Bottom Railway when it was built; for many years a member of the board of directors of York County Agricultural Society, and is a life member of the same; one of the projectors and is now president of the Chanceford Turnpike Company and a director; was a director of the York City Market until its completion, when he resigned; is vice-president of the Penn Mutual Horse Insurance Company of York, and is largely engaged in the real estate business. Mr. Loucks was married January 5, 1843, to Sarah Ann, daughter of Col. Michael Ebert, of Spring Garden. She was born March 18, 1822. Their eldest son, Alexander, resides in Manchester Township, and was married to Catharine Wambaugh. They have four children: Harry, William, Annie and Isabel. George E., the second son of Z. K. and Sarah Ann Loucks, was married to Susan Jane Myers. He resides at Hellam Station. Edward, the third son, is at home. Z. K. Loucks, Jr., the fourth son, is a law student in Philadelphia, and graduated with high honors from the College of New Jersey, at Princeton. Isabella, the only daughter, was married to John W. Kohler, and died at the age of twenty-seven, leaving two children: William I. and Edwin. Mr. Loucks, as a business man, has had an active and prosperous career. He is possessed of good judgment, keen discrimination and excellent financial and executive abilities. In politics he was originally an active Whig, cast his first presidential vote for Gen. Harrison, and was an enthusiastic advocate of Henry Clay's election. He is now an ardent advocate of the principles of the Republican party.

CASPER LOUCKS, born in York County, June 4, 1834, is a son of William and Elizabeth (Spangler) Loucks, and assisted his father, who was a farmer and distiller, until twenty-six years of age, then managed the home farm himself five years, removed to York in 18— and engaged in the manufacture of all kinds of crackers and cakes for five years; subsequently erected a building and removed to his present location, southwest corner of South George and Maple Streets, where he opened a pop manufactory and beer-bottling establishment, and is doing an extensive business. He was married March 24, 1861, to Annie M., daughter of Israel Fissel, and they have seven children: Elizabeth, William, Ida May, Katie, Mary, Edward and Charles. Mr. Loucks has been an active member of the Reformed Church for many years.

FRANKLIN LOUCKS, born in York County September 27, 1834, is a son of Peter and Maria Loucks, was brought up on his father's farm in West Manchester Township, and followed farming on the homestead until 1869, then moved to York and engaged in business as a member of the firm of Fahs, Smith & Co., dealers in coal, and, subsequently, dealt also quite extensively in grain, flour and feed. At the end of five years he severed his connection with that firm, formed a partnership with Bender Bros. in the flour, feed and grain business; sold his interest in the firm in 1882; bought a lot on West Philadelphia Street, and erected a commodious warehouse, where he has built up an extensive trade in the same business. He was married February, 1857, to Mary A., daughter of Adam and Eliza Smyser, and they have had five children: Eliza (deceased), Charles A. (deceased), Anna and Sallie and William F. He is a member of the Lutheran Church.

GEORGE W. S. LOUCKS is a prominent young business man and identified with the development of the manufacturing interests of York. He was born in Baltimore, Md., September 29, 1856, and with his parents came to York County, in 1865. He received his education in the schools of York County, finishing his studies at the York County Academy. After finishing his studies he engaged with P. H. Glatfelter at paper manufacturing, continuing until 1878 when he became an assistant of his father, who had purchased an interest in the York Manufacturing Company, and in 1881 he became a partner. This company is extensively engaged in the manufacture of steam engines, water-wheels and mill machinery, and employs about forty hands. Mr. Loucks was united in marriage May 23, 1883, with Anna N. Lord of Baltimore, Md. Mr. Loucks is a Knight Templar and also an encampment member of the I. O. O. F.

HUGH W. McCALL, attorney at law, was born in Lower Chanceford Township, York Co., Penn., June 15, 1839, is a son of James L. and Sarah D. (Whiteford) McCall, and is of Scotch-Irish and English descent. The father of Mr. McCall was born in Lower Chanceford Township, January 9, 1806, and his mother was born in Harford County, Md., in 1805. The McCall family has been identified with the history of York County for more than 150 years, and the maternal grandfather of our subject was a soldier in the war of 1812. Receiving an academical education, Mr. McCall went, in 1861, to Mansfield, Ohio, and took up the study of law, under Judge Thomas W. Bartley, ex-governor of Ohio. Our subject in 1862 enlisted in Capt. Miller's company, which was at that time ordered to the defense of Cincinnati which was threatened by Kirby Smith; in this capacity he served for thirty days, and returned to Mansfield and resumed his legal studies, which he continued until 1863, when he came to York County, where he raised and organized Company A, of the Twenty-first Pennsylvania Cavalry, commanded by Col. W. H. Boyd, until he was severely wounded at Cold Harbor. Mr. McCall was commissioned captain February 19, 1864, and this position he held until the close of the war. He completed the study of the law in the office of Hon. Thomas E. Cochran of York, and was admitted to the bar August 27, 1866, and has since continued the practice of his profession. He is a Republican, and in 1868 was a delegate of the National Republican Convention at Chicago. He was married in 1871 to Miss Rachel E. Kell, a native of Franklin County, Penn. Their children are as follows: James S., born August 15, 1872; Hugh C., March 17, 1874, and Samuel K., April 9, 1876. Mr. and Mrs McCall are members of the Presbyterian Church.

DR. HENRY MILLER McCLELLAN, deceased, was a prominent physician of his day. He was born October 12, 1809, in York, Penn., and was a son of Robert and Sarah (Miller) McClellan. Robert McClellan died March 12, 1813, and his widow was subsequently married to Dr. William Jamison, of York, with whom our subject prosecuted his medical studies. He was also a student of the Medical College of Baltimore, and a graduate of that institution. He began the practical duties of his profession immediately after graduation, and until his death was untiring in his devotion to his duty. He was a skillful practitioner and achieved an enviable reputation and a large practice. Dr. McClellan was for many years prominently identified with the Presbyterian Church, of which he was an elder, treasurer and valued member. As a citizen, he was just and honorable to all, and his death, which occurred August 7, 1869, was sincerely regretted by all. His wife, with whom he was united May 7, 1835, was Miss Catherine Louisa Smyser, a daughter of Philip A. and Susan L. Smyser of York. She died July 9, 1884, and was the mother of seven children, only two now living, Catherine J. and William H.; the latter is one of the prominent business men of York, and is engaged in the hardware and grocery trades.

G. W. McELROY, district atorney of the county of York, was born in Lancaster County, July 23, 1824. He is a son of Daniel and Rebecca (Wishard) McElroy, and is of Scotch-Irish origin. He is the youngest of nine children, only two of whom are living. His father was born in the county of Donegal, Ireland, and his mother in Glasgow, Scotland, and came to America and settled in Lancaster County, Penn., where they died. Our subject received a common school education in Lancaster County, and was afterward educated in the higher branches, under the kind favor and continued patronage of his brother, A. McElroy, Esq., who died at Chestnut Hill, Philadelphia County, in the summer of 1876. In 1841 he became the principal of the Ephrata Academy, which position he held for three years and then read law under Col. Reah Frazer, at Lancaster. He was admitted to the Lancaster bar in 1846, and practiced there a number of years, during a part of which time he edited the Lancaster *Intelligencer*, and then went to Meadville, Crawford Co., Penn., where he remained until 1853, and then returned to Lancaster and continued practice until 1860. In 1861 he enlisted in Company A, First Pennsylvania Artillery, and was about to be promoted when he was taken ill and was brought to the York Hospital, but regaining his health, was placed in the commissary department, and there continued until 1864, when he was honorably discharged. He was admitted to the York County bar December 20, 1864, and in 1883 was elected district attorney of York County. He was married in 1866 to Miss Anna M. Fisher, a native of York, and has had eight children born to him. He is a Democrat.

JOHN T. McFALL, hatter and dealer in gents' furnishing goods, was born in Union County, Penn., in 1842, and is a son of Thomas and Eliza (Mensch) McFall, and is of Scotch-German extraction. His father was born in Northampton County, Penn., but subsequently removed to Union County, where he died in 1846. The mother of our subject still resides in that county. Mr. McFall was educated in the public schools. He first engaged in the painting business. In 1860 he left his native county and went to Chester, Delaware County. There he remained for nine years, and in 1869 came to York and engaged in his present business. He makes a specialty of fine goods and ranks as the principal hatter and gents' furnisher in York, and is doing a successful business. His marriage took place in 1866, to Miss Mollie E. Johns, a native of Adams County. They have two children, viz.: Wayne G. and Edith M. Mr. and Mrs. McFall are members of the Lutheran Church.

DR. MATTHEW J. McKINNON, son of Michael W. and Ann L. (McCall) McKinnon, was born in February, 1832. The father was a native of Hartford County, Md., and the mother of York County. Penn.; the father was a tanner and farmer. Dr. McKinnon began his education in the common schools of York County, which he attended until the age of ten years ; then entered the academy of York, where, after completing a course of study, he entered Franklin College, at New Athens, Ohio ; after finishing his collegiate course he began the study of medicine under Dr. A. S. Baldwin, of York County, and subsequently entered the University of Maryland, at Baltimore, and graduated March, 1853 ; practiced one year and then went to Shirleysburg, Huntingdon Co. Penn., and practiced until 1861 ; was then commissioned surgeon in the army ; served until January, 1863 ; then resigned and began the practice of his profession at Hagerstown, Md. He remained there until March, 1870, then removed to Chanceford Township, York Co., Penn., and practiced until October, 1873 ; then removed to York, where he still resides and continues the practice of his profession. Dr. McKinnon was a member of the school board of Huntingdon County, Penn.; a member of the school board of Hagerstown, Md.; a member of the town council of Hagerstown three years ; served three years in the school board of York, and was elected a member of the legislature in the fall of 1884, which position he still holds. He married in May. 1857, Amelia J., daughter of Daniel Schindel, of Hagerstown, Md., and to this union were born six children : Carrie, Annie, Robert B., John W., Walter S., Margaret H. The Doctor is a member of the asssociation known as the A. O. M. P.; a member of the Masonic fraternity ; a member of the American Medical Association, and York County Medical Society, and also a member of the Presbyterian Church, of York.

WILLIAM MACK, a native of Germany, was born in 1841. Learning the trade of cooper and brewer he has followed it all his life. He immigrated to America in 1861. He has since been engaged at his trade in New York, Lancaster, Philadelphia, and since 1869, in York. Since 1878 he has been engaged in the bottling business, in connection with that of a cooper. Mr. Mack was married in 1863, to Annie Rinehart, also of German ancestry. They have seven living children : Charles W., Annie, Lizzie, Fred, William, George and Frederike.

HON. LEVI MAISH. This gentleman is one of York's most distinguished sons, and one who has most heroically hewn out his own pathway along the rugged highway of life. He was born in Conewago Township, York Co., Penn., November 22, 1837. His father, David Maish, a most estimable farmer, is now deceased. His mother, Salome Nieman Maish, is still living. The Maishs were among the original settlers of York County, coming here from Chester County with the Quakers, who were among the pioneers in the red lands of the upper end of York County. The subject of this sketch, Col. Levi Maish, received the rudiments of his education in the common schools of his native place and afterward entered upon a course of study at the York County Academy. He was a close student and retired reluctantly from the academy to learn the trade of machinist, April, 1855. Desirous of completing his education and entering upon a professional life he abandoned his apprenticeship in the summer of 1857, and prosecuted his studies with renewed energy. For two terms he taught school in Manchester Township, York County, and also one term in York Borough. In 1861 he took up the study of the law under D. J. Williams, Esq., at the time an able practitioner at the York bar. Being of a patriotic turn of mind, in 1861, unable to resist the call to arms, he raised and organized a company of volunteers from among the young men of his town and vicinity, which, with three other companies from York County and six from Carlisle, Penn., formed the famous One Hundred and Thirtieth Regiment Pennsylvania Volunteer Infantry. In the organization of the battalion, he was elected lieutenant-colonel, and August 17, 1862, went with his regiment to Washington, and was stationed in the defenses of the capital. Very soon afterward Gen. Pope met with disaster at Manasses and the One Hundred and Thirtieth Regiment was attached to the Army of the Potomac, and participated in Gen. McClellan's pursuit of Gen. Lee into Maryland. While actively engaged in the thickest of the fight at Antietam, he received a ball in the right lung, from the effects of which he suffered, terribly, and narrowly escaped death. The ball was never extracted and he still carries it in his lung as a reminder of that sanguinary conflict. Again, at the battle of Chancellorsville, he was dangerously wounded, this time in the hip by a minié ball. The colonel of his regiment, H. I. Zinn, was killed at the battle of Fredericksburg, December 14, 1862, when our subject was promoted to the colonelcy of the regiment, and for a time commanded the brigade to which his regiment was attached at the battle of Chancellorsville, the general commanding having been captured. On May 21, 1863, he was mustered out of service at Harrisburg, the period of his enlistment having expired. Previous to resuming the study of law, he attended lectures in the law department of the University of Pennsylvania; in 1864 passed a highly creditable examination and was admitted to the bar. His talents and pleasant manners soon attracted to him a good practice. His party in October, 1866, elected him to the lower house of the State legislature of Pennsylvania, and was re-elected in 1867. He was a member of the committee of ways and means and that of local judiciary. He served also on the special committee to present the Hancock chair to the city of Philadelphia. Col. Maish on entering the political field in his county identified himself with the reform wing of the Democracy, and labored zealously with the friends of that element to attain the satisfactory results which were secured and an end put to the extravagance and corruption so flagrant at the time. In 1871, when the question of the adoption of the new constitution was being agitated, Col. Maish was a zealous advocate of this praiseworthy and desirable movement, and took no mean part in the discussion which resulted in the adoption of that constitution. In 1872, in company with the late Hon. Thomas E. Cochran and C. B. Wallace, Esq., he was appointed by the legislature of Pennsylvania, to reaudit the accounts of all the county officers, a duty he performed with great ability, judgment and discretion, and for which he was much complimented. The duties of this appointment were very complex, and from the delicate nature of the work, liable to make a man not endowed with the capability and foresight of our subject, forever afterward unpopular with his party. In August, 1874, he was nominated by the Democracy of the Nineteenth Congressional District, composed of the counties of York, Adams and Cumberland, as its candidate for congress and was elected by a very handsome majority. He served in the forty-fourth congress upon the committee of agriculture and coinage, weights and measures, with distinction. He was re-elected in 1876 to the forty-fifth congress and was placed second on the committee of military affairs, and again on that of coinage, weights and measures. It was at this session of congress, that he especially distinguished himself, and won the respect and admiration of the leading men of the nation by the display of his abilities, honesty of purpose and devotion, not only to the principles of the Democratic party, but his great reverence for constitutional liberty and work for the best interests of the republic. We shall here briefly refer to some of Col. Maish's work in congress which brought him prominently before the country as a man of genius and ability.

HIS SPEECH ON THE PENSION BILL.

On July 29, 1876, a bill having been reported by the Committee on Pensions, providing for the payment of pensions to pensioners of the government from the time of their discharge from the service to the time at which their pensions were arbitrarily commenced by the Pension Bureau, otherwise called the Arrears of Pension Act, Col. Maish made a speech in the house of representatives, in advocacy of the bill, which speech was not only considered a very able effort, but one which attracted great attention in the house and all over the country for the originality of the views presented in it, and was also the subject of many complimentary letters from the soldiers of the Union.

By a rule of the pension office, pensions began from the time of the last material evidence furnished. This sometimes procrastinated the claim from one to ten years after the application for a pension was made, varying in accordance with the diligence of the pension office and the good luck of the claimant in expediting his claim. In extenuation of this unjust method of the pension office, Hon. John A. Casson, of Iowa, and Gen. Hurlburt, of Chicago, members of the house at the time, took the ground that the pension was a mere matter of gift or grace. Col. Maish delivered his admirable speech in reply to this proposition, and showed that the pension of the soldier from the acts of congress, under which he enlisted, was as much a contract as the promise of the government to pay its bonds to those who loaned their money to carry on the war; and the government having contracted to pay its soldiers certain pensions for disabilities incurred in the service, such pensions could not be postponed at the caprice of the pension office for an indefinite length of time. The argument was conceded to be unanswerable. The bill became a law, but subsequently similar enactments were largely extended to cases not covered by the principles advocated in the speech of Col. Maish.

SPEECH ON THE ELECTORAL BILL.

February 8, 1877, immediately after the consummation of the fraud of 1876, which resulted in the defeat of the people's choice: Hon. Samuel J. Tilden, and the seating of Rutherford B. Hayes, Col. Maish proposed an amendment in the house of representatives, to the Constitution of the United States, which had for its object the changing of the method of electing the president and vice-president of the United States. To guard against the evils of disputed elections, it proposed to abolish the election of electors and provide for the election of the president by a direct vote of the people.
The amendment is as follows:

ARTICLE XVI.

Article II, Section 1, paragraph 2, to be made to read as follows:
"Each State shall be entitled to a number of electoral votes equal to the whole number of senators and representatives to which the State shall be entitled in congress."
The first division of the twelfth amendment to the Constitution, ending with the words "directed to the President of the Senate," to be struck out, and the following substituted:
"The citizens of each State who shall be qualified to vote for representatives in congress shall cast their votes for candidates for president and vice-president by ballot, and proper returns of the votes so cast shall be made under seal, within ten days, to the secretary of State or other officer lawfully performing the duties of such secretary in the government of the State, by whom the said returns shall be publicly opened in the presence of the chief executive magistrate of the State, and of the chief justice or judge of the highest court thereof; and the said secretary, chief magistrate, and judge shall assign to each candidate voted for by a sufficient number of citizens a proportionate part of the electoral votes to which the State shall be entitled, in manner following, that is to say: they shall divide the whole number of votes returned by the whole number of the State's electoral vote, and the resulting quotient shall be the electoral ratio for the State, and shall assign to candidates voted for one electoral vote for each ratio of popular votes received by them respectively, and, if necessary, additional electoral votes for successive largest fractions of a ratio shall be assigned to candidates voted for until the whole number of the electoral votes for the State shall be distributed; and the said officers shall thereupon make up and certify at least three general returns, comprising the popular vote by counties, parishes, or other principal divisions of the State, and their apportionment of electoral votes as aforesaid, and shall transmit two thereof, under seal, to the seat of Government of the United States, one directed to the president of the Senate and one to the speaker of the house of representatives, and a third unsealed return shall be forthwith filed by the said secretary in his office, be recorded therein, and be at all times open to inspection."
Article II, Section 1, paragraph 4, to be made to read as follows:
"The congress may determine the time of voting for 'president and vice-president and the time of assigning electoral votes to candidates voted for, which times shall be uniform throughout the United States."
Strike out the words "electors appointed," where they occur in the twelfth amendment to the Constitution, and insert in their stead the words "electoral votes."

Again at the following session of congress in October, 1877, Col. Maish introduced his amendment.

In the *N. American Review* of May and April, 1877, ex-Senator Charles R. Buckalew. reviewed at length the amendment proposed by Col. Maish, and advocated its adoption in a very able article. The amendment was reported favorably by a committee of the house, but the report was made so near the end of the session that its final consideration was not reached. The proposition received very general approval and indorsement by the press of the country, and the colonel received many compliments for his introduction of the measure.

The glaring defects of our present system of electing a president and vice-president was called into view at the presidential election of 1884; the contest, having resolved itself upon the issue in the State of New York, her entire electoral vote, was, after many days of uncertainty and doubt (which disturbed the business of the country, after a heated contest, and rekindled the embers of bitter strife), finally declared to have been cast in favor of Grover Cleveland, by a majority of a little over 1,000, in an aggregate vote of nearly 1,000,000. This circumstance revived the interest in the necessity for a change in our general method óf election, and Col. Maish's amendment found many friends and warm advocates in the newspapers of the country. Ex-Senator Buckalew, during the contest, in an able interview, published in the Philadelphia *Times*, presented its merits very forcibly, and the Pittsburgh *Post*, shortly after the election, in a long and able editorial, zealously advocated its adoption.

It was during the closing days of the forty-fourth congress that Col. Maish made himself especially popular and prominent by his arduous duties upon that important committee of "powers and privileges of the house." This committee was the one which investigated and exposed the frauds of the Louisiana Returning Board, of which the notorious James Madison Wells was the president. Hon. J. Proctor Knott, now governor of Kentucky, was the chairman of this committee, and he assigned to our subject the laborious duty of preparing a very large portion of the testimony taken during the investigation of those frauds. It is also a well-known fact and much to the credit of Col. Maish, that in a great measure it was owing to his shrewdness and sagacity, that J. Madison Wells' attempt to sell the vote of Louisiana was discovered.

At the close of the forty-fifth congress, in 1878, his term having expired and, under the rules of the district, the nomination going to Cumberland County, he was succeeded by the Hon. Frank E. Beltzhoover, of that county. After leaving congress, Col. Maish devoted himself to the practice of the law, which he temporarily abandoned to take his seat in congress, and has ever since devoted himself assiduously to the interests of the large clientage he enjoys, and is at present the counsel of the board of commissioners of York County. On October 31, 1883, Col. Maish was married to Miss Louise L. Miller, of Georgetown, D. C., daughter of Benjamin F. Miller, who, prior to the war of the Rebellion, was a very successful merchant of Winchester, Va. A son has blessed this union, who at this time is but an infant.

S. M. MANIFOLD, superintendent of the York & Peach Bottom Railroad, is a native of Hopewell Township, and was born in 1842. His ancestors are of Scotch-Irish and English origin, and were early settlers in the southern portion of York County. Upon his father's side, his grandfather was Henry Manifold, a farmer of Hopewell Township, and upon his mother's, Samuel Martin, a well-known Presbyterian minister, and a resident of Lower Chanceford Township. His parents were Joseph and Rebecca (Martin) Manifold, the former a native of Hopewell and the latter of Lower Chanceford Township. They resided in the lower end of York

BIOGRAPHICAL SKETCHES.

County all their lives. The mother died in 1860, and the father in 1884. They were the parents of six children (four of whom are living): Samuel N. (being the eldest), Margaret J., Keziah A. and William F. (a farmer of Lower Chanceford), Mrs. Rosanna Dougherty (deceased) and Alexander (deceased). Our subject was reared upon a farm and obtained a common school education. He remained engaged in agricultural pursuits until 1863, when he enlisted in Company A, Twenty-first Pennsylvania Cavalry, and was in active service until the close of the war, participating in several severe battles, the principal of which were Cold Harbor, the battles before Petersburg, Poplar Grove Church and with Gen. Warren when he destroyed the Weldon Railroad. When he was mustered out he held his commission as second lieutenant, and for four months subsequently was engaged in the provost marshal's office at Campbell Court House. Returning to his home he engaged in farming in Lower Chanceford until 1872, when he accepted a subordinate position with the engineer corps, then surveying the York & Peach Bottom Railroad. Possessing no practical knowledge of the business of this period, he so applied himself to its study that he was soon after made assistant engineer and subsequently chief; under his charge, the last twenty miles of the road were built, and the Peach Bottom Railroad, on the east side of the river, completed. Soon after the road was finished, in 1878, he was appointed superintendent, which office he still holds; under his supervision all of the many improvements have been made, and the improved condition of the road fitly attests to his executive ability. Mr. Manifold was united in wedlock in 1874 with Miss Sallie Gregg, a native of Chester County, Penn. They have three children living: Howard, Roscalmo and Myra. The family are members of the Presbyterian Church.

CHARLES H. MARTIN, the "artist tailor," is one of the progressive young business men of York. He is a native of York born in 1860, and a son of Jacob F. and Emma (Weiser) Martin. His father was a native of Lancaster County; his mother, a native of York, is a daughter of Martin Weiser and a descendant of an old York County family. His father came to York about 1850, established himself in business as a merchant tailor and was a resident until his death, in 1880. Charles H. received his education in the schools of York, graduating from the high school in 1877. He began his mercantile career as a clerk in the dry goods house of Alexander Fishel, where he was employed two years. He next engaged with Myers & Hoffman as trimmer, remaining with that house one year and a half, when he went to Reading and accepted a position as assistant cutter with Myers & Heim, remaining there two years. He then returned to York and formed an association with F. N. Michaels, and embarked in business as merchant tailor. January 1, 1883, their business relations were dissolved by Mr. Martin purchasing his partner's interest, and he thus established himself in business alone. Mr. Martin has achieved an enviable reputation and successful business results. He carries a large line of all goods suited to his trade, and is the artist of his own productions. He is liberal and progressive in all affairs of public benefit and improvements, and one of the rising young men of York.

LOGAN A. MARSHALL, wholesale liquor and wine dealer, was born in Warrington Township, October 26, 1837. He is a son of James and Elizabeth (Ulrich) Marshall, and is of Scotch-German descent. His father was born in Edinburgh, Scotland, in 1794, and at twelve years of age came to America and settled in the "Upper End" of York County, where his death occurred in 1879. The mother of Mr. Marshall was born in this county in 1794. The first years of our subject were spent on the farm. He came to York in 1863 and engaged in the hotel business, which he continued one year and then began the wholesale liquor business. In 1865 he went to Indiana and remained in the West until 1876, when he returned to York, where he has since resided. He was married in 1860 to Miss Cecelia Picking, of Dover, daughter of William S. Picking, who for fourteen years was a clerk in the house of representatives at Harrisburg. They have had six children, two of whom are living: Annie M. and Neonia E. Mr. Marshall is a Mason and one of the successful business men of York.

EDMUND W. MEISENHELDER, M. D., was born in Dover, York Co., Penn., February 22, 1843, is a son of Dr. Samuel and Josephine S.(Lewis)Meisenhelder, and of German and English extraction. His father was born near Dover, York Co., Penn., in 1818, and mother in York County in 1823. His paternal grandfather was Jacob Meisenhelder, an early settler of Dover Township. His paternal grandfather died about the year 1843. His father, after practicing medicine for thirty-five years in this and Adams County, died in 1888. Our subject was educated at Pennsylvania College, at Gettysburg, and was graduated with highest honors in 1864. He began the study of medicine under his father in 1865, attended lectures at Jefferson Medical College and was graduated in 1868. He began practice at East Berlin, Adams County, and after three years removed to York. In 1870 he married Miss Maria E. Baughman, a native of York County. Three children are the result of this union: Robert L., Edmund W. and Samuel B. Was a member of Company A, (Pennsylvania College Company) Twenty-sixth Regiment Pennsylvania Volunteers, under the "emergency" call of Gov. Curtin, during the rebel invasion of 1863. In 1864 the Doctor enlisted in Company D, Two Hundred and Tenth Pennsylvania Volunteers; was commissioned second lieutenant in 1865, and was discharged May 30, 1865. Dr. and Mrs. Meisenhelder are members of the Lutheran Church.

JAMES L. MENOUGH was born at Pittsburgh, Penn., September 11, 1852, and is the son of Samuel H. and Louisa (Bott) Menough, natives of York County. His father died when he was but six years old, and James made his home with his uncle, Michael Bott, of Dover Township, until he arrived at the age of seventeen years. He then became an apprentice to Jacob Seacrist to learn the carpenter's trade, and with him continued four years. He then located at Reading, Penn. Upon his return to York he was engaged with Nathaniel Weigle for a period of seven years. He then embarked in business for himself, subsequently in association with Peter F. Yost, adding a planing-mill and facilities for doing all kinds of work in their line. Emanuel Yessler subsequently purchased the interest of Mr. Yost, and the firm of Menough & Yessler has continued up to the present writing. They are doing a thriving trade and are honorable business men. Mr. Menough was married in 1878 to Miss Anna, daughter of Franklin and Mary (Smyser) Loucks, of York. They have one child, Luther D. Mr. and Mrs. Menough are members of Christ's Lutheran Church.

FRANK G. METZGER, secretary and general passenger agent of the York & Peach Bottom Railway, is a native of Yocumtown, Penn., born November 26, 1852, a son of William B. and Emma G. (Ginder) Metzger. He is of German descent and is a representative of one of the old families of York County. His father was born in this county in 1828. In 1871 subject began studying telegraphy and for some time continued as an operator. In 1874 he graduated at Eastman's Business College, at Poughkeepsie, N. Y., and for four years afterward was book-keeper for Elcock, Metzger & Co. In 1878, in partnership with his father, he engaged in the boot and shoe business, at Dillsburg, and continued until 1881. In 1879 he was elected clerk of the commissioners of York County, being the first Republican ever elected to that office in this county. His term of office expired in 1882, and that same year he accepted his present position. His marriage took place in 1876 to Maggie Kister, of Goldsboro, Penn. They have one child, Pearl.

E. J. MILLER, dealer in boots, shoes and clothing, was born in York County, Penn., in 1844, a son of Jacob and Leah (Jacoby) Miller, and is of German descent. His mother died in 1864 and his father in 1881. E. J. Miller began life for himself as a manufacturer of cigars. In 1864 he enlisted in Company D, Two Hundredth Pennsylvania Volunteers, and served one year In 1868 he engaged in the boot and shoe business, which he has since continued and now carries one of the most complete lines of boots and shoes in York. In 1884 he, in partnership with George S. Billmeyer, engaged in the clothing and merchant-tailoring business. Mr. Miller married Angeline Mathias, daughter of David Mathias, and three children have been born to this union. In politics Mr. Miller is independent.

J. S. MILLER, M. D., is a native of Hopewell Township, York County, where he was born in 1856. His parents are David and Sarah (Winemiller) Miller, both natives of Hopewell Township, and descendants of old families of the county. The father of our subject is a farmer, and his earlier years were passed as an assistant upon the old homestead. He received a good education attending the Stewartstown Academy, and the York Collegiate Institute. In 1876 he began the study of medicine, reading with Dr. Thomas M. Curran, of Cross Roads, York County. He remained with his preceptor until 1880, in which year he graduated from the College of Physicians and Surgeons, of Baltimore. He immediately located in Paradise, Springfield Township, where he practiced three years, subsequently traveling for six months, through the Middle and Western States. He then entered John Hopkins University at Baltimore, as a student in biology and chemistry. While in Baltimore he also took a special course under Dr. Clinton McSherry, on diseases of the heart, throat and lungs. Dr. Miller located in York in July, 1884, where he is earnestly engaged in practice. He is devoted to his profession, is a close student and a worthy young man.

WILLIAM MITZEL, wholesale and retail dealer in groceries, fruits and confectioneries, was born in Chanceford Township, in 1822, and is the eldest of five children born to Philip and Lydia (Sailor) Mitzel. His great-grandfather, Peter Mitzel, was born in Germany, and came to America previous to the Revolutionary war, in which he was a soldier. The grandfather of our subject was Michael Mitzel, who was born in Codorus Township in 1777, and who died in 1845. The father of our subject was born in Codorus Township in 1800, and his mother in Chanceford Township in 1805. The latter is still living and is the only daughter of William Saylor. Her mother was a Siechrist. Both the Saylor and Siechrist families came from Germany in the early history of York County, and both have numerous descendants. The early life of Mr. Mitzel was spent at Mitzel's Mills, now known as Felton Station, where he was educated at the private schools of Chanceford Township. He served an apprenticeship at the miller's trade and in 1840 began general merchandising at Mitzel's Mills, where he remained four years, and then removed to Hopewell Township. In 1856 he went to Stewartstown, and in 1864 came to York and engaged in his present business. The marriage of Mr. Mitzel took place in 1848, to Miss Keturah Sumwalt, a native of Baltimore, and daughter of Jacob and Dorcas Sumwalt, whose ancestors came from Germany and located at Baltimore prior to the Revolution. Her grandfather, Adam Hendrix (formerly spelled Hendricks), was a descendant of the family of that name who settled in York County as early as, or prior to, 1720, and who were among the first English settlers west of the Susquehanna Rivers. They have had three children, two now living: Francis A. and William A. Mr. Mitzel is a Democrat and cast his first presidential vote for James K. Polk Mrs. Mitzel is a member of the Methodist Episcopal Church.

JOHN A. MORRISON, fruit and produce dealer, was born in Hopewell Township. York Co., Penn., to William E. and Eliza D. (Beaty) Morrison, and is the eldest son in a family of nine children. His father, also, was born in Hopewell Township in 1812. The great-grandfather of our subject was Michael Morrison, a native of Scotland, who came to America prior to the Revolution, in which he was a soldier. The grandfather of Mr. Morrison was a soldier in the war of 1812, and his father in the Rebellion. In 1864 Mr. Morrison enlisted in Company B, Two Hundred and Ninth Pennsylvania Volunteers, and served one year. Returning from the service he served a regular apprenticeship at the milling trade, which he continued seven years. In 1873 he came to York and engaged in the grocery business, which he followed until 1875, and then established his present business. He is the most extensive fruit dealer in York. The marriage of Mr. Morrison took place in 1869, to Miss Sarah A. Bowman, a native of Hopewell Township. They have three children: Margaret J., John W. and Ida K. Politically Mr. Morrison is a Republican. He has a good business education, and is an energetic and enterprising gentleman. Mr. and Mrs. Morrison are members of the Methodist Episcopal Church.

M. J. MUMPER. The Keystone Chain Works are owned and operated by two representatives of the oldest families in the county—M. J. Mumper and David Trout. Mr. Mumper, the senior proprietor, and a practical workman, is a native of Adams County, and a descendant of the Mumper family of the northern end of York County. He learned his trade in Dillsburg, commencing at the age of sixteen years, and has followed it since in Dillsburg and York. The present business plant was first started by Addison Sheffer, of York, upon a very limited scale, between King and Market Streets, in 1870. In 1880 Mr. Mumper, under the firm name of Mumper & Walker, bought the works, and these partners continued together one year, when Mr. Walker withdrew. In 1882 Mr. Mumper sold an interest to David Trout, and the present firm was established. In the spring of 1884 their works were destroyed, and they erected extensive buildings in West York. The works have been steadily on the increase, and are under the personal supervision of Mr. Mumper. They are now selling from $40,000 to $50,000 worth of goods in all the markets of the United States. They have in their works about thirty employes. Mr. Trout is a native of Hopewell Township, and previous to his present co-partnership was a farmer of York County.

JOHN S. MUNDORF, news-dealer and fruit merchant, is the son of George W. and Henrietta Mundorf, and was born and reared in York. After receiving a public school education, he engaged as clerk in a dry goods store, and then for three years was clerk in the York postoffice; he then engaged in handling newspapers, periodicals, etc., receiving subscriptions for all foreign and American issues; subsequently adding foreign and domestic fruits and country produce, in which he deals at wholesale and retail. He is active and progressive, having started in business on a store box, which he has developed into his present extensive and lucrative

BIOGRAPHICAL SKETCHES.   37

trade. He was married, in 1876, to Jennie A. Evans, who has borne him three children: Edgar, Blair and Percy. Mr. Mundorf is a member of the Masonic fraternity, and, with his wife, of the Episcopal Church

SOLOMON MYERS, justice of the peace, was born in Adams County, March 14, 1829, and is a son of John and Elenor (Hummer) Myers, natives respectively of Adams and York Counties, and of German and English descent. The father, a farmer and carpenter, came to York in 1850, and engaged in hotel-keeping, which he followed until 1866, when he retired. He died August 29, 1868, followed by his widow, November 9, 1871. Of the seven children, born to these parents, five are living: Solomon, Julia (Smyser), Harriet (Mundorf), Matilda (Spangler) and Sarah Ellen (Brubaker). The deceased were Lee H., who died in May, 1884, and Sarah Jane, who died in infancy. John Myers had held the rank of captain in the State militia twelve years, and for three years, as a Republican, served as county commissioner. Both he and wife were connected with the Lutheran Church. Solomon Myers was reared a farmer in Adams and York Counties until twenty-one years old. He received a good education, and for thirteen years taught school in York County—nine years in the borough. In 1861, as a member of the Worth Infantry, of York, he was assigned to the Sixteenth Regiment, Pennsylvania Volunteers, as second lieutenant of Company A; was advanced to the first-lieutenancy, and was mustered out after a service of three and one-half months, when he organized a company, which was attached to the Eighty-seventh Regiment as Company E, and of which he was captain; he served in all the engagements of his regiment, excepting the battle of the Wilderness, when he was on detached duty, and was mustered out October 14, 1864. In 1861, also, he was elected justice of the peace, but was then unable to serve on account of military obligations; on his return from the war, however, he entered upon the discharge of the duties of the office, and has since served, with the exception of one term. Since 1882 he has been dealing in pianos, organs and musical instruments generally, and carries a general stock from all the leading makers. Mr. Myers is treasurer of a lodge of Free Masons, and for a number of years was a representative to the Grand Lodge of the I. O. O. F. of the State. He was married December 8, 1872, to Margaret A., daughter of John Orwig, of Shrewsbury.

HENRY NEATER, treasurer of York County, Penn., was born in 1836, son of J. Frederick and Willemina Neater. His parents, natives of Germany, first came to Maryland, but in a very short time left Maryland and came to York County, Penn., where they lived until they died at an advanced age —nearly eighty years. They had four children (one son and three daughters); they are all living in York. The son at an early age, fourteen years, went at his trade of blacksmithing at Mr. William Shetter's, where he worked a few years, when he was employed by Mr. Palmer, where he finished his trade of coachsmith, and worked for Mr. Palmer up to the time he took his present office as treasurer of York County. Mr. Neater is a straight-out Democrat, and has been from boyhood on. He became a voter in 1857, and has never missed a single election. He cast his first presidential ballot for Stephen A. Douglas. He has held the office of assessor and councilman, and in 1884 was elected treasurer of York County. In 1857 he married Miss Annie Fahs, a native of York County, and eight children have been born them; two are dead. The surviving ones are William H., Edward C., George B., Franklin, Frederick and Bertha. Mr. Neater is a member of the I. O. O. F., and he and family are members of the United Brethren Church.

JOHN NEIMAN, the fifth of thirteen children of George and Mary (Rupert) Neiman, was born July 2, 1820, on the old Neiman homestead. He was reared to farming, and on December 29, 1842, married Cassandria Heilman, daughter of George and Eve (Deisinger) Heilman, of Manchester Township. Eleven children were born to them: Melvina, William, Louis, George, John (deceased), Eli, Henry, Cary (deceased), Maggie (deceased), Ellen and Amanda I. Our subject's brothers and sisters were Cassandria (widow of Jacob Hake), Sarah (widow of David Maish), Eliza (wife of Jacob Shettel), Elizabeth (widow of Samuel Shettel), George, Mary (wife of Solomon Shettel), Rebecca (wife of Peter Altland), Lavina (deceased), Samuel, Adam, Susanna (wife of Jacob Rudy) and Leah (wife of William Metzger. Mr. Neiman is well and favorably known throughout York County as president and director of the Dover Fire Insurance Company. He has resided in York since 1874.

G. W. NOEDEL, of the firm of Noedel & Co., bottlers, is a native of Germany, born in 1822, son of Simon and Eliza (Brandan) Noedel, and is of German descent. His parents were both natives of Germany, and lived there until they died; the father in 1835, and the mother in 1836. Our subject was educated at the Latin schools in Germany. In 1848 he engaged in general merchandising, and in that continued until 1851. After the Revolution he immigrated to America, and settled in Baltimore, Md., where he resided twenty-three years, and was engaged in the wholesale wine and liquor business. In 1874 he removed to York County, Penn., and settled on a farm five miles from York, and here he resided until 1877 when he came to York, his present place of residence. On coming to York he began his present business, in which he is very successful. Mr. Noedel was married, in 1853, to Miss Bertha V. Gumpel, a native of Germany. They have one son—Theodore W. Mr. Noedel is a Republican and a man of a public enterprising spirit. He resides in comfort at Cottage Place.

D. K. NOELL, as the name implies, is of French descent, although his father, Jacob Noell, came to America from the east bank of the Rhine, to which his ancestors had fled from religious persecution in France. There are several families of this name in York County, who are generally Catholics, while the family of D. K. Noell were Protestants. His father, Jacob Noell, came to America in 1795, and located in York, Penn. During the war of 1812, when the British menaced Baltimore, Jacob Noell joined Capt. Michael Spangler's company of Independent York Volunteers, which marched to Baltimore, and was engaged in the battle of North Point, September 12, 1814. Mr. Noell was seriously wounded in this battle by a musket-ball passing through his body from left to right, just below the nipples, and from the effects of which he died, leaving a widow and six children poor and helpless, indeed. The children, as soon as they could do any work, were put out to earn their own living. Daniel, the subject of this narrative, at the age of ten years was sent to the country, where, on a farm, without a trade or schooling, he grew to manhood as a common farm laborer. The only books in the family in which he lived were the Bible, the almanac and an old geography. These he studied so well and so often, as to become quite an adept in either. In fact he got the Bible almost by heart, and learned to know every natural and political division, city, town river, etc., on the globe, and the manners, customs, religion and government of all its inhabitants. In 1838 he found his way into the service of William R Gorgas, in Cumberland County, Penn. Here he found many books, especially the histories of men and nations, and being fond of reading he applied himself so diligently that in a short time he knew the histories and biographies of all the nations, and their founders. In fact he was seldom seen without a book, pamphlet or newspaper from which, during idle moments, he could gain some knowledge. Happening one day to find an English grammar in Mr. Gorgas' library, he asked permission to study it. This being granted, he soon made himself acquainted with that study, after which he applied himself to the study of arithmetic, geometry and algebra, in all of which, without a teacher, he became so proficient that, as a teacher, in which he is now engaged, he stood unexcelled. Mr. Noell taught for twenty-two years in the same school-house, thus showing his ability and the high appreciation in which he was held by those whom he served. In 1855 he was elected prothono-

tary, and in 1862 county superintendent of the schools of Cumberland County. In 1845 he married Anna Lukens, a graduate of the Harrisburg (Penn.) High School, who greatly aided him in his various pursuits of knowledge. They have had seven children, only three of whom are now living.

Their four sons, all became naval officers or dets for naval service. Cadet Engineer Michael D. Noell died from a fall on shipboard in 1878, aged nineteen years. He was a bright and promising youth, accurate in mathematics and ready in all studies requiring deep thought. Charles W. Noell, becoming tired of the sea, is now in the service of the Northern Central Railroad, while Jacob E. Noell, as lieutenant-commander, is now in charge at League Island Navy Yard, Philadelphia, Penn. He is quite an intelligent officer, having been in all parts of the world, from which for twelve years,

he sent very interesting and instructive letters, which were published in the York *Democratic Press*, and read with unusual interest by all parties. York Noell is a lieutenant on the United States steamer "Swatara," now in the Caribbean Sea. Mr. Noell's children were all born in Cumberland County, where he lived, taught school and was married. But in 1871, after an absence of forty-one years, he moved back to York, his native town, after which he called one of his sons, thus showing that he never forgot the town that gave him birth. Thus D. K. Noell has made himself, without friend, school or even favorable circumstances, a man of worth, wealth and intelligence. He never went to school, he never learned a trade, had no relations or friends in the world who would or could help him. All he got of men he paid full value for by the sweat of his brow. He honestly worked at all and everything that might offer, when he needed work. Sometimes he was a miner, quarryman, welldigger, riverman, boatman, cooper, etc., but never without a book from which to study, and which, at last, brought him to teaching and a fortune. In 1841, with a small slate and an arithmetic, he traveled 100 miles on foot, through snow, slush and ice, from Harrisburg to Wilkslane, Penn., and ciphered nearly all the way. And in this way he mastered all the branches necessary to a good English education. Being a man of perseverance and indomitable will, he always executed what he undertook. What a lesson this affords for young men! What encouragement for effort, perseverance and sobriety! What a strong proof of the fact that he who wills may conquer!

HERMAN NOSS, son of John and Elizabeth (Leckrone) Noss, was born in December, 1831. His parents were among the early settlers of York County. His father was a miller by trade, and followed milling for a number of years in West Manchester Township, and subsequently engaged in the mercantile business. He still resides in West Manchester Township. Herman Noss attended the schools of York County until the age of sixteen; he then served three years' apprenticeship at the harness-making business, under the instruction of John W. Small, and worked at the business for Mr. Small for twenty-six years and nine months. He began the lumber and coal business in 1878, in York, which business he has carried on extensively to the present time. He was elected treasurer of York County in the fall of 1873, and served two years; he also served as school director six years. He married in the spring of 1858. Sarah J., daughter of Peter and Christiann (Small) Grimm, natives of York. To this union were born six children, viz.: William S., George B. M. (deceased), Mary V., John W., Adela, Harry P. William, the eldest, assists his father as clerk in the lumber and coal business. Mr. Noss and wife and two of his children are members of the Rev. J. O. Miller's German Reformed Church.

H. L. NEUMAN, engaged in the wholesale manufacture of ice cream, and the manufacture of agricultural implements, is a native of Conewago Township, and the son of Jacob and Elizabeth Neuman, natives of this county. After leaving the home farm, H. L. Neuman engaged as a clerk in a dry goods store in York, where he remained until 1861, when he enlisted in the Eighty-seventh Pennsylvania Volunteers, served three years, and near Richmond was seriously wounded in the leg. Returning to the county, he engaged in the confectionery business, under the firm name of Neuman & Wiest, for nine years, and then engaged in the wholesale manufacture of ice cream. In 1874 he also engaged in the manufacture of agricultural implements, which he still continues. He was married in 1867 to Miss Amanda Wambaugh, of York, and there have been born to him four children: Edward N., James W., Margie and Daisy M. Mr. and Mrs. Neuman are members of the Reformed Church, and Mr. N. is a member of the G. A. R.

PHINEAS PALMER, born in Bucks County, Penn., May 1, 1824, is a son of Phineas and Sarah Palmer, natives of the same county. At the age of twelve he left the paternal roof to seek his fortune. In 1840 he apprenticed himself to Joseph Stewart, carriage-maker of Trenton, N. J., served five years, and then, in the fall of 1845, came to York and worked nearly five years at journey work, and in October, 1850, established a manufactory, which he has ever since conducted, being now one of the oldest and most extensive carriage-makers in the borough. In November, 1847, he married Miss Susan, daughter of William Lenhart, of York County, and there have been born to him twelve children, of whom the six surviving are Milton L., Emma E., Franklin P., Sarah K., Lucy and Harry P. Mr. Palmer is a member of the order of A. F. & A. M.

F. J. PALMTAG, son of John and Bertha (Henise) Palmtag, was born May 27, 1859, in York County, Penn. His parents were born in Wurtemberg, Germany. John Palmtag has for many years been extensively engaged in the manufacture of soaps and candles, in connection with the chandlery business. F. J. Palmtag, the subject of this sketch, although a young man, has a thorough knowledge of the soap and chandlery business, and has for several years managed the business for his father.

JOHN F. PATTON, proprietor of the City Drug Store, so well known to the citizens of York County, is of English and Scotch-Irish ancestry. His grandfather, John Patton, was born in County Antrim, North Ireland, and his grandmother, Margaret (McGowen) Patton, in County Tyrone. Soon after their marriage, they immigrated to America, and located, in the year 1780, in Chester County. They had fifteen children—twelve boys and three girls. Both grandparents died at the age of eighty years, or upward. The father of our subject, Ebenezer Patton, was the eighth son. In early life he learned the trade of shoemaking, and moved to Chanceford Township, this county, and in 1820 was married to Rebecca Smith, of Lancaster County. The other brothers and sisters located in Chester, Lancaster and Berks Counties, and the family became very numerous. Ebenezer Patton died at the age of forty-nine, and the mother, with her eight children, moved to Wrightsville, where she died in the year 1852. John F. Patton, the fourth son of this family, was born in Lower Windsor Township, December 15, 1839. He received his educational training in the common schools. In 1853 he came to York and engaged as a clerk in a dry goods store. In the spring of 1856 he entered the drug store of Dr. Jacob Hay, Sr., to learn a business for which he has since proven himself so admirably fitted. He entered the wholesale drug establishment of Thomsen & Block, of Baltimore, in 1859, remaining there until 1866. During that year he went to St. Louis, but, on account of sickness, stayed there but a few months, and returned to Baltimore. In the year 1869 he began the drug business for himself in a small room on the north side of West Market Street, York, on the same site of his present handsome and elegant store building. In 1873 he moved his store to the large business room of Martin Bender, nearly opposite the Motter House. He always prospered in business, continually enjoying a large and increasing trade. The familiar name of "City Drug Store" was found in the columns of every newspaper in the county, and on all the conspicuous advertising places that could be obtained. His industry and close and attentive application to business were worthy of admiration. They were the cause of his unrivaled prosperity. But the disastrous flood of June, 1884, played sad havoc with his store, and the owner narrowly escaped with his life. The contents were almost a total wreck. He had already begun the erection of the new City Drug Store, a three-story brick building, with a large and commodious store room, which he stocked and fitted up on a more extensive scale than ever, in September, 1884. In this place he has now an extensive and encouraging trade. Mr. Patton is an enterprising, public-spirited citizen, and a member of St. Paul's Lutheran Church, of York.

DR. EDWARD H PENTZ was born January 24, 1826, and is the son of John and Salania Pentz, natives of York County. The subject of this sketch had the advantage of an education, and began a course of studies preparatory to his profession under the instructions of Dr. Theodore Haller. He subsequently went to New York and graduated at the Medical University of New York, about the year 1848. He then returned to York and began the practice of his profession, and through his skill and devotion to the duties relative to his profession soon built up a good practice in the borough of York and the surrounding country. He devoted his time and energy to his profession until a few months before his death. He died November 30, 1873. Dr. Pentz married, April 14, 1853, Miss Josephine, daughter of Charles and Anna M. (Spangler) Weiser, of York. To this union was born one son, Bransby C., who is a photographer, and at present writing is doing an extensive business in York, having one of the finest appointed studios in southern Pennsylvania, and is noted for his superior work.

J. TURNER PERKINS, M. D., a native of Prince George County, Md., was born in 1854. He is of English and Scotch ancestry, and a son of James T. and Susan M. (Travers) Perkins. His father is a large planter and a resident of Maryland. Dr. Perkins received superior educational advantages, and was graduated from the Maryland Agricultural College, A. B. Ph. D. In 1874 he commenced his medical studies at Baltimore, having for his preceptor Prof. Nathan R. Smith. He was graduated from the University of Maryland in 1877, as M. D., and for one year was an assistant to his preceptor. He located in York in 1878, where he has been in constant practice since, and has achieved a reputation as one of the leading physicians and surgeons of York County. Dr. Perkins has taken three special courses in surgery at Baltimore, and has been surgeon in the Baltimore Marine Hospital and of the city almshouse. He is a member of the York County Medical Association, of which he has been vice-president, and is a Royal Arcanum Mason. In 1883 Dr. Perkins was married to Miss Nora Salmon, daughter of Maj.-Gen. George Paris Salmon, of the English Army, a native of Scotland.

F. MARVIN T. PFLIEGER, chief clerk in the Northern Central & Pennsylvania Railway freight office, was born in 1855 and is of German descent. The Pflieger family is well known in the history of York County. Mr. Pflieger was educated at the public schools and York County Academy, and in 1869 entered the employ of the firm now known as Thomas Chambers & Co., as messenger, and in 1870 was promoted to the position of book-keeper. Here he remained until 1875, when he engaged in the railway business. In 1880 he was made chief clerk, and still holds that position. He was married, in 1876, to Ida J. Keech, daughter of W. L. Keech. They have two children. Mr. Pflieger is a stanch Democrat.

HENRY PRESAW, son of Henry and Barbara (Smith) Presaw, was born near Hanover, January 20, 1832. Henry, the subject of this sketch, is the youngest in a family of six children. He learned the trade of blacksmith and followed it for many years. At the breaking out of the war he enlisted in Company I (Capt. Russell), First Maryland Cavalry. He was in the first raid made by Gen. Stoneman in the Shenandoah Valley, and was also in the battles of Winchester, Rappahannock Dam, Briscoe Station, Gettysburg, Malvern Hill, Front Royal, Maryland Heights and Brandy Station. At an engagement on the Weldon Railroad, Mr. Presaw lost his left leg (August 16, 1864), by a minie ball, and had his leg amputated the same day. He was sent to Beverly Hospital, New Jersey, and remained there about six weeks, and then removed to the hospital at Broad and Cherry Streets, Philadelphia, and remained there about three months, when he was honorably discharged. Few soldiers from this section have seen more hard service than the subject of this sketch. January 20, 1872, Mr. Presaw married Catherine Mate, of York, Penn.

THOMAS RAMSAY, justice of the peace, is a native of Baltimore, born October 14, 1842. His parents were William and Mary (Kilgore) Ramsay, the former a native of Baltimore, and the latter of York County. His father was engaged in the mercantile business in Baltimore until 1852, when he removed to York County where he continued in business until his death. The subject of this biography was the eldest of four children, and although quite young upon the death of his father, assisted his mother in conducting the business left by his father, devoting his leisure to study. He entered the high school of York at the age of fourteen, and when sixteen began teaching in York County. He subsequently entered Duff's Commercial College at Pittsburgh and graduated in 1863. Being offered a professorship in this college he accepted and remained one year, resigning to accept a position as chief clerk tendered to him by an extensive oil refinery at Pittsburgh, which position he held one year, the works being destroyed by fire. Returning to York, he was engaged at several vocations until 1875, when he was appointed deputy clerk of the courts, which position he held two terms. In April, 1881, he was appointed justice of the peace by Gov. Hoyt to fill a vacancy in the Sixth Ward, and subsequently he was elected to the same office for a term of five years, which position he is now creditably filling. Mr. Ramsay is a member of the I. O. O. F., the I. O. R. M. and the order known as the Seven Wise Men. In 1876 Mr. Ramsay was married to Miss Helena Hemler, of Adams County, Penn.

E. A. REESE, foreman of the smith and plow department at Farquhar's, was born in Eutaw, Ala., February 1, 1851; he is a son of Edward and Charlotte (McKinstry) Reese, and is of Scotch-Irish descent. After receiving a common school education he learned coach and carriage-making, and continued that work in his native State until 1874, when he came to York, and for a time worked at pattern making for A. B. Farquhar, and about two years later he was made foreman of the smith and plow department, where he has since continued. He has under him about fifty men. In 1859 he married Miss Louisa M. Buckingham, a native of Piqua, Ohio, and a daughter of Ferdinand Buckingham. They have one child, Edwin B. Politically Mr. Reese is a Democrat. Mrs. Reese is a member of the Trinity Reformed Church.

WILLIAM G. REICHLEY, general merchant, was born in York, July 15, 1852, is the son of Jacob and Sophia (Bilber) Reichley, and is the second of seven children. The parents of our subject were born in Germany, came to America in 1847, and settled in York, where the mother died in 1880. Mr. Reichley received a common school education at the schools of York. Subsequently he clerked in a store for five years. In 1870 he began the general merchandise business in York. His marriage occurred in 1871, to Miss Kate Heindel, a native of York County, and a daughter of P. B. and Catherine Heindel. Of four children born to them two are living: Nettie M. and William J. Mr. Reichley is a Democrat and takes great interest in politics. He and wife are members of the Lutheran Church.

FREDERICK REINDEL is a native of Bavaria, Germany, was born in 1838, and is a son of Dr. Thomas and Kuninguda Reindel. His father was born in Germany and died there. His mother still resides in that country, and is seventy-four years of age. The subject of this sketch was educated at the public schools of Germany. At fourteen years of age he joined the Bavarian Army, in which he spent fifteen years. In 1870 he came to America, and settled in Baltimore, Md., and engaged in the barbering and hair dressing business. There he remained some time and then came to Hanover, and continued the same business. In 1874 he came to York and continued the same business, until about five years ago. Since that time he has been engaged in the wine and liquor business. He was married in 1870 to Miss Julia Ulrici, a native of Bavaria. They have two children, Harry and Clara.

THE REISINGER FAMILY are of the early settlers of York County. Carl, Gotlieb and Jacob, three brothers, came to this country in 1767, and settled at Lexington, Mass. At the breaking out of the Revolution they joined a company organized by Benedict Arnold, and were engaged at the first battle of Bunker Hill. Jacob was killed or drowned at Long Island. Carl and Gotlieb served through the war, to the battle of Yorktown, where Lord Cornwallis surrendered the British troops to Gen. Washington. Carl and Gotlieb then came to York County. Carl married a daughter of Gen. Boyer, and had born to him nine daughters and one son, Samuel Reisinger. Samuel married a daughter of Conrad Gipe, and raised a family of seven daughters and four sons. The names of the four sons are William I. Reisinger, George Reisinger, Henry Reisinger and Adam Reisinger. Henry Reisinger was elected recorder of deeds, of York County, in 1866. William I. Reisinger, the eldest of the four sons, married a daughter of Henry Hartman and had five sons, Samuel H. Reisinger and William F. Reisinger, who served during the late Rebellion, and O. DeWitt Reisinger, Calvin J. Reisinger and Elmer E. Reisinger and two daughters. William I. Reisinger was an active worker in the Democratic party from his early life. He joined the York, Penn., Rifle Company, which was ordered out by the governor in 1844, and took part in the Philadelphia riots in 1849. He took an active part in organizing the Worth Infantry Company, which was commanded by Capt. Zeigle up to 1861. At the breaking out of the Rebellion the company was attached to the Sixteenth Pennsylvania Regiment. Capt. Ziegle was made colonel, for three months' service. William I. Reisinger was quartermaster-sergeant of the said regiment. After the three months' service he raised forty men for the Ringgold Cavalry and failed in getting a commission; organized a company of 109 men and gave the command to Daniel Herr, with the under-

BIOGRAPHICAL SKETCHES.   41

standing that he should be major, but took first lieutenant. After a short time Capt. Herr resigned and he became the captain, and served as such in Company I, Eleventh Pennsylvania Cavalry up to October 15, 1864, when he was compelled to quit the service on account of his ill health. During his service he received four wounds, but none of a serious character, and was in bad health for some years after his return from the war. In 1875 he was elected a justice of the peace in York, and in 1881 was re-elected, and was well spoken of as a justice.

E. A. RICE, son of William H. and Sarah (Julius) Rice, eldest of three children, was born June 14, 1863, in Dover Township. He was reared on a farm and received his education in the public schools of Paradise Township, and four years at East Berlin Normal School. He began teaching in Paradise Township; after teaching three terms removed to York in 1882, where he has since resided, teaching the Penn Street Primary School one term, then promoted to teach No. 65 Secondary School; has just finished his second term here and received a professional certificate from Prof. Shelley. Mr. Rice also attended the State Normal School, at Millersville, Penn. He is a young man of pleasing address, conscientious in the discharge of his duty and highly esteemed by all who know him. His father was born in Codorus Township, and brought up on a farm. September, 1862, he married Sarah Julius, daughter of Peter and Maria (Shaffer) Julius, of Dover Township. Three children were born of this marriage: E. A. (our subject), Annie M. and Charles P. His maternal ancestors were among the earliest settlers of Dover Township.

J. F. ROHRBACH, Jr., dealer in all kinds of hardware, paints, oils and groceries, is a native of Codorus Township, born in 1851, son of J. F., Sr., and Julia A. (Geisleman) Rohrbach. In a family of twelve children he is the third, and is of German descent. His parents are natives of this county. Formerly Mr. Rohrbach was a farmer, but at about nineteen years of age he accepted a clerkship in the hardware store of Hantz & Bro., of York, and here remained twelve years. In 1883 he began his present business, which has since increased from year to year until now he does an extensive trade. By the flood of 1884 he lost about $3,000. He was married, in 1875, to Miss Emma Meckly, who died in 1881. In 1883 he was united in marriage to Miss Ida Neiman. daughter of John Neiman. Mr. Rohrbach has fought his every battle, and through energy he has been victorious. He was educated at the public schools. Mr. and Mrs. Rohrbach are members of the Lutheran Church, and are highly respected citizens.

JOSEPH ROOT, a native of New Hampshire, was born October 31, 1811, and is the son of Joseph and Lydia (Croak) Root. He received a good academical education, and at the age of nineteen began teaching in Vermont, and was thus employed for five consecutive terms of five months each. He was next employed by Alfred Blake, scale-maker, as a traveling salesman, and subsequently, in 1839, engaged in the manufacture of scales on his own account. In 1841 he formed a partnership at York with Emerson J. Case, who died in 1881, but the high reputation achieved by the firm for the superiority of its scales had induced Mr. Root to retain the name of the old firm. Root & Case, under which he still conducts the business. In the spring of 1850 Mr. Root married Miss Marion, daughter of Joseph Parkhurst, of Vermont, and to his nuptials have been born two children: Jabez H. and Helen M. Mr. Root is a member of the Presbyterian Church and also of Mt. Zion Lodge I. O. O. F.

PROF. GEORGE W. RUBY, Ph. D. (deceased), was a native of Lower Windsor Township, York County, and was born July 4, 1824, to Henry and Catherine (Rathfon) Ruby. He was of German descent. The parents of Dr. Ruby were also York County born, and the family dates at least 100 years in this county. Dr. Ruby first attended school at Lititz, Penn., then entered Marshall College, at Mercersburg, Penn., and from that college graduated with honors in the class of 1848. He first taught school at Middletown, Md. In 1850 he came to York, and was immediately elected principal of the York County Academy. This position he filled for thirty consecutive years. During his administration more than 5,000 pupils received instruction from him. Prof. Ruby was married, December 14, 1848, to Miss H. Mary Hassler, a native of Franklin County, daughter of Jacob and Elizabeth (Keiffer) Hassler. The Hassler family came from Germany many years ago and settled in York County. To Dr. and Mrs. Ruby were born thirteen children, only four of whom survive their father: Henry J. John C., William H. and Samuel. Dr. Ruby was a member of the German Reformed Church. His life was one of much usefulness, and in his death, which occurred November 16, 1880, the county lost one of its greatly respected citizens and honorable men. Mrs. Ruby is a member of the German Reformed Church and an amiable Christian lady.

WALTER B. RUBY, detective and constable, is a son of Joseph and Sarah (Barnhart) Ruby, was born at Wrightsville, Penn., October 20, 1844, is one of fourteen children, and is of Scotch-German descent. The father was born in Somerset County, Penn., January 20, 1809, and died in York County, in 1871; the mother was born in York Couny, in 1811. In 1845 the Ruby family came to York. Mr. Ruby received a common school education, and at fourteen years of age began for himself in life; for some time he was news boy on the Northern Central Railroad. In August, 1862, he enlisted in Company K, One Hundred and Thirtieth Pennsylvania Volunteers, but on account of physical disability, was discharged in December of the same year. In January, 1864, he enlisted again in the One Hundred and Eighty-seventh Pennsylvania Volunteers, Company B, and was discharged at the close of the war. In 1874 he was given a position on the York police force, where he continued until 1879, and has since that time been acting in his present capacity. In 1880 and 1881, he was made foreman of the Laurel Fire Company. His marriage occurred in 1872, to Miss Sarah J. Fishel, of York County; he is a Democrat, and a member of the I. O. O. F., and I. O. H.

DANIEL A. RUPP, retired merchant, is a native of York, Penn., born in 1825, son of Daniel and Lydia (Small) Rupp, and is of German descent. His parents were both natives of York County; the father was born in 1776, and the mother in 1786. His paternal grandfather, Gotlieb Rupp, also a native of York County, was a soldier in the war of the Revolution. The Rupp family has been known in the history of this county for more than a century, and has long been prominent in the business circles of York. Daniel A. Rupp was educated at the York County Academy. In 1844, he in partnership with his brother, David Rupp, who died in 1871, engaged in general merchandising in York County, under the firm name of D. & D. A. Rupp. Mr. Rupp continued however until 1868, when he retired from active business life. He was married, in 1850, to Miss Sarah Dietz, a native of York County, and daughter of Jacob Dietz, a prominent builder and contractor of York, who was the principal contractor of York County Court House. To his marriage have been born two children: Harry and Anna V. Mr. and Mrs. Rupp are members of the Presbyterian Church.

DAVID RUPP, proprietor of the York Steam Soap Works, is a native of York, and a son of David and Henrietta (Harry) Rupp, natives of the county and of German descent. David Rupp, Sr., was for many years engaged in the dry goods trade in York, subsequently retired, and died in 1875; his wife is also deceased. They were the parents of nine children, of whom two are living. our subject and Lydia S., wife of H. S. Myers, of York. David Rupp, our subject, in 1876 engaged with P. H. Sprenkle and C. F. Ford, in the manufacture of quercitron extract for dyeing, remaining with them five years, and then conducting the business two years alone. In 1879 he embarked in his present enterprise in association with J. R. Busser, whose father had originated the soap works. They were in company together three years, when Mr. Rupp took full charge, enlarged the works, and now has a capacity of 100 boxes, or 75,000 pounds per day, consisting of laundry and fine toilet soap, which is principally sold in the State of Pennsylvania. Mr. Rupp has been a Director of the York County National Bank, and is now a director of the Opera House and West End Improvement Company. He was married, in 1882, to Annie E. Riter, of Philadelphia, and is the father of two children: Michael R. and David.

JOHN CHARLES SCHMIDT, chain manufacturer, is a native of Carlisle, Penn., and was born March 14, 1859. His parents, Henry D. and Louisa (Carson) Schmidt, were natives of York county. Mr. Schmidt received superior educational advantages, attending the schools of York, until 1868, when his parents removed to St. Paul, Minn., where his studies were continued until 1873, when the family returned to York. He next entered the York Collegiate Institute, and in 1875 accompanied his father to Europe, and passed one year in the educational institutions of Stuttgart, Germany. Upon his return to York, he entered the mercantile house of P. A. and S. Small, where he continued until 1881. He then embarked in business, establishing a chain manufactory, in which field of enterprise he has been very successful. He employs about fifty workmen, and his works have a capacity of manufacturing 50,000 pounds of chain daily, which is shipped all over the United States, and exported to Cuba and Mexico. The enterprising and progressive spirit of Mr. Schmidt has added much to the business interests of York. He is a director of the York Gas Company, also a director of the York National Bank, and for several years has been identified with St. John's Episcopal Church.

CAPT. EDWARD L. SCHRODER was born in York, York Co., Penn., and is a son of Emanuel and Mary (Laucks) Schroder, and of German and Scotch origin. His father was born in York in 1803, and his mother in York County, 1809 Our subject was educated in the York public schools and the York County Academy. He learned the trade of cabinet-making. He was a member of the Worth Infantry Military Company (Capt. Thomas A. Zeigle), when that company was called in service April 20, 1861. He entered the service; the company became Company A, Sixteenth Regiment, and served until mustered out July 80, 1861. October 22, 1861, he enlisted in Company F, Fifth Maryland Volunteers, for the term of three years, was appointed sergeant-major of the regiment, commissioned second lieutenant of Company A, March 16. 1862, and first lieutenant of Company H same year (December 10, 1862), and captain of Company I, April 7, 1864. He took part in the historic engagement between the "Monitor" and "Merrimac," was at Antietam and Winchester, Va., June 13 to 15, 1863, was taken prisoner of war on June 15, and was for eighteen months in Southern prisons. He spent eleven months in the famous Libby Prison at Richmond, Va., was under fire of Union batteries at Charleston, S. C., was paroled at Columbia, S. C., and sent to 'Camp Parole, Annapolis, Md., December 15, 1864, and on January 28, 1865, was honorably mustered out of the service. His marriage was solemnized July 1, 1878, to Miss Kate Laucks, daughter of David Laucks, of Berks County, Penn. In politics he is a Republican, is a Mason and Knight Templar, and member of I. O. O. F., also a member of Post 37, G.:A. R., has been senior vice commander and post commander and an aide-de-camp on the staff of the commander-in-chief of the G. A. R. of the United States, and director Western National Bank.

FREDERICK T. SCOTT, who for more than thirty years, has been permanently identified with the business interests of York, was born in Baltimore County, Md., about fourteen miles from the city, in 1824. His father, Thomas Scott, was a native of North Ireland, and early in life immigrated to America, settling in New York, where he was married to Margaret Lintz, a native of that State. Removing to Maryland they remained there until their deaths. Thomas Scott, the father, was one of the contractors on the first railroad that led out from the city of Baltimore. Four children were descendants: John (now deceased, was for thirty years an employe upon the Northern Central Railroad; for a long time a conductor; died at Hanover Junction); William (who died in 1869 at the same place, was also a conductor upon the same railroad about thirty years); Jane Lewis (the only daughter, died in 1861, in the State of Ohio). The subject of this sketch, at the age of eleven, went to Baltimore and was employed for six years as a bar tender. He then served an apprenticeship for over three years in the machine shops of the Baltimore & Susquehanna Railroad (now Northern Central Railroad). Here he became a skillful machinist, and, having thoroughly mastered his trade, remained for five years as an employe. He then embarked in business for himself, manufacturing cars and mill work, but his enterprise was doomed to disaster. In 1850 he lost heavily by fire, and in 1852, when employing seventy five hands, he was forced to suspend, losing every dollar of his property on account of the strike on the Baltimore & Ohio Railroad, which forced, in thirty days, the price of iron from $55 to $90 per ton. He then sought a new field for business operations, and in 1854 removed to Glen Rock, this county, where he established the Glen Rock Machine Shops, manufacturing upon an extensive scale, cars, paper-mill works, agricultural implements and general machinery This enterprise added greatly to the material interests of the town, and at times as many as forty-five hands were employed in his works. In 1861, upon the outbreak of the civil war, he sold out his interests at Glen Rock at a great sacrifice, removed to York and engaged with the Northern Central Railroad as master machinist of the company's car and locomotive shops. This responsible position he filled with signal ability, and with eminent satisfaction, until 1875, when he resigned. Mr. Scott then again embarked in business on his own account, and his latter efforts have met with success. He has established a large and lucrative trade in coal, lumber and railroad ties in York, and, in connection is manager of extensive granite quarries, at Goldsboro, York Haven. Upon his farm, which consists of 194 acres, are also large deposits of brown stone, which is quarried to a large extent. He has a steam saw-mill upon his farm, and is engaged in farming in Codorus Township, where he owns a valuable, finely improved farm, which, with valuable real estate in York, is the result of wise business enterprise. Mr. Scott was elected resident director of the York County Alms-house, in 1873, and instituted many valuable reform measures in the management of that institution. His independence of action and prudent management won for him the

admiration of the tax-paying people of the entire county, regardless of political preferences. He had the land connected with the alms house surveyed and, together with the other members of the board of directors, introduced a new code, rules and regulations, setting forth the duties of the different officers by whom the institution is governed, which received the approval of the State board of public charities, the grand jury and the court of common pleas of the county. In the exercise of his public duties Mr. Scott evinced the same prudent and practical knowledge which has made his private affairs eventually successful. For nearly forty years Mr. Scott has been a member of the I. O. O. F. and is at present a member of Harmony Lodge, No. 855, and also of the encampment of the Grand Lodge of Maryland. He is a member of York Lodge, No. 266, of A. F. & A. M., and also of the order of K. of P. He is president of the York Building and Loan Association, president of the Star Building and Loan Association, and a president of the Penn Mutual Relief Association, of which he served as president for a number of years. He is enterprising in all matters of moral advancement, and the architect of his own fortunes. Mr. Scott was united in marriage February 10, 1848, with Miss Elizabeth A., daughter of Jacob and Henrietta Pein Cook. They have been blessed with seven children: Jacob F., Henrietta M., Emma L. (deceased), Cecelia N. (deceased), Oscar W. (deceased), Calvert C. and Winfield W. The family are members of Trinity Reformed Church of York.

JACOB SEACRIST, one of the leading contractors and builders of York, was born in York County, October 29, 1829, his parents being Henry and Anna (Daley) Seacrist, both of whom are natives and citizens of the county. Jacob received the educational advantages of the common schools until he was fourteen years of age, when he was engaged upon a farm, at which he was employed until he attained his majority. He then was apprenticed to learn the carpenter's trade with Samuel Kohr, and having mastered it, worked at this branch of industry until 1863. Being desirous of extending his business relations, he erected a planing-mill in York, and began contracting and building on an extensive scale. Having superior advantages, he has taken a leading position among the builders of York, particularly in school and church structures. Mr. Seacrist is still actively engaged in business, and is a representative of the enterprising school of citizens. He was united in marriage in July, 1855, with Miss Mary E. Kepler, of Baltimore. Eight children have been born to them: Adam W., Annie K., Jacob K., Mary E., George H., Lucy M., Oliver V. and Harry E. Mr. Seacrist is a member of the I. O. O. F., K. of P., and with his wife a member of the Methodist Episcopal Church.

AMBROSE H. SEIFFERT, general accountant for the firm of Baugher, Kurtz & Stewart, was born in Dover Township, York County, December 1, 1838, and is the second in a family of seven children born to John and Elizabeth (Henise) Seiffert, of German descent. The parents of Mr. Seiffert were born in Dover Township, where they now reside. His paternal grandfather was John Seiffert, a native of Pennsylvania, but in 1833 he moved to Ohio, where he died. The boyhood of our subject was spent on the farm. He was educated at the public schools of Dover Township and York County Academy. In 1857 he began teaching school, at which he continued until 1872, when he accepted his present position. He was married in 1865 to Miss Mary A. Daron, a native of Manchester Township, born June 9, 1845, and daughter of George and Lydia Daron. They have four children, viz.: John H., George R., Franklin M. and Maggie M. Mr. Seiffert is an earnest supporter of the Democratic party. In 1884 he was elected to represent the Fifth Ward in the borough council, and re-elected in 1885, and upon the organization of the council was chosen assistant chief burgess for the ensuing year. Mr. and Mrs. Seiffert are members of the German Reformed Church.

PROF. WILLIAM H. SHELLEY, superintendent of the public schools of York, was born on the Mansion farm, which he now owns, on the Hill Island in the Susquehanna River. He entered the York County Academy when quite young, spent several years as a student in that institution, and there laid the foundation of a broad and liberal education. He began teaching in West Hempfield Township, Lancaster County, and taught there two years, three years in Columbia Borough, and three years as assistant to Prof. George W. Ruby, in York County Academy, during which time he completed a full collegiate course, and received special native instruction in French and German. Failing health at that time prevented him from graduating at Dickinson College. He went to the State of Michigan, and for three years filled the chair of Latin and Greek, and two years the chair of mathematics, in Albion College. While occupying these positions he was a diligent student, and became very proficient in the branches which he taught. The honorary degree of master of arts was conferred on him by the Iowa Wesleyan University, and later he received the full State certificate for the classical course, an honor conferred upon him by the State Normal School at Millersville, Penn. While spending his summer vacation in York, during the year 1870, he was unanimously elected the first superintendent of schools of York, which position he has since continuously held with great honor to himself and great benefit to the educational interests of the town. As an organizer of schools, Prof. Shelley has few equals Under his able administration, the public schools of York have regularly improved and prospered. He is thoroughly familiar with both the theory and the practice of his chosen profession, and has illustrated by his practical work both the science and the art of teaching. He also takes an active interest in church and Sunday-school work.

GEORGE E SHERWOOD, ex-representative and justice of the peace, was born in Virginia, August 17, 1843, and is a son of Lewis and Minnie (Koch) Sherwood, both natives of Germany. His father came to this country as a political refugee in 1834, settling at Hampton, Elizabeth Co., Va., where he bought a large plantation, upon which he resided until 1855, when he removed to Baltimore, Md. Our subject was educated at Baltimore, and upon the breaking out of the late civil war, he responded to the call for volunteers, and enlisted as orderly sergeant in the First Virginia Scouts, under Gen. Rosecrans; served likewise in Sanno's Scouts, Twenty-sixth Pennsylvania Infantry, and Ninth Pennsylvania Cavalry, and served until the close of the war. He rose from the ranks to captain, and participated in the following battles: Winchester, Red House, Morefield, Gettysburg (where he was taken prisoner), Nashville, Savannah and Lister's Ferry. He received his discharge at Newburn, N. C., June 11, 1865, and on the 16th day of July of the same year came to York, where he has since been a resident. Mr. Sherwood, upon his arrival in York, assumed the editorship of the York German *Gazette*, one of the leading Democratic papers in the county, filling the position with marked ability. In 1873 he was elected town clerk of York, and filled that position until 1881. He was elected to represent his district in the State legislature in 1876, and was re-elected in 1878, and attained high rank as a representative. In 1883 he was elected justice of the peace in the Fourth Ward of the borough of York, and is still administering the duties of that office in an efficient manner. He is a politician of influence, and has been a leading member of the I. O. O. F. for many years ; is District Deputy Grand Master, and D. D. Grand Patriarch, treasurer of Humane Lodge, and of Mount Vernon Encampment, and a member of the order of Red Men, Knights of Pythias, Union Brotherhood, G. A. R., and Knights of the Mystic Chain. He was the founder of the York Public Library, of which he is president ; was trustee of the Rescue Fire Company, and agent for P. B. Wright & Sons and other steamship lines. Mr. Sherwood has been twice married ; his union with Sarah A., daughter of Maj. R. J. Winterode, of Williamsport, Penn., occurred July 6. 1866. She died April 20, 1875, leaving three children, two having died. December 26, 1876, he was united to Lucy A., daughter of Peter and Charlotte Flickinger, of Hanover, Penn.; to this union there have been born five children, three of whom are deceased.

LEWIS A. SHIVE was born in York, December 27, 1818, and is a son of John and Sallie (Bupp) Shive. The father of Mr. Shive was one of seven children, and was born in 1798 and died in 1877, and his mother was born in 1794 and died in 1858. His grandfather, Ludwick Shive, was born in York, in 1761. The Shive family came originally from Germany. At fourteen years of age the subject of this sketch began learning the cabinet-maker's trade under his father. In 1841 he began the furniture business in York, and has since been engaged in that business. He was married in 1841, to Miss Harriet Hamm, of Dover Township, and daughter of Samuel Hamm. Ten children were born to this union, six of whom are living, viz : Philip, Walter, Charles, Lewis. Sallie and Samuel. Mrs. Shive died in 1873. Mr. Shive is a member of the Lutheran Church, and for many years has taken much interest in church affairs.

W. H. SITLER, attorney at law, ex-prothonotary of York County, is a native of Lower Windsor Township, was born January 24, 1849, and is a son of Jacob and Elizabeth (Burg) Sitler. His paternal grandfather was Abraham Sitler, an early settler of York County. Two brothers, John and Matthias, on account of religious persecution, were banished from Germany and came to America, and from one of these our subject is descended. Our subject received his education at the public schools of York County. In 1875 he began the study of law, and was admitted to the bar, December 17, 1877. Politically he is a Democrat, and for many years has taken an active part in politics. In 1881 he was elected prothonotary of York County, and most efficiently he filled the office for three years. Prior to his election to this office he was deputy prothonotary several terms. His marriage occurred in 1878, to Miss Celia T. Erury, a native of York County, who has borne him two children : Mable O. and Horace J. Mrs. Sitler is a member of the Reformed Church.

DAVID SMALL was born in York, May 3, 1812, and was the son of Peter Small, a prominent citizen and master-builder, who died when David Small was twelve years of age, leaving five children: Daniel, John, David, Margaret (who became the first wife of Henry Welsh, Esq.,) and a half-sister named Sarah, intermarried with Lewis Templein, now living in Ohio, and the sole survivor of the family. At the tender age in which we find him at his father's death, he was taken by Mr. Welsh, his brother-in-law, and initiated into the mysteries of printing in the office of the York *Gazette* then published by King & Welsh ("next door below the German Reformed Church, Main Street") the latter becoming a partner in its publication in May, 1824. After the manner of the enterprising news boys of the present day, he was not slow to take advantage of opportunities as they presented themselves at that early date, and took pride in relating how he had taken part in contributing his professional skill to the demands of the citizens on the occasion of the visit of Gen. La Fayette to York, in 1825, of which he had a distinct recollection to the last. Mr. Welsh, in 1829, disposed of his share of the *Gazette* to George A. Barnitz, Esq., and subsequently became proprietor of the Pennsylvania *Reporter*, at Harrisburg, and was elected State printer. Mr. Small left York with Mr. Welsh and became foreman of the State printing. Owing to bad health, however, he was compelled to leave Harrisburg, and on the 1st of April, 1836, became part owner of the *Gazette*, with Hon. Adam J. Glossbrenner, continuing uninterruptedly in the proprietorship until his death, nearly half a century. In his salutatory to the readers of the *Gazette*, on assuming his share in the proprietorship, he tersely concluded: "The undersigned will not trouble the reader with a long string of promises—believing in the old adage that 'large promisers are generally small performers.' He would much rather be judged by his acts than by his promises to act," and this peculiar announcement at the beginning of his business career will be recognized as characteristic of his whole life. Before Mr. Small left Harrisburg, he became united in marriage with Miss Adeline Sprigman, daughter of Solomon Sprigman, bookbinder, of that city, the ceremony having been performed by Rev. A. H. Lochman, D. D., of York, then a resident of Harrisburg. In his wedded life he was assisted with good counsel and the encouragement and comfort of a helpmeet in every emergency, rearing a family of three boys, whose conduct in life has caused their parents but little jar in the family circle. In 1839 Mr. Small became postmaster at York for the unexpired term of Daniel Small, his brother, under President Van Buren, and was succeeded by George Upp, Jr., under President Tyler, in 1841. Mr. Small was tendered a continuance of the postmastership under Mr. Tyler, but having contributed nothing to the elevation of that gentleman to the presidency, declined to become a supporter and beneficiary of his administration. In 1845, however, he was appointed to the same position by President Polk, again by President Pierce, and was continued by Mr. Buchanan. The appointment of editors as postmasters has been tabooed, generally, by the government in the early days, but in the person of Mr. Small the custom was broken, and under the persuasive eloquence of prominent Pennsylvania politicians, the Hon. Amos Randall, postmaster general under President Polk, made the way clear for many prominent and intelligent officials, who have sprung from the editorial staff, with great benefit to the service, and without detriment to the interests of professional brethren, who, it was feared, would suffer in the prompt dispatch of the mails, by narrow-minded competitors. In 1861 he was elected director of the poor, and served four terms successively. In 1862 he was elected chief burgess of York, and continued for nine successive terms, and in 1876 he was a presidential elector on the Tilden ticket. He was a director of the York National Bank about thirty years, and of the Farmers' Insurance Company about ten years. As a printer Mr. Small stood well in his profession. He was practical, and in his early days one of the fast compositors of southern Pennsylvania. As an employer he was kind, not exacting, dignified, but approachable, and solicitous for his employes, and always commanded their respect and good-will. His standing in the Democratic party in York County, while in health, was at the fore-front, and while not a brilliant leader, was a wise counsellor, and much of the grand Democratic majority in the county is owing to his wisdom and tact; and, although prominent in politics, he never permitted himself to be named before a county convention for office except for director of the poor, in which he was solely governed by a desire to contribute to the welare of the unfortunate class who come within the ministration of that office, and it is to his credit that his memory is still retained in gratitude by many of those who participated in the humane treatment experienced in the days of his directorship. Mr. Small died August 8, 1885, and, as a mark of respect to the deceased, Chief Burgess Heiges issued the following proclamation:

"By the death of David Small on Saturday last, York has lost one of its most prominent and honored citizens. In view of his long and useful public career in various positions of trust and responsibility in this community, and on account of his exemplary private life, and because of his having so acceptably filled the office of Chief Burgess of York for nine consecutive years, I have directed the borough flag to be suspended at half mast until after the funeral of David Small, Tuesday afternoon, August 11, 1885, and I recommend a suspension of business, as far as possible, from 3¼ to 4¼ p. m. of said day, and especially on the part of all offices and employes of the borough; and I further direct that the bells on the engine houses be tolled between the above mentioned hours as tokens of respect for the memory of the deceased.

"GEORGE W. HEIGES,
"*Chief Burgess.*

"YORK, PENN., August 10, 1885."

The funeral of Mr. Small took place on Tuesday afternoon, the services commencing at his late residence at 3½ o'clock, Rev. J. O. Miller, of Trinity Reformed Church, officiating. The remains were interred in the family lot at Prospect Hill Cemetery, attended by a large concourse of relatives and friends. In accordance with an expressed desire in life, the employes of the York *Gazette* printing-office acted as pall-bearers. Thus closes the career of a useful man who has left his impress for good upon the community, and leaves one land-mark less to connect the past with the present; leaves a void in the family and social circle, and many regrets among those who knew him best and had cause to remember his many kindnesses in word and deed; and to whom it will be gratifying to know that his end was peace, and his departure without a struggle, entering into a rest he longed for, as the rest which endureth forever. [The above sketch is comprised of extracts from an obituary notice in the York *Gazette* of Tuesday, August 11, 1885.]

LUTHER A. SMALL, ex-chief burgess of York Borough, and son of David and Adaline Small, was born August 16, 1843. He is the youngest in a family of four children and is of German origin. He received his education at the York public schools and the York County Academy. At eighteen years he began learning the printer's trade, and since then his life has been that of a printer and editor, and he is connected with the *Gazette* Printing Company. The marriage of Mr. Small with Miss Susan Groff was solemnized in 1865. Mrs. Small is also a native of York. They have one child, Emma V. Mr. Small is a thorough Democrat, and for quite a number of years has taken an active part in political affairs. During the years 1881 and 1882 he was a member of the town council. In 1883 he was elected chief burgess and re-elected in 1884. He is a member of the I. O. O. F. and I. O. R. M.

REV. J. C. SMITH, of York, is now the oldest itinerant minister in the Pennsylvania Conference of the church of the United Brethren in Christ. He was born in Franklin County, Penn., January 22, 1819. His grandparents came from Switzerland in 1750, and settled near Chambersburg. Mr. Smith is next to the youngest of eight children. He attended the schools of his native section first, and afterward entered an academy at Uniontown, Md.; then engaged in teaching, and was licensed to preach February 28, 1843, and ordained February 26, 1846. His first circuit in Franklin County had twenty-six appointments, each of which he visited every four weeks, by traveling 150 miles. The first year of Mr. Smith's labors brought 100 members into the church, among them John Dickson, now bishop of the Pennsylvania Conference. He next went to the Harrisburg circuit, then to Littlestown circuit, during which time through his preaching Revs. J. S. Wentz, L. W. Craumer and W. B. Raber became members of the church and afterward successful ministers of the Gospel. His next appointment was at York, where he served several different times. He is now a highly respected and honored citizen of the town. Few itinerant ministers of the Gospel have had so varied an experience as Rev. Mr. Smith. He has been an earnest, faithful and devoted worker in the cause of the church, and has served many other appointments, the work of which our limited space here cannot describe. He has been presiding elder of York for several years, was a member of the board of education in York, and filled many other positions of trust. His reminiscences, published in the church journals, are read with great interest. He was unceasing in his interest to furnish facts and statistics of church history for this work.

WILLIAM SMITH, one of the leading druggists of York, is a native of Lancaster County, where he was born in 1822. He decided upon a mercantile career and, in 1834, entered the drug store of C. A. Morris, now deceased, but who was an old and valued citizen and business man of York. Having become thoroughly acquainted with the drug business and possessing good business qualifications, he was admitted as a partner in 1846, and continued in this relation until 1872, when he became the head of the firm, having in association with him G. P. Yost, who had been one of the chief clerks of the firm of C. A. Morris & Co., since 1859. Horace Smith, a son, was admitted as a partner, April 1, 1879; he has also become thoroughly acquainted with the business by long service. The firm is finely located on East Market Street, and are doing a large wholesale and retail business.

GIBSON SMITH, dealer in grain, flour and coal, was born in Cumberland County, Penn., in 1823, is a son of Abraham and Sarah (Smith) Smith, and is of German origin. At the age of four years, Mr. Smith came with his parents to York County, and the family made settlement in the "upper end." In 1856 our subject began his present business. He was married in 1852 to Miss Susan Fahs, daughter of John Fahs. To this union have been born two children. Edgar F., born in York County, in 1854, was educated at the public schools, at York County Academy and Pennsylvania College, at Gettysburg; graduating from that institution, he went to Germany and after two years received a degree from the University of Goettingen. He is now professor of natural science at Wittenburg College at Springfield, Ohio. Allen J. was born in 1865, in York, Penn. He has received a liberal education and is now attending lectures at the University of Pennsylvania.

REV. REINHART SMITH was born in the county of Shopfheim, grand dukedom of Baden, Germany, near the river Rhine, May 15, 1836, to Joseph and Rosina (Ruetchli) Smith. He was educated at the public schools and received a good German education. In 1854, in company with his parents, he came to America, landing at Castle Garden, New York, September 4. The family proceeded to Lehigh

County, Penn., and thence moved to Shelby County, Ohio, where his parents died in 1855. Early in life our subject was forced to make his own way, and for a time worked upon a farm, and then entered a hat factory as clerk. He studied privately from 1855 to 1860 with Rev. A. Linbagh, Reading, Penn., while he was clerk. In 1860 he entered the theological seminary at Mercersburg, Penn. Completing his labors at the seminary, he was licensed to preach, and since that time has been actively engaged in the ministry. In 1863 he removed to Sullivan County, and the first year received for his services $197.85. In 1866 he came to York County and accepted the pastorate of the Reformed Church at Dallastown, and there remained until 1868, when he removed to York and here has since resided. The marriage of Rev. Smith was solemnized, in 1863, to Miss Anna Hoelker, of Philadelphia. Mrs. Smith died in 1864 and our subject was next married, in 1866, to Miss Hannah C. Shaffer. They have five children, viz.: Aaron F., Anna A., William R., Charles S. and Emma A.

S. MORGAN SMITH, inventor of Smith's Success Turbine Water-wheel and manufacturer of mill machinery, was born February 1, 1830, in Davie County, N. C., second son of John W. and Sarah Purden (Beauchamp) Smith. He is of English-French descent. His parents were born in Davie County, N. C., his father in 1811 and mother in 1816. By occupation his father was a farmer and yet resides in his native county. His mother died in 1866. The paternal grandfather of Mr. Smith was also born in Davie County, N. C., and his great-grandfather in Frederick, Md., and his great-great-grandfather was a native of France, who emigrated from England to America and settled in Frederick City, Md. The subject of this sketch was educated at the public schools of Davie County, N. C., and the Moravian College at Bethlehem, Penn., from which he graduated in 1861. During his collegiate course he prepared himself for the ministry, and from 1861 to 1866 was pastor of a Moravian Church. In 1866 he went to Canal Dover, Ohio, and had charge of a congregation at that place for five years. In 1871 he quit the ministerial work, on account of a serious throat trouble, and returned to York. About 1871 Mr. Smith began giving his attention to the invention of water-wheels and the manufacture of mill machinery. He was united in marriage, in 1862, to Miss Emma R. Fahs, a native of York County. Children have been born to this marriage as follows: Charles E., Stephen F., Beauchamp H., Sarah P., Susan E. and Mary D. In 1864 Mr. Smith was elected chaplain of the Two Hundredth Pennsylvania Volunteers, and served until the close of the war. He is a Republican, and a member of the G. A. R. Mr. and Mrs. Smith are members of the Moravian Church.

THE SMYSER FAMILY. On the 17th of February, 1715, by the historic little village of Rugelbach, in the kingdom of Wurtemburg, now Germany, was born Mathias Smyser, the ancestor of the Smyser family in York County. His father, Martin Smyser, was an industrious peasant, and a member of the Lutheran Church. The boyhood days of the son were spent in the schools of his native place, and assisting the father in tilling the soil and weaving. The visit of William Penn to Germany to invite the industrious peasants of that country to his new province across the sea, caused many thousands to emigrate. On September 21, 1731, the good ship "Britannia," with Michael Franklyn as captain, set sail from Rotterdam, stopping at Cowes to pay proper obeisance to the English flag and government, thence to Philadelphia, freighted with 267 German emigrants, 141 of whom were males, and 126 females. Among them were Mathias Smyser, then but sixteen years old, his mother, Anna Barbara, aged fifty, his sister, Margaret, aged twenty, and his brother George, aged nine. It was just at the time of their arrival that the first permanent settlements were being made west of the Susquehanna, and we next hear of him as a weaver, among the original settlers of Kruetz Creek, in York County. Having received money from Germany, he obtained a land warrant from the proprietors, and took up a large tract of land near the present village of Spring Grove, about the year 1740. Being anxious to have near neighbors, Mathias divided his plantation into smaller tracts, and presented all except one to new immigrants. Whether his brother, who had now grown to manhood, was the recipient of one of these farms, is not known, but they did live near each other, on different tracts of land, for some years. He eventually found that he had parted with his best land, so he sold the remainder, and purchased a tract of 400 acres from Mr. Henthorn, about three miles west of York, on what is now the Berlin Road, erected buildings and moved there on May 3, 1745. He remained there until his death in 1778, about the time his distinguished son was fighting the battles of the new government. His brother George also disposed of his property, and bought a farm north of York, where he resided several years, but eventually moved to Virginia, and thence to Kentucky, where many of his descendants now reside. Mathias Smyser left to survive him three sons: Michael, born 1740; Jacob, born 1742; Mathias, born 1744. Anna Maria, next to the youngest daughter, was born 1757; Susanna, the youngest, born 1760. The dates of the births of the other daughters, Dorothy, Sabina, Rosanna and Elizabeth, cannot be ascertained. Michael, the eldest son, became a conspicuous personage during the Revolutionary war.

COL. MICHAEL SMYSER, the eldest son, was born in 1740, and was long and extensively known as a highly respectable farmer and tavern keeper in what is now West Manchester Township, near the site of his father's home. He owned a farm of 200 acres. Though not favored with a liberal education, he was known as a man of discriminating mind and sound judgment. He was early associated with the Revolutionary patriots, and was a useful man in the councils of that day, as well as on the field of battle. He was one of a committee of twelve from York County, who raised money in 1775 to send to the inhabitants of Boston, when the port of that city was closed by the British, collecting £6 12s 1d from his own township. If the American cause had failed, every one of that committee would have forfeited his life on the scaffold of the enemy. He joined the Continental Army as a captain in Col. Michael Swope's regiment of York County volunteers, and was captured by the enemy in the engagement at Fort Washington, north of New York City, on the 16th of September, 1776. Several months of distressing imprisonment followed, during which time he was unremitting in his efforts to alleviate the sufferings of others, and bold and animated in the advocacy of his country's cause. After his release and return home, in 1778, he was elected a member of the house of representatives of Pennsylvania from York County, and from that time to 1790 was seven times re-elected to the same position. From 1790 to 1795 he represented his county in the State senate, being the first person to fill that position under the State constitution of 1790. Here, his warm attachment to our political institutions enabled him to act with honor to himself and his constituents. After the war he turned his attention to agricultural pursuits, and kept a tavern. He died in the year 1810, and his remains are interred near those of his father in the graveyard of the First Lutheran Church of York.

He left three sons and four daughters, namely: Peter, Elizabeth, Sarah, Jacob, Mary, Michael and Susan.

JACOB SMYSER, the second son of Mathias, the immigrant, was a prosperous farmer, and for some years a justice of the peace. In 1789 was elected a member of the house of representatives of Pennsylvania, and soon after died at the age of fifty-one years. He left seven sons and one daughter, viz.: Henry, Jacob, Martin, John, Daniel, Catherine, Peter and Adam.

MATHIAS SMYSER, the youngest son of the immigrant, resided on the mansion farm of his father, where he quietly pursued the useful and respectable occupation of an agriculturist. He was a man of the strictest integrity. He was in the Revolutionary war as a teamster, driving a baggage wagon. He lived to the age of eighty-four years, much longer than the other two of these brothers, and left five sons and two daughters, namely: Catharine, Polly, George, Jacob, Mathias, Philip and Henry. A centennial celebration was held by the descendants of Mathias Smyser, the elder, on the mansion farm now owned by Samuel Smyser, in West Manchester Township, on May 3, 1845. It occurred on Saturday, and was a bright and pleasant day. The meeting organized by electing George Smyser president, Jacob Smyser (of Michael) and Martin Ebert, vice presidents, and Philip Smyser and Rev. S. Oswald, secretaries. After a sumptuous dinner, the exercises were opened by Prof. Charles Hay, now of Gettysburg, and an address was made by the venerable president, who yet remembered seeing his aged grandfather, whose location on that spot, 100 years before, they were then celebrating. A series of resolutions was passed, letters read from absent ones, an historical narration prepared by Philip Smyser was read, and an address delivered by Rev. S. Oswald. The following beautiful sentiment is an extract from his speech: "My thoughts while here have been made up of some sort of pleasant mingling together of the present, the past and the future. At one time my imagination carries me back 100 years. I look up, I look around me, but I see naught except the blue vault of heaven, and a dark, dreary forest, enlivened only by the sweet warbling of the feathered songsters, and the rapid darting of the squirrel among the wide-spreading branches of the forest oak. I look again and see a solitary adventurer, firmly treading this thick forest; the sturdy oak falls before the ax wielded by his vigorous arms; and soon where once that forest stood now waves the golden grain. But with the rapidity of thought I am carried back to this hour, and here I see a numerous assembly, the descendants of that hardy adventurer, congregated to celebrate the day which dates the flight of a century, since first he called these lands his own." Prof. Charles Hay made a short address, after which a resolution was adopted christening the old homestead "Rugelbach," in honor of the birth-place of their ancestor. The meeting adjourned recommending "that future generations hold a similar celebration in the year 1945, and further, that we entertain the hope that this homestead of our ancestor be held in the name of Smyser." At this meeting, a committee was appointed to ascertain the number of descendants of Mathias Smyser, the elder, then living, reported as follows: Descendants of Col. Michael Smyser, 244; of Jacob Smyser, 177; Mathias Smyser, 160; Dorothy, married to Peter Hoke, 240; Sabina, married to Jacob Swope, of Lancaster County, 54; Rosanna, married to George Maul, who moved to Virginia, 66; Elizabeth, married to Leonard Eichelberger, who lived near Dillsburg, 116; Ann Mary, married to Martin Ebert (whose father came from Germany in the same vessel with her father), 64; and Susanna, married to Philip Ebert, 47; in all, 1,162.

JOSEPH SMYSER was born in West Manchester, three miles west of York, on the Ruegelbach farm, in 1811, is a son of Matthias and Elizabeth (Eyster) Smyser, and the third eldest in a family of four children, viz.: Elizabeth, Sarah, Joseph and Samuel; the three last named are now living within the same square, in York, Penn.; and Elizabeth died in the year 1829. The early life of our subject was spent on the farm. In 1844 he moved to York, where he has since resided. The marriage of Mr. Smyser took place, in 1835, to Miss Sarah Weaver, a native of Adams County, Penn. To this union have been born five children, three of whom are still living: Catherine L. E., Ellen S. and Alice M. Politically Mr. Smyser is a Republican. Mr. and Mrs. Smyser are members of the Lutheran Church.

SAMUEL SMYSER, retired farmer, was born in West Manchester Township, on the old Smyser homestead in 1813, to Matthias and Elizabeth (Eyster) Smyser, and is of German origin. Mr. Smyser worked on the farm for his father until he was twenty-five years of age, when he began life for himself and continued farming for twelve years. In 1863 Mr. Smyser came to York and here has since resided. He now owns the old Smyser homestead, which has been in the family for 140 years, and where the family centennial was held in 1845. The marriage of Mr. Smyser occurred, in 1866, to Miss Rebecca M. Lewis, daughter of Dr. Robert Lewis, of Dover. Mrs. Smyser was born in Dover, in 1825. The father of Mrs. Smyser died in 1846, and her mother in 1867. Mr. Smyser is a Republican. Mr. and Mrs. Smyser are members of the Lutheran Church and are among the prominent people of York.

DR. HENRY L. SMYSER was born in York, December 8, 1825, and is a son of Michael and Eliza (Lanius) Smyser. He is descended from German stock. His father was born in York in 1799, was a tanner, and died in 1874. Here also his mother was born in 1802, and died in 1882. Dr. Smyser is a representative of one of the first families of York County. Having received a common school education, he, in 1844, began the study of medicine under Dr. J. W. Kerr, and in 1847 graduated from the University of Pennsylvania at Philadelphia, and afterward located in Jackson Township, York County, and there remained one year. In 1849 he went to California, remained two years, and then returned to his native county. In 1855 he went to Europe and entered the Russian Army as contract surgeon, and was appointed to the rank of major. At the end of the war he returned to York County, and for distinguished services he received from the Emperor Alexander II the decoration of St. Stanislaus and also a medal commemorative of the war. He enlisted in the war of the Rebellion in 1862, and here also was a contract surgeon. He did faithful and efficient service at the hospital in York. In 1860 he was married to Emma E. Rieman, of York, daughter of John Rieman. Two children, Ella N. and John R., are the result of this union. Dr. and Mrs. Smyser are members of the Lutheran Church.

ALEXANDER D. SMYSER, son of Daniel and Catherine (Weist) Smyser, fifth of six children, was born April 3, 1848, in Jackson Township. He was reared to farming, and resided in Jackson Township until 1881, when he removed to York. He married Louisa Yost, daughter of Peter Yost, of York, Penn. One child—Clayton—was born to them. May 26, 1881, he married Amanda Metzler, daughter of George and Mary (Fishel) Metzler. Two children were born to this marriage: Harry E. and

Bertha. (See history of Smyser family for our subject's ancestral history.)

HAMILTON SPANGLER (deceased), a native of York, the third of four children of Samuel and Mary (Dinkel) Spangler, was born April 10, 1810. Mr. Spangler was educated at the York County Academy. In 1838 he began farming; continued at this occupation for ten years, then retired from active business life. While farming Mr. Spangler resided near Shrewsbury, York County, and owned two of the best farms in that township. In 1861 he married Miss Ann Eliza Connellee, a native of York, daughter of Col. James S. and Sarah (Danner) Connellee, early settlers of York. The father of our subject was born in York County in 1773; Mary Dinkel, his mother, was born in the same county in 1783. Mr. Spangler's maternal grandfather was a soldier, and did gallant service for his country, in the Revolutionary war. Baltzer Spangler, his paternal grandfather, served also in that struggle. Our subject had one sister, Eliza, the wife of Jacob Hoke, of Havre de Grace, Md. His brothers were Samuel (deceased) and Washington (deceased), who died at the early age of sixteen. The father of Mrs. Spangler, Col. James S. Connellee, was born in Westmoreland County, Va., in 1788; was reared and educated in the city of Richmond, Va. Col. Connellee was a progressive and prominent citizen of York in his day. He was a leading member and vestryman in the Episcopal Church for many years; member of the York Lodge of Freemasons, and one of the first men in York to offer his services to his country in the war of 1812. He was the youngest of four sons; Thornton, William and Daniel were the names of his brothers. He died on the 23d of April, 1839. Sarah (Danner) Connellee, the wife of Col. Connellee, was the daughter of Abraham Danner. The Danner family were among the pioneer settlers of York, and the history of York County will show that Michael Danner was the intimate friend and adviser of the Penn family. (See History of York County.)

ADAM SPANGLER was born in York, April 12, 1839, and was the fifth of the six children of Samuel and Elizabeth (Frank) Spangler, of York, Penn. Mr. Spangler attended the public schools of York, and also the York County Academy. He learned the hatter's trade with his father, and worked at it ten years. He then began building, and erected sixty-four houses, also a large planing-mill and sash factory, 80x90 feet, well-equipped for doing all kinds of work for builders, and supplied with a thirty-five horse-power engine. Mr. Spangler owns at present forty houses and thirty-five building lots. He is a self-made man, having begun life without a dollar. No man has done more toward improving his native town than our subject, and he is a descendant of one of the oldest families of York, about two miles from which borough his grandfather was born. His mother still lives at the advanced age of eighty-seven, and enjoys remarkably good health. His grandfather, Frank, was a soldier in the war of 1812. January 26, 1859, Mr. Spangler married Jane Gipe, daughter of Philip and Catherine Gipe, of York, Penn.; there have been born to them seven children: Susan, Elizabeth, Adam, Mary (deceased), Mary Ann, Robert and David. Mr. Spangler is a member of Keystone Conclave, No. 12, I. O. H., of York.

J. W. SPANGLER, inventor and manufacturer, was born in Jackson Township, York County, in 1842. For nearly thirty years he was employed upon his father's farm, subsequently engaging in business, as a partner, with the firm of Crider & Bro. in the publishing business. After one year's association with this firm he embarked in connection with Samuel Fry in the manufacture of cotton comforters and quilts, which partnership lasted one year. He then formed the company of J. W. Spangler & Bro., J. C. Spangler being the partner. This firm continued until 1882, notwithstanding being burned out in 1876. They next began the manufacture of agricultural implements, and have so continued. Our subject is a natural mechanic, and notwithstanding the fact of never serving an apprenticeship, has taken out thirteen patents, each of them being valuable. Their principal work now is in the manufacture of Spangler's Fertilizer Feed, Improved Corn Planter, Lime Spreader, and the building of feed cutters. Mr. Spangler's many other inventions include a washing machine, and last, but important, is his "lightning hitch," a paragon of simplicity in hitching or unhitching a horse. Mr. Spangler is yet young in years, and will doubtless add more improvements to the benefit of mankind He is an excellent business man, and a moral citizen. Mr. Spangler was married, in 1882, to Laura S. McKinley, of York They have one child, Julia Estelle, and are members of the Reformed Church.

B. F SPANGLER, M. D., was born in Jackson Township, York County, February 21, 1844, to Rudolph and Sarah (Harbaugh) Spangler, and is of German descent. His father was born in 1800, and his mother in 1807. His father died in 1851. The boyhood of Dr. Spangler was spent on the farm. His literary education was acquired at the common schools and the York County Academy. In 1865 he began the study of medicine, and the following year entered Jefferson Medical College at Philadelphia, graduating in 1868, and the same year began the practice of his profession in York, which he has since continued. The marriage of Dr. Spangler was solemnized in 1868, to Miss Ada E. Nes, daughter of the late Hon. Henry Nes. They have two children: Theresa J. and Chauncy K. Dr. Spangler is a Republican, and one of the directors of the Drovers' and Mechanics' National Bank, and assisted in its organization. August 7, 1862, Dr. Spangler, at the age of eighteen years, enlisted as a private in Company K, One Hundred and Thirtieth Pennsylvania Volunteers, and was mustered out as fourth sergeant at the expiration of term of service in May, 1863. He participated in the battles of Antietam, Fredericksburg and Chancellorsville. Dr. and Mrs. Spangler are members of the Presbyterian Church.

EDWARD WEBSTER SPANGLER was born in Paradise Township, York County, February 23, 1846. As a country boy he performed boy's work on his widowed mother's farm, and during four months in winter attended free school. Never relishing agricultural labors he abandoned them at the first opportunity and at the age of thirteen became a student at the York County Academy. After a year's study he entered as a clerk in one of the leading dry goods houses in York. In August, 1862, at the age of sixteen years, he responded to the call of President Lincoln for nine months' volunteers, and enlisted as a private in Company K, One Hundred and Thirtieth Regiment Pennsylvania Volunteers. After a two months' service, in the Army of the Potomac, he received his first baptism of fire at the battle of Antietam, in which his company lost in killed and wounded one-third of its number engaged. Mr. Spangler fired the eighty rounds with which he was equipped, and finding use for more took ten rounds from the cartridge box of a dead comrade, eight of which he discharged before his regiment was relieved. During the engagement the stock of his rifle was shattered by a Confederate bullet. At the battle of Fredericksburg, his division—the third of the second corps—made the initial and sanguinary charge on Mary's Heights. His colonel was killed at the first fire. At Chancellorsville his division was thrown into the breach to arrest the victorious

Confederates in their pursuit of the routed Eleventh Corps. During the terrible Saturday night, May 2, 1863, Mr. Spangler's company was fighting nearly all night on the plank road at the foot of the knoll on which our artillery was massed, and in front of which Stonewall Jackson was mortally wounded. The next morning, Sunday, his division was compelled to give way, and his general of brigade, Hays, was taken prisoner. Although in the fore-front of every battle, Mr. Spangler was unharmed in each. The term of enlistment having expired, the regiment returned home and was disbanded. After his return he was appointed deputy United States marshall of York County. He was in service but a few weeks when his leg was broken by the kick of an abandoned Confederate horse and, being incapacitated for active duty, resigned. Upon his convalescence he resumed his studies at the York County Academy, during which he also registered as a student at law. After attending a course of lectures in the law department of the University of Pennsylvania, at Philadelphia, t he was admitted to the York bar, March 4, 1867. He soon acquired a very lucrative practice which he has ever since retained. He has been admitted to practice in the neighboring county courts and in the United States district court, and is an active practitioner in the supreme court during the week appointed for the argument of York County cases. He has studiously eschewed politics, save his filling the office of president of the York Republican Club, in 1881, which position he subsequently resigned, having joined the independent wing of his party. In 1881 he was one of the principal promoters in the building of York's beautiful opera house, and superintended its first year's management. He has also taken an active interest in suburban development, and laid out his real estate, extending from George Street to Cottage Hill, into building lots, which are propinquitous to nearly all of York's manufactories, and are made accessible by the construction of the new and handsome Beach Street iron bridge, in the procuration of which he was mainly instrumental. In January 1882, Mr. Spangler purchased the *York Daily* and *Weekly* Printing House, with daily and weekly editions, and extensive job department. With the valuable assistance of his two able publishing partners he at once introduced into these issues new life, features and methods, resulting in the large increase in their circulations and carrying them to the fore-front of successful inland journals. Mr. Spangler possesses great energy and executive ability, is a sound and able advocate, and a pungent and forcible writer.

JACOB R. SPANGLER, M. D., is a son of Rudolph and Sarah (Harbaugh) Spangler, was born in Jackson Township, November 22, 1850, and is of German origin. The father of Mr. Spangler was a native of the same county, born in 1800, and died in 1851. Our subject worked on the farm during the summer and attended the public schools during the winter. In 1867 he entered the Millersville Normal School, and subsequently the York County Academy. In the fall of 1871, Mr. Spangler began the study of medicine in the office of Dr. B. F. Spangler, in York, and afterward entered Jefferson Medical College at Philadelphia, from which he graduated March 11, 1874, and immediately began the regular practice of his profession in York, where he has since continued. He is a thorough Republican and manifests much interest in politics. During the year 1880 he was the health officer of York. He is a man of much public spirit and a most successful physician.

CHARLES FREDRICK SPANGLER, M. D., was born in York. York County, December 31, 1859, to Harrison and Mary Spangler, and is of German descent. Dr. Spangler derived his earlier education from the public schools of the borough. In July, 1876, he began the study of medicine under the preceptorship of Dr. C. M. Nes. In 1879 he entered the Jefferson Medical College, of Philadelphia, graduating with honors in 1881. Being an ardent lover of the profession, blessed with a retentive memory, studious, a hard worker, his association with that institution was attended by marked distinction. His social qualities inviting the confidence of the faculty, responsible duties were assigned to him, affording exceptional opportunities for acquiring practical knowledge. His acknowledged thorough mastery of the various branches, with a comprehensive manner of imparting information to his associates, gave him a foremost position `n a class of 600. He began the practice of his profession at Spring Grove, York Co., Penn., subsequently locating permanently in York, August, 1881, where he has the pleasure of attending to a large and lucrative practice. In 1880 he was married to Miss Frances H. Wilson, of Franklin County, Penn. One child has been born to this union, Joseph. Politically the Doctor is of Democratic propensities. At the general election in 1884, he was elected coroner of York County by a handsome majority, receiving the largest vote on the ticket and carrying the Second Ward, which is largely Republican. He is a member of the Lutheran Church and a contributor to various city medical journals.

PETER B. SPRENKLE was born in North Codorus Township in 1837, is the son of George and Elizabeth (Bare) Sprenkle, the fourth of six children, and of German descent. Our subject remained at home and worked at milling and attended school at Cottage Hill; taught under S. B. Hayes and H. Griffith. In 1865 he went to Illinois, and remaining two years returned to York County and settled in his native township, where he remained several years and then came to York, where he has since remained. On coming to York he engaged in the grain business, which he continued for some time. Mr. Sprenkle was married in 1878 to Miss Rebecca Fishel, born in Springfield Township (but a resident of York, Penn., at time of marriage), and daughter of Charles Fishel. Mr. Sprenkle is a Republican and a Mason. Mrs. Sprenkle is a member of the Moravian Church. At present Mr. Sprenkle is engaged in North Codorus Township manufacturing ground flint. The firm is composed of D. B. and P. B. Sprenkle, Enos Frey and George Motter. The name of the firm is Sprenkle Bros. & Co. The firm was organized October, 1884.

R. S. STAHLE, M. D., was born in York in 1858, is a son of Col. J. A. and Mary E. (Spangler) Stahle, and is of German descent. At the age of sixteen he entered York Collegiate Institute, and graduated in 1880. He began the study of medicine in 1879 under Jacob Hay, M. D. In the fall of 1880 he entered the University of Maryland and graduated in 1882. In the spring of 1881 he entered the Baltimore Infirmary as clinical assistant, and after, was acting chief of clinic in the surgical department of the Baltimore Infirmary, and was also engaged practicing in Baltimore City during his services in the hospital. In 1883 he came to York and is now in the regular practice. In politics he is a Republican.

W. GUY STAIR, jeweler and dealer in watches, clocks and spectacles, was born in Hanover, York Co., Penn., in 1860, and is a son of William and Maria (Boadenhamer) Stair. Mr. Stair is the oldest in a family of four children, and is of German extraction. His father was born in Hanover, and his mother in Berlin, Adams Co., Penn. The Stair family has long been known in the history of York County. By occupation the father of Mr. Stair is a painter, and a resident of Hanover. At eleven years of age our subject began serving an apprenticeship at the jeweler's trade, at which he has since continued to work. In 1884 he came to York and engaged in his present business, which is successful beyond his expectations. He makes a specialty of the famous Rockford watches. The marriage of Mr. Stair occurred, in 1883, to Miss Anna M. Miller, a native of Penn Township, and a daughter of Jacob Miller. They have one child—Willie J. Mr. and Mrs. Stair are members of the Lutheran Church.

D. F. STAUFFER is one of the leading cracker bakers of the State. He is a native of York County, where he was born February 18, 1844. He is a son of Rev. Frederick and Mary (Forry) Stauffer, who were also natives of the county, his father being for more than forty years a minister of the Mennonite Church, eighteen of which he served his denomination as bishop. Our subject was reared and received a common school education in his native county. In 1867 he engaged in the milling business, which was conducted by him until 1870, when he embarked in his present enterprise. Mr. Stauffer has succeeded in establishing a large trade, which is extended to adjoining States. His manufactory for baking cakes and crackers is a model one of its kind, and is managed and superintended by him in person. He is a liberal and deserving citizen of the county. On July 31, 1870, he was married to Miss Lucinda, daughter of Samuel and Susan Wagner, who are also natives of York County. They have been parents of eight children, seven of whom are now living: Bertie, Callie, Harry, Nettie, Maggie, Annie, Elsy M. (deceased), and William H.

JOHN W. STEWART, proprietor of the York Book-bindery, was born in Philadelphia, August 18, 1831, is a son of James A. and Mary B. (Bell) Stewart, and is of English-Scotch origin. His father was born in Maryland in 1803, and his mother in Delaware in 1806. Our subject was educated at the public schools of Philadelphia. At fifteen years of age he was bound as an indentured apprentice at book-binding, which apprenticeship lasted until he had gained his majority. In 1855 he began business for himself in his native city, and continued therein until about 1861. During the late war he was employed in the United States Navy Yard at Philadelphia; he then resumed his former occupation, and remained in Philadelphia until 1867; then came to York, and here has since resided, and successfully carried on the book-binding business. This bindery was established in 1860, though for a number of years very little business was done, and it was not until Mr. Stewart came to York, that the industry began to flourish or gave much promise. The establishment is supplied with all the modern machinery and improvements adapted to all classes of work. Mr. Stewart was married, in 1856, to Miss Caroline Matthews, a native of New York. To this union have been born nine children, three of whom are deceased. In politics Mr. Stewart is a Democrat.

WILLIAM R. STOUCH, wholesale dealer in boots, shoes and notions, is a native of York Township, York Co., Penn., and was born March 12, 1816, son of Leonard and Susan (Rinehart) Stouch, and of German extraction. His paternal grandfather emigrated from Germany and settled in Dover, York County. Subject's father was born in this county in 1780 and died in 1856. At thirteen years of age William R. Stouch came to York, Penn., where he remained until 1833, when he went to Baltimore and there served a four years' apprenticeship at coach-making. He then returned to York and engaged in the manufacture of coaches, but on account of ill health was compelled to abandon this business. In 1850 he went to Philadelphia, and for twenty years was salesman in a dry goods house, after which he returned to York, in 1869, and established his present business. He was married, in 1842, to Margaret, daughter of George and Mary Holder. Mrs. Stouch was born in York, in 1819. By this union they have three children: George L., Emma M. and Rex M. H. Mr. Stouch is a Democrat and is a member of the I. O O. F. Mr. and Mrs. Stouch are members of the St. Paul's Lutheran Church.

C. A. STRACK, furniture dealer and undertaker, is a native of York, Penn., born March 4, 1843, son of Charles A. and Caroline (Funk) Strack. The father was a native of Saxony, Germany, born in 1810, and the mother was born in 1806. In 1838 the ancestors of our subject emigrated from Germany to America and settled in Baltimore, Md., and in 1839 removed to York, where subject's father died in 1855. At the age of twelve years our subject began learning the cabinet-maker's trade under an elder brother, and in this capacity continued five years, after which he became general manager of the furniture and undertaking business. Mr. Strack's father was one of the early furniture dealers of York. In 1878 subject purchased his mother's interest in the business, and since that time has been doing business for himself. He was married, in 1865, to Mary M. Heckert, a native of York. Six children were born to this union: Carrie S., Emma J., Charles P., Rebecca B., Samuel H. and Fannie M. Mr. Strack is a Democrat, and has been a member of the borough school board and identified with the numerous associations of York. He and his wife are members of the Trinity German Reformed Church.

JOSEPH ROSS STRAWBRIDGE, attorney at law and junior member of the law firm of Geise, Zeigler & Strawbridge, was born in Fawn Township, this county, July 25, 1858, son of John and Grizella (McDonald) Strawbridge, residents of the "Lower End," and prominent people of York County. His maternal grandfather, Aquila McDonald, was an officer in the war of 1812. Our subject was reared on the farm. He attended the Farm Grove Academy, afterward attended Stewartstown English and Classical Institute during 1874–75, and graduated from the York Collegiate Institute in 1880, and from Lafayette College in 1882. During the years 1877 and 1878 he taught school in Adams County, Ill., and was principal of Fawn Grove Academy, York County, Penn., in 1882–83. He was registered as a law student August 25, 1882, was admitted to the bar August 28, 1884, and December 9th of the same year became a member of the firm with which he is still connected. He is a Democrat.

CAPT. E. Z. STRINE, attorney at law, and a native of Strinestown, Conewago Township, was born June 11, 1842, to Peter S. and Rebecca (Zeigler) Strine, and is of German descent. His father was born in Mount Pleasant, York Co., Penn., July 25, 1815, and his mother in Shrewsbury Township, 1817. His paternal grandfather was John Strine, a native of York County, and his great grandfather was born in Germany, came to America, settled in York County, and was a soldier in the Revolutionary war. The father of our subject died in 1854. From 1862 to 1871 Capt. Strine was engaged in the mercantile business in York. In 1871 he began the study of law under E. D. Zeigler, and in 1873 was admitted to the York County bar, since which time he has been in active and successful practice. His marriage was solemnized in 1865, to Miss Addie E. Dehoff, a native of York County. They have two children: Emma A. and Ulysses S. G. For ten years Capt. Strine has been commander of the York Grays, Company A, Eighth Infantry, National Guard of Pennsylvania. Capt. and Mrs. Strine are members of Trinity Reformed Church.

OLIVER STUCK, Esq., the subject of this sketch, is practically a self-made man, and who by perseverance, thrift and industry has made his mark in the world, achieving success in his profession of journalism, while many others, lacking the invincible qualities of pluck and industrious habits, and not content to live a life of self-denial, have failed. From a very tender age he has been a hard worker, and very painstaking with everything he undertook, and the success with which he has met in life is all owing to the habits of industry and frugality he formed in his youth. Oliver Stuck was born in the borough of York, September 19, 1817. His father was Capt. Charles Stuck, a carpenter by occupation. Capt. Stuck was a member of the famous company of volunteers who marched to the defense of Baltimore, under Capt. Michael H. Spangler, on August 29, 1814, and were attached to the Fifth Maryland Regiment, and participated in the battle of North Point, September 12, 1814 The company received the thanks of Gen. Stricker, commanding, and the officers of the Fifth Regiment, for their gallantry in action. Capt. Stuck was, after his return from the war, always very active in the militia of the State, and commanded a company for a number of years. Capt. Stuck was a man much respected and held in high esteem by his fellow-citizens for his many virtues and kindness of heart. He died at the age of forty-eight years. Jacob Stuck, the grandfather of our subject, with his father, were among the earliest settlers of the thriving and populous township of North Codorus. The records of the courts, and deeds held by the land-owners now living in this township attest the fact of the Stucks holding large grants of territory in this section, and which they disposed of by deed to the progenitors of those now holding the farms in this section of York County. When the titles to these lands were vested in the Stucks, the country was very sparsely settled, and the soil of the small portion cleared not very productive, consequently the value was small in comparison to that of these broad and fertile acres at this writing. Jacob Stuck came to York to reside at a very early age, over a century and a half ago, where his descendants have ever since resided As the name implies, the Stucks are presumably of German descent, though the present generation cannot trace their nationality to any authentic source, other than to the fact that the township of North Codorus was settled by Germans, and the Stucks being among the first settlers, it is but fair to presume they were of that nationality. The name is distinctively German, and properly written to give it the broad German pronunciation, it should be with two dots over the letter ü, making the name Stück, though the ordinary English pronunciation makes it sound like the word stuck. The mother of Oliver Stuck, our subject, was Rebecca Snyder Stuck, a most estimable lady, who lived to the advanced age of eighty-two years, dying in the year 1877. October 15, at the home of her daughter, in Sunbury, Northumberland Co., Penn. Oliver Stuck, at the early age of scarcely twelve years, was apprenticed to the printing business with Messrs. King & Barnitz, then proprietors of the old York *Gazette*, June 20, 1829, serving an apprenticeship of five years very faithfully. At the expiration of his term of service he worked in the same office as a journeyman for a number of years, after which he went to Harrisburg, and worked in the State printing office on the legislative record. There being no railroad in those days between York and Harrisburg. Mr. Stuck used to walk the twenty-six miles' distance intervening between the two points, in his frequent visits home to his parents, whose principal support he was. From the early age at which he entered upon his apprenticeship, it will be observed that he did not possess the advantage of securing an education in the schools, and really attended school very little, gleaning all the knowledge he possesses in that great college, the printing office, and by the reading of useful books. His ambition was to become the editor and proprietor of a newspaper, and with that end in view he applied himself vigorously to work, and his efforts were finally rewarded with success. In the year 1839 he became one of the editors and proprietors of the York *Democratic Press*, by the purchase of a half-interest in the paper, and continued as such until he became finally the sole proprietor by purchasing his partner's interest, and has conducted the paper in his own name and interest ever since. The *Press* espoused the principles of the Democratic party, and as an exponent of those principles, and a disseminator of news, has proved a very acceptable paper to the people; and its editor, by hard work and the practice of the most rigid economy, has made it a success financially. (For a full history of the *Democratic Press* see article under that head in this volume.) In the year 1843, April 17, he was married to Margaret Gilberthorp, daughter of the late William Gilberthorp, deceased. He has reared a family of six children (two sons and four daughters), one of which, the eldest, is Edward Stuck, the editor of the York *Age*. Oliver Stuck has held several important positions of honor and trust. In November, 1852, he was appointed State agent, on the Philadelphia & Columbia Railroad, by the board of canal commissioners, of Pennsylvania, the State, at that time, owning what is now known as the Pennsylvania Railroad. This position he held until August, 1857—when the road passed out of the hands of the State into the possession of the present owners by purchase—with credit to himself and an unimpeachable record as a faithful and efficient officer. During his connection with the railroad he still devoted all his spare moments to editing his newspaper, and upon retiring from the road gave his entire attention to the newspaper business. He kept the *Press* fully abreast of the times, and succeeded in placing it beside the most influential weeklies of the State. He has always taken an active part in the politics of his county, and was the champion of the reform wing of the Democracy, denouncing the methods of those who did not consider holding office a public trust, but simply for their own pecuniary advantage. Against all politicians of this class he wielded his pen, denouncing the extravagance and corruption which disgraced the records of office-holders and reflected upon the fame of the Democratic party. Much of the credit for the healthy state of affairs in this county is due to his efforts, through the *Press*, to bring about this great and wholesome change, and to the sterling gentlemen who rallied around his paper in its work for reform. In June, 1880, he was nominated by his party as their candidate for register of wills of York County, and ran on the same ticket with Gen. Hancock for president, receiving the highest vote of any candidate upon the ticket. He entered upon the duties of his office in January, 1881, and filled it acceptably to the people, and at the end of his term was complimented by the auditor-general of Pennsylvania, for the excellent manner in which the affairs of the office were administered.

WILLIAM STUCK, steward of the York County Alms-house, was born in Springfield Township, York County, January 19, 1826; is a son of Charles and Rebecca (Snyder) Stuck, is the fifth in a family of fourteen children, and is of German descent. His father was born in York in 1793, and his mother in the same county in 1797. His father was a soldier in the war of 1812. His grandfather was one of the first settlers of York, and carried on distilling. Our subject received a common school education, and at fourteen years of age began life for himself. In 1842 he began learning the carpenter's trade, and in 1850 he began for himself, and thus continued until 1872, when, on account of ill health, he was forced to abandon his occupation. In 1875 he was elected steward of the alms-house, which position he continues to hold, and under his stewardship the house and farm have been most successfully and satisfactorily managed. He was married May 30, 1849, to Miss Sarah Gilberthorpe, a native of York, born in 1826. He is a Democrat, and has been a member of the borough council. He was made a Mason in 1861, and a member of the I. O. O. F. in 1847. He is an elder in the German Reformed Church, of which Mrs. Stuck is also a member.

A. DUNCAN THOMPSON, clerk of the commissioners of York County, was born in Hopewell Township, April 30, 1842, to Archibald and Rosana (Morrison) Thompson, and is of Scotch-Irish descent. The parents of Mr. Thompson were also born in Hopewell Township; the father in 1807, and the mother in 1821. His paternal grandfather was Alexander Thompson, a native of York County, and a soldier in the Revolutionary war and of 1812. The boyhood of our subject was spent on the farm, where he attended the public schools in the winter and labored on the farm in the summer. In 1862 and in 1863 he attended the Stewardstown Academy, and subsequently taught school. In 1867 he began farming for himself, and so continued until 1881, when he came to York. In 1866 Mr. Thompson was married to Miss Annie E. Trout, a native of Hopewell Township, and daughter of Samuel and Catherine Trout. To this union have been born three children: Mary A., Margaret A. and James S. In 1868 Mr. Thompson was elected assessor of Hopewell Township; in 1879 he was elected school director, and in 1881 was elected clerk of the commissioners, re-elected in 1883, which position he now occupies. He is a most efficient officer, and one that has the confidence of the people of York County. Mr. and Mrs. Thompson are members of the Presbyterian Church.

JOHN J. VANDERSLOOT, a stanch business man of York, is a native of the county, and was born November 24, 1836. His father, Rev. Frederick W. Vandersloot, was a minister of the Reformed Church, and for over fifty years a faithful and conscientious Christian worker in York County. Our subject received a good education, having had the advantages of the schools of York and the York County Academy. He began his mercantile career when sixteen years of age in York, where he was employed for seven years. He was next employed by C. E. Morgan & Company, of Philadelphia, where he remained until 1861, when he returned to York and began business for himself. He has, by energy and application, established a leading and extended trade in dry goods, notions, queensware, etc., and is a citizen of the progressive type. Mr. Vandersloot was married October 12, 1869, to Miss Leanora V. Jaeger, of Philadelphia. They have four children: Catherine A., Mary A., Sarah C. and William J. The family are members of the Reformed Church, in which Mr. Vandersloot has taken a leading part, having been a deacon and elder, and a teacher in the Sabbath-school for over twenty years.

DR. EDWARD F. WAGNER, son of Ernst and Barbara (Fahs) Wagner, was born June 26, 1860, in York, Penn., where he was reared. He attended the public schools of York, passed examinations for the high school, but left York and went to Northampton County, attended one year Nazareth Hall Cadet School, at Nazareth, Penn., then went to the Moravian Theological Seminary, at Bethlehem, Penn. (His course here was in the classical department. In 1878 he returned to York and began reading medicine with Dr. J. W. Kerr. After three and one-half years he went to Jefferson Medical College, at Philadelphia, and graduated rom this institution March 29, 1834, and at once began the practice of medicine, at York, Penn. Dr. Wagner graduated with honorable mention for his thesis.

W. H. WAGNER, M. D., was born in Dover Township, December 26, 1853, is a son of Joseph and Levina (Lauer) Wagner, and is of German origin. His father was born in Adams County, Penn., in 1824, and his mother in York County, in 1829. Our subject was reared a farmer, and at eighteen years of age began teaching school, and taught seven years. In 1878 he began the study of medicine in the office of Dr. J. R. Spangler, afterward attended lectures at Jefferson Medical College, at Philadelphia, and graduated in 1881. He then began the practice of his profession in York, He was married in 1883, to Miss Mattie J. Stuart. a native of Philadelphia, and a daughter of James and Elizabeth Stuart. The Doctor and Mrs. W. are members of the Lutheran Church, and in politics he is a Republican.

C. B. WALLACE was born in Chester County, Penn., October 14, 1819, and is the son of Thomas and Mary (Jackson) Wallace, natives respectively of Chester County, Penn., and Maryland. The elder Wallace was a farmer and a justice of the peace of Chester County, and there he and wife died. C. B. Wallace was reared a farmer, but received a good education, and for a time was engaged in teaching school. In 1846 he commenced reading law with Thaddeus Stevens, of Lancaster. In 1847 he came to York, taught school in the county, and read law under Judge Durkee. In February, 1849, he was admitted to the York County bar, and has ever since been in active and successful practice. He has been identified with all progressive measures, and for six years has been a school director of York Borough. February 6, 1848, he married Frances A. Levergood, daughter of Jacob and Fanny Levergood, of Wrightsville, and to this union have been born three children, viz.: Mary A. (wife of Edward M. Vandersloot, of York), Clayton J. (who is engaged in the wholesale boot and shoe trade with Mr. Vandersloot), and Louisa L. Mrs. Wallace and family are members of the Presbyterian Church.

WILLIAM WALLACE, a retired business man, is a native of Hopewell Township, born in 1822, son of James and Catherine (Gemmil) Wallace. His parents are both natives of this county ; the father born in 1789 and the mother in 1800. The family is of Scotch-Irish descent. Mr. Wallace began business running a woolen-mill and manufacturing woolen goods, which he continued until 1845. He then engaged in the mercantile business at Freeland, Baltimore Co., Md., where he remained until 1874, when he returned to his native township and there continued merchandising. Mr. Wallace was one of the projectors of the York & Peach Bottom Railway, and in 1874 removed to York and gave his entire attention to this enterprise, acting as secretary and treasurer. This position he held until 1882, when, on account of failing health, he was compelled to resign. He was married, in 1846, to Jennet Gemmil, of Chanceford Township, this county. To them were born three children : James W., Mary A. and Katie A. Mrs. Wallace died September 11, 1881, a member of the United Presbyterian Church. Mr. Wallace is a Republican. He is a member of the Masonic fraternity and of the United Presbyterian Church.

CAPT. H. B. WALTMAN, foreman of the machine department at A. B. Farquhar's, is a native of Mount Joy, Lancaster Co., Penn., was born November 25, 1838, is a son of Henry and Helena (Bupp) Waltman, and is of German descent. His father was born in 1798, and his mother in 1801. The former died in 1848 and the latter in 1875. Our subject was educated at the public schools of Mount Joy. In August, 1861, he enlisted in Company G, Ninth Pennsylvania Cavalry. He was commissioned second lieutenant November 9, 1861; first lieutenant August 8, 1862, and captain in 1864. He participated in the battles of Clarksville, Tenn., Crab Orchard, Chickamauga, Dandridge, Lafayette Grove, Waynesborough, Raleigh and many other minor engagements. He was honorably discharged at Lexington, N. C., in July, 1865. Prior to this service he had served a four-years' apprenticeship at the machinist's trade, at Mount Joy, Penn. In 1866 he went to Harrisburg, and for two years was in the employ of W. O. Hickok, and then for more than one year had charge of Wilson Bros'. Works, at the same place; he then went to Wheatland, Penn., and subsequently to Erie, Penn., and was for nearly three years in the employ of the Erie, Philadelphia & Reading Railway, and then came to York, where he has since resided. In 1877 he took charge of the machine department at A. B. Farquhar's, and in this capacity still continues. He was married, in 1876, to Miss Sarah J. Harmon, of Harford County, Md., a daughter of Michael Harmon. They have two children: Daisy H. and Harry J. Mr. Waltman is a Republican, a member of the G. A. R., and during 1882 was commander of Sedgewick Post No. 37.

NEVIN M. WANNER, attorney at law, was born at Washingtonville, Ohio, May 14, 1850. He entered Heidelberg College, at Tiffin, Ohio, in 1866, and after remaining there two years went to Franklin and Marshall College at Lancaster, Penn., from which institution he graduated in 1870. In that year he entered the law department of the University of Pennsylvania, where he remained two years. He read law under Erastus H. Weiser, of York, Penn., and Gen. B. F. Fisher, of Philadelphia, Penn., and was admitted to the bar at York, August 28, 1872, since which time he has been in active practice, and is now one of the leading lawyers of York County. He is a Democrat, and one of the leaders of that party in this county. He was married, in 1882, to Amelia D. Croll, a native of York County, and daughter of John R. Croll, deceased. Mr. Wanner is a member of the Reformed Church, and Mrs. Wanner of the Lutheran Church.

PROF. ATREUS WANNER, principal of the York High School, is a son of Rev. Aaron and Rebecca (Miller) Wanner, and was born in Washingtonville, Ohio, September 26, 1852. His parents and grandparents were natives of Pennsylvania. He graduated at Franklin and Marshall College, of Lancaster, Penn., in 1873, and in the spring of 1876, after having in the meantime taught school elsewhere, accepted the position of assistant principal of the York High School. In 1880 he was elected principal of the same school, which position he has since filled with marked ability. He is one of the most successful educators in this part of Pennsylvania. He was married, June 21, 1882, to Miss Clara J. Eckert, daughter of Henry and Elizabeth C. Eckert, of Gordonville, Lancaster Co., Penn.

JOHN B. WANTZ, son of Lewis W. and Lyddie (Bentzel) Wantz, was born March 19, 1836, in Heidelburg Township, and in his youth divided his time between the common schools and farm work. His first work was in the flour-mill, after which he began his trade as carpenter with Rogers & Wilt, of Dover. After learning his trade he worked at journey-work two years, when the civil war of 1861 broke out, when he began work for the United States Government at Aquia Creek, Va., also at Washington, D. C. He then returned home and superintended an ore mine for a year, and afterward began building and contracting in York, Penn. August 23, 1868, our subject married Susanna Buhler, of Manchester Township, daughter of Andrew and Sarah (Hake) Buhler. Six children were born to this union: Lizzie E., Emerson H. (deceased),

Charles (deceased), Sadie Ellen, Carrie May (deceased) and Louisa A. A. Our subject's grandfather, Frederick Wantz, came from Alsace, Germany, to York County, when a young man, and settled in Heidelberg Township, where our subject's grandfather, Philip Wantz, was born, and died in his eighty-third year. Mr. Wantz has been one of the leading builders of York for many years, having erected many of the finest residences in the western part of the borough.

CHRISTIAN WARNER, son of Conrad and Barbara Warner, was born in Germany, May 7, 1847, and came to this country in 1851, with his parents. He enlisted August 11, 1864, in the Two Hundredth Regiment, Pennsylvania Volunteers, which formed a part of the First Brigade, Third Division, Ninth Army Corps, of the Army of the Potomac. He was with his regiment when they participated in the battles of Butler's Front, Fort Steadman, and the battles before Petersburg on the 1st, 2d and 3d of April, 1865, and at the surrender of Lee at Appomattox. He was mustered out of service at Alexandria, Va., May 30, 1865. In 1867 he began working at his trade of blacksmith, which he has followed since. Mr. Warner has been inspector of elections for his ward for six years, and was a member of the K. of M. C. (now disbanded), and for four years was a trustee of the Laurel Fire Company. He is an active Republican, and was an officer of the Young Men's Republican Club in 1880, and of the P. K. in 1884. Mr. Warner was married March 5, 1868, to Sarah Jane Smith, daughter of Henry and Sarah (Roller) Smith. They have had born to them four children: Willie (deceased), Emma L., Lillie May and Harry Elmer.

GEORGE WEHRLY is a native of Lancaster County, Penn., where he was born in 1827. His father, Francis Wehrly, was a native of Germany; his mother, whose maiden name was Barbara Brenner, was born in Lancaster County. His father was by trade a weaver, subsequently engaging in the mercantile business. He removed to York County in 1845, settling in Strinestown, Conewago Township, where he resided until his death, which occurred in 1878; the mother died in 1881. They were the parents of five children, our subject being the third child. He attended the common schools, and at the age of sixteen became a teacher, and taught seven years continuously in Lancaster County. He then embarked in the mercantile business at Strinestown with his brother Daniel, continuing four years. In 1854 he came to York and for one year was assistant recorder of the county. Removing to Emigsville he was an assistant of John Emig in the commission and forwarding business for three years. In 1857 he was elected recorder of York County, and served a three-years' term. His next business venture was in the wholesale liquor trade, in which he was engaged twelve years in Lancaster and York Counties. Returning to York he became proprietor of the Ginder House, and in 1883, he assumed the management of the Pennsylvania House, where he is located at this writing. Mr. Wehrly is a deservedly popular host and citizen, and is well-known and esteemed all over the county. He has served as councilman in Lancaster seven years; was postmaster at Emigsville and Strinestown, and in all has been progressive and honorable Mr. Wehrly was married, in 1849, to Miss Elizabeth A. Glatfelter, of Lancaster County. They have four children living: Mary E. (wife of William P. Frailey, of York), Filie Gracey (of Philadelphia), Ida K. (wife of E. D. Bentzell, of York), and Anna C. Mr. Wehrly is one of the leading Democrats of York County.

NATHANIEL WEIGLE, a leading contractor and builder, was born in York County, April 12, 1823, and is the son of Martin and Charlotte (Lightner) Weigle, natives of York County. Mr. Weigle attended the common schools at York and subsequently attended the York County Academy one session. He then apprenticed himself to learn the carpenter trade under the instruction of Jacob Gotwalt, of York; after finishing his trade he worked at journey-work until 1860. He then began business for himself; his first prominent contract was for the building of the present Presbyterian Church; he subsequently contracted for and built the German Reformed Church, the Presbyterian Chapel, St. Paul's Lutheran Church and Chapel, remodeled Dr. Lochman's Church, built the York Opera House, and many of the finest and most prominent private dwellings in York. In connection with his contracting he has established a large and well-appointed planing-mill, furnished with all the machinery for preparing all kinds of church, school and building material. Mr. Weigle has extended his business relations to many of the surrounding towns and cities, and has achieved a reputation which is highly creditable. He is a worthy citizen, a member of the Masonic fraternity, and of the I. O. O. F. He has been prominently identified with the Lutheran Church and Sunday-school, for many years having served as deacon and elder. Mr. Weigle has been twice married. He was first united with Miss Catherine Gotwalt, of York County, in January, 1847, she died in 1864. Three children are living; Charlotte E., Henrietta B. and Annie K. In January, 1874, Mr. Weigle was married to Mrs. Mary J. Smyser, daughter of Jacob Weiser, of York.

THE WEISER FAMILY. On a proclamation of Queen Anne, of England, in 1708, owing to internal dissensions in Germany, about 4,000 Germans were transported to Holland in 1709, and thence to England. They encamped near London, when, in the following year, Gov. Robert Hunter, of New York, who was then in England, and about to sail for his own country, invited with him about 3,000 of these Germans or Palatines to the town of New York, and they were soon afterward located on what was called the Livingstone District of that State, and turned their attention to agriculture. A chief of the Mohawk Indians, who had about this time visited England, presented to Queen Anne a tract of his land in Schoharie, N. Y., and in 1713 about 150 families were transferred through the wilderness to that place. Among these emigrants was the father of Conrad Weiser, with his wife and seven sons and daughters. He is the great ancestor of the Weiser family in this country. His Christian name is not for a certainty known. From one of his sons, the Weisers, of York County, are descended. The colony at Schoharie did not prosper. They commenced improving lands and building houses, and labored until 1723, when they were partly dispersed, owing to defects in their titles to lands. They then began to search for a new home, and began wending their course in a southeasterly direction, till they struck the Susquehanna. Here they made canoes, in which they floated down the river to the mouth of the Swatara, and thence to the fertile spot in Berks County, along the Tulpehocken Creek, where they settled among the Indians, in the fall of 1823. The father of Conrad Weiser having become familiar with the Mohawk language, was an interpreter, and remained at Schoharie until 1729, when, with his wife and four children, all that were then living, he also came to the Tulpehocken. It was his design to now devote all his attention to farming, but on many noted occasions his services as an interpreter were demanded by the authorities of Pennsylvania. He was a man of great benevolence. It was through him the Moravian people were made so attentive to Indian natives. He died and was buried in Berks County.

Conrad Weiser, his eldest son, was a justice under the king, and also an Indian interpreter. In 1736 he was sent to treat with the Six Nations of New York concerning a war that was to break out between them and the Indians of Virginia. He was visited, August 14, 1752, by Count Zingendorff, at Tulpehocken, who here met a numerous embassy of sachems of the Six Nations. The Count preached the gospel to the Indians. At the conclusion of his remarks to them he said concerning Weiser: "This is a man whom God hath sent, both to the Indians and to the white people, to make known his will unto them." For a quarter of a century he attended all the important Indian treaties. In connection with the governor of Pennsylvania, Benjamin Franklin and several other persons, in 1752, he was appointed one of the trustees of the public schools, which were established through the efforts of Rev. Michael Schlatter; one of these schools was, about this year, started in York. During the French and Indian war he was lieutenant-colonel of a battalion of Pennsylvania soldiers. After an eventful and very useful life he died among his friends at Wormelsdorf, Berks County, on the 13th of July, 1760, at the age of sixty-four. His remains were interred and still rest in an historic old graveyard near that town. He left seven children, who, by marriage, were related to the Muhlenbergs.

Samuel Weiser, a descendant of the Tulpehocken settlement, came to York in 1780, and immediately commenced the business of a hatter in a building on the present site of Jacob Wilt's jewelry store on East Market Street. He continued this business until 1822, but opened a dry goods store in 1808 on the corner still occupied by his descendants. During the war of 1812 he employed about fifty workmen making hats, and sent wagon loads of them every Monday morning to Baltimore. He died in 1834, aged seventy-four years, and his remains were interred in the graveyard adjoining Christ's Lutheran Church. They have since been removed to Prospect Hill Cemetery. He was married to Eve Phfleager, and had eight children: Samuel, Jacob, Charles, Daniel, Catherine, Eliza, Margaret and Cassandra. Samuel, the eldest son, succeeded his father in the manufacturing of hats until 1840, when he bought a farm one-half mile south of York, and died there in 1856. Augustus, his eldest son, died on the farm; Albert is living in Preston, Minn., engaged in the jewelry and drug business; Æmilius is located in Decorah, Iowa, in the drug business; Louisa was married to John Ensminger; she is now dead; Alexander died unmarried; Catherine, married to John C. Rupert; Margaret, married to Josiah Poorbaugh, of Berrin, Somerset Co., Penn.; Annie, married to David Ziegler, of York; Florence, now dead, was married to Martin Bender, of York; Helen, unmarried, living in York.

Jacob, second son of Samuel Weiser, Sr., went into the dry goods business in 1818 with his brother Charles, which he continued until 1836, when he engaged in the lumber trade with his brother, Daniel P. Weiser. He was director in the York County Bank, York Water Company, and York & Susquehanna Turnpike Company, each for many years. He died in 1874 at the advanced age of about eighty-three years. He left two children: Franklin S., who succeeded him in the lumber business, and Jane, married first to Jacob Smyser (deceased), and now to Nathaniel Weigle.

Daniel, fourth son of Samuel Weiser, Sr., was a tanner and currier for many years, and afterward formed a partnership with his brother Jacob in the lumber business. He died about 1855, leaving three sons: Gates J. Weiser (lately deceased), David Weiser and Oliver P. Weiser. Charles Weiser, father of John A. and Charles S. Weiser, who are prominently identified with the business interests of

BIOGRAPHICAL SKETCHES.

York, was born in 1796, and was the junior member of the dry goods firm of J. & C. Weiser, commencing business in 1818 and continuing until 1846. In 1856 he founded the banking-house in his own name. In January, 1860, his son, Charles S. Weiser, became a member of the firm. In January, 1867, the present firm, Weiser, Son & Carl, was formed. For a number of years he was a director in the York Bank, and president of the York & Gettysburg and York & Susquehanna Turnpike Companies. He was a member of Christ's Lutheran Church under Dr. Schmucker, and one of the founders of St. Paul's Lutheran Church. He died in 1867, aged seventy-one years. He lived for twenty-five years on the property now owned by Jere Carl, Esq. He was married to Anna A., daughter of Gen. Jacob Spangler, and left nine children: John A., Erastus H., Horace, Charles S., George (who died in infancy), Josephine (married to Dr. Pentz), Theodosia E. (unmarried), Arabella (now deceased), Amelia (married to M. S. Green), Adaline (married to Jere Carl). John A. Weiser, eldest son of Charles Weiser, was born July 31, 1824. He received his education in York County Academy. He began his mercantile career in 1838 as a clerk in his father's store, and remained in the same position until 1846, when he succeeded his father in the business. This he continued until 1883, when his two eldest sons succeeded him. The present firm name is H. P. Weiser & Bro. The same store, in the same location, has been continued in the Weiser name since its organization in 1808. Mr. Weiser has been exceptionally prosperous as a merchant, and his name is very familiarly known in York County. Possessing rare business qualifications, he has been prominently connected with other interests in the town and county. He was one of the founders of, and is still one of the directors of, the Farmers' National Bank, and was for many years a director of the York County Bank. He has been president of the York & Gettysburg Turnpike Company since 1881; treasurer of the York Gas Company since 1850; manager and treasurer of the York & Susquehanna Turnpike Company since 1867. He was married first to Miss Georgiana Eichelberger (now deceased) in 1851. Of this marriage there was one son—Harry—born in 1852, now senior member of the mercantile firm of H. P. Weiser & Bro. In 1859 he was married to Miss Mary Jane Upp. The children by this marriage are Bertha, born in 1860; George U., in 1861; P. Sterrett, in 1864; Louisa, in 1865, and Annie S., in 1867. He resides in his delightfully situated home at 210 East Market Street, surrounded by all the comforts and conveniences of life.

Erastus H. Weiser, second son of Charles Weiser, was born in 1826. He received his preparatory education at York County Academy and Pennsylvania College at Gettysburg. He afterward entered Yale College, and graduated in the class of 1849; read law with John G. Campbell, Esq., and had a lucrative practice in this profession before the York Court until the time of his death in 1871. He was married, in 1852, to Miss Annie Franklin, daughter of Walter Franklin, Esq., of York, who is now also dead. They had two sons: William F. Weiser, in the banking firm of Weiser, Son & Carl, and Charles, a student in Collegiate Institute. He was an earnest and devoted worker, and an elder in the Presbyterian Church at York, and a teacher in the Sunday-school.

Horace S. was educated at Yale, and read law with Judge Fisher. He practiced at the York bar for a few years, then removed to Decorah, Iowa, and founded the Winneshiek County Bank in 1854, and conducted the same successfully until the time of his death in 1875.

Charles S. Weiser was born in 1838, and educated in the schools of York and in York County Academy. He began the banking business as a partner with his father in 1860, and is now the senior member of the firm of Weiser, Son & Carl, which bank is described elsewhere in this book. For several years he was a member of the firm of Weiser & Bender, engaged in the lumber business in Center County, Penn. The following list of positions of trust and honor held by him gives conclusive evidence of his business capacity and integrity: treasurer of the York Water Company, of the York County Academy, of the York Hospital and Dispensary, of the Society for the Prevention of Cruelty to Animals, of the York County Mutual Fire Insurance Company, of the Board of Home Missions of the General Synod of the Evangelical Lutheran Church in the United States, of the Theological Seminary at Gettysburg, of the Charles A. Morris fund of $7,000 for St. Paul's Lutheran Church, and vice-president of the Orphan's Home and director in the York & Susquehanna Turnpike Company. Mr. Weiser was married, in 1866, to Miss Isadora Brown, daughter of the late William Brown, Esq., of York. They had one child—Charles, who died in infancy. He and his wife are members of the St. Paul's Lutheran Church, and also teaches in the Sunday-school. He is a member of the Masonic fraternity, and resides in a comfortable and convenient home at 225 East Market Street.

FRANKLIN S. WEISER, a prominent manufacturer of York, was born in the county September 25, 1825, and a son of Jacob and Sarah Weiser. His father being engaged in the mercantile business, our subject was early instilled with business ideas, being an assistant of his father. He received a good education, having the supplementary advantage of the York County Academy. At the age of eighteen he began an apprenticeship to learn the carpenter's trade, and subsequently followed that trade for five years in Baltimore, Md. Returning to York he formed an association with Jacob Weiser in the coal and lumber business, which continued until 1900, when he became the sole owner. He has since continued in this business, and has also become a manufacturer of cigar and paper boxes. Mr. Weiser is a progressive business man; has been a director of the York County Bank and of the York & Chanceford Turnpike Company, and also prominent in the Lutheran Church. Mr. Weiser was married, March 25, 1852, to Barbara S., daughter of Jacob Stahle, of Manchester Township. They have had born to them six children: Robert S., deceased; Sarah K., deceased; Jacob S., deceased; Harvy K., William H. and Eugene F.

GATES B. WEISER was born in York in 1852, and is a son of Gates J. and Elmira (Brown) Weiser, the former of whom was born in 1824, and died in 1883. Gates J. was educated at the York County Academy. When a young man he engaged in the lumber business with his father, Daniel Weiser, and after the death of the latter formed a partnership with John M. Brown. Retiring from business for a few years, he again engaged in the lumber business with Small, Bender & Co., as one of the firm. This firm was afterward changed to Bender & Weiser. Subsequently they established a business in Center County, Penn., the firm being known as Weiser & Bender. In 1875 he returned from Center County to York, Penn., and retired from business, selling his interest in the firm of Bender & Weiser to his two sons, James M. and Gates B., and known as Weiser Bros. After the death of James M. in 1876, G. B. bought his interest, and continued under the same firm name until 1883. G. B. Weiser was married, in 1884, to Miss Minnie M. Blummer, a native of Philadelphia. They have one child—Isadore E. He now resides in a beautiful residence at Prospect Hill. In politics Mr. Weiser is an Independent.

YORK BOROUGH.

JOHN H. WELLENSIEK, whip manufacturer of York, was born February 10, 1825, and is the son of Herman and Catherine Wellensiek, natives of Germany. The subject of this sketch was born in Germany. He remained at home and assisted his father on the farm until he was sixteen years of age. He received the advantages of a common school education, and immigrated to this country in the year 1845, locating at York, and engaged as an apprentice to learn the whip manufacturing business. He spent three and one-half years learning that trade. He then learned the carpenter trade under the instruction of Lewis Kuehn, of York, and after finishing his trade he went to Philadelphia and engaged as carpenter and builder. In a very short time he acquired a reputation that placed him among the leading builders of the city. He remained in Philadelphia until 1875, when he then returned to York and engaged in the whip manufacturing business. He leased a piece of ground for a term of years, and built a large brick building, put in the necessary machinery, and in a short time established quite an extensive business, having at the present several hands employed. Mr. Wellensiek was married, November 25, 1860, to Miss Mary, daughter of Gottleib and Barbara Brietling, natives of Germany. To this union were born six children: Katie, Albert, Anna, John, Mamie and Harry. Mr. Wellensiek is a member of the Lutheran Church, also a member of Walker Lodge No. 306, I. O. O. F., of Germantown, Philadelphia, Penn.

PETER WELLER, marble dealer, was born in Germany in November, 1824. His father, Jacob, came to this country while Peter was quite young, and located in Spring Garden Township, where he took up a tract of land. Peter assisted his father on the farm, and in the meantime attended the common school. He remained on the farm with his father till he was twenty years of age, when he learned the shoe-making trade, and followed it about three years. About the year 1878 he formed a co-partnership with Edward Evans, and engaged in the marble business at York. The firm of Weller & Evans subsequently by mutual consent dissolved partnership, and Mr. Weller has continued the business in his own name. Mr. Weller married, in April, 1850, Miss Matilda, daughter of George Loucks, of York. Mr. Weller is a member of the Penn Mutual Relief Association, and has for several years been a member of the Lutheran Church.

ALBERT A. WELSH was born in York November 13, 1838, and is a son of George and Sarah (Wilt) Welsh, natives of the same borough. He received a common school and academical education, and then engaged at butchering with his father, which business he has followed ever since, being now one of the oldest butchers in York, and at the present time his place of business is No. 131¼ East Philadelphia Street, York, Penn. January 29, 1860, he married Miss Catherine, daughter of John and Magdalena Lutman, of York, and to this union have been born twelve children. But of twelve, only seven children, Thomas Ivin, George Lincoln, John Lutman, Mary Magdalena, Charles Augustus, Carrie Verginnia and Albert, are living at the present time. Mr. Welsh is a member of the Conewago Tribe, No. 87, I. O. R. M., and has served as deacon of the Reformed Church, as well as assistant superintendent and superintendent of the Heidelburg Sabbath-school, of York.

DAVID H. WELSH is the son of Charles and Eliza Welsh, natives of York County, and was born in York Borough August 13, 1845. He was educated at the common schools, and afterward learned coachsmithing, which trade he followed for about five years after finishing his apprenticeship. He then engaged in the ready-made clothing, gents' furnishing and merchant tailoring business, in which he has achieved an enviable reputation, doing first-class work and carrying a line of ready-made and piece goods. September 17, 1878, he married Miss Frances K., daughter of Col. J. A. Stahle, of York. To this union five children have been born, viz.: Edward S. (deceased), James A., Fannie M., David H. (deceased) and Nellie V. Mr. Welsh is a member of Mt. Zion Lodge, I. O. O. F., and also of the Reformed Church.

T. KIRK WHITE, special agent and adjuster for the Phœnix Assurance Company, of London, was born in Cecil County, Md., September 18, 1826, son of Abner and Esther (Kirk) White, and of fourteen children (eleven living) he is the ninth. His father was born in England, and came to America at about twenty years of age, and settled in Chester County, Penn. Here the mother of our subject was born February 4, 1792, and died in Morgan County, Ohio, at the advanced age of eighty-four years. His father died in Lancaster County in 1847. At twelve years of age subject began life for himself. For some time he worked on the farm, and then learned the machinist's trade, and while thus employed he sustained physical injuries from which he has never recovered. In 1845 he entered Strasburg Academy, at Lancaster, Penn., where he remained two years, and then for a number of years taught school, and was one of the leaders in establishing the first district institute in Lancaster County, Penn., in 1851. In 1855 Mr. White came to York, and established what was known as the Pennsylvania Commercial College, which he conducted until the beginning of the late war. In 1861 he was elected justice of the peace and held the office until 1865, when he began the insurance business. In 1872 he was made special agent of the Home, of New York, and with that company remained until 1882, when he was given his present position. His marriage was solemnized April 17, 1849, to Miss Susan J. Smith, daughter of William and Nancy Smith, of Lancaster County. They have had seven children, five living, as follows: Anna M., Walter B., George C., Charles S. and Harry C. Mr. White is a Democrat, and a member of the I. O. O. F.

PETER WIEST, dealer in dry goods and notions, is a native of Jackson Township, York Co., Penn., born in 1818, son of John and Elizabeth (Eyster) Wiest, being the fourth of eight children. His father was born in what was then Paradise Township in 1787, and died in 1837. His mother was born in 1790, and died in 1833. The great-grandfather of our subject was a native of Germany, and immigrated to America about 1730. The Wiest family has been identified with the interests of York County for more than 100 years. At eighteen years of age Mr. W. came to York, and for some years attended the York County Academy. In 1840 he began the general merchandising at Dover, Penn., where he continued for more than a year, and then in the spring of 1843 returned to York, and has since been continually engaged in the mercantile life. For almost half a century he has been one of the successful and reliable business men of York. Mr. Wiest was married, in 1844, to Miss Catherine Lenhart, a native of Dover Township. They have children as follows: Edward F., Emma E., George L. and Harry S. The sons are now engaged in the dry goods business with their father. Formerly Mr. W. was a Whig, but of late years he has been independent in politics. Mr. and Mrs. Wiest are members of the Reformed Church, having joined as early as 1836.

WILLIAM T. WILLIAMS was born in York County July 31, 1815, and is a son of Ezekiel and Elizabeth Williams, both of whom were natives of Berks County, Penn. He was educated at the common schools, and assisted upon his father's farm until he was twenty-four years of age. He then learned the weaver's trade, at which he was engaged for five years. He subsequently engaged in schoolteaching, which he continued for nine years, learning (in the meantime) surveying. He was elected justice of the peace in 1858, in Washington Township, and served two years. In 1870 he removed to York, where he has since resided. In 1875 he was elected justice of the peace for the Fifth Ward, and is still administering the duties of a magistrate. Mr. Williams was united in marriage with Miss Catherine Gross, daughter of Peter and Catherine Gross, both natives of York County. They have six children: David G., Levi G., William F., Peter G., Henry L. and Mandilla. The family are members of the Lutheran Church, of which Mr. Williams has been an elder, and for many years prominent in the Sabbath-school.

PROF. D. G. WILLIAMS, superintendent of schools for York County, is a native of Dover Township, where he was born in 1840. He is of Welsh and German descent, and son of William T. and Catherine (Gross) Williams, both natives of York County, and parents of six children, our subject being the eldest: Levi, Mandilla, Franklin W. (a resident of Iowa), Peter and Lewis (both of whom are living in Ohio). Prof. Williams received meager educational advantages in his youth, having access only to the common schools, and eleven weeks in a county normal. The education which he has since obtained has been acquired by liberal reading and constant studious application. He has been a teacher nearly all of his life; the few years which he devoted to business convinced him that his duty in life was in the field of education, and as an educator he has been signally successful. He commenced teaching early in life, and was thus engaged for thirteen consecutive terms in York County. He then went to Indiana, where he taught one term, and then engaged in the mercantile business. In 1867 he returned to York, and for about five years was engaged in business. He then resumed teaching, and continued until he was elected to the office which he now holds. Prior to his election he was for four years connected with the public schools of York Borough during which period he was a member of a prominent literary association. He assumed the duties of his office in 1878, succeeding W. H. Kain, and in the administration of the arduous and responsible labors of this position, he has developed executive attributes of superior order. Prof. Williams is an earnest and indefatigable worker, and under his supervision the schools of the county have maintained a high degree of excellence. In 1863 Prof. Williams was united in marriage with Miss Sarah Ellen Myers, of Dover Township. They have had seven children: William P., Ida M., Lillie D., Charlie M., Harry L., Elmer L. and Maud E. Prof. Williams and wife are members of the Lutheran Church.

HON. DAVID F. WILLIAMS (deceased) was born in York, January 28, 1823; he was educated at York County Academy, and from 1844 to 1855 was in partnership with Oliver Stuck, as editor and proprietor of the York *Democratic Press*. During the years 1848, 1849 and 1851, he represented York County in the State General Assembly. In 1858, he went to Pittsburgh and became a partner in the publication of the Pittsburgh *Gazette*, which he conducted two years, and then went to Philadelphia, and from 1860 until 1866 held a position in the custom house. In 1869 he was appointed Assessor of Internal Revenue for what was then the Fifteenth District of Pennsylvania, and continued in the revenue service until 1876. He was married in 1853 to Miss Anna M. Smyser, a native of York, and to him were born four children. He died October 14, 1881. For many years he was president of the York County Bank.

JACOB A. WILT, jeweler, was born in York in 1843, and is the son of Peter E. and Eliza M. (Wisenall) Wilt. He is the youngest in a family of two

children, and is of German descent; was educated at the public schools of York and York Academy, and in 1860 began serving a four-years' apprenticeship at the jewelers' trade, under the direction of C. A. Keyworth. In 1864 he went to Washington and remained some time, and then returned to York and continued his vocation, but subsequently formed a partnership in the jewelry business with his old employers. In 1881 Mr. Wilt began business for himself, and still continues in the jewelry business, and is one of the most successful jewelry merchants in York. Our subject's marriage was solemnized March 28, 1866, to Miss Kate C. Hagger, a native of Baltimore, Md., and daughter of John W. and Lavinia Hagger. Mr. Wilt is a Democrat and cast his first presidential vote for McClellan. He is a member of the I. O. O. F., K. of P., and R. M.

GEORGE WASHINGTON WINEHOLD, dealer

in fine groceries, canned fruits, etc., was born in York County in 1848, son of Joshua and Rufina (Ilges) Winehold. He is of German descent and a representative of one of the oldest families of York County. His father was born in York Township in 1813, and his mother in the "lower end" in 1817. The paternal grandfather of our subject was George Winehold, also a native of York Township, born in 1786. The father of Mr. Winehold died in 1863. When about five years old, Mr. Winehold removed with his parents to York, where he was educated at the public schools of York and York County Academy. In 1866 he began business for himself. The systematic order in which everything in his store is arranged is unexcelled in York. For some years Mr. Winehold has taken much interest in the Laurel Fire Company, of which he was formerly secretary, and now for two years has held the office of vice-president. He is a Democrat and has represented the First and Sixth Wards in the borough council. The mother of Mr. Winehold now resides with him.

GEORGE WOGAN, deceased, was a native of Manchester Township, York Co., Penn., was born April 14, 1800, and was a son of George and Rebecca (Lowe) Wogan. He is the youngest in a family of seven children, and of Scotch-Irish descent. He remained at home and worked on the farm for his father until 1825, when he began life for himself. At the death of his father, he inherited the old Wogan homestead in Manchester Township, and continued farming until 1861, when he retired from active life, and removed to York, where he lived until his death, which occurred April 20, 1878. His marriage was solemnized December 16, 1834, to Miss Margaret Hay, a native of York County, and a daughter of John Hay, the elder. Politically Mr. Wogan was a Republican. He was one of the leading and greatly respected citizens of York County. Mrs. Wogan is a representative of one of the old families of York County. Her father died in 1866, and her mother two years previous. To Mr. and Mrs. Wogan were born three children, viz.: Rebecca L. (deceased), John H. and Anna H.

EMANUEL YESSLER, a member of the firm of Menough & Yessler, contractors and builders, was born July 4, 1836, in Dover Township, York County, and is a son of Jacob and Susan (Harbaugh) Yessler, farmers of Dover Township. Emanuel was an assistant upon the farm, attending the common schools, until he became eighteen years of age. He then became an apprentice to Jacob Gotwald, learning the carpenter trade. He remained with Mr. Gotwald for several years. In 1863 he went to Washington, D. C., and was in the employ of the government about three years, working at his trade. Returning to York he was, for fifteen years, in the employ of Mr. Weigle, subsequently becoming associated with James L. Menough, in the planing-mill and general contracting business. The business of Menough & Yessler has been prosperous and their trade extended. Mr. Yessler was married December 24, 1866, to Miss Mary, daughter of John and Mary Miller, natives of the county. Two children have been born to them: Harry E. and Jennie M. Mr. and Mrs. Yessler are members of the Lutheran Church, of which he has been an active member for several years, serving as deacon, elder, and treasurer of the Sabbath-school.

PETER F. YOST, son of Abraham and Maria (Feiser) Yost, was born in York Township, January 29, 1829, on the farm now owned and occupied by Frank Deitz. His father removed to Dover Township, when our subject was four years old. Subject was reared a farmer. February 20, 1851, he married Sarah Bott, daughter of Peter and Elizabeth (Smyser) Bott, of West Manchester Township. One child has blessed this union—Louisa Jane, deceased wife of Alexander Smyser; one child, Clayton A. Smyser, was born to them. Mr. Yost, for a short time was in the firm of Menough & Yost, builders and carpenters. The handsome residence he now occupies he built in 1880, and also the adjoining residence for his sisters in 1878. Our subject's father was born May 5, 1792, and died August 31, 1855, aged sixty-three years, three months and twenty-six days. His mother died September 23, 1859, aged sixty-eight years, five months and eighteen days. Subject's sister, Rachel Yost, died June 11, 1854, aged thirty-eight years, seven months and fifteen days. Mr. Yost moved to York from Dover Township in 1876. The Yost family was among the earliest settlers of York Township.

CHARLES YOST was reared on his father's farm in York Township, and worked on the farm and attended school when a boy. He married Sarah Lower, of Dover Township, a union productive of four children: Eliza, William, Sarah Ann (deceased) and Ellen Jane. Subject, by close attention to business and untiring industry, has secured for himself a handsome competence. He owns one of the best farms in Manchester Township, also one in Newberry Township, and a fine residence in the borough of York, beside other property.

HIRAM YOUNG. The Youngs' family history in this country dates as far back as 1735 and 1740. About that time Hiram Young's great-grandfather, Alexander Shaeffer, landed in America, and located on the mountains, which then formed a part of Lancaster, but which are now included within the limits of Lebanon County. A short time after his arrival here he purchased about 1,200 acres of land in the valley, and founded what is now known as Shaeffertown. His wife, Anna E. Engle, bore him six children. One of them, Henry Shaeffer, was a captain in the army of the Revolution; was afterward associate judge of the court at Harrisburg, and at the time of his death, which occurred in 1805, was an acting justice of the peace. His daughter, Maria, married Frederick Oberlin, and their daughter, Sarah, became the wife of Samuel Young, of Lancaster County. Two sons and one daughter were the fruit of this marriage, among whom was Hiram Young, the subject of this sketch. Hiram Young was born in Schaeffertown, Lebanon County, May 14, 1830. Some time after this event his parents moved to Lancaster County, where they remained a few years. His father having died in Lancaster County, his mother afterward returned to her parents in Schaeffertown. Up to his fifteenth year Mr. Young attended the public schools of that place, and being studiously inclined, mastered the different branches then taught. About this time he went to Lancaster and served four years with Judge Emanuel Shaeffer as an apprentice to the saddler's trade. In the month of February, 1850, he obtained a position in John Gish's book store, and remained with him until he secured a more lucrative one in the large establishment of Judd & Murray, with whom he acted as employe for several years. After leaving Judd & Murray he entered the Lancaster High School with a view of preparing himself for a regular collegiate course, but after some time, finding his means limited and difficulties in the way, abandoned the undertaking, and returned to the book business. In this he obtained employment in the publishing house of Uriah Hunt & Son, of Philadelphia, and afterward with Lippincott, Grambo & Co, now J. B. Lippincott & Co. After several years' experience in Philadelphia he returned to Lancaster City, and purchased a small book store, entering into partnership with John Shaeffer. About two years afterward a consolidation was made with the firm of Murray & Stokes, under the firm name of Murray, Young &

Co., Mr. Stokes retiring. After several years in the book business in Lancaster, Mr. Young retired, and in the year 1860 came to York, and purchased the book store of B. Franklin Spangler, now deceased, and founded the firm of Pierce & Young. In 1862, after largely increasing the business, he sold out his interest to Mr. Pierce, and opened another store on West Market Street, and in 1865 removed to the building No. 10, East Market Street, now occupied by him for the publication of the *Evening Dispatch*, the *Weekly Dispatch*, and the *True Democrat*. June 7, 1864, the first number of the *True Democrat*, now *Weekly Dispatch*, was issued by him, it being a four-page, eight-column paper, advocating the Union cause and Republican principles, and taking a prominent part in furthering the local interests of the town and county. The *True Democrat* rapidly became one of the leading weekly papers of the county, and soon obtained a large circulation. Neither labor nor expense was spared by Mr. Young to make his paper acceptable in all families without distinction of party. May 29, 1876, the first number of the *Evening Dispatch* was issued. A strong assistant editorial and reportorial force was employed, and the news of the day, both local and telegraphic, was carefully gathered together and published. This evening paper met with a hearty welcome and liberal patronage from the public, and has always been and now is one of the most widely read dailies in York County. In his position as publisher of these two papers, Mr. Young took a lively interest, and devoted his best energies and personal attention to the details of the business. In this his former experience in the book publishing business was a most valuable aid in his work. Mr. Young has always taken an active part in the politics of the county, and with pen and voice labored for the Union cause and the triumph of Republican principles. In 1881 he was prominently named as a candidate for the office of State treasurer, and in this received the endorsement of leading papers of the commonwealth. He has many warm friends, but like others occupying similar positions, some enemies. Where he is best known he is recognized as a stanch and sincere friend, and as such deserves the support not only of his own party but the public generally. Mr. Young was married September 3, 1857, to Miss Mary E. Shriener, of Columbia, Lancaster County. Five sons were born to them, one of whom died in infancy; Edward, Charles, William and John, the survivors, all learned the printing business, and have been of great assistance to their father in the conduct of his large and extensive newspaper business. He has had an active business life, a large portion of which has been spent as a bookseller and publisher, and in his present editorial position he takes pride in advancing measures for the public good, both for his immediate constituency and the country at large. He now has the satisfaction of having two well-established and successful newspapers, with extended and growing influence, and can look back upon a most successful business experience, and forward to still greater triumph in the future.

EDWARD D. ZIEGLER is a son of Rev. Jacob Ziegler, of the borough of York. His father is a minister of the Reformed Church; he is still living and has reached the ripe age of seventy-five years. His mother is Anna Mary Danner, of York, and is still living. Mr. Ziegler is a graduate of Pennsylvania College, located at Gettysburg, Penn., having graduated from that institution of learning in the year 1865. Immediately upon leaving college he was employed by Dr. George W. Ruby, as assistant teacher in the York County Academy, in the borough of York. At this place he was employed in teaching for a period of three years, imparting instruction in the Latin language, in algebra, geometry, mathematics and English grammar. During this time he prosecuted the study of the law under N. L. Fisher, Esq., and was admitted to the York County bar in November, 1868. He was a candidate for and elected to the office of clerk of the county commissioners soon after his admission to the bar. In this position he served during one term of two years. At the expiration of his term of office he was honored, by the county commissioners of the county of York, by a unanimous election as their counsel, and was reappointed for a period of three years. In June, 1880, he was a candidate before the Democratic county convention for the nomination for district attorney of the county. He was nominated by the convention and elected by the people at the election following, and served in the office for three years. He continued in the practice of his profession alone until 1885, when he associated himself in the practice of the law with Frank Geise and Joseph R. Strawbridge, Esqs. From boyhood he was fond of politics, and there has been no campaign, county, State or national, in which he has not prominently figured. He has several times been elected delegate to State conventions of the Democratic party, and at the Allentown State convention, in the spring of 1884, was chosen as the delegate of the Nineteenth Congressional District to represent it in the national Democratic convention, which met in Chicago in July of the same year, and nominated Cleveland and Hendricks for president and vice-president of the United States.

HANOVER BOROUGH AND PENN TOWNSHIP.

HORACE ALLEMAN, M. D., was born in Lancaster County, in 1824; is a son of John and Elizabeth (Mockert) Alleman, and is of German origin. His father was born in Dauphin County, Penn., in 1793, and his mother in Lancaster County, Penn., in 1797. His father, when a young man, settled in Lancaster County, where he died in 1866; his wife having died one year previous. The Alleman family was one of the early families of Dauphin County, and among the prominent people. Dr. Alleman was educated at Emaus Institute in Dauphin County, and at Pennsylvania College at Gettysburg. He began the study of medicine, in 1846, in the office of Dr. Nathaniel Watson, of Lancaster County, and afterward graduated at the Pennsylvania Medical College, Philadelphia. In 1848 he began practice at Elizabethtown, Lancaster County, remained there some time, and then removed to Safe Harbor, Lancaster County, and in 1859 came to Hanover; here he has since remained. He was married, in 1847, to Miss Rebecca B. Winnemore, a native of Lancaster County. They have six children. He is Republican, and he and wife are members of the Lutheran Church. He is one of the leading physicians of York County.

JACOB E. BAIR, cigar manufacturer, of Hanover, was born at that place July 18, 1831. He is a son of John and Julia (Snyder) Bair, of York County. His father was a tanner by trade, and followed it through life. Jacob E. received a good common school education, and assisted his father in the tanning business until 1848, when he began the manufacture of cigars at Hanover, which occupation he has followed since. He owns quite an extensive cigar manufactory, and is assisted by his sons. Most of the time he employs quite a number of hands. July 3, 1855, he was married to Catherine Grim, daughter of Henry D. and Elizabeth Grim, of Virginia, and has had eight children: Julia A., John H., Cecilia and Edmonia (twins, the latter deceased), John J. C., Howard E., Jacob H. and Robert L. Mr. and Mrs. Bair are members of the Reformed Church.

G. MILTON BAIR was born in Hanover in 1850, is a son of Edward and Deliah (daughter of George and Mary Gitt), and is of German origin. His parents were born in Hanover, the father in 1810, and the mother in 1813. His paternal grandfather was John Bair, who was also born in Hanover. His father, a saddler, died December 13, 1883. Our subject was educated at the public schools of Hanover, and Dickison College, at Carlisle, Penn., and graduated from the latter in 1867. In 1868 he engaged in the mercantile business, continued for nine years, and then engaged in the life, fire and accident insurance business, and in this still continues. He was married, in 1871, to Miss Emma C. Welsh, daughter of G. W. Welsh, a prominent politician of York County. They have two children: Edward W. and Ray W. He is a Republican, and he and wife are members of the Lutheran Church.

FABER BANGE, D. D. S., was born June 9, 1854, in Hanover; is a son of Dr. W. H. and Sarah (Faber) Bange, and is of German descent. His father was born in Hanover, in 1819, and his mother in 1823. Dr. William H. Bange, father of subject, was the second son of the late John Bange, who was one of the old settlers of Hanover. Dr. William H. Bange was prominently connected with the town of Hanover for forty years, was one of the first members of Emanuel's Reformed Church, and took great interest in the Sabbath-school; he was a member of the I. O. O. F., and a man of sterling worth. His death took place in 1882. The mother of subject died in 1868. Subject was reared in Hanover, and received a common school education. At sixteen he began the study of dentistry under his father, and subsequently began the practice, which he still continues. He is most successful, and for over ten years has been practicing in Hanover. He is a Republican, a member of the I. O. O. F., and of Emanuel Reformed Church.

ALBERT F. BARKER, proprietor of the Diller House, Hanover, was born January 20, 1841, near Littlestown, Penn. His parents, Joseph and Cassia (Diehl) Barker, natives of Chester and York Counties, were married in York County and removed to Adams County, where all their children, fourteen in number, were born, of whom only six are now living. Mr. Barker acquired his education in the public schools of his native town. His studies were pursued with a view to the medical profession, but he abandoned it at the age of seventeen, at the request of his father. He clerked in mercantile establishments and hotels in Pennsylvania and Maryland, and during the last war he volunteered as a nurse to attend the sick and wounded at the second battle of Bull Run, had charge of a ward in general hospital, but was several times detailed for field hospital duty. He was in the service about four months. He was married at Uniontown, Md., January 30, 1864, to Miss Ellen R. Carlisle, a native of Maryland. Their only child died in infancy. He embarked in the mercantile business in Littlestown in 1864, and followed it fourteen years. He then retired from the business and for about four years traded in cattle, etc. In March, 1888, he bought out the Diller House, which he refitted and refurnished and converted into a first-class hotel. His father died in Littlestown, Penn., at the age of sixty-nine years, leaving an estate of several thousand dollars, of which he has charge as administrator. His mother is still living at the old homestead, aged about seventy-one years. Mr. Barker is a member of the I. O. O. F. and of the order of Red Men. He had been an active Republican for many years of his life, and was postmaster at Littlestown from 1864 to 1878.

ALBERT M. BARNITZ (deceased) was a native of York; was born. August 25, 1835, son of Jacob and Catherine (Wagner) Barnitz, and was of German extraction. His education was gained at York public schools, and York County Academy. He subsequently read law under Hon. Thomas E. Cochran. On account of ill health he was compelled to abandon his studies and sometime later engaged in the jewelry business, which he continued until the death of his father, when he took charge of the brewing business which had been established by his father. Later he resumed the jewelry business, and in this enterprise continued until his death. He married Miss Martha Wirt, a daughter of the late Jacob and Amelia Wirt, of Hanover, June 12, 1862; to this union were born two children: Jacob Percy and Emma Wirt. Politically Mr. Barnitz is a Republican, and for many years manifested much interest in political affairs. He was a member of the Episcopal Church. His death occurred November 29, 1869. His remains now repose in Prospect Hill Cemetery, at York. He was a man of pronounced merit, and ever wielded an energetic and enterprising influence. In 1869 Mrs. Barnitz removed to Hanover, where she has since resided. She is also a member of the Episcopal Church, and a most amiable woman.

S. T. BASTIAN, real estate, insurance, collection and general agent of Hanover, Penn., was born in Allentown, Penn., in 1858, and is the son of Jonas and Eliza (Smith) Bastian, one of the oldest families in Lehigh County. He was educated at the public schools, spent a few years at a collegiate institute at Hackettstown, N. J., and then at the Allentown Business College, from which he graduated. He then engaged with the *Allentown Daily Bulletin* as a reporter for one year; then he clerked a few months in a dry goods store, and in 1878 he came to Hanover and engaged as clerk for Grove & Carver, dealers in dry goods, etc., with whom he remained about three years and a half. In 1882 he formed a partnership with J. H. Flickinger, in the real estate and fire insurance business, from which Mr. Flickinger, retired in the spring of 1883, since when Mr. Bastian has successfully conducted the business and built up a good reputation. He is also advertising agent for the Northern Pacific Railroad Company for southern Pennsylvania; is correspondent for several daily papers, and is generally considered a very enterprising young man, who will meet with success in everything he undertakes.

J. H. BITTINGER, M. D., of Hanover, is a lineal descendant in the generation of Adam Bittinger (Biedinger) who, in 1736, emigrated from Alsace, Germany, to America, landed in Philadelphia, and settled first in Lancaster County, and in 1753 purchased a tract of land three miles northwest of Hanover. Adam Bittinger died in 1768, leaving a widow (Sabina) and children as follows: Nicholas, Henry, Michael, Peter, Marrilas, George, Adam, Christian, Frederick and Eva. Nicholas Bittinger, the eldest son, was born in Alsace, grew to manhood in America, and, as early as 1743, was one of the members of the council of the "Evangelical Lutheran Church of the Conewago," now St. Matthew's, of Hanover. For a time, when the church was without a pastor, he was licensed by the synod to read sermons from the pulpit and conduct other religious services. In 1775 he became a member of the Committee of Safety for York County, and served during a part of the Revolution. He became captain of a company of associators, and entered the military service. He was very successful in the accumulation of property, and at the time of his death, on May 2, 1804, owned several good farms within six miles of Hanover, and a number of choice tracts of land in Franklin County. His remains were interred at Abbottstown. He had a family of nine children—two sons, John and Joseph, and seven daughters. Joseph, the great grandfather of our subject, was born February 26, 1773. In the year 1798, he became the owner of the tract of land purchased by his grandfather, Adam Bittinger, in 1753. He died July 26, 1804, at the early age of thirty two years, and left a widow and five sons, viz.: John, Joseph, Henry, Frederick and George. His second son Joseph, the grandfather of Dr. J. H. Bittinger, was born November 13, 1794, married Lydia Bear, of Hanover, in 1819, and died September 27, 1850, on the old homestead of Adam Bittinger, the immigrant. He left twelve children, viz.: William, now residing in Abbottstown; Henry, born 1821 and died 1879; Joseph, graduate of Pennsylvania College and of Andover Theological Seminary, became pastor of a Presbyterian Church in Cleveland, Ohio, and Pittsburgh, Penn., was a fine speaker, an elegant writer and a doctor of divinity; died in 1885, and his remains were interred at Hanover. The other children were Ellen, Edward (died in Chicago), Rebecca, John, Quincy (graduate of Dartmouth College and Andover Seminary, pastor of Congregational Church at Haverhill, N.H.), Daniel, Annie, Howard, Nicholas (now in Florida) and Charles Lewis, now in Florida. Dr. J. H. Bittinger, the subject of this sketch, was born in Berwick Township, February 3, 1852, and is a son of Henry Bittinger. For a time he attended Pennsylvania College, taught school in Illinois and in Pennsylvania. In 1871, while in the wholesale foreign and domestic fruit business with his uncles, George and Charles, in the city of Chicago, their entire establishment was burned by the disastrous fire that destroyed over $200,000,000 worth of property, and 7,450 buildings. Dr. Bittinger returned to Hanover in 1873, began to read medicine, entered the Jefferson Medical College of Philadelphia and graduated in 1878, began practicing in Hanover, where he soon prospered in his profession. After two and one-half years of successful practice he removed to Philadelphia, where he did a lucrative business. In 1882 he returned to Hanover, and the same year was married to Miss Clara E. Bucher. They have one child—Lida. Dr. Bittinger is an active practitioner, is well read, and thoroughly versed in his profession and now enjoys a large practice. He is a member of the State Medical Society, American Medical Association and the York County Medical Society.

CHARLES C. BOWMAN is a native of the city of "brotherly love," was born in 1831, and is a son of Charles and Sarah (Sultz) Bowman, of German descent. His father was born in the same city in 1800, and died in 1874; his mother died in 1864. When a mere boy he left Philadelphia and went to New York City, remained a short time and then went to Newark, N. J.; fourteen years of age found him at sea, which he sailed six years, and has traveled around the world from west to east once, and for a number of years he was in the employ of the United States government. In 1851 he came to Hanover and engaged in the manufacture of cigars, but at the end of one year he went to Newark, N. J., and there remained until 1864, when he returned to Hanover, and here has since resided. Mr. Bowman was married in 1852 to Miss Dorothea Grimes, a native of Germany. To this marriage have been born thirteen children. Politically Mr. Bowman is a Democrat. He is one of the substantial and successful business men of Hanover. He is a Mason and K. T. and a member of the I. O. O. F. and I. O. R. M., and Mr. and Mrs. Bowman are members of the Reformed Church. He is at present one of the building committee of the Trinity Reformed Church which is being erected in Hanover and was one of the founders of said church, which is nearly completed. He is closely connected with Hon. Daniel Fox, ex-mayor of Philadelphia, Penn.

HON. PHILIP S. BOWMAN, eldest of the seven children of John and Catharine (Stambaugh) Bowman, was born February 15, 1846, in Jackson Township, formerly Paradise Township, and is of German descent. The father was born March 29, 1822, in Heidelberg Township; the mother was born in Paradise Township. Our subject was reared a farmer, and educated at the common schools, and at the Manchester Academy, Carroll County, Md., and at the normal school at Millersville, Lancaster Co., Penn. For five years from 1863 he taught school. In 1871 he engaged in the grain and produce trade at Hanover, and two years later resumed farming. In politics he is a Democrat, and in 1869 was elected assessor of Heidelberg Township. In 1873 he was elected assistant assessor; in 1874, school director; in 1876, representative of York County, and in 1878 was re-elected in each of the two last cases by more than a party vote. In the legislature he took an active part in opposing the Pittsburgh Riot Bill, which was defeated. In 1881 he was elected secretary of the Farmers' Mutual Fire Insurance Company, of Paradise, York Co., Penn., of which company he is also a director. In 1885 he was elected justice of the peace, and for the past two years has also been engaged in surveying. In 1867 he joined the Odd Fellows, and in 1872 was made a Free Mason, being now W. M. of Patmos Lodge No. 348. He is also a member of Howell Chapter No. 199, and York Commandery No. 21. He was married, in 1867, to Miss Lydia E., daughter of Samuel and Julia Ann Keller, born September 23, 1846, in Heidelberg Township. Four children have blessed this union, viz.: Milton E., Martha E., Ira A. and Oscar R. Mr. and Mrs. Bowman are members of the Lutheran Church.

JOHN BUTT, a cigar manufacturer of Pennville, Penn Township, York County, was born December 25, 1825, in York County, and is the only child of John and Eva (Zeigler) Butt. His father was a hatter by trade, and followed the same until his death. Our subject was brought up a farmer, and received a common school education, most of which he acquired by himself, as he lost his father when an infant. Until his seventh year he remained with his mother. He then made his home with Daniel Diehl, with whom he remained until he became of age. Early he learned the trade of shoemaking, and followed it for fourteen years. November 4, 1848, he was married to Joanna Bankert, a daughter of Daniel Bankert, deceased. To them were born six children: Zepania, Matilda, Austin, deceased; Elaranda, deceased; Milton and an infant, deceased. In 1849 Mr. Butt removed to the place where he has since resided, and has carried on the manufacture of cigars for thirty years. He and wife are members of the Methodist Episcopal Church of Hanover. Mr. Butt takes great interest in educational matters, and is considered a liberal, public-spirited citizen Politically he is a Republican.

CAPT. A. W. EICHELBERGER. The subject of this sketch is an honored representative of the Eichelberger family. The great-grandfather of our subject. Philip Frederick Eichelberger, son of John and Maria Barbara Eichelberger, who was born April 17, 1693, in Itlingen, near Sinzheim, then in the Grand Duchy of Baden, now in the Empire of Germany. He was married November 11, 1714, to Anna Barbara Doerners. On May 11, 1728, he received from the authorities of Itlingen a testimonial of his good character and honorable standing, the original of which is now in possession of Edwin S. Eichelberger, Esq., a great-great-grandson, residing in Frederick, Md. On the 22d of June, 1728, himself, wife and four children, together with thirty other Palatinates and their families, 100 in all, embarked in the good ship "Albany," and set sail from Rotterdam, Holland, for the land of their adoption. Lazarus Oxham was shipmaster, or captain, of this vessel, which landed September 4, of the same year, at Philadelphia. On September 13, 1748, he obtained a land warrant from the proprietaries of Pennsylvania for 175 acres of land in Manheim Township, Lancaster Co., Penn. Upon this tract he took his family, cleared and cultivated the land, built a house and prospered to such an extent that only two years later he obtained grants for 140 acres additional, located in Conestoga and Manheim Townships of the same county. He remained in Lancaster County until 1754, when, on April 28, 1761, he purchased a warrant of Conrad Low for 220 acres of land in Manheim Township, York Co., Penn. He died September 19, 1776, aged eighty-three years five months and two days. His remains now slumber in the historic old burying ground, about one mile north of Hanover. The children by his first wife were Martin, Frederick, Anna Margeret (married to Vincent Keefer), Barbara (married to Andrew Hoke) and Elizabeth (married to Jacob Smyser). His first four children, as above stated, were born in Germany. These children, after marriage, located in and around York. Martin, the eldest of the sons, was present at York when the town was laid out in 1741, and purchased Lot No. 120. He was one of the original members of the first Lutheran Church in York; was commissioned a court justice under King George III in 1760, the first year of his long reign, and also under constitution of 1776, being prominently identified with the early history of York, where he died in 1781 or 1782. The children of Martin were George, Frederick, Jacob, Bernard, Martin, Susanna (married to Daniel Barnitz) and Mary (married to William T. Coale). George and Jacob were prominent in collecting goods and money for the Revolutionary army. George was appointed quartermaster of the militia of York County in 1776. He was a member of the Provincial Convention, which was held at Philadelphia the 23d of January, 1776. He had been high sheriff of York under the king from 1768 to 1771. He died in York about the year 1781. Jacob was sheriff of York County, elected in 1804. He subsequently removed to Reisterstown, Md., where he died in 1832, aged eighty-nine years. Frederick, the second son of Martin, was a large land-holder. He lived in Bottstown, near York. His children were John, Thomas, Daniel, George, Bernard, William, Charles and Sarah. He died at his son's house, one and one-third miles west of York, in 1824, aged eighty-four years. Martin, the youngest son of Martin, during the Revolution, when less than eighteen, took a horse and rode to Boston, and joined Capt. Swope's company, which had left York before. He obtained a lieutenancy in Capt. Nichols' company, and on his transfer to the commissary department succeeded to the command of the company. He served with much credit during the war, and subsequently accompanied the expedition to Wyoming to repel the incursions of the Indians. He remained in the army until 1783. As a recognition of his services and exemplary character, he obtained the office of weighmaster at the port of Baltimore, which position he held for forty-five years. He died in that city October 2, 1840, in the eighty-second year of his age. Among his sons was Otho W. Eichelberger. He was one of the oldest merchants in Baltimore; was in business at No. 1 Howard Street for over fifty years. He died January 30, 1879, in the eightieth year of his age. Jesse, another son of Martin, was killed in Fort McHenry, at Baltimore, in 1814. Frederick Eichelberger, the second son of the immigrant, although born in Germany, soon imbibed the spirit of American patriotism. He lived near York, and was a justice during the time of the Revolution. The children by the second marriage of Philip Frederick Eichelberger were Adam, Leonard, Jacob (grandfather of our subject) and Lewis. Adam, the eldest, was a captain of a company of Associators of York County during the Revolution, and was also active in collecting money and supplies for the army. He was married to Magdalina Bechtel. Their children were Frederick, Michael, Samuel, Adam, Joseph, Susanna, Salome and Magdalina. He obtained possession of the homestead in 1766, which then contained 220 acres, including the mill place, which at that time was situated in Manheim but is now in Heidelberg Township, about three miles east of Hanover on the York road. The mill, which is in close proximity to the Hanover & York Railroad, is now owned by George Jacobs. In addition to the occupation of farmer, Adam was also a tavern-keeper. He was a prominent and influential citizen, and died in 1787, aged forty-eight years and seven months. The home place has been kept in the family up to the present time, and is now occupied by Charles Eichelberger, a great-grandson. Leonard, the second son of Philip Frederick Eichelberger, by the second wife, was a farmer. He was married to Elizabeth Smyser, and had four sons: Jacob, Frederick, George and John; and six daughters: Mary, married to Barney Welty; Sarah, to Frederick Welty; Susan, to Lewis Shearer; Lydia, to Daniel Bailey, and Elizabeth, to H. Richenbaugh. Jacob lived in York, was sheriff of York County, elected a member of the legislature in 1807 and a justice in 1829. He had three daughters: Eliza, married to Dr. George L. Shearer, of Dillsburg; Maria, to James McCosh, and Catherine, to Enoch Young. Frederick was a farmer, and lived near Dillsburg until the last year of his life, when he moved to Frederick City, Md. He married Catherine Baker; was a member of the legislature in 1815-16-17, and of the senate in 1819. He had no children, and died in 1836. George, the third son of Leonard, removed to Frederick County, Md., and was register of wills for thirteen years. He married Sarah Grayson. His sons were Niles, Grayson, Hervy and Allen. Grayson was secretary of State under Gov. Grayson, and was also a member of the senate of Maryland. Edwin, son of Grayson and great-great-grandson of the immigrant, is now a lawyer in Frederick City, Md. John, the fourth son of Leonard, was a farmer and justice. He lived in York County, and was a member of the legislature in 1825. His children were John and Alexander. Jacob, the third son of the second wife of the immigrant, resided in the town of Hanover. He was engaged in farming and keeping tavern. He was married to Anna Maria Reiniker. He died in 1811. His remains were first interred in St. Matthew's Lutheran graveyard, and were afterward removed to Mt. Olivet Cemetery. He left but one son, Jacob, the father of our subject, who became quite prominent in the borough of Hanover for a great many years. He was a merchant and farmer, and kept a public house which was long known as the "stage office," now the "Central Hotel." He was the first president of the Maryland Line Turnpike Company, and was active in organizing the Hanover Savings Bank, of which he became president in 1835, and served with great acceptance for a number of years. He died in 1843. He was first married to Elizabeth Nace. By this marriage he had three daughters: Louisa, mar-

BIOGRAPHICAL SKETCHES.

ried to George Trone; Maria, to Jacob Young, and Elizabeth, to Michael Barnitz. In the year 1806 he married Miss Maria Wirt, daughter of Christian Wirt, of Hanover. By this marriage he had eight children: Matthew, who now resides in Gettysburg; Jacob, who died in the State of Alabama in 1881; Henry, a farmer, residing in Hanover; Catherine Maria, married to S. A. McCosh, died in Georgia in 1868; Capt. A. W.; Rufus, president of the Hanover Saving Fund Society; Amanda, married to A. F. Gitt, of New Oxford, and died in 1871; and Amelia, the youngest, who is now living with her brothers in Hanover. Lewis, the fourth son of Frederick, lived in Adams County, Penn. He left one son, Adam, and three daughters, all of whom are now dead. Capt. A. W. Eichelberger was born in Hanover December 6, 1819. His father gave him the advantage of the best schools the town afforded. He remained at home until May, 1838, when he was apprenticed to learn the carpenter's trade with Conrad Moul, at Westminster, Md., where he remained three years and returned to Hanover. In 1843 he traveled overland to the State of Georgia to visit his elder brother, Jacob. Whilst there he arranged for the shipment of carriages and damask coverlets to that State, which business he continued for several years, and subsequently purchased, jointly with his brother, the Wehadkee Flour and Sawmills in the State of Alabama, and has since held his interest in the same, except during the civil war, when the property was confiscated by the Confederate government, and returned to him after the war. From 1845 to 1852 he spent his winters in the South, looking after his interests there, and his summers in Hanover, devoting his time to farming his own and his mother's land, to making purchases for shipment South, and in drilling an infantry company of citizen soldiers, called the "United Blues," and afterward a cavalry company known as the "Fourth Dragoons." As a military officer he was a universal favorite. In his early life, was a devoted Whig, and took an active part in the political campaigns of 1844 and 1852, and took the stump as a speaker on those occasions. He is now a Republican. He has never married. In the year 1872 he, together with three other public-spirited citizens, presented the beautiful fountain which now adorns the Centre Square of Hanover, and adds so much to the attractions of the town. He is a regular attendant at St. Mark's Lutheran Church, and a liberal contributor to all objects of benevolence and charity; takes a lively interest in the public welfare of his native town, and is universally popular among his neighbors and fellow citizens. In 1853, on account of his administrative and executive abilities, he was at the age of thirty-four elected president of the Hanover Branch Railroad Company, and still holds the same position, being in term of continuous service the oldest railroad president in the United States. This road was afterward, through his influence, consolidated with the Gettysburg Railroad. He is now president of the Baltimore & Hanover, Bachman Valley, Berlin Branch and Baltimore & Harrisburg Railroad Companies, all of which are described in another part of this work. In his industrious career in the railroad business, he has constantly kept in view the material interests of his native town and surrounding country, and the prosperity of the roads over which he presides. The town of Hanover will long remember him for his industry, liberality and devoted interest in her material welfare.

OLIVER T. EVERHART, second son of George and Catherine Everhart, was born May 18, 1832. He received his preliminary education at the Manchester (Md.) Academy, and thus prepared himself for the Sophomore class of 1851 at Marshall College, at Mercersburgh, Penn. This college was afterward removed to Lancaster, Penn., and being united to Franklin College, the name was changed to Franklin & Marshall College, and from this institution our subject was graduated in 1854. He read medicine under Dr Henry E. Beltz, of Manchester, Md., and attended medical lectures at the University of Maryland, from which he graduated in 1856. The same year he located in Goldsboro', York County, and began the practice of his profession. During the late war Dr. Everhart was assistant surgeon at the Chambersburgh and Camp Curtin Hospitals. In 1867 he removed to Shrewsbury, Penn., and thence in 1869 to Marysville, Penn., where he remained nine years, and then came to Hanover, and here has since continued to reside. He was united in marriage in 1859 to Miss Sarah, daughter of Rev. Jacob G. Kister. Mrs. Everhart died in 1860; and Dr. Everhart, in 1864, married Miss Anna C. Shelly, daughter of Michael Shelly. To this marriage have been born four children. Dr. Everhart is a successful physician and enjoys a lucrative practice. He is a Democrat. Dr. and Mrs. Everhart are members of the Trinity Reformed Church.

JOSHUA F. FLICKINGER was born in York County, Penn., July 15, 1854. His parents were Abraham and Sarah (Wertz) Flickinger, of York County. He remained with his father until he was twenty-one years of age, when he engaged in the insurance business two years. In the spring of 1879 he formed a partnership with C. E. Bowman, for the sale of agricultural implements. Mr. Flickinger belongs to the I. O. O. F. and is also a Mason.

DAVID GARBER, a prominent horse dealer of Hanover, Penn., was born in Lancaster County. Penn., November 14, 1836, and is a son of Samuel and Rebecca (Davis) Garber. In the year 1846 he had already engaged in the stock business and followed it eight years. He then removed to Hanover, Penn., where he engaged in the livery business, and in connection with this in buying and selling horses. In 1870 he purchased the Central Hotel at Hanover, which he owns and lives in at the present In 1856 he was married to Anna Elizabeth Bair, daughter of John and Lydia (Young) Bair, of Hanover. They have two children: Ida Alice and Annie May. Mr. Garber is a Knight Templar in the Masonic fraternity.

D. B. GROVE, M. D., is a son of Jacob and Louisa C. (Shriver) Grove. His grandfather, George Grove, was a wagon-maker in Hanover. His maternal grandfather, Henry Shriver, resided in Littlestown, Adams County. Dr. Grove was born in Hanover May 29, 1860, and was educated in the public and private schools of his native town. He then entered a drug store in Baltimore as a clerk, but on account of declining health, for the time, retired from that position and returned to his home. After recuperating his health his attention was directed to homœopathy. Being a thorough convert to that mode of medical treatment he began to study medicine, and in 1881 entered the Homœopathic Medical College of New York City, and was graduated in 1883. While in that institution he was elected quiz-master in medical jurisprudence, an honor conferred upon him by his fellow students. He joined the American Society of Homœopathy in 1884, and attended its sessions that year at Deer Park, Md. In 1885 he was elected surgeon of the Hanover Junction, Hanover & Gettysburg and Hanover & Baltimore Railroads. Dr. Grove is devotedly attached to the practice of medicine, and as a result thereof soon secured a lucrative business.

JACOB F. GUNDRUM, teacher and composer of music, and justice of the peace of Hanover, was born in Alsfeld, Hesse Darmstadt, Germany, December 22, 1837, and is a son of Jacob and Sophie (Strecker) Gundrum. His father was a preceptor in his native country over fifty years, and upon his retirement received from his king a gold cross, order of merit. When quite young he began the study of music in his native city, and at the age of sixteen years he entered the seminary at Freidberg, near Frankfort-on-the-Main, from which he graduated in the class of 1856. The same year he taught music a few months and then came to America, and went directly to Wisconsin, where one of his sisters resided, with whom he remained until the war broke out. In April, 1861, he enlisted at Mineral Point, Wis., in Company I, Second Wisconsin Volunteers, for three months, but re-enlisted shortly after for three years, June 11, 1861. He was soon transferred to the band, and with his regiment he participated in the battles of Blackburn's Ford, July 18, 1861, and the first Bull Run, at the latter receiving a slight wound. He served with the regiment until September, 1862, when all bands were mustered out. During this part of service he took part in all the engagements which Gen. McDowell had in Virginia, until the second battle of Bull Run, after which he returned to his own State to organize a brigade band, and re-enlisted November 9, 1863, in the brigade known as the "Iron Brigade of the West," and with the brigade was in all the battles from that time until the war closed, receiving an honorable discharge June 12, 1865. February 5, 1865, he was married at Gettysburg, Penn., to Susan Herr, a native of Lancaster County, and had five sons, two of whom died in infancy. The living are Harry F., Charles A. and J. Willie. After the close of the war he came to Gettysburg, where he began teaching music, forming a class also at Hanover, to which latter place he removed in 1867, and has since resided there, teaching music and dealing in pianos and organs. Although in politics a Democrat, he was elected in 1861 justice of the peace of Hanover Borough for five years. He is a member of the G. A. R. and of the society of the "Iron Brigade." His wife died November 12, 1882. Mr. Gundrum has also been a successful composer of music.

REV. JOHN H. HARTMAN, resident pastor of Leshey Reformed Church, and three other congregations, was born in Bavaria, Germany, September 9, 1848. His parents were Peter and Wilhelmina (Fetzer) Hartman, who came to this country in September, 1852, bringing with them their two boys and one daughter, and located in Tamaqua, Schuylkill Co., Penn., where they have since resided, and where two more sons have been born. Rev. John went to school in his boyhood, and also worked in the coal mines as slate picker, after which he worked at the barber's trade in Philadelphia. When about twenty years of age he attended Palatinate College, at Myerstown, Penn., where he spent two years and a half. From there he went to Heidelberg Theological Seminary, at Tiffin, Ohio, from which he graduated in 1874. His first charge was the Trinity Reformed Church at Tamaqua, Penn., which he served six years; then Lehighton, Carbon Co., Penn., where he was in charge four years and three months. He came to Hanover, April 23, 1884, and assumed the pastorate of "Leshey" charge. He was ordained by a committee of Lebanon Classis at Tamaqua, Penn., March 10, 1874. On June 4, 1874, he was married at Canfield, Ohio, to Mary A. Berger, a native of Switzerland, who lived at the time of her marriage at North Georgetown, Ohio. They have five children: John Edwin, Charles Reuben, Minnie Eliza, Mary Elizabeth and Oliver Samuel. Both husband and wife were brought up in the Reformed Church. Rev. H. preaches in German and English.

DANIEL JACOB HAUER, D. D., was born in Frederick, Md., March 3, 1806; is the son of George and Catherine (Shellman) Hauer, and is of German descent, his ancestors having come from Lorraine. Dr. Hauer received his elementary training in the public schools of Frederick, Md., and prosecuted his classical studies at Frederick College. In 1826 he began the study of theology under Rev. D. F. Schaffer, D. D., and three years later he was licensed *ad interim* to preach by the synod of Maryland and Virginia. His labors for some time, as missionary, were within the confines of Virginia, and then he accepted a call from congregations in Guilford and Orange Counties, N. C. In 1829 he was ordained by the synod of North Carolina, at Wythe Court House, Va. In 1828 he accepted a call from several churches in Montgomery, Roanoke, Floyd and Botetourt Counties, Va., and there he remained until 1882, when he removed to Lovettsville, Loudoun Co., Va., where he labored until 1845, when he came to Jefferson, Md. In 1853 he was called to the Manchester charge, Maryland. The degree of doctor of divinity was conferred upon him in 1859 by Irving College, in Carroll County, Md. From 1862 until 1872 he was pastor of the Abbottstown, New Oxford and East Berlin congregations in Adams County, Penn., together with St. Peter's Church, in York County. In 1872 he took charge of the Manheim charges, York County, and in 1881 of the Spring Grove charge of his present pastorate. In 1855 he was elected president of the Maryland synod, and in 1862 of the Melancthon synod of Maryland. He is the only survivor of the founders of the synod of Virginia. He has spent fifty-nine years in actual ministerial labor, and though he is passing into the sere and yellow leaf, his years sit lightly upon him. His marriage occurred, in 1828, to Miss Henrietta Warner, of Baltimore, Md. Of seven children born, three yet survive. Dr. Hauer is one of the prominent clergymen of York County, and a leading citizen of Hanover.

WILLIAM HELTZEL, ex-editor of the Hanover *Citizen*, and a leading Democratic politician of York County, was born at New Lisbon, Ohio, May 13, 1840, and is a son of Hon. Nicholas and Mary (Knepley) Heltzel. The Heltzel family is of Scotch-German lineage. The father of Mr. Heltzel was born in York County in 1805, and his mother in Georgetown, D. C., in 1818. The father of our subject has long been one of the prominent men of Adams County, Penn., and during the years 1867 and 1868 he represented that county in the general assembly. Mr. Heltzel was educated at the public schools, and at New Oxford College, in Adams County, Dr. Pfeiffer, principal. In 1859 he began serving an apprenticeship to the printing trade in the office of the Gettysburgh *Star*. For some years he did journey work, but spent most of his time in the *Patriot* office at Harrisburg. During the time spent at Gettysburgh he was also a law student under Hon. Moses McClain. In November, 1865, he came to Hanover and purchased the Hanover *Citizen*, which he conducted until 1879, when on account of ill health he was forced to abandon journalistic work. He has been a life-long supporter of the Democratic party, and for many years he has taken an active part in politics. He was married, in 1865, to Miss Mary E. Doan, a daughter of Dr. George Doan. Four children have been born to this marriage, viz.: Milton, Albert, George N. and Alda M. He is a Mason and a member of the Reformed Church.

REV. HENRY HILBISH, pastor of the Second Reformed Church of Hanover, is a native of Freeburgh, Snyder Co., Penn., was born September 13, 1836, and is the sixth in a family of seven children born to Henry and Elizabeth (Keller) Hilbish, and is of German descent. His parents were born in Montgomery County, Penn., the father in 1790, and the mother in 1801. The former died in 1858, and the latter two years prior. His great-grandfather was one of three brothers who were born in Germany and came to America in 1749, and settled in Montgomery County, Penn., and there the grandfather of Rev. H. was born. Rev. H. was educated at Freeburgh, Snyder Co., Penn. He studied theology under a private tutor, and at the age of twenty-one entered the ministry. He preached one year in his native county, and then went to Dauphin County; he there preached some time and then went to Berks County, and thence to Ohio, where he remained until 1880, when he came to Hanover, and here has since been, and is a most efficient and successful clergyman, and was the leading spirit in the erection of the Second Reformed Church of Hanover. He was married, May 10, 1858, to Miss Mary Whitmer, a native of Juniata County, Penn., and has had born to him eight children.

DR. CHARLES A. KAIN, born in York County, April 17, 1852, is a son of John and Susanna (May) Kain. He attended the common schools, and began teaching in the various schools of the county at the age of seventeen. After teaching about five years he began a course of study under Dr. J. M. Kilmore, of York County, preparatory to his profession of veterinary surgeon. He located in Manchester, York County, and in 1882 removed to Hanover, where he has since practiced his profession. He was married, in 1878, to Miss Caroline, daughter of Henry and Sarah Bower. They have two children: Herbie B., born in January, 1879; and Charles E., born April, 1880. The Doctor is a member of the Lutheran Church.

STEPHEN KEEFER was born in West Virginia, November, 29, 1816, and is a son of Joseph and Mary Keefer, natives of the same State. He remained at home with his parents until the age of eighteen, when he was apprenticed to learn the carpenter trade, and remained at this business twelve years. He then moved to Hanover, and was engaged for thirteen years in the grocery business, where he laid the foundation of an ample fortune. Mr. Keefer was elected a director of the First National Bank of Hanover, when it was organized, which position he held four years; he was then elected cashier and served six years, but resigned this position to seek a more active vocation. He then became prominently identified with the railroad interest of this section of York County, becoming a director in the Hanover Junction, Hanover & Gettysburg Railroads, and Baughman Valley, Berlin Branch and Hanover and Baltimore and Baltimore & Harrisburg Railroads; is a director of the Hanover Gas Company, helped to organize the Hanover Water Company, and is now president and general superintendent of it. At the organization of the Hanover Agricultural Society, he was elected president. Always having been an ardent supporter of the Republican party, he was elected county commissioner in 1880, and performed the duties of that office with signal ability, showing an extensive knowledge of business. In this official capacity he made many warm friends in both political parties of York County. His marriage to Catherine, daughter of David and Susan Bixler, occurred December 24, 1842. His second marriage was to Miss Susan, daughter of Rudolph and Elizabeth Forry, of York, Penn., and was solemnized May 18, 1858. Mr. Keefer is a member of the Reformed Church, and his present wife of St. Mark's Lutheran Church of Hanover. He has always been a public spirited citizen and has done much to improve the material interests of Hanover. He was elected burgess of Hanover, February, 1885.

ARNOLD KLEFF, hotel keeper, was born on the river Rhine, near Seegburg, in Prussia, Germany, April 9, 1831, and came to America August 27, 1847, where he landed at Baltimore. Until 1865 he was clerking for Canfield Bros. & Co., jewelers, and traveled for them six years. In 1868 he opened the Montour House at Westminster, Md., and conducted it four years, after which he commenced dealing in agricultural implements and traveled a great deal in the South until 1874, after which he removed to New York City, where he began dealing in notions. In 1875 he returned to Baltimore—to Canfield-Bros. & Co., and in 1877 he took charge of the Diller House at Hanover, Penn., which he kept until 1880, when he leased the Central Hotel, at the same place, which he has kept since. May 12, 1853, he was married at Baltimore to Annie McGraw, of that city, who died in 1860, leaving two children: John N. and William (deceased). January 26, 1864, he was married to Gertrude Voshell, a native of Maryland, and of French descent. They have five children: Harry V., Annie H., Gertrude H., Arnold J. and Charles. The family are members of the Catholic Church. The father of Mr. Kleff came to America on a visit in 1854, but returned to Germany, where he died.

BARTON H. KNODE, editor and publisher of The Hanover *Citizen* and *Der Hanover Citizen* (the latter being published in German), was born at Jones' Cross Roads, Washington Co., Md., April 19, 1851. He was educated at the public schools, but had little opportuity for attendance even at those institutions—his father being a farmer, subject's assistance was required in that capacity. He served an apprenticeship on the Boonesborough (Md.) *Odd Fellow*, beginning in 1868. After his apprenticeship, he held positions on the Baltimore *American* and Baltimore *Sun*, as a compositor, afterward obtaining a position in the Government printing department of Washington, D. C., solely on his abilities as a first-class compositor. In that office his abilities were justly recognized by promotion, until he was finally placed on "bill" work and "rule and figure" work, the highest grade of general composition. In the early spring of 1875 he was compelled to resign his position because of the failure of his health. Retiring to the country home of his parents, however, by the careful and tender nursing of a true and affectionate mother, he was soon fully restored to his accustomed good health. In the early summer of that year he made his first venture in journalism by taking charge of the Mechanicstown (Md.) *Clarion* during its proprietor's protracted illness. Mr. Knode conducted the *Clarion* for eight months in a most successful and profitable manner, when the establishment was sold. In December, 1875, he purchased the Littlestown (Penn.) *News*, and conducted that paper with credit and ability until June, 1879, when he succeeded to the proprietorship of the two papers which he now so ably conducts. Since having charge of these two journals he has conducted them in the same channel as his illustrious predecessor (Mr. William Heltzel) and enjoys the confidence, esteem and respect of his neighbors, acquaintances, and the political party (Democratic) whose principles he loves and advocates. Mr. Knode's acquaintances include a large circle of eminent men of both political parties, and his influence at home and throughout the country is extensive and much sought after. He has been a member of the order of A. F. & A. M. since 1875, and has for many years been an active member of the I. O. O. F., having "passed through the chairs" in both the subordinate and encampment branches.

FRANCIS A. H. KOCH, a physician of Hanover, Penn., was born in York, Penn., August 31, 1830. His parents, Dr. Francis and Nancy (Hiestand) Koch, were of the pioneer families of the county. His great-grandfather, who came from Germany, settled in Dover before York Borough was laid out. He has two brothers and three sisters, one of whom is younger than himself. His early education he received at the York County Academy, and at the age of twenty he began reading medicine with his father. In 1849 he entered the University of Maryland, in Baltimore, and graduated in 1852. He first practiced in York, but removed to Hellam Township; returning, however, to York in two years, and after a few months' stay removed to Liverpool, York County, where he practiced two years, then going to York again, and from there, in one and a half years, to North Codorus, where he remained sixteen years. In 1871 he came to Hanover where he has since resided. In 1857 he was married at York, Penn., to Annie M. DeHuff, daughter of Abraham DeHuff, of Dillsburg, and has had seven children: Abram (deceased), Virginia, Annie E., Helen G., Francis Abram, Susan and Edward William. He is a member of the Masonic Lodge of York, of the York County Medical Society, and was three times elected chief burgess of Hanover.

REV. J. C. KOLLER, pastor of St. Matthew's Lutheran Church, Hanover, Penn., was born October 24, 1839, in Springfield Township, York County, a few miles northeast of Glen Rock. His parents were Henry and Anna Mary Koller. He spent his early years on the farm, and in teaching school, and entered the preparatory department of Pennsylvania College, Gettysburgh, in the spring of 1860, and graduated in 1865—the valedictorian of his class. He took a full course in the Theological Seminary at the same place, and was licensed to preach the Gospel by the West Pennsylvania Synod at Chambersburgh, in September, 1867. He soon after became pastor of the Glen Rock Evangelical Lutheran Church, and remained there until the spring of 1877, when he entered his present field of labor as pastor of St. Matthew's Church, which was organized in 1738. It is the second church of that denomination, in point of age, in York County, and with its communicant membership of 725 persons, and nominal membership of over 1,000 persons, is the largest congregation of the Lutheran denomination in the county. Mr Koller is a faithful and earnest worker, a close student and a devoted pastor. He was married to Alice C., daughter of William Heathcote, June 1, 1869. They have one daughter and three sons.

JOSEPH LEIB, general freight and ticket agent of the Hanover Junction, Hanover & Gettysburg Railroad, was born in Hopewell Township, York County, April 14, 1829, and is the son of John and Mary (Purkey) Leib, both natives of York County and of German descent. His grandfather, Christian Leib, also a native of the county, was a soldier in the Revolutionary army, and his father was a soldier in the war of 1812, and participated in the affair at North Point near Baltimore, being one of 100 men, who went as defenders from his neighborhood. He outlived them all and died at the age of eighty-four. The Purkey family were, at an early day, quite numerous in the county, but Mr. Leib's mother, who died at the age of seventy-five, was the last of her father's family in its limits, the rest having emigrated probably to the west. Joseph Leib is the sixth son of a family of eleven children, ten of whom are living—nine sons and one daughter. Four of the sons are railroad men; an elder brother, John S., has been treasurer of the Northern Central Railway since 1854, and two others are in Baltimore. The other members of the family are farmers, one in Kansas, the rest in York County. Mr Leib was educated in the common schools, and followed farming until 1855, when he began railroading as clerk in the Baltimore freight office of the Northern Central Railway, and in less than a month was appointed agent of the same company at Hanover and filled that office until 1876, when he was appointed general ticket agent of the Hanover Junction, Hanover & Gettysburg Railroad, and in 1883 was appointed general freight agent. His duties embrace the general freight, ticket and auditing departments of the company. He was married at New Freedom, Penn., in 1857, to Julia A., daughter of Peter Free, for whom that town was named. They have two children: Wilbur F., a railroad man by profession, and Josephine H. The family are members of the Methodist Church, of which Mr. Leib is a trustee. He is recording scribe of Hanover Division, No. 84, S. of T.

REV. JAMES H. McCORD, resident minister of the Methodist Episcopal Church at Hanover, was born in Lewistown, Penn., January 15, 1837; his parents, James and Mary (Willis) McCord were natives of Mifflin County, Penn., and of Irish and English descent, respectively. They had four children—two sons and two daughters—of whom Rev. J. is the third now living. He was brought up and educated at the public schools at Lewistown and at the academy. When about sixteen years old he entered Dickinson's Seminary at Williamsport, from which he graduated in three years as A. B. He had intended to study law, but being taken sick he abandoned that idea and began to prepare for the ministry. He at once entered conference and at the end of two years was ordained deacon and after four years, elder. He served as deacon for two years in Frederick City, Md., and as elder in Baltimore City three years, and Huntingdon Methodist Episcopal Church for two years: at Danville, Penn., three years; Clearfield, Penn., two years; while at the latter place he completed the church, which cost $35,000. He then went to Tyrone for two years; Waynesborough, three years; Gettysburg, three years; Duncannon, Penn., one year; New Cumberland, Penn., three years; and in April, 1884, he came to Hanover. During this time over 1,250 persons were taken into the church. While in Baltimore he married more couples than any other minister—300 in three years. He was married at Clearfield, Penn., March 13, 1871, to Clara Foley, daughter of Judge W. C. Foley. They have one child, Maggie. Rev. McCord is a member of the R. A. M. of Frederick City. He has repeatedly given lectures before collegiate institutes.

FRANKLIN G. McKINNEY, proprietor of the Franklin Hotel, York Street, Hanover, was born in Adams County, Penn., in 1842, and is a son of John and Barbara (Wills) McKinney, of Irish and German descent respectively. Brought up on a farm he received a common school education and at the age of nineteen began the trade of blacksmith, which he followed eight years in Hanover, to which place he came in 1855. In 1876 he became a brakeman and afterward conductor on the Baltimore & Hanover Railroad. In 1883 he bought and took charge of the Franklin Hotel; which he has since conducted He was married in 1861 to Miss Lydia Low, and they have three children: Annie, Martha and William. Mr. and Mrs. McKinney are members of the Catholic Church. In politics he is a Democrat. He began life a poor boy and has successfully made his own way in the world.

JOHN A. MELSHEIMER, M. D., a promising young physician of Hanover, Penn., was born at that place January 18, 1858. His parents were Lucius F. and Lucretia C. (Forney) Melsheimer, of York County, and of German descent. John A. is their only living child. His early education he received at the schools of Hanover; later he attended Dickinson's Seminary at Williamsport, from which he graduated as A. B., in 1877. He then began to read medicine with Dr. Snively, of Hanover, with whom he studied for two years and then entered Jefferson Medical College, from which he graduated in 1883. Coming back to Hanover he stayed with his old preceptor, Dr. Snively, for one year, and then, in April, 1884, began the practice of medicine under his own name. The Doctor is very much attached to his profession and devotes all his attention to it. December 23, 1884, he was married to Ella Trone, daughter of George E. and Amelia Trone (deceased), of York County.

REV. JOHN A. METZGER, A. M., resident pastor of West Manheim charge (composed of St. Bartholomew's, St. David's and St. Paul's Churches), was born at Liverpool (now Manchester Township), York County, April 5, 1855. His parents were Zachariah and Maria (Feiser) Metzger, of York and Adams Counties, and of German and Polish descent respectively. Rev. John A. is the youngest of three children (one son and two daughters, one of the latter having died), and until his fifteenth year remained on his father's farm, attending the public schools. After that he attended the Millersville normal schools. When about nineteen years of age he entered the York Academy to prepare himself for the Pennsylvania College at Gettysburg, which he entered at twenty-one years of age with a view of studying for the ministry. He graduated in 1880, and then entered the Theological Seminary, where he remained until 1883. He came to Hanover in July, 1883, to take charge of the congregations. Three months previous to this he had already accepted the call, and had been licensed to preach in 1882, but in September, 1883, he was ordained as a regular minister of the gospel at Carlisle, Penn. September 25, 1883, he was married at Gettysburg, Penn., to Mary C. Culp, of Gettysburg, of German descent, and like her husband a Lutheran. Rev. Metzger devotes his whole time and attention to the ministry. Having to attend three congregations, and to preach in German and English, his duties are necessarily many and burdensome, yet with the spirit of a true Christian, he attends to all his duties with a cheerful spirit.

SAMUEL B. MYERS, son of John and Susan (Bechtel) Myers, was born July 28, 1821, on the homestead, where he has always resided, having been reared to farming. October 10, 1844, Mr. Myers married Magdaline Baer, daughter of David and Polly (———) Baer. Thirteen children were born to them: David (deceased), Emanuel, Maria (deceased), Susanna, John, Ezra, Sarah (deceased), Elizabeth, Samuel, Abraham, Daniel, Magdaline and Isaac (deceased). Daniel and Abraham are school-teachers; at present they are at the State Normal School at Shippensburg, Penn. September 6, 1881, our subject married Barbara Baer, daughter of Jacob and Barbara (Keagy) Baer, of Heidelberg Township. Marlin Myers, the grandfather of our subject, came from Lancaster County; his wife's maiden name was Annie Dooner. Mr. Myers is well and favorably known in his section of the county, and is one of Penn Township's best citizens.

MAHLON H. NAILL was born in Taneytown, Carroll Co., Md., February 13, 1843. His parents, William W. and Harriet (Kehn), were natives of Maryland, and of German descent; they were married in Carroll County, Md., where the father carried on cabinet-making for a few years, but removed to Ohio in 1849, where he died in 1851, leaving a widow and two sons, of whom Mahlon H. is the eldest. After the death of the father the widow removed to Hanover, where she has since resided, and where she brought up her sons. There she was married to Samuel Trone, of Hanover, and has one daughter—Catherine—now the wife of W. S. Gallatin. Mahlon H. began to learn the cigar-making trade when about eleven years of age, and followed it until 1877, working for his step-father, who was a cigar manufacturer. His education he received at the public schools of Hanover. June 17, 1863, he enlisted in Company I, Twenty-sixth Pennsylvania Volunteer Militia, and served during the "emergency." Some three or four days before the battle of Gettysburg he took part in a skirmish near that place. May 20, 1869, he was married at Hanover to Mary E. Long, daughter of Henry Long, of Hanover, and has six sons: Harry C., George E., Irvin T., Maurice W., Elmer M. and Mahlon C. Mr. Naill and wife are members of the St. Mark's Lutheran Church of Hanover. Mr Naill is a member of the Friendly Circle No. 19, B. U. H. F., of Pennsylvania; is one of the orginal stockholders of the Hanover Agricultural Society; was twice elected assessor, and has held the office of postmaster since 1877, having been first appointed by President Hayes.

H. C. RUTH, D. D. S., was born in York County, in 1853; is a son of Henry and Louisa (Hoff) Ruth, and is of English descent. His parents were also born in York County. His great-grandfather came from England, and was an early settler in York County. Our subject received a common school education, and in 1869, began the study of dentistry in Hanover under Dr. H. C. Derr, and now has established an extended and successful practice. He was married, in 1877, to Miss Ella S. Stine, a native of Hanover, and a daughter of John R. Stine, and is now the father of two children: J. Harry and Austin S. The Doctor and Mrs. R. are members of St. Mark's Lutheran Church, of Hanover, Penn.

AMBROSE SCHMIDT, born in Germany, January 11, 1824, is a son of Andrew and Catherine (Meisener) Schmidt, both natives of Germany. He came to this country with his parents in 1842, and settled in the borough of York. Having served an apprenticeship at the trade of mason in Germany, he engaged in stone cutting and building soon after his arrival at York. He assisted in tearing down the old county jail at York and building the new one. He continued at his trade until 1866, when he removed to Hanover, Penn., and engaged in the business of beer brewing, to which he subsequently added beer bottling and pop manufacturing, which business he has profitably conducted to the present. Mr. Schmidt was married, August 2, 1849, to Miss Margaret, daughter of Anthony and Margaret Boll. Six children have blessed this union, Catherine, born April, 1850 ; Margaret, February 1852 ; Adam, December, 1854 ; Mary, April, 1857 ; John, August, 1859 ; and Ambrose O., October, 1863. Mr. Schmidt and his family are all members of the Catholic Church.

JAMES R. SCHMIDT, ex-recorder of York County, was born in 1830, is the son of Joseph W. and Catherine (Knaub) Schmidt, and is of German descent. His father was born at Martinsburgh, Va., in 1794, and when a young man came to York County. The subject of this biography, in 1846, began the drug business in Hanover, continued for a time and then went to Middletown, Butler Co., Ohio, remaining there one year; he then returned to Hanover, and again engaged in the drug business. In 1862 he was drafted and was in the employment of the government almost one year, acting in the capacity of hospital steward. He is a Democrat, and in 1876 was elected recorder of York County, and served three years. He was married in 1860 to Miss Rebecca Sherman, a native of York County. To this marriage five children have been born. Mr. Schmidt is one of the representative men of Hanover, and a member of the I. O. O. F.

HENRY M. SCHMUCK, of the firm of Schmuck & Sons, lumber and coal dealers, and president of the First National Bank of Hanover, was born at Hanover, September 26, 1824, is a son of Joseph and Christiana (Felty) Schmuck, and is of German descent. His father was born in York County, and in 1812 established the first English newspaper in

Hanover, which was known as the Hanover *Guardian*. His death occurred in March,1829. The grand father of this subject was Michael Schmuck His maternal grandfather was Henry Felty, a cavalry officer in the war of the Revolution. Our subject was educated at Hanover Academy, and from 1841 to 1847 was employed in the dry goods store of Isaac Baugher, Emmittsburg, Md. In 1847 he went to Charleston, S. C., and until 1848 was in the employ of C. & E. L. Kerrison, wholesale dry goods dealers. In 1852 Mr. Schmuck engaged in the lumber and coal business in Hanover, and in this has since continued. In 1880 he was elected president of the First National Bank of Hanover. He was married in 1851 to Miss Amanda Reid, of Cincinnati, Ohio, and a daughter of Patrick Reid. Eight children have been born to this union, viz.: Joseph H., Blanch A., William A., Eugene R., Helen V., Emma E., Minnie C. and Percival. Mr. S. is a member of the Emanuel Reformed Church.

JACOB H. SCHRIVER is a native of what is now Penn Township, York County, was born November 14, 1842, is a son of Henry C. and Maria M. (Felty) Schriver, and is of German descent. His father was born in Adams County, Penn., and his mother is a native of York County. Mr. Schriver was educated at the public schools of Hanover. At twenty-five years of age he began life for himself, and for a time clerked in a store, and later engaged in mercantile business. In 1874 he began his present occupation as liveryman, in which he has been successful. He has the most extensive livery in Hanover, and in connection carries on an exchange and sale stable. In 1866 he married Miss Ella C. Gitt, a native of Hanover. Two children have been born to this union, viz.: Harry G. and M. Grace. Mr. Schriver is a Republican, and a member of the Reformed Church, of which his wife is also a member.

HENRY SCHWALM, proprietor of the Mansion House, Hanover, Penn., was born September 24, 1842, in Kurhessen, Germany, and is the elder of two children born to Henry and Anna M. (Nau) Schwalm, also natives of Germany. Henry received a good German education. He immigrated to America, landing at Baltimore, May 25, 1868, and two days after came to Hanover, where he has since resided. He is a tanner by trade, and worked for one man fourteen years, and quit the trade and embarked in the hotel business. He had owned and managed a restaurant for seventeen months, after which he sold out and purchased the good will and fixtures of the "Mansion House," his present stand, where he is now doing a flourishing business. He was united in marriage to Miss Elizabeth Stutz in 1867. Five children have blessed this happy union: John H., Harry (deceased), George E. (deceased), Mary E. and Alice G. He and his wife are both members of the Reformed Church. He is a member of the Friendly Circle No. 19, B. U. (H. F.) of Hanover Lodge No. 318, K. of P., and of Minnewakuru Tribe No. 250, I. O. of R. M. He was constable of Hanover from 1876 to 1880, the last year police of the borough. In politics he is a Republican, takes great interest in educational matters, and is a liberal, public-spirited citizen.

LEWIS D. SELL, justice of the peace of Penn Township, York County, was born in Adams County, Penn., March 20, 1853. His parents, Henry and Lucinda (Heagy) Sell, were natives of Adams County, of German descent and reared a family of six children—five sons and one daughter—the latter now deceased. When Lewis D. was but two and a half years of age, his parents removed to York County and settled near Hanover, where they engaged in farming, which they followed until 1877. Lewis D. was brought up on the farm, and assisted his father until sixteen years of age. His education he received at the common schools, and at the normal schools of York County. After leaving his father's farm, he began teaching school in Manheim Township, and taught about eleven years in York County, spending his vacations at farming. He was married at Littlestown, Penn., May 24, 1874, to Henrietta A. Aulabaugh, of York County; they have four children: Emma Lucinda, Harry Samuel J. Tilden, Lewis Absalom, and Tempeth A. Jackson Snively. The family are members of the Trinity Reformed Church of Hanover. Mr. Sell is a member of the K. of P., and has been chancellor and commander. In 1880 he was appointed justice of the peace by the governor of Pennsylvania, and in the following year, he was elected to that office and is the present incumbent. In 1884 he was a candidate for clerk of the court. In 1883 he was a delegate to the State convention. He is an active Democrat and has often represented his township in the county conventions. He is also a stockholder in the Hanover Agricultural Society.

EDGAR SLAGLE, retired merchant, was born at Willow Grove Farm, Adams County, Penn., April 6, 1824, is a son of Michael and Eliza (Weaver) Slagle, and is of German descent. His father, a farmer, was also born in what is now Adams County, and his mother in Lancaster County, Penn. Mr. Slagle received a common school education and was reared on the farm. In 1842 he was appointed to a clerkship at the Duncannon Iron Works in Perry County, Penn. There he remained until 1850. In 1852 he began the hardware business in Hanover in partnership with Samuel Shirk. In 1879, Mr. Slagle retired from business, after many years of success. He was married in 1856 to Miss Anna E., daughter of Henry and Lydia Schriver, and a native of Adams County. They have had four children, viz.: Calvin S., Ida E., Mary L. and Edgar (deceased). He is a Republican and manifests great interest in political affairs. He is a member of the I. O. O. F. Mr. and Mrs. Slagle are members of the Reformed Church. His son, Calvin, now a minister in the Reformed Church, is located at Cessna, Bedford County, Penn. He graduated from Franklin and Marshall College, Lancaster, in 1879, and from the theological seminary at Lancaster in 1882. His marriage was solemnized in 1882 to Miss Kate, daughter of Rev. Dr. Thomas Apple, president of Franklin and Marshall College.

MALCOLM O. SMITH, editor and proprietor of the Hanover *Herald*, and a well known local historical writer, was born in York in the year 1846, and is a son of William W. and Charlotte (Stair) Smith; he received superior educational advantages, attending the York public schools, the York Classical and Normal Institute, Eastman's Business College at Poughkeepsie, N. Y., and the Pennsylvania College of Gettysburg; also has had a practical experience of five terms as teacher of select and public schools. In March, 1865, he enlisted in Company D, One Hundred and Third Pennsylvania Volunteers, and was in service until August of the same year. Having previously learned the trade of a printer, Mr. Smith began his journalistic career in 1870, establishing the Glen Rock *Item*, which he successfully conducted until he sold out in 1872, and in that year established the Hanover *Herald*, of which he is still the editor and proprietor. Mr. Smith is an able writer and has made his journal especially attractive by publishing historical matter of interest concerning the early "Annals of Hanover," and "Early History of York County," etc., to the careful compilation of which he has devoted much time and earnest labor. Many incidents, facts and much valuable history, as preserved by him, appear

BIOGRAPHICAL SKETCHES.

in appropriate chapters in this work. The Pennsylvania College bestowed on him in 1873, the honorary degree of A. B. Mr. Smith is a citizen of progressive ideas, and one of the most successful newspaper men of York County. He has taken an earnest interest in the affairs of the Grand Army of the Republic, and served as Commander of Maj. Jenkins Post, No. 99, at Hanover, for the first three years of its existence. He is secretary of the Hanover Agricultural Society, in the organization of which society he was especially active. His marriage with Miss Louisa H. S., daughter of Dr. F. E. Vandersloot, of Gettysburg, occurred in 1867. Three children, all of whom died in early childhood, were the fruits of this union.

ALOSYUS SMITH was born in Mount Pleasant Township, Adams County, in 1830, is a son of Joseph and Mary (Lawrence) Smith, both natives of Adams County, and is of German descent. His paternal grandfather was Charles Smith, a native of Germany, who came to America and settled in Adams County, where he died in 1832. Subject's father was born in 1792, and his mother in 1800; the former died in 1857; the latter in 1864. Mr. Smith was reared on the farm, and in 1849 came to Hanover and learned the blacksmith trade, and worked at it nine years; then began coach-making, which he followed twelve years; he then began the lumber business in 1872, and then the livery business and dealing in horses and mules. He was married, in 1854, to Miss Agnes Hember, also a native of Adams County, and has had born to him thirteen children. He is a Republican and with his wife a member of the Catholic Church.

A. J. SNIVELY, M. D., was born in Franklin County. Penn., in 1844; is a son of John and Catherine (Keefer) Snively, and is of Swiss origin; the father was born near Greencastle, Franklin County, in 1799; the mother was born in the same county in 1802, and died in 1854; the father died in 1853. The Snively family emigrated from Switzerland to America in 1707, and settled in Lancaster County, in the Province of Pennsylvania. Dr. Snively was educated in the public schools of Chambersburg. In 1859 he entered West Branch High School at Jersey Shore, Lycoming Co., Penn., and was there prepared for the junior class at Princeton College. In 1863, he enlisted in Company D, Second Pennsylvania Infantry, and served one year. In 1864 he was acting assistant-surgeon at Beverly, N. J. He graduated from the Bellevue Hospital Medical College, at New York, in 1866; located at Williamsburg, Blair County, where he was in practice two years, and then came to Hanover in 1867, where he has resided ever since, and has established a large and successful practice. He was married, in 1875, to Miss Mazie E. Gitt, daughter of J. W. Gitt, of Hanover, and is the father of two children: John U. and Roie I. He is a Free Mason, and a Republican.

NATHAN STAMBAUGH, veterinary surgeon, at Hanover, Penn., was born in Jackson Township, York County. Penn., in 1840, and is a son of Henry and Leah (Myers) Stambaugh, of York County. Until fourteen or fifteen years of age, he stayed with his father on the farm, and then learned the blacksmith's trade at Abbottstown, Penn., and followed it for about twelve years. He began the study of medicine when fourteen years old. In 1872 he came to Hanover and began cigar-making, which he followed five years. Since 1879, he has devoted his whole time to veterinary surgery, and has a large practice in York and Adams Counties. When twenty years of age he was married at Abbottstown, to a Miss Livingston, who died in 1869, leaving three children. In 1871, he married a Miss Leas, who died in a few months. In 1872 he married at New Oxford, Penn., Mrs. Catherine Shultz, widow of Jacob W. Schultz. Her maiden name was Lichty, of York County. In 1862 he enlisted in Company K, One Hundred and Sixty-fifth Regiment Pennsylvania Militia, and served nine months. He next enlisted at Harrisburg in Company C, Two Hundred and Second Pennsylvania Volunteers, in August, 1864, and served one year as color-sergeant. He took part in three battles: White Plains, Hanover, Court House, and Manasses Junction, beside numerous skirmishes. Dr. Stambaugh and wife are members of the Reformed Church. He is also a member of the I O. O. F., K. of P., and B. H. G. F., of Post 99, G. A. R., and is also a stockholder of the Hanover Agricultural Society.

F. G. STARK was born in Prussia in 1835; is a son of Frederick L. and Anna E. (Kraemer) Stark, and the eldest in a family of four children. The father of Mr. Stark was born in the town of Berleburg, in the district of Westphalia, and his mother is a native of the same town. Our subject's paternal grandfather was a native of Germany, but came to America and here died. The father of Mr. Stark also came to America, and settled in Hanover. When our subject was about one year old, he was brought to America by his mother, who was accompanied by her brother, Henry Kraemer, her husband having come some months previous. Mr. Stark was educated at the public schools of Hanover. At a very early age he began learning the jeweler's trade under his father. In 1857 he went to Littlestown, Adams Co., Penn., and engaged in the jewelry business, which he continued for some time, and then came to Hanover, and here continued the business for a few months, then sold out and went to Europe in 1859, and for some years worked in many of the principal cities in Germany and Switzerland. Returning to America in 1862, he again began the jewelry business in Hanover. He makes a specialty of fine watches, clocks, jewelry and spectacles, etc. The marriage of Mr. Stark took place in 1871, to Miss Alice L. Gitt, daughter of Joseph S. (C. E.) and Anna Gitt, of New Oxford, Penn One child has been born to him—George W., February 22, 1872. Mr. Stark is a Republican, and one of the leading business men of Hanover. Mr. Stark is a member of the Reformed Church; Mrs. Stark is a member of the Methodist Episcopal Church.

W. C. STICK, an active business man of Hanover, was born in this county in 1850. He is the fifth of a family of seven living children born to Henry and Mary (T man) Stick, natives of York County, and of German descent. Our subject passed his early life in Codorus Township as a farmer and teamster. He has been an active business man all his life and since 1879 a resident of Hanover, in which year he engaged in selling agricultural implements, and in which branch he has been extensively engaged since. He is also the general agent for the celebrated D. M. Osborne Mower and Reaper Company, and as their representative travels extensively. Mr. Stick has done much to promote the business interest of Hanover, and is a member of the town council. He is one of the originators of the Hanover Agricultural Fair Association, of which he is now vice-president. His large reaper parade of 1881 was an event of local importance. In 1885 he originated the idea of an agricultural implement exhibit, and opened the new fair grounds, on the 3d, 4th and 5th of June, to a large attendance and a successful exhibition. Mr. Stick was united in marriage, in 1872, with Lamanda Rohrbaugh, of Carroll County, Md. They have one child living, John W. C., and are raising an orphan child—Harry Lee Shields. Mr. and Mrs. Stick are members of the Reformed Church. Mr. Stick is a member of the I. O. R. M.

DAVID S. TANGER, of the firm of D. S. Tanger & Son, hardware dealers, of Hanover, was born in Lancaster County, May 29, 1831, and is the second of two children of Jacob and Esther (Snavely) Tanger. His father was of Scotch descent and his mother of German extraction, both natives of Lancaster County. Jacob Tanger, by a previous marriage, had seven children. In his early life he was a mason but abandoned this trade and for many years conducted a distillery, which he also discontinued, and engaged in farming, which occupation he followed until his death. David S. Tanger, the subject of this sketch, and now a prosperous and influential merchant of this town, upon the death of his mother, when he was only one year old, became a member of the family f his grandfather, Jacob Snavely, with whom he lived until the age of fourteen years. After returning to his father's home for one year, he began to learn the trade of wagon-making, and followed it three years. He then removed to Petersburg, Adams County, and engaged in the mercantile business as a salesman, remaining there until 1852, when he located in Hanover. Here he began the business of carriage-making, which was an important industry of Hanover. At the expiration of five years he quit the carriage business and was elected high constable of his adopted town, serving four years during the time of the civil war, and was an ardent advocate of the Union cause. In 1864 he engaged in the hardware trade, which he has conducted with unabated success since he began, and is now enjoying a large and prosperous business, with his son, John, as partner. He was married to Susanna C. Rupp, February 22, 1855. Their children were Fannie E., married to Samuel Hostetler; John Carroll, his present partner in business, and Mary R., deceased. His wife died November 9, 1859. November 13, 1863, he was married to Lizzie Harnish The children, by this marriage, were Grant S. (deceased), Frank L., Annie Sue (deceased), Eva L., David A., Lizzie C. and Viola G. The family are members of the Reformed Church. Mr. Tanger has repeatedly been elected chief burgess, a member of town council, and school director of Hanover. He is a liberal, public-spirited citizen, and takes an active interest in education. He became a member of the Masonic fraternity in 1861.

EPHRAIM A. TRIMMER, born in York County. January 10, 1833, is a son of John and Catharine (Masemore) Trimmer, both natives of York County. At the age of eighteen he went to Hampton, Adams County, where he learned the trade of mill-wright, which he followed until 1867, when he opened a grocery store in Hanover. Since 1874 he has been engaged in the fire insurance, agricultural implement and fertilizer business. He was married January 25, 1856, to Miss Sarah Ann, daughter of Jacob K. and Sarah Weiser, and they have had seven children: Hamilton M., John W., Jacob C. (deceased), Ida C., Etta F., Weiser G., and Samuel P. Mr. and Mrs. Trimmer are both members of the Lutheran Church.

CHARLES L. TRONE was born in what is now Penn Township, York County, October 24, 1848; is a son of Charles and Mary (Reed) Trone, and is of German-English descent. He is one of six children living in a family of fifteen. The father of Mr. Trone was also born in York County, and his mother in Baltimore City, Md. His father was a machinist, and lived and died in York County. Our subject was brought to Hanover Township by his parents when one year old, and was here educated at the public schools. He remained at home until twenty-one years of age, and then began for himself. For a number of years he was in the lumbering business, and then learned the upholsterer's trade and carried on that business nine years. In 1863 he was sutler of the Seventy sixth Pennsylvania Volunteers. Coming home he resumed his former business, and at that continued until 1880, when he began the grocery business, and this he s'ill continues. In 1869 he married Miss Mary Swartz, a native of York, and daughter of Peter and Elizabeth Swartz. To this union have been born four children, three of whom are living: Curtis J., William S. and Lizzie M. Charles S. is deceased. Mr. Trone is a Democrat, a member of the school board. A Mason, and with his wife a member of St. Matthew's Lutheran Church.

ALEXANDER C. WENTZ, A. M., M. D., now a practicing physician of Hanover, was born in Manheim Township on the 14th day of July, 1855. His father, Edward R. Wentz, is a great-great-grandson of Valentine Wentz, who was born in Partenheim, Germany, July 10, 1717; was married to Barbara Jenawein in 1749, soon after immigrated to America and located in Manheim Township, York County. He is the ancestor of the Wentz family of Pennsylvania and Maryland, and died in April, 1788, leaving six sons, five daughters and twenty-nine grandchildren. The mother of Dr. Wentz, Margaret Couldren, is a native of Adams County, and is of Scotch-Irish descent. The Doctor is the elder of two children now living. His sister is married to Dr. Wesley C. Stick, of Glenville. He spent his youth at school and on the farm, and in 1873 entered Pennsylvania College at Gettysburg, from which institution he graduated in 1879. In the fall of the same year he entered the medical department of the University of Pennsylvania, and from that institution received the degree of Doctor of Medicine in the spring of 1882. Soon after graduating he began the practice of his chosen profession in the borough of Hanover, where he has met with encouraging success. Dr. Wentz was married, June 1, 1882, to Clara Bertron Ulp, daughter of the late John J. Ulp, wholesale dry goods merchant of Philadelphia. Her mother, Harriet K. (Porter) Ulp, is a descendant of the Annekajan family, originally from Holland. Dr. Wentz is a member of the Lutheran Church and his wife of the Episcopal Church. He is a member of the Phi-Kappa-Psi College fraternity of the State and county medical societies, and is one of the chiefs of Minnewakaru Tribe No. 250, I. O. R. M.

DAVID E. WINEBRENNER, packer of hermetically sealed fruits and vegetables, was born in Hanover August 25, 1839, is a son of Henry and Sarah (Forney) Winebrenner, is the second in a family of six children, and is of German descent. His father was born in Hanover also. His mother was a daughter of Adam and Rachel Forney, first settlers of York County. In 1857 Mr. Winebrenner began learning the tanner's trade under his father. In 1865 he engaged in business in partnership with his father and brother, P. F. Winebrenner, the firm being known as H. Winebrenner & Sons, and this continued until 1867, when P. F. Winebrenner retired, David E. continuing the business with his father until 1884. In 1874 he began packing fruit and vegetables in partnership with his brother, H C. Winebrenner, the firm being known as Winebrenner Bros.; this continued until September, 1882, since which time he has been alone. For ten years he carried on tanning in connection with his other business, and also conducts a canning establishment at Baltimore. He was married, in 1864, to Miss Elia B. Shriver, a native of Union Mills, Carroll Co., Md., and a daughter of Andrew K. and Catherine (Wirt) Shriver. He has had born to him three children, viz.: Helen S., M. Katherine and David E., Jr. He is politically a Republican, and with his wife a member of the Emanuel Reformed Church. Mr. Winebrenner also served a short time in the late war in Company I, Twenty-sixth Pennsylvania Volunteer Infantry.

HENRY WIRT, the ancestor of the Wirt family

BIOGRAPHICAL SKETCHES. 71

of Hanover, was born in Germany, immigrated to this country and arrived at Philadelphia February 9, 1738. Nothing is definitely known of him from the time of his arrival in America until the year 1750, when he purchased the farm now owned by John Kehr, near Iron Ridge Station, on the Hanover & York Railroad. He was appointed constable of Manheim Township, in which his property then lay, in 1750, and served in that office several years thereafter. He was naturalized April 10, 1762, and died the latter part of the year 1764, leaving a widow, two sons—Jacob and Christian—and several daughters. The house built by him is still standing. Jacob, the eldest son, remained nearly all his life on the farm, and died unmarried in Hanover at an advanced age. Christian, the other son, was born May 12, 1763, and at an early age was apprenticed to Henry Felty, of Hanover, to learn the trade of a saddler, and after serving his apprenticeship went to Baltimore, but soon returned to Hanover, and in 1787 commenced business for himself as a saddle and harness maker, which he continued very successfully until the year 1800. He then bought the property on the Diamond at Hanover, long known as Wirt's Corner, from Col. Richard McAllister, and opened a general store. This received his close attention, and by good management he was enabled to retire from business in 1816, with what was then considered quite a large fortune. He was never engaged in active business after this, but was always ready to encourage all public and private enterprises, having the public good for an end. He was married to Eve Catharine Gelwix, daughter of Charles Gelwix, and died March 2, 1842. His sons were Henry, Jacob and William, and his daughters were Mary, married to Jacob Eichelberger; Catharine, married to George Emmert; Lydia, married to Adam Forney, and Deliah, married to Dr. George W. Hinkle. Henry Wirt, son of Christian, was born October 9, 1789, and received what educational training the town afforded in those days. He and one other pupil were the only ones in Hanover who studied English grammar in his school-boy days. He entered his father's store at a very early age, and gave the business his entire attention. For some years during the sickness of his father, the whole care of the large business rested entirely upon him. He was married March 9, 1815, to Catharine, second daughter of John Swope, and in the spring of 1816 succeeded his father in business at the old stand, which he continued eleven years, and in 1827 retired to private life. He took great interest in all the movements that were then made for the advancement of the educational, spiritual and material interests of his native town. He with several others were instrumental in establishing the first Sunday-schools in Hanover, and after very determined opposition, succeeded in putting the common schools in operation in Hanover during the year 1835. He was very much interested in the question of railroad connections to his native town. When the construction of the York, Wrightsville & Gettysburg Railroad was projected, he used all his powers to have it pass through Hanover. He heartily encouraged the building of the Hanover Branch Railroad, was the heaviest subscriber to its stock, and was a member of the board of managers for many years. He was for a long time a director in the bank of Gettysburg, the Hanover Saving Fund Society and was president of both turnpikes that extended from Hanover. He died in the spring of 1859, aged about seventy years, leaving a widow, who died in 1876, six daughters and one son (Henry) to survive him. Henry Wirt, son of Henry and Catharine (Swope) Wirt, was born in Hanover February 23, 1827. He received his education in the schools of his native town. Early in life he entered his father's store and at the age of twenty years began the mercantile business for himself, which he continued until 1850, when he retired from active business. He has served as chief burgess of Hanover two terms, secretary and director of the Hanover Branch Railroad Company, president of the Hanover Saving Fund Society for eight years, and in the year 1885, is a director in the National Bank of Gettysburg, director of the Hanover Saving Fund Society, a charter member and director in the Hanover Water Company, secretary of the Berlin & Hanover Turnpike Company, president of the Hanover & Maryland Line Turnpike Company and a member of the board of trustees of Franklin and Marshall College at Lancaster, to which institution he recently gave the first $5,000 toward creating an additional professorship in the theological department of that institution. Mr. Wirt was about fifteen years a member of the school board of his native town, and while serving in that office, was constant and earnest in his efforts to advance the cause of public education. He was married October 26, 1854, to Louisa, daughter of Mathias N. Forney, who was a prominent citizen of Hanover and one of the projectors of the Hanover Saving Fund Society. Mrs. Wirt's mother, Amanda (Nace) Forney, was the daughter of George Nace, also a prominent and influential citizen. Mr. and Mrs. Wirt are members of Emanuel Reformed Church of Hanover, of which he has been elder for sixteen years. Jacob Wirt, second son of Christian and Catharine Wirt, was born February 24, 1801. He began the dry goods and general merchandise business for himself in 1827, succeeding his brother, at his father's stand, and continued at the same place eleven years. He then engaged in the lumber and coal business for a short time. When the Hanover Branch Railroad Company was organized, in November, 1849, he was chosen its president, served one year and then resigned. He was elected a director of the same corporation in 1860, and continued until 1865. For a number of years he was president of the Hanover Saving Fund Society, which position he held until his death, and was recognized as an excellent financier. In politics he was a Whig originally, and afterward a stanch Republican. He was an ardent supporter of all enterprises that contributed to the welfare of his native town. He was a member of the Reformed Church. Mr. Wirt was married to Amelia Danner, November 20, 1827, and died November 8, 1869. Their children were Emma C., born May 28, 1829 (married to Dr. John A. Swope, of Gettysburg and now her representative in congress from the district to which York County belongs), deceased; Alexander Christian, born November 13, 1831, deceased; Jacob, born February 28, 1834, deceased; Eliza Ann, born May 10, 1836 (married to George W. Forney, of Hanover; they have two children, J. Wirt and Nettie A.); Martha, married to Albert Barnitz, of York (he died leaving two children: J. Percy and Emma W. Mrs. Barnitz lives in Hanover); Danner, born October 21, 1840, deceased; Reuel, born July 20, 1842, deceased; Calvin Clay, born April 12, 1844 (engaged in banking business in Baltimore; married Miss Ellen Buehler, of that city, and returned to Hanover. He died at the age of thirty years); Florence Amelia, born March 29, 1846, deceased. Robert Millard Wirt, the youngest son of Jacob and Amelia Wirt, was born January 16, 1853. Attended the schools of Hanover and afterward Pennsylvania Military Academy, at Chester, Penn. He was married June 24, 1875, to Miss Bertha B. Barnitz, daughter of Dr. C. S. Barnitz, of Middletown, Ohio. They have three children: Amelia D., Charles B. and Robert O. Mr. Wirt and family are members of the Reformed Church. He is a director of the Hanover

Saving Fund Society, secretary of the Hanover Junction, Hanover & Gettysburg Railroad, secretary and treasurer of the Hanover Water Company and treasurer of the Baltimore & Hanover Railroad Company.

FREDERICK W. WOLFF, a musician of some note and a resident of Baltimore, Md., was born in Hanover, Penn., November 17, 1858, and is the only son of Philip C. and Susanna (Snyder) Wolff, of York County. The father, a German by birth, engaged in the manufacture of buckskin gloves at Hanover about 1833, and continued the same until his death in 1883. The mother, of English descent, is also a resident of Baltimore. Frederick W. began the study of music, when quite young, at Hanover, where he remained until twelve years of age, when he moved with his parents to Baltimore, and there received a collegiate education. Desiring to perfect himself in the study of music, he went to Leipzig, Germany, where he took a three years' course in the Conservatory of Music, and is an alumnus of that institution. Besides being a very successful teacher of music he is also dealing extensively in real estate in Hanover, Penn.

CHARLES M. WOLFF was born near Hanover, Penn., in October, 1847, is a son of J. George and Eleanor (Bittinger) Wolff, and is of German-French extraction. He was educated at the Pennsylvania College, at Gettysburg, and graduated from that institution in 1871. Subsequently he went to Pottsville, Penn., and for five years conducted a newspaper, known as the *Tremont News*. He began the study of the law in Pottsville, Penn., under ex-Atty.-Gen. Francis W. Hughes. In 1877 he returned to York County, and the same year was admitted to the bar in York and Adams Counties, and has since been in the active practice of his profession. He is a member of the I. O. O. F., and is an energetic citizen. The father of our subject was born in Adams County, and is now engaged in the grain business at Gettysburg.

CHARLES YOUNG, born in Hanover, March 3, 1880, is the fourth child and third son of a family of four sons and two daughters. His parents, George and Susan (Sholl) Young, were natives of Hanover, and of German descent. His father was a farmer, and died in 1867, in the seventieth year of his age. Charles Young attended the public schools until sixteen years of age, assisted on his father's farm until twenty, then went to Middletown, Ohio, where he carried on a hardware and iron store, and bought grain for eight years, and farmed four years more; then returned East, and remained until his father's death, after which he went to Kansas City, Mo., remained in that section about seven months, when he again returned to Hanover, and soon afterward engaged in the lumber and coal business, which he still follows. He was married in Middletown, Ohio, in December, 1852, to Miss Susan Zearing, a native of Warren County, Ohio, and of German descent. They have had four children: Louisa Catherine, who died aged about eight months; William Z., who died at the age of twenty-two; Ida S. and Emily L. The family are members of the Methodist Episcopal Church, and Mr. Young is one of the stewards of the Hanover congregation. During Lee's invasion of Pennsylvania, Mr. Young served in the militia of his State. He served the borough as school director one term of three years; as councilman two terms, and was elected chief burgess in February, 1884. He is a Republican in politics, and is a member of the Masonic fraternity.

REV. WILLIAM KNOX ZIEBER, D. D., who for many years has been a prominent and influential clergyman of the Reformed Church, was born at Reading, Penn., September 26, 1825. His parents, Philip and Catharine (Bruckman) Zieber, are natives of Reading. They brought up a family of ten children—six sons and four daughters. The father was a merchant in his native city for forty years. The subject of our sketch attended private schools; at twelve years of age he had a fair English education, and knew something of Latin. During this time he was a classmate of Hon. Hiester Clymer. From the age of twelve to eighteen years he was a clerk in his father's store. He entered Marshall College, at Mercersburg, Penn., at nineteen, and graduated in the classical course in 1848. Three years later the degree of master of arts was conferred upon him. He entered the theological seminary of the Reformed Church immediately after leaving college. He was licensed to preach in 1849, and went to Easton, Penn., where he was assistant preacher, and a teacher of a private school. He was ordained in 1850, and during the next year removed to Miamisburg, Ohio; he was pastor there for three years, and at Tiffin, Ohio, five years. The succeeding two years he was engaged in the home missionary work, and in the meantime traveling in the far West in the discharge of his duty. In July, 1859, he came to Hanover, Penn., to take charge of the Emanuel Reformed Church, which position he held until May, 1882, when, from over-work, he was compelled to resign on account of physical disability. Rev. Dr. Zieber was married at Mercersburg, Penn., on September 25, 1850, to Miss Sarah Good, a native of Pennsylvania, and a sister of Rev. William James Good. Five children were descendants: Annie, Blanche, Bertha, Grace and Paul. Bertha is teaching in a female seminary at Hagerstown, Md. Grace is also a teacher in a kindergarten in Philadelphia, and Paul is a druggist in the latter city. During a ministry of twenty-two years, in Hanover and vicinity, Dr. Zieber preached exclusive of lectures 3,106 times, baptized 700 persons, added to his church 496 members, officiated at 379 funerals, performed the marriage ceremony 254 times, and collected for benevolent purposes $12,000, which went to home missions, orphans' homes, and for the preparation of young men for the ministry. Dr. Zieber is well read in all departments of literature, a theologian of recognized ability, and has done much to improve the moral, educational and social interests of Hanover. His home is a model of refinement and culture.

FRANK A. ZIEGLER, Pennsylvania Railroad agent at Hanover, was born in Littlestown, Adams Co., Penn., February 27, 1844, and is a son of Charles H. and Margaret (Brothers) Ziegler, of Adams County, and of German descent. His father, who died in 1879, had been in the employ of the Pennsylvania Railroad Company as collector of tolls on the Pennsylvania Canal at Clark's Ferry, and subsequently at Middletown, from the time the canal passed into the hands of the Pennsylvania Railroad till within four years of his death. The last two years he spent as bridge toll collector at Wrightsville. Frank A. is the eldest of seven children, and grew up principally in his father's office. At the age of fifteen years he began learning telegraphy, and soon after occupied a place as operator in his father's office at Clark's Ferry, but remained only six weeks, and went to Harrisburg, where he was until August 22, 1863, when he enlisted in Company A, One Hundred and Twenty-seventh Pennsylvania Volunteer Infantry; he served nine months, and was honorably discharged at Harrisburg. On his return he took his old position as operator in his father's office, which he kept until 1870, when he was transferred to Middletown, and at the end of two years went to Alexandria, Va., where he was clerk in the freight office of the Pennsylvania Railroad. After a few months he was appointed agent and operator at Bowie, on the Baltimore & Potomac Railroad, which position he held for three years, and then was removed to Baltimore

BIOGRAPHICAL SKETCHES.

City as clerk in the car record office of the Northern Central Railroad. At the establishment of the Frederick division of that line he was transferred to the superintendent's office at York, and remained there from 1875 to 1879, when he came to Hanover, where he has since held the office of the agent of the Pennsylvania Railroad. In July, 1881, he, in company with D. P. McKeefer, established the telephone at Hanover, but sold out to the Pennsylvania Telephone Company. In 1866 he was married, in Dauphin County, to Ellen Garman, of that county, and has had five children: George S., Grace G., Carrie M., Mary C. and Carl E. The family are members of the Methodist Episcopal Church. Mr. Z. is a Mason, a member of the I. O. O. F., in which latter he is a trustee, and a member of the G. A. R. In 1883 he was elected councilman of his ward, but was defeated as chief burgess in 1884.

FRANCIS S. ZINN, junk dealer of Hanover, Penn., was born in Austria in 1847, and is the eldest of two sons of George J. and Theresa (Hergesell) Zinn, natives of Austria. The father was a major in the Austrian army for eighteen years; he came to this country in 1858 and settled at Hanover; in 1862 he enlisted in Company G, One Hundred and Sixty-sixth Regiment Pennsylvania Volunteers, for one year, and died in 1879. Francis S. was brought up at Hanover, where he received a good German and English education, which enabled him to teach a German school in New York State one term. In 1868 he was married to Belinda Parr, who died, leaving five children: Ida K., George W., Otto J., Harry W. (deceased) and Rosa J. Mr. Zinn belongs to the Lutheran Church of Hanover; is a Mason and a member of the I. O. O. F., commander of Encampment No. 47, of Hanover. In politics he is an active Democrat, and has held the offices of assessor, school director, district superintendent of schools of Heidelberg and Penn Townships, and in 1880 was enumerator of the census for the same townships. Before engaging in his present business he followed farming.

WRIGHTSVILLE BOROUGH AND HELLAM TOWNSHIP.

JAMES A. ARMSTRONG, M. D., was born in Lisbon, Ohio, January 8, 1839. His parents were James and Margaret (Knepley) Armstrong, of Ohio and District of Columbia, and of Scotch-Irish and German descent respectively. Until his fourteenth year he lived on the farm, receiving his primary education at the schools of New Oxford, Penn. At the age of twenty he entered the office of Dr. Pfeiffer, of New Oxford, and remained there for two years, going from there to Abbottstown, where he read with Dr. Pepper for three years. After practicing and continuing his studies for a few years, he entered the University of Pennsylvania at Philadelphia, from which institution he graduated, in the spring of 1871, as medical doctor. After practicing a year in Philadelphia, he discovered his health to be failing, and discontinued for about one year, devoting his whole time to the recuperation of his physical forces. In 1873 he removed to Hellam, where he has since been practicing his profession with success. He was married, at Abbottstown, in 1876, to Miss M. Wolf, and had born to him six children, three of whom died in infancy. The living are Ernest A.,

Mary E. and Margaret L. Dr. Armstrong is a member and deacon of the Lutheran Church, and was school director three years, and is a member of the State Medical Association, and of the York County Medical Society, of which he was vice-president at one time.

THEODORE D. BAHN was born July 14, 1833, on the Dosch farm, half a mile south of East Prospect, York Co., Penn. His parents were Henry and Maria (Dosch) Bahn, and soon after subject's birth removed to Marietta, Penn.; when he was about one year old they removed to Lewistown, Mifflin Co., Penn., thence to the Comfort Farm, five miles west from Lewistown; thence, in his fifth year, to a farm in Juniata County, and in his seventh year to McAlistersville, same county, where his father engaged in the tanning business, and died in our subject's thirteenth year. When Theodore was fourteen, his mother died, leaving a family of six small children, he being the eldest and only boy. All were subsequently well cared for by kind friends, he with his eldest sister being taken into the family of his uncle, Jacob Dosch. At the age of fifteen he removed with his uncle to the then far West, arriving at Galena. Ill., on the 1st of December; thence they traveled by team to Fayette County, Wis., where they settled. He remained with his uncle, working at the carpenter's trade and farming at intervals, until he was eighteen years of age, when he went into the Wisconsin pineries, where he spent one year working at shingle-making; returning again to Fayette County, he worked at his trade and farming, until the spring of 1857, when he removed to Lodi, Columbia Co., Wis., continuing at his trade in the summer and teaching school in the winter until April 18, 1861, when he enlisted in Company H, Second Wisconsin Volunteers, for three months, going into camp at Madison, where the regiment was drilled until the 11th of June, when he, with the entire regiment, re-enlisted for three years (being promoted in the meantime to the position of fifth sergeant) and on the same day embarked for the seat of war. He participated in the first Bull Run battle, when he received a gunshot wound in the right shoulder; was granted a furlough for two months, returned home and in due time joined his regiment. He participated in all the battles in which his regiment was engaged (except those of second Bull Run and Antietam, at which time he was on detached duty in the engineer corps), up to the battle of Gettysburg, where he was severely wounded in the left side during the first charge of the famous "Iron Brigade," within thirty yards of he spot where Gen. Reynolds fell. With considerable difficulty and severe pain he reached the court house, then being used as a hospital, where he remained until the close of the battle; he was then transferred to the United States General Hospital, at York, Penn., where he remained until February 11, 1864, when he was pronounced unfit for field service, and transferred to the Second Battalion Veteran Reserve Corps, Company 108, with the rank of first sergeant. He was assigned to duty as clerk in the office of the surgeon in charge of the above-named hospital, where he remained until June 11, 1864, when he was honorably discharged. He returned to his Western home, where, on the 21st day of July, the third anniversary of the first Bull Run battle, he was married to Miss Hattie C. Bartholomew. Resuming his trade, he worked for the government at Duvall's Bluff, Ark., on hospitals for six months; returning again to Lodi, Wis., he pursued his trade until the fall of 1869, when he removed to the city of Milwaukee, where he was engaged in a sash, door and blind factory until the spring of 1872, when he removed to Cedarburg, where he engaged in the same business until the fall of 1874, when he came to Wrightsville, and entered the employ of his brother-in-law, John Beidler, in the lumber and hardware business. In 1880 he entered the millinery, trimming and fancy goods business, in which he is still engaged, with very fair prospects of success. At present he holds the position of "Post Commander" of Lieut. R W. Smith Post, No. 270, G. A. R., and is a member of the E. Lutheran Church and Sunday-school.

JOHN BEIDLER. The subject of this sketch is one of the most prominent and active of the business men of Wrightsville, and is now engaged in the hardware business. For many years he carried on the lumber business in Wrightsville, and his trade extended through York and Adams Counties in Pennsylvania, and Frederick and Harford Counties in Maryland, and from his extended business connections he is well and favorably known throughout this whole region of country. He has recently placed the lumber business in the hands of his eldest son, Harry B. Beidler, and devotes his attention to the hardware business. Mr. Beidler was born in the year 1836, on the farm now owned by him, about two miles from Wrightsville, in Hellam Township. This farm has been in the uninterrupted possession of the Beidler family since the year 1744, having been conveyed, in that year, by patent from John Penn, Thomas Penn and Richard Penn, to Ulrich Beidler, the great-great-grandfather of John Beidler, and has been transferred from one generation to another of his descendants until it reached the present owner. Ulrich Beidler, above mentioned, was one of the first of the German settlers of the Creitz'Creek Valley, though we have no record of the exact date of his arrival. The records of the family show that he and his wife Barbara left three sons and three daughters. One of the daughters, Anna, was married to Henry Strickler, and was the maternal ancestor of many of the Stricklers now living in the valley. Barbara, another daughter, was married to Jacob Blasser. We have no record of the descendants of the other daughter, Frena, or of the two younger sons, Peter and Jacob, though it is more than probable that descendants of Jacob Beidler, who, it is known, left children, may be found. The eldest son of Ulrich Beidler, Daniel Beidler, and who inherited the home farm, married, and with his wife Barbara, had a family of one son and eight daughters, all of whom lived to grow up and become heads of families of their own. Of the daughters, Barbara was married to Joseph Erb, of Warwick Township, Lancaster County; Magdalena, to Jacob Witmer, of Cumberland County; Anna, to Daniel Flury; Frena to Jacob Grove, of Hawkins County, N. C.; Elizabeth to Nathan Barns, of Washington County, Penn.; Mary to Melchoir Bringalf, and Catharine to —— Berntheisel. Daniel Beidler the second, the only son, who was born March 6, 1770, married Susanna Fitz, and on the death of his father, Daniel Beidler the first, came into possession of the homestead, paying to his sisters their respective shares of their father's estate. He had six children, namely: Jacob, born in 1804; Barbara, born in 1805; Daniel, born in 1807; Baltzer, born in 1808; Anna, born in 1809, and John, born in 1810. John died when less than a year old, and before the death of his father. Daniel Beidler the second died suddenly, at York, August 5, 1816, and the farm passed into the possession of his widow, Susanna, and his children. Jacob, Barbara, Daniel, Baltzer and Anna. With the exception of Baltzer these all died without having married. Jacob died in 1824, Anna in 1861, Susanna (widow of Daniel Beidler the second) in 1862, Daniel in 1872, and Barbara in 1880, leaving Baltzer Beidler the only survivor and sole heir to the estate left by his father, Daniel Beidler the second. Baltzer Beidler was married in 1834 to Elizabeth Stoner. They had but two children: John, the subject of this sketch, and Susan, who was born August 11, 1838, and died May 10, 1842. Mrs. Elizabeth Beidler died January 12, 1841, in the twenty-seventh year of her age. Baltzer Beidler died May 4, 1884, aged seventy-five years ten months and six days, when the estate passed to John Beidler, the only heir. John Beidler, the only son of Baltzer and Elizabeth Beidler, was born in Hellam Township, York County, February 10, 1836, and received a common school education. For a short time, in early manhood, he engaged in teaching in the public schools of the county. In the year 1859 he was married to Miss Mary E. Bahn, of Hellam Township, and soon after his marriage he removed to Wrightsville and engaged in the lumber business. At this time, Wrightsville was the center of a large lumber trade, and wagons came from all points south and west for a distance of twenty, thirty and forty miles, to the number often of as many as thirty in a single day, to be loaded at his yards. A few years ago Mr. Beidler opened a large hardware store at the corner of Front and Locust Streets, and he has since placed the lumber business in the hands of his son, Harry B. Beidler. Mr. Beidler has one daughter and three sons living: Cordelia S., Harry B., Daniel and Elmer J. His residence is in Hellam Township, adjoining the borough of Wrightsville.

GEORGE E. BERGER was born in York Township, York County, April 11, 1852, and is the youngest son in a family of seven children of Joseph and Lehna (Yaney) Berger, of York County. He was brought up on the home farm, and received his education in the district schools of his neighborhood. At fifteen years of age he left home and worked at various occupations until the spring of 1871, when he began learning the trade of blacksmithing with his brother Isaac, in Longstown, York County, and remained there two years, after which he came to Stony Brook and followed his trade for eighteen months, then entered the employ of Christian Stoner, at Stoner's Station, where he remained eighteen months; then opened a shop of his own, which he conducted until 1881, when he came to Hellam, where he has since been engaged for himself. He was married April 6, 1879, to Hannah Keller, daughter of Jacob Keller, of York County, and has by this union two children: Lillie D. and Maud.

HENRY BIRNSTOCK was born in Saxony, Germany, November 4, 1837; came to this country in 1854 and located at York, where he at once apprenticed himself to D. D. Doudel, to learn the trade of tinsmith. In April, 1861, he enlisted at York, in Company A, Sixteenth Pennsylvania Volunteers, for three months, and in August, 1861, re-enlisted in Company I, Seventy-sixth Pennsylvania Volunteers, for three years; with the exception of the last six months in the Army of the Potomac, he served in the Army of the South Atlantic, and participated in the engagements of Fort Pulaski, Pocataligo, S. C. (in which he was slightly wounded), Fort Wagner, James Island, Cold Harbor (Army of the Potomac), Chapin's Farm and front of Petersburg. He was mustered out at Harrisburg as first sergeant in November, 1864, having served three months over time. On his return to York he entered again the employ of Mr. Doudel, with whom he worked until 1869, when he moved to Wrightsville, where he has since successfully carried on the manufacture of tin and sheet iron ware and roofing, and the stove business. He is a director of the Wrightsville Town Hall Company, the Wrightsville & Chanceford Turnpike Company, and the Wrightsville Hardware Company; is a member of the school board, and also a member of the Masonic order, I. O. O. F. and the G. A. R. He and wife belong to the Lutheran Church. In the borough he has

BIOGRAPHICAL SKETCHES.

served three terms as chief burgess, and one term as councilman. In 1865 he was married at York to Barbara Wisman, of York, who has borne him eight children, of whom five are living. Silas M., Harry D., Charles F., Willie W., Mary E.; Laura N., Freddie and Calvert were the names of the deceased.

JACOB A. BLESSING was born in Lower Windsor Township, March 20, 1848. His parents were Alexander and Charlotte (Kauffelt) Blessing, of York County, and descendants of a very old family. Their only child is Jacob A. He was educated at the public schools, and in 1870 began business for himself in Hellam Township in the manufacturing of cigars, and in the mercantile business in company with J. W. Gable; the partnership, however, was dissolved in 1872. In 1873 he began the manufacture of cigars at Hellam for himself, and in 1879 he opened the "Hellam House," which building he had erected. He manufactures from 400,000 to 500,000 cigars per annum. May 1, 1870, he was married in York Township to Ellen Sakemiller, of Hellam Township, and has three children: Annie, Walter and Grover. Mrs. Blessing is a member of the German Reformed Church. Mr. Blessing, although a young man yet, possesses good business qualities and is highly esteemed. In 1882 he was assessor of Hellam Township.

CHRISTOPHER C. BURG was born in Lower Windsor Township, March 15, 1829. His parents were P. W. and Eliza (Dosch) Burg, natives of Amsterdam, Holland, and York County, respectively. The former died in 1856, and the latter in 1848. They had four sons and two daughters. Christopher is the second son. He was brought up on the farm, and educated at the public schools. His father owned a mill, where Christopher spent five years of his early life. From his twenty-fourth to his thirty-fourth year he was engaged in canal boating. Since 1872 he has been engaged in farming, four years in Spring Garden Township, and since in Hellam Township, two miles west of Wrightsville, on his fine farm of 106 acres. In March, 1854, he was married to Mary Hauser, daughter of John Hauser, deceased; and has had born to him five children: P. W.; Sarah, John L., Mary E. and Alfred W. Mr. Burg and family belong to the Lutheran Church; he is an active Republican, and from 1865 to 1872 he held the office of justice of the peace of Wrightsville. His first presidential vote was cast for John C. Fremont.

JAMES CLARK CHANNELL, M. D., was born in Fawn Township, York County, October 11, 1843. His parents were John and Mary (Clark) Channell of Fawn Township, of Scotch-Irish and Scotch descent, respectively. They had ten children, of whom Dr. Channell is the fourth. He spent his early youth on the farm, and received his early education in the public school, and later at the York Normal School, and at the Stewartstown Academy. He entered the University of Pennsylvania, at Philadelphia, in 1868, and graduated in 1871, with the degree of M. D. Prior to entering the college he had taught school for six years. August 7, 1862, he enlisted at York in Company I, One Hundred and Thirtieth Pennsylvania Volunteer Infantry, and served his full term. He participated in the battles of Antietam, Fredericksburgh and Chancellorsville. At Antietam he was slightly disabled by a spent ball. Through exposure and marching he also contracted varicose veins, from which he has never recovered. He next entered the service as second lieutenant of Company D, One Hundred and Ninety-fourth Pennsylvania Volunteer Infantry. Returning he commenced the study of medicine and began the practice in 1871, at State Hill, York County. He left there in 1879, traveled to some extent, and finally located at Wrightsville, where he has since practiced his profession. In 1875 he was married at New Brunswick, N. J., to Elizabeth F., daughter of Dr. Frank W. Clement. of Philadelphia. Dr. Channell belongs to the Presbyterian Church, is a member of the K. of P. and Post 270, G. A. R., and a correspondent for different newspapers.

STEPHEN A. COPENHAFER was born November 15, 1856, is the son of John H., and Mary Copenhafer, of Manchester Township, and is of German and English descent. His boyhood was passed on the farm and in attending school. One year he spent in learning milling with Jacob Musser, of Lancaster County, then two years with Benjamin Small of Mt. Wolf; then he worked a year for F. U. Gantz, in Lancaster County, and then he returned to Mt. Wolf and for four years ran a mill on his own account. In 1883 he came to Hellam and rented a mill from Z. K. Loucks, in which he now carries on the business in its different branches. March 13, 1869, he married Emma S., daughter of M. L. Duhling of Manchester Borough. Mr. Copenhafer is a member of the Lutheran Church, and his wife of the United Brethren.

MONROE P. DECKER, son of John and Mary Decker, of Glen Rock, this county, was born February 5, 1860, and passed his earlier years in attending school and working on the home farm. January 6, 1879, he began to learn stone-cutting with L. B. Sweitzer, remained with him over three years, and April 1, 1882, removed to Wrightsville and commenced business for himself, now employing three hands and turning out some fine work in marble, which he ships to various points. December 12, 1880, he married Emma M., daughter of Henry and Louisa Strayer, of Springfield township, and to this union have been born three children: Phebe Ellen, Elsie Viola and May Irene. Mr. Decker has been a member of the German Reformed Church since 1879; is a member of the Riverside Lodge No. 503, A. F. & A. M., and of Chihuahua Lodge No. 317, I. O. O. F. He is of German descent through his great-grandparents.

JONAS DEISINGER, M. D., was born in Paradise Township (now Jackson), York County, April 18, 1833. His parents were Jacob, and Salome (Davis) Deisinger of York County, and of German descent. They had eleven children, of whom Jonas is the eldest now living. His first twenty years he spent on his father's farm, receiving his education at the neighboring schools. For the next three years he attended select schools at York and other places, and taught during the winter in the common schools of this county. At the age of twenty-three he began to read medicine with Dr. C. S. Picking, and in 1858, entered the medical department of Pennsylvania College at Philadelphia. From 1861 to 1868 he practiced medicine at Hellam. In 1866 he entered the University of Pennsylvania and graduated in the class of 1867. After graduating he returned to Hellam, where, with the exception of about three years, he has been since. In the fall of 1862, he was married at Hellam to Maria Mann, of York County. The Doctor is a genial gentleman, fond of his profession, and has acquired a lucrative practice; he is a member and an elder of the Reformed Church of the United States, was a school director two terms, is a member of the York County Medical Society, once president of the same, and is also a member of the State Medical Association.

DAVID DETWILER was born in Lancaster County, January 27, 1818. His parents were Joseph and Susan (Garver) Detwiler, of Pennsylvania, and of German descent. They had seven children, of whom David is the eldest. He was brought up as a farmer, and educated at the common schools. He was married, in 1849, in Hellam Township, to Sarah Stoner, a native of Pennsylvania, who has borne him five children, four of whom are living: Paul, Anna, David S. and Ellen. Mr. Detwiler is quite a prominent man in his community. He owns 140 acres of land, on which he resides; is at present auditor of Hellam Township, a director of the Susquehanna & York Turnpike, and Wrightsville & Chanceford Turnpike Companies. He was one of the organizers of the Wrightsville Hardware Company, and for many years one of the directors. He is very wealthy, and since 1879 has retired from active business life, and resides in his magnificent home he built on the hill just at the edge of the town of Wrightsville.

PAUL DETWILER, son of David Detwiler, was born near Wrightsville, October 25, 1852. His mother was Sarah (Stoner) Detwiler, of Pennsylvania. He was reared on the farm and educated at the district schools, and after becoming of age worked for two years for his father, and then in partnership with his brother began farming near Wrightsville, and continued until 1879, when they dissolved, and he kept on farming alone. He was married, October 21, 1879, to Lizzie J. Emig, daughter of Eli Emig, an old and respected citizen of York County. Two children have been born to this union: Martha, deceased; and Sarah. In the spring election of 1884; Mr. Detwiler served as judge of election. He and wife are members of the Lutheran Church.

PETER DIETZ, Sr., was born in Hellam Township July 14, 1812. His parents were Peter and Susannah (Lieppart) Dietz, of York County, and of German descent. They had a family of seven sons and two daughters, of whom Peter, Sr., was the third son. He was brought up on a farm, and educated at the German schools of his native township. His whole life was devoted to farming, from which he retired in 1872, residing nearly all the time in the township in which he was born. In 1836 he was married in lower Windsor Township to Mary Luppert, who died in 1873, aged about sixty-two years, leaving a family of eleven children: Rebecca, Susan, Jacob, Mary, Elizabeth, Peter, Rachel, Michael, Daniel, Levi (deceased) and Sarah (deceased). The family belong to the German Reformed Church. David Newcomer was born in Hellam Township in 1841. His parents were John and Lena (Lehman) Newcomer, of York County, and of English and German descent, respectively. He was brought up on the farm and educated in the public schools. Learning the shoe-making trade, he has followed it ever since. He was married, in May, 1870, to Elizabeth Dietz, and had two children: Annie and Sadie, deceased. Mr. Newcomer was a school director one year.

WILLIAM DIETZ, the eldest of the three sons of Frederick and Martha M. (Strickler) Dietz, of York County, was born in Hellam Township, March 25, 1847, and received a good common school education. He has always followed the occupation of farming, in Hellam Township. In October, 1877, he was married to Fannie Baer, daughter of John and Leah Baer, of York County, and has had born to him three children: Amos, Leah and Paul.

ANDREW J. DUDEN was born at York, Penn., January 25, 1841, and is the only child of John A. and Sarah (Jack) Duden. His father died in 1846, aged forty-seven years, but his mother is still living, aged about eighty-two years. He came to Wrightsville, in 1847, and remained about ever since, receiving his early education here. At the age of fifteen, he began learning the trade of wheelwright, and worked at it until twenty-two years of age, excepting the time he served in the army. September 23, 1861, he enlisted at Harrisburg, in Company I, Seventy-sixth Pennsylvania Volunteer Infantry, and served eighteen months in the department of the South. At Pocataligo, he was wounded by a rifle ball in the right cheek. He carried the ball for six years in his neck, when it was discovered that it had lodged against his collar bone, and was removed. On account of the wound, he lay in the hospital five months, and finally was discharged on account of disability. He was virtually sergeant-major at the time he was wounded, but did not receive the appointment until after his discharge. In 1870, he engaged in the planing-mill business at Wrightsville, in company with Mr. Zorbaugh, in which business he is engaged at the present day. He was one of the organizers of the Wrightsville Hardware Company, and is the present secretary; also of the Wrightsville and Chanceford Turnpike Company and of the Wrightsville Hall Association, and is director of the latter. He has held various borough offices: burgess, councilman and school director, for several terms. November 24, 1864, he was married at Wrightsville, to Emma Mann of the same borough, and has had three children: Charles F., Sally M., and Ralph. Mrs. Duden is a member of the Presbyterian Church. Mr. Duden is a Mason, a member of the I. O. O. F., and officer of the day of the G. A. R. He sold out the planing-mill, April 1, 1884, and is going to Columbia, to engage in pulverizing rock flint. He is also proprietor of a cigar box factory, and manufactures annually about 225,-000 boxes, employing about twenty hands.

GEORGE D. EBERT, whose portrait appears in this work, was born in Manchester Township, December 24, 1824; his parents were Michael and Lydia (Diehl) Ebert, of York County, and of German descent. They had five children, of whom George D. is the third. He was brought up on a farm in Spring Garden Township, and was educated at the public schools. At the age of twenty-three years he left home, and in 1849 was married to Sarah Smyser, daughter of Michael Smyser, who has borne him three children: William Winfield, Amanda and Agnes. Mrs. Ebert died March 19. 1884, aged fifty-nine years. Mr Ebert removed to Hellam Township in 1850, on a farm of 185 acres, upon which he has resided since. He has held every township office, and in 1880 represented the county in the State convention. As guardian and administrator he has been very successful in settling up estates. He was one of the organizers of the Wrightsville Hardware Company, the Wrightsville Furnace, of the First National Bank (of which he is director), and of the Wrightsville *Star* and the *True Democrat* at York; he is also a member of the Riverside Lodge, A. F. & A. M., and of the I. O. O. F., and the family are members of the Lutheran Church. In 1867 Mr. Ebert made a voyage to Europe and remained there several months. His father, Michael Ebert, was in the war of 1812, and held a commission as colonel. Mr. Ebert is also very largely engaged in raising and dealing in tobacco. A Republican in politics, he stands very high in his community, and enjoys the respect of all who know him.

WILLIAM EMENHEISER was born in Lower Windsor Township, August 31, 1846, to Samson and Mary Emenheiser, of German descent. His rudimentary education was received at the public schools, during his early life on the farm. In 1864 he taught a term, and the following summer he attended the Normal School at Millersville; then attended the Normal Institute at York two terms; then in 1869 returned to Millersville for one term, and the same year received his professional certificate; in 1871 he received his permanent certificate. He has taught public school sixteen terms, and three terms of select school. August 12, 1869, he married Elizabeth, daughter of Charles and Magdalena

Sprenkle, and of the seven children born to this union four are living: Willie Edwin, Maggie, Anna and Edith. Mr. and Mrs. Emenheiser are members of the Lutheran Church at Kreutz Creek; he has charge of the church property of about ten acres, which he keeps under cultivation, and is sexton and organist, as well as assistant superintendent of the Sunday-school; he is also agent for the White Sewing Machine Company.

JOHN A. EMIG was born in Hellam Township, March 13, 1851. He was reared on the home farm in Hellam Township, and received his education in the district schools; until he was twenty-five years old he assisted his father on the farm, after which he began burning lime. At the death of his father, in 1877, he was appointed one of the executors of the estate, and has managed the settlement until the present day. In the spring of 1881 he purchased the farm of 122¼ acres, upon which he now resides. January 8, 1880, he was married to Clara Strickler, daughter of Henry Strickler, of Spring Garden. They have had three children: Florence, Henry (deceased) and Walter.

HENRY W. EMIG, a prominent young farmer, was born in Hellam Township January 20, 1849. His parents were Eli and Magdalena (Crider) Emig, of York and Lancaster Counties respectively, and of German descent, and parents of ten children, of whom Henry W. is the second. He was reared on the farm and educated at the public schools. At the age of twenty-two he began farming for himself on the place which he now owns and occupies. His father, who died in 1877, aged fifty-eight years, owned six large farms at the time of his death; his mother still lives in Hellam Township, aged about sixty-two years. Three sisters and four brothers reside in York County, the latter engaged in farming. The farm upon which Mr. Emig resides, was purchased by him in October, 1883; besides this, he owns five farms, which came from his father. He is much interested in educational matters and public improvements, and like the family, belongs to the Reformed Church.

JOHN W. GABLE was born in Windsor Township, York County, June 4, 1847, and is the seventh of nine children, and the third son of Jacob and Annie M. (Jackson) Gable, of York County, and of German and English descent, respectively. The first thirteen years he spent on his father's farm, and from that time until twenty-two years of age, was engaged as clerk in different mercantile establishments in York County. He was educated at the common schools and one term at the commercial school at Poughkeepsie, New York. Between the age of eleven and thirteen years, he worked at shoe-making and learned the trade. At the time he began the mercantile business for himself, in 1869, he also began manufacturing cigars, and now manufactures and handles about 2,000,000 to 3,000,000 of cigars annually. In connection with his mercantile business he owns and works a farm in Spring Garden Township. Mr. Gable is one of the organizers of the Eureka Building and Loan Association of York. He was married September 23, 1875, in Hellam Township, to Elizabeth Hiestand, daughter of Henry A. Hiestand. To this union were born two children; a daughter, Susan Hiestand, and a son, Chauncey E., who died August 4, 1881, aged about six months. He is a member of the Lutheran Church at Kreutz Creek; superintendent of the Sunday-school, and is an enterprising and very popular business man. In 1874 he was appointed postmaster at Hellam, which office he still holds.

JACOB GOHN, son of George and Magdalena Gohn, of Hellam Township, was born November 20, 1825; is of German descent, and was reared on the home farm. In March, 1847, he began butchering in partnership with Thomas Harris, but one year later dissolved the partnership and united with his brother, John Gohn, with whom for seven years he was engaged in the same business, and one year in the cattle trade. From 1856 to 1867 he was in the mercantile trade under the firm name of Heppenstall & Gohn, and for two years thereafter was with Levi and George Lehman, under the firm name of Gohn & Lehman. William Witman then came in and business continued until 1871 under the style of Gohn, Lehman & Co., and then was changed to Gohn & Witman; as such it continued until March, 1876, since when Jacob Gohn has been in business alone, carrying a large stock of groceries, dry goods, boots, shoes, hardware, etc., having rebuilt and enlarged his storeroom in 1879. With Mr. James Cook, Mr. Gohn was the originator of the Wrightsville National Bank in 1862, of which he is a director, as well as director of the Wrightsville Hardware Company; he was also a large stockholder in the furnace. January 11, 1855, he married Martha, daughter of John and Sarah Heppenstall, and of the seven children born to this union, the only son is dead, and six daughters living: Sarah, Mary Martha, Carrie May, Laura Silvers, Minnie and Nellie Levingston. Mr. and Mrs. Gohn are members of the Lutheran Church, and Mr. Gohn of Riverside Lodge, No. 503, A. F. & A. M. Mrs. Martha Gohn is of English descent; her parents came from England about 1812.

WILLIAM F. HIESTAND was born in Spring Garden Township, May 4, 1814. His parents were Abraham and Nancy (Fitts) Hiestand, of Lancaster County, were of German descent, and had a family of four sons and four daughters, of whom William F. was the youngest son and seventh child. There are at present only our subject, one brother (Abraham), and one sister (Mrs. Wilson) living. Mr. Hiestand was reared on a farm and received his education in the district schools of York County. In 1866 he was married, in Lancaster, to Rebecca Doll of York County, and of German descent, and to their union were born eight children: Herby A., Annias F., William, Mary E., Susanna, Franklin C., Bird J. and Margaret. Mr. Hiestand came to Hellam Township in 1866, owns thirty-eight acres in Hellam Township and 207 acres in Heidelberg Township, is retired at present on his homestead in Hellam Township, and owes his prosperous condition to his own energy and industry. He is a very liberal man, especially to churches and benevolent organizations, and takes a great interest in school matters, having been a school director. He has at present eight grandchildren living in York County.

ISAAC HINKLE, son of Henry and Sarah Hinkle, of Lancaster County, was born March 4, 1832, grew to manhood on the home farm and was educated at the district schools. For five years, from 1858, he farmed for Hahn & Himes, at Woodstock, and then, in 1863, moved to Mr. Miflin's place, known as the "Woodbine Farm." In 1879 he bought his present place of about 133 acres, on which are a good stone dwelling and a large bank barn, and here he largely carries on farming and also dairying. In 1858 he married Elizabeth, daughter of Jacob and Elizabeth Kauffman of Lancaster County. Besides being a successful agriculturist, Mr. Hinkle is a stockholder in the Wrightsville and Chanceford turnpike company, and in the Wrightsville Hardware Company. Mrs. Hinkle is a member of the Lutheran Church at Wrightsville.

DANIEL L. HOKE was born in Hellam Township, August 22, 1849. His parents were George and Jane (Kendrick) Hoke, of York and Philadelphia, respectively, and of German descent. They had five children, of whom Daniel is the youngest. He was brought up in a hotel and has always followed the hotel business. November 10, 1875, he was married at Columbia, Penn., to Pauline E. Baker, daughter of Peter and Susan C. (Trainer) Baker, of Marietta and Columbia, Penn., and has had born to him four children: Daniel, Helen (deceased), Jane and Teresa. Mr. Hoke is a Master Mason and a very enthusiastic and popular Democrat. He has thrice been elected a member of the council of Wrightsville, and is a member at present. He was one of the organizers of the Wrightsville Hardware Company. August 1, 1884, he purchased and opened the Union Hotel at Wrightsville.

SAMUEL F. HOLLINGER was born in York Township, near Dallastown, May 16, 1844. His parents were Daniel and Elizabeth (Flinchbaugh) Hollinger. He was reared on the home farm and educated at the district schools. In the spring of 1865 he went to Lancaster County and farmed about one year, when he returned to York Township, and assisted his father on the farm for two years. In the fall of 1868 he began learning the trade of millwright with Jonathan Geesey, of Dallastown; remained with him for two years, and then worked at his trade for four years. In 1874 he began milling at Henry's Mill, in Hopewell Township, where he remained two years, going from there to Yost's Mill in York Township for two years, then to the Ness Mill in Springfield Township for two years; then to the Tunnel Mill in the same township for one year; then to Diehl's Mill near York for three years, and in April. 1884, came to Strickler's Mill near Hellam, where he is at present engaged. He was married February 23, 1878, to Emeline Lehman, daughter of J. W. Lehman of York County, and has had three children born to him: Lizzie (deceased), Millie and Annie (deceased).

WILLIAM J. HOUCK, justice of the peace, was born in York City, April 20, 1855. His parents were John and Genevieve Houck, of Germany, who had seven children, of whom William J. is the youngest. He remained in York with his parents until 1866, when he went with them to Baltimore, where he attended the Catholic schools. In 1869 he returned to York, and began learning the trade of shoe-making with Philip H. Amig, served an apprenticeship three years and six months, and then worked for himself for three years. He was married February 5, 1875, to Mary A. Cramer, daughter of Charles Cramer, of York, and to this union three children have been born: William J., Charles E. and Fannie L. In March, 1876, he removed to Des Moines, Iowa, where he followed his trade but a short time, returning again to Hellam Township, where he opened a shoe store, in which business he is at present engaged. In the spring of 1878 he was elected justice of the peace of Hellam Township, and was re-elected in 1883. The family belong to the United Brethren Church, and are now co-operating in the construction of a new church edifice for that denomination in the village of Hellam.

JAMES L. JAMISON, M. D., son of William and Catherine Jamison, of Wrightsville, was born January 20, 1855. Until the age of fourteen his boyhood was passed at Wrightsville; he then went to Philadelphia, where he was in the employ of Dr. F. Getchell until seventeen years of age, when he returned to Wrightsville, and entered the employ of Kerr, Cook & Co., lime burners. October 29, 1873, he entered the preparatory department of Lincoln University, graduated therefrom in June, 1875, and the following September entered the collegiate department, from which he graduated June 3, 1879. His summer vacation of 1875 was spent in the Catskill Mountains; that of 1876 at Newport; that of 1877 at Cape May, and that of 1878 was spent in canvassing Newark and Elkton, Md. In June, 1879, he returned to Wrightsville, studied medicine under Dr. D. A. Stubbs, of Oxford, Chester County, entered Jefferson Medical College in the fall of 1879, graduated March 30, 1882, and in June began his profession in his native town, where he has since built up a large practice. August 27, 1884, he married Francenia, daughter of Peter and Carrie Baldwin, of Lower Oxford, Chester County. The Doctor is a member of the Presbyterian Church of Lincoln, and the Alumni of Jefferson Medical College. He has had the care of his mother since boyhood, his father being infirm.

W. H. KERR was born in Wrightsville, October 19, 1828. His parents were Matthew and Jane (Wilson) Kerr, natives of Ireland and York respectively, and the mother of Scotch descent. They had a family of eight sons and one daughter, of whom William H. is the sixth. He was educated at Wrightsville, and at the age of nineteen years he commenced boating on the Susquehanna and Tide Water Canal, and continued it for fifteen years. In 1861 he began the business of lime burning under the firm name of Robert W. Kerr & Co. In 1865 the firm changed to James L. Kerr & Co., and in 1871 to Kerr, Cook & Co., in 1879 to Kerr, Weitzel & Co. During all these changes, the subject of this sketch retained his interest in the firm, being most of the time on the road, selling or collecting for the firm. October 25, 1857, he was married to Eliza Beaverson of Wrightsville, and has twelve children, seven of whom are living: Kate, Sarah B., Gertrude, Matilda G., Eliza B., Harry B. and Sewell. Mr. Kerr and family belong to the Presbyterian Church. Although living all his life in York County, he has never been drawn as a juror, nor had he ever been in court as a witness in any case. About half his time is spent in traveling, in the interest of the firm. His father died in 1859, aged sixty-eight years.

JACOB KLINE was born in Lower Windsor Township, May 6, 1842. His parents were Henry and Eliza (Flury) Kline of York County, and of German descent. They had nine children, of whom Jacob is the fifth. He remained on the farm until twenty-two years of age, receiving his education at the public schools. When twenty-six years of age he began the business of cigar-making at Wrightsville, which he followed for a number of years. In 1873, in company with Henry Keller of Lower Windsor, he began the manufacture of cigars at Wrightsville, and has followed it since with success. In 1876 he built the large brick building on Hellam Street in Wrightsville, where the firm have their factory. They at first employed about twenty hands in the factory, but now have about fifty-three hands. In 1880 he erected an additional brick building, remodeling the first and raising the whole to a three-story building, in which he opened, in the same year, a general merchandising business They manufactured about 2,500,000 cigars in 1883. He was married at York, in 1867, to Eliza Lebernight, of York County, and has had six children born to him: John Henry (deceased), Martha Jane, William Edward, Howard Smith (deceased), Maggie May (deceased) and Eliza Bertha. Mr. Kline is a member of the I. O. O. F., and with his wife, of the Methodist Church. He was twice member of the Wrightsville Borough council.

SAMUEL R. KOCHER was born in York County, May 18, 1844. His parents were Christian and Mary (Abel) Kocher, of German descent, who had three children, of whom Samuel R. is the eldest. He was brought up on a farm, and educated at the public schools; he followed farming until 1881, although he began other business for himself before he was twenty-one years of age. In 1870, he began a cigar manufactory in Lower Windsor Township, and in 1871 he opened up in Wrightsville, but continued the country factory until 1879, In 1878, he erected the building which he has since occupied at Wrightsville. He is also engaged in

BIOGRAPHICAL SKETCHES.

packing tobacco and is considered the largest dealer in the leaf in the county. He packs about 1,000 cases of tobacco, and manufactures from 4,000,000 to 5,000,000 cigars annually, employing about 100 hands. He was married May 26, 1864, to Susan, daughter of Daniel and Anna (Sherick) Lefer, of Lower Windsor Township, and has three children; Emma D., Samuel C. and Annie M. Mr. Kocher was the originator of the Wrightsville & Chanceford Turnpike Company, of which he was the first president, and still holds that office. He owns about fifty acres of land about three miles below Wrightsville, and two shad fisheries, and also has one-half interest in 345 acres of choice land in Orange County, Fla., containing a grove of 200 bearing orange trees, and within convenient railroad facilities. He is treasurer of the Riverside Lodge of Masons, and a member of S. of T., and was a judge of elections and assessor, and is altogether a prominent and active business man. Mr. Kocher's grandfather, George Kocher, came from Wurtemberg in 1817, bringing with him his brother John and sister Rosana, and, arriving at Philadelphia, he moved to Peckway Creek, Lancaster County, where he lived several years, when he moved to Hellam Township, York County, (near Stoner's Station). He lived several years in Hellam, when he again moved to Lower Windsor Township, on the road leading from Wrightsville to Margaretta Furnace. Mr. Kocher's father was born at Peckway, Lancaster County, in 1818. Mr. Kocher has three uncles: George, living in Perry County; Emanuel, living near Dayton, Ohio, and Jacob, living in Nebraska. He also has a brother, Henry P., living in Dayton, Ohio; a sister married to Mr. Shultz, is living in Lower Windsor Township. The portrait of Mr. Kocher appears elsewhere as a representative of the tobacco interest of York County.

AARON M. LEHMAN was born in Springfield Township April 3, 1862. He is the second son and third child of a family of eleven children, and was reared and educated in Springfield Township. At twenty years of age he began learning the miller's trade with S. F. Hollinger, and at present is milling vt Strickler's Mill. He was married October 4, a883, to Almira A. Gruver, daughter of Peter Gruler of Paradise Township.

GEORGE E. LOUCKS was born in Spring Garden Township December 10, 1850. His parents were Z. K. Loucks and Sarah Ann (Ebert) Loucks, of York County, of whom he was the fourth child. His youth was spent at farming, and his education was received at York, and one term at the Pennsylvania College at Gettysburgh, at which institution he prepared himself for his profession, but owing to feeble health was obliged to abandon his studies, and until his twenty-eighth year he worked about the farm. In 1878 he was appointed agent of the Pennsylvania Railroad, at Hellam, which position he has held ever since, devoting his whole time and attention to it. He was married in his native township March 7, 1878, to Mary J. S. Myers, daughter of Samuel Myers. Mr. and Mrs. Loucks belong to the Lutheran Church at York, at which place also his father, Zachariah K. Loucks, president of the First National Bank, and one of the wealthiest men of York County, has his residence.

CAPT. FRANK J. MAGEE, justice of the peace, was born at Wrightsville, December 8, 1837, and is the second son of James F. and Rosanna (Hinkle) Magee, of Chester and York Counties respectively, and of Irish and German descent. He received his primary education at the public schools of Wrightsville, and in 1855 he entered Georgetown College (D. C.) and graduated in 1859. Returning to Wrightsville he took charge of all the public schools for two years as principal. November 28, 1861, he entered the military service as second lieutenant of Company I, Seventy-sixth Pennsylvania Volunteer Infantry (Col. Power), and served three years and three months. He was promoted to first lieutenant and captain, and served on the staffs of Gens. Terry, Ferry, Ames and Strong, participating in the battle of Olustee, Fla., the Sumpter campaign, and all battles along the coast, except Beaufort, N. C. At the battle of Cold Harbor, in 1864, he joined the Army of the Potomac, and served with that army until the expiration of his term of service. Returning to Wrightsville, he again took charge of the schools till 1871, when in the fall of that year he was elected to the legislature from York County on the Democratic ticket. On his return he was elected justice of the peace and has held that office since. At present he is regulator of the borough, president of the Wrightsville Hardware Company, director of the Wrightsville Iron Company, has been secretary of the school board for the past nine years, and captain of the "Wrightsville Grays" National Guard since 1872; is commander of Post 270, G. A. R., J. W. of Riverside Lodge, No. 503, A. F. & A. M., and was also editor of the Wrightsville *Star* in 1867–68–69–70. He was married at Wrightsville August 6, 1867, to Martha H. Smith, daughter of R. W. Smith, Esq., and has two children, Robert S. and Helen M.

HENRY MILLER was born in Lower Windsor Township June 10, 1823. His parents were Henry and Magdalena (Smith) Miller, of Lower Windsor Township, who had six children, of whom our subject is the youngest. He was reared and educated in the same township, and at eighteen years of age he began learning the carpenter's trade with his brother, George Miller, with whom he remained two years. He followed his trade for twenty-five years, and then began farming in Lower Windsor Township, which he continued four years, and then commenced building panel fences, at which he is still engaged. In 1888 he came to Hellam Township and purchased a small farm, and engaged in the manufacture of cigars, a business he had previously conducted in connection with his other enterprises, having now an experience therein of about twenty years. His present output is about 300,000 per year. He was married to Catherine Dellinger, and has had five children, three of whom are living. He and family are members of the Lutheran Church.

WILLIAM H. MILLER was born in Windsor township April 18, 1838. His parents were Peter and Magdalena (Deckman) Miller, and his grandparents Peter and Mary (Murphy) Miller. His great-grandparents came to York County during the Revolution. He is the eldest son and fourth child in a family of seven children, and was educated in the public schools of his neighborhood, York County Academy, and an academy in Lower Chanceford. For fourteen terms he taught school in Lower Windsor Township, after which he followed the Tide Water Canal for four years. In 1865 he began farming in Lower Windsor Township and continued for seven years. He was married January 21, 1864, to Leah Stine, daughter of Valentine and Sarah Stine, of York County, and has had born to him eight children: Minnie, Preston H., Arthur C., Olivia (deceased), Persifer O. (deceased), Jennie, Winfield S. H. and Addie. In the spring of 1875 he removed to Wrightsville, where he was engaged in auctioneering for two years; he then removed to Hellam Township where he at present resides, dealing in sewing machines, agricultural implements, fertilizers, and is also engaged in auctioneering and fire insurance business.

AMBROSE MILLER, son of George and Susan Miller of Lower Windsor Township, was born February 19, 1860, and passed his boyhood on the farm, attending school during the winters. From the age of eighteen years until his majority, he served an apprenticeship at blacksmithing with Henry S. Heindle of Hellam Township. In 1881, he came to the village and worked for a year for James Ray, whom he then bought out, and is now receiving an encouraging patronage in custom work.

JOHN W. MINNICH, was born in Wrightsville, Penn., January 16, 1849. His parents were Michael and Anna (Upp) Minnich, of York County, and of German nationality. They had four children, of whom John W. is the second. He spent his youth mostly at school, and at seventeen years of age he entered Pennsylvania College at Gettysburgh, where he remained about two years studying for the ministry, which he afterward abandoned. In 1868 he went West as a carpenter, stopping two years at Pittsburgh, Penn. He drifted as far west as Atchison, Kas., where he remained nine months; he also was eighteen months at Caledonia, Ohio. On his return from the West, he again remained two years at Pittsburgh, as assistant foreman in a door and sash factory. In the winter of 1874, he returned to Wrightsville, and engaged in the undertaking and carpentering business, which he followed until 1882, when he added the furniture business. Retiring, however, from the furniture business in February, 1884, he in company with R. W. Weller, purchased the Wrightsville Builders' Mill, and from April, 1884, has carried on that business. He is also interested in the Wrightsville Hardware Company, and was one of its organizers. February 12, 1874, he was married at Abingdon, Md., to Emma McComas, who bore him one child (Anna), and died March 7, 1876, aged twenty-three years. Mr. Minnich is a member of the Lutheran Church, and of the Masonic order, and has served as school director three years, and borough assessor for two years.

SAMUEL M. MYERS, was born in West Hempfield Township, Lancaster Co., Penn., December 25, 1835. He was the fourth of the twelve children of Jacob and Magdalena (Myers) Myers, of Lancaster County, where he was brought up, receiving a good common school education. At twelve years of age he began to work on the farm of Andrew Brubaker, and remained with him six years, after which he began to learn painting with Samuel Coffman, which he continued for about one year. October 8, 1856, he was married to Fannie Kuhns, daughter of Jacob Kuhns of West Hempfield Township, and was blessed with a family of four boys and five girls—two boys and two girls still living. After his marriage he worked three years for John Bowers of Lancaster County. On the 5th of August, 1864, he enlisted in Company A, Two Hundred and Third Pennsylvania Volunteers, under Capt. J. B. Bauchman, and took part in the engagements at New Market road, Virginia, and at Fort Fisher, N. C. He was honorably discharged in June, 1865, and returned to Lancaster County, where he was engaged in farming and tobacco raising until March, 1881, when he removed to York County, and is at present engaged in farming and fruit raising. Mr. Myers is a member of the Osceola Tribe, No. 11, of R., M., of Columbia, Lancaster County, is a member of Post 122. G. A. R., and was at one time constable of West Hempfield Township.

GEORGE A. REBMAN, M. D., was born in West Manchester Township, York County, July 6, 1852. His parents were Jacob and Catherine (Heindle) Rebman, of Pennsylvania, and of German and English descent, respectively. He was brought up on a farm, and educated at the public schools and at the York County Academy. After leaving school he taught in public schools till about twenty-two years of age, when he entered the office of Dr. Hay, at York, and began to read medicine, which he continued for something over a year. He then entered the University of Maryland, at Baltimore, and graduated in 1876, with the degree of M. D. In May, of the same year, he located at Wrightsville, where he has since practiced his profession with great success. He was married January 13, 1880, at Wrightsville, to Ella K. Detwiler, daughter of David Detwiler, and has two children—David and one unnamed. The Doctor is very much attached to his profession, has acquired a lucrative practice, is a prominent member of the Lutheran Church, and is the owner of a magnificent home property in Wrightsville.

S. L. REISINGER was born in Hellam Township. November 24, 1852. His parents were Samuel and Elizabeth (Smith) Reisinger, of York County, who had seven children, of whom S. L. was the second son. He received his education at the common schools, and, in 1876, began learning the trade of cigar maker in Hellam Township, which occupation he has followed since. November 4, 1880, he was married to Arabella R. Upp, daughter of Jacob and

BIOGRAPHICAL SKETCHES.   81

Mary Upp, of Wrightsville, and has two children: Elsie B. and May E. Mrs. Reisinger is a member of the Methodist Episcopal Church.

LUTHER L. REWALT, M. D., was born in Middletown, Penn., December 25, 1839. His parents were William and Catherine (McKinley) Rewalt, of Pennsylvania, and of German and Scotch-Irish descent, respectively. They had only this one son and one daughter. Until the age of ten Luther L. attended the public schools, and the following five years at Eman's Institute at Middletown. At the age of fifteen he entered the preparatory school at Litiz Academy, where he remained four years. He then began reading medicine at Halifax, Penn., with Dr. Wright, and then read with Dr. Filbert, at Columbia. At the age of twenty he entered the medical department of the University of Pennsylvania, at Philadelphia, from which institution he graduated in March, 1861, with the degree of M. D. At the outbreak of the Rebellion he received the first surgeon's commission issued by Gov. Curtin, and was assigned to the Twenty-fifth Pennsylvania Volunteer Infantry, a three months' regiment, and served until the end of his term. Returning to Wrightsville he practiced medicine until August, 1864, when he was appointed acting assistant surgeon, United States army, by Dr. John Campbell, United States army surgeon at Philadelphia, which position he held but a few months. Returning to Wrightsville he resumed the practice of his profession until January 27, 1865, when he entered the Twenty-first Pennsylvania Volunteer Cavalry, as assistant surgeon, and remained to the end of the war. He again returned to Wrightsville, where he has since located, practicing his profession, except one year, which he spent in Philadelphia. He was married April 6, 1863, to Mary Jane Magee, daughter of James F. Magee (deceased), of Wrightsville, and had five children: James W. Mary F., Annie M., William H. (deceased), and Francis J. The family are members of the Methodist Episcopal Church. The Doctor is surgeon of the G. A. R. Post, at Wrightsville, and a past member of the school board. He is a man of fine scholastic attainments, and devotedly attached to his profession, and is respected by all.

REV. L. K. SECRIST, eldest son of William and Salome Secrist, was born in Conewago Township, York County, February 6, 1829. When he was five years old his parents moved to Warrington Township, same county. There he worked on the farm, until preparation for the gospel ministry occupied his time and attention. One year was passed in study with Rev. James M. Harkey, pastor of the Lutheran Church at Rossville, four years in Pennsylvania College, Gettysburgh, and one year in the study of theology with Rev. D. Sell, at Berrysburgh, Dauphin Co., Penn. He entered the ministry in 1855, and up to the present served the following charges: Fisherville, Dauphin County; Salona, Clinton County; Boalsburg, Centre County; Blain, Perry County; Wrightsville and Kreutz Creek, York County—the last since 1872. He was united in marriage with Miss Catherine, daughter of David Hobaugh, September 4, 1856. Death having severed the sacred bond, he married Miss Mary J., daughter of William Howard, May 27, 1862. Of ten children, four sons—Arthur H., Maurice B., Mason E. Orville K.—are living.

GEORGE K. SCHENBERGER was born in Clark County, Ohio, September 3, 1841. His parents were Samuel and Sarah (Kauffelt) Schenberger, of German descent. Their ancestry were among the first settlers of the "Canadochley" Valley, and his parents emigrated to Ohio, probably in 1839. George K. is the eldest of three sons, and spent his younger days on the farm, but at the age of ten years came to Wrightsville, where he entered the public schools, having left Ohio when five or six years old. In August, 1862, he enlisted in Harrisburg in Company B, One Hundred and Thirtieth Pennsylvania Volunteer Infantry, and served nine months. He was promoted to orderly sergeant, and participated with the Army of the Potomac in the battles of Antietam, Fredericksburg and Chancellorsville. In the last named he was wounded (May 3, 1863), being shot through the shoulder. Returning, he entered the Columbia Bank at Columbia in 1864 for three months, but in 1865 engaged as clerk in the First National Bank at Wrightsville, and in 1873 was elected cashier, which position he still holds. In politics he is a Republican.

CALVIN G. SMITH was born at Wrightsville November 27, 1839. His parents were Robert W. and Martha (Herr) Smith, of Pennsylvania, and of German descent. They had eight children, five sons and three daughters, of whom Calvin G. is the fourth. He was brought up in Wrightsville and finished his schooling before he was fourteen years of age. He then spent one year in a store at Wrightsville and one in an iron foundry. At the age of sixteen he entered the office of the *York County Star* at Wrightsville, which paper was started, owned and edited by his father. He there learned the printing trade, and followed it a few years In 1861, in company with W. S. Boyd, he engaged in the mercantile business, in which he retained an interest for about three years. During the war he served a term in the army, and after the war he, in company with Capt. Magee, bought out the *Star* and ran it a few years, selling out to his partner and engaging in the coal business in 1872 at Wrightsville. He was one of the incorporators of the Wrightsville & Chanceford Turnpike Company and the Wrightsville Cemetery Association, and is secretary of the former and secretary and treasurer of the latter. In December, 1869, he was married, in York, to S. Anna Kauffelt, daughter of Henry Kauffelt, Esq., and has four children: Henry K., Robert Grier, Amy Lanius and Paul. He and wife belong to the Presbyterian Church. In 1874 Mr. Smith was appointed bank assessor by State Treasurer Mackey.

THE STONER FAMILY. Henry Stoner (deceased) was born in Hellam Township, in December, 1800. His father was Christian Stoner, and his grandfather was also Christian Stoner, who settled on a tract of 177¼ acres in 1761, which has since been the Stoner homestead. He attended the subscription schools of his neighborhood, and was married to Anna Strickler. They had ten children: Mary, Sarah, Henry, Samuel, Jacob, Annie, John, Eliza, Rudolph and Emanuel. His occupation was that of a farmer, which he followed until his death, from paralysis, March, 1872. He was a member of the Dunkard Church. Henry Stoner was born November 30, 1830, and educated at the common schools. He served as a school director for two years. November 3, 1857 he was married to Sarah Farhinger, daughter of David and Christiana Farhinger, of York County, and had eight children, six of whom are living. John Stoner was born August 7, 1838, and educated in the common schools. He always took a lively interest in education, and served in the school board in Hellam Township for some time. Emanuel Stoner was born June 23, 1843, received a good common school education, and later attended the normal school at Millersville for one session. David Stoner was born in Hellam Township and was the youngest son of Christian and Mary (Herr) Stoner, pioneers of York County. He was educated in Hellam Township, and engaged in farming.

JOHN STONER, Sr., was born in Hellam Township, December 1, 1820. His parents were John and Magdalena (Strickler) Stoner, of York County, and of German descent. They had eight children, all

6

of whom died except our subject, and a brother. His life was spent at farming and milling, and his education was received at the township schools. In 1842 he was married at Lancaster, Penn., to Sarah Landes, daughter of Samuel Landes, of York County, and has had born to him six children: Anna, Mary, Henry L., John, Jr., Samuel and Malinda. The family belong to the Dunkard Church. Mr. Stoner has twice been supervisor of Hellam Township and once assessor.

JOHN STONER, JR., son of John and Sarah Stoner, was born March 30, 1849, was reared a farmer, and was educated in the public schools. For several years he assisted in his father's mill, and in the spring of 1873 took charge of the home farm. In the fall of 1877 he bought his present property of sixty acres at Stoner's Station, on which he has a fine dwelling, a large barn, four tenements, a blacksmith shop, and a two-story stone warehouse 30x60 feet, the property costing him about $16,- 000 at public sale. He deals largely in grain, flour, feed stuff, coal, lime, etc., and leaf tobacco. October 17, 1872, he married Sarah E., daughter of Daniel and Sarah Smyser. The result of this union has been three children: Harry S., Margie E. and Howard S.

JACOB STRICKLER was born January 6, 1811. His parents were John and Catharine (Garver) Strickler, of Hellam Township. He was reared on the farm in Hellam Township, is the eldest son, and was educated at subscription schools. He was married to Elizabeth Dietz, daughter of George Dietz, of York County, and had three children: Alfred (living), Ellen (deceased) and Anna (deceased). The farm on which he resides contains 190 acres of well improved land.

BENJAMIN STRICKLER was born in Hellam Township, in December, 1821. His parents were Benjamin and Mary (Freet) Strickler, and had three sons and five daughters, of whom Benjamin, Jr., is the eldest now living. He was brought up on a farm and educated at the common schools. At the age of twenty-three he began life for himself. In 1854 he was married, in Hellam Township, to Elnora Bahn, who has borne him six children, one of whom, Albert W., died at the age of twenty-four years, the living are Byron B., Edward M., Elmer D., Mary E., and Flora R. Mr. Strickler owns a fine farm of 126 acres; and has held various Township offices, such as assessor of the township, judge of elections, inspector, and school director several terms. Mr. Strickler is a member of the Reformed Church. Mr. Strickler's ancestors were among the first persons to obtain permits from Samuel Blunston, agent of the Penns, to settle on this side of the Susquehanna River. They settled in Kruetz Creek Valley as early as 1782, and were in the valley when Capt. Cressap and his band of Marylanders encroached upon the right of the Pennsylvania settlers. The father of Mr. Strickler died in 1866, aged seventy-one years; the mother died in 1876, aged seventy-seven years.

MILTON SULTZBACH was born in Hellam Township, December 26, 1839. His parents were Frederick and Lydia (Gibson) Sultzbach, of Hellam Township, and Cumberland County, and of German and Scotch descent, respectively. They had eleven children, of whom they reared eight. Milton was the third child. He was educated at the public school and has worked all his life at farming, and in a tan yard. At the age of twenty-five he began business for himself. His father died August 17, 1863, aged forty-nine years, but his mother is still living and is now sixty-three years old. Mr. Sultzbach belongs to an old family of pioneers, and is now residing on the same homstead, which had been in the family for many years, and always was handed down from father to son, as was the present tannery, of which Milton took charge in 1864, and which was established by his grandfather. Mr. Sultzbach is a prominent member of the Masonic order and is universally respected.

JOHN A. THOMSON, M. D., was born in Franklin County, Penn., November 3, 1823. His parents were Alexander J. and Margaret M. (Kerr) Thomson, and of Scotch descent. They had a family of five sons and four daughters, one daughter, only, being older than the subject of this sketch, who was educated a Fayetteville Academy, spending part of his time clerking in a store, farming and teaching the high school at Fayetteville. While engaged in teaching he devoted some of his time to reading medicine, and in 1849 entered Jefferson Medical College, at Philadelphia, from which he graduated in 1852, and at once began the practice of medicine at Wrightsville, where he has since been, and holds a high rank in his profession. He was married at Athens, Penn., May, 1855, to Elizabeth Satterlee of Bradford County, Penn., and has one child, John A., who was late resident marine surgeon at Jefferson College, Philadelphia, and is now practicing medicine at Germantown, Penn. Dr. Thomson is at present surgeon for the Pennsylvania Railroad, was chief burgess for two years, for a number of years school director, and one of the directors of the Columbia National Bank. His wife and son are members of the Presbyterian Church. He has always enjoyed a large practice in his profession, and is one of the influential citizens of his town.

JOHN E. WEITZEL was born in Hellam Township February 24, 1828, the only child born to John and Elizabeth (Poff) Weitzel. He was brought up on the farm and educated at the public schools. At seventeen years of age he began learning the blacksmith trade at Wrightsville, and served as apprentice four years. When about twenty-one years old he engaged as foreman in Elwine's brickyard, which position he held until 1859, when he purchased the yard. In 1865 he engaged in the lime burning business in addition to brick-making, and continued until 1882, when he sold the brickyard, but retained and continued the lime burning business in the name of Kerr, Weitzel & Co. In 1850 he was married at York, Penn., to Carrie Elwine, of York, and had eight children, five of whom are living: Henry E., John L., Carrie May, Emma L. and George B. Mr. Weitzel is a very active business man; he is a director of the First National Bank of Wrightsville, president of the Wrightsville Hall Association, and the man who, through his energy, made the latter enterprise a success. He was school director three times, and councilman twice. He also owns a branch lime business in Lancaster County, which he managed from 1865 to 1875. In 1883 he burned and handled about 250,000 bushels of lime. He and wife are members of the Lutheran Church.

WILLIAM WITMAN was born in Dauphin County March 8, 1839. His parents were John and Mary (Koutsman) Witman, of Dauphin County, and of German and English descent. They had twelve children, of whom William W. was the eighth. He was brought up on the farm, and spent ten years of his minority in making bricks. At twenty years of age he learned the trade of wheelwright, at which he worked for two years. He then spent seven years on the Northern Central Railroad as conductor and division foreman. In 1868 he engaged in the dry goods business with Jacob Gohn, at Wrightsville, but dissolved partnership in 1876. In company with a brother he then bought out a mercantile establishment at Wrightsville, which they conducted together two years and a half: his brother then retiring, he has carried on the business by himself since. In 1862 he was married at Chambersburg, Penn., to Kate Deck, daughter of Christian

BIOGRAPHICAL SKETCHES.

Deck, of Chambersburg, Penn., and has had born to him four children, three of whom are living: William F., Ida May and Horace M. Mr. Witman is Past Grand of the Odd Fellows, and he and wife are members of the Lutheran Church, while he is superintendent of same Sabbath-school, and elder in church council.

JOHN WILSON, deceased, was born in 1807 and died in 1860. He was brought up about Wrightsville and Columbia, and educated at Wrightsville. He was railroad contractor in Virginia at the time of his marriage, in 1839, at York, to Sarah Hiestand, daughter of Abraham Hiestand, of York County, and had born to him twelve children, one of whom died in infancy, and two after arriving at age. The living are Mary, John, Stephen, Webster, Frank, Thomas, Tempest, Emma and Sarah. In 1844 he removed to Hellam, where he spent the remainder of his life, dying at the age of fifty-three years. Mr. Wilson was a prosperous farmer, and at his death left his family well provided for. His widow is descended from the pioneer families of York County, and aunt of Gen. A. Hiestand Glatz. Mrs. Wilson herself is a woman of fine accomplishments, rare merits and womanly excellence.

JACOB WELTZHOFFER, son of Henry and Catherine Weltzhoffer, of Wrightsville, was born January 31, 1849, was educated at the public schools, and in 1869 went to learn printing and journalism with Magee & Smith, of the Wrightsville *Star*. In 1874 he joined Mr. W. W. Moore in the publication of the journal named, and six years later sold his interest to his partner, and took a commercial course in the Pierce Business College of Philadelphia. He next acted as book-keeper for Keller & Kline, of Wrightsville, for a year and a half, and in 1883 rebought the *Star*, which he still owns and edits to the entire satisfaction of his subscribers, and the public in general. October 24, 1882, he married Eliza H., daughter of Henry and Sarah A. Harris, of Wrightsville. Mr. and Mrs. Weltzhoffer are members of the Presbyterian Church, in which both sing in the choir, and of which Mr. W. is an elder as well as an active worker in the Sunday-school. Mr. W. has a good publication, with remunerative circulation, is an enterprising, energetic and liberal citizen, and is a stockholder in the Wrightsville & Chanceford Pike.

CARROLL TOWNSHIP.

SAMUEL ALTLAND, son of Philip Altland, of Warrington Township, was born October 28, 1836, and assisted on the home farm until 1854, when he began brick-making, which he followed for nine years, and then for four years engaged in car-building at Hanover, this county. In 1869 he began farming in West Manheim Township, but in 1870 came to near Williams Grove, in this township, and farmed until 1874, when he moved to one-half mile south of Dillsburg, bought from the heirs of John Pentz, and made brick and farmed until 1880, when he was elected sheriff, on which he removed to York County Prison, in order to discharge his official duties. January 24, 1861, he married Lydia, daughter of Peter and Elizabeth Fickes, of Carroll; of the eight children born to this union, two died; Philip Alvin, the eldest, was deputy sheriff under his father the last two years of his term; Jeremiah Henry was turnkey. At the time of his election to the shrievealty, Mr. Altland had served four years as constable, and one term as assessor of Carroll Township. On retiring from the office of sheriff, in which he had been ably assisted by Mrs. Altland as matron, Mr. A. retired to his farm near Dillsburg, but soon sold out and moved to the town and bought a dwelling and livery stable on York Street, and another dwelling and livery stable on Harrisburg Street; he also owns a tract of seventeen acres of woodland in Warrington Township, from which he is clearing the timber; also a tract of six acres in Carroll Township, and a five-acre lot in Dillsburg Borough, on which he has a brick-yard.

ALFRED D. ALTLAND, first of the three children of Daniel A. and Elizabeth Altland, of Mechanicsburg, was born October 16, 1857, and is of German and English descent. From 1872 until 1875 he clerked for J. A. Kauffmann, of Mechanicsburg, and then embarked in business with his father, under the firm name of D. A. Altland & Son. In 1880 he started trade at Lisburn, Cumberland County, but in 1882 removed to Dillsburg, where he now has a large dry goods and grocery store, doing a business of $16,000 per annum. January 8, 1880, he married Mary E., daughter of George and Mary Wilson, of Shepherdstown, Cumberland County, and to this union has been born one child—Lettie—now four years of age.

GEORGE P. ARNOLD, son of Micah and Mary Arnold, of this township, was born June 30, 1826, and is of German descent. He was reared on a farm, but in 1861 entered upon the study of medicine under Dr. Michael Frees, of Mechanicsburg, with whom he remained one year, then attended the New York Home Medical College five months, and also received private instruction at Bellevue Hospital. He became a very successful practitioner, and was particularly so during the epidemic of diphtheria of 1865 and 1870. He carried on farming for ten years in connection with his practice, owning two farms, one of sixty-six acres near Dillsburg, on which he resides, and one of seventy-five acres, three miles distant. In 1850 he married Sarah, daughter of David and Catherine Law, of Franklin Township, and became the father of nine children, six of whom are living—four boys and two girls. Of the boys, two are farmers, one is a carpenter, and one is in business in New York; three are married. The Doctor and his wife are members of the Franklin Lutheran Church. The Doctor is a school director, and is a stockholder in the Dillsburg & Mechanicsburg Railroad, and in the smelting furnace.

W. D. BAILEY, M. D., is a representative physician of York County, and a descendant of celebrated pioneer ancestry. The grandfather of our subject, John Bailey, was of Scotch-Irish descent. His wife was Mary Nelson, of English descent. They were both born in Monaghan Township, where they resided until their deaths. He was a farmer, surveyor, and a worthy citizen. The father of our subject, S. N. Bailey, attained prominent distinction. He was born in Monaghan Township in 1809, reared upon a farm and educated at the common schools. He was a close student and a great reader, which, with high natural ability and keen power of observation, enabled him to acquire a liberal education. Learning surveying in early years, he made it the principal business of his life. About 1835 he came to Carroll Township, locating in Dillsburg, where he resided the remainder of his days. He was engaged in farming for a short period, subsequently devoting his attention to surveying and school teaching. He served several years as county surveyor, and for a number of years was a justice of peace. In 1843 he was elected to represent his district in the State legislature, serving three years with ability and honor. Col. Bailey was also connected with one of the early militia companies from

CARROLL TOWNSHIP.

which he derived his title, and by which he was always called. In 1836 he was married to Miss Margaret Mumper, daughter of John and Jane (Beelman) Mumper, a native of Carroll Township, and also a descendant of a well known and old time family. Three children were born to them: John M., a leading practitioner of law at Huntington, Penn.; D. Bigler, a lawyer of ability (died in York in 1881), and the subject of this sketch. Col. Bailey was a clerk under Adjt.-Gen. Banks, and his successor at Harrisburg for eight years. He entered the service in 1862, and was elected lieutenant-colonel of the Twelfth Pennsylvania Reserves, and was in service nearly one year when he resigned. Col. Bailey died at Dillsburg in 1872, after a long and useful career. His widow resides at Dillsburg. W. D. Bailey was born in Dillsburg January 3, 1837. He received a good education, attending the schools of his native town, and also received the advantage of the Tuscarora Academy. After teaching one term he began the study of medicine with Drs. G. L. & J. M. Shearer, of Dillsburg, now deceased. Under their instructions he remained three years, attending in the meantime the University of Pennsylvania, from which he graduated in 1862. He began his practice in York, continuing until the spring of 1863, when he entered the service and was appointed assistant surgeon of the Seventy-eighth Pennsylvania Volunteer Infantry, joining his regiment at Murfreesboro, Tenn. In 1864 he was promoted to surgeon of his regiment, with rank of major. He participated in the battles of Hoover's Gap, Tullahoma, Chickamauga, Buzzard Roost, Dalton, Resaca, New Hope Church, and in various minor engagements. His regiment was under the command of Gens. Thomas, Rosecrans and Sherman, and was a part of the Fourteenth Army Corps. In November, 1864, he was mustered out, his term of service having expired. Upon his return he went to Oil City and resumed his practice, remaining there about one year. In 1866 he returned to Dillsburg, where he has since resided, and established a large and lucrative practice. Dr. Bailey has always identified himself with all measures of public improvement, is liberal and honorable in all of his relations of life, keeps well abreast with the advancements of the age. In his profession Dr. Bailey takes an honorable pride, and with its progress is well conversant. He is a member of the York County Medical Society, of the State Medical Society, and a member of the York Lodge, No. 266, A. F. & A. M. He has served in various offices in his township, and is one of the honored citizens of York County. Dr. Bailey was married, in 1879, to Miss Josephine F. Logan, daughter of Col. Henry Logan, of Carroll Township. This union has been blessed with two children: William B., deceased, and Martha L. The family have always been connected with the Presbyterian Church.

SAMUEL NELSON BAILEY, son of Daniel Bailey (deceased) was born in this township, June 14, 1840, was reared on a farm and received a good education, including three years' instruction at Tuscarora Academy. On his return from the latter he assisted in filling up the quota for the draft sent to Harrisburg by the township. In 1866 he married Mary Ann, daughter of Jacob Urich, of Cumberland County, and went to housekeeping on the old homestead of 135 acres; this land he purchased in 1869, and still resides thereon, with his wife and two children: Logan W. and Frank E. In 1876 he embarked in the grain, coal and phosphate trade in partnership with his brother, M. J. Bailey. Our subject has served two years as auditor, and in the spring of 1882 was elected justice of the peace.

MUMPER JOHN BAILEY, son of Daniel Bailey (deceased), of this township, was born January 31, 1844. He was educated in the schools of the neighborhood, and at Academia, Juniata County, and from 1864 until 1868, taught school in Franklin Township, this county, Hampden Township, Cumberland County, on the eastern shore of Maryland, and again in this township. From 1871 to 1875 he was engaged in mercantile business in Dillsburg, under the firm name of Spahr & Bailey, carrying a stock valued at $10,000; in 1876, in partnership with his brother, under the firm name of S. N. Bailey & Bro., he entered the commission and grain business and dealing in phosphates, at the corner of Church and Second Streets, opposite the depot, and is doing a thriving trade. December 23, 1880, he married Matilda M., daughter of Philip Zeigler, of Monroe Township, Cumberland County. Mr. Bailey has served as school director, and as clerk of the town council, and is a stockholder in the Dillsburg & Mechanicsburg Railroad Company.

P. D. BAKER, M. D., was born in Carroll Township November 19, 1848, and is a son of Daniel and Margaret (Lehmer) Baker. Great-great-grandfather Baker was a native of Germany, and great-grandfather Daniel Baker a native of Paradise Township, this county. Grandfather Daniel Baker was also born in Paradise Township in 1792; was a weaver and died in 1853. The father of our subject is also a weaver, and followed his trade in Paradise Township until 1842, when he came to Carroll Township, where he is engaged in farming. Dr. P. D. Baker was reared on the farm until sixteen years of age; he then attended the normal school at Dillsburg, and the York County Normal School and the York County Academy, and subsequently taught in the common schools and in the academy a number of terms. In 1870 he began the study of medicine under Drs. G. L. & J. M. Shearer, of Dillsburg, and during the sessions of 1872-73-74 attended lectures at the University of Pennsylvania at Philadelphia, graduating in the spring of 1874, since when he has been in constant practice in this township. To the Doctor's marriage with Miss Kate Kershey, of Washington Township, in 1874, two children have been born: Daniel T. and Maggie J.

DANIEL W. BEITZEL, son of William Beitzel, of Warrington Township, was born June 20, 1848, and was reared on the farm, attending school in the winter. In 1869 he studied at the York County Normal School, and in 1870 at the York County Academy. He had taught, however, in Washington Township in 1868, and during the winters from 1869 to 1873 taught in Warrington Township. He began his business career in 1872 by clerking for Emig & Bahn, at New Freedom. In the spring of 1874 he was elected teller of the Dillsburg Bank, filled the position four years, and in February, 1878, engaged in the dry goods business in partnership with J. B. Metzger. Four years later Mr. Metzger sold his interest to Michael Bender, and the firm of Beitzel & Bender now carry a stock worth about $14,000. January 17, 1883, Mr. Beitzel married Jennie E., daughter of Matthew Porter, of Carroll Township. Mr. and Mrs. Beitzel have been members of the Presbyterian Church since 1877. Of this church Mr. B. is at present a trustee, and he has been treasurer of the Sunday-school since 1878. He was made chief Burgess of Dillsburg in 1876, and borough treasurer in 1881. In the spring of 1882 he was elected justice of the peace. He is a member of M. W. Sackett Lodge, No. 89, Dillsburg, and of Central Lodge, No. 19, Harrisburg, and is a charter member of the Pennsylvania Marble, Mining & Manufacturing Company of Dillsburg.

WILLIAM B. BEITZEL, son of William and Leah Beitzel, of Warrington Township, was born October 14, 1851, and is of German descent. He was reared a farmer, and received his earlier education at the public schools. In 1873 he attended the normal school at Shippensburg, and in 1874 the National Normal School at Lebanon, Ohio, graduating in the business department of the latter institution in the same year. He taught two terms of school in York Township, two in Warrington, two in Upper Allen, Cumberland County, one in Warren County, Ohio, and one term in this township. From January 15, 1878, to May 18, 1880, he was editor of the Dillsburg *Bulletin*. In June, 1880, he became a clerk in the office of the Cumberland Valley Railroad Company at Dillsburg; January 1, 1882, he became agent for that company and for the Adams Express Company. He received an appointment as notary public from Gov. Hoyt in November, 1881, and was reappointed in 1884 by Gov. Pattison. Since 1876 he has been a member of the United Brethren Church.

JACOB S. BENTZ, son of Jacob L. and Elizabeth Bentz, of Warrington Township, was born April 28, 1836, and is of German descent. He attended school and assisted on the home farm until 1854, and then served an apprenticeship of two years at carpentering with his uncle, Andrew Bentz; he next worked a year with Henry Arnold, and then started business for himself, employing five or six hands, for about four years. For some time thereafter he farmed on the old homestead; in 1869 he bought a farm of 107 acres near Dillsburg, of Henry Arnold, on which he built a large barn and other out-buildings, and removed and enlarged the dwelling. Mr. Bentz has had born to him four children, of whom two sons, one a farmer, the other a merchant, are still living. With his wife he is a member of the Lutheran Church at the Barrens. He has served as supervisor, school director and auditor, and three years ago was elected county commissioner.

CHRISTIAN BOWMAN, son of John and Martha Bowman, of East Lampeter Township, Lancaster County, was born July 26, 1811, and was brought to Monaghan Township, this county, at the age of four years, in 1815. He was reared on the home farm until 1832, when he learned the cooper's trade, at which he worked eleven years. In 1843 he began farming in Monaghan Township on Jacob Coover's place, remained two years and then bought 125 acres near Filey's Church, on which he lived until 1869, when he came to Carroll Township and bought a thirty-five-acre tract, on which he erected a new dwelling, in which he now resides. In 1834 he married Susan, daughter of Jacob and Elizabeth Coover, of Monaghan Township. This lady died in April, 1852, having borne her husband twelve children, of whom six—twin girls and four boys—still survive. In 1858 Mr. Bowman married Margaret, daughter of Frederick and Margaret Asper, and to this union was born one son—Frederick—who died at the age of twenty months and eight days. Mr. and Mrs. Bowman are members of the Union Reformed Church at Filey's. Mr. B. is a large stockholder in the Harrisburg & Potomac Railroad

JOHN COOK, son of John and Hannah Cook, of this township, was born August 18, 1813, and is of Welsh descent. He was reared a farmer and remained with his father thirty-one years after he attained his majority; but on the 24th of April, 1849, married Lydia M., daughter of John and Lydia Walker, of Warrington Township. For many years Mr. Cook drove a team during the winter to Baltimore, Chambersburg, Lancaster, Harrisburg and Carlisle. At the death of his father he bought the homestead of 100 acres, of which eighty-five are under cultivation and fifteen in timber, and in 1869 erected a fine barn. He still resides on the place. Mrs. Lydia Cook died March 3, 1873, the mother of four children, viz.: Eliza Ann, married to A. B. Shearer; William Ramsey, married to Mary M. Herges, and superintendent of the home farm; Fanny N., at home; and Ruth Emma, a school teacher. The family are members of the Warrington Friends' Meeting.

GEORGE W. COOK, son of Hezekiah Cook, of Warrington Township, was born June 30, 1862, and was reared on the home farm, had his winters being devoted to the district school, and also to a select school at Franklintown. In September, 1880, he went to Poughkeepsie, N. Y., where he passed eleven weeks at Eastman's Business College. On his return he was appointed teller of the Dillsburg National Bank, and a few years later was elected cashier, which position he still holds. March 23, 1882, he married Nannie M., daughter of William Beitzel, of Warrington Township, and the union has been blessed with two children: May and Ralph. Mrs. Cook is a consistent member of the United Brethren Church at Mt. Zion.

JOHN FLEMING was born January 12, 1835, and is the second of the five children of Abraham and Susanna Fleming, of this township. He passed his boyhood in attending school in winter and assisting on the farm in summer. His mother died in 1862, and his father in 1873. In 1864 he assumed charge of the homestead, which comprises 123 acres, and contains a good house and barn, and is now the property of his two sisters and himself. In 1862 he married Catherine, daughter of Jonas Huntsberger, of Monaghan Township. Five children were born to this union; of these, three are living: Abraham Huntsberger, Arthur Eugene and John Newton Patterson. They have also one adopted daughter, Minnie Dehia, aged about eighteen. Mr. and Mrs. Fleming have been members of the Church of God at Mt. Pleasant since 1861.

JOHN B. FIRESTONE, son of Aaron Firestone, of this township, was born October 20, 1851, and passed his boyhood on the farm and in attending school. In his twenty-second year he began attending the York County Normal School, which he attended two terms. He also taught school the winter of 1875-76 in Dover Township, and the following year he taught in this township. In 1881 he took charge of the primary school at Dillsburg, and the following year was promoted to the charge of the grammar school, which he taught two terms, and was then re-elected, but declined to accept the position of teller in the Dillsburg National Bank. Prof. Firestone has been a member of the United Brethren Church at Beavertown since 1877.

J. O. HOFFMAN, M. D., was born in York County, August 21, 1854, and until 1871 assisted on the home farm and attended the district school. From 1871 to 1872 he attended select schools, and taught alternately; from 1872 to 1873 he worked in his father's mill; from the summer of 1873 to the summer of 1875 he attended various seminaries and taught school, working the ensuing winter in the mill; from the summer of 1876 to 1880, he was a student in the Millersville State Normal School, teaching at various points in the meantime. In the spring of 1880 he began reading medicine under Dr. J. H. Marsden, of York Springs, author of Marsden's "Midwifery," editor of the obstetrical department of the *Homœopathic Observer*, and an authority in obstetrics. From 1880 to 1883 our subject attended three courses of medical lectures of nine months each, and during the last two years was assistant in the homœopathic hospital of the university. June 28, 1883, he was graduated with the degree of M. D. from the University of Michigan, and in October following located at Dillsburg, where he has established a satisfactory practice and makes a specialty of eye and ear treatment. September 25, 1884, he married Miss Kate Klugh, of Dillsburg.

JOHN KUNTZ, son of John and Susanah (Harbold) Kuntz, was born in Adams County in

CARROLL TOWNSHIP.

1835, and is of German descent. At the age of fifteen he began the carpenter's trade with Jacob Haybarger, serving three years. He then began business for himself and has since followed the trade in connection with farming and lime-burning, and for twenty-three years he has kept eighteen men in his employ. His farm comprises forty acres under cultivation and ten acres in timber. He has been largely interested in the copper business, and has traveled through New Jersey, New York, West Virginia, Virginia, Ohio, Indiana, Illinois, Iowa, Minnesota, Wisconsin and Michigan, inspecting ore. He was also one of the organizers of the Dillsburg Copper, Lead & Iron Company, of which at present he is director. In 1858 he married Anna M., daughter of Barnet M. Myers, of Franklin Township, and to this union two children have been born: Lewis Carroll and Susannah E. (deceased). Mr. and Mrs. Kuntz are members of the Evangelical church. He was one of the principal men connected with the building of the church in Beavertown, and in 1881 was elected local minister.

A. J. LEHMER is the son of Cornelius and Eve (Koch) Lehmer, and was born in Carroll Township March 23, 1863. His great grandfather, John Lehmer, was born in Adams County, Penn., in 1725, and by occupation was a miller. Philip Lehmer, subject's grandfather, settled in Washington Township at an early day, and was the owner of several large tracts of land in Washington, Carroll and Franklin Townships; he was married to Margaret Bushey, and with his wife was a member of the Lutheran Church. Peter Koch, the maternal grandfather of A. J. Lehmer, was a native of Perry County, Penn.; his ancestors were early settlers in New York State, whence they came to Perry County, from which county Peter removed, when a young man, to Warrington Township, this county, and engaged in farming; he married Eve, daughter of John Smith, of Washington Township. Cornelius Lehmer followed farming in Carroll Township until 1882, when he retired from the active duties of his calling; with his wife he is a member of the Lutheran Church. A. J. Lehmer was reared a farmer, received a liberal education at the common schools, and at the age of eighteen became a school teacher in Dover Township. In the spring of 1882 he entered the Normal School at Kutztown, Berks County, and the following winter resumed teaching in Carroll Township. In the summer of 1883 he attended Coleman's Business College, Newark, N. J. In the winter of 1883-84 he taught the grammar school in Lewisberry, York County. In 1884-85 he was connected with the York County Historical Society.

COL. HENRY LOGAN (deceased) was born near Dillsburg, York County, Penn., April 14, 1784. His father, Henry, and his grandfather, John Logan, immigrated to this country from Coot Hill, Monaghan County, Ireland, in 1749, and settled in Cumberland Valley, and afterward patented a tract of land called Logania, in York County, which is still in possession of their descendants. Henry's first public act was to volunteer as a private in the war of 1812 for the defense of Baltimore. After the close of the war he was chosen captain of the Tenth Company, Ninetieth Regiment, Second Brigade, Fifth Division of Pennsylvania Militia, composed of men from York and Adams Counties, August 1, 1814, he was commissioned by Gov. Simon Snyder, lieutenant-colonel in the same regiment for seven years. He represented York County in the State assembly of 1818 and 1819, and in the State senate from 1828 to 1831. In 1834 he was elected a member of the Twenty-fourth Congress, and re-elected by an increased majority to the Twenty-fifth Congress in 1836. He was in Washington during the exciting times of Jackson's second administration, of whom he was a great admirer and personal friend. About 1840 he was elected a county commissioner, and during his term of office succeeded in clearing the county of its large indebtedness, and was perhaps the last commissioner who saw the county entirely free of debt. Col. Logan was a strong Democrat. He was the leader of his party in the county, and it was largely owing to his influence that the Democrats attained the supremacy in the county which they have ever since held. He lived in a better political era than the present, and often said that although he had been so frequently honored by his fellow-citizens, he had never asked a man to go as a delegate or vote for him. He was a self-made man; had few opportunities of receiving a school education, but was a constant reader and a good writer. When a young man he organized a debating society, to which he afterward attributed much of his success. He was a man of sound judgment and good common sense, and of remarkable general intelligence. When he once made up his mind nothing could shake his purpose or his conviction. His counsels were sought by his acquaintances, and his advice was of great value to his neighbors. For many years he was a director of the Carlisle Deposit Bank, and of the Allen & East Pennsboro Mutual Fire Insurance Company. He took a deep interest in the common schools and served frequently as school director. He was also an ardent advocate of the American Colonization Society. Col. Logan was a man of strong physical constitution, standing six feet tall, and of commanding appearance. He was an early riser, hard worker and knew no fear. A man of plain tastes, of frugal habits, but indomitable will, energy and perseverance, he succeeded in acquiring a comfortable fortune, owning at the time of his death over 700 acres of land. His marriage with Martha O'hail occurred February 22, 1825. She was born January 29, 1800, and was also of Irish descent. Her ancestors were early settlers of the northern portion of the county. They had eleven children, seven of whom survive them. She was a woman of great force of character, of sincere piety, and for many years a patient sufferer. Her death occurred January 28, 1866. Col. Logan died December 20, 1866. Both were members of the Presbyterian Church, and regretted by all who knew them. The children are as follows: Jane (now the widow of William M. Beetem, for many years cashier of the Carlisle Deposit Bank), James J. (a farmer of Carroll Township), Mary A. (wife of Abram Williams, a prominent farmer of Cumberland County), Martha W., Josephine F. (wife of W. D. Bailey, M. D., of Dillsburg), Rev. William Henry Logan (pastor of the Presbyterian Church of Millerstown, Penn.) and John N.

JOHN N. LOGAN was born April 17, 1846, in Carroll Township, York Co., Penn. He received his education by commencing in the common schools of his native township, and preparing for college at the Tuscarora Academy, then under the care of Dr. J. H. Shumaker. His sophomore year was spent in Dickinson College, Carlisle, Penn., from which he entered the junior class of Princeton College in 1867, and graduated from that institution in 1869. He returned to his farm and spent two years farming, during which time he became prominently identified with the railroad enterprises then projected through the northern part of the county, and was one of the most influential men in the building of both the Harrisburg & Potomac and the Dillsburg & Mechanicsburg Railroads. He began the study of law in 1872, but gave it up to accept the cashiership of the Dillsburg Bank, which was organized in 1873, and changed into a National Bank in 1878. Mr. Logan remained in this responsible position till 1884, having served

BIOGRAPHICAL SKETCHES. 87

eleven years as cashier of the two institutions, and left the bank in a most flourishing condition. Mr. Logan is also engaged in mining, and has been one of the most successful men in the iron ore business in the upper end of the county. He owns one of the finest magnetic ore mines in the State. His mine has been worked for eleven years, and large quantities of ore taken from it, and it is supposed to be practically inexhaustible. Mr. Logan has also been largely interested in the promotion of the leading industries in the upper end of the county. He was justice of the peace for ten years. He has always been an ardent supporter of advanced education, and is at this time president of the Chautauqua Literary and Scientific Circle of Dillsburg, Penn. He has also been active in social and moral interests; was president of the Upper District Sabbath School Association during 1872–73, and corresponding secretary for many years. He is an elder in the Presbyterian Church of Dillsburg, Penn., and has been superintendent of the Sabbath-school for ten years. He was married, November 26, 1874, to Miss Ella May Coover. They have four children living: James J. Logan, Jr., Frederic Welty Logan, Helen Martha Logan and Caroline E. Logan.

ALEX B. METZLER, son of Henry and Catherine Metzler, of Dover Township, was born in July, 1845, and is of German descent. After a preliminary education in the public schools, in 1864, he attended at Cottage Hill College, this county. In 1865 and 1866, he clerked for John A. Weiser, and in 1867 for Stine & Harish; the latter year also he entered the shoe trade with his father, and continued until 1876, when he bought his father's interest and continued for himself, in Dover, until 1882, when he came to Dillsburg and bought out Levi Gross, of the Howard House, which he continues to conduct. September 22, 1872, he married Lucinda, daughter of John and Lydia Kunkel, of Mt. Royal. To this marriage have been born four children: Nora K., Lizzie I., Henry A. and Amanda J. Mr. Metzler is a member of the Hanover Lodge, No. 327, I. O. O. F., is a Democrat, and a popular landlord.

CHARLES MILLER, second son of Michael and Eliza Miller, of Windsor Township, was born December 8, 1820, and through his great-grandfather is of German descent. He was reared on the home farm, but at the age of eighteen went into his father's mill, where he worked four years. In 1842 he married Catherine, daughter of Daniel and Elizabeth Kauffman, of Spring Garden Township. In 1845 he moved to Warrington Township, where he owned a saw, grist and clover-mill. In 1850 he bought twenty acres of mill property on this railroad, one-quarter mile from Dillsburg, and carried on sawing and grinding. He has been a member of the Franklin Reformed Church, and has filled the office of deacon and trustee for many years. He has also served as assessor, school director and assistant assessor. He is a stockholder in the Dillsburg & Mechanicsburg Railroad, and also deals largely in grain, coal, plaster and phosphates. He stands six feet three and one-half inches high, and has had born to him seven children, of whom five are living.

MICHAEL B. MUMPER, the fifth of the eleven children of John and Jane Mumper, of Carroll, was born August 20, 1812, and was reared on the home farm. From the age of fourteen until thirty he drove a team to Baltimore, Wheeling, etc., and then engaged in the cattle trade. February 6, 1848, he married Eliza, daughter of Jacob and Elizabeth Coover, of Monaghan Township, and then engaged in farming. Of the two children born to this union Annie only is living. In 1855 Mr. Mumper bought his present farm, and built a good dwelling, barn and tenement. Mr. Mumper has reared four orphan boys, all of whom are doing well. For many years Mr. and Mrs. Mumper have been members of the Presbyterian Church, of which Mr. Mumper has been a trustee for fifteen years.

SAMUEL MUMPER is a son of John and Jennie (Beelman) Mumper, of Monaghan Township, was born March 16, 1825, and grew to manhood on the home farm, attending the district and select schools in his youth. In 1866 he began farming on the old homestead, which he soon after purchased, and remodeled the dwelling and built a new barn, carriage house and other out-buildings. The place comprises 110 acres, all under cultivation. February 7, 1867, he married Mary E., daughter of George and Lizzie King, of Washington Township. To this marriage have been born three daughters: Bertha M., Annie K. and Katie L. Mr. and Mrs. Mumper are members of the Dillsburg Lutheran Church, having joined about 1878. Mr Mumper is a prosperous agriculturist and has also been largely engaged in extracting iron ore, etc., having spent all his life in this vicinity, with the exception of a trip, in 1866, to Ohio, Indiana, Kentucky, and other parts of the country.

ROBERT McCALL NELSON, son of Samuel P. and Margaret Nelson, was born February 3, 1844, and paternally is descended from the British admiral, Lord Nelson; his maternal grandfather, Bailey, was a native of Ireland. Our subject was reared on the home farm, attending school until his majority, and in 1879 taking charge of the home place. The same year he married Annie (Caroline), daughter of Robert C. and Lydia (Livingston). The only child born to this union is now deceased. The farm contains 135 acres, ten in woodland, the balance under cultivation, and improved with substantial buildings.

JOHN O'HAIL, son of Hugh and Elizabeth O'hail, was born November 3, 1827. His great-grandfather, John O'hail, came from Ireland and settled near Dillsburg in 1754. The family were Covenanters, and the grandfather of our subject, Edward O'hail, was an elder in the Presbyterian Church. Our subject was reared on the farm, and educated at the public and private schools. He became a teacher, and from 1846 until 1866, taught at various points in this and Cumberland Counties. In 1867 he clerked for the Trindle Spring Paper Mill; in 1868 he resumed his profession as teacher, and from 1874 to the present time he has conducted the O'hail School. His professional certificates were received in December, 1859, from Dr. A. R. Blair, county superintendent, and December 30, 1870, from S. G. Boyd, county superintendent; his permanent certificate, dated August 28, 1871, was received from J. P. Wickersham. Mr. O'hail has served as inspector of elections, and is a stockholder in the Harrisburg & Potomac Railroad. From 1846 to 1871 he was a member of the United Presbyterian Church at Carlisle, and is now a member of the Presbyterian Church at Dillsburg, and has been a Sunday-school teacher and superintendent since 1848. In politics he is an ardent Republican.

JACOB PETERMAN, son of John and Sarah Peterman, of this township, was born May 24, 1820—his great-grandfather having come from Germany. He was reared a farmer, and in 1850 took charge of the homestead for his father. In 1851 he married Eliza Mary, daughter of Christopher and Rachel Marks, of Newberry Township, and to this union have been born four children, of whom two boys and one girl are living. The daughter is married to John Mechling; the eldest son married Mary Smyser, and the youngest son married Mary Walker. In 1867 Mr. Peterman inherited the homestead of 120 acres—ninety five acres under cultivation and twenty-five acres in timber; in 1874 he erected a new dwelling, barn, etc.; he also bought from the heirs a farm of eighty acres, improved with a good house and barn, and from the heirs of his brother John, he bought a farm of 100 acres in Warrington Township, also improved with buildings. Mr. and Mrs. Peterman have been members of the United Brethren Church since 1863; of this church Mr. Peterman has been steward, and he has also served the township as school director for three years.

LEWIS J. PRESSEL, son of John and Abigail Pressel, of Washington Township, was born February 9, 1830, and is of German descent on his father's side and of English on his mother's. He was reared to manhood on the home farm, attending select school in the winters. He learned surveying and subsequently taught school in Lower Allen Township, Cumberland County, and also in this township. He began farming on the home stead in 1857, and the same year married Sarah, daughter of Henry and Catherine Reiff, of Monroe Township, Cumberland County, and to this marriage have been born six children, of whom two boys and three girls survive. In 1874 he built on the homestead, which consists of 100 acres, a fine new dwelling, and out-buildings. Mr. Pressel, wife and all the family are members of the Lutheran Church at Filey's, of which he has been deacon and elder a number of years; he was also superintendent of the Northern Sunday-school several years, and has filled a number of township offices.

HENRY W. PRESSEL is the fourth child of John and Abigail Pressel, of this township, and is of German and English descent. John Pressel, now deceased, settled in Carroll Township in 1831. Our subject grew to manhood on the home farm, attending school in the meantime. In 1853 he began teaching and followed that profession at various points until 1860. He also learned the theory of surveying. In 1857 he began farming on the southern part of the old homestead, putting up a new dwelling in 1857, and a barn in 1862. December 27, 1857, he married Annie E., daughter of Samuel and Elizabeth Plank. Mrs. Pressel died April 7, 1875, the mother of seven children, five of whom are still living. Mr. and Mrs. Pressel joined the Lutheran Church at Filey's in 1861, and of this church, for a number of years, Mr. Pressel has been both deacon and elder. He has also served in different offices—township assessor and township clerk several times. He is an I. O. O. F., a K. of P., an agent of the fire insurance company and a stockholder in the Harrisburg & Potomac Railroad and several other companies. He retired to private life in the spring of 1884, but still owns 104 acres of clear land, on which there are two sets of buildings, and one-half interest in 124 33-100 acres clear land in Cumberland County, on which there is one set of buildings; also twenty-four acres timber-land.

CHARLES W. SHEFFER, son of David and Sarah Sheffer, of Dillsburg, was born June 15, 1846. In 1860 he began learning coach-making of his father, and in 1872 went to Dover, where for about six years he worked for Brown & Strayer. On his return to Dillsburg he erected a fine dwelling house and a large coach-maker's shop, and has succeeded in establishing a large and lucrative trade in the borough and surrounding country in buggies, spring wagons, hacks, phaetons, etc. He was married in 1868 to Mary Baish, daughter of Joseph and Mary Baish; of the two children born to this union—a boy and a girl—the girl only is living. Mrs. Sheffer is a member of the Lutheran Church.

JOHN A. SMITH, son of John Smith of Dillsburg, was born August 30, 1834, and is of German descent. At the age of fifteen he began learning tinsmithing with his father, who died three years later. John A. and his brother, Thomas, then continued the business until 1861, when John A. bought his brother's interest. In 1873 his brother Andrew came in, but retired in 1876. In 1872 our subject had enlarged the shop, and also built a residence for his mother near by; he also erected a dwelling on Main Street opposite the public school building. In 1864 he married Catherine, daughter of William Spahr, of Dover Township, and this marriage is graced with three children: Laura, William and John. Mr. Smith has been a successful business man and has filled various positions of public trust. He served one year as chief burgess, and has also served as judge of elections and councilman, and has been school director nine consecutive years. At present he is treasurer of the school board; he is also a stockholder in the Dillsburg & Mechanicsburg Railroad.

MARTIN SMYSER, son of Henry and Eve Smyser, of Adams County, was born February 6, 1810, and is of German descent through his great-grandfather. He grew to manhood on the home farm, and in 1831 married Mary, daughter of Christian and Margaret Hostler; he settled near Dillsburg and has resided here ever since, with the exception of four months passed in Michigan. Mrs. Smyser died in 1879, the mother of five children—two boys and three girls. The second son, George W., is a resident of Russell County, Kas. Mr. Smyser is a member of the Lutheran Church of Dillsburg, in which he has served as deacon and trustee; he has also served his township in the capacity of supervisor, inspector and clerk. He is a prosperous farmer, and on his premises are two valuable ore mines.

JEROME B. STARRY is the sixth of the eleven children of John P. and Sarah A. (Chronister) Starry; was born in Adams County in 1841, and is of German extraction. He was reared on the farm and educated in the common schools and at the high school at Carlisle. At the age of fourteen he came to York County and began teaching in the common schools under the superintendent, A. R. Blair, and for twenty-eight years has followed the profession. For two and a half years, however, he served his country in the late war as sergeant in Company A, Twentieth Pennsylvania Cavalry, and took part at Cold Harbor, Petersburgh, the capture of the Weldon Railway, Five Forks and at other points. After his return he began farming in connection with teaching, and now has a place of twenty-two acres in this township. In 1869 he married Jennie E., daughter of James L. Livingston, of Cumberland County, and became the father of three children: George W., Irvin B. and H. F. (deceased). He has been a member of the Lutheran Church since sixteen years old.

LEWIS HYERS WATTS, son of Hiram and Sarah Ann Watts, of Upper Allen Township, Cumberland County, was born June 21, 1850, and is of English and German descent. He was reared on a farm, but received a good education, and during the winter of 1870-71 taught school in Penn Township, and in the winter of 1872, in Lower Allen Township, Cumberland County. In the summer of 1873 he began reading medicine with Dr. J. W. Rupp, of New Cumberland; then began the drug business at the same place; he came to Dillsburgh in February, 1874, and opened on the corner of Baltimore and Harrisburg Streets; twenty months later he removed to opposite the Nelson House, on Baltimore Street, remained there four years and four months, and then took his present store on the same street, where he has met with abundant success. August 8, 1871, he married Mary F., daughter of David H. and Mary Miller, of Northumberland County; to this union have been born two children: Leon Lewis (deceased) and Amy Alda. Mr. and Mrs. Watts are members of the Presbyterian Church.

JOHN WILLIAMS, son of James Williams, of Monroe Township, Cumberland County, was born February 5, 1815, and is of Welsh descent. He was reared a farmer and married, in 1846, Lucinda Nelson. In 1847 he settled on fifty acres at the mouth of Dogwood Run, and engaged in farming and milling. He has had born to him a family of seven children—four sons, still single, now living on the home place. Mr. and Mrs. Williams are members of the Monaghan Presbyterian Church at Dillsburgh. Mr. Williams has served as school director, auditor, assessor and judge of elections.

CHARLES WILLIAMS, son of John and Nancy Williams, was born June 18, 1840, and is of Scotch-Irish extraction. He was reared a farmer, and in 1864 began on his own account on sixty-four acres on the roads leading from Harrisburg to York and from Sidonsburg to Dillsburg. In the fall of 1862 he was drafted and assigned to Company C, One Hundred and Sixty-sixth Pennsylvania Infantry, as corporal; was stationed at Suffolk in the Third Army Corps, under Gen. Peck, and was mustered out in July, 1863, at Harrisburg. He was engaged in butchering from 1870 to 1878, in connection with farming, and in 1877 opened a general store. He is a Jeffersonian Democrat; he served as school director in Monaghan Township three years, and in Carroll six years, and in the fall of 1884 was elected to the legislature by over 3,800 majority. Since 1861 he has been a member of Filey's Lutheran Church, and has been deacon, elder and trustee many years; he has been actively connected with the Sunday-school since boyhood, and in the conventions at the upper end held the offices of president and secretary and chairman of the executive committee. In 1861 he married Margaret A., daughter of Thomas and Sarah Burtnet, of this township, and of the seven children born to him four are living: Mary Jane, Henry Wesley, Catherine Elizabeth and Martha Elverta.

CHANCEFORD TOWNSHIP.

DANIEL CONRAD is a native of Lancaster County, Penn., born in 1828, and is a son of Daniel and Mary (Erisman) Conrad. His grandfather, Daniel Conrad, was a native of Lancaster County, Penn., and a soldier in the Revolutionary war. He had three sons and four daughters. At the age of eighteen years our subject was apprenticed to the wheelwright's trade, and after serving three years began business for himself at New Danville, Lancaster Co., Penn., where he remained until 1860. He then removed to Chanceford Township, York County, and purchased a farm, and is now engaged in farming and keeping hotel. Mr. Conrad was married, in 1855, to Miss Martha Zercher, of Lancaster County. They have four children: Elvina, Benjamin F., Daniel W. and Henry. Mr. Conrad is a member of the German Reformed Church.

THOMAS G. CROSS, son of James and Elizabeth (Grove) Cross, was born on the old homestead in Windsor Township, York County, August 14, 1818. His grandfather, James Cross, was a native of the "Emerald Isle," and came to America at twelve years of age with his parents, who were among the first settlers of York County. Several of the older members of the Cross family were soldiers in the early wars, and held some of the first civil official positions in York County. Thomas Cross, great-grandfather of our subject, came from Ireland to the United States about 1752, locating in Windsor Township, where he took up about 500 acres of land. He died in 1776, leaving three sons: John, who served in the Revolution, settled in the West; James, who remained upon the old homestead and followed farming, served in the French and Indian wars and the whisky insurrection, died in 1845, leaving six children—three sons and three daughters—James, the father of our subject, being the eldest. He followed farming, and served as justice of the peace for twenty-five years. He died in June, 1872, leaving two sons and four daughters. Thomas G. Cross was educated at the common schools and York County Academy, and also spent some time at Chanceford Academy. At seventeen years of age he began teaching, and followed that occupation for thirteen years, and for four years was engaged in mercantile business. In 1851 he settled where he now resides and engaged in surveying and general farming. He served as justice of the peace for ten years, and 1857 was director of the poor for York County, serving until 1860, during which period the county hospital was erected. In 1866 he was elected county prothonotary, and served three years. In 1872 he returned to his farm, where he now lives. He was married, in 1849, to Miss Martha J. Campbell, daughter of John S. Campbell, of Lower Chanceford Township. Seven children have blessed this union: Almira A., Elizabeth J., Maggie E., Emma M., Nettie S., Otho W. and Thomas C. Mr. and Mrs. Cross and all their children are members of the United Presbyterian Church.

THE CURRAN FAMILY. John Curran was a son of David Curran, who emigrated from Ireland to America and settled where Jefferson, Md., is now situated. This property afterward passed into the hands of John Curran, who subsequently sold it to Thomas Jefferson, and removed to Chanceford Township. John Curran had ten children: Samuel, John, David, Jacob, Charles, Sophia, Sarah, Elizabeth, Margaret and Catherine. John Curran died in 1819. Samuel Curran had seven children: Andrew, John, Henry, Samuel, Joseph, Mary and Margaret. Andrew Curran, a son of Samuel and Mary (Wise) Curran, was born January 29, 1829. At the age of twenty-three he began serving an apprenticeship at the stonemason's trade at Dallastown, Penn., and continued this trade for several years. In 1855 he removed from York Township and settled on his present farm. He was married in 1854 to Miss Catherine N. Young, daughter of Jacob Young of York Township. This marriage has been blessed with four children: Mary C., Joseph A., Margaret A. and Samuel H. Mr. Curran is a member of the German Reformed Church, and his wife belongs to the Lutheran Church. John Curran, a son of Samuel and Mary A. (Wise) Curran, was born September 14, 1832, in the old family homestead, which he now owns and where he resides; he is a farmer and grows tobacco extensively. In 1859 he married Miss Sarah A. Wise, daughter of John Wise of Chanceford Township. They have five children: John S., William F., Joseph W., George A. and Mary M. Mr. Curran has held various official positions in his township. He is agent for the Southern Mutual Insurance Company of York. He is a member of the German Reformed Church. Henry Curran, son of Samuel and Mary A. (Wise) Curran, was born on the old homestead in 1834, and remained at home until 1863, when he went to Montana, and engaged in mining. In 1870 he returned to Chanceford Township and engaged in farming and merchandising at Collinsville. He remained there some time and then removed to Brogueville, where he continued business for seven years, and then sold his interest and began business where he now resides. He is also engaged in farming, and has 180 acres of land.

CHANCEFORD TOWNSHIP.

He was married, in 1877, to Miss Maria Trout, daughter of Judge Valentine Trout. Three children have blessed this marriage: Ivy M., Mary E., and Sarah J. He is a member of the German Reformed Church and his wife of the Presbyterian Church. Samuel Curran, son of Samuel and Mary A (Wise) Curran, was born October 29, 1836, and reared and educated in his native township. He remained on the homestead farm until thirty-three years of age, when he purchased a farm adjoining that of his father, and there he remained eight years. In 1881 he purchased his present farm, where he now resides. He was married in 1869 to Miss Mary A. Sechrist, daughter of Charles Sechrist, of Chanceford Township. Mr. Curran's second marriage was in 1879 to Mrs. Catherine E. McNaughton. They have three children: William H., George S., and Jacob E. Mr. and Mrs. Curran are members of the Lutheran Church.

HENRY DIETZ was born March 2, 1852, and is a son of Frederick and Magdalena (Strickler) Dietz, natives of Hellam Township, York Co., Penn. At the age of nineteen years he began learning the miller's trade, which he followed until 1877, when he purchased a farm of 143 acres in Chanceford Township and is now engaged in general farming. He was married in 1874 to Miss Henrietta Burg of Lower Windsor Township. They have one child, Martha.

LEVI C. FRY was born in Chanceford Township, York Co., Penn., March 25, 1843, and is a son of John and Christina (Blouse) Fry, also natives of this township. His grandfather, John Fry, was a native of Lancaster County, Penn. He was reared on the farm, and in 1861 enlisted in the Eighty-seventh Pennsylvania Volunteers. He was at the battles of Winchester, Kelly's Ford, Mine Run, Wilderness, and was wounded at Locust Grove, November 27, 1863, and also took part at Horse Shoe Bend, Spottsylvania, Cold Harbor and Bermuda. At the battle of Petersburg he was captured, June 22, 1864, and was confined at Bell Island, Castle Thunder, Libby and Andersonville prisons. He was released April 28, 1865, and discharged June 18, 1865. After the war he returned to Chanceford Township, and engaged in farming. Mr. Fry was married, March 22, 1866, to Miss Cevella A. Hoover, daughter of Philip and Elizabeth Hoover, of Manchester Township. Mr. Fry has served as township auditor, and is a church member.

ROBERT S. GEMMILL was born in 1840, and is a son of James and Mary A. (Norris) Gemmill, the latter a daughter of John V. Norris, of Harford County, Md. William Gemmill, subject's grandfather, was a native of Hopewell Township, York County. He had seven children, of whom the father of Robert S. was the second son, who was twice married, and who died in 1859. Robert S. remained at home until his twenty-first year, when he purchased a farm and began general farming. He now owns a farm of 126 acres of well improved land, and is one of the successful farmers of Chanceford Township. In 1861 he was married to Miss Margaret I. Andrews, daughter of Robert Andrews, of Chanceford Township. This union has been blessed with eight children: Franklin P., James N., Robert A., Mary L., Hugh L., William W., Annie P. and Flora L. Mr. and Mrs. Gemmill are members of the Presbyterian Church. Joseph W. Gemmill, brother of Robert S., was born December 4, 1845, on the old Gemmill homestead. At the death of his mother he inherited a portion of the home farm, and bought the remainder and engaged in farming. He now has 150 acres of good land. He was married December 27, 1870, to Miss Emma C. Good, daughter of Jesse B. Good, of Hopewell Township. They have four children: Lottie I.,

James L., Sarah E. and Alfuah M. Mr. and Mrs. Gemmill are members of the Presbyterian Church.

THE GRAHAM FAMILY. Thomas Graham, a soldier of the American Revolution, was born in 1751, and emigrated from Ireland in 1768. He was married July 16, 1778, to Miss Hannah Hooper, who bore him eleven children—five sons and six daughters. Thomas Graham died in 1832. Robert Graham, a son of Thomas, inherited the Graham homestead. He followed farming, and in 1839 was appointed postmaster, and held that office (from which Grahamville originated) until 1860. He was married in 1839, to Miss Sarah F. Clarkson, of Chanceford Township, who died May 28, 1859, leaving four children: Andrew C., Thomas L., James C. and Hannah E. Mr. Graham's second marriage was in 1860 to Miss Jane M. Stewart, who died in 1880. Mr. Graham represented York County in the State legislature during the years 1842-43 and held many township offices, and was a prominent merchant. For many years he was an elder in the Presbyterian Church, of which he was a member at the time of his death in January 20,1875, aged eighty-one years one month and fifteen days. Thomas L. Graham is principal of the academy at Elkton, Cecil Co., Md., and is a Mason. James C. Graham was born August 22, 1845, on the old homestead, and is by occupation a farmer. He was married, November 28, 1878, to Miss Ella A. Shaw, of Hopewell. They have one child—Robert. Mr. Graham is a Mason. The Graham family have been identified with the history of York County for more than a century, and the members of the family have always figured prominently in the affairs of the county.

JAMES W. KILGORE, son of Robert N. and Mary E. (Wilson) Kilgore, natives respectively of Chanceford Township and of Maryland, was born February 22, 1851. His grandfather, John Kilgore, was a native of Lower Chanceford Township, and was married to Margaret Nelson, by whom he had five sons and three daughters. Our subject received his education at the public schools and York County Academy. In 1875 he engaged in general merchandising at Brogueville, under the firm name of Curran & Kilgore, and continued business for some time, but at the death of Mr. Kilgore's father, in 1877, he sold his interest in the store and took charge of the old homestead. In 1883 he again entered the mercantile business in partnership with a Mr. Grove. In 1880 he was elected justice of the peace. His term expired May 1. 1885. Mr. Kilgore owns a farm of 150 acres, which he operates in connection with merchandising.

JACOB K. KOHLER was born in 1831, in Conewago Township, York County, and is a son of John and Anna Maria Kohler, natives of Manchester Township. His grandfather, Baltzar Kohler, was a farmer and tavern keeper at Manchester, then known as Liverpool. He had six children, of whom the father of Jacob K. was the youngest. At nineteen years of age Jacob K. began learning the miller's trade, and afterward followed the milling business for fifteen years. In 1858 he came to Chanceford Township, and for a time worked at his trade. In 1873 he purchased his present farm. He was married, in 1857, to Miss Eleah Scheaffer, of Hopewell Township. They have two children: Albert J. and Emma L. Mr. Kohler has been school director of Chanceford Township.' Mr. and Mrs. K. are members of the Lutheran Church.

MICHAEL LYMAN, son of Michael and Sarah (Kline) Lyman, was born in Lancaster County, Penn., in 1823. His father was born in Centre County, and his mother in Lancaster County, Penn. Our subject remained in his native county until 1847, when he came to York County and entered the employ of the Tide Water Canal Company, and

BIOGRAPHICAL SKETCHES.

was located in Lower Chanceford Township. Here he continued to work for three years, and then began boating, which he continued until 1870, when he removed to York Furnace and engaged in the hotel business. He remained there until 1884, when he removed to Shank's Ferry and entered the hotel business. Mr. Lyman was married in 1845, to Miss Elmira Raymond, of Dauphin County, Penn. They have seven children: Jacob, Æneas, Ella, Joseph, Charley, Lilly and Theodore. Mr. Lyman is a member of Lodge No. 125, of the Brotherhood of the Union.

THOMAS McCULLOUGH was born in Chester County, Penn., in 1818, and is a son of Thomas and Ann McCullough. The father of our subject was born in Harford County, Md., and the mother in Chester County, Penn. Mr. McCullough first learned the manufacturing of machinery and edged tools of every description, and followed auger-making for a number of years. His native home was Kennett Square, and his early days were spent in company with our esteemed and much loved friend and poet, Bayard Taylor. In 1856 he removed to Chanceford Township, York Co., Penn., and engaged in farming and boating. When the tocsin of war was sounded, he offered his life and interest in the defense of his country's honor. They received him, and chartered his boats at Baltimore to convey soldiers across the Southern rivers, and he many days lay defenseless under the enemy's fire on the Pamunkey until the malarial fever drove him home. Mr. McCullough married Miss Eliza Porter, of New Garden Township, Chester Co., Penn., in 1848. Mrs. McCullough died November 3, 1883. Mr. McCollough is a member of the Methodist Episcopal Church.

WILLIAM MOORE, son of John and Elizabeth (Ellison) Moore, was born January 20, 1846, on the old family homestead in Chanceford Township. His grandfather, Samuel Moore, a native of Scotland, came to America and settled in Chanceford Township. He died in 1836. He had eight children—four sons and four daughters—the father of our subject being the eldest son. John Moore, subject's father, was by occupation a cooper, and died in 1878, leaving three children: William, Samuel H. and John A. Our subject served a three-years' apprenticeship at carpentering, and for seventeen years worked at that trade. Mr. Moore is now engaged in general farming. He was married, in 1868, to Miss Mary E. Shaw, of Chanceford Township. They have three children: Lemon S., Maggie S. and Ida E. Mr. Moore is a member of the Methodist Episcopal Church.

JOHN MURPHY is a son of James and Mary (Smith) Murphy, natives of Chanceford Township, York County. His paternal grandfather was born in Ireland and immigrated to America prior to the American Revolution, in which he was a soldier. He was married, in 1778, to Miss Barbara Pretz, of this township, by whom he had six children. He died in 1808. James Murphy, his eldest child, had nine children—four sons and five daughters. John Murphy, our subject, was born in 1813 on the old Murphy homestead, which adjoins his present farm. He was engaged in boating and school teaching for some years. He was married, in 1844, to Miss Leah Smith, daughter of William Smith, of this township. They have had eight children: Charles W. (deceased), James S., Samuel H. (deceased), John R. S., George W. (deceased), Mary C., Hester A. and Thomas W. Mr. Murphy has held the offices of auditor and assessor.

GEORGE B. MURPHY is a son of Joseph and Alice (Cunningham) Murphy, natives of York County, Penn. His grandfather, Joseph Murphy, came from Ireland in 1794. Our subject was born on the old Murphy homestead, January 13, 1848, where he now lives. At the death of his mother, in 1877, he purchased the home farm. In 1870 he engaged in the mercantile business, and since 1877 has been engaged in farming, in connection with that business. He was married on February 12, 1874, to Miss Sarah Gemmill, daughter of Robert Gemmill. They have two children: Robert E. and Joseph R. In 1882 Mr. Murphy was elected school director for three years. He and wife are members of the Presbyterian Church.

BENJAMIN FRANKLIN PORTER, M. D., son of Benjamin and Ruth (Wilson) Porter, was born in Mill Creek Hundred, Newcastle Co., Del., May 19, 1827, being the fourth of a family of seven children. His father removed to New Garden Township, Chester County, when the subject of this sketch was three years of age, where they continued to reside until their removal to York County. His father had no brothers and but one sister, who died early in life, and his grandfather Porter, who was an officer in the Continental army, died about the year 1790. His mother was the eldest daughter of John and Elizabeth (Beverley) Wilson, and his grandmother, Elizabeth, was the daughter of Samuel and Ruth (Jackson) Beverley, of Kennet and East Marlborough Townships, Chester Co., Penn. Samuel and Ruth Beverley had two daughters, Elizabeth, as above mentioned, and Mary, afterward married to William Gause. They had six sons and five daughters. The early life of Dr. B. F. Porter, the subject of this sketch, was divided between attendance at school and his duties as a farmer's son, until his fifteenth year, when he entered the academy of his friend and neighbor, the late Enoch Lewis, where his advancement was very rapid. Mathematics was his delight, and when he left school to enter Delaware College, his preceptor considered him fully prepared to do all kinds of civil engineering. Having to depend upon his own resources in a great measure, for his further advancement, he taught in the common schools of Chester County, and in Newcastle County, Del., the last year being in a select school. In the spring of 1851 he entered the office of Dr. J. R. McClurg as a medical student. After more than the usual course of study—for under the advice of his friend, the late Dr. Porter, of Wilmington, Del., he devoted considerable time to hospital training and experience—he graduated with the degree of doctor of medicine from the Jefferson Medical College of Philadelphia, on March 10, 1855. Immediately after graduation he came to Chanceford Township to treat and care for a sister who was in feeble health, and finally made it his permanent home; and from the day on which he was vested by the State of Pennsylvania with the powers "*exercendi, docendi, et scribendi, ubi rite vocati fueritis,*" and that too, "*inter nos et ubique gentium,*" he practiced his profession among all classes, faithfully, earnestly and circumspectly, and has always enjoyed a large patronage. Always an ardent friend of popular education, and believing that the heritage of liberty, as bequeathed to us by the fathers of the republic, is dependent for its perpetuation upon the intelligence of the people, he served his township twelve years in succession as a school director, in which he gave his time and energies freely to the improvement and elevation of the people's colleges—the common schools. In 1868 he was elected a member of the house of representatives of the commonwealth of Pennsylvania, and in 1869 was re-elected to the same position, and as an evidence of the acceptability of his services, at the expiration of his second term his fellow-members presented him with a handsome gold-headed cane, as a testimonial of esteem and regard. On August 20, 1861, he married—Sarah Jane Bigler becoming his life partner. They have one son living: David B. Porter, who is just entering his twenty-third year.

JOSEPH W. REED was born in Chanceford Township, in 1844, and is a son of Samuel and Sarah J. (Wiley) Reed, natives respectively of Chanceford and Fawn Townships, York County, Penn. His great-grandfather emigrated from Ireland to America prior to the war of the Revolution, and held a commission in 'the Continental army. He was also one of the signers of the Declaration of Independence. The grandfather of our subject had six children, of whom the father of Joseph W. was the eldest son. Joseph W. Reed, in 1871, purchased his present farm of 112 acres, where he has since lived and been engaged in general farming. He married Miss Mary S. Bigler, daughter of David Bigler, of Windsor Township. They have three children: Sarah J., Charles F. and Ralph M. In March, 1865, Mr. Reed enlisted in the One Hundred and Third Regiment Pennsylvania Volunteers, and served until the close of the war. Mr. and Mrs. Reed are members of the Presbyterian Church.

JAMES P. ROBINSON is a son of Nehemiah and Maria (Pennington) Robinson, natives of Maryland, and was born in Cecil County, Md., September 22, 1840. At six years of age he came with his parents to York County, and settled at York Furnace, in Lower Chanceford Township. The earlier years of his life were spent at various occupations. In 1872 he removed to New Bridgeville and engaged in general merchandising and hotel business. Here he remained until 1878, when he went to Long Level in Lower Windsor Township and continued the same business. In 1882 he returned to New Bridgeville, where he still resides, and engaged in the same business. He was married January 1, 1867, to Miss Sarah A. Schall, daughter of John Schall. They have six children: Maggie R., Ida J., Rose, Sarah E., Samuel T. and Clara B. In 1884 Mr. Robinson was elected to the State legislature. He is a member of the I. O. O. F. Mr. and Mrs. Robinson are members of the Evangelical Lutheran Church.

JOHN K. SCHENBERGER, son of Frederick and Lydia (Whitman) Schenberger, was born on the old family homestead in Chanceford Township, March 19, 1833. His parents were also born in York County. His early life was spent on the farm, and at twenty-five years of age he began learning the carpenter's trade, at which he worked for eight years. In 1873 he engaged in general merchandising, which business he has since continued in connection with farming. He was appointed postmaster at New Bridgeville in 1864, which position he still retains. He was married April 12, 1857, to Miss Elizabeth Loucks, daughter of Samuel Loucks, of Windsor Township. They have five children: Ida A., John W., Frederick H., William J. and Latta S. Mr. Schenberger has held various township offices.

JAMES TAYLOR, son of Robert and Jane (McKee) Taylor, was born in Lower Chanceford Township, in 1826. His parents, who were born in Ireland, immigrated to America in 1820, and settled in Lower Chanceford Township. Mr. Taylor, by occupation, is a farmer, and is now engaged in superintending a farm for John Small. He was married to Miss A. (daughter of George) Waltermyer, of Hopewell Township. This union has been blessed with six children: George W., James F., Catherine J., Joseph T., John H. and Wesley McK. Mr. Taylor is a member of the Chanceford United Presbyterian Church.

ARCHIBALD THOMPSON (the ancestor of the Thompsons in York County) came from Scotland, and was a Scotch Covenanter, some of his ancestors being compelled to live in caves during the persecution. He married Margaret Wallace, daughter of Alexander Wallace, who came to York County in 1730, and in whose house Old Guinston Church was first organized. Archibald Thompson and Margaret Wallace had four children: Alexander, single; James married Samuel Collins; James, single, and Joseph, who married Mary Purdy, the daughter of Archibald Purdy and Agnes Gilliland. Joseph Thompson, born February 2, 1762; died December 19, 1815. Mary Purdy, born 1766; died 1834. They had ten children as follows: Archibald married Jane Kirkwood, Joseph married Jane Martin, Nancy married Robert Anderson, Alexander married Margaret McKinley, James married Rosanna Kerchner, Margaret married William Reed, Mary married Thomas Grove, William married Mary Ann Hoopes, Samuel H. married Elizabeth Shenberger. Andrew Purdy married Elizabeth Donaldson and had eight children, of whom William R. Thompson, of the banking firm of Semple & Thompson, corner Fourth Avenue and Wood Street, Pittsburgh, Penn., is the eldest. Andrew Purdy Thompson studied for the ministry, and was sent by the Associate Church as a missionary to the island of Trinidad in the West Indies. After three years absence, he came home and has been almost uninterruptedly engaged in the work of the American Bible Society. William R. Thompson, of Pittsburgh, was born in Alleghany City, in 1845. During the civil war, he entered the Union army. Since 1865 he has been engaged in the banking business; was seven years cashier of the Mechanics National Bank of Pittsburgh, and afterward its president. He is now the active member of the banking firm of Semple & Thompson.

WILLIAM THOMPSON is a son of Archibald P. and Jane (Kirkwood) Thompson, the latter, a native of Harford County, Md. The father of our subject, a farmer, was born in Chanceford Township, York County, and was the eldest son in a family of ten children, and for a number of years was captain in the State militia. Our subject was born on the old Thompson homestead in 1819, where he grew to manhood. He remained on the farm until 1850, when he engaged in merchandising at Bald Eagle, in Fawn Township, and there remained three years. He then returned to Chanceford Township, and again engaged in farming, which occupation he has since continued. He was married in 1848, to Miss Sallie E. Gemmill, daughter of John Gemmill. They have four children: John G., Archibald P., James D. and Sallie M. Mr. and Mrs. Thompson are members of the United Presbyterian Church.

SAMUEL WORKINGER, son of Jesse Workinger, present sheriff of York County, Penn., was born February 9, 1843. He was married in 1866, to Miss Agnes R. Warner, daughter of Jacob Warner, of Chanceford Township. They have one child, Alice M. Mr. Workinger is a leading citizen, and has held positions of public trust in Chanceford Township.

CODORUS TOWNSHIP.

LEVI BAHN, son of John and Polly Bahn, nee Schwartz, of Springfield Township, was born March 22, 1820, in Shrewsbury Township. He was reared on his father's farm until his nineteenth year, then went to his trade of carpenter with John N. Miller, of Shrewsbury Township, and followed his trade since that date, except four years when engaged in milling. He built the mill which Henry M. Bort-

BIOGRAPHICAL SKETCHES.

ner now owns and operates. January 22, 1843, he married Margaret Bortner, daughter of Jacob and Catherine (Snyder) Bortner, of Codorus Township. Twelve children have been born to this union: Cassie, deceased; Rebecca and Levi, twins; Louis, Elizabeth; Matilda, deceased; John, Catharine, Sarah J., Louisa, Jacob and William H. Mr. Bahn has been the leading builder of Codorus Township for the past forty years, nearly all the large barns and dwellings having been erected by him. The first meeting house ever built in Glen Rock was put up by Mr. Bahn. He is descended from one of the old families of the township. Mr. Bahn is a member of Fishel's (Lutheran) Church. His grandfather, Frederick Bahn, was only four years old when he came to York County.

HENRY M. BORTNER, son of Michael and Catherine (Marckel) Bortner, of Codorus and Shrewsbury Townships, respectively, was born January 3, 1821, in Codorus Township, and is the second son in a family of eight children, viz.: Jared M., Henry M., Jonas M., Noah M.; Sarah, wife of Solomon Wherly; Liddie, widow of Henry Bahn; Cassie Ann, wife of Peter S. Smith; and Catherine, wife of Adam S. Smith. June 14, 1846, our subject married Henrietta Dubs, daughter of John and Elizabeth (Rohrbach) Dubs, of Codorus Township. Thirteen children have been born to them: Albert D., Louisa J.; Henry D., deceased; Henrietta D.; Leminda, deceased; John D.; Sarah, deceased; Josiah D., Amanda D., George D., Edgar D., Laura D. and Alice D. Our subject was reared on his father's farm, and received the advantages of the common schools of his township. He followed weaving for seven years, having learned it from his mother, and then went to learn the trade of miller, June 8, 1844, with Jacob Bortner, ex-commissioner of York County; Ephraim Fair was his miller. After working there four years, our subject bought the mill property of Michael Krout, at what is now Seitzville. He operated this mill four years, then bought Abraham Thoman's mill in Shrewsbury Township, now Honeytown, where he followed milling twelve years, and then moved to his present mill, and after three years' stay here rented a farm and followed farming five years, when he relinquished that occupation to accept the office of treasurer of York County, having served the full term to the entire satisfaction of the people. In 1875 he removed to the mill property, where he now lives, at Pierceville. He still runs the mill to its full capacity. Our subject's father, John Michael Bortner, died October 21, 1870, in his ninetieth year. His mother died October 9, 1888, in her fortieth year. Subject's paternal grandparents were Ludwig Bortner and Ablona (Florschner) Bortner, and were among the pioneer settlers of Codorus Township. Mr. Bortner is a member of Fishel's (Lutheran) Church; has been assessor of his township ten consecutive terms, also school director for nine years, and is one of the leading and most respected citizens of Codorus Township.

JONAS M. BORTNER, son of Michael and Catherine (Marckel) Bortner, of Shrewsbury Township, was born December 17, 1824, in Codorus Township. He received the ordinary common school education available at that day, and was reared on the farm. In February, 1849, Mr. Bortner married Catherine Bortner, daughter of Jacob and Catherine (Garwick) Bortner, of Codorus Township. This union has been blessed with eleven children: Lewis, Adeline (deceased), Levi, Sarah (deceased), Caroline, Henry (deceased), Nathaniel, Richard, Amanda (deceased), Maria and Harris. Mr. Bortner has been constable for eighteen years, and is one of the most popular and best known men in Codorus Township. The mill now owned and operated by him was built in 1839,

by Jacob Bortner, generally known as old Commissioner Bortner, and, except an interval of two years, this mill has been in the Bortner name ever since. Mr. Bortner is a prominent member of the Reformed Church.

S. B. BRODBECK, only son of George and Leah (Bossert) Brodbeck, of Codorus Township, was born May 21, 1851, in Jefferson, Codorus Township, and to Prof. Gray's school at Glen Rock, he entered his father's store, and at the death of his father, in 1874, continued the business for Brodbeck estate until 1879, when he began business in his own name. July 4, 1875, Mr. Brodbeck married Eliza Weaver, daughter of Jacob and Eliza (Gettier) Weaver, of Manchester, Carroll Co., Md. Four children have been born to this union: Rose E., George W., Lettie May and Sadie. Our subject's father, George Brodbeck, was a prominent citizen and one of the leading business men of his section of York County. He was postmaster and also treasurer of Codorus Township for many years, and was leader of the choir at the Stone Church from the time he settled in the township until his death. His success in life was due to his own efforts. The subject of this sketch, though comparatively a young man, is widely known, and doing a large mercantile business, having a branch store and postoffice at Brodbecks (Green Ridge Station) on the Hanover & Baltimore Railroad. He is a member of the Stone (Reformed) Church.

HENRY GABLE, son of Henry and Annie (Gertrude) Gable, was born June 17, 1839, in North Codorus Township, and was brought up on a farm. January 23, 1864, he enlisted in York, Penn., in Company B, One Hundred and Eighty-seventh Regiment Pennsylvania Volunteers. He was wounded in left thigh and leg, in the discharge of his duty at Weldon Railroad, Virginia, June 18, 1864, and was taken to Division Hospital, and thence to City Point Hospital, Virginia. June 30 he left there for Findley Hospital, Washington, D. C. Our subject's sister came to Washington and secured his transfer to the hospital at York, Penn. On July 25, 1865, he was again transferred to the Citizens' Hospital, Philadelphia; July 26 to the Chestnut Hill Hospital; he left the Chestnut Hill Hospital October 17, 1865, for the Christian Street Hospital, where a piece of bone came out of his leg, December 10, 1866, and a second piece of bone came out on September 3, 1872. Mr. Gable is a well known and respected citizen of Codorus Township.

LEWIS K. GLATFELTER, son of Charles and Leah (Klindinst) Glatfelter, is the third child in a family of eleven children, and was born October 20, 1843, in North Codorus Township, where he was reared on his father's farm; when a boy, his time was devoted to school and farm work. February 15, 1863, he married Isabella, daughter of John B. and Elizabeth (Behler) Kerchner, of North Codorus Township. This marriage has been blessed with seven children: Franklin (deceased), Emma J., Lucy, Alice (deceased), Miranda (deceased), Paul (deceased) and Rose (deceased). Our subject's father, Charles Glatfelter, died in his sixty-fifth year, and his mother was sixty-seven when she died. Mr. Glatfelter owns an excellent farm of 100 acres, well stocked and under good cultivation; also owns an adjoining farm of sixty acres that he farms in connection with the home farm. The Glatfelter family is one of the oldest and most numerous in York County. The subject of this sketch is a man of wide influence in his township, and a prominent member of Shaffer's Church.

E. W. HEINDEL, son of George and Leah (Winehold) Heindel, of Shrewsbury Township, was born October 17, 1832. He was brought up to and followed farming until 1879, when he built Green

Ridge Mill, at Green Ridge Station, Codorus Township, on the Hanover & Baltimore Railroad. April 15, 1859, Mr. Heindel married Elizabeth Rife. May 2, 1867, he married his second wife, Annie Dubs, of Adams County, Penn. This marriage has been blessed with two children, Tirza Jane (deceased), and Elsie A. Mr. Heindel is the owner of a farm containing 218 acres, about sixty acres being in woodland. He has been school director three years; was director on the B. N. R. R., the time it was built, for eight years, and ticket agent for eight years. He has by his own exertions and good management acquired a handsome competency, and is one of the solid men of Codorus Township.

DR. H. C. JONES, son of H. B. and Mary Ann (Zimmerman) Jones, was born August 9, 1842, in Codorus Township (near the Maryland line). The Doctor is the third in a family of nine children. He was reared on a farm and mill and attended private school in Baltimore County, Md., and for several years the Manchester Academy, in Manchester, Md. He began to read medicine with Dr. H. Baltz, of Manchester; he then continued under Prof. N. R. Smith, of Baltimore, and after three years of close reading attended two courses at the University of Maryland, also taking private instruction between courses. He graduated in 1865, and immediately began the practice of medicine at Menge's Mills, and after five years' stay removed to Jefferson borough, his present location. Dr. Jones is a member of the I. O. O. F., No. 327, Hanover Lodge, and has been burgess of Jefferson. September 29, 1867, he married Sarah F. Hershey, daughter of Abraham and Eliza (Forry) Hershey, of Heidelberg Township. Seven children have blessed this union: infant daughter, deceased; Minnie, two infant sons, deceased; Henry H., Pius H., and Honora E. Dr. Jones is devoted to his profession, has a lucrative practice, and is one of Jefferson's best citizens.

DR. JOHN D. KELLER, son of Henry S. and Henrietta (Wherly) Keller, of Codorus Township, was born February 24, 1852. After attending school at home until his tenth year, he went to York County Academy for two years, then to Glen Rock School under Professor Gray two years. He taught school for three terms, two in Codorus Township and one in Springfield Township. He began reading medicine with his father during the summer months; then attended lectures at the Hahnneman Medical College in Philadelphia, where he graduated March 10, 1874. He began the practice of medicine at Melrose, Md., and after three years' practice removed to his present location at Glenville, Codorus Township. October 10, 1875, he married Sarah Lippy, daughter of Benjamin Lippy, of Carroll County, Md. One child has been born to them —Albertus H. B. Our subject's father, Dr. H. S. Keller, was born in West Manheim Township; his family were John D., Henry J., Elizabeth S., Daniel W.; Henrietta, deceased; William E. A.; Anna Mary, deceased; infant, deceased. Our subject's mother died, and his father married Margaret Doll, daughter of Henry A. Doll, of Manheim Township. Four children have been born to this marriage: Catherine, Jesse; Tobias, deceased; and Lydia, deceased. Our subject has been a hard student, devoted to his chosen profession, and as a reward of this has a large and lucrative practice.

REV. W. H. KETTERMAN, son of George and Anna May (Bush) Ketterman, of Dover and North Codorus Townships respectively, was reared on the farm and attended school in his native township until his sixteenth year, when he began teaching school; taught five terms in "Lesh's" Church, North Codorus Township, and one term at "Auchey's" Schoolhouse, Jefferson Borough. Easter day, 1876, Rev. K. married Lydia M. Hamm, daughter of Daniel and Lydia (Lau) Hamm, of North Codorus Township. Four interesting children have blessed this union: Paul, George and Daniel (twins), and Annie. Our subject is the ninth child in a family of twelve children, and he is loved and honored by his people, to which, his first charge, he was called twelve years ago, and it is not too much to say that no charge in York County has made such rapid progress in same length of time. When Rev. Ketterman came to this field twelve years ago, the salary at the stone church, comprising 160 members, paid between $60 and $80; Schaffer's paid about $13; Jefferson about $30. These churches now pay about five times that amount, respectively; the collections for benevolent purposes then were from $12 to $20 per year at the stone church, now they are from $120 to $150 a year; the same relative increase has taken place in the other two churches; all due to the wise and energetic management of the reverend pastor.

JESSE SHAFFER, son of John and Margaret (Overmillèr) Shaffer, second in a family of eleven children, was born in Hopewell Township in 1811, and was reared on his father's farm. He married Catherine Klinefelter, daughter of George and Elizabeth (Diehl) Klinefclter. Five children have blessed this marriage: Rebecca, Elizabeth, George, Catherine and Jacob. Mr. Shaffer has resided at his present home for the last forty years. His farm contains 164 acres of excellent land, about forty acres of woodland. In 1862 he built the Shaffer gristmill, which has been in operation continuously ever since John Shaffer, our subject's father, attained the ripe old age of eighty-two, when he died in Hopewell Township; his wife died in her fifty-eighth year. Mr. Shaffer is one of the leading members of Shaffer's Church. He has been closely identified with this church since it was built, having aided largely by his means and time in its construction.

CONEWAGO TOWNSHIP.

GEORGE ENSMINGER, Esq., was born in Manchester Township, eldest son of Samuel Ensminger and grandson of John Ensminger, great-grandson of Conrad Ensminger, and great-great-grandson of Heinrich Ensminger, who came from the Palatine by the ship "Samuel, of London;" landed at Philadelphia, Penn., August 17, 1738, and settled near Lewisberry, this county. George Ensminger, Esq., the subject of our sketch, lived in Dover Township from the time he was three years old, and was educated in the public schools of said township and worked on the farm until August 12, 1863, when he joined the army and became a member of Company I, One Hundred and Forty-third Regiment Pennsylvania Volunteers. He participated in the battles of Haymarket and Wilderness. In the latter he was unfortunately captured by the Confederates, was a prisoner of war at Danville, Va., Andersonville, Ga., and Florence, S. C., for a term of nine months and twenty-two days. After being paroled joined his regiment, and was mustered out with the regiment June 12, 1865; returned home and worked on the farm till the fall of 1869; traveled west to Ohio and Michigan, and returned to the oil region of Pennsylvania and worked in the oil fields till the fall of 1870; returned to York County, worked on the farm till the spring of 1872. He entered the York County Academy under the instructions of Profs. Ruby and Heiges; taught school in the winter and went to school at the York County Academy during summer, and taught the summer of 1874 as assistant teacher to Prof. Ruby. Moved to Conewago Township in the spring of 1875 and taught school. Was elected justice of the peace in 1877, but did not take up his commission. Was elected justice of the peace again in the spring of 1880 by the votes of both parties; followed surveying and conveyancing in connection with his office, teaching school in the winter till the spring of 1884, teaching twelve terms in succession, when he was appointed United States Storekeeper and Gauger, in which vocation he is at present (1885) engaged. The genealogy of the Ensminger family is as follows: Heinrich Ensminger, father of Conrad Ensminger and others; Conrad Ensminger, born in 1745 and father of John and others, died July 13, 1788, buried at Quickel's Church; John Ensminger, father of Samuel, Jacob, John, Henry, Elizabeth and Mary, born in 1783, died in 1862; Samuel Ensminger, father of George (the subject of this sketch), Samuel, Albert W. and Jacob W., was born March 9, 1811, died April 9, 1879.

HENRY H. KOCHENOUR was born in Manchester Township January 18, 1829, and is a son of Henry and Catherine (Hoffman) Kochenour, natives of York County. Martin Kochenour, grandfather of subject, was also a native of York County, was a distiller, and afterward a school teacher and musician. Subject's father was born in 1803, and was for many years proprietor of a grist-mill and fifty-six acres of land in Manchester Township, and two farms in Conewago, in which latter township he now resides. His wife died in 1882. Henry H. Kochenour was reared to farming and milling under his father. He received a liberal education, and for twelve winters taught school and music in Conewago Township. In 1864 he enlisted in Company D, Two Hundredth Pennsylvania Volunteer Infantry, took part in the engagement at Fort Steadman and the siege of Petersburg, and at the close of the war returned to Conewago and engaged in milling, which he followed ten years. In 1866 he married Susan Machlin, who died in 1867 at the age of twenty-two, leaving one child—Susan L. In 1868 Mr. K. married Catherine Stough, a daughter of John Stough and a native of Dover Township. To this union has been born one child—Henry A. Mr. and Mr. Kochenour are members of the Lutheran Church.

DOVER TOWNSHIP.

SOLOMON BOYER was born in Manchester Township, October 28, 1819, and is a son of Peter and Sarah (Heidlebaugh) Boyer, both natives of York County. The grandfather of our subject, Frederick Augustus Boyer, came from Germany before the American Revolution, in which he took part and afterward married a Miss Shull, of York County, and died at the age of ninety-six. Subject's father was born in 1789, was a millwright and farmer, remained in active business life until seventy years old and then retired, dying in 1881 at the age of ninety-two. Solomon Boyer was reared on the farm, and also worked as a millwright with his father five years. He has been a resident of Dover Township since seven years of age, and is now the owner of two good farms of 108 and 104 acres, respectively, and also a tract of thirty acres, on which he resides. In 1843 he married Elvisa, daughter of Henry L. Lenhart, of Dover Township. Three children have resulted from this union: Edwin, deceased; Amanda L. Zinn, in Missouri, and Aaron, who resides on one of his father's farms. In 1880 Mr. Boyer was elected by the Democratic party director of the poor of York County, for three years. He is a member of the Lutheran Church, while his wife belongs to the Reformed Church.

MARTIN EMIG was born in Dover Township March 29, 1840, and is the eldest of the seven children born to George B. and Anna M. (Ziegler) Emig. The father was born in 1814, was a miller, and for ten years operated the Emig Mill on Conewago Creek, and also managed the mill on the Little Conewago for six years; he was also engaged for fifteen years in mercantile pursuits. He died in 1876, the owner of 150 acres of land along the Conewago and also a large grist and saw-mill. In 1877 our subject bought the mill, and has been doing a successful business ever since. In 1865 he married Susan Swartz, a daughter of Charles Swartz and native of Washington Township, and to this union have been born two children: Elizabeth J. and George E. Henry Emig, brother of Martin Emig, was born August 12, 1848. At his father's death he purchased the old homestead of 120 acres of improved land, which he has ever since cultivated. In 1880 he entered the mercantile business. In 1878 he married Clarissa Julius, daughter of John Julius, of Dover Township.

DR. J. M. GROSS was born in Dover Township January 19, 1844, and is the sixth in a family of twelve children born to Samuel and Susanah (Smyser) Gross, natives of York County and of German descent. Subject was reared a farmer and educated at the common schools, at the York County Academy and at the Pennsylvania College at Gettysburgh, from which last, after a three years' course, he graduated with the degree of A. B. and later with the degree of A. M. He next studied medicine with Dr. J. J. Zitizer, of Carlisle, and with Dr. Ahl, of Dover, in the meantime attending lectures at the Jefferson College, Philadelphia. He graduated from this institution in 1872, and in 1874 began practice in partnership with Dr. Ahl, and a year later on Dr. Ahl's removal to York, succeeded to the joint practice, which he has since increased and is now doing a lucrative business. In 1875 he married Louisa A., daughter of Daniel Smyser, of York County.

GEORGE N. LECKRONE is a native of Dillsburgh, York Co., Penn., was born November 22, 1839, and is the son of Leonard and Hannah (Nesbit) Leckrone, of York County. The father was born in 1812, was a tinner, and died in 1864. Our subject spent his early days on a farm, and at the age of sixteen came to Dover, where he held the position of assistant postmaster for six years. He now owns a fine dwelling in town and also nineteen acres of land within the borough. He is a member of the German Reformed Church, and a highly esteemed citizen.

DR. WILLIAM LENHART, a native of Dover Township, and son of William and Susan (Hamm) Lenhart, was born January 20, 1824, is of German descent, and the fifth in a family of seven children. He remained on the home farm until his thirtieth year, but in the meantime acquired a good education and was engaged in the practice of medicine. He then combined farming with veterinary practice and in 1861 relinquished farming and confined himself to his practice as a veterinarian, in which he met with flattering success until his retirement in 1883. He is the owner of 130 acres adjoining the town of Dover, a half interest in 114 acres in the township, a fine residence in the town, and also of the Dover cemetery. The Doctor has held several borough offices and in politics is a Democrat. He is a member of the German Reformed Church and is a bachelor.

DR. CHARLES LENHART was born in

Dover Township, April 9, 1852, and is the fourth of seven children born to John and Rebecca (Emig) Lenhart, of German descent. John Lenhart was born December 27, 1813, and died April 7, 1885. Our subject was reared on the farm until twenty-one years of age, when he began the study of medicine with his uncle, Dr. William Lenhart, with whom he remained until 1883, when he entered the Columbia Veterinary College of New York City, graduating in 1884, when he established himself in business with every prospect of success. In 1879 he married Emma J. Bond, daughter of W. H. Bond, of York, and to this union have been born two children. The father of our subject was born in 1812, and is living on his farm of 160 acres in this township, having retired from active life in 1869; the mother of our subject died in 1868, at the age of forty-two.

DR. EDMUND L. MELSHEIMER was born in Dover Township, April 28, 1823, is the son of Dr. Frederick E. and Sarah (Kimmel) Melsheimer, and is of German descent, his paternal grandfather having come to this county in 1778. He was a Lutheran minister, and died in 1816, aged seventy years. Grandfather Kimmel was a native of Washington Township, was a farmer by occupation, a potter by trade, and was owner of several tracts of land in Washington Township. Subject's father was born in Hanover Township in 1781, was a physician and died in 1872, aged ninety-one, his widow, also a native of York County, died in 1874, aged eighty-three years. Both were members of the Lutheran Church, and were the parents of six children, of whom our subject is the fifth. Our subject was educated in the district school of Dover Township, at the York County Academy and the New Oxford College, in Adams County, and then for seven winters taught subscription schools in his native and other townships. His medical studies were pursued under his father for a number of years, and then a year at Oxford, Penn., under Dr. Pfeiffer, a learned German physician, after which he attended the Pennsylvania Medical College, at Philadelphia, from which he graduated in the spring of 1850. He opened practice in Washington Township and Wellsville, in Warrington Township, but eventually settled in Davidsburg, Dover Township, where he has met with abundant success. In 1851 the Doctor married Miss Mary A., daughter of Joseph Underwood; this lady died in 1852, the mother of one child. In 1855 the Doctor married Sarah F. A., daughter of George Massmore, and to this union have been born five children—Mary E., Laura G., Flora R., Rosa L. and George F. E. Mr. and Mrs. M. are members of the Lutheran Church.

HENRY H. SPAHR was born in Warrington Township, August 28, 1834, and is the sixth of the nine children of George and Rebecca (Myley) Spahr, both natives of York County. The father was a miller and farmer, owned 142 acres of land in Warrington Township, and died in 1878, at the age of seventy-seven. Our subject was reared on the farm until nineteen, when he went to Chicago and clerked a year and a half; on his return he taught school seven terms in Warrington, Dover and Paradise Townships; in 1876 he was elected justice of the peace for Dover, and still holds the office; in 1859 he married Miss Rosa M., daughter of Dr. F. E. Melsheimer, of Dover Township. Mr. Spahr is owner of twenty-five acres of improved land in Dover, on which he resides. He is an active Democrat, and with his wife is a member of the Lutheran Church.

Z. B. TOOMEY is a native of Conewago Township, was born February, 1847, and is a son of John and Henrietta (Core) Loomey, being the third in a family of eleven children. He was reared until eighteen years of age on the home farm in Newberry Township when he enlisted in Company K, One Hundred and Ninety-second Pennsylvania Volunteers. He was engaged in the battles of Winchester, Culpepper Court House, Cedar Creek, Woodstock and various minor engagements, and at the end of eleven months returned to the farm. He next engaged in the cigar business in Newberry, where he enjoyed a very lucrative trade. In 1883 he took charge of a hotel at Dover, which he conducted in connection with the cigar business for two years. In 1872 he married Catherine Nailor, a native of West Manchester Township, and a daughter of Daniel Nailor. To this union were born four children: William L., Amanda E., Anna L., and Louisa (deceased). Mrs. Toomey died in 1881, at the age of twenty-nine, and in 1882, Mr. T. married Miss Emma Leathery, a native of Dover Township.

JESSE YOST was born July 19, 1833, in Dover Township, and was reared on his father's farm. He married Margaret Bowersox, daughter of John Bowersox, of Dover Township. Mr. Yost is a prosperous farmer and one of Dover Township's best citizens. He is a member of Strayer's Lutheran Church.

FAIRVIEW TOWNSHIP.

HENRY ATTICKS was born in Fairview Township, York Co., Penn., December 16, 1833. His parents, Henry H. and Elizabeth (Peterman) Atticks, were natives of York County, Penn., and had nine children, five living: Susanna, Henry, Sarah A., Catharine and George; four deceased: William, Jacob, John and Elmira. The father was a cabinetmaker and carpenter by trade, and followed farming, together with his trade, in Fairview Township. He owned a large tract of land, and was one of the leading farmers of his time. Subject's great-grandfather came from Germany and settled in eastern Pennsylvania. The grandfather, Henry Atticks, a native of York County, Penn., was a blacksmith, and followed farming, together with his trade. He died in Fairview Township, in 1844. Our subject at twenty-two years of age began farming on C. Hursh's farm, in Fairview Township, and remained one year; then worked one year on the farm and driving team for Mr. Boyer. In 1857 he went West, and engaged in farm work for two years in Kansas, Illinois and Ohio. In 1862 he married Harriet Greenfield, daughter of Jacob Greenfield, who was county commissioner three years. They have three children: George B., Charles E. and Jacob H. Mr. Atticks has a finely improved farm of 114 acres. He is a Democrat.

GEORGE W. ATTICKS was born in Fairview Township, York Co., Penn., February 5, 1842, son of Henry H. and Elizabeth (Peterman) Atticks, natives of York County, who had nine children. The father was a carpenter and cabinet-maker by trade, and followed farming, together with his trades, in Fairview Township, where he always resided. He owned six farms at one time, amounting to 378 acres of land. He was school director for many years, and died in 1873, aged seventy-two years. George W. was reared on the farm, and traveled in the West four years. In 1870, his father deeded him a farm, and he has since followed farming. He owns two farms of ninety and sixty-seven acres respectively, which he inherited. In 1869 he married Lucinda Fluke, daughter of David Fluke, native of Ashland County, Ohio. They have two children: Lee and Kelsey. Mr. Atticks is a Democrat.

BIOGRAPHICAL SKETCHES.

HENRY M. BITNER was born in Fairview Township, York Co., Penn., April 24, 1823, son of Samuel and Annie (Mish) Bitner, natives of Lebanon County, Penn., and parents of nine children: Elizabeth, deceased; Margaret, deceased; Catharine, Anna, Samuel, John, Henry M., Matthias and Sarah A. Subject's father was born in 1786, and came to Fairview Township in 1812, where he afterward owned a farm of 200 acres of land. He was a member of the German Reformed Church, and died in 1857, aged seventy one years. Henry M. was reared on the farm, and after his father's death, began farming for himself, and has since followed that occupation, owning 126 acres of land in Fairview Township, and twenty-two acres of timber land. His son now manages this property, which is the old homestead. In 1871, Mr. Bitner moved to Cumberland County, Penn., where he now resides, and owns fifty-five acres of finely improved land. In 1857, he married Rebecca Cassel, a native of Dauphin County, Penn., and by this union they have four children: William H., residing on his father's farm, in Fairview Township, and Samuel L., Joseph M. and Henry C., at home.

LEWIS CLINE was born in Newberry Township, York Co., Penn., March 10, 1836, and is the fourth of ten children born to Andrew and Margaret (Foster) Cline, natives of York County, Penn., and of German and Irish descent, respectively. Andrew Cline was a hatter by trade, but gave that up and began farming, which he followed until his death. Lewis was reared a farmer, and at the age of twenty-one began teaching school, which he followed for two terms. He continued farming until he was thirty-one years old, when he took charge of his father's mill, on shares, and since his father's death has operated the mill in his own name. He enlisted August 4, 1862, in Company K, One Hundred and Thirtieth Pennsylvania Volunteer Infantry, and took part in the battle of Antietam, where he was wounded in the left arm. He was with his regiment at Chancellorsville where he took no part in the battle, but carried water to the wounded. He was discharged May 21, 1863, on the expiration of his term of enlistment. He is now a pensioner and receives $64 yearly. In 1871 he married Elmira Mordorf, and they have three children; Clara, Rosaline and Edith. Mrs. Cline is a daughter of Levi and Susanna (Leiby) Mordorf, natives of Cumberland County, Penn. Mr. Cline is doing a good business in his mills, which have three run of buhrs, one on wheat and two on feed. On the date stone of these the Lewisberry Mills is carved in antique letters the following: "Samuel Kniselley, Mason IOHN HARMN & ELIZ his WIFE, October ye 11, annd 1785, in the 10th year of Amrn. Independcy." Mr. Cline is a Republican.

CHRISTIAN GARVER was born July 24, 1818. in Fairview Township, York Co., Penn., son of Christian and Nancy (Horsht) Garver, the former a native of Lancaster County, Penn., the latter of Fairview Township. His grandfather, Garver, a native of Switzerland, came to America at an early day and settled in Lancaster County, Penn., where he followed farming. Subject's father was born in 1775, came to York County when about twenty-five years of age, and settled in Fairview Township, where he owned several fine farms, and was also engaged in distilling. He retired from active life a few years previous to his death in 1849, at the age of seventy-five years. Our subject was reared on the farm, and in 1845 began farming for himself, which occupation he followed ten years. He then retired from active work, and has since resided in New Market, Fairview Township. He owns a finely improved farm of 160 acres, and a fine residence in New Market. In 1845 he married Elizabeth Miller, daughter of Tobias Miller, of Cumberland County, Penn. They have had four children: Anna Baughman, Benjamin (deceased), Elizabeth (deceased), and Christian M. The latter lives on his father's farm.

JOHN M. HART was born October 16, 1822, in Fairview Township, son of Isaac and Elizabeth (Moore) Hart, natives of this county. His great-grandfather, Jacob Hart, was born in Germany, came to America at an early date, and settled in York County, Penn., where he engaged in farming. Subject's grandfather, John Hart, was born in this county, and was a large landowner. He died in 1849, aged about eighty years. Isaac Hart, subject's father, was born in 1788, was a farmer by occupation, and died in 1839. His wife was born in 1799, and died in 1876. They had seven children: Sarah J., John M., Joseph K., Jacob, Andrew, Robert L. (deceased), and Elizabeth. John M., at the age of twenty-five years, bought a farm of 125 acres in Fairview Township, on which he followed farming from 1849 to 1884, when he retired from active life. He has a finely improved farm, and has made all by his own industry and energy. In 1870 he married Mary E. Lloyd, daughter of William and Amanda (Anderson) Lloyd, the former a native of Chester County, the latter of Cumberland County, Penn. Mr. Hart has been a director of the Second National Bank of Mechanicsburgh, Penn., for fifteen years, and was elected president of that establishment January 1, 1884. Mrs. Hart is a member of the Methodist Church.

SAMUEL B. HOFF was born in Fairview Township, York Co. Penn., February 25, 1838, son of Henry H. and Elizabeth (Boyer) Hoff, natives of Heidelberg Township, York Co., Penn. The father was born in 1792, followed coopering, and afterward engaged in farming in Heidelberg and Fairview Townships. He owned 165 acres of land, where Samuel B. now resides, besides a large amount of other property. He was a Democrat. He died in 1865. His wife, who was born in 1799, is still living in Lisburn, Penn. They had five children: Jeremiah (deceased), Elizabeth, Magdalena, Henry and Samuel B. Subject's great-grandfather, Hoff, served in the Revolutionary war, and was taken prisoner by the British. Subject's great-grandfather, John Boyer, was one of the first settlers in Heidelberg Township, to which he came over 108 years ago. Samuel B. Hoff was reared on the farm in Fairview Township, where he resides, and at the age of twenty-two years began farming for himself. In the spring of 1865 he sold his stock, and spent two months in Ohio, Indiana and Illinois, after which he returned to York County, Penn., where he has since remained. He owns a finely improved farm of 165 acres, and 20 acres of woodland. Mr. Hoff is a school director. He was elected prothonotary of York County on the Democratic ticket November 4, 1884, by a majority of 3,504, for a term of three years. In 1868 he married Mary Jane Anderson, born February 26, 1845, daughter of William and Mary (Wiley) Anderson, of Monaghan Township. By this union they have had five children: Harry and Willie, twins (deceased), Charles (born July 16, 1870), Leroy (born March 6, 1875), and Morris (born August 26, 1882. Mr. Hoff has a box which was made by the Indians in Lancaster County, Penn., and which has been handed down from his great-grandfather, Boyer.

JACOB HURSH, March 18, 1767, obtained a grant for 300 acres of land near "Lofty Mountain" in Newberry, now Fairview Township. In 1789 Peter Hursh, with his family of wife, five sons and six daughters, moved to York County from Lancaster County, and purchased 600 acres adjoining lands of Jacob Hursh, a part of which called "Fortune" was originally granted to Richard Ashton in 1734, by one of Samuel Blunston's permits. Four-

FAIRVIEW TOWNSHIP.

teen hundred and sixty pounds currency were paid for the entire tract. It was divided into four plantations, and conveyed to four surviving sons, each son receiving one tract. These lands have since remained almost entirely in the possession of the lineal descendants to the fifth generation, who are engaged in farming the coveted land-marks of their ancestors. They are valuable limestone lands, and very productive. Some of the descendants of the family have immigrated to Cumberland, Adams, Franklin and Fulton Counties, Penn. Those who remained in Fairview Township have always been among her leading citizens.

DR. GEORGE R. HURSH, a lineal descendant, was elected a member of the house of representatives of Pennsylvania from York County in 1868, and re-elected the following year. He was born February, 6, 1835, in Fairview Township, and was brought up on his father's farm. At the age of sixteen he attended the Cumberland Valley Institute, after which he made the study of medicine his choice, and having attended the required course of lectures in Jefferson Medical C llege, at Philadelphia, he graduated in that institution March 7, 1857. He has since been continuously engaged in the active duties of his profession, until the spring of 1884, when he began to devote a part of his time to the delightful and healthful pursuits of agriculture on his farm in Fairview Township, York County.

J. A. KANN was born December 16, 1837, in Fairview Township, York Co., Penn., son of Daniel and Eliza (Hutton) Kann, natives of York County, Penn. His grandfather, Daniel Kann, immigrated to America from Germany at an early day and settled near York, Penn. He was a member of the Lutheran Church. Daniel Kann, subject's father, was born in 1809, came to this township with his parents when ten years old. followed farming, and owned about 400 acres of land. He was a member of the Church of God, and died in 1876. He had seven children: Anna, Priscilla, Jacob J., Margaret, Daniel, Ellen and Christiana. J. A. Kann remained on the home farm till he was twenty-three years old, when he began farming for himself. In 1873 he bought his father's farm of 115 acres, and in 1881 retired from active life and moved to Lisburn, Cumberland Co., Penn., where he now resides, owning four lots and a fine residence in that town. In 1864 he married Rachel Strominger, daughter of John and Rachel (Kilmore) Strominger, natives of Fairview Township. Mrs. Kann is a member of the Methodist Church.

MARTIN KAUFFMAN was born in Lancaster County, January 1. 1826, and is the son of Michael and Barbara (Mosser)Kauffman. His grandfather, Michael Kauffman, was also a native of Lancaster County. Subject's father was born in 1791, in Lancaster County, but moved to Fairview Township, York County, where he possessed 140 acres of land, and where he followed farming until fourteen years prior to his death in 1872. He was a member of the Mennonite Church, and the father of eight children. Martin Kauffman worked on the home farm for his father until thirty years of age, when he purchased the homestead and conducted it until 1883, when his son took charge—Mr. K. retiring to New Market. He was married in 1857 to Mary, daughter of Samuel and Catherine Strickler Landis, and has had born to him three children: Emma, Samuel and Kate.

HENRY KILMORE was born in Fairview Township, York Co., Penn., February 6, 1834, son of Joseph and Eve (Peterman) Kilmore. Subject's grandfather, Henry Peterman, was a farmer, and was born in Carroll Township, this county. Joseph Kilmore, subject's father, was born in 1797, and at fifteen years of age moved with his parents to this township, where he followed farming, and owned 135 acres of land. He died in 1871, and his wife in 1862, aged forty-nine years. They were members of the Winebrennerian Church. They had ten children, of whom Henry, David, Mary J., Susan, Joseph and William are living, and John A., Adeline, Catharine and Dora are deceased. Our subject, at the age of twenty-two years, began learning the carpenter's trade, which he followed for fifteen years, and in 1864 began coach-making in Fairview Township, and has since been doing a prosperous business in building buggies, wagons, sleighs, etc. He has a two-thirds interest in the homestead farm, and has a fine home near the farm. In 1856 he married Sarah Fink, daughter of John Fink, of Newberry Township. They have had fifteen children, ten living: Charles, Anna M., George O., Harry, John A., Joseph, Jennie, Lerne, Himen and Minnie, and five deceased: Cora M., Bertha, Ella, Florence and Walter. Mr. and Mrs. Kilmore are members of the Lutheran Church.

D. P. KILMORE was born in Fairview Township, February 12, 1836, son of Joseph and Eve (Peterman) Kilmore, also natives of the same township, and parents of the following children: Henry, David P., Mary J., John (deceased), Susanna, Adeline (deceased), Joseph, William and Elizabeth (deceased). His great-grandfather Kilmore, came from Germany at an early date to America, settling in Adams County, Penn., and engaged in farming. He was a member of the Lutheran Church and a soldier in the Revolutionary war. Subject's grandfather, David Kilmore, was born in 1767, in Adams County, Penn.; followed farming chiefly. owning 200 acres of land in Fairview Township, and died in 1853. He was a member of the Lutheran Church, and in politics a Democrat. Joseph Kilmore, subject's father, followed farming all his life, and owned a farm of 136 acres in Fairview Township. He was a Democrat and a member of the Lutheran Church. D. P. Kilmore, at the age of twenty-two years, began farming for himself, and has since followed that occupation. In 1872 he bought a farm of 115 acres in Fairview Township, where he now resides. In 1864, he married Sarah J. Nailor, daughter of Jacob Nailor, of Fairview Township. They have two children, Ira J. and Ray. Mrs. Kilmore is a member of the Church of God. Mr. Kilmore is a Democrat and has held several township offices.

JOHN GEORGE MAISCH, the ancestor of a numerous family of descendants, was a native of Germany. On the 16th of October, 1751, he set sail from the port of Rotterdam, Holland, with 106 passengers in the sailing vessel "Duke of Wellington," which paid respects to England by stopping, at Cowes, and two months later landed at Philadelphia with its load of emigrants. He first settled in Chester County, Penn., but soon after arriving immigrated to the Quaker settlement in the northern part of York County, and purchased a tract of land in Fairview Township, now owned by George Lefever. Some of his descendants joined the Society of Friends. Joseph, his eldest son, married Barbara Leidy. Their children were David, Samuel, Joseph, Frederick, Barbara and Martha. The father died in Fairview; the sons all moved to Indiana. David, second son of the immigrant, married Sarah Stickel, sister of Hon. Jacob Stickel, who was a member of State Constitutional Convention of 1838. Frederick, the youngest son of John George Maisch, was a soldier of the Revolution, and died of camp fever at Valley Forge, during the winter of 1777-78. He left one son, who moved to New Philadelphia, Ohio, and was killed by accident. Children of David Maish, son of John George Maisch: Jacob, George, David, Susan, intermarried with John Spangler; Polly, intermarried with Michael Wollet ; Hannah, intermarried with David Crone, of West Virginia; Sarah, intermarried with George Moser; Jacob, married

BIOGRAPHICAL SKETCHES.

Lydia Sibhart. They had three daughters: Mary Ann, Mrs. Zachariah Heindle; Ellen, Mrs. Benjamin Heindle; Susan, Mrs. Sebastian Stevens; George, married Lydia Moser, daughter of George Moser. They had children: David, George W., Thomas Jefferson, Sarah, Mary, Emma, Ellen and Amanda. David married Salome Neiman, daughter of George Neiman, of Conewago Township, a man of large landed estates, who died a few years ago, at the age of eighty-nine years eleven months twenty days, leaving 184 lineal descendants. David had three sons, George H., Levi and Lewis.

GEORGE H. MAISH, Des Moines, Iowa, son of David Maish and Salome *nee* Neiman. was born in Conewago Township, this county, September 30, 1835. Being ambitious to engage in active business life, at the age of seventeen he secured a position as salesman in the extensive mercantile establishment of P. A. & S. Small, of York, with whose service he continued for nine years. He was married on October 1, 1857, to Miss Charlotte E. Weaver, of York, the only daughter of Jeremiah Weaver. In 1861 he engaged in the coal business in York with John M. Brown, forming the firm of Brown & Maish, in which business he continued until 1865, when he was chosen teller of the York National Bank, continuing in this position in a very acceptable manner for four and a half years. In 1869, he, with his family removed to Des Moines, Iowa, where he arrived July 22, 1869. Here he engaged in the drug business with his brother-in-law, Charles A. Weaver. In the fall of 1875 he, with other gentlemen, organized the Iowa National Bank of Des Moines, of which he was chosen cashier. In January, 1885, at the earnest solicitation of many friends, he accepted the presidency of the State Insurance Company of Des Moines (the largest insurance company in Iowa having a cash capital of $200,000), to the management of which he is giving daily attention, in connection with his duties as cashier of the Iowa National Bank. His church connection is with the English Lutheran Church of Des Moines. In political sentiment Mr. Maish has been identified with the Republican party since its organization. Of eight children born to Mr. and Mrs. Maish, seven are now living. Charles Edward died when two and a half years old; William Weaver, Annie Kate, Harriet Jane and Albert George were born in York, Penn., and Mary Martha, Georgie Elizabeth and Lottie Salome were born in Des Moines, Iowa.

CAPT. LEWIS MAISH was born July 2, 1840, in Spring Garden Township, York County, within a few miles of York. At the age of sixteen he was apprenticed to learn the machinist's trade at the Variety Iron Works, York, Penn.. where he remained until the breaking out of the Rebellion. In September, 1861, he took an active part in the raising of a company for the Thomas A. Scott Regiment (afterward numbered Eighty-seventh Regiment Pennsylvania Volunteer Infantry). On the organization of the regiment he was elected second-lieutenant of Company B, and soon after the regiment was called into active service, and May 26, 1863, he was promoted to first-lieutenant, and October 25, 1863, to captain of his company. June 23, 1864, Capt. Maish was taken prisoner, while the lines of the army were being established in front of Petersburg, Va., and taken to Richmond, and confined in Libby Prison for a few days, after which he was taken, with about 3,000 other prisoners, to the State of Georgia. About 250 of the above being officers were left at Macon, (the principal military prison at that time for officers), the remainder being taken to Andersonville. During the nine months of the captain's prison life he spent about one month at Macon, two months at Savannah, Ga., about two months in the jail yard at Charleston, during the siege of that doomed city, and four months at Columbia, S. C.; a few days at Charlotte, N. C. From the latter place, in company with two companions (Capt. H. C. Smyser, of Baltimore, and Lieut. Anderson, of Philadelphia), he made his escape into the Union lines. Incidents of the captain's military and prison life, in connection with his escape, would make too large a volume to attempt here. Capt. Maish was mustered out of service March 24, 1865, having served his country three and one-half years. After the close of the war Capt. Maish returned to his native town, and resided there with his wife whom he had married at Winchester, Va., and remained for one year, and then spent one year in the South. In September, 1867, he located in the city of Minneapolis, Minn., where he is now residing, and engaged as an active member of the Variety Iron Works, in the manufacture of machinery.

JACOB MILEY was born in Cumberland County, Penn., July 21, 1827, son of Jacob and Catherine (Miller) Miley, natives of Lebanon County, Penn. His grandfather Miley came from Germany at an early date, settled in Lebanon County, Penn., and followed farming and distilling. He drove a team during the war of 1812-14. Subject's father was born in 1790, was a miller by trade and engaged in distilling in Lebanon County, Penn. In 1828 he moved to Cumberland County, Penn., where he followed farming and milling. He died in 1842, aged fifty-two years. He had nine children: William (deceased), Ellen, Nancy, Richard (deceased), Martha, Lydia, Levi, Jacob and Kate. Our subject at seventeen years of age began learning the tanner's trade, serving three years' apprenticeship, and worked at that trade eight years. He then bought a farm in Cumberland County, Penn., where he remained three years, and in 1864 removed to York County, and bought 103 acres of improved land in Fairview Township. He also engaged in sawing timber three years. Mr. Miley owns 222 acres of timber land in Perry County, Penn. In 1859 he married Susan Hursh, a native of York County, Penn., and daughter of Christian Hursh. They have three children: William, John and Laura.

JOHN R. MOORE was born in Fairview Township, April 15, 1840; son of John and Mary (Stettler) Moore, the former a native of Fairview Township, the latter of Newberry Township, York Co., Penn. His grandfather Moore was born in York County, Penn., January 9, 1777; was a farmer by occupation and died February 29, 1852. His wife, Hannah (Sutton) Moore, died November 8, 1863, aged eighty-five years. Subject's grandfather Stettler was a native of York County, and a potter by trade. His wife was also a native of York County, Penn. John Moore, subject's father, was born in 1811, was a farmer by occupation, and owned 170 acres of land in this township. He held the office of justice of the peace in this township for a number of years; was elected commissioner of York County on the Democratic ticket in 1850, and in 1869 elected associate judge of York County, Penn , but died before the expiration of his term, after serving about three years. He was a member of the Methodist Church, and died July 31, 1874. His wife died March 10, 1883, aged seventy years They had the following children: Hananiah, Henry S., John R., Logan C., Hannah E., Jacob A., Sarah J. and William (deceased). Our subject remained on the home farm till he was twenty eight years of age, when he bought a farm of seventy acres from his father, and has a finely improved place. December 31, 1867, he married Anna M. Nailor, a native of Cumberland County, and daughter of Jacob Nailor, a native of York County, Penn. They have two children, William E. and Flora J. Mrs. Moore is a member of the Church of God. Mr. Moore is a Democrat.

HENRY R. MOSSER was born in Fairview Township, York County, July 14, 1828, to Benjamin H. and Elizabeth (Rupley) Mosser. Dr. Benjamin Mosser, subject's great-grandfather, was a native of Berne, Switzerland. Henry Mosser, subject's grandfather, a blacksmith, farmer and preacher for the Dunkard Society, settled in Fairview Township in 1800; he married Susanna Neff, whose father owned the Columbia Ferry which Washington crossed when congress was convened at York; and on one occasion, this lady, when a child of ten years, had the honor of sitting on Washington's knee while her mother was preparing breakfast. One of her children, Dr. Daniel Mosser, became Bishop of the Mennonite Reformed Church of Lancaster County; another son, Rev. Joseph Mosser, is in Salem, Ill. The father of our subject was born in 1802, was a farmer, owning 200 acres of land, also a lumber merchant; he was a prominent Whig, and was a member of the convention which nominated Gen. Scott for the presidency. He died in 1859, aged fifty-seven; his widow died in 1877, aged seventy-five years. Henry R. Mosser was reared on the home farm, and at the age of twenty-one joined his father in the lumber business; his father withdrew in 1857, and from 1864 to 1868 the firm was known as Mosser & Coover, at New Cumberland. In 1852 Mr. Mosser married Margaret A., daughter of Jacob Yocum, of York; her mother was a daughter of Gen. A. Duncan. To this union were born two children: Mettie and Rev. Benjamin H. In 1859 Mrs. M. died, and in 1863 Mr. Mosser married Jennie, daughter of John G. Miller, and to this union also two children have been born, Annie and John C. The family are members of the Methodist Episcopal Church.

MICHAEL SHULER was born in Manchester Township, York County, Penn., June 8, 1811, a son of John and Rebecca Baker Shuler, the former a native of Berks County, Penn., and the latter of Manchester Township, York County. His grandfather Shuler was a native of Berks County, Penn., and a farmer by occupation. His grandfather Baker, who came from Germany at an early day and settled in York County, owned a large mill and finely improved farm in Conewago Township. Subject's father came to York County and settled in Manchester Township, where he owned 212 acres of improved land. He was a member of the Reformed Church and died in 1844, aged sixty-six years. He had six children, of whom Michael and Daniel are living, and George, John, Eliza and Rebecca are deceased. Michael was reared on the farm, and when thirteen years old moved with his parents to Conewago Township. At the age of eighteen he began learning the blacksmith's trade, serving two years' apprenticeship. He then began business for himself in Manchester Township, where he remained twelve years. In 1848 he moved to Fairview Township, where he followed farming, together with his trade, for many years. In 1862 he retired from active work. He has a farm of 149 acres, with fine residence and buildings, where he resides, another farm where his son lives, and also thirty-six acres of improved land. In 1833 he married Jane Seward, daughter of John Seward. Mrs. Shuler was born in Lancaster County in 1815. They have had ten children: Anna, John, Charles H., Eliza J., Michael (deceased), Mary A., Ellen N., Amanda, Adeline and Henrietta. Mr. and Mrs. Shuler are members of the Lutheran Church.

FAWN TOWNSHIP.

JOHN H. ANDERSON, son of Joseph R. and Elizabeth (Wilson) Anderson, of Hopewell Township, York County, Penn., and Harford County, Md., respectively, was born September 9, 1835, on the homestead now owned by his brother. His father was born in Hopewell Township in 1803, and lived there nearly all his life. John H. Anderson lived with his parents until 1868, when he bought his present farm of 120 acres, and has resided there since. He was married, in 1868, to Elizabeth Wilson, daughter of David and Jane Wilson, of York County, Penn., and has three children: Joseph C., Henry M. W. and David R. Mr. Anderson is a member of the school board, and a member of the Presbyterian Church of Centre.

REED W. ANDERSON, son of Joseph R. and Elizabeth (Wilson) Anderson, was born on the old homestead December 24, 1840. The father was a native of York County, Penn., and the mother of Harford County, Md. Our subject now owns and occupies the old homestead place, which consists of 161 acres of land. He was married January 14, 1875, to Martha A. Brown, daughter of Milton and Sarah Brown, of Lancaster County, Penn. By this union they have been blessed with two children, Annie M. and Nora B. Mr. Anderson is a member of the Presbyterian Church of Centre.

JOHN ANDERSON, son of Robert and Nancy (Payne) Anderson, natives of York County, was born in 1834 in Fawn Township, York County, where he has always resided. He was married, in 1861, to Margaret E. Grove, daughter of Jacob Grove, of Hopewell Township. This union has been blessed with four children: Mary A., Robert P., Margaret J. and Thomas Franklin W. In 1863 Mr. Anderson purchased the farm on which he now resides, and which contains 132 acres. He is at present a school director; he is a member of the Methodist Episcopal Church of Zion. His wife died in 1883.

BENJAMIN P. ANDERSON, son of Robert and Nancy (Payne) Anderson, of York County, was born in Fawn Township, this county, in 1843. His parents were born in York County, and lived there until they died; the father dying in 1877 and the mother in 1859. Mr. Anderson owns a farm of 130 acres, where he has always lived. In 1871 he was married to Elizabeth M. Anderson, daughter of James Anderson, of York County. They have three children living: James C., Mary B., and Robert P. Mr. and Mrs. Anderson are members of the Presbyterian Church of Centre.

ROBERT BARTOL, son of George and Mary (Bayless) Bartol, natives of Harford County, Md., was born December 23, 1814, in Harford County, Md. He remained with his parents until he was sixteen years of age, when he learned the tanner's trade in Baltimore. He moved to York County, Penn., in 1834, and bought a farm of 136 acres, which he has since cultivated in connection with tanning. He was married in 1841 to Mary Kurtz, who died in 1864. His second marriage was in 1871 to Mary Quinlan, daughter of Philip and Mary Quinlan, of Harford County, Md. He had twelve children, ten of whom are living: Sarah, George, James, Robert, Charles, Mary E., John, Corinne M., Nathaniel, Robert, Imogene and Joseph. Mr. Bartol has held several prominent school positions in the Township. He is a brother of Judge Bartol, chief justice of the court of appeals of Maryland.

ROBERT BLAIN was born February 11, 1805, on his present farm of 100 acres, which he inherited at the death of his father, and where he has since resided. He is a son of William Blain,who came to York County, Penn., in 1800, and settled in Fawn Township, where he resided until his death in 1829. He followed farming, and also did quite a large business in distilling. Robert Blain was married in 1872 to Mary Tarbort, daughter of William Tarbort, of Fawn Township. By this union they have been blessed with two children: Robert S.and Elizabeth.

JOHN A. BOYD, son of Dr. Thomas Boyd, of Lancaster County, Penn., was born January 5.1811, in Fawn Township, where he has since lived, with the exception of three years, which he spent in Harford County, Md. His father died in 1836. In 1861 Mr. Boyd was married to Margaret Anderson, daughter of Nathaniel Anderson, of York County. Penn. Mr. Boyd moved to his present farm of 116 acres with his parents in 1824, and at the death of his father inherited the farm, and has lived on it ever since.

ROBERT D. BROWN, son of John and Susanna (Ray) Brown, natives of York County, Penn , and Ireland, respectively, was born May 2, 1816, on the farm of eighty acres, on which he now lives, and where his father was also born. The father died in 1843, and the mother in 1853. In 1856 Mr. Brown was married to Julia Marsteller, daughter of Henry Marsteller, of York County, Penn., she died in 1862, leaving four children: Susan, Henry T., Robert D. and James W. Mr. Brown's second marriage was in 1864, to Caroline Mitchell, daughter of Joshua and Beulah (Wilson) Mitchell, of Lancaster County, Penn.; by this marriage four children have been born to them: Clement L., Mary E., John and Carrie L. Mr. Brown was county commissioner for four years.

JOHN CHANNELL, son of Abel and Jane (Anderson) Channell, of York County, was born December 17, 1814, in Fawn Township; his father died in 1868. John Channell was married in 1836 to Mary Clark, daughter of James Clark, of York County, Penn. They have nine children living: Elizabeth, Jane, Agnes, James, Samuel M., Sarah, Rosa Anne, Joseph and Annie. Mr. Channell lived in Fawn Township all his life, and has held the offices of school director and supervisor. He is a member of the Presbyterian Church of Chanceford. The farm on which he resides contains about 185 acres, and was purchased by him in 1842.

ANDERSON CHANNELL, son of Isaac and Mary (Anderson) Channell, of Fawn Township, York Co., Penn., was born January 26, 1818, on the old homestead. The father died in 1830, and the mother in 1874. Our subject was married in 1840 to Martha M. Thompson, daughter of Israel and Phœbe (Ewing) Thompson, of York County, Penn. By this union they have had thirteen children: Alex. E. John A.. Phœbe E., Clarissa A., William T., Mary F., Sarah V., James F., Henry C., Thomas I., Rosa B., Isaac M. and Etha M. In 1844 Mr. Channell purchased the farm upon which he resides, and which contains 100 acres. He has held the offices of assessor and supervisor of the township. Two of his sons were in the army during the late war: John A. Channell, Company I, One Hundred and Thirtieth Regiment Pennsylvania Volunteers, who served from 1862 till the close of the war, and was severely wounded, and William T. Channell, who enlisted in the One Hundred and Eighty-seventh Regiment Pennsylvania Volunteers, in 1863, and served until the close of the war.

WILLIAM HENRY DEVOE, son of John DeVoe, of Harford County, Md.. was born in Harford County, Md., October 10, 1828. He was educated at the Deaf and Dumb Institute in Philadelphia, and after leaving the school, began learning harness-making, in 1845, at Jarrettsville, He was married, in 1856, to Martha Bonnister, daughter of Joseph Bonnister, of Harford County, Md. They have six children: Sarah P., Mary M., Henry C.,

John, William A. and James F. Mr. Devoe purchased his present residence and one-half acre of land in Fawn Grove, in 1855, and has since resided there, doing a good business in harness-making. Mr. and Mrs. DeVoe, are members of the Methodist Episcopal Church, of Harford County, Md.

WILLIAM FLEMING, son of Robert Fleming, a native of Ireland, was born in Ireland in 1828; came to this country in 1846, and settled in Fawn Township, York County. He was married, in 1854, to Agnes Keady, daughter of John Keady, of York County. They have five children: Robert G., John K., Samuel B., Agnes J. and Margaret R. In 1856 Mr. Fleming bought the farm on which he now resides and which contains forty-two acres, and, with the exception of a few years, he has since resided there. He is a member of the Presbyterian Church, of Chanceford.

JOHN B. GEMMILL,son of Benjamin and Mary (Brown) Gemmill, of York County, was born January 19, 1838, and resided on the homestead with his parents until 1861. His father died in 1878, and his mother in 1879. He was married, in 1860, to Agnes M. Workman, daughter of John and Rebecca Workman, of Baltimore, and formerly of York County. In 1874 he was elected member of the legislature, re-elected in 1876 and served four sessions. He has had five children, one of whom is dead. The living are Milton C., Willie B., Benjamin M. and Ellis H. He also has an adopted daughter—Molly Rinely. Mr. Gemmill is a member of the Centre Presbyterian Church; he has been treasurer for thirteen years and trustee for six years. He has also held important offices in the township, and takes great interest in schools. He served several terms as township school director and was one of the originators of the Fawn Grove Academy. He is a director in the Stewartstown Railroad. During his legislative career he was devoted to his work and faithfully represented his constituents. He is an ardent advocate of the principles of the political party which he represents. In 1885 he was elected a director of the Codorus and Manheim Insurance Company.

CHARLES H. GIESEY, son of John and Catharine (Zellers) Giesey, of York County, was born December 10, 1836, at Shrewsbury, Penn. He remained with his parents until 1853, when he went to Hanover, Penn., and learned the cabinetmaker's trade. In 1855 he returned to Shrewsbury, where he remained two years after which he went to Baltimore, and remained there five years. He returned to Shrewsbury in 1860 and remained there until 1878, when he went to Hopewell Township and resided there two years. He came to Gatchellsville in 1880, bought a hotel property and four acres of land and has since resided there. He was married in 1861 to Rebecca Brenise, daughter of William and Lydia Brenise, of York County. Mrs. Giesey died in 1875, leaving three children: John B., Lydia B., and Charles B. Mr. Giesey's second marriage was in 1882 to Mrs. Mary Brooks, daughter of David Workinger, of York County, Penn.

CHARLES GROVE, son of John Grove, of York County, Penn., was born in 1808, in York County. He was married, in 1835, to Elizabeth Leib, daughter of Joseph Leib, of York County. Mrs. Grove died in 1880, leaving nine children: John W., Mary E., Henry P., Laura E., Charles L., Jacob W., Francis N., Christopher T. and Catherine J. Mr. G. purchased his present farm of 250 acres in 1849 and has since that time resided on it.

DR. JOHN A. HAWKINS, son of John and Susan (Thompson) Hawkins, was born in Harford County, Md., June 30, 1831. His parents came to York County in 1868; his ancestors were English, and include the Chalk and Thompson families of

FAWN TOWNSHIP.

Maryland, the former of which located in the early colonial times, on Winter's Run, about sixteen miles from the Pennsylvania line and exercised no inconsiderable local influence in their day. The family name, Hawkins, was brought to this country by three brothers, who first trod American soil at Elk Ridge Landing, Md., shortly before the Revolution. The youngest of these, Nicholas, had a son, John, who, in turn, was father of the subject of this sketch, and who was widely known throughout his county, having at one time represented it in the legislature of the State. Dr. Hawkins received his preliminary education at Belle Air Academy, and graduated from Maryland University at Baltimore, in 1852. He practiced medicine successfully in Baltimore County, Md., for one year, and then at the instance of some friends was induced to remove to York County, where he has since resided and where he is now enjoying a large practice. In 1855 he was married to Hannah A. Jones, daughter of Asa Jones, of Fawn Grove, a strict member of the S. of F. He has two children: Charles A. and Vallandigham. In 1884 he purchased a small farm within the borough limits of Fawn Grove, for the purpose of establishing a hennery, which he is now conducting in connection with his practice. Both the Doctor and his wife are members of the Methodist Episcopal Church.

FELIX C. HERBERT, son of Gideon and Mary Herbert, of York County, Penn., was born in 1803, in Harford County, Md., and came to York County, Penn., when very young. He moved to his present farm of seventy acres, in 1825, and has lived there since. He was married, in 1825, to Rachael Harrison, who died in 1855, leaving eight children: William Richard, Sarah, Mary J., Salome, Rebecca, Elfie and Henry. His second marriage was in 1857, to Anabel M. Boyd, daughter of Dr. Thomas Boyd, of Lancaster County, Penn. Mr. Herbert has held the offices of commissioner and auditor of York County. He is a member of the Methodist Episcopal Church of Fellowship. Mr. Herbert has always taken a prominent interest in local politics, frequently representing his township in Democratic conventions. He voted first for Andrew Jackson for president.

THOMAS H. HERBERT, son of Richard Herbert, of Baltimore County, Md., was born in 1832, in Baltimore County, Md. He came to York County, Penn., in 1857, and settled in Fawn Township. He was married, in 1857, to Melissa Jones, of York County, Penn. They have seven children: Oscar A., Milton J., Mamie M., Maggie, Wilburt J., William D. and Annette. Mr. Herbert purchased his present residence and one acre of land, in 1864. He is a member of the Methodist Protestant Church of Fawn Grove. At present he holds the office of justice of the peace. His son, Milton J., who was born in 1860, in Baltimore County, Md., came to York County, Penn., with his parents, and has since resided there. He learned the blacksmith trade in 1881 and carries on an extensive business.

JOSEPH HOSTLER is a son of George and Mary (Noon) Hostler, natives of York County, Penn., and was born March 28, 1822. His parents dying when he was yet an infant, he was brought up in the family of his eldest brother, in Shrewsbury Township, until his sixteenth year. He then went to Groves Mills and learned the blacksmithing trade and worked there for two years. He was married October 21, 1845, to Sarah E. Herbert, daughter of Gideon and Mary (McCurdy) Herbert, of Harford County, Md. By this union they have been blessed with three children: Israel T., John J. and Araminta E. Mr. Hostler has held the offices of supervisor and auditor of Fawn Township. He is a member of Whiteside Chapel, of Fawn.

ROBERT B. HYSON, son of John and Margaret Hyson, natives of York County, was born December 28, 1854, in Hopewell Township, this county. He remained with his parents on the homestead until 1870; then spent about five years in Ohio; returned to Pennsylvania in 1874, when he engaged in general merchandising business at Mount Pleasant, Penn., where he remained three years. He then came to Gatchellville in 1879, and has since remained there. He was married in 1880. Mr. Hyson is at present justice of the peace of Fawn Township. He is a member of the Presbyterian Church at Centre, and it may well be said stands second to none in the rank of business men of southern York County.

DANIEL C. ILGENFRITZ, son of Daniel Ilgenfritz, was born March 3, 1828, in York, Penn. The father, also a native of York, Penn., died in 1833, and the mother in 1874. In 1851 Mr. Ilgenfritz was married to Susan Neff, daughter of Daniel Neff, of Windsor Township, York Co., Penn. They have two children living: Edward and Mary E. The farm on which Mr. Ilgenfritz resides, contains 100 acres, and was purchased by him in 1875, since which time he has resided on it. He is a member of the order of Red Men of York, Penn., and also a member of the Lutheran Church of York, Penn.

GEORGE W. JAMISON, son of William and Margaret (Murphy) Jamison, natives of Pennsylvania and Ireland, respectively, was born September 16, 1830, in Carroll County, Md. He came to York County, Penn., in 1832, and after remaining two years, went to Chester County, Penn., where he remained until 1850. He then returned to York County, and purchased his present farm of seventy acres, upon which he has resided since. His father was born in Philadelphia, and his mother was born in Ireland, and came to this country when a child. Mr. Jamison was married, in 1868, to Catharine Wayne, daughter of Thomas Wayne, of York County, Penn. They have had eight children: Sarah, Mary Jane, Margaret M., Amanda, Alexander, William H., George G. and Emma Belle. He has held the office of assessor of Fawn Township.

ASA JONES is a son of Asa and Hannah (Riley) Jones, natives of York County, Penn., and Baltimore, Md., respectively, and was born July 17, 1833, on the farm of 120 acres, where he now resides. His father died in 1862, but the mother of our subject is still living. Mr. Jones was married, in 1863, to Elmira E. Powers, of Lancaster, Penn., who died in 1866, leaving two children: Inza M. and Laura M. His second marriage, was, in 1867, to Alice J. McCurdy, daughter of A. C. McCurdy, of York County. Mr. Jones is an extensive dealer in agricultural implements and stock.

JOSHUA R. JONES. A notable instance of a successful business career is presented in the life of Joshua R. Jones. Born of Quaker parentage, in the village of Fawn Grove, August 28, 1837, he spent his summers during his boyhood working on his father's farm, and his winters attending the neighboring schools. At this period of his life he displayed that buoyant vigor and exuberance of animal spirits, which with him have always formed prominent characteristics. If there was a rabbit to be chased Joshua was always there to lead the crowd. One year was spent in a Friends' school in Loudon County, Va., presided over by the venerable Samuel U. Janney. His studies were completed at the Pennsylvania State Normal School, at Millersville. After teaching one year, he entered another school, a rough one, but replete with valuable experience, and especially adapted to the study of human nature. He became a book agent. After canvassing with success for three years in the East and West, he opened an office as general agent in Balti-

BIOGRAPHICAL SKETCHES.

more, but removed to Philadelphia in 1864, where he is now operating under the style and title of the National Publishing Company. His business has grown with great rapidity, as the imposing appearance of the new establishment at 724, 726 and 728 Cherry Street will attest. About 200 hands are constantly employed in the manufacture of his large stock of family Bibles, albums and miscellaneous books. Twenty-four large presses, and a number of small ones, are used in printing his publications. Mr. Jones is quick to see a business point, and quick to act upon it, decided in forming his plans and energetic in executing them. He seldom fails to estimate aright the selling qualities of a book, and rarely publishes one that does not have a sale of from 50,000 to 250,000 copies. Still comparatively a young man, he applies himself closely to business, and is ever watchful over its details. The National Publishing Company is now one of the largest subscription book houses in the United States. Mr. Jones' career affords a striking example of the results of American "push." His progress has been steady and rapid until, it may be truly said, he has come to be a marked man in his calling.

DANIEL T. KELLER, son of Daniel Keller, of York County, Penn., was born in 1847, in Lower Windsor Township, York Co., Penn., where he remained and received a common school education. In August, 1872, he went to Ohio, and there went to high school seven months, in Clyde, Sandusky County, to superintendent Ginn, and then taught school for three terms, and worked on the farm the remainder of his stay in Ohio; was married, in 1878, to Nancy Dice, formerly a native of Pennsylvania, and in 1879 he came back to York County with his family, and in 1883 he purchased his present residence, and one and a half acres of land, where he has since resided, running a cider-mill in connection with farming. They have three children: Elsie, Iva and Emory.

HENRY KUNKEL, son of Michael and Elizabeth (Myers) Kunkel, natives of York County, Penn., was born September 2, 1814, on the homestead in York County. His mother died when he was very young, and he was brought up in the family of his uncle, Jacob Markey, where he lived until nineteen years old, when he went to York, Penn., and learned the shoe-maker's trade. He was married, in 1838, to Ruth White, of Harford County, Md., who died in 1852, leaving six children. His second marriage was in 1853, to Sarah V. Herbert, daughter of Phœnix Herbert, of Harford County, Md. By this union they have had five children. Mr. Kunkel has now eight children living: Elizabeth H., Mary J., Salome E., Felix H., Michael J., Jacob M., John T. and Annie R. Mr. Kunkel owns a farm of fifty acres, and also carries on general merchandising.

M. H. McCALL, son of Matthew and Amanda (Manifold) McCall, of York County, Penn., was born September 24, 1843, in Indiana County, Penn. He came to York County when only five years old, and lived with Alexander Manifold until fifteen years of age. The father was a graduate of Jefferson College, and died in 1849; the mother died in 1850. In 1862 our subject enlisted in Company I, One Hundred and Thirtieth Pennsylvania Volunteers, and served nine months. He then enlisted in the First Battalion Pennsylvania Volunteers, and was promoted to first lieutenant. He afterward enlisted in the One Hundred and Eighty-seventh Pennsylvania Volunteers, in which regiment he was first lieutenant and regimental quartermaster, and served until the close of the war. He is now engaged in a general mercantile business at Gatchellville. He was married, in 1869, to Amanda Livingston, daughter of Andrew Livingston, of Chanceford Township. They have one child—Hugh L. Mr. McCall has been postmaster of his town for twelve years. He is a member of the Masonic fraternity, and of the Presbyterian Church at Chanceford.

DR. D. MORGAN McDONALD, son of Thomas B. and Elizabeth (Thompson) McDonald, of York County, Penn., was born in Lower Chanceford Township June 4, 1852. His father, who was then residing in that township, engaged in smithing; he moved to Hopewell Township in 1858. At one time he held the position of auditor for three years. Our subject received his early education at the Pleasant Grove Academy, and in 1873 went to Ohio and read medicine with Dr. Gemmill, finally graduating from the Eclectic Medical Institute at Cincinnati in 1876. He first practiced medicine in New Market, Md., where he remained until 1881. He then moved to Fawn Township, York County, in February, 1882, and succeeded to the practice of Dr. Wright, of Gatchellville, and has since remained here. He was married, in 1877, to Ella G. Warfield, daughter of David A. Warfield and Sarah E. (Curran) Warfield, of Wrightsville. They have two children: Reba E. and Thomas W.

RICHARD McDONALD, son of Robert and Lydia (Payne) McDonald, of York County, was born in 1833 in Hopewell Township, and has always resided in York County. He was married in 1867 to Mary McWilliams, daughter of James McWilliams, of York County. They have five children: Richard T., Robert G., May C., Harriet and Margaret A. Mr. McDonald purchased the farm of 150 acres, on which he lives, in 1865.

HENRY S. MERRYMAN is a son of Nelson and Sarah (Davis) Merryman, of Baltimore, Md., and was born September 6, 1839, in Harford County, Md. He remained there until 1861, when he enlisted in Purnell's cavalry, Company A, called Purnell's Legion, and served until the close of the war, when he returned to Harford County, where he remained until 1871. He then came to Fawn Grove and established a general merchandising business, in which he is still engaged. He was married, in 1866, to Jane A. Webb, a daughter of William and Margaret Webb, of Fawn Grove. By this union they have five children: Carrie E., Harry C., Nelson, William E. and Corinne. Mr. Merryman is a member of the Methodist Episcopal Church, of Harford County, Md.

JOSEPH MILNER, son of Cyrus and Sarah (Carter) Milner, of Delaware and Harford Counties, Md., respectively, was born March 11, 1808, in Lancaster County, Penn. His great-grandfather came from England to Pennsylvania with William Penn, on his last visit in 1699. The parents of our subject came to York County in 1856, and settled in Fawn Township, where they resided until their death. The father died in 1859 and the mother in 1860. Joseph Milner remained in Lancaster County, Penn., until 1830, when he went to Illinois, where he stayed two years. He then returned to Lancaster County in 1832, and followed teaming in connection with farming. In 1854 he came to York County and purchased his present farm of 144 acres, where he has since resided. He was married in 1840 to Joanna B. Hamilton, daughter of Robert and Elizabeth Hamilton, of York County. By this union they had six children, three now living: Robert H., Lewis H. and William G. Mr. Milner has held the offices of treasurer and supervisor of this township. George D., the second son, died in the rebel prison at Salisbury, N. C., during the war in 1864. Mr. Milner is a member of the Society of Friends, who have a meeting house at Fawn Grove. Lewis H. Milner, son of Joseph and Joanna B. (Hamilton) Milner, was born October 3, 1844, in Lancaster County, Penn. He enlisted on June 17, 1863, in Company B. One Hundred and Eighty-seventh Pennsylvania Volunteers, and served until the close of the war, when he returned to the homestead where he has since resided.

DAVID PYLE, son of Abram and Harriet (Payne) Pyle, of Chester County, Penn., was born March 8, 1835, in Chester County, Penn. He came in 1851, to York County, Penn., with his parents, who settled in Fawn Township, where they remained until their death. He was married, in 1857, to Huldah J. Torbert, daughter of Andrew and Susan (Jones) Torbert, of Fawn Grove. By this union they have had two children, of whom one is living—Abram. Mr. Pyle holds the position of collector of Fawn Township at present. Abram Pyle, son of the above, is a miller by trade, and is engaged with J. R. Wiley, at Rock Run Mills.

BENJAMIN F. PYLE, son of Isaac and Cassie (Brooks) Pyle, natives of Chester County and Lancaster County, Penn., respectively, was born April 11, 1857, on the same farm that he now occupies. His parents came to York County, Penn., in 1854, and settled on a farm of fifty acres in Fawn Township. The father died in 1876, but the mother is still living on the homestead. They had seven children. Mr. Pyle follows the trade of carpenter, in connection with farming. He was married, June 5, 1884, to Ella A. Wilson, daughter of Josiah and Elizabeth (Lutz) Wilson, of York County, Penn.

CORNELIUS PRALL, son of Isaac R. and Ann B. (Rhodes) Prall, natives of New Jersey and Baltimore, Md. respectively, was born November 30, 1833, in Fawn Township, York County, Penn. His parents came to York County, Penn., in 1830, and settled in Hopewell Township. The father died in 1880, and the mother in 1865. Mr. Prall was married, in 1856, to Margaret Zigler, daughter of Peter Zigler, of York County, Penn. They have four children: Margaret M., Annie S., Delfinia H. and Chambers R. Mr. Prall purchased his present farm of forty-eight acres in 1869. The family are members of the Methodist Episcopal Church, of Prospect.

ANDREW M. SCOTT, son of Robert and Susan (Morrison) Scott, of York County, was born October 19, 1855, in Fawn Township, where he has always resided. His father and mother are both deceased, the former dying in 1876, and the latter in 1871. At the age of nineteen our subject began learning the wheelright's trade, and has been established in his present location since 1878. He was married, in 1881, to Sarah E. Enfield, daughter of Andrew Enfield, of York County, Penn. They have no children. Mr. Scott owns the dwelling and one acre of land, where he resides, which he purchased in 1880. He is a member of the Methódist Protestant Church, at Fawn Grove. He has been auditor, and is at present constable of the township.

JOHN STRAWBRIDGE (deceased), son of John and Rachael (Alloway) Strawbridge of York County, Penn., was born in 1804, in York County, Penn. He purchased the farm near New Park, containing 150 acres, in 1835, and remained there until his death in 1878. He was married in 1840 to Grizella McDonald, daughter of Aquilla McDonald, of York County, Penn. This union was blessed with nine children: John C., Mary E., Rachael., Aquilla M., Richard A., Sarah J., Franklin P., Louisa and Joseph. Mrs. Strawbridge died on the homestead in 1877. Aquilla M. and Franklin P., sons of John Strawbridge, inherited the homestead at the death of their parents, and carry on the farm, with their sister Sarah J. as housekeeper. Mr. Strawbridge held various offices in the township, and was postmaster for thirty years.

JOHN B. THOMPSON, son of James Thompson, of York County, was born at Muddy Creek Forks, York Co., Penn., February 15, 1828. His father removed from Upper Chanceford Township to Fawn Township in 1830, settling on property now owned by W. R. & J. B. Thompson, and known as Bald Eagle, there he remained until his death in 1860. John B. Thompson was married in 1860 to Elizabeth Channell, daughter of John Channell, of York County. They have five children: Mary B., John, Samuel G., Joseph and William R. Mr. Thompson has held the office of school director, and has been postmaster of Bald Eagle for ten years. In connection with farming he carries on a woolen-mill, manufacturing cloth, blankets, etc.

WILLIAM R. WEBB, son of William and Margaret (Channell) Webb, natives of Fawn Township, York Co. Penn.; was born in Fawn Grove, January 27, 1858. His parents always resided in Fawn Township; the father died in 1878, leaving a widow and four children: William R., Abel J., Mary S. B. and Jane A. M. At the age of sixteen years William R., began learning the cabinet-maker's trade and worked at it until 1878, when he came into possession of an undertaking and cabinet business, which was left him by his father, which business he now conducts. He was married January 25, 1883, to Jesse A. McElvain, a daughter of Josiah McElvain, of Lancaster County, Penn., and they have one child, Mary A. Mr. Webb is the owner of a hotel stand and several building lots in Fawn Township.

JAMES R. WILEY, son of Thomas and Isabella (Irwin) Wiley, of York County, Penn., was born February 15, 1852. His grandfather, James Wiley, was one of the earliest settlers of York County, Penn. Thomas Wiley, subject's father, owned a farm of 100 acres and founded the Rock Run Mills, now owned and worked by his son James R. The latter began learning the milling trade when sixteen years of age, and has followed it since. He also runs a saw-mill. Mr. Wiley is a member of Centre Presbyterian Church, and holds the position of trustee.

JOHN C. WILEY, son of Samuel and Ellen (Anderson) Wiley, of York County, Penn., was born April 16, 1853, on the homestead of 112 acres, which he now owns. His father died in 1859. In 1879, Mr. Wiley was married to Louisa Strawbridge, daughter of John and Grizella (McDonald) Strawbridge, of York County, Penn. This union has been blessed with three children: Samuel J., Nellie B. and an infant. In addition to the 112 acres on the homestead Mr. Wiley owns ninety-eight acres. He is a member of the Presbyterian Church, of Centre. He has held the office of auditor for three years.

FRANKLIN TOWNSHIP.

JACOB W. ALBERT was born in Adams County, Penn., in 1821, a son of Rev. J. E. and Catherine (Wentz) Albert, of Adams and Perry Counties, respectively. His great-grandfather came from Germany, and was sold to pay his passage across the ocean. The grandfather was a farmer in Adams County, Penn., and owned a large tract of land, which was divided into eight farms. He was a member of the Reformed Church. The father of subject was a German Reformed minister in Adams and York Counties for many years. He owned three farms in Adams County of 175 acres, seventy-five and fifty acres, respectively. He had twelve children: Susanna, Ezra (deceased), Elizabeth, Jacob W., Mary (deceased), Josiah (deceased), Ephraim, Appolonia (deceased), Hiram, Samuel, Rebecca and Catherine. Jacob W. Albert managed his father's farm when he was seventeen years old, and has since followed farming, owning ninety-eight acres of finely-improved land in

BIOGRAPHICAL SKETCHES.   105

Franklin Township, where he resides. Like his ancestors, he belongs to the Reformed Church. In 1844 he married Leah Bup, daughter of Frederick Bup, of Franklin Township. They have three children: Catherine, Sarah and Abraham F.

LEWIS ARNOLD was born in Warrington Township, York County, Penn., September 30, 1844, and is a son of Daniel and Anna (Straley) Arnold. His grandfather was a native of York County, and engaged in farming in Washington Township, having a farm of 150 acres. His father was a miller by trade, and followed it and farming in Dover and Warrington Townships. In 1869 he purchased twenty-three acres of land in Adams County, which he farmed till his death in January, 1872. He had seventeen children; Rebecca, William (killed in the battle of the Wilderness in 1864), Solomon, Samuel, Stephen, Sarah, Frank, Lewis, Jacob (deceased), Henry, Louisa (deceased), Maria, George, Aaron, Mary A., Amanda and Daniel L. Lewis Arnold, when eighteen years old, began learning the tanner's trade, which he followed six months, when he enlisted, in September, 1863, in Company G, One Hundred and Forty-third Regiment Pennsylvania Volunteers, under Gen. Warren, and took part in the following engagements: Wilderness, Spottsylvania, Laurel Hill and North Ann River. In the last engagement he was wounded in the leg, May 23, 1864. On the following day his leg was amputated, and he was removed to Mt. Pleasant Hospital, at Washington, where he remained until April 25, 1865; he then returned home and engaged in the cigar manufacturing business in Cumberland County, Penn. In 1866 he came to Franklintown, and in 1868 began learning the shoe-maker's trade which he still follows. He has a fine home in Franklintown. In 1870 he married Lydia M. Ditmer, daughter of Henry and Mary (Wierman) Ditmer, of Franklin Township. By this union they have had five children; Mary E., James D., Henry D., Clayton S. and Richard L. Mr. and Mrs. Arnold are members of the Union Baptist Church.

CHRISTIAN BENDER was born in 1828 in York County, and is a son of Lewis and Catherine (Hershey) Bender. His grandparents were natives of Lancaster County, Penn., but came to York County at an early day. His father was also a native of Lancaster County; his mother was born in York County. They owned a farm of 165 acres, which the father farmed until a few years before his death. They were active members of the United Brethren Church, and left eight children: Mary, Christian, Henry, Elizabeth, Sarah, Lydia, Michael and Catherine. Christian Bender followed farming until his marriage, when he engaged in threshing, farming and teaming, which he is still following. He owns ninety-three acres of well cultivated land in Franklin Township, also a small farm of twenty-eight acres half a mile from the home farm, and twenty-eight acres of mountain land. In 1851 he married Elizabeth Mumper, a daughter of Michael Mumper, a prominent farmer of Franklin Township, who died in 1859. They have five children; Samuel H., Mary E., Edward L., Lilly E. and Sallie. Nearly all the family belong to the United Brethren Church. Mr. Bender has been a director of the Dillsburgh and Mechanicsburgh Railroad for fourteen years.

JACOB BRANDT was born in 1827 in Carroll Township, York County, and is a son of Jacob and Rachel (McClure) Brandt, of York County, who, like the grandparents, followed farming. Jacob Brandt was reared a farmer, and has always followed that occupation. He owns 275 acres of some of the best land in the township, adjoining which he owns a small place of five acres, where his son David lives; he is the owner also of thirty acres of mountain land, several building lots in Dillsburgh, three places in Adams County, and a fine building in Mt. Holly, Cumberland Co., Penn. In 1848 he married Sarah Smith, a daughter of John S. Smith, who came from England in 1827. They have had the following children: Mary E. (deceased), David, John, Saran E (deceased), Albert, Harry C. (deceased). They all belong to the Evangelical Church, in which Mr. Brandt was steward for ten years. In connection with his farming, he also deals in horses and mules, and has been for twenty-one years quite extensively engaged in that trade.

LEVI CHRONISTER was born in Adams County, Penn., in 1831, a son of Jonas and Margaret (Sowers) Chronister, of Adams and Cumberland Counties, Penn., respectively. His grandfather was a native of Adams County and a farmer, which occupation he followed until his death in 1836. His farm contained about 400 acres, and was situated in Reading Township, Adams County. He was drafted for the army in 1812. Jonas Chronister was a farmer and teamster. He owned several town lots in Hampton, Adams County, and a farm of thirty acres on which he lived. He died from an apoplectic stroke April 3, 1881, aged seventy-seven years. A brother of subject's grandfather was killed in the Revolutionary war. Levi Chronister remained on the farm until his seventeenth year. When the common school system was adopted in Pennsylvania he was one of the first teachers in Reading Township, Adams County, where he taught twenty-one terms. In 1852 he entered Dickinson College at Carlisle, Penn., where he attended two sessions, about 300 students being then there. Before going to Carlisle he worked at blacksmithing, but being disabled by a kick from a horse, he in 1851 learned the trade of a wheelwright, at which he worked eleven summers, teaching school in the winter. He was elected justice of the peace in Reading Township, and held that office for fourteen years. In 1868 he moved to Franklin Township, where he engaged in teaching school, settling up estates, fire insurance, and served as justice of the peace. He was married, in 1856, to Amanda Picking, daughter of William S. Picking, of Dover Township. They have had two children: Albert W. (deceased) and William P. Mrs. Chronister died in 1864. In 1868 Mr. C. married Susannah Mumper, daughter of George Bollinger, of York County. Mr. Chronister has taught school for thirty-seven winter terms.

EDWARD DICK was born in 1829 in York County, and is the son of George and Mary (Nagle) Dick, of Adams County, Penn., who settled on the property now owned by the son in 1831. The father was engaged in farming and the mercantile business, and during the time the jail was building at York he was commissioner for York County, after which he retired from active business in 1851. He was a progressive farmer and merchant, and a director of the Dillsburgh Bank. He owned about 180 acres of well improved land. In all public affairs he took a lively interest until his death in 1876. His wife survived him only two years. They were members of the Lutheran Church and had seven children: Catherine, Edward, Christian, all living; Lydia Ann (deceased), Elizabeth (deceased), Mary Jane (deceased) and Sarah E. Edward Dick has always been identified with the old homestead. He, like his father, is one of the most progressive business men of the township. He owns 230 acres of improved land, and about 100 acres of mountain land. Besides farming he is engaged in the mercantile business, owns a grist and saw-mill, and since 1853 has been postmaster at Clear Spring. He has been school director for nine years. January 22, 1857, he married Elizabeth A. Myers, of Adams County, who, like himself, is a member of the Lutheran Church. They have four children: John

H., George W., Charles E., James A. (deceased) and Lottie M., some of whom are already assisting their father on the farm, in business and in the mill.

REV. S. DILLER is a native of Cumberland County, Penn., born in 1840, a son of Samuel and Catharine (Richwine) Diller, of Cumberland County. His grandfather was a farmer and owned several hundred acres of land in Cumberland County. His father, Samuel Diller, was also a farmer and weaver by trade; he owned 500 acres of good land in York County, divided into seven farms, and about 100 acres of mountain land. He came to Franklin Township in 1867, and remained here until his death in 1873, at the age of sixty-four years. He had eleven children: Mary A., Sarah A., Catherine A., Julia A., Simon, Joseph (deceased), Susan A. (deceased), Cyrus, Priscilla A., S. C. and Rosa A. Subject remained on the farm in York County, until the age of twenty-eight years, when he went to the Lutheran Missionary School at Selin's Grove, Penn. He then began active work in the United Brethren ministry at the Carlisle Spring Circuit in Cumberland County, where he remained two years; next he went to Dover Circuit, York County, where he remained four years; then took Yocumtown charge for one year, In the conference of 1883, he chose the local ministry. In 1865 he married Lydia A. Morrett, daughter of George Morrett, of Cumberland County. They have two children: George S., and Luther O. Mr. Diller is an ardent worker in the cause of education, the church and Sunday-schools. He owns several fine tracts of land with all the necessary improvements.

SAMUEL C. DILLER was born in Cumberland County, Penn., in 1849, and is a son of Samuel and Catharine (Richwine) Diller, of Cumberland County. His grandfather, Diller, was a farmer in Cumberland County, and owned about 200 acres of land. The father was a weaver by trade but also followed farming, owning about 600 acres of improved land, which were divided into seven farms, also 100 acres of mountain land. He came to Franklin Township in 1867, where he remained until he died, in 1873, at the age of sixty-five years. He had eleven children: Mary A., Sarah A., Catherine A., Julia A., Simon, Joseph (deceased), Susannah A. (deceased), Cyrus, Priscilla, S. C. and Rose A. Samuel C. Diller assisted his father on the farm until he was twenty-one years of age, when he took one of his father's farms and began farming for himself. In 1877 he sold his farm to John Arnold, and in the spring of 1878 went to Michigan with his family, where he remained ten months, engaged in laboring. In the following spring he returned to Franklin Township, where he purchased sixty-two acres of improved land and commenced farming again, working sometimes at the carpenter trade. Like his ancestors, Mr. Diller is a musician and sometimes teaches music. He was married, in 1873, to Susan Bender, daughter of Joshua Bender, of Snyder County, Penn.

AARON B. ELICKER was born in 1841 in Warrington Township, York County, Penn., a son of Valentine and Jane (Blackford) Elicker, natives of Adams and York Counties, respectively. His father was a native of Adams County, Penn. Subject's father followed farming for about thirty years, although he was a carpenter by trade. He owned 220 acres of well-improved land in Warrington and Washington Townships. He was a member of the U. B. Church, and was a liberal supporter of the same. He possessed more than ordinary musical talent. He died in 1862 at the age of sixty-seven years, leaving a widow and six children to mourn his loss. Aaron B. was brought up on the farm, attended the common schools and afterward an academy. In 1862 he began farming in Warrington Township, and in 1864 taught school in Franklin Township, to which he removed in 1866 and commenced farming, which he followed for nine years. He then moved to Dillsburgh where he remained four years; renting his property there, returned to Franklintown, now a borough (his buildings and part of his farm of forty acres are within the borough limits), where he resumed farming. In 1866 he married Susan E. Miller, daughter of William B. Miller, of Carroll Township. They have two children: William M., eight years old, and Olive M., four years old. Subject served the offices of town council, assessor, inspector, and was elected school director in 1884 for the term of three years. The family attend the Presbyterian Church, of which Mrs. Elicker is a member.

JOHN ERNST was born in 1829, in Franklin Township, York Co., Penn., son of John and Catharine (Ritter) Ernst, of Lancaster and Adams Counties, respectively. His father and grandfather were farmers, and took a lively interest in church and public affairs. The father owned 119 acres of well-improved land in Franklin Township. He had six children: Daniel (deceased), Susannah, Mary A., Daniel, Caroline (deceased) and John. The latter was brought up on the farm, and has since followed farming. Besides the home farm of 119 acres, he owns another, adjoining, of 157 acres of well-improved land and about forty acres of woodland. He owns also six valuable properties in Dillsburgh, among which is a large warehouse occupied by the Baily Bros. Mr. Ernst is a Lutheran in religion. He has never been married.

JOHN HUMMER was born in West Manchester Township, York Co. Penn., in 1817, son of John and Eve (Ziegler) Hummer, of German descent. The grandfather came from Germany when very young, and settled in West Manchester Township, where he remained until his death. John Hummer, subject's father, was a miller, and followed that occupation in West Manchester, Dover and Codorus Townships, Both he and his wife died in Dover Township. Our subject was reared in West Manchester Township, following farming. In 1843 he removed to Adams County, where he remained one year. Returning to York County, he continued farming until 1846, when he commenced huckstering, which he continued in connection with farming for thirty-five years. He then sold out and purchased the farm upon which he now lives, containing about 160 acres, which he has highly improved. He also owns the Lucas Grove Mills, which belong to the farm. In 1844, he was married to Julia Ann Sowers, of York, who died in 1880, leaving six children: George S., Sarah E., Mary A., Lillie, John and Charles E. The family belong to the Reformed Church of Franklin Township.

CAPT. JOHN KLUGH, is a native of York County, Penn., was born May 11. 1816, and is a son of George and Hannah (Arnold) Klugh, of Lancaster and York Counties respectively. His grandfather came from Germany, and settled in Lancaster County, where he engaged in farming. George Klugh was a carpenter, and followed his trade in Franklin Township until 1878. when he died at the age of eighty-four years. He was blessed with the following children: John, George, Henry, Frederick, Peter, Joseph, Clarissa and Philip (deceased). Capt. Klugh remained at home until his fifteenth year, when he began learning the carpenter's trade which he followed for thirty years. In 1860 he began mercantile business in Franklintown, where he was also postmaster. In 1864 he was elected captain of Company I, Two Hundred and Ninth Regiment Pennsylvania Volunteers, and with his regiment, was engaged in the battles of Hatcher's Run, and Fort

BIOGRAPHICAL SKETCHES. 107

Steadman. In the latter engagement he was wounded in the arm; being disabled for further duty, he returned home and resumed the mercantile business. In 1881 he sold his stock of goods to his son-in-law, George Lehmer, and commenced farming, owning about 250 acres of improved land; 100 acres of wood land, and 234 acres in Washington Township. He also owns two houses and ten lots in Franklintown, all of which he accumulated by hard labor; held the office of jury commissioner, and is also a justice of the peace. He was married in 1848, to Henrietta Ritter, daughter of Henry Ritter, one of the earliest settlers of York County, they have the following children: Mary, Alice, Harry, John and Milton B. They belong to the Lutheran Church in Franklintown, to which Capt. Klugh has given the ground, and is otherwise interested in the erection of a new church.

GEORGE LEHMER is a native of York County, and was born October 1, 1844, a son of Cornelius and Eve (Koch) Lehmer, of York County. His grandfather, Philip Lehmer, also of York County, was a farmer, owning about 500 acres of land in Washington, Franklin and Carroll Townships. Cornelius Lehmer was also engaged in farming, and is still living in Carroll Township. He had seven children: Mary, George, Leah (deceased), Sarah (deceased), James (deceased), Philip H. and Andrew J. George Lehmer was brought up on the farm, assisting his father until the age of sixteen years, when he enlisted, October 1, 1862, in Company D, Eighty-fourth Regiment Pennsylvania Volunteers, and with his regiment engaged in the battles of Fredericksburg and Chancellorsville, where he was wounded in the right arm; he was in the engagements of Mine Run, Wilderness, Spottsylvania, Cold Harbor, North Ann River, Petersburg, Mine Explosion and Richmond. At the close of the war he returned home, and in 1868 went to Michigan, where he served two years as an apprentice at carpentering; returning to York County, he followed painting and carpentering four years. In 1872 he married Mary Klugh, daughter of Capt. John Klugh, one of the most prominent men of this township. Mr. Lehmer became a partner with his father-in-law in the mercantile business, and in 1881, took charge of the business himself, at which he has since been very prosperous. In the spring of 1884 he and J. S. Bentz, of Carroll Township, went into business in Washington Township, thus making him one of the four leading business men of this section of the county. In 1880 he was licensed enumerator of Franklin and Washington Townships, and in 1863 was appointed mercantile appraiser of York County. He has had six children, five living: Ralph F., Viola, Walter S., Hattie, Georgia (deceased), and Morris.

ROBERT C. LIVINGSTON was born in York County, Penn., in 1815, a son of William and Margaret (Cook) Livingston, of York and Cumberland Counties respectively, and of Scotch descent. His grandfather came from Scotland in a very early day and settled in York County. The father, a cooper by trade, followed farming in York County for many years, and died in 1846 at the age of sixty-eight years. He had the following children: James (deceased), Mary, William, Ellen (deceased), Robert C., Hugh (deceased), and George (deceased). Robert C. Livingston was brought up on the farm until the age of eleven years, when he went to live with William Diven, Esq., with whom he remained until the age of twenty-one years. During that time he learned the tanner's trade, which he followed for thirty-one years in Adams County, Penn. He owns about eighty-one acres of well cultivated land in Franklin Township, where he resides. In 1838 he married Lydia Beles, daughter of Josiah Beles, of Adams County: James. Caleb, Robert A. (deceased), Lorah M. (deceased), Mary E., Lydia J., Anna C.,

Margaret D. (deceased), Ida C. (deceased), and Fletcher (deceased), are the children born to this union. Mr. Livingston is a member of the Presbyterian Church, and his wife a member of the Episcopal Church. The eldest son, James, was a soldier in the late war, and their third son, Robert, died when in the service.

JOSEPH MENGES was born in 1830 in Jackson Township, York Co., Penn., son of Daniel and Elizabeth (Bullinger) Menges, of York County. His grandfather was a native of York County, Penn., and owned three fine farms in the county, but retired from active life several years before his death, in 1839, at the age of seventy-four years. The father, Daniel, was brought up on the farm, and in 1841 he removed to Adams County, and purchased 170 acres of improved land, and forty acres of woodland. He had a family of five children: Joseph, Henry, Susannah, Emanuel and Franklin. Joseph Menges went to Adams County with his parents in 1841, when only eleven years old, and worked on the farm until he was twenty-five years old. In 1855 he removed to York County, where he now resides, and possesses about 105 acres of finely cultivated land, and twenty acres of woodland, the greater part of which he made by his own industry and economical habits. Like all of the Menges family, he belongs to the Lutheran Church. In 1855 he was married to Elizabeth Coulson, daughter of William Coulson, of Adams County. They have five children: Sadie, Mary, Alice, Marshie and Josie. Mr. Menges takes an active part in school and township affairs.

EDWARD W. MUMPER is a native of Franklin Township, York County, was born in 1832, a son of Michael and Elizabeth (Weaver) Mumper, natives of York County, Penn., and Maryland, respectively. His grandfather, Mumper, owned a large tract of land in Carroll and Franklin Townships, and was engaged in farming and distilling. He was a member of the German Reformed Church. Grandfather Weaver was in the war of 1812, and in Baltimore when Gen. Ross was killed. Michael Mumper, father of Edward W., was a farmer and teamster, and followed these occupations in Franklin Township until his death in 1839, at the age of sixty-nine years. He owned 500 acres of improved land, and 100 acres of woodland, divided into four farms. He was a member of the Reformed Church and had the following children: Samuel (deceased), Rebecca (deceased), Mary (now living), Michael (now living), John (deceased), Elizabeth (now living), Edward W. (now living), and Lewis (deceased). Edward W. Mumper began farming for himself in 1852, and continued until 1880, when he retired from active work. He owns 120 acres of improved land, and twenty acres of woodland. In 1852 he married Susannah Myers, daughter of Barney Myers, of Franklin Township. They have two children: William, who manages the home farm, and Mary E. Mrs. Mumper died September 15, 1883, a member of the Reformed Church, of which Mr. Mumper is also a member. In October, 1884, he married Henrietta Rice, of Adams County.

REV. HENRY SEIFERT, of the Evangelical Lutheran Church, of Franklintown, was born in York County August 21, 1822, and is a son of Michael and Polly (Leimbauch) Seifert, who were descended from old families of York County. The father was a farmer of Dover Township, where he resided nearly all his life. He died April 29, 1864, and the mother died September 21, 1850. He was a Lutheran; and the mother a Reformed. Rev. Henry Seifert was brought up on his father's farm until he was seventeen years of age, attending the common schools. He then, for eleven years, worked at the trade of coverlet weaving and dyeing, afterward attending the Pennsylvania College and Seminary at Gettysburg for four and one-half years. In 1855 he went to Bedford County, where he entered the Lutheran ministry, preaching there for four years and a half. He then went to Monroe County, where he was pastor of the Hamilton charge for nine years. Returning to his native county he took a charge at Rossville for two years; then in Centre County for two years; thence to Somerset County, where he had charge three years. In 1876 he returned to York County and assumed the charge of Clear Spring around Franklintown, where he has ever since been preaching. He has charge of four congregations, two in Adams County and two in York County. At one time he had charge of nine congregations, whom he faithfully served. He is now building a church in Franklintown. He was married December 25, 1843, to Harriet Meisenhelter, daughter of John and Mary (Klinefelter) Meisenhelter, of York County. They have seven children: Clara E., Martin L., David I., Mary J., Ellennora M , John M. and Charles H.

JOHN T. SMITH was born in York County in 1831, and is a son of John W. and Hannah (Thoman) Smith, natives of York County. His grandfather, also a native of York County, was a distiller and farmer in Manheim Township. Subject's father was also engaged in farming and milling in Shrewsbury Township. He removed to Washington Township in 1840, where he again engaged in farming until his death in 1877. He left four children: John T., Jacob T., Elizabeth A., Jesse T. (deceased). John T. Smith has been engaged in farming all his life, and owns ninety-three acres of improved land with fine buildings. He belongs to the German Reformed Church, and takes a great interest in church and school matters. In 1860 he was married to Anna Hollinger, daughter of George Hollinger, of Adams County; she was born July 23, 1839, and died March 27, 1888. They had ten children: William H. (deceased), Lizzie J. (deceased), George C., Susan E. (deceased), John A. (deceased), Adam, Charles E., Caroline, Rebecca (deceased), and Mary C.

GEORGE SPAHR was born 1834, in Washington Township, this county, son of William and Catharine (Miley) Spahr, of the same township. His grandfather lived in Carroll Township, York County, and was a farmer by occupation. Subject's father was a farmer and lived in Washington Township, owning a farm of 130 acres. He was a Lutheran and died in Carroll Township, at the age of eighty-four years. He had eight children: Cornelius, Henry, Martin (deceased), William, Caroline, George, Catharine and Lizzie. George Spahr was brought up as a farmer in Washington Township, but removed to Franklin Township in 1860, where he still resides and owns a farm of 110 acres of fine land. He also owns twenty-two acres of land in Washington Township. In 1855 he married Catharine Pressel, daughter of Joseph Pressel, of Washington Township. They have three children: William, Nancy and Milton U. Mr. Spahr is an active member of the Lutheran Church.

MOSES STRAYER is a native of York County, Penn., born February 14, 1808, son of Peter and Mary (Spahr) Strayer, of York County. His grandparents were born in Germany; they came to this country at an early day and settled in Dover Township, York County. The father was a farmer in Dover Township, having a farm of about 800 acres of well-improved land, which he farmed until fifteen years before his death, at the age of eighty-six years. He took an active interest in church and school matters, gave the ground upon which Strayer's Church is built, and was a leading member of the building committee. He had ten children: Catharine (deceased), Daniel (deceased), Peter, Samuel, Jacob, Susannah, Moses, Eve (deceased), Sarah (deceased) and Henry (deceased). Moses Strayer is a farmer and a tanner by trade, and followed these occupations for forty-nine years, but has now retired from business. He owns 300 acres of improved land, embracing three farms, one in Franklin Township, one in Adams County and one in Washington Township. He has also a house in Dillsburgh. In 1833, he married Susannah Sheffer, daughter of Samuel Sheffer, of Washington Township, York County. She died June 14, 1881, at the age of sixty-four years, leaving eight children: Cornelius, Mary, Samuel, Lizzie, George, Catharine, Nancy and Annie. Mr. Strayer is a Lutheran. His wife belonged to the U. B. Church. His grandfather, who has been dead ninety-four years, is buried at Strayer's Church, in Dover Township.

HEIDELBERG TOWNSHIP.

ANDREW R. BRODBECK, traveling salesman and manufacturer of fertilizers, was born April 11, 1860, in Jefferson, York Co., Penn., a son of Jesse and Lucy Ann (Renoll) Brodbeck. His grandfather was a farmer and distiller, who owned and lived on the old Snyder property (now Brodbeck's) at Jefferson, and died at the age of fifty years. He left five sons, of whom the youngest was Jesse Brodbeck, who all his life lived on the home farm, and died in 1871, at the age of thirty-three years, and Lucy Ann the mother of A. R. died in 1878 at the age of thirty-seven years, leaving four sons, of whom A. R., the subject, is the eldest. His brothers were Nathaniel (deceased), Adam (deceased), and Jesse, who is living with Andrew Brodbeck on the home farm. A. R. Brodbeck spent his early life on the farm, and shortly after his father's death, went to his uncle, George Brodbeck, a merchant in Codorus Township, where he remained two years. At the age of eighteen he began teaching at Codorus Township, and for three years taught there and in other townships. In 1879 he took a trip west as far as Kansas. In the same year he married Ellen Thoman, daughter of Jacob and Mary Ann (Snyder) Thoman, of Heidelberg Township. They have three children: Estella, Wilson and Mary Ellen. In 1880 he purchased the Hildebrand property at Porter's Sideling and, in 1885, the Slagle property in Hanover, where he is now residing. Mr. and Mrs. Brodbeck belong to the Reformed Church at Jefferson. He has been organist for different churches.

CHARLES F. EICHELBERGER was born in York County, Penn., July 2, 1834. His great-great-grandfather came from Wittingen, near Ziosheim, in Wurtemberg, Germany, in 1728, located first in Lancaster County, and then came to York County, Penn., and settled on the property now owned by Charles F. Eichelberger, embracing at that time Jacob's Mill and the adjoining property. He died in Hanover in 1776, aged eighty-three years. He was married twice. The eldest son of his second wife, Adam, lived on the home farm, and also died there. Michael, the grandfather of the subject, was the second son of a family of five sons and three daughters. He had four children: Adam (former sheriff), George, Michael and Polly. George, the father of Charles F., bought the homestead from his brother Adam, in 1827, and afterward bought the Miller property. After he lived there some time he moved to Hanover, where he lived a retired life until he died, in

1869, aged sixty-nine years. Charles F. Eichelberger's early life was spent on the farm. He was married February 25, 1858, to Susan Menges, daughter of Daniel and Elizabeth (Bollinger) Menges, of Adams County, Penn. They have had four sons and five daughters: Martin D., Ira M., George D., William H., Sarah (deceased), Emma J., Clara Ann, Ada E. and Jennie. After his marriage he lived on the Miller farm for two years as tenant, and then took the farm and lived there four years more. After that he sold some of his property and bought the homestead farm on the York Road, owned by his brother Adam, containing about 200 acres of well-improved land. The family are members of St. Matthew's Lutheran Church, of Hanover, Penn., in which Mr. Eichelberger has held the offices of elder and deacon. He was superintendent of Mt. Carmel Sunday-school for four years. He is a Democrat, and has held a number of offices in township and county

JOHN F. HERSHEY was born in Heidelberg Township, York Co., Penn., October 24, 1845, a son of Benjamin and Barbara (Forry) Hershey, who were of Swiss descent. His great-great-grandfather, Andrew Hershey, born 1698, came to this country when quite young, and settled in Lancaster County, Penn. He died December 25, 1754. Tradition says he owned and was buried on what is known as James Buchanan's farm, near Lancaster City. His son, John Hershey, came to York County, and settled on land that had been taken up by Andrew Hershey, in the eastern part of Heidelberg Township. He died in 1795, and was buried in Garber's graveyard, near Menges' Mill. His son, John Hershey, took the homestead farm (Menges' Mill), where he lived all his life. He was one of the defenders of 1812, and died in 1829. His son, Benjamin, the father of John F. Hershey, was born in 1808, and spent his early life on the farm, and working in mills in Ohio, Maryland and Pennsylvania. He was married in 1844, to Barbara, daughter of John and Annie Forry. After his marriage he bought a farm one-half mile west of Menges' mill, where he lived until his death (1877), his widow surviving him but five years. Both are buried in Garber's graveyard. John F. Hershey's early life was spent on the farm. He was married December 17, 1868, to Susan M. Miller, daughter of Jacob and Susan (Mause) Miller, of Heidelberg Township. They have had four sons: J. Jacob, Joseph (deceased), Charles and Alvin. Mr. Hershey owns one tract of land, about 106 acres, which he has brought to a high state of cultivation.

JESSE KRAFT, a representative of one of the old families of York County, miller and farmer of Heidelberg Township, was born August 5, 1828, in Manheim Township, York County, son of George and Mary (Loucks) Kraft. Subject's great-grandfather was born on the ocean, when his parents were immigrating to America. They landed at Baltimore, and resided there. Subject's grandfather, Frederick, lived in Baltimore as proprietor of a hotel until 1810, when he came to York County, and founded the town of Kraftstown, which, since Jefferson's presidency, is known as Jefferson. He was born December 6, 1773, and died July 20, 1836. Subject's father, George, was ten years of age when his parents came to Jefferson. He was married in 1823, and soon after commenced teaching. Subsequently he removed to Manheim Township, continued teaching, and opened up a small store, remained in Manheim, farming and merchandising about ten years; then returned to Jefferson and opened up in general merchandising and dry goods. He was associated in business there with a son-in-law, Jacob Spangler. He subsequently retired from business life, and lived in retirement until his death in 1868, being sixty-eight years old. He was a prominent Democrat, and at one time represented his district in the State Legislature. His wife died in 1872. Jesse Kraft is the third child of a family of six—three sons and three daughters. Subject's early life was passed as an assistant of his father; educated in schools of the day; married, in 1851, to Lucinda Baughman, of Manheim Township. This union was blessed with ten children—four sons and six daughters. Subject farmed for about ten years near Jefferson, when he exchanged his farm for the Mummert Mill property, lying in Heidelberg Township, where he is still residing, engaged in farming and milling. He is a prominent member of the Lutheran Church of Jefferson, and has been deacon and elder of the church at different times for over twenty-five years; active in Sunday-school, etc. He is one of York County's well-known citizens and highly esteemed. He is a Democrat, but not active in politics.

PETER H. MENGES was born in north Codorus Township, York Co., Penn., November 27, 1835, son of Peter and Nancy (Hershey) Menges, of German and Swiss descent, respectively. His great-grandfather came from Germany when quite young, and settled about five miles west of York, some time before the Revolutionary war. He is buried at Wolf's Church in West Manchester Township. The grandfather, John Menges, was a farmer, and settled in that part of the home section now owned by Andrew Menges, in Jackson Township. He had a family of thirteen children, and died at the age of sixty-nine years. Peter Menges, Sr., the fifth child of this family of thirteen children, was born July 1, 1802, and spent his early life on the farm, and then learned the milling trade in Cumberland County, Penn. After his marriage he moved to his father's farm in North Codorus Township, which he farmed for eleven years, then came to Heidelberg Township, and purchased the farm and property (Menge's Mill) where he passed the remainder of his life. He died October 10, 1883, and is buried at Lichey's Church, of which church he was elder for nearly twenty years. During the last twenty years of his life, he devoted his time to the good of the church. Throughout the whole community he was known as "Old Father Menges." Two of his sons are living: Peter H. and John. The latter was born in 1824, and is a minister of the Evangelical Lutheran Church. He was educated at Mount Joy, Lancaster County; was received into the ministry by the "Old Pennsylvania Synod" in 1851, and has since filled various charges in Lancaster and York Counties. In 1880 he became pastor of Grace Evangelical Lutheran Church, at West Philadelphia. With a few members he built a Mission Church, and now he has a large membership and a successful Sunday-school. Peter H. Menges' early life was spent on the farm and at milling, receiving his education at subscription schools, finishing at the public school at Columbia, Penn., and the high school of Mount Joy, Penn. For eleven years afterward he was engaged as a teamster, hauling lumber, merchandise, etc., between Littlestown and Susquehanna River. He was married, January 24, 1860, to Kate Hinkle, daughter of Isaac and Elizabeth Hinkle, of Lancaster County, Penn., of Irish and German descent. They have had seven children—three sons and four daughters: John, Alvin, Willie, Annie, Mary (deceased), Pacie (deceased) and Minnie. After marriage they moved to the homestead farm, as tenants, where they remained ten years, after which Mr. Menges engaged in the milling and produce business. After the construction of the H. & Y. R. R., he purchased and built the property known as Menges' Mill, store and warehouse, creating thereby a good market for produce. He was an active participant in the construction of the above railroad. He and family are members of the Lutheran Church at Lichey's (now Spring Grove), in which he was a deacon eight years, and Sunday-school superintendent for nearly twenty-five years. In 1875 he was a delegate to the Sunday-school convention at Philadelphia. He has held the office of internal revenue collector Fifteenth Division of Pennsylvania, in 1863 and 1864, and school director in the township.

E. D. MILLER was born in Lower Windsor Township, York Co., Penn., December 8, 1854, a son of Michael and Catherine (Stein) Miller, also of that township. His great-great-grandfather, Michael Miller, came to this country in youth, settled in Windsor Township, near Red Lion, and died before the Revolutionary war, and is buried at Freysville Cemetery in Windsor Township. Subject's grandfather, Michael Miller, lived on the homestead farm near Red Lion, and was at that time known as the tallest man in York County; he was a miller and died in 1866, aged eighty-two years. The father of our subject is now living in Windsor Township, and was born in 1821. He is a farmer and owns four tracts of land. He was for a number of years a director of the Western National Bank of York, and is also interested in the First National Bank at Wrightsville, and the city market of York. They had six children: E. D., Michael W., Calvin Edward, David G., Mary (deceased), Fanny A. and Sarah J. E. D. Miller's early life was spent on the farm and attending public schools. He afterward taught school in different townships, and was clerk for Emig & Bahn at New Freedom, Penn., for three years. He was married, December 26, 1876, to Laura C. Sweeney, daughter of Daniel and Hester Ann (Kohler) Sweeney, of Freeland, Baltimore Co., Md., of Scotch-Irish descent. In the spring of 1877 he commenced the mercantile business at Nashville, York County, where he kept store two years, and then came to Menges' Mill Station, where he is still keeping store, postoffice and express office. He has been a member of Friendly Circle No. 17, of Hanover, Penn., since 1881, and is a member of the German Reformed Church. His wife is a member of the Methodist Episcopal Church. Since 1883 he has also established a store at Iron Ridge, in which he has one-half-interest.

AARON D. RENOLL, was born in Heidelberg Township, York Co., Penn., March 11, 1844, and is the son of Henry and Mary (Danner) Renoll. His great-grandfather was Daniel Renoll, who died in 1800, aged seventy-six years. Subject's grandfather, Henry Renoll, was born February 12, 1767, was twice married, and died in 1824, aged fifty-seven years, leaving a family of six sons and four daughters. Henry Renoll, the father of Aaron D., bought a tract of land near Porter's Sideling in 1830, which he improved and made his home until his death. He was born in Codorus Township, in 1805, and died at the age of seventy-five years. He had three sons and four daughters: Henry (deceased), Emanuel D., Aaron D., Harriet (deceased), Anna, Mary and two sisters who died in infancy. Aaron D. received his early education in the common schools and afterward attended the York County Academy under Prof. Ruby, for one term. During the winter of 1866-67 he taught school in Heidelberg Township. October 13, 1867, he married Rebecca Rudisill, daughter of Jacob and Elizabeth (Miller) Rudisill, of North Codorus Township. They have three children: Emma Jane, Ellen J. and Lillie A. After his marriage Mr. Renoll moved to the homestead farm, where he lived as a tenant for fourteen years. He then bought the farm, and in 1882 bought the Bollinger property (Half Way House), on the York road. He is a member and deacon of the Lutheran Church. His wife is a member of the German Reformed Church. Mr. Renoll takes an active part in prayer meetings and Sunday-schools.

AARON S. THOMAN, was born September 25, 1842, in Heidelberg Township, York Co., Penn.; son of Jacob and Mary Ann (Snyder) Thoman, of Swiss descent. His great-grandfather, Jacob Thoman, came from Switzerland when very young and settled in Lancaster County, Penn., west of the Susquehanna. He afterward came to York County, where he took up a section of land in the eastern part of Heidelberg Township, and remained there with his ten children, three of whom, Henry, Rudolph and Abraham, received the home farm. The latter, the grandfather of our subject, lived on the home farm, during his life. He had nine children, one of whom, Jacob, the father of Aaron S., received the home at his father's death, and resided on it during his life. Jacob Thoman had five sons and three daughters: Henry (deceased), Aaron S., George, Abraham, Jacob, Lydia, Elizabeth and Ellen R. Aaron S. Thoman spent his youth on the farm, receiving his education in subscription schools. He made three different tours through the Western States. He was married, May 12, 1870, to Fanny Hohf, daughter of David and Elizabeth (Baehr) Hohf, of Heidelberg Township, who died July 2, 1871. His second marriage was October 5, 1873, to Sarah Bollinger, daughter of Samuel and Eliza (Forry) Bollinger, of this township. He retired from farming and is now living on the old home farm, which contains about 150 acres of fine cultivated land. He and his wife are members of the German Reformed Church at Leichey. They have one son, Paul B. aged eight years.

JOHN B. TRONE was born August 27, 1827, and is the eighth of twelve children of George Trone, of Heidelberg Township. His grandfather, Abraham Trone, came from Germany and received a grant of 250 acres of land from the Penns, May 14, 1767. This land was located in what was then Manheim Township, now the central part of Heidelberg Township, near Smith's Station. Abraham Trone was a Revolutionary hero. He was married twice and had a family of seven children. George, the father of John B., was the first son of the second wife. He lived on the homestead farm until his death at eighty years of age, and was buried at the Mennonite Meeting House (Baer's), of which denomination he was a minister. John B. Trone spent his early life on the farm, receiving his education in subscription schools. At the age of eighteen he began learning the trade of blacksmithing, and continued it at Trone's Stand, Smith's Station, for twenty-two years. His first marriage was to Eliza Shutt, daughter of Joseph Shutt, of Heidelberg Township. They had five children: Valentine, Franklin (deceased), John S., Lizzie and Mary (deceased). His second marriage was, May 20, 1866, to Annie Rohrbaugh, daughter of George and Sarah Rohrbaugh, of this township. They have had six children: Charles, Joseph, George, an infant (deceased), Sarah and Alla Mary. Mr. Trone is now farming near Smith's Station. He is a member of the German Reformed Church, is a prominent Democrat and has held various offices of trust and profit in church and township. His son, John S. Trone, a dealer in general merchandise at Smith's Station, and a teacher, was born August 1, 1856, in Heidelberg Township. He taught school for several years, and is now a successful merchant and also a justice of the peace of Heidelberg Township at Smith's Station.

E. K. WALTERSDORFF was born April 21, 1836, in Heidelberg Township, York Co., Penn., son of Daniel and Catharine (Carver) Waltersdorff. His father came from Germany at the age of twenty-one years, and settled in Maryland, where he married Elizabeth Garrett, who died, leaving four sons and three daughters. After twenty years of residence in Maryland he removed to Heidelberg Township and there married again, having three sons and one daughter by this union. He was a defender of 1812, and died in 1863 aged ninety three years. E. K. Waltersdorff spent his early life on the farm and attended subscription schools till he was eighteen years of age. He was married, September 30, 1855, to Catharine Bricker, daughter of John and Christiana (Warner) Bricker, of Manheim Township. They have had eleven children— eight sons and three daughters: Samuel A., James H., George W., an infant (deceased), Emanuel D., John F., Aaron E., William H. (deceased) Emeline (deceased), Eleanora and Alice Catharine. He worked his father's farm until 1877, when he moved to Heidelberg Township, to the Heistand farm, where he is now living. George W., the third son, was born July 4, 1862, and spent his early life on the farm. In 1881 and 1882 he attended York County Academy. He has taught school successfully in different townships, and is now a teacher in Heidelberg Township, and is living with his father.

HOPEWELL TOWNSHIP.

SILUS ALTHOUSE, son of George and Maria (Silfeus) Althouse, was born August 8, 1844, in Lancaster County, Penn., but removed to Hopewell Township with his father in 1852. He was brought up in this township, and at nineteen years of age commenced farming for himself. In 1873 he purchased the farm on which he now resides, containing 145 acres, and engaged in farming. He was married, February 11, 1866, to Mary J. Householder, daughter of Henry Householder, of Hopewell Township. They have the following children: Catherine L., Emanuel F., Henry H., Bethey A. and Abbie G. Mr. and Mrs. Althouse are members of the Presbyterian Church of Stewartstown.

JOSEPH W. ANDERSON, son of Joseph R. and Elizabeth (Wilson) Anderson, of York County, Penn., was born February 5, 1837, in Fawn Township, York County. He lived on the farm with his parents until 1871, receiving his education at the public schools of the township. February 23, 1871, he was married to Louisa Gemmill, daughter of Benjamin Gemmill, of Fawn Township. They have three children: Marion E., Howard Wilson and Joseph Ray. Mr. Anderson purchased his present farm of 202 acres in 1870, and has resided there ever since, dealing in phosphates in connection with farming. He and his wife belong to the Presbyterian Church of Hopewell Church.

HENRY ANSTINE, son of Henry and Elizabeth (Miller) Anstine, of Hopewell Township, was born March 22, 1833, and is the tenth of thirteen children. Until he was twenty-six years of age he remained on the home farm, attending the public schools of the township, after which he purchased a portion of the homestead farm, where he has since resided and gradually enlarged his farm until he now owns about eighty-eight acres, with fine farm buildings. January 17, 1856, he married Catherine Grove, daughter of Henry Grove, Esq., of Hopewell Township. They have five children: James R., Mary V. G., Ella E., Lottie E., George McC. In 1875 he was elected supervisor of his township, and re-elected the following year. In the fall of 1884 he received the Democratic nomination for commissioner for three years, and was elected. The family are members of the Methodist Episcopal Church at Stewartstown.

MRS. MARY J. ARTHUR, widow of Richard Arthur, and daughter of A. S. and Rebecca (Turner) Jordan, of Hopewell Township, was born in Hopewell Township, York Co., Penn., May 10, 1826. She was married, in 1851, to Richard Arthur, son of John and Clemence (Thompson) Arthur, who was born in Harford County, Md., in 1825. He came to York County in 1854, and engaged in farming near Stewartstown, and after remaining there two years removed to Iowa, and engaged in stock-raising. He enlisted, in 1862, in Company B, Twenty-second Regiment Iowa Volunteers, and held the position of orderly sergeant. He was wounded at the battle of Vicksburg, from the effects of which he died, June 1, 1863. His widow returned to York County, Penn., in 1867, and purchased the residence she now occupies. She has three children: John S., T. Frank and Rebecca A. John S. is engaged in farming and canning in Baltimore County, Md. and T. F. Arthur is a dentist in Baltimore, Md. Mrs. Arthur's brother was a medical doctor in Baltimore.

JOSEPH H. BELL is a son of David and Hannah (Norris) Bell, of York County. He was born in January, 1817, and reared in Hopewell Township, and has been engaged in farming, carpentering and also butchering. In 1843 he was married to Sarah J. Thrue, who died on June 7, 1876. They had eleven children. In 1881 he married Lizzie (Walter) Myer, of Hopewell Township. They have two children. Mr. Bell is a member of the Protestant Methodist Church.

CORNELIUS COLLINS, son of John and Margaret (Gemmill) Collins, was born November 6, 1813, and was educated at the public schools of Hopewell Township. He remained on the home farm until 1848, when he married Elizabeth S. Gordon, daughter of Andrew Gordon, of Hopewell Township, who emigrated from Ireland and settled on land which now forms a part of his son-in-law's farm. The grandfather of Mr. Collins came from Scotland. Mr. Collins has a family of six children: Andrew G., John W., Alexander D., Mary E., Samuel C. Mrs. Collins died October 30, 1865. One of the sons, John W., is a resident of Cheyenne, Wyoming Territory, and is cashier for Martin E. Post & Co., bankers; Andrew G. is in Hebron, Neb., and is president of a banking house; Alexander is cashier of the Shrewsbury Savings Bank; Samuel is at home with his father, and helping him on the farm, which contains about 202 acres of cultivated land and forty acres of timber. Mr. Collins' second marriage was to Balinda J. Manifold, of Hopewell Township, daughter of Solomon Manifold; she died January 29, 1872, leaving one daughter—Sarah E. Mr. Collins is a member of the United Presbyterian Church of Hopewell Township.

WILLIAM S. DOUGLASS, son of David and Ann (Brannon) Douglass, natives of Chanceford and Fawn Townships, respectively, was born in Hopewell Township in 1832, and was reared and educated at the public schools in the same township. At the age of eighteen years he learned the plasterer's trade, and at the age of twenty-one he returned to the homestead and assisted his father in farming. In 1882 he engaged in the hotel business at the old stand at Mt. Pleasant, formerly kept by his father for fifteen years. In addition to keeping hotel he does some farming, having, in 1878, purchased a farm of forty acres in Hopewell Township. In 1863 he was married to Lavinia Minnich, daughter of Joseph Minnich, of Hopewell Township, and has six children: Samuel S., Emma J., Mathew W. William S., John McN. and Clarence. In 1864 he received the commission of second lieutenant in Company B, Two Hundred and Ninth Regiment Pennsylvania Volunteers, from Gov. Curtin, and was discharged in 1865. He participated in the battles of Bermuda Hundred, Hatcher's Run and Fort

HOPEWELL TOWNSHIP.

Steadman. In 1865 he was appointed storekeeper and United States gauger for the Fifteenth District of Pennsylvania, and held that office until 1868. Mr. Douglass is an active business man. His hotel, which is conveniently located, offers all the comforts a traveling man wants, and shows plainly that Mr. Douglass knows how to keep a hotel.

JUDGE ADAM EBAUGH, son of John and Sarah (Flowers) Ebaugh was born August 4, 1806, on the homestead. His grandparents, on mother's side, were natives of England and Alsace, respectively, who settled near Philadelphia. His grandparents on father's side (John Jacob) came from Switzerland in 1740, and settled in what is now Carroll County, Md. His parents had twelve children, of whom he is the seventh son, the father dying in 1833. After being educated at the public schools he took charge of the farm and mill property, which his father had willed to him, and has since been principally engaged in farming and milling. In May, 1833, he married Willie E. Bosley, daughter of B. and Susan (Brooks) Bosley, who died in June, 1834. In 1837 he married Elizabeth Anstine, daughter of Henry and Elizabeth Anstine, of Hopewell, and had ten children: John, William C., Sarah A., Elizabeth R. (deceased), Mary E., Nancy E., Isabella A., Adam B., Martha J. F. (deceased) and Barbara L. Mr. Ebaugh has always been an active politician. He was drum-major for seven years of the Sixty-fourth Pennsylvania Militia; was afterward elected lieutenant of the Jackson Grays, of Shrewsbury, and elected captain of the Mechanicsburgh Rifles, which office he held for twelve years, during which time his command was called out to suppress the riots, at Philadelphia, in 1848. February 6, 1834, he was appointed justice of the peace by Gov. George Wolf. In 1837 he was elected assessor of Hopewell Township; he served sixteen years as school director, and in 1840 was elected to the legislature for 1841-42. In 1843 he was elected senator, and served in 1844-45-46. After that he was appointed State agent for the York & Cumberland Railroad by Gov. Bigler, and held that position for six years. In 1856 he was elected associate judge for five years, and was re-elected in 1861 for five years more. He served in about twenty county and five State conventions. Mr. Ebaugh has voted for fifty-seven years, and has always been a sterling Democrat. He is a member of the Masonic order, York Lodge No. 266, and of Mt. Zion No. 74, of York I. O. O. F., and is a member of the Baptist Church at Hopewell. At his advanced age he is in excellent health.

DR. JOHN L. FREE is a son of Peter and Naomi (Lowe) Free, of Baltimore County, Md., and was born in that county March 5, 1821, and came with his parents, in 1823, to Shrewsbury Township, where they settled and resided until the father's death in 1860. He received his early education in the schools of Shrewsbury, took up the study of medicine in 1844, and graduated from the University of Maryland in 1848. He first practiced medicine in Dillsburgh and New Freedom until 1849, when he went to Philadelphia and attended a course of lectures. In 1850 he moved to Stewardstown, built his present residence, and established an extensive practice, which he enjoys to the present day. In 1852 he was married to Martha J. Jordan, of Hopewell Township, who died in 1871. His second marriage was, in 1873, to Jennie A. Wiley, of Hartford County, Md. They have four living children; Jennie A., Evans M., Naomi E. and Lizzie E. He and his wife are members of the Methodist Episcopal Church. Dr. Free was one of the founders of the English and Classical Institute, located at Stewartstown, of which he has been a trustee since its organization, now over thirty years. He also took an active part in securing a charter from the legislature, constituting the borough of Stewardstown. Since his residence here it has been a prosperous, growing place. Three churches have been built, and with the railroad nearly completed to New Freedom, its further prosperity seems assured.

CORNELIUS GEESEY, son of Samuel and Sarah (Reichard) Geesey, of York Township, was born May 12, 1849. He remained on the homestead until he was nineteen years of age, when he began learning the trade of stone-mason, at which he worked for two years, and afterward followed bricklaying for eight years. In 1876, in company with John Kohler, he purchased a farm of 197 acres at Chanceford, and engaged in farming for five years, after which he removed to Winterstown, and purchased a hotel, which he has kept ever since. He is also engaged in manufacturing ice cream. He was married, in 1875, to Mary Ness, of York Township. They have three children: Laura, Sarah E. and Francis. Mr. and Mrs. Geesey are members of the Lutheran Church.

JOHN C. GEMMILL, son of Joseph and Margaret (Collins) Gemmill, was born April 4, 1822. His great-grandfather, William Gemmill, was a native of Scotland and immigrated to America some time previous to 1750, settling in Hopewell Township, York Co., Penn., a part formerly known as Shrewsbury Township, taking up about 1,000 acres of land. Joseph Gemmill, father of John C., was born April 26, 1794, on the farm now occupied by his son. He was at one time engaged in distilling liquors. He reared six children, of whom John C. was the eldest, and who was brought up on the farm. Joseph Gemmill, who had been in the war of 1812, died in 1868, and at his death the farm of 200 acres came into the possession of his son, John C., who in the same year was married to Rosanna McKinley, daughter of Stephen McKinley, of Chanceford Township. They have four children: Ulysses C., Jeanetta B., A. A., Ada, and John M. Mr. Gemmill was drafted during the late war, in 1861, but was exempted on account of disability. He is a member of the Masonic Lodge of Shrewsbury, and the family are members of the Presbyterian Church of Stewartstown. He has a clock in his possession which was made by John Gemmill, in Carlisle; it belonged to his great-grandfather, and has always remained in the family.

JOHN S. GEMMILL, son of Robert and Elizabeth (Dorris) Gemmill, of York County, Penn , was born December 13, 1844, on the farm where he now resides. His grandfather came from Scotland and settled on a farm of 135 acres, near New Park, Penn. The father of John S. was born in 1807, who was brought up on a farm, and finally moved to a farm of 145 acres, which is now owned by his son, and where he died in 1878. John S. was reared on a farm and has followed farming since. He was married, in 1872, to Rachel B. Robinson, daughter of William Robinson, of Harford County, Md. They have eight children: Nettie B., Mary E., William James, Charles C.. Edith P., Edna L., Robert B. and Joseph S Mr. and Mrs. Gemmill are members of the Presbyterian Church of Centre. Robert Gemmill, subject's father, was at one time commissioner of York County, Penn., for three years, and has also held several minor township offices.

JOHN K. GREEN, son of Giles T. and Deborah (Kirkwook) Green, natives of Harford County, Md., was there born September 6, 1829. His parents came to York County, Penn., in 1830. His father settled at Grove's Mill, where he carried on blacksmithing. He died in 1864, and the mother died in 1847; he left eleven children by his first wife, of whom John K. is the fifth child. The latter lived with his grandparents until fifteen years of age, when he came to York County. In 1851 he began learning the carpenter's trade, which he has since followed. In 1862 he enlisted in Company H, Seventh Maryland Vounteers, and served until the close of the war, participating in the battles of the Wilderness, Cold Harbor, Five Forks and Petersburgh. In January, 1864, he was promoted to the rank of first lieutenant, which rank he held to the close of the war. He came to Stewartstown in 1853, where he has since resided, and owns some very valuable properties in the town. He was married, October 12, 1854, to Alice A. Fulton, daughter of Hugh and Jane Fulton, of Hopewell Township, and has two children: Hugh T. and Ida May (Ritchie). Mr. Green is a member of the G. A. R., of Stewartstown, has been justice of the peace of the borough for five years, and at present time holds the office of notary public.

ANTHONY GRIME (or as he is familiarly called Webster Grime), son of Daniel and Catherine (Snyder) Grime, was born February 12, 1825, in York Township. He received a common school education and taught school for ten terms in York, Windsor and Springfield Townships. At the breaking out of the Rebellion Mr. Grime promptly responded to his country's call, and enlisted in Company C, Eighty-seventh Regiment Pennsylvania Volunteers (August 27, 1861), and was with his regiment until taken prisoner June 22, 1864, in front of Petersburg. He was taken to Libby prison, then to Castle Thunder and Belle Island; was taken to Danville; after a short stay was removed to Andersonville, remaining a prisoner of war from June 22, 1864, to March 31, 1865. After being honorably discharged he returned to his native county, where he has since resided. He has, for many years, been the weekly correspondent of the *Pennsylvanian*, and for some time correspondent of the *Weekly Republican*, *Gazette* and *True Democrat* for Hopewell and surrounding townships.

WILLIAM HAMMEL was born in Baltimore, Md., and is a son of Jacob and Margaret (Gruber) Hammel. His mother was a native of Philadelphia, Penn. His father was born in Germany, and immigrated to this country in 1821, settling in Baltimore, Md. Our subject, at the age of nineteen years, began learning the trade of coach painter, and served three years apprenticeship. In 1865 he came to Hopewell Township, and purchased a farm of 150 acres. In 1867 he returned to Baltimore, and engaged in the wholesale liquor business. He has one of the finest places in the township.

JESSE HAMMER, SR., son of George and Catherine (Purkeypile) Hammer, was born November 3, 1819. His father was a native of Germany and immigrated to this country at an early date, and settled in Baltimore, where he engaged in the butcher business. He died when his son Jesse was very young, and two years later the mother removed to Hopewell Township, York Co., Penn., where the son, Jesse, was reared and educated in the public schools. When Jesse was eight years old his mother died, and he was adopted by his uncle, Moses Leib. At the age of twenty-one years, Mr. Hammer was married to Mary A. Winemiller, daughter of John Winemiller, of Hopewell Township. In 1847 he purchased a farm of 130 acres, where he now resides. They have three children living: Catharine A., Mary J. and George W. Mr. and Mrs. Hammer belong to the Presbyterian Church of Hopewell Center.

J. C. HAMMOND, son of Henry and Sarah (Coulson) Hammond, natives of Baltimore County, Md., was born in Hopewell Township, York County, May 12, 1834. His grandfather, Philip Hammond, came to York County in 1815, settling in Hopewell Township. Henry Hammond, subject's father, was born July 3, 1793, came to York County in 1815, and settled in Hopewell Township, where he resided until his death in 1873. He held the office of commissioner from 1865 to 1868. The mother of our subject is still living at the age of eighty-seven years. J. C. remained on the home farm until 1876, when he engaged as clerk, with James Fulton, of Stewartstown, with whom he remained four years. He is now a dealer in agricultural implements, also has a book store and circulating library. In 1867 he was appointed mercantile appraiser for the county, and held that office one year. He owns two valuable properties in Stewartstown, an interest in a farm of 360 acres in Baltimore County, Md., and has an interest in a farm of 100 acres in Harford County, Md.

DR. CHARLES G. HILDEBRAND, son of Dietrich and Maria (Leider) Hildebrand, natives of York County, Penn., was born in Loganville, York County, December 31, 1859. His father, also born at Loganville, is a shoe-maker by trade, and in 1864 was elected justice of the peace, which office he still holds. He had a family of three children, of whom Charles G. is the eldest. Our subject was educated at the public schools, and at the age of fifteen years began teaching. After teaching three years he entered the York Collegiate Institute, where he remained one year. He then studied medicine with Dr. G. P. Yost, of Loganville, for three years, after which he took two courses of lectures at the College of Physicians and Surgeons, at Baltimore, graduating in 1881. He located at Winterstown the following April, and has since resided there, enjoying an extensive practice. In 1878 he married Kate Feigley, daughter of Martin Feigley, of Loganville. They have two children: Esther M. and Robert L. Dr. Hildebrand is a member of the York County Medical Society and the American Medical Association. He has been one of the council of Winterstown, and at present is school director. His wife is a member of the Brethren Church of Springfield.

JAMES C. JORDAN, son of Joseph and Mary (Cowden) Jordan, was born July 8, 1832. His mother was a daughter of Matthew Cowden, of Harrisburg, Penn. His grandfather, Thomas Jordan, a native of Ireland, immigrated to this country in 1760, and settled in what is now known as Hopewell Township, and on the same property now owned by his grandson. He was a prominent man in the county in his day; was justice of the peace for many years. He was married first to a Miss Hood, of Cecil County, Md., who left one child, John Jordan. The second marriage was to Ann Dixon, of Pennsylvania, and they had six children. Subject's father died when James C. was fifteen years old. At twenty-one years of age, James C. took the management of the home farm, having purchased his brother's share. In 1879 he engaged in canning fruit and vegetables, which he carried on to a large extent. He was married, March 12, 1857, to Mary Mitchell, daughter of Joseph and Margaret Mitchell, and grand-daughter of Rev. Dr. Morton, of Chanceford. They have eight children: Mary M., Joseph M., Thomas M., Annie M., James F., Samuel M., Ralph R. and George I. Mr. Jordan was one of Gov. Pollock's aides in 1856, with the rank of lieutenant-colonel, Mrs. Jordan died in 1876. Mr. Jordan is a member of the Masonic fraternity, and is also a member and elder of Centre Presbyterian Church, of Hopewell. His father was a soldier in the war of 1812. Mr. Jordan now owns 300 acres, which descended to him from his grandfather, who on arriving here took up about 500 acres.

J. R. W. KEESEY, son of Jacob and Catherine (Hyson) Keesey, of Hopewell Township, York County, Penn., was born in said township, May 17, 1855. At the age of ten years he moved to Chanceford Township with his parents. In 1872 he returned to Hopewell Township, and began learning the milling business with his grandfather, Hyson, in whose employ he remained until 1877, when he entered the mill and carried on the business four years. In 1881 he purchased a store property and twenty-two acres of land at Mt. Pleasant, and carried on a general merchandise business for two years; then he sold his stock of goods and leased the store. He then followed the carpenter's trade for six months, after which he again leased Hyson's Mill, where he has since been doing a very extensive business. In 1881 he was married to Effie Hyson, daughter of Robert Hyson. of Hopewell Township, and has one child, Walter O. H. Mr. and Mrs. Keesey are members of the Presbyterian Church, of Hopewell.

GEORGE W. KERLINGER, son of Henry and Catherine (Ehrhart) Kerlinger, was born in Loganville, Penn., July 6, 1855, and is the sixth of a family of seven children. The father came from Maryland and the mother was a native of Adams County, Penn. Henry Kerlinger, subject's father, purchased the present farm in 1864. He built a tannery and established an extensive tanning business, which he carried on until 1883, when he retired from active business and removed to Stewartstown, where he is now residing. George W. attended school in Loganville and in Hopewell Township. He was married, in 1880, to Mary V. Anstine, daughter of Henry Anstine, of Hopewell Township. They have two children: Harry A. and Nellie E. In 1884 Mr. Kerlinger was elected township clerk for a term of one year and was re-elected for 1885. He is a member of the Methodist Episcopal Church of Stewartstown.

ANDREW LEIB, son of John and Mary (Perkey) Leib, of Hopewell Township, York Co., Penn., was born April 8, 1821. His grandfather, Christian Leib, a native of York County, was in the Revolutionary war, and came to Hopewell Township after the war. He settled three miles from where his grandson now lives, and took up and purchased about 1,500 acres of land. He left four children. Andrew Leib, our subject, was born on the homestead, and is the second son in a family of twelve children. He was married, in 1852, to Rachel Wilson, daughter of William and Margaret Wilson, of Hopewell Township, and settled near Stewartstown, where he purchased a farm. Subsequently he removed to his present farm of thirty-four acres. They have three children: Mary, Margaret J. and Sarah E. Mr. Leib was school director for ten years. He and his wife are members of the Methodist Episcopal Church. His father was in the war of 1812.

JESSE P. LEIB, son of John Leib, of Hopewell Township, was born October 30, 1836, on the farm occupied by his father. He was married, in 1866, to Mary Sellers, daughter of Levi Sellers, of Hopewell Township. They have five children: Mary E., Annie L., Everett S., Harry C. and Jessie. The place where he resides now and where he was born, was purchased by him in 1878, and contains seventy-eight acres. Mr. and Mrs. Leib are members of the Presbyterian Church of Stewartstown.

SAMUEL C. LIGGIT, son of William and Grizzella (Collins) Liggit, of Hopewell Township, York County, was born May 17, 1837. He was brought up on the homestead in Hopewell Township, where he remained until his twentieth year, when he began learning the trade of miller with his brother. In 1860 he was engaged in milling at Peach Bottom. In September, 1864, he enlisted in the Ninth Pennsylvania Cavalry, and served until the end of the war, being with Gen. Sherman on his "march to the sea." In 1865 he purchased the mill property, where he now resides, and is engaged in milling.

He also owns about forty acres of land, which he farms. In March, 1864, he was married to Mary Gemmill, daughter of David Gemmill, of Hopewell Township. They have seven children: Martha G., Florence G., Sarah C., William A., Laura J., Joseph E. and Cornelius W. Mr. Leggit is a member of the E. B. Morrison Post 387. G. A. R. He and his wife belong to the Guinston United Presbyterian Church of Chanceford.

MRS. HARRIETT R. LONG is the widow of William S. Long, son of John and Harriet (Steel) Long, who was born in Lancaster County, Penn., in 1818, and died in 1869. He was engaged very extensively with his brother, Hugh H. Long, in milling. Mrs. Long was born in Hopewell Township, York Co., Penn., April 2, 1829. Her father, Archibald S. Jordan, was a paymaster in the war of 1812. He had ten children, of whom Mrs. Long was the sixth child. She was married in 1856, but has no children. Her husband was prominently engaged in raising troops in the late war, and was a highly esteemed citizen. After his death his widow returned to Stewartstown to the homestead, but subsequently located in the village, where she now resides.

THOMAS B. McDONALD, a son of John and Catharine (Winand) McDonald, was born in Fawn Township, York Co., Penn., March 3, 1828. His father came to York County, Penn., from Harford County, Md., when young, and located in Hopewell Township, where he followed the trade of a shoemaker. He afterward removed to Fawn Township, where he remained a number of years, and then returned to Hopewell Township, where he remained until his death in 1881. He had nine children, of whom Thomas B. is the fifth. Our subject was reared in this township, and in 1847 began learning the blacksmith's trade in Chanceford Township, and, with the exception of a few years, has since followed that trade. In 1851 he was married to Elizabeth J., daughter of Alexander Thompson, of Lower Chanceford Township. They have three children: Dr. David M., John A. and William T. Mr. McDonald held the office of assessor one year and was elected county auditor in 1881, and still holds that office. He and his wife are members of the United Presbyterian Church of Hopewell.

WILLIAM H. McDOWELL, son of William and Sarah (McLean) McDowell, was born in Windsor Township, York Co., Penn., November 15, 1812, and is the third of a family of eleven children. The father also was born in Windsor Township, and the mother in Hopewell Township. His father was in the war of 1812. Our subject was reared by John Anstine, and at the age of twenty-one years became engaged in the iron furnaces, with which he was connected for nearly twelve years, working at different furnaces. In 1849 he purchased his present farm of 101 acres near Stewartstown, where he has since resided. In 1845 he was married to Catherine Hilderman, daughter of Adam Hilderman, of Hopewell Township. They have seven children: Elizabeth, William H., Jacob, Agnes, Franklin, Adam and Maggie. In 1845 Mr. McDowell engaged in distilling liquors, which he followed for three years, and also distilled apples on his farm. He has held the offices of auditor and supervisor in the township. He and his wife belong to the Reformed Church of Mount Pleasant.

ADAM McDOWELL, son of William and Catherine (Hildebrand) McDowell, was born in Hopewell Township, York Co., Penn., March 16, 1859. He remained on the homestead, following farming until 1884, when, in March of that year, he established a cigar factory at Stewartstown, Penn., and is doing an extensive business. May 9, 1884, he was married to Amanda Meier, daughter of John Meier, of Hopewell Township.

BIOGRAPHICAL SKETCHES 115

JOHN A. MANIFOLD, son of Salem and Lizzie T. Manifold, was born in Fawn Township, York Co., Penn., March 9, 1830. His great great-grandfather, Edward Manifold, emigrated from England before 1776. Subject's father was born December 6, 1799, in Fawn Township, York County, but spent the latter part of his life in Hopewell Township. He had eleven children, of whom John A. is the eldest. While the latter was yet a child, his parents moved to Hopewell Township. In 1850 he began learning the carpenter's trade, and moved to Indiana in 1854, where he remained six years. He then went to Missouri, where he remained six years, returning to Hopewell Township, where he has since resided. He married Emeline Diling, of Indiana, and they have four children living: Eliza M., Franklin S., Cora W. and Alonzo J. The farm on which Mr. Manifold resides, and which contains seventy-six acres, he purchased in 1865. He, his wife and family are members of the Methodist Episcopal Church of Zion.

WILLIAM MARTIN was born February 15, 1814, in Franklin Township, York County, and is a son of John and Elizabeth (Lehmer) Martin, of Franklin Township. In 1846, he removed to York, Penn., where he engaged in the hotel business for eight years; then moved to Liverpool, now called Manchester, where he kept a hotel for some time. He then returned to York, and engaged in mercantile business. In the fall of 1860 he was elected sheriff of York County, and held that position three years. In 1863, he came to Hopewell Township, purchased twenty-four acres of land, and has since been engaged in farming. He was married, October 14, 1832, to Miss Cassandra Small, daughter of Joseph Small, of York. Mr. Martin is a member of the I. O. O. F. He and wife are members of the Lutheran Church.

DR. JOSEPH R. MARTIN, son of James and Eliza (Morrison) Martin, of Lancaster County, Penn., was born September 14, 1838, in Lancaster County, Penn. He received his early education in the public schools of his township, and at the age of twenty years commenced the study of medicine with his brother, Dr. John Martin, at Georgetown, Penn., and graduated from Jefferson Medical College, Philadelphia, in 1862. The same year he received a commission as assistant surgeon of the One Hundred and Twenty-fourth Pennsylvania Volunteers. On leaving the service, in 1863, he located in Penningtonville, and commenced the practice of medicine. In the fall of 1864 he received an appointment as surgeon of the officer's hospital at Alexandria, Va., and remained there until the close of the war. He then returned to Penningtonville, and in the spring of 1869 removed to his present place of residence. He was married in 1866 to Abbie J. Smith, of Hopewell Township, daughter of Rev. H. Smith. They have six children living: Sarah J., Annie L., Harriet B., Dwight C., Jonewell and John R. Dr. Martin is a member of the Masonic fraternity No. 343, Skerret Lodge of Cochransville, Penn. He and wife are members of the Stewartstown Presbyterian Church.

HENRY S. OVERMILLER, son of Frederick and Mary (Snyder) Overmiller, natives of Hopewell Township, but later residents of Loganville, was born in Loganville, Penn., August 2, 1844, and is the twelfth in a family of thirteen children. He was reared and educated at Loganville, and remained with his parents until 1865, when he engaged in the mercantile business at Hartley Postoffice, where he remained for two years, doing a thriving business. In 1867 he engaged in farming in Windsor Township, but exchanged the farm in the fall of the same year, and moved to a farm near Dallastown, where he remained eight years, and in connection with farming followed the mercantile business and huckstering. He then went to Dallastown Station, on the Peach Bottom Railroad, where he again engaged in the mercantile business, and was also postmaster and agent of the York & Peach Bottom Railroad. He remained there two years, and in 1878 moved to Virginia, where he purchased a farm, which he cultivated for three years. He then moved back to York County, Penn., and purchased a store at Mount Pleasant, Hopewell Township, where he has since resided, and has built up an extensive business. He also works a farm of twenty-two acres. He was married, in 1865, to Hannah M. Althouse, daughter of George Althouse (deceased), of Hopewell Township. They had seven children; George F., Oscar H. (deceased), Virginia L., Daniel W., Wilburt F., Tyburtus J. and Silvanus.

JACOB SAYLOR, son of Jacob and Elizabeth (Ramsay) Saylor, was born in Manchester Township, York Co., Penn., December 25, 1837, and is the fifth of a family of nine children. His father and mother were born in Manchester Township—the latter died in 1858. Jacob Saylor, our subject, at the age of twenty-one years, began farming, which he followed two years. He then learned blacksmithing, and worked in the car shops at York for two years. In 1863 he went to Illinois, and worked at farming for two years, and then returned to York, Penn.; was again employed in the car shops until 1867, when he began selling machinery as traveling salesman. In 1870 he rented the hotel property near Stewartstown, known as Patterson's Hotel, where he remained three years, and gained an enviable reputation as a first class hotel keeper. In 1875 he rented the Douglass hotel, near Winterstown; remained there only one year, when he removed to the Plank Road, and engaged in smithing for one year. In 1877 he rented a hotel at Winterstown one year, and then rented Snyder's hotel, where he also remained one year, after which he removed to the present hotel property at Cross Roads where he has since been located, and is enjoying an extensive trade. In connection with keeping hotel he is also dealing in agricultural implements and horses. He was married, in 1859, to Henrietta Albright, daughter of John Albright, of York, and has four children; William E, George B., Emma K. and Clara E. His wife died August 4, 1868. His second marriage was in 1869 to Mary Jane Portner, daughter of Mrs. Mary Portner, of Cross Roads, and they have one child—Henry Irving. In 1880 Mr. Saylor was elected constable of his township, and held that office four years. He and wife are members of the Lutheran Church, of Mount Pleasant. He is now building a hotel on property which he owns at Felton Station, on the York & Peach Bottom Railroad, where he intends locating

WILLIAM SECHRIST, son of John and Elizabeth (Grove) Sechrist, of York County, was born December 24, 1819. At the age of seventeen years he was apprenticed to John Gemmill, in the manufacturing of woolen goods, and at the age of twenty-two years entered into partnership in that business with Benjamin Hank, who lived four miles from Wrightsville, in Windsor Township. In 1850 he bought out John Gemmill, and in 1852 built a new factory, known as Keseling's Mills, in Hopewell, and remained there until 1867, when he sold out to George Keseling, and then removed to his farm, where he now resides, having bought of Arthur I. Edie. His farm contains 143 acres of well-improved land. He was married, January 17, 1850, to Anna M. Becker, daughter of John Becker, late justice of the peace of York. They have three children living.

JAMES M. SMITH, son of Robert M. and Liza (Griffith) Smith, was born September 17, 1845, in Chanceford Township, York Co., Penn. His parents were natives of Hopewell Township and Chanceford Township, respectively, and his grandmother a native of Ireland. He was educated at Stewartstown Academy and at Shrewsbury, and in 1865 commenced teaching school. After teaching one term in Hopewell Township, he took a course at Easton's Commercial College at Poughkeepsie, N. Y., where he remained about four months. He then entered Waynesburg College, where he remained one year, being compelled to discontinue on account of poor health. Returning home he remained on the homestead one year, and then entered a general store at Stewartstown, where he remained only five months, and then returned to the homestead for two years. In 1872 he was married to Jennie E. Kerlinger, daughter of Henry Kerlinger, of Hopewell Township. They have three children: Clayton C., Annie F. and Olive E. After his marriage he attended his father's farm during harvest for three years, after which he returned to his present farm of 300 acres. In connection with farming, he also deals in phosphates and agricultural implements. Mr. and Mrs. Smith are members of the Presbyterian Church of Hopewell.

WILLIAM C. SMITH, son of Sampson and Eleanor (McAllister) Smith, of Hopewell Township, York Co., Penn., was born in that township, October 22, 1848, and received his education at the public school and at Stewartstown and Shrewsbury Academies. He remained with his parents on the homestead until 1871, when he engaged as a clerk in the store of Mr. Logan, at Cross Roads, and remained there one year. In 1872 he was appointed collector of county, State and school taxes, which office he held for two years. In 1874 he purchased a building lot at Cross Roads, erected a dwelling house and store, and in 1875 established a general merchandise business, and has built up a very extensive trade. In 1877 he was married to Louisa M. Zellers, daughter of Levi Zellers, of Hopewell Township. They have no children. Mr. Smith was elected justice of the peace in 1881, which office he still holds; was also school director for one year in 1877, and auditor for three years, and in 1880 was engaged in taking the census of the township. He and wife are members of the Presbyterian Church of Stewartstown.

REV. THOMAS LOVE SPRINGER, son of Stephen and Mary Elizabeth (Love) Springer, of Newcastle County, Del., was born August 25, 1849, is the eldest of five children; two of his brothers are practicing physicians in Delaware. He received his education at the public schools and the Newark Academy. In 1867 he entered Lafayette College, at Easton, Penn., and graduated in June, 1871; in September, 1871, he entered Princeton Theological Seminary, from which he graduated in April, 1874. During the vacation of his junior year he preached in a Congregational Church in Maine. During his next vacation he preached in a Presbyterian Church in Illinois. In November, 1874, he was called to the pastorate of the Hopewell Presbyterian Church, and was ordained and installed by the Presbytery of Westminster, December 1, 1874, and is still pastor of said Church. November 9, 1875, he was married to Mary Gould Bowker, daughter of Frederick and Rachael A. Bowker, of Chester. They have three living children: Courtland Bowker, born May 15, 1878; Mary Cronham, born April 12, 1881, and James Love, born October 22, 1883.

ROBERT F. STABLER, son of Jared and Margaret J. (Koller) Stabler, of Shrewsbury Township, was born in Shrewsbury Township, York Co., Penn., September 26, 1851. His father was born in 1820, and carried on the lime business in York County for a number of years, subsequently removing to Railroad Borough, where he engaged in milling and dealing in grain, which occupation he still follows. Robert F. received his education at the public schools of the township and at the academy of Shrewsbury and New Freedom. In 1869 he began learning the milling trade in his father's mill at Railroad Borough, where he remained until 1872, when he engaged in railroading and farming for three years. In 1875 he came to Hopewell Township, and engaged in milling. He remained there five years, after which he went to Stewartstown, and kept a feed store for three years, and then went back to Ebaugh's Mills, where he has since resided, having charge of a grist and saw-mill. He was married, in 1871, to Artilda Kunkel, daughter of A. W. Kunkel, of Shrewsbury Township. They have six children: Charles W., Clara L., Addie E., Minnie S., Daniel A. and Mary Ann. Mr. Stabler is a member of the Brotherhood of Stewartstown, and his wife is a member of the Lutheran Church.

ADAM F. STRAYER, son of David W. and Lydia (Strayer) Strayer, was born in Lancaster County, Penn., February 25, 1846, came to Hopewell Township in 1848. His father was born in Hopewell Township in 1829, and has always resided there, with the exception of a few years spent in Lancaster County. Adam F. received his education at the public schools and at Pleasant Grove Academy. He remained on the farm until 1863, when he enlisted in Company C, Twenty-first Pennsylvania Cavalry, for nine months; after which he enlisted in Company B, One Hundred and Eighty-eighth Pennsylvania Volunteer Infantry. In the battle of Chapin's Farm he was wounded in the right arm, which was subsequently amputated. After the close of the war he followed school teaching, and taught in this township eleven years. In 1881 he was elected justice of the peace for the borough of Winterstown, which office he still holds. In 1867 he was married to Sarah E. Snyder, daughter of Jacob Snyder. They have no children. In 1868 he was appointed postmaster, which office he held until 1881. He and wife are members of the U. B. Church at Winterstown.

ARCHIBALD THOMPSON, son of Alexander and Elizabeth (Duncan) Thompson, of Hopewell and Fawn Townships, respectively, was born June 7, 1804. His grandfather, Archibald Thompson, a native of Hopewell Township, settled on the present homestead before the Revolutionary war. Subject's father was a soldier in the Revolutionary war, and served under Capt. Moffett. Our subject was reared on the homestead where he always lived. He was married, February 15, 1827, to Hannah Meats, of Hopewell Township, who died July 16, 1839. July 29, 1841, he married his second wife, and has eight children: Alexander, Samuel H. S., James G., Archibald J. G.,John M., Margaret J. A., Ellen M. E., and Elijah P. For twenty-five years he was connected with his father in the manufacturing of cider brandy. He has held two military commissions, captain and first lieutenant; was appointed by Gov. Porter justice of the peace of Hopewell Township, and served ten years. Besides these offices he has held nearly all the public positions in the gift of the people of the township. From his father he inherited 285 acres of land, on which two of his sons are living: Samuel H. S. and Archibald J. G. Samuel H. S. was married in 1880 to Catharine A. McDole, of Hopewell Township; she died in 1884, leaving two children: Archibald W. J. and Anna S. M. Archibald J. G. married Susan F. Baird, of Hopewell Township, and has two children: Ethel and Ralph B. Mr. Thompson is a member of the Presbyterian Church of Hopewell and Stewartstown, and has been an elder and one of the builders of the church.

WILLIAM THOMPSON was born in Chanceford Township, York Co., Penn., January 1, 1841.

His parents were Archa and Elizabeth (Heffner) Thompson, natives of Maryland and Pennsylvania, respectively, and of English and German descent. They reared a family of two sons and six daughters, and buried four children in infancy. William Thompson, the eldest living of this family, was reared on a farm. In 1862 he was married in his native township to Margaret Jane Blouse, daughter of Solomon Blouse, of the same township, and of German descent. They had twelve children, two of whom died: Rebecca, six years of age, burned to death by accident; Wellington, deceased, aged two years. Those living are Elizabeth, William James, Annie, Ella, Mary, Fannie, Andrew Leib, Jesse R., Georgie, Nettie and Llewellyn. Mr. Thompson owns 149 acres of well cultivated land in Hopewell Township, which he has been farming since 1863. He has been assessor, has been a delegate to the Democratic county conventions, and is connected with a building and loan association at York, Penn. His father who lives in Shrewsbury Township, is now seventy-four years of age.

JAMES H. TROUT, son of Abram and Violet (Morrison) Trout, of Hopewell and Peach Bottom Townships, York Co., Penn., was born July 29, 1849, in Harford County, Md. He received his education in the Harford and York County public schools. He came to York County in 1868, and in 1872 was married to Lizzie Hendricks, daughter of Thomas Hendricks, of Hopewell Township. They have two children: Violet C. and Jesse H. Mr. Trout purchased the farm on which he resides, which contains about sixty-five acres, in 1877.

WILLIAM VENUS, son of Henry and Anna (Sykes) Venus, natives of York County and the north of England, respectively, was born in Shrewsbury Township, September 3, 1843. He was educated at the public schools of the township, and at the age of twenty-three years engaged as a clerk in a store, and one year later he removed to Carroll County, Md., where he engaged in the milling business with his father. In 1868 he returned to Shrewsbury and engaged in the carpenter business. In 1870 he again engaged in the mercantile business in Hopewell Township, and in 1875 he moved to Winterstown, where he opened a general store. In 1877 he sold out and removed to Shrewsbury Township, where he engaged in his old business—storekeeping. In March, 1877, he removed to Hopewell Township, where he is at present engaged in keeping a general store. He was married, in 1870, to Elizabeth Gladfelter, of Shrewsbury Borough, and has six children: James A., Charles H., Sadie B., Annie C., Daniel E. and an infant.

JAMES W. WALLACE, son of William and Jeannette (Gemmill) Wallace, was born April 26, 1847, in Harford County, Md., where his parents resided, with whom he came to York County, Penn., when only three years old. His parents were born in York County, Penn. Until 1873 he remained on the homestead farming, after which he purchased a merchandising business, formerly owned by his father. In 1882 he built a dwelling house, and in 1884 a store. In connection with the store, he works a farm of ninety-five acres. In 1872 he was married to Sarah A. McCall, daughter of Matthew McCall, of Fawn Township, and has three children: Margaret J. A., Anna M. and Marion A. Mr. and Mrs. Wallace are members of the United Presbyterian Church of Hopewell. Mr. Wallace was appointed postmaster of Hopewell Centre in 1875, which office he still holds.

WILLIAM H. WINEMILLER, son of Joseph and Mary (Souder) Winemiller, of Hopewell Township, was born November 13, 1834. His grandfather, Jacob Winemiller, was the third son of one Winemiller who, it is supposed came from Switzerland and located in Hopewell Township, and who owned about 1,200 acres of land. The father was engage in farming and milling in Hopewell Township and died in 1861, leaving five children, of whom William H. is the third. He was reared on the homestead, educated at the public schools and studied veterinary surgery. He practiced for six years at Shrewsbury Station, but in 1874 he returned to the homestead, which he had inherited from his father, and commenced farming, which he has followed since in connection with veterinary surgery. In 1860 he was married to Rebecca Ziegler, daughter of Peter Ziegler, Hopewell Township, and has eight children: Edward P. (a teacher in the public schools of Harford County, Md.), Mary A., Joseph G., Calvin D., Eva J., Oran F., Oscar M. and Raleigh W. Mr. Winemiller enlisted in the late war in the One Hundred and Forty-ninth Regiment Pennsylvania Volunteers, in the fall of 1863, and was discharged in the spring of 1864. He and members of his wife's family belong to the Presbyterian Church at Stewartstown.

WILLIAM L. WINTER, son of John and Mary (Gibbs) Winter, of Stewartstown, Penn., was born January 1, 1848, and was reared in Stewartstown. At the age of fifteen years he enlisted in the Twenty-first Pennsylvania Cavalry, and was discharged at the close of the war at Lynchburg, Va. He was engaged in the battles of the Wilderness, Petersburg, Weldon Railroad, Five Forks and others. At the close of the war he returned to Stewartstown and began learning the trade of blacksmithing with Thomas Cole, at the carshops of Glen Rock, and in 1874 engaged in business for himself in coach-making and general blacksmithing. He held the office of assessor for two terms, and in the spring of 1884 was elected justice of the peace for Stewartstown. He is the only Republican ever elected in that town. In 1869 he was married to Lily Keesey, of Chanceford, daughter of Jacob Keesey, Esq. They have four children: Annetta B., Mary M., Minnie M. and Charles. Mr. Winter is a member of E. B. Morrison Post No. 387, G. A. R., of Stewartstown. Mrs. Winter is a member of the Methodist Episcopal Church of Stewartstown.

LEVI ZELLERS, son of Bartholomew and Rose A. (Miller) Zellers, of Loganville, Penn., was born at Stewartstown, Hopewell Township, in 1817. He was reared and educated in the same township, where he has lived on the homestead, which he and his brother inherited at the death of his father, subsequently buying his brother's interest in the farm (136 acres). In 1888 he was married to Lavina Edie, of Hopewell Township, who died in 1877, leaving six children: Lydia A., Andrew, William, Mary, Louisa and Samuel. Mr. Zellers is a member of the Stewartstown Presbyterian Church. He is now living with his son, William, who bought the farm from him in 1882. William Zellers was born in 1843, and in 1875 was married to Esther J. Anderson, of Hopewell Township, and has one son, James Lee Zellers.

JACKSON TOWNSHIP.

G. W. BAHN, M. D., is a native of York County, Penn., and was born in Spring Garden Township, in 1856. His parents, Samuel L. and Susan (Tyson) Bahn, are also natives of York County, and representatives of old families of the county. Our subject was educated in the common schools of his day, supplemented by a course at the Normal School of York and Emigsville Academy. In 1878 he commenced the study of medicine under

JACKSON TOWNSHIP.

Dr. J. B. Kain, now of York, Penn. He remained with Dr Kain three years, attending medical lectures at the University of Maryland, at Baltimore, in the meantime. In 1881 he graduated from this institution and commenced the practice of his profession in Spring Grove, where he is now engaged in active and successful practice. Dr. Bahn married in 1880, Miss Alice E. Sitler, of East Prospect, Lower Windsor Township. They have one child living—Edith M. Dr. Bahn is a member of the Mount Olivet Lodge No. 997, I. O. O. F., of Spring Grove, and, with his wife, a member of St. Paul's Lutheran Church. The Doctor is also a member of the York County Medical Society.

C. W. BAUER, one of the leading merchants of Spring Grove, is a native of Germany. He came to America in 1873, and located at York, where he entered the employ of J. L. Getz, with whom he remained ten years. In 1884 he removed to Spring Grove, and embarked in the general mercantile business in partnership with Frank Raab, which partnership has since been dissolved. He carries a large stock of goods and has succeeded in establishing a first-class trade. Mr. Bauer is an agreeable gentleman, possessing fine business attributes, and ranks among the leading citizens of the borough. He was appointed justice of the peace in 1884, and is now administering the duties of that office. Mr. Bauer formed a matrimonial alliance, in 1880, with Miss Lydia Raab, of York, Penn. They have one child—Lottie. Mr. and Mrs. Bauer are members of St. John's Lutheran Church of York.

Z. L. BOWMAN, son of Henry L. and Clara (Loucks) Bowman, fourth of seven children, was born December 24, 1854, in Heidelberg Township, and after attending school in his native township, his first work was at Glatfelter's Paper Mill, at Spring Grove. He worked at this mill for ten years, then began the manufacture of all kinds of powder in 1882. Mr. Bowman married Annie E. Menges, daughter of P. H. and Katie (Hinkle) Menges. Two children bless their marriage—Bessie and Willie. The Spring Grove Powder Mill, owned and operated by P. H. Glatfelter. Z. L. Bowman and M. S. Johnson, is doing a thriving business, although but recently put in operation. They manufacture all kinds of powder, and they have a large trade in York and adjoining counties for all their powder.

P. M. BRINGMAN is a native of York County, and is the son of John and Anna M. (Bowersox) Bringman. The father and grandfather, John and Jacob, were also natives of York County, and the grandfather, George Bowersox, a native of the same. John Bringman died in March, 1880; his widow, Anna M. resides in Spring Grove, and is the mother of six living children: Amanda Rudisill, George, P. M. (subject), Annie, Jacob and John. Our subject was reared in Jackson Township, and was educated at the common and normal schools and at the Academy of York, and for a number of years followed the profession of teaching in Jackson; in 1879 he began teaching in Spring Grove, where he still resides. He is a member of the I. O. O. F. of Spring Grove, and, with the family, a member of the English Church.

EDWARD GLATFELTER, superintendent of Spring Grove Paper Mills, is a son of Charles and Louisa (Fishel) Glatfelter, and was born in 1839, in Spring Garden Township. He was reared on a farm, and until twenty-five years of age, remained upon the farm as an assistant of his father. He then operated the old homestead farm for a period of nine years for himself, after which he became the general agent of the Weed Sewing Machine Company, for York and Adams Counties, continuing this business two years. He then removed to Spring Grove, and entered the employ of his brother in the paper-mills as a laborer. In 1879 he became the superintendent of the mills, which position he has ably filled up to the present writing. In 1863 he was united in marriage with Sarah A. Herman, a native of West Manchester Township. This union has been blessed with five children: Laura Z., Harvey E., Lucy K., Nettie J. and Sadie E. Mr. and Mrs. Glatfelter, with their two eldest children, are members of St. Paul's Lutheran Church.

HENRY HOKE was born in this township in 1822, to Michael and Barbara (Fishel) Hoke, natives of York County. His grandfather, Casper Hoke, who married a Miss Emig, was a blacksmith by trade, but was following farming at the time of his death. Subject's mother was descended from one of the oldest families of the county and died about 1828, the mother of eight children: Elizabeth, Magdalena, Margaretta, Joseph, Michael, George. Henry and Susanna. By a subsequent marriage, Michael Hoke had born to him three children, Eliza, Abraham and Nancy. The father of these died about 1868, and his widow about 1880. Our subject was reared a farmer, and in 1845 began on his own account, following agriculture until 1882, when he left his farm of 115 acres in charge of his son, Jacob, and moved to Nashville and engaged in a general mercantile trade, in which he is quite prosperous. In 1844 he married Anna, daughter of Christian Hershey, of Jackson Township. This lady died December 1, 1883, the mother of twelve children, of whom Joseph is deceased. The living are Elizabeth Sprenkle, William, Emanuel, Henry, Sarah N. Bott, Eliza, Jacob, Amanda, Martin, George and Michael. Mr. Hoke is a school director and a member of the Reformed Church, in which he has been a leader of the choir for over thirty years.

WILLIAM H. HOKE, son of Henry and Annie (Hershey) Hoke, was born in Jackson Township, October 26, 1846. His early days were passed on the farm and in attending the district school until nineteen. In the spring of 1869 he began life on his own responsibility, and in 1874 purchased his present homestead of 138 acres. This farm is noted for its iron ore, a number of shafts having been sunk, and is productive in wheat, corn and Havana and Connecticut tobacco. Mr. Hoke also gives considerable attention to the culture of Italian bees, and finds a ready market for several hundred pounds of honey annually. August 23, 1868, Mr. Hoke married Sarah, daughter of Peter and Catherine (Wiest) Spangler, to which union the following children have been born: Phares Henry, Alice Jane, Lilly Ann. William Edward, Emma Elverta (an infant daughter), Naomi Sarah, Nettie Savilla, Lucy Viola and Ada Anna. Mr. and Mrs. Hoke are members of the Emanuel Reformed Church, of which Mr. H. has been organist since 1879.

M. HOKE, M. D , is a native of York County, Penn., and was born in Jackson Township in 1859. His parents, Henry and Anna (Hershey) Hoke, are both natives of York County, and descendants of old families of the county. Our subject was reared in his native county, and attended the common schools, and also York County Academy. About the age of eighteen years he commenced the study of medicine with Dr. J. Wiest, then of Jackson Township, but now one of the leading practitioners of York, Penn. Under the tutelage of Dr. Wiest he remained three years, attending lectures at the Jefferson Medical College, of Philadelphia, in the meantime, and graduating from that institution in 1881. He also attended a special course of anatomy in 1880. In 1881 he located in Spring Grove, and commenced the practice of his profession, which is continually increasing. He was married, in 1883, to Miss Harriet Schwartz, of York County, Penn. Dr. Hoke is a member of the German Reformed Church, and his wife of the Lutheran Church.

WILLIAM S. JOHNSTON, a descendant of old

representative families, was born in Spring Garden Township, in 1834. His great-grandfather was a pioneer of the county, a farmer and one of the founders of the Episcopal Church of York, in the church-yard of which he lies buried. His grandfather, William Johnston, was a farmer of Spring Garden Township, where he resided until his death; he was the father of eleven children, two of whom are now living; Mrs. Mary Hantz and Sarah, both residents of York. Samuel Johnston, the father of our subject, was born in Spring Garden Township, where he resided until 1838, when he removed to Jackson Township, where he became a leading farmer and resided until his death, which occurred in 1872. The mother of our subject, Mary Smyser, was a daughter of Michael Smyser, of West Manchester Township, and a descendant of an old family of the county. She was the mother of two children: William S. and Mary (deceased). The mother died in 1857. Our subject was reared upon a farm, and in the field of agriculture he has devoted the entire attention of his life. Mr. Johnston has been a resident of Jackson Township since he was four years of age; he became the manager of the old homestead farm in 1857, and in 1872 he became the inheritor, upon the death of his father. This farm consists of 200 acres of superior land, finely improved, the most of the improvements having been made by our subject; he also owns a tract of land in Codorus Township. Mr. Johnston is one of the solid, substantial citizens of York County; he is enterprising in all matters of public improvement, and one of the esteemed citizens of the county. Mr. Johnston was married, in 1857, to Miss Julia Bott, a daughter of Jacob Bott, of Jackson Township, and of an old family. Three children have been born to them: Sarah Smyser, William Allen (deceased at the age of eighteen) and an infant daughter. The family have always been members of the Lutheran and Episcopal denominations.

M. W. LAU is a native of York County, and was born in West Manchester Township in 1844; his father Michael Lau, was a native of York County, and a farmer of West Manchester Township, until his death. Catherine (Wolf) Lau, mother of our subject, is still living. Our subject was reared on a farm and followed farming for fourteen years, seven years in Paradise and seven in Heidelberg Townships. In 1876 he became the agent of the White Sewing Machine Company, which business he has successfully conducted up to the present writing; he is also the general agent for York County for the Reid Creamery, for which valuable machine he has established a large sale. Mr. Lau became a resident of Spring Grove in 1879, where he has since resided. He assisted materially in the movement for the incorporation of the town, and was one of the first election officers. He has served as councilman since Spring Grove became a borough, was the manager and superintendent of the building of the schoolhouse, and is always a public spirited and progressive citizen. Mr. Lau was married, December 20, 1866, to Miss Lucinda Fishel, daughter of Michael Fishel, of Jackson Township. She died July 14, 1876, leaving three children: Charles K., Henry H. and Minnie K. His second marriage occurred June 1, 1879, when he was united with Miss Elizabeth Ellen Senft, daughter of Isaac Senft, of Codorus Township. They have two children—Luther M. and Paul F. Mr. and Mrs. Lau are members of St. Paul's Lutheran Church. Mr. Lau has been earnestly identified with his church, and has served as deacon since the organization of the church at Spring Grove.

W. H. LOCKEMAN, dealer in agricultural implements and wagons, who has recently begun business in Spring Grove, is a young man worthy of encouragement, being thoroughly acquainted in the business in which he has embarked. He is a practical machinist, having worked in some of the best shops in the country. He learned the trade of blacksmith with his father, Frederick Lockeman, of York County.

HENRY K. MARKEL is a native of Shrewsbury Township, and was born in 1833. His great-grandfather was a soldier in the war of the Revolution. His grandfather, Martin Markel, was also a resident of York County. His parents, Henry and Catherine (Kunkel) Markel, were natives of York County, and farmers of Shrewsbury Township, where his father died in 1850; his mother still resides there. Our subject was reared upon the farm, and at the age of eighteen learned the shoe-maker's trade at Glen Rock, and followed that occupation five years in his native township. He next learned the carpenter's trade, which he followed fourteen years, learning in the meantime the machine trade at Glen Rock. He then farmed for twelve years in Codorus Township, and in 1881 came to Spring Grove and established a general machine, repair and jobbing shop, and is now doing a successful and remunerative business. Mr. Markel is a skilled general mechanic. He has served as a councilman and assistant assessor of Spring Grove Borough. In 1852 he married Miss Louisa Bailey, of Shrewsbury Township. They have six children living: Elnora, Sarah J., Mary A., William, George and Ida. Mr. and Mrs. Markel are members of the German Reformed Church.

GEORGE MENGES, a successful and representative business man of York County was born in Jackson Township in 1848. He is descended from two old families of the county, his parents, Andrew and Caroline (Klinepeter) Menges, natives of the County. His father is a farmer, and George, until the age of twenty-five, continued at home as an assistant. He then farmed the homestead for seven years, also extracting iron ore from the beds upon the land. At the expiration of this period he removed to Spring Grove, and embarked upon a more extended field of business, establishing a general trade in coal, lumber, grain, phosphates, etc., in which field he has been eminently successful, and is now enjoying a large patronage. He was the prime mover and worker in securing the incorporation of Spring Grove into a borough, and was the first burgess; he also takes an active interest in the schools and is now serving upon the school board. Mr. Menges has done considerable in building up Spring Grove, and owns several tenement houses and considerable other property, and is recognized as one of the leading citizens and business men of the county. In 1872 he married Miss Amanda Martin, of Jackson Township. They have one child living—Lillie. Mr. and Mrs. Menges are members of the Lutheran Church at Spring Grove.

GEORGE. W. METZGER, M. D., son of Solomon and Rebecca (Bower) Metzger, was born in Manchester Township, February 8, 1855. He attended the common schools until about thirteen years of age, when he entered the Millersville State Normal School, and studied for two years. In 1874 he commenced reading medicine with Dr. J. B. Kain, of Manchester Borough, and was under his instruction for two years; he then entered Jefferson College, Philadelphia, from which he graduated in 1877. The spring of that year he began practice in Jackson Township as successor to Dr. Christian Picking, and has here been very successful, now owning a brick dwelling, with several acres of ground, on the Gettysburgh pike, one and one-half miles west of Thomasville. June 17, 1877, he married Mary Elizabeth, daughter of Abraham Yost, and has had born to him by this union: Alemena K., John L., Sallie R. and Lizzie. The Doctor has been a school director since 1883, and he

JACKSON TOWNSHIP.

and wife are members of the St. Paul's Lutheran Church, of West Manchester.

JOHN ROTH, son of John and Elizabeth (Spangler) Roth, was born October 3, 1828, and was brought up on his father's farm. February 10, 1856, he married Susan Schwartz, daughter of John and Catharine (Myers) Schwartz, of Jackson Township. Nine children were born to them: Emma, Jacob (deceased), Ellen, Henry (deceased), Moses (deceased), Ida, Amanda, Susanna and John. Mr. Roth's ancestors were probably the first settlers in that neighborhood. His great-grandfather took up land where our subject now lives, and this land has been in the Roth family continuously down to present time. (See history of Roth's Church in this volume.)

L. A. ROTH, M. D., was born in Adams County, Penn., in 1849, and is the youngest of the nine children born to Jonas and Barbara (Kauffman) Roth. The father of our subject was born in Jackson Township in 1800, was a farmer, and about 1822 removed to Adams County, where he died in 1871; his widow, Barbara Roth, died in 1884. Subject's paternal grandfather, Abraham Roth, whose grandparents emigrated from Switzerland about 1720, and located in York County, was an old settler of the county, and was a farmer and Mennonite minister and bishop. L. A. Roth was reared a farmer and received his education at the common schools and at the normal school at Millersville three years, and afterward taught school. In 1865 he served six months with the One Hundred and Third Pennsylvania Volunteer Infantry, Company C, through North and South Carolina, and elsewhere, and at the age of eighteen commenced the study of medicine with Dr. Thrall, of Burlington, N. J., remaining with him seven years—three in partnership. He graduated from a New York medical college and filled the chair of anatomy for three years in the New York Hygeio-Therapeutic Medical College (founded in 1852 and chartered by the New York legislature in 1857), and for two years practiced in Adams County. In 1878 he located, in partnership with Dr. John Wiest, in Jackson Township, where he has since enjoyed a good practice. In 1878 he married Miss Rosa, daughter of ex-Sheriff Jacob Plank, of Adams County, and has had born to him two children: Leroy and Ralph.

GEORGE SEILER is a native of Adams County, Penn., and was born in 1837. His parents were Charles and Sarah (Bollinger) Seiler. They subsequently became residents of York County, where they remained until their death at Spring Grove. The father died in 1881, the mother, in 1877. Three children are now living, of whom George is the youngest. He learned the miller's trade with his father, and followed that occupation about twenty years in York County. He subsequently learned the trade of painter with Garrett Bros., of Williamsport, and has followed it until the present time with marked success. Mr. Seiler became a resident of Spring Grove about 1874, where he has since resided, and been identified with all its progress. He was one of the leaders in securing the incorporation of the town, and was the first assessor, and one of the first election officers. Mr. Seiler was elected chief burgess of the borough in 1884 (February), and is a member of Mount Olivet Lodge No. 997, I. O. O. F. In 1858 he married Eliza Raber, of North Codorus Township, who died January 8, 18—, leaving two children: Mary E. and Charles H. R. Mr. Seiler was united to his present wife April 3, 1882. Her maiden name was Belle Zehring, and she is a native of Jefferson Borough, York County. Mr. Seiler is a member of St. Paul's Lutheran Church, of Spring Grove, and his wife of the German Reformed Church of Jefferson.

JOHN K. SHAFFER, a son of John and Polly (Kerr) Shaffer, was born in Heidelberg Township, July 6, 1829. His ancestors were among the early settlers of York County. His grandfather, John Shaffer, a native of York County, at the age of eighteen, was enrolled for service in the Revolutionary army. He resided in the county all of his life, and died at the advanced age of ninety-five years. The father of our subject lived in the county until his death, at the age of eighty years. John K. was reared on a farm, and learned the trade of blacksmith from his father. This occupation he has always followed in connection with farming. He is a skillful and efficient workman, and for the past five years has conducted his business in the borough of Spring Grove. Mr. Shaffer married Elizabeth Moul. She is the daughter of Henry Moul, of Heidelberg, and also a descendant of an old family of the county. The town of Moulsville (near Hanover) was settled by her ancestors. Five children have blessed their union: Martin, Jacob (deceased), Henry (deceased), Caroline Baker and Annie Kessler.

MICHAEL D. SMYSER, son of Daniel and Catherine (Weist) Smyser, was born March 27, 1842, in Jackson Township, where he was reared on his father's farm. In 1867 he moved to Franklin Township, and after fifteen years residence he returned to Jackson Township, and removed to his present home in Spring Grove in the spring of 1885, and began business in grain, all kinds of feed, flour, coal, phosphates, etc. Mr. Smyser is the owner of valuable real estate in Spring Grove, having 110 feet of ground fronting on Main Street, and extending back to Glatfelter's Sideling, on which are erected four buildings on Main Street, two warehouses, etc. In addition to this Mr. Smyser owns a house and lot on Water Street and a lot on Main Street, and is building a new warehouse in place of the old one. April 15, 1866, Mr. Smyser married Magdaline Menges, daughter of Andrew and Caroline (Klinepeter) Menges, of Jackson Township. This marriage was blessed with four children: Henry Howard, Edith Ellen, Andrew Willard and Ada May. In the late war Mr. Smyser enlisted in Company H, Two Hundredth Regiment Pennsylvania Volunteers, and was with the regiment at Butler's Front, Fort Stedman, Petersburg, at the surrender of Petersburg, and also at the surrender of Lee's army. He was mustered out of service at Alexandria, Va., and honorably discharged at Harrisburg at the close of the war. Our subject's grandfather was Michael Smyser. His grandmother's maiden name was Wolf.

I. C. UMBERGER, a native of Dauphin County, Penn., was born in 1853. He first learned the trade of stone cutter at Baltimore. He was in the employ of the Nevada Central Railroad, at his trade, a period of eight years, and in 1883 became a resident of Spring Grove, embarking in the bakery business with W. J. Dyer, which partnership was dissolved after a few months—Mr. Umberger retiring from the firm. He then started his present business, the green grocery and provision business, together with shipping poultry, butter, eggs, etc. Mr. Umberger has established a thriving trade, and is an enterprising and respected citizen. He was united in marriage, in 1873, with Lizzie A. Schock, a native of Maryland. They have two children living: John and Irene. Mr. Umberger is a member of Humane Lodge No. 342, I. O. O. F., of York, and with his wife is connected with the Methodist Episcopal Church of York.

GEORGE G. WAGNER, son of John and Elizabeth (Glatfelter) Wagner, was born in Codorus Township, January 15, 1850. His grandfather, Jacob, a farmer and a native of the county, died about 1870; John Wagner died about 1880. George G. Wagner assisted on the home farm until about sixteen years old, when he took a two years' course in Manchester College and then became a clerk. In 1875 he opened a store at Menges' Mill, twelve miles west of York, and continuing three years; in 1878 he opened at Spring Forge, where he is now doing a successful general trade, and where, in 1882, he was appointed assistant postmaster. March 25, 1875, he married Alice Jane, daughter of Jesse and Malinda Kraft, and to this union have been born Alvertus, Mabel Pauline, Irvin Jesse and Lottie Elmira. Mr. Wagner is the owner of a good brick dwelling and store-room combined at Spring Forge, and with his wife is a member of the Lutheran Church.

N. G. WAGNER, son of John and Elizabeth (Glatfelter) Wagner, was born in 1851, in York County. His grandfather, Jacob Wagner, was also a native of York County, and died in Manheim Township. John Wagner, the father of our subject, was a farmer through life; his widow is still living in Spring Grove. Our subject was reared on a farm, but in October, 1876, entered into mercantile business, which he carried on in Manheim Township, and at other points, until 1881, when he came to Spring Grove, where he is now carrying on a large trade. In 1872 he married Alice J. Bortner, of Codorus Township, and by her has six children: Janeva, Charles, Henry T., Mary, Minnie A. and Bessie. Mr. Wagner is a member of Mt. Olivet, No. 997, I. O. O. F., and with his wife a member of the St. Paul's Lutheran Church at Spring Grove.

JOHN WIEST was born in Jackson (Paradise) Township, July 19, 1810, and is the son of Michael, a native of the township and Magdalena (Myers) Wiest, of Adams County, Penn. His great-great-grandfather, Wiest, came from Switzerland, and settled as a farmer in Jackson (Paradise) Township. John Wiest is the third in a family of five children, consisting of himself and four sisters: Catherine (Mrs. Michael Emig), Elizabeth (Mrs. Henry Rebert), Mary and Eliza (Mrs. Charles Rebert). Elizabeth died February 19, 1880, and Mary died in 1878. Mr. Wiest's homestead comprises twenty-two acres, one-half mile northwest of Spring Grove, beside which he owns a farm of 150 acres in Carroll County, Md. He has held the office of school director of his township several terms and that of township auditor one term; he was also for several years captain of a militia company with headquarters near Nashville, same township, and since early manhood has been a member of Roth's Reformed Church, in which for many years he has served as elder. February 8, 1838, he married Elizabeth, daughter of Jacob and Sarah Maus, of Carroll County, Md., and to his union with her have been born Eliza, Michael, Jacob, Henry, John, Magdalena, Peter, Mary and Levi D. Levi David Wiest was born January 20, 1859; was reared on the home farm. In 1874 he entered upon a four years' course at the York County Academy. In the winter of 1876-77 he taught school in Jackson Township, and in 1879 entered Pennsylvania College at Gettysburgh, where he passed two years in the classical course. In 1881 he entered the University of Michigan at Ann Arbor, and for two years followed the study of civil engineering, which he has adopted as his life profession.

LOWER CHANCEFORD TOWNSHIP.

REV. ALEXANDER S. AIKEN, pastor of Airville United Presbyterian Church, was born February 3, 1846, near the village of Princeton, Lawrence Co., Penn. His elementary education was received in the schools of his native township. In 1865 he entered the Westminster College, Penn., and graduated from that institution in 1870. He completed his theological course in Allegheny City. April 15. 1873, he was licensed to preach, and was ordained April 29, 1875, by the presbytery of Big Spring, Penn. At the age of nineteen he enlisted in the Sixteenth Pennsylvania Cavalry, was promoted to sergeant of Company I, and served until the end of the war. January 1, 1875, Rev. Mr. Aiken became pastor of the congregation over which he now presides with such signal ability and success. He was joined in marriage April 5, 1882, with Miss Mary J., daughter of George and Sarah (Cummins) Porter, of Huntingdon County, Penn. They now reside in the newly erected parsonage of the Airville congregation. Rev. Mr. Aiken is finely educated, and is a gentleman worthy of encouraging success in the ministry.

JOHN HARVEY ANDERSON, son of Isaac and Eliza M. (Barnett) Anderson, was born September 3, 1853, in Lower Chanceford Township, and was educated in the public schools. At the age of seventeen years he began to learn the carpenter's trade, which he pursued until 1875, when he commenced farming. In 1882 he began the business of canning fruits, as manager for the firm of Kilgore & Co. He was married, in 1876, to Ida Kilgore, daughter of Samuel Kilgore. They have two children: Samuel and Hugh. Mr. Anderson is a lineal representative of one of the first settlers of his township.

JAMES E. ANDERSON, son of Isaac J. and Eliza M. (Barnett) Anderson, of Lower Chanceford Township, was born March 15, 1856, upon the old homestead, where he was reared and educated. Mr. Anderson has, for the past eight years, had charge of the old homestead farm, which consists of eighty-three acres of valuable land. He was married, October 20, 1881. to Sally, daughter of R. S. Scott, of Lower Chanceford Township. They have one child—Robert R. Mrs. Anderson is a member of the Union Chapel of Lower Chanceford Township.

JOHN BAIR, son of John and Elizabeth (Miller) Bair, natives of Lancaster County, Penn., was born May 25, 1816, in Lancaster County, where he was reared and educated. In 1845 he came to York Furnace, Lower Chanceford Township, and engaged in the manufacture of charcoal iron, and conducted a general merchandise business. In 1850 he added to his other business lumber manufacturing, saw-milling and lime burning, and in 1855 he added the sale and purchase of grain, phosphates and general railroad merchandise. In 1855 he began the subscription and erection of the York Furnace Bridge, being president of the company. The bridge was destroyed in 1857 by ice and wind. Mr. Bair was married, in 1855, to Susan Groff, of Lancaster County, daughter of David Groff. They had two children: Robert Cabeen and Lizzie. In 1863 Mr. Bair accepted a position on the staff of Maj. R. W. Shenk, Pennsylvania Volunteers. He is a Knight Templar.

JAMES BOYD (deceased), son of John Boyd, who emigrated from the north of Ireland about 1774, and located in Chester County. When twenty-eight years old James Boyd moved to Wrightsville, and engaged in the lumber business with his brother Robert. He came to Lower Chanceford in 1855, and purchased the John Kilgore farm, containing 600 acres, and began farming, which he continued until 1865, when he built the "Oakland Valley Mills," located about one mile from McCall's Ferry. He was married, in 1844, to Ann C. Schroeder, a native of Germany, who immigrated to this country with her parents at the age of twelve, and settled at Stoney Run, near York. They had

LOWER CHANCEFORD TOWNSHIP.

five children: Robert, James M., John C., Isaac N. and Martin L. Mr. James Boyd, who died March 17, 1883, was a prominent member of the Lutheran Church of Wrightsville, before moving to Lower Chanceford, and took an active interest in erecting the church of his denomination in that town. He was afterward prominently identified with the erection of the Methodist Episcopal Church at Centreville. Mrs. Boyd resides at the home near Centreville.

ISAAC N. BOYD is a son of James and Ann C. (Schroeder) Boyd, of Lower Chanceford, and was born March 12, 1853, at Wrightsville, and at the age of twenty-five commenced the study of medicine with Dr. Jacob R. Spangler, of York. He graduated from the College of Physicians and Surgeons of Baltimore, and in 1880 commenced the practice of medicine in Lower Chanceford Township, where he is also engaged in farming and milling, and at the mill built by his father. He was married, March 16, 1881, to Mary E. Vanhyning, of Chanceford Township. They have two children: Lulla A. and Minnie K. Dr. Boyd is a representative citizen, and served as tax collector for his township in 1882–83.

ROBERT BOYD, son of James and Ann C. (Schroeder) Boyd, was born at Wrightsville December 4, 1846, and was educated at the public schools. At the death of his father he became manager of the homestead property, being executor of his father's estate. In 1879 and 1880 he was inspector of elections; in 1881 he was elected road supervisor of Lower Chanceford Township, and re-elected the next year. He was married, September 28, 1865, to Martha J., daughter of Daniel Robinson, of Dauphin County. They have had nine children: James F., Isaac N., John E., Annie C., Maggie J., Lizzie J., Robert D., Jesse W. and Bertie M. Mr. Boyd is a member of Harbor Lodge No. 333, I. O. O. F., of Safe Harbor, Lancaster County. He and his family are members of McKendrie Methodist Episcopal Church of Lower Chanceford. Mr. Boyd is a descendant of a highly respected family, who settled in Lancaster County about 1835.

ELLIS CHANDLEE was born February 29, 1832, in Lower Chanceford, to Veazey and Jemima (Kilgore) Chandlee, natives of Cecil County, Md., and Lower Chanceford, York Co., Penn., respectively. The former was born in 1804, served an apprenticeship to watch and clock-making in Baltimore, and in 1826 came to Lower Chanceford, York Co., Penn., and located on a farm. Ellis Chandlee remained on the homestead until the age of twenty-two. He then taught school two years; then clerked in a store two years; then followed store keeping for himself until 1865. He was elected justice of the peace in March. 1866, which office he still holds. Mr. Chandlee was married, July 3, 1856, to Mrs. Caroline C. Kilgore, a native of Lower Chanceford; their children are Harriet A. and Edmund G, Mrs. Chandlee died March 8, 1878, and June 7, 1881, subject married Mrs. Susan Main. a native of Lower Chanceford Township. Mr. Chandlee. is engaged in the raising of tobacco, in connection with his office of justice of the peace.

JAMES CHANDLEE, son of Veazey and Jemima (Kilgore) Chandlee, was born November 21, 1837, and remained at home until eighteen years of age, when he learned the trade of a wheelwright. He followed this trade and boating on canal until he purchased the home he now owns, containing sixty-nine and a half acres. He married, in 1867, Ann Clayton, daughter of Harlan and Rebecca Clayton, of Lower Chanceford Township. Their children are Carry, Franklin, Edith, Emory, Goldsmith, Edgar and Harlan (deceased). Mr. Chandlee was elected road supervisor for his township in March, 1884, and has performed the duties of his office very acceptably.

SAMUEL CHANDLEE, son of Veazey and Jemima (Kilgore) Chandlee, was born September 20, 1839, and remained on his father's farm until twenty-two years of age. He was then engaged in the lumber business for twelve years, after which time he purchased the farm of Daniel Gordon, of Lower Chanceford Township, containing 150 acres. Since then he has followed farming. January 26, 1882, he was married to Elizabeth Barton, daughter of Jarrett Barton, of Peach Bottom Township. Their children are Mary Jamima and an infant, Grover Cleveland Chandlee. Mr. Chandlee is an enterprising citizen of his township and a prosperous farmer.

JOHN V. CHANDLEE, farmer, was born January 7, 1844, and spent the first twenty-five years of his life on his father's farm, and upon the latter's death purchased the homestead, which comprises eighty-seven acres. He was married, October 10, 1878, to Laura Kilgore, of Lower Chanceford Township. Their children are Ira W. and Walter V. Chandlee. Both parents are members of the Presbyterian Church.

B. F. CHANDLEE, of Lower Chanceford Township, is a son of Veazey and Jemima (Kilgore) Chandlee, and was born August 30, 1840. He remained on the farm until 1865, when he enlisted in the One Hundred and Ninety-fifth Regiment Pennsylvania Volunteers, and remained in the service until January, 1866, when he returned home and engaged in boating four years. At the expiration of this time he purchased a farm of 140 acres, which he is now cultivating, and is also engaged in canning fruits and vegetables. He was married, December 21, 1871, to Nancy J. Anderson, daughter of Isaac and Eliza M. (Barnett) Anderson. They have four children living, viz.: Jemima, Isaac, A. Veazey, and William Herbert. Mrs Chandlee died in 1881. Mr. Chandlee is a member of Chanceford Presbyterian Church.

WARREN B. CHANDLEE was born in Lower Chanceford Township, May 18, 1853, the son of Veazey and Jemima (Kilgore) Chandlee. He began business in 1881, as a clerk in the store of Fry Brothers at McCall's Ferry. In 1888, he became proprietor of the hotel at this place. He was married, February 10, 1880, to Lydia A., daughter of Elias Fry. They have one child, named Martha J. In 1884, Mr. Chandlee was elected selectman of his native township.

W. H. CLAYTON is a son of Harlan and Rebecca (Emmitt) Clayton. natives of Delaware, and of English and Scotch-Irish ancestry. His parents first moved to Lancaster County, and then to York County in 1847, and located in Lower Chanceford on the farm now owned by the son. His father built Clayton Mill, and followed the business of miller and farmer until his death in 1868. His mother is still living. Mr. Clayton is the first son in a family of nine children, whose names are Anne E. Chandlee, Susanna M., William H., Joseph N., now in Iowa; Pitner E., in Washington Territory; Plummer H., in Washington Territory; John R., in Iowa; Ella Chandlee, in Missouri; and Mary F. Russell. Our subject was born in 1847, in Lancaster County. He remained on the farm until sixteen years old, when he removed to Chester County, returning home on the death of his father. He is now the owner of a grist-mill and thirty-eight acres of land. In January, 1873, he married Miss Henrietta G. Connelly, of Maryland. They have four children; Flora, Harlan, Nellie and Mary. Mr. Clayton and wife are members of the Salem Methodist Episcopal Church.

THOMAS J. COLLINS is a son of C. M. and Martha J. (Porter) Collins. His father was born in Lancaster County in 1798, and came to Lower Chanceford Township about 1808 with his parents,

BIOGRAPHICAL SKETCHES.

David and Dorcas Collins, who purchased about 300 acres of land about two miles from McCall's Ferry. Mr. Collins is a third son of a family of ten children, and was born August 6, 1839. His father, in connection with his farming interest, for many years conducted the blacksmithing business. The sons were trained on the farm, and educated at the schools of the district. In 1862 our subject enlisted in the One Hundred and Thirtieth Regiment Pennsylvania Volunteers for nine months, and participated in the battles of Antietam and Fredericksburg. At the expiration of his term of enlistment he returned home, but soon afterward re-entered the service, enlisting for three years, or during the war, and joined the Twenty-first Regiment Pennsylvania Cavalry. They were sent immediately to the front, and did valiant service in the terrible battles of the Wilderness, Cold Harbor and Petersburg. Mr. Collins had the honor of being present at the time Gen. Lee surrendered to Gen. Grant at Appomattox, on April 9, 1865, and was wounded at the engagement at this place. At the close of the war he returned home to Lower Chanceford, and in 1868 took charge of the homestead farm of 120 acres, which he bought. He has one surviving sister, Sarah J. Collins, who resides with him.

SARAH A. (CHANDLEE) COLVIN, daughter of Veazey and Jemima (Kilgore) Chandlee, was born May 1, 1834. On February 7, 1867, she was married to Robert R. Colvin. Their children are Veazey C. and Robert Lee Colvin.

WILLIAM C. COLVIN is a son of Gen. Robert Colvin, who commanded a company of soldiers that marched from the lower end of York county to the defense of Baltimore in 1814, of which company William Cowen, of Lower Chanceford, is the sole survivor. Gen Colvin married Margaret Gibson. Their son, William, was born October 13, 1817, in Fawn Township; remained with his father until 1842, when he engaged in farming with Mr. Hughson, and afterward embarked in the mercantile business at McCall's Ferry In 1849 he purchased seventy-five acres of land, the present site of Centreville, and subsequently built the fine hotel building and store-house now so well known in that section of the county. Mr. Colvin is one of the prominent and influential men of the lower end. He kept the hotel for many years, but discontinued and rented the stand a few years ago. His hotel is known as one of the best stopping places for travelers in York County, and during the summer season is known as a resort for pleasure seekers from the towns and cities. Mr. Colvin was married to Mary Ann Colt, daughter of Charles and Nancy (Stewart) Colt. Her mother was a native of County Tyrone, Ireland, and her father of Chester County, Penn. They have three daughters and one son; Hannah J., Helen A., Daisy and Cyrus H. Colvin, who owns and manages a livery and exchange stable in Lancaster City.

JOHN M. EASTON, son of Hezekiah and Hetty (McGuire) Easton, was born at Fort Loudon, Franklin County, April 29, 1846, and was educated at Chambersburgh. In 1864 he entered the service of the government in the quartermaster's department under Col. R. E. M. Newport, at Baltimore, where he remained until the fall of 1867, when he was transferred to Fort Gibson, under Capt. Amos S. Kimball. He returned to Baltimore in 1868, and began the study of telegraphy with the Franklin Telegraph Company. October 16, 1869, he took charge of the office at Centreville. The name has since been changed to Airville. He now owns a farm of thirty-eight acres. Mr. Easton is a member of the Telegraphers' Mutual Benefit Association, and in connection with his office work has charge of thirty-seven miles of the company's lines of six wires, which cross the lower end of York County. He also has charge of the National Transit Telegraph office, connected with the United Pipe Line, which also crosses York County, thence to Baltimore. March 24, 1874, he was married to Addie Johnson, daughter of Jonathan Johnson, of Airville. They have four children, viz.: Thomas H., John W., Mary J. and Clarence C. Mr. Easton and wife are members of the Presbyterian Church of Chanceford. His wife is a descendant of one of the first settlers in the lower end of the county.

DR. S. J. FINLEY, son of John and Mary (Cameron) Finley, was born November 21, 1880, on the homestead in Lower Chanceford, where he remained until he was twenty years old, when he went to Baltimore and studied medicine with Dr. C. M. Roberts. After he graduated he commenced to practice medicine in Peach Bottom and Lower Chanceford in 1853. In 1863 he was married to Josephine Cameron, of Owego, N. Y., and has five children: John A., Mary O., Sylvester J., Lillian F., and Robert C. His wife's parents were James and Adelia (Dwight) Cameron, of Owego, N. Y. Dr. Finley owns about fifty acres of land and is engaged in farming, in connection with the practice of his profession.

L. W. FINLEY, son of John and Mary (Cameron) Finley, was born in Lower Chanceford Township in 1833. His grandfather, William Finley, came from Castle Fin, Ireland, in 1803, and settled in New York State, where he engaged in farming, but in 1810 removed to York County and settled on a farm, where he died. His son, John, the father of L. W., inherited the farm, and was married December 20, 1827. The subject of this sketch was born on the old farm and has made it his home ever since. At the age of fourteen he assisted his father on contracts, and at the age of twenty became his partner until his father died. Since then he has filled a large number of contracts, principally in bridge building. He has entered into large contracts with York County, other places in Pennsylvania, Maryland and Virginia. In March, 1856, he was married to R. A. Gordon, daughter of Daniel and Ruth Gordon, of Lower Chanceford Township, who died in 1860, leaving two children, John M. and Mary A. In November, 1867, he married Mary E. Lewis, daughter of John Lewis, of York County. John Finley, the father of subject, was born in 1805, on the farm in Lower Chanceford, and died in 1866. He was an extensive contractor on railroads and canals, also in bridge-building His first contract was on the Tide Water Canal. L. W. Finley owns 104 acres of good land; is an enterprising man and a Master Mason.

SAMUEL D. and MILTON L. FRY are the sons of Elias and Martha (Groff) Fry, natives of Lancaster, who came to Lower Chanceford Township about the year 1846. The father was engaged on the Susquehanna as a pilot for rafts, at which business he gained an enviable reputation on account of his ability. The sons were brought up in the township where they now live, and at the ages of twenty-seven and twenty-three, respectively, engaged in a general mercantile business at McCall's Ferry, which they now continue. Samuel D. was married to Emma Bennington, of Peach Bottom Township. They have two children: Charles and Lydia. Milton L., born in 1860, was married, in 1881, to Corrinne Kilgore, a member of the Presbyterian Church. They have one chil l—Bessie. In 1880 Samuel D. was appointed postmaster, and still holds the office.

WILLIAM GALLAGHER, deceased, was born in Armstrong County, Penn., and September 23, 1858, was united in marriage with Miss Ann E. Bryan. They resided in Armstrong County until 1861, when they located in York County, where Mr. Gallagher died. Mrs. Gallagher was born in Bryansville, York County, April 26, 1837, and is a daughter of Dr. James T. Bryan, a native of Maryland, who located in York County when thirty years of age, where he enjoyed a large personal acquaintance, and an extensive practice until his death. Mrs. Gallagher has two children: Guy B. and Caroline. Mrs. Gallagher is a consistent church member.

JESSE GILBERT was born in Lancaster County and is a son of Joshua and Elizabeth (Valentine) Gilbert; his mother, a native of Chester County, and his father of Lancaster County. He grew to manhood in his native county. At the age of twenty-eight years he removed to Chester County and engaged in farming in connection with which he carried on pump-making for three years. At the expiration of that time he came to Lower Chanceford, purchased a farm of 167 acres, which he has since cultivated, and in the meantime has been engaged in selling fruit trees and ornamental shrubbery. He has held the office of township auditor. January 3, 1861, he was married to D. Anna Hunter, daughter of Alexander and Mary P. Hunter, of Lancaster County. Mr. Gilbert is a member of the Society of Friends, and belongs to the Meeting at Fawn Grove.

WILLIAM M. GROVE, farmer, is a son of Jacob and Martha (Tosh) Grove, who were natives of Fawn Township, and moved to Lower Chanceford. Jacob Grove, the father, had eleven children and was first married to Agnes Workman. William M. Grove, who is a son by a second marriage, was born October 8, 1856, in the township where he now resides. At the death of his father he became the owner of the homestead farm of 139 acres. He was married, January 31, 1884, to Mary E., daughter of E. McVey, of Cecil County, Md. His wife is a member of the Presbyterian Church at Airville.

WILLIAM ILGENFRITZ (deceased) was born in 1812, in York Borough, where he received his early education. His parents were Daniel and Elizabeth (Deitch) Ilgenfritz. At the age of fifteen he was employed as a clerk in the prothonotary's office of York County. He was afterward elected to fill that office himself for two terms. In 1864 he removed to Lower Chanceford, and purchased a farm of 500 acres at the present site of Woodbine, on the Peach Bottom Railroad. He was joined in marriage to Elizabeth B. Donalson, of Baltimore, on November 28, 1839. Their children are Alice C., William J. and James E. He was a member of the I. O. O. F. William J. Ilgenfritz, the eldest son, was married, January 11, 1883, to Miss Annie J. Boyd. They have one child—William Boyd.

HUGH W. KILGORE, son of Levi and Jeannette (Cunningham) Kilgore, was born May 3, 1813, on the old homestead in Lower Chanceford Township, on the night Havre de Grace was burned by the British. His grandfather, Thomas Kilgore, was a native of Ireland, immigrated to America and settled in Peach Bottom Township, where he followed the trade of wheelwright and farmer, remaining there until his death, leaving a family of eight children: Solomon, William, Levi, Keziah, Mary, Hiram, Jehu and Joshua. His grandmother, Hannah (Ankrem), was born in Lancaster County, and was of Irish descent. His mother was born on the ocean, when her parents were emigrating from Ireland to America. His father was born in Peach Bottom, and also married there. He followed distilling apple brandy, but finally came with his brother William to Lower Chanceford, where they bought a piece of land (which is now in possession of his son) and commenced farming, and engaged also in shad fishing, and added more land to their farm, until they owned at one time 500 acres. They lived together in a large stone house until their death, the father of our subject leaving five children: Hugh W., Thomas, Andrew, Mary and Samuel. Hugh W. resides on the old homestead, and has had a busy life, being engaged in farming, boating, shad fishing and saw-milling. At present he owns 280 acres in Lower Chanceford Township, and thirty-two acres in partnership with S. W. Kilgore. In addition to this he owns an interest in the fisheries on the Susquehanna River. He was married to Sarah J. Pegan, of Lancaster County, daughter of Andrew and Jane (Leper) Pegan, of Scotch-Irish descent, and they have seven children: Alvin L., James A., William R., Laura, Margaret S., E. Milton and Luella J. Although well up in years, Mr. Kilgore is still vigorous. He is an elder in the Presbyterian Church of Chanceford, and was for many years a school director.

WILLIAM K. KILGORE, son of Joshua and Ellen (Boones) Kilgore, of Peach Bottom Township, was born July 3, 1831. He remained with his parents until twenty years of age, when he began learning the trade of wheelwright with John S. Kilgore, one of his cousins, in Lower Chanceford Township, with whom he remained two years and then went West, where he stayed a few years. In 1877 he purchased the farm of Alexander Snodgrass, containing about 145 acres, and followed farming since. September 25, 1857, he was married to Elizabeth E. Snyder, of Peach Bottom, and had nine children: Amanda A., Clarkson B., Eva J., Harvey E., William H., James W., Emily R., Harriet A. and Charles V.; two died in infancy. Mrs. Kilgore is a daughter of Jacob and Mary A. (Wales) Snyder, and like her husband belongs to the Salem Methodist Episcopal Church.

HUGH T. KYLE, son of Joseph Kyle, of Chester County, Penn., and Matilda (Scotten) Kyle, of Philadelphia, was born November 27, 1833, in Peach Bottom Township. At the age of fifteen years he engaged in boating, and followed it for twenty years. In 1870 he purchased the farm on which he now resides, and which contains 225 acres. He was married, in 1862, to Sarah Jane Gilbreath, and to them were born two children: Bertram B. and Mary Jane. His wife died in 1865. In 1871 he was married to Mary L. Snyder, of Lower Chanceford. Their children are Lydia D., Sarah E., Annie B., Hugh H. and Lulu B. Mr. Kyle has taken an active interest in the affairs of his township and has served as school director for several years.

REV. JOHN JAY LANE, son of John and Sarah (Wilson) Lane, was born March 21, 1818. His father was a native of Virginia and his mother of Chester County, Penn. His father came to Lower Chanceford Township in 1812; prior to this he was engaged in tanning in Harford County, Md.; he purchased 190 acres of land in Lower Chanceford Township, and commenced farming. John Jay remained on the farm until 1831. He entered Jefferson College, at Cannonsburg, Washington Co., Penn.; then studied theology at the Western Theological Seminary, at Allegheny, Penn., and finished his studies in 1849. After teaching school for two years, he became professor of Latin in Franklin College, at New Athens, Ohio, for two years. His first charge was at Fairview, Ohio, then Wrightsville, Penn., where he was pastor of the Presbyterian Church for fifteen years; then he returned to Rockhill, Ohio, and was in charge of the Presbyterian Church for ten years, after which he returned to the homestead, which he bought from his brother and sister, containing 182 acres. He was married, in 1847, to Lucy Grimes, of New. Athens, a graduate of the Female Seminary of Pittsburgh, Penn., who died in 1866, leaving the following children: Sarah B., Ashed G., Flora, Bertha V. and Latimore N. (deceased). The elder son, Ashed, is now pastor of the Presbyterian Church

BIOGRAPHICAL SKETCHES. 125

at Crestline, Ohio, and married Miss Maggie Nelson, on October 14, 1882; he has one son named Latimore C. Lane. John Wilson, the grandfather of J. Jay Lane, on the maternal side, was a soldier of the Revolutionary war, during most of the campaign; was in several battles, one of them the battle of Brandywine. A brother of his was taken prisoner by the British, and held at Philadelphia until he, with two others, broke prison and returned to the American army after knocking down the guard. Also his paternal grandfather, Joseph Lane, was in the same army of the Revolutionary war and died in the hospital caused from fever caught in the service of his country, his own father being quite a small lad at that time was near losing his life by the Hessians who came over to this country to fight for England, some of the descendents of whom still live in a portion of this county.

JANE M. LINDSAY is the daughter of John and Mary (Snodgrass) Lindsay, representatives of highly respectable families of Scotch-Irish origin, whose ancestors were among the early emigrants from the north of Ireland to America. The Lindsay family is quite numerous in Pennsylvania, and some of them have attained considerable distinction in the history of the State. Robert and Mary Lindsay, grandparents of Jane M. Lindsay, came to Lower Chanceford during the latter part of the last century. They had two children: John H. and Mary A. The former, who was the father of the subject of this sketch, was born in York and moved to Lower Chanceford Township in 1811, and purchased the farm which his daughter now owns. He was married in 1821, and had two children: Jane M. and Mary A. Lindsay. The youngest sister is dead. Miss Jane Lindsay was born August 31, 1823, and at the death of her father inherited the farm on which she has resided since her birth. She is an active worker in the church, and an influential member of the Pine Grove Congregation.

FREDERICK McSHERRY, son of Joseph and Annie (Burkholder) McSherry, of Lower Chanceford and Lancaster County, respectively, was born and educated in Lower Chanceford Township. His father was engaged at the blacksmith trade at Lower Chanceford. At the age of twenty-six years, Frederick McSherry engaged in the mercantile business at Airville, formerly McSherryville, and has since followed the same business. He was born June 26, 1819, at Lower Chanceford, and was married, May 30, 1849, to Tolitha M. Smith, daughter of Peter and Cassey McCleary, of the same township. They have ten children living: Joseph L. B., William R., Napoleon B., Smith B., Edmond E., Ella F., Elmer N., James A., Jackson McC. and Nelson M. January 1, 1867, he was appointed postmaster at McSherryville and kept that office for two years. He was also township auditor and bank tax collector.

WILLIAM MANIFOLD, farmer, is a son of Joseph and Rebecca (Martin) Manifold, natives of Hopewell and Chanceford Townships, respectively, was born February 8, 1852, in Hopewell Township. In 1859 he removed with his parents to Lower Chanceford, where he now resides. In 1880 he became the owner of his father's farm of 130 acres which he occupies in companionship with his two sisters—Margaret and Keziah. His mother was a daughter of Rev. Dr. Martin, for many years pastor of Slate Ridge and Chanceford Presbyterian Churches.

NELSON MICHENER, a son of Isaac and Rebecca (McHenry) Michener, natives of Bucks County, Penn., was born June, 1809, upon the old homestead. In 1882, he moved to Delaware County, Penn., and, 1836, was employed upon the construction of the Tide Water Canal. In 1841 he purchased a farm of 103 acres, located in Lower Chanceford Township, where he has since been engaged in general farming and the practice of veterinary surgery. Mr. Michener was married to Eliza Halderman, February 3, 1831, daughter of John and Catherine Halderman, of Bucks County. Mr. Michener is a member of the Methodist Episcopal Church of Lower Chanceford.

T. Z. H. MURPHY, born in Chanceford Township, February 9, 1840, is a son of George and Rebecca (Hughs) Murphy, natives respectively of York County, Penn., and Hartford County, Md. He entered his father's store as clerk at the age of seventeen, and remained eleven years; at the age of twenty-eight formed a partnership with Robert Reed, and opened a store at Collinsville; bought his partner's interest in the store, and continued the business at that place until 1872; in 1875 went into business at Woodbine, his present location, dealing in general merchandise, grain, coal, fertilizers, etc.; has been postmaster at Woodbine since 1878; is a school director in Lower Chanceford Township, and a trustee of the Presbyterian Church of Chanceford Township; was married June 29, 1868, to Margery McVey, daughter of Henry McVey, of Lancaster County, and they have seven children: Eugene, Harry, William, Hughs, Charley, Elizabeth and Margery.

THOMAS J. NEELY (deceased) was a son of William and Jane Neely, natives of Ireland, who emigrated from that country to the United States, and settled in Lancaster County in 1833. He was born November 11, 1836, and at the age of twenty-three, located in Centreville, Lower Chanceford Township, and engaged in stock-dealing, and the purchasing and selling of valuable horses. He was a well known business man of York County, and a successful and esteemed citizen. He was married, in 1861, to Hannah J. Colvin, daughter of William C. Colvin, of Centreville, who died February 23, 1883. Mr. Neely died May 30, 1884. Four daughters are descendants: Lizzie J., Maggie C., Mary A. and Cora.

BENJAMIN PEDAN, before the time of the Revolutionary war, became a prominent and influential citizen of the lower end of the county. He was appointed justice of the peace for his township under the first constitution of the State of Pennsylvania, in June, 1777, and in the year 1790, was one of the five representatives of York County who helped to frame the second constitution of the State. For many years after this event he served as justice. In 1805, he was elected a member of State legislature. In the taxable list of Chanceford Township for the year 1783, he was assessed for 307 acres of land, one slave, five horses, six cows and six sheep. Benjamin Pedan was married to Jane Giffin, and came from Frederick County, Md., in 1772, bought 307 acres of land, added eighteen adjoining acres, and at the time of his death, in 1813, owned 325 acres and a number of slaves. He was an elder in the Presbyterian Church. He had eleven children. His first wife having died, he married a second time. John Pedan was the ninth child by the first marriage, and was born June 7, 1780, in Chanceford Township (now Lower Chanceford), where he remained until his death in 1840. His father died in 1813. John Pedan was married to Nancy Campbell, who was a native of Stewartstown, Ireland, and immigrated to America about 1800. John Benjamin Pedan grew to manhood on his father's farm in Lower Chanceford, and received his educational training in the public schools of his native township. In 1863 he enlisted in Capt. Stevens' company of ninety-day men, who entered the service during Lee's second invasion of Pennsylvania. In 1864 he purchased the farm of 140 acres, on which he now resides. Samuel M. Pedan, Esq., whose portrait appears in this work, was a son of John and Nancy (Campbell) Pedan, was born on the old homestead, and there lived and died; he was for fifteen years known as a prominent justice of the peace of his township. He was a man of excellent character and sterling worth. He served in various positions of honor and trust among the people of the lower town. His death, while he was yet in the prime of life, on February 11, 1882, was deeply felt by a large circle of friends and acquaintances. He was never married. The other members of the family of John Pedan are Margaret J., Martha E., Allie E., Annie A. and Charles J.

JOSEPH PEIRCE, merchant of Airville, is a son of George and Jane Peirce, of Chester County, Penn. He received his early education in the excellent schools of his native township—Brandywine. He was employed as a clerk in a store and also taught school. At the age of eighteen he became a partner with his brother-in-law, A. C. Sin, in farming and storekeeping. He afterward entered the employ of a Philadelphia business firm as a salesman. In 1855 he moved to York Furnace, in Lower Chanceford, and purchased the mercantile stock and rented the store stand of John Bair & Co. In 1866, he purchased a farm of sixty acres from J. J. McSherry, of Airville: To this farm he has added eighty-five acres. At the same time he began the general mercantile business, which he is yet conducting at Airville. He has been postmaster for twenty five years. His marriage with Lydia, daughter of Hartly Potts, of Bucks County, took place in 1852.

CYRUS PLETT, a son of Thomas and Elizabeth (Ferguson) Plett. natives of Lancaster County, was born in York County, August 1, 1839. He was reared on the old homestead farm, and at the age of eighteen learned the carpenter's trade, which occupied his attention for a number of years. Mr. Plett is now engaged in the lumber business and farming. He was married, December 23, 1869, to Maggie Painter, a native of York County. They have four children: Thomas E., Eugene C., Everett B. and Etna G.

WILLIAM G. ROSS (deceased) was the son of Hugh and Rebecca (Glenn) Ross. Hugh Ross, son of William and Margaret (Evans) Ross, was born May 10, 1785, in Lower Chanceford Township. He succeeded his father as justice of the peace, which office he held about forty years, and resigned the position in 1861. He was married to Rebecca Glenn. They had three children, viz.: William G., James E. (now living in Missouri) and Rebecca I. H. William G., the eldest son, was born September 29, 1830, on the "Ross Homestead" in Lower Chanceford. He received his early educational training in the schools of his native township, and afterward entered the Chamberlain Commercial College in Baltimore, where he graduated. Upon the death of his father, in 1873, he succeeded him as the owner of a large estate of 650 acres. He married Miss Julia A. McConkey, daughter of Maj. James and Mary A. (Ramsay) McConkey, of Peach Bottom. They had three children, two of whom—Marian and Hugh—survive. Mr. Ross died in 1884. He studied farming as a science and practiced it as an art, and at the time of his death owned one of the most valuable tracts of land in York County. The large and abundant crops brought him in a handsome revenue as a reward for his judicious labors. For many years he was a director of the York & Peach Bottom Railroad, and was also one of the directors of the First National Bank of York, and served in various other positions of honor and trust. As a gentleman and neighbor he was universally esteemed and respected and was a noble representative of true manhood. For many years he was a member and an active worker in Chanceford Presbyterian Church, to which his honored ancestors belonged.

DAVID SHENK was born at Spring Forge, this county, and was a son of George Shenk, of the same place. David Shenk came to Lower Chanceford in 1888, and was married, in 1837, to Magdalena Brown, who is now living upon the homestead. They had six children: Daniel, Henry, Mary J., Sarah E., John and William. He was a forge-man by trade and died February 14, 1879.

DANIEL SHENK was born in Codorus Township, January 1, 1838, and is the son of David Shenk, who was born in 1816, at Spring Forge, Codorus Township, and who, March 22, 1837, married Magdalena Brown, subject's mother, who was born in Codorus Township in December, 1813, and became the mother of six children: Daniel, Henry, Mary Jane, Sarah Elizabeth, John and William. David Shenk was a forge-man by trade and died in 1879. At the age of seventeen, Daniel Shenk began learning carpentering with Jarrett Borton, of Peach Bottom, and at the age of twenty-six, engaged in business on his own account in Lower Chanceford, as builder, and still continues in that occupation. April 17, 1862, he married Elizabeth J., daughter of Harman Snyder, of Lower Chanceford. To this union have been born seven children: Eleanor Ann, John, David Herman, Sarah Alice, Emma Florence, Henry Francis and Lydia Louisa. Mr. and Mrs. Shenk are members of the Pine Grove Presbyterian Church.

JOHN SHENK, boatman and farmer, son of David and Magdalena (Brown) Shenk, was born March 16, 1846, and lived at home with his parents until the age of sixteen, when he engaged in boating on the Susquehanna and Tide Water Canal. He continued this occupation until 1880, when he settled on a farm of ninety-three and one-half acres, which he had some time before purchased in Lower Chanceford, and engaged in cultivating it. He was married, February 13, 1878, to Mary C. Poteet, daughter of Jesse Poteet. Their children are Jesse and Beatrice Myrtle.

ROBERT SMITH, one of the prosperous farmers of the lower end of York County, was born on Christmas Day, 1820, in Lower Chanceford Township. He is a son of James H. and Jane (Smith) Smith. At the age of four years he was adopted by his uncle, Robert Smith, and at his death inherited the excellent farm near Airville, which he now owns. November 16, 1843, he married Sarah R., daughter of Henry Manifold, of Hopewell. They have five children living: Robert H., J. Hume, Lizzie T., Samuel H. and J. Charles. The subject of this sketch is a son of Capt. James Hume Smith, a veteran of the second war with Great Britain, in 1812, who died in 1834. The farm which Mr. Smith now owns was originally deeded to his great-grandfather by the proprietors of Pennsylvania about 1740. Ever since that time, this valuable farm has been owned by a lineal descendant who bore the same name as his great grandfather, Robert Smith. This is one of the very few farms in the county owned by a descendant of the first settlers.

DR. WILLIAM F. SMITH, physician and surgeon, of Airville, son of Dr. William F. and Maria L. (Clarkson) Smith, whose ancestors were among the first settlers in this section of York County, was born here January 13, 1836. He lived with his parents until the age of twenty years, when he began the study of medicine with Dr. John Atlee, of Lancaster City. He graduated with the degree of M. D., in the medical department of the University of Pennsylvania, March 14, 1861. During the civil war he entered the army as assistant surgeon of the One Hundred and Fifth Regiment Pennsylvania Volunteers, which position he resigned October 5, 1862. In the spring of 1863, he joined the Twenty-eighth Regiment Pennsylvania troops, and was promoted to the position of surgeon of the Seventy-third Pennsylvania Regiment, and remained in the service until the close of the war in 1865. In this capacity he had rare advantages for gaining a thorough and practical knowledge of the science of surgery. During the campaign on the peninsula in Virginia, he had charge of the Division Hospitals of Gens. Kearney and Geary, of the Second Division of the Twentieth Army Corps. He was married October 31, 1865, to Hannah M. Murphy, daughter of George S. and Rebecca Murphy. They have three children: Rebecca M., Mamie L. and William C. Since his return from the army, he has practiced in Airville and the surrounding country with abundant success. Dr. Smith is a gentleman of more than ordinary degree of educational training and intellectual culture. He is a public-spirited citizen, and much honored and respected in his community. In 1872 he was nominated on the Republican ticket for State senator, a position which he would have filled with eminent ability. Dr. Smith and family are members of the Chanceford Presbyterian Church.

EDMUND M. SMITH, son of Peter and Cassandra (McClary) Smith, was born at Centreville, April 15, 1838. At the time of his father's death, he inherited the homestead property of seventy-seven acres, on which he has since resided and skillfully farmed. He was married, November 16, 1864, to Emeline Mundorff; they have six children, viz.: Peter M., Cyrus, Curtis H., Hannah J., Ross and William F. Mrs. Smith is a daughter of Jonathan and Hannah (Wade) Mundorff. of Lower Chanceford, and was one of a family of ten children as follows: William, Mary A., Hannah J., Susan, Jonathan, Barbara, Amanda, John W., Emiline and Margaret. Her father died in 1866, aged 'sixty-one years, and her mother in 1880, aged seventy-eight years.

ALEXANDER SNODGRASS was born November 9, 1825, in Lower Chanceford, and is a son of Joseph and Hannah (Smith) Snodgrass. His mother was a daughter of John Smith, of the same township. At the age of nine years he went to live with John McCleary, at Bridgeton. He began learning the blacksmith's trade when seventeen years of age, and followed it four years. At twenty-one he engaged at boating on the Susquehanna Canal and continued eighteen years, and then purchased a farm of fifty acres in Lower Chanceford, where he now resides. He later purchased a farm of 128 acres in the same township. Mr. Snodgrass was married, June 26, 1854. to Corinna McConkey, daughter of Jesse McConkey, of Peach Bottom Township. He and his wife are members of the Union Chapel of his township.

ROBERT G. SWEENEY was born in Lower Chanceford Township, York County, May 18, 1812, and removed to Peach Bottom in 1840, where he purchased a farm of forty-eight acres, on which he still resides. In connection with farming he works at blacksmithing. His father, James Sweeney, was a native of Ireland, who immigrated to Chanceford Township at the age of sixteen years, where he subsequently married Miss Jennet Gibson. a native of York County. Mr. Sweeney is a quiet, respectable citizen, who attends closely to his own business, but takes an active interest in politics.

GEORGE UREY (deceased), son of George and Barbara (Mundorff) Urey, was born December 8, 1811, in Lower Chanceford. His grandfather came to that township about 1700, and purchased a tract of land now known as Centreville. Subject was reared, educated, lived and died on the homestead. In 1838 he married Annie E. Kline-Young, of Chanceford Township, and had three children: George, Annie E. and Peter. His wife died in 1841, and in 1843 he was married to Margaret Hevner, of Chanceford Township, and had four children:

Mary, Elias W., Barbara E. and Benjamin T. His second wife died in 1850, and in 1852 he married Mrs. Catherine Urey, of Lower Chanceford. He died May 2, 1875. He was a farmer, and was also engaged on the Tide Water Canal. Elias W. Urey, son of George and Margaret (Hevner) Urey, was born on the homestead in Lower Chanceford Township, February 9, 1845, and was educated at the puplic schools of his township. In 1873 he engaged in the hotel business at York Furnace, and in 1877 he began boating and followed this until 1880; then kept hotel at McCall's Ferry until 1883, when he came back and took the hotel at York Furnace, which he still keeps. March 12, 1867, he was married to Ella Mehaffey, of Lancaster County, and has two children living: Emma and John M.

WILLIAM WILSON, son of James and Mary (Bunting) Wilson, was born January 22, 1824, in the township where he now resides. His father was a native of Lancaster County and his mother of Chester County. His father was drowned on the 17th of March, 1836. After Mr. Wilson grew to manhood he was a pilot on the Susquehanna River for a period of thirty years. For a number of years he was proprietor of the hotel at McCall's Ferry. In 1854 he was married to Mary E. Ayers, of Lower Chanceford. They have six sons and daughters, viz.: William T., Hannah M., James M., Clarkson F., Sarah E. and Jo. Ellen. Mr. Wilson took the census of Lower Chanceford for the year 1860, has been inspector of elections, township assessor and road supervisor, and is the present assessor of his township. James M. Wilson, his son, was born in 1861 at McCall's Ferry, and married Sarah Stokes of the same township. They have one child, John

---

LOWER WINDSOR TOWNSHIP.

JOHN E. BEARD, Esq., son of Joseph and Susan Beard, of Heidelberg Township, York County, was born in Lancaster County, Penn., November 11, 1813. At eighteen years of age he was apprenticed to the tanner's trade with Jacob Bayler, of York, Penn., and served until twenty-one years of age. He then worked for some time with John Kline, of Marietta. His father bought forty acres of land and a tannery, and in 1846 our subject began business for himself, renting the tannery from his father. After a few years he bought the property from his father, increased his facilities for doing business, and introduced steam into his tannery in 1845 or 1846. He has been in business ever since 1836, with the exception of eleven years, during which his sons carried on the business. At present his son Henry is associated with him in business. They tan about 1,300 hides annually. Mr. Beard was married in 1839 to Nancy, daughter of John Gehly, of Windsor Township, and they had five children, of whom two sons and two daughters are living. Mrs. Beard died in 1850. Mr. Beard's second marriage was in 1856, to Maria, daughter of Henry Leber. By this union they have three children: Emma, Elmira and George. The latter is teller in the bank at Cheyenne, Wyoming, and receives a salary of $1,500 a year. Mr. Beard was elected justice of the peace five times. He was appointed assistant assessor of internal revenue, and served four years; was elected county commissioner for one term. Mr. Beard is a stockholder and director in the Wrightsville National Bank. He is a member of Lodge No. 74, I. O. O. F., York, Penn.

ABDIEL BORTNER, justice of the peace, was born March 27, 1851, son of Jesse and Mary A.

LOWER WINDSOR TOWNSHIP.

Bortner, and is of German descent. He was reared on the farm, and received his education at the public schools, afterward attending the Millersville Normal School in 1870. He then engaged in mercantile business in Manheim Township, near Hanover, Penn., for four years, and sold the "Domestic" Sewing Machine for one year. In 1876 he moved to East Prospect, built a slaughter house and engaged in the butchering business. He also owns a house and lot in East Prospect. He was elected justice of the peace in 1882. He served as constable two years, and has been school director since 1884. Mr. Bortner was married, October 24, 1870, to Anna M., daughter of Isaac and Sarah Glatfelter, of Springfield Township. By this union they have one son, Franklin M., born May 30, 1873. Mr. Bortner has been a member of the Lutheran Church since 1870, and is at present a member of the Canadochley congregation.

JOSEPH B. BUDDING, son of Levi and Cassie Budding, of Wrightsville, Penn., was born May 6, 1854. He left home at five years of age and lived with his uncles, Levi Kauffet and George Kauffet, until he grew to manhood. In 1873 he embarked in the mercantile business at Yorkana, starting in a small room with a capital of $1,600. In 1878 he began the manufacture of cigars, employing about ten hands, and now handles about 6,000,000 cigars annually. He also deals in leaf tobacco. In 1880 he took his brother Jacob into partnership with him in the store. Mr. Budding was married, October 8, 1878, to Emma J., daughter of John E. and Maria Beard, of Lower Windsor Township, York County. This union has been blessed with three children, of whom one son and one daughter are living. Mr. Budding is a stockholder in the York City Market House, and in the York *Tribune* Company. He was the first postmaster at Yorkana, when that office was established in 1876.

JACOB K. BUDDING, son of Levi and Catharine Budding, of Wrightsville, was born January 27, 1857, is of German descent, and was reared on the home farm. He was educated at the district school and also attended the normal school at Millersville. In 1880 he entered into partnership with his brother, Joseph B. Budding, in the mercantile business at Yorkana, at which point he is at present assistant postmaster.

HENRY BURG was born August 11, 1834, son of Henry and Catherine Burg, of East Prospect, York Co., Penn. He taught school three terms, and in 1864 engaged in the dry goods business, which he continued six years. In 1870 he bought a farm of 100 acres near East Prospect, on which he erected new buildings, and where he has since resided. Mr. Burg was school director three terms, and was also assessor. He is a member of Winona Lodge No. 944, I. O. O. F., of East Prospect, and also a member of the Lower Windsor Grange Lodge No. 565, of Lower Windsor. October 1, 1857, he married Rebecca, daughter of Samuel and Rebecca Gilbert, of East Prospect. By this union they have been blessed with seven children. Their son, Harris W., a graduate of Eastman's College, Poughkeepsie, N. Y., has clerked three or four years, and taught school five terms. Mr. and Mrs. Burg are members of the Evangelical Church of East Prospect.

WILLIAM BURG, son of Henry and Catharine Burg, of Lower Windsor, was born April 8, 1836, and grew to manhood on the homestead. In 1857 he began for himself on the Ruby farm, on which he resided four years, and then returned to the homestead, where he remained eleven years. In 1870 he bought a farm of 200 acres near East Prospect, put up a fine dwelling, bank-barn and outbuildings, all modern in their plan, and a tenement house, and then went to Marion County, Kas., where he remained eight months, when he returned and resumed farming. He first married Catharine Ruby, who died within a year; his next marriage was to Leah, daughter of Samuel and Rebecca Gilbert. This lady also died; the mother of eleven children. Mr. Burg's third marriage was to Mary, daughter of Henry and Rebecca Gilbert, of East Prospect, and to this union have been born five children. Mr. and Mrs. Burg are members of the Evangelical Church at East Prospect.

A. H. CRALEY, son of George and Julyann Craley, was born March 16, 1845, in York County, Lower Windsor Township. He spent his youth on the farm and attended the public schools. August 10, 1864, he was married to Eliza Daron; the same year he went to Union County, Ohio, where he spent a year farming on Darby Plains. He returned to Craleyville in 1865, and commenced the manufacture of cigars, and manufactures about 600,000 a year. He married, February 14, 1867, Susan, daughter of John and Magdalena Poff, of Lower Windsor Township. Mr. Craley again married, October 22, 1870, another daughter of John and Magdalena Poff, named Rebecca. Mr. Craley had only one child, a daughter, by his first wife. She is named Alice. The two first wives are dead, and Mr. Craley and his third wife, Rebecca, have been members of the Church of Christ since about 1874 or 1875. Mr. Craley has been postmaster at Craleyville since the office was established at that place. He is of German descent; his ancestors came over as Hessians during the Revolution, and remained. Mr. Craley engaged one year in the mercantile business; he owns ten acres of land with fine buildings thereon.

JOHN W. DERINGER, son of John and Elizabeth (Young) Deringer, was born at Woodstock Forge, April 25, 1847, and at the age of two years was removed by his parents to East Prospect. At thirteen he left his home and worked on a farm until he was eighteen years of age, when he went to learn carpentering with P. W. Keller, with whom he remained three years. From 1868 to 1879 he worked for his father-in-law, H. E. Stein, of Lower Windsor. In 1879 he quit his trade and began the manufacture of cigars, employing about eight hands, and having purchased about five acres of land near Yorkana and built a house and cigar shop upon it. December 24, 1868, he married Julia A., daughter of H. E. and Elizabeth Stein, of Lower Windsor. They have adopted a daughter—Flora S. Wallick. Mr. and Mrs. Deringer are members of the Evangelical Church. Mr. Deringer joined in 1868, and since 1874 has been an exhorter; at present he is an exhorter and steward.

EMANUEL DETWILER is a son of John and Susan Detwiler, of Lower Windsor Township, York Co., Penn., and is of German descent. At the age of fifteen years he began driving a team and followed that occupation three years, after which he followed boating on the Tide Water Canal three years; then farmed three years, after which he engaged in mercantile business at the Five Mile Level for a few years and then returned to the farm. He now owns two well-improved farms in East Prospect. Mr. Detwiler also carried on lime-burning two years. At twenty-one years of age he married Mary, daughter of John and Eliza Anstine, of Lower Windsor Township. This union has been blessed with seven children, of whom the following are living: Alice, born July 3, 1862, married to Prof. M. H. Seitz, of Glen Rock; Elmer Ellsworth, teacher, born January 12, 1864; Charles Wesley, born November 30, 1865; Albert Franklin, born March 6, 1867; John Irvin, born May 12, 1869, and Ellie Octavia, born August 23, 1873. Mr. and Mrs. Detwiler are members of the Evangelical Church at East Prospect, of which Mr. Detwiler was trustee.

BIOGRAPHICAL SKETCHES.

G. W. FERREE was born November 3, 1855, and is the son of John and Mary Ferree, of Lower Windsor. He was reared a farmer, but at the age of twenty began the trade of milling with Adam Dellinger, of Hellam, remained a year and then went to William Mundis. In 1878 he engaged in the raising of tobacco and the manufacture of cigars; in 1879 he rented Emig's Mill near Margaretta Furnace and is still engaged in milling. He sells largely in Columbia and drives a good custom trade. June 31, 1877, he married Amanda, daughter of Henry and Susan Brubaker, of Lower Windsor. His two children are Harry, born December 13, 1878, and Mary, born June 9, 1880.

WILLIAM O. HAINES is the son of William and Mary Haines, of York Township; was born February 26, 1833, and was reared to manhood on the farm, commencing for himself at the age of thirty-two, near Wrightsville, where he remained nine years, when he removed on Daniel Leber's place, near the mill, and there resided three years. He then rested a year, after which he bought a farm containing sixty-four acres, remodeled the buildings and made other improvements. In 1863 he married Catharine, daughter of John and Eliza Anstine, of Lower Windsor, and to this marriage children have been born as follows: Flora E., January 23, 1865; Lorenzo D., April 22, 1868, and Charles W., July 7, 1870. Mr. and Mrs. Haines are members of the Evangelical Church at East Prospect.

WILLIAM A. HAINES, son of John and Elizabeth Haines, of Lower Windsor Township, York Co., Penn., was born October 29, 1852. His great-grandfather was born in Germany and came to America at an early date. Our subject, at the age of nineteen years, began learning the coach and wagon-making trade with Chas. Schazberger, of East York, and served an apprenticeship of three years. In 1874 and 1875 he was foreman for George Schleenstine, of East Prospect, and afterward commenced business for himself at Margaretta Furnace, where he remained two years. In 1877 he bought a house and two lots in East Prospect, where he built a shop and has since been doing a successful business, building stages, sleighs, buggies, etc. October 28, 1875, he married Sallie E., daughter of George and Rebecca Freed, of East York. By this union they have two children: Hattie R., born January 11, 1879, and Henry A., born December 29, 1881. Mr. Haines has been leader of the Prospect Cornet Band since its organization.

JOHN W. KINARD, M. D., son of Simon and Catherine Kinard, of Lower Windsor Township, York County, Penn., was born at Wrightsville, Penn., February 15, 1857. His early life was spent on the farm, and attending the public schools, and the York County Academy, after which he attended the State Normal School, at Millersville, four terms. He began teaching school at the age of seventeen, and taught two years in Lower Windsor and two years in Hellam Township. He then began the study of medicine under Dr. Jacob Hay, of York, and also studied under Dr. Bigler, of Windsor. He took a course of lectures in the University of Maryland, from which he graduated March 1, 1882. He located at Craleyville in the spring of 1882, and built up a large practice there. In the spring of 1884 he bought out Dr. Wiles, of East Prospect, and has been very successful in the practice of his profession. He was married, September 27, 1883, to Isabella, daughter of Jacob and Margaret Weidman. Dr. Kinard is a member of the Winona Lodge, No. 944, I. O. O. F., of East Prospect. As a surgeon, he is heroic and dexterous. December 30, 1882, he removed a fibroid tumor from Mr. O.'s back, administering chloroform and performing the operation unaided, which was done in twenty-five minutes; the tumor, when removed, weighed nearly two pounds. January 10, 1883, he removed from Miss F.'s left axilla a carcinoma

tumor, which was cut therefrom in thirty minutes, he having but the assistance of his medical student; the tumor weighed nearly one pound; he also cut a congenital tumor, of twenty-seven years standing, weighing five ounces, from Mrs. D.'s nose. He also performed a number of minor amputations, all of which resulted in a complete and rapid recovery. There are few who have made medicine such a success as this young physician. He also took a course of lectures in the Philadelphia Polyclinic and College for Graduates in Medicine, from which he graduated June 20, 1885.

SIMON P. KINARD, assistant postmaster, is the son of Simon and Catharine Kinard, and was born November 28, 1859. He was reared to farming and was educated at the common schools and at the York County Normal School at Wrightsville, and was afterward a teacher for three terms in Lower Windsor and one term in Spring Garden Township. April 10, 1882 he embarked in the mercantile business at Craleyville, which he still conducts in conjunction with the 'manufacture of cigars, having added the latter in 1883, and now turning out 120,000 per year; he also owns one acre of ground and his house and store. December 31, 1883, he married Mary, daughter of George and Elizabeth Silar, of Lower Windsor.

DANIEL W. LEBER, JR., son of Daniel and Anna Leber, of Lower Windsor Township, was born July, 22, 1846, and until nineteen years of age passed his time in attending school, and assisting on the home farm. In 1865 began milling at River View Mill and continued in the business about fourteen years. In the spring of 1879 he assumed charge of the old homestead, on which he still resides and which consists of forty-two acres, improved with a stone dwelling and bank-barn erected by himself and enriched with a mine of hematite, January 1, 1874; he married Mary, daughter of John Strickler, of Hellam Township, and by this union is the father of the following children: John, Flora, Nettie, Charles, Lester, Elsie, Daniel Wesley, Harry and Mary Ellen. The parents are both members of the Evangelical Church at East Prospect, and are of German extraction.

JOHN LEBER, son of Daniel and Anna Leber, was born January 25, 1838, in Lower Windsor Township, and is of German descent. Reared a farmer, in the spring of 1860 he commenced on his own account on his father's place near East Prospect; he remained there four years, then moved to another farm of 180 acres belonging to his father near Trinity Church. June 17, 1859, he married Anna Louisa, daughter of Daniel and Sarah Keller, of Lower Windsor. The children born to this marriage are Georgianna (married to Ed. Emig, son of John Emig), Cordio, Josephine and Charles. Mr. Leber is the owner of a fine brick dwelling house and stable on Hellam Street, Wrightsville, and has led a prosperous life. With his wife he is a member of the Evangelical Trinity Church.

DAVID D. POFF, son of John and Magdalene Poff, of Hellam Township, was born November 28, 1845, and is of German descent. February 16, 1864, he enlisted in Company A, Twenty-first Pennsylvania Cavalry, and took part in all its engagements and marches until his muster out, July 18, 1865. He was married, November 2, 1865, to Lydia, daughter of Jacob and Wilhelmina Howard, of Lower Windsor, and had born to him one child: Flora Ida, June 17, 1866. Mr. Poff is member of the I. O. O. F. and G. A. R.; he has filled the offices of supervisor and school director three years; he is a stockholder and director in the Chanceford Turnpike Company; he has served as juryman of the supreme court at Philadelphia; has been three times sent to the county convention, and has been five times on the county committee. In 1881 he bought his present farm of fifty acres on which he has erected fine buildings.

H. H. SPRENKLE, son of John and Betsy Sprenkle, of Hellam Township, was born September 22, 1841. At an early age he started for himself by teaching two terms of school at Dover, and one term in Lower Windsor Township. In 1871 he began milling at Hellam, and two years later moved to Margaretta, where he followed the same business for five years. He next engaged in the tobacco trade, first buying leaf and then starting the manufacture of cigars. October 29, 1861, he married Priscilla, daughter of John and Nancy Beard, of Yorkana. This lady died April 6, 1874, the mother of five children, and her remains were interred at Canadochley. Mr. Sprenkle's second marriage was to Clara A., daughter of John and Rebecca Bentz, by whom he had born to him four children. Mr. Sprenkle is a Jeffersonian Democrat, and takes an active interest in local politics; he has served as assessor in Hellam Township and is a member of Winona Lodge, No. 944, I. O. O. F., at East Prospect; his wife is a member of St. John's Episcopal Church, York.

HENRY E. STEIN, son of Henry and Julia A. (Slenker) Stein, was born September 23, 1827, and is of German descent. He lived upon the home farm until he was eighteen years of age, when he began the carpenter's trade with Jacob Streavig, with whom he remained two and a half years, working one year as a journeyman. In 1849 he began business on his own account, and since that time has erected about 175 churches, dwellings, barns, etc. In 1849, also, he married Elizabeth, daughter of Elizabeth and Jacob Gohn, of Lower Windsor. To this union have been born four daughters and one son, viz.: Julia A., wife of J. W. Deringer, of Yorkana; Mary, wife of Henry May, same place; Eliza Jane, William H. and Amanda. Mr. Stein owns about ten acres of land, on which he has erected a fine dwelling and other buildings. He has served as township auditor and also as trustee of the Evangelical Church, of which, with his wife, he is still a member.

JACOB R. WALLACE, ESQ., second son of Jacob and Susan Wallace, of Windsor Township, York Co., Penn., was born February 28, 1833. His early life was spent on the farm, after which he worked at the carpenter's trade two years. He then attended Millersville Normal School two years, also a select school in York, Penn., and in 1859 attended school at Cottage Hill. He taught school twenty-five terms: one term in Lancaster County, Penn., in 1874; sixteen terms in East Prospect, Penn., and eight terms in Lower Windsor Township. During the summers of 1874 and 1875 he also taught a select school, to prepare teachers, with M. J. Blessing as assistant. He was for ten years captain of a boat on the Tide Water Canal. In 1860 he was assessor in Windsor Township, in 1864 in Lower Windsor Township, and in 1882 in East Prospect Borough. He took the enrollment in Windsor Township in 1861, and the census of Windsor, Lower Windsor and East Prospect in 1870. In 1858 he was elected justice of the peace in Windsor Township, but declined to serve; and in 1874 was elected to the same office in East Prospect Borough, and re-elected in 1879 and 1884. He is a surveyor and conveyancer, is director of the Loan and Building Association of Frystown, and agent for the York, Spring Garden and Dallastown Insurance Companies. He is a Republican, was a candidate for auditor and was a delegate to the State convention, nominating H. M. Hoyt, for governor. He was treasurer for the County Institute for nine or ten years, and four years a member of the committee on permanent certificates. He has been secretary for the town council of the borough of East Prospect since the spring of 1875, and is secretary of the school board of East Prospect. In 1857 he married Susan, daughter of William and Magdalena Sprenkle, of Chanceford Township, and by this union they have two children: Linnie A., born October 20, 1862, and Florence Eugenia, born October 18, 1868. Mr. Wallace is a member of Winona Lodge No. 944, I. O. O. F., of East Prospect.

MANCHESTER TOWNSHIP.

REV. ISAAC H. ALBRIGHT, A. M., was born in Cumberland County, Penn., April 9, 1853. His parents were Michael and Fannie (Huntsberger) Albright, who were of German descent. They had three sons and one daughter—Isaac H., being the eldest. Until his nineteenth year he remained on the farm, studying at public and preparatory schools, teaching school one term himself before entering college. In 1872 he entered Lebanon Valley College, Penn., and graduated in 1876 as A. B. He pursued his studies under private instructors for two years, especially in the study of German and Hebrew languages, and was made A. M. in 1879. He entered college with a view to medicine, but being converted he changed his mind and studied for the ministry. His first charge was at Manheim, Lancaster County, where he remained three years, from 1876 to 1879. From there he went to Spring Garden, Lancaster County, where he stayed three years, and in the spring of 1882 came to Mount Wolf, where he had charge of six congregations—Mount Wolf, Manchester, Emigsville and others, all in York County; stayed there three years. From there he went to York, to the first United Brethren Church, where he is pastor now. He was married, February 15, 1872, in Dauphin County, Penn., to Kate H., daughter of George and Mary Uhler. To this union three children were born: John W., Mary Bertha and George Henry. Rev. Albright belongs to the United Brethren Church, and during his ministry 250 members have been added. He conducts services in the German and English languages. Besides attending to his pastoral duties, Rev. Albright also teaches instrumental and vocal music.

HENRY ALTLAND was born in Manchester Township, October 7, 1849. His parents are John and Mary Magdalena (Stoughl) Altland, natives of Dover Township, and of German descent. They had two sons and one daughter, of whom Henry is the youngest son. In his youth he learned the trade of blacksmithing with his father, but abandoned it when he became of age. He attended the public schools, York County Academy and Guntzler's Commercial College. When he became of age he commenced to teach in the public schools, and taught about twelve years. In 1876 he took the secretaryship of the Dover Mutual Fire Insurance Company, of York County, which office he still holds. March 17, 1872, he was married at York to Louise Lehr, of Manchester Township, daughter of Charles B. Lehr. They have five children: Kurvin Wilson, Walter Grant, Mabel Alberta, Oscar Henry and Park Caleb Wogan. Mr. Altland is a Lutheran. belongs to the Red Men of York, has held various township offices, was elected justice of the peace in 1875, and since. He is an active Republican and quite a political speaker. His father died in 1883, but his mother, now sixty-five years of age, is still living.

SAMUEL L. BAHN, farmer and auctioneer, was born in Spring Garden Township, December 2, 1820. His parents, Adam and Mary (Liebhart) Bahn, were natives of Spring Garden and Hellam Townships, respectively, and of German descent. He is the sixth child and third son of a family of ten children. After attending the schools of his native place he began the occupation of farming (and auctioneering in 1850) which he still pursues. He is a member of the Evangelical Association, was many years a class leader and for twenty years a steward in that denomination. Since 1882 he has been an exhorter in the Emigsville Chapel, and has been superintendent of the Union Sunday-school for nearly a quarter of a century. In May, 1847, he was commissioned first lieutenant of the Sixth Company, Third Regiment First Brigade of the Pennsylvania Militia, by Gen. Daniel A. Stillinger, and served until the militia was disbanded. Was once elected assistant assessor, and twice judge of elections of Manchester Township, and is a stockholder in the York City Market and Gettysburgh Turnpike Company. In 1875 he removed from his farm in Conewago Township to his present home on a tract of twenty-three acres, beautifully located, and in addition to the work of attending it, is representing the Farmers Mutual Insurance Company of York, and for several years the Conewago & Dover Insurance Company. He was married in York, December 5, 1841, to Susan Tyson, daughter of Daniel Tyson, of Spring Garden. They have had ten children: Amanda, Susan, Mary A., Daniel T., John A., Samuel F., Frederic M., George W., William H. N. and Elmer E.

SAMUEL F. BAHN, son of S. L. and Susan (Tyson) Bahn, sixth of ten children, was born October 3, 1852, was reared on his father's farm; went to his trade of miller when about eighteen years of age, at Menges' Mills, at which he worked four years at Meyer's Mills; then took charge as manager of George Small's farm near York. October 2, 1873, Mr. Bahn married Amanda Stair, daughter of George and Catherine (Merchandall) Stair, of Manchester Township. Their marriage was blest with four children: William H., Edward F., Hettie May and Sarah S. Mr. Bahn is engaged in truck and flower business, is also agent for fruit trees; is extensively engaged in the poultry business. His exhibit of all kinds of fancy and rare fowls for years at York County and Lancaster County fairs is well known to the people.

GEORGE W. BARNHART is the son of Elijah and Margaret Barnhart, of York County, and was born January 16, 1858. He was reared a farmer, but afterward learned milling and began the latter business on his own account in 1881, on the Codorus at Rudy's Mill, subsequently removing to Wolf's Mill, near Mt. Wolf. November 20, 1880, he married Ellen E., daughter of Levi and Mary Becker, of Jackson Township, the result of the union being four children: L. Nevin, Vertie (deceased), Daisey and Mabel Matilda. Mr. Barnhart has been a member of the American Mechanics' Association and is an adherent of the Lutheran Church.

HENRY S. BEAR, justice of the peace, was born in Conewago Township, York Co., Penn., May 6, 1825. His parents, Jacob S. and Elizabeth (Stover) Bear, were natives of York County, and of German descent. They reared three sons and three daughters, of whom Henry S. is the eldest. Until the age of seventeen, he lived on the farm and enjoyed a common school education; after that he taught school about eight years. November 11, 1851, he was married in Manchester Township, to Elizabeth Lichtenberger, who died June 19, 1874. They had twelve children, two of whom died before their mother: George E., aged nine, and Annie K., aged four and a half years. One, Clara Ann, the wife of Eli Gross, died in 1877. The remaining nine are Stephen A., merchant; Charles H., merchant; Elizabeth, teacher in Illinois; Mary Margaret, wife of W. H. Kauffman; Sallie Frances, who is still at home; Willie Lincoln, teacher; Fannie Leah, at home; Carrie Irene, at home and Jennie Laura. Our subject was next married, December 3, 1882, in Manchester Borough, to Adaline Schriner, widow of John Schriner, and daughter of Henry Frank, and a native of Lancaster County, Penn. Henry S. and his wife belong to the Lutheran Church. He came to Manchester Township in 1871, where he engaged in merchandising

MANCHESTER TOWNSHIP.

for five years. Since that time he has been engaged in conveyancing, surveying and insurance. He also held the office of school director in Conewago Township for about six years, and that of justice of the peace about twelve years. In the spring of 1884 he was re-elected justice of the peace of Manchester. In politics, he is an active Republican.

STEPHEN A. BEAR, born in Conewago Township, April 24, 1853, is the eldest son of Henry S. and Elizabeth (Lichtenberger) Bear, of York County. His parents removed to Manchester Borough when he was seventeen years of age. He was educated in the common schools, supplemented by a two-years' course of the State Normal School at Millersville. He taught two terms in the public schools at Conewago and Manchester Townships. He worked on the farm when a boy, but began clerking at Manchester when the family moved there, and clerked altogether about six years for different merchants. He was married at Manchester Borough, February 29, 1880, to Amanda J. Warner, daughter of D. Warner, Esq., contractor and native of Manchester. They have had three children: Carrie Irene, Elizabeth and Charles Henry. July, 1883, in partnership with his brother, Charles H., he purchased C. H. Bishop's mercantile business in Manchester, and has since carried on the leading business in general merchandise at this place. Since April, 1883, he has been postmaster of Manchester. He is a Republican and has served one term as borough treasurer. He is a stockholder in the Drovers and Stockholders National Bank of York. He is a district president of the P. O. S. of A., and has held all the offices in order. He devotes all his time to his store at Manchester, while his brother is employed as clerk in a large dry goods house in York.

DAVID BENTZEL is the sixth of ten children of David and Elizabeth (Meisenhelder) Bentzel, and was born May 3, 1815, in Dover Township, on the Bentzel homestead, now occupied by Samuel Bentzel. David received a limited education, and went to his trade of miller September, 1834, at his present location. In 1850 he went to Illinois, and worked at Big Thunder Mill, in Boone County, seven months. He then returned home to his present mill, where he has since remained. He married, April 2, 1842, Sarah Eisenhart, daughter of John and Catherine (Myers) Eisenhart, of Dover Township. Six children were born to their union: Henry D., died in California; Edward D., David E., Leah (deceased), Nancy, wife of Henry W. Jacobs; Catherine, wife of Peter Binder. Subject's grandfather and grandmother came from Germany —landed at Baltimore, and came soon to Dover Township. Subject's uncles and aunts are Henry Bentzel, Elizabeth (deceased), Catherine, wife of John Ailman; Barbara, wife of John Kump; Mary, deceased. Subject was director of the poor in 1868-69-70. David E. Bentzel is engaged in the manufacture of cigar boxes, and has twelve hands constantly employed in his factory, which is known as the Eureka Cigar Box Factory. He ships to Lancaster and Adams Counties, besides those he sells to York County. He commenced here in October, 1884, with a capacity of 400, and has since increased to 1,500 per day. David E. was married, August 12, 1877, to Louisa E. Stough, daughter of Valentine and Elenora (Fissel) Stough. The following named children were born to their union: B. Frank, James Simpson, Africa, David V. (deceased), Felix S. S. and Annie Amanda. Mr. Bentzel is an active business man, and belongs to the Lutheran Church of Dover (Strayer's). He was enumerator of the census in Dover Township in 1880.

DR. CHARLES H. BISHOP (deceased), was a son of Charles and Elizabeth Bishop, natives of the eastern shore of Maryland, where the Doctor was born, April 19, 1812. He came to York Haven with his parents when a small boy, there went to school, and embarked in the mercantile business, when a very young man, taking his father's store in Manchester Borough. After several years in the mercantile business, he began to read medicine, and attended lectures at Philadelphia, and graduated there. He began practice at the village of Manchester, where he continued in his chosen profession for thirty years. Dr. Bishop died on May 28, 1875. His widow still lives in Manchester. Her maiden name was Anna Frey, daughter of Frederick and Margaret (Kissinger) Frey, of Spring Garden Township. To this marriage one child was born—Charles Halleck. Dr. Bishop was one of the leading and most influential men of his section of the county. He had a large and lucrative practice, and was held in high esteem as a conscientious physician.

JOHN G. DIEHL was born in Manchester Township, June 13, 1851, is the third son in a family of three sons and one daughter. His parents, Charles H. and Sarah (Gross) Diehl, natives of York County, were of German descent. He was reared on a farm until he was fifteen years of age, and educated at New Berlin Academy. After teaching school a few months, he began cigar-making at the age of nineteen, followed the business a short time, and then learned painting, which he followed off and on for eight years, and clerked a few months for G. H. Wolf at Mount Wolf, where he has resided since 1870. He was married in Mount Wolf, December 26, 1872, to Elizabeth, daughter of Samuel Dietz, and a native of York County. Two children—Minnie and George—resulted from this union. In June, 1884, Mr. Diehl formed a partnership with Israel Finfrock in the manufacture of fancy and common cigars. He is a member of the United Brethren Church; is a stockholder in Dover Fire Insurance Company, and has served one term as assessor of Manchester Township.

JACOB DOLL, born in Spring Garden Township, May 24, 1851, is the eldest of three children of Henry and Susanna (Dissenberger) Doll, natives of York County, and an old Pennsylvania family. He spent the first twenty-six years of his life on the farm, and received a good education. He was married at York, Penn., May 11, 1875, to Anna C. Coleman, a native of New Holland, Penn., and a daughter of Matthias Coleman (deceased lumber dealer), and has had four children, of which number two are dead: John Albert, died at the age of three months, and George Henry, died at the age of ten months. The living are Lillie Mary and Susie. From 1877 to 1879, our subject was an invalid. In 1879 he began the manufacture of cigars at his father's house, near Starview, from which he removed in the spring of 1880, to New Holland, where he has since carried on the same business, employing eight hands, and has also a factory at Starview, employing four hands. He makes about 700,000 cigars per year. He is something of a German scholar, but devotes his whole time to the manufacture of cigars.

JOHN DRAYER, retired merchant, is a son of Jacob and Catherine (Cockley) Drayer, who were parents of seven children, four now living: Susanna, Henry, John and Mary; three deceased: Jesse, Eliza and Elizabeth. He was reared on the farm, and when old enough began learning the tailor's trade in Frystown. In 1844 he engaged in general merchandising, in connection with tailoring in Manchester. He was appointed postmaster by President James K. Polk, and afterward received the appointment for the same office from James Buchanan and Andrew Johnson. December 24 1843, he married Sarah Frey, daughter of Samuel and Annie (Kissinger) Frey, of Spring Garden

Township. To this union were born nine children: Annie, David C., Charles P., Samuel M., Sallie A., Willie F., Flora J. and Ella M. Mr. Drayer is a member of the I. O. O. F., and attends the Lutheran Church. The family name was originally spelled Dreher.

MARTIN LUTHER DUHLING, justice of the peace, was born in Manchester Township, April 9, 1820. His father was Martin Duhling, a native of England, and his mother, Barbara Quickel, born in York County. Until his fifteenth year, our subject remained on the farm, and then learned the pottery trade, which he followed twenty years. He was educated at the public schools, and at seventeen years began teaching, and taught thirty-two winters in York County. At twenty-one years of age he married Elizabeth A. Bentz, daughter of John Bentz, of Manchester. They had seven children, four of whom are now living: William H., of York, now of Edgar, Clay Co., Neb.; Sarah Catherine, wife of George Mathias, of New Cumberland; Emma S., wife of Stephen Copenhefer, miller, at Hellam, and Lillian Jane, at home. The three who died were John Clay, thirteen years; Annie, two years; Maria, wife of H. M. Everhart, twenty-six years. Mr. Duhling formerly belonged to the Lutheran Church, but left it in 1868 to connect himself with the United Brethren Church, in which he is assistant class leader. Since 1870 he has been secretary of the Quarterly Conference. In 1844 he was captain of the militia of Hellam District. He was a member of the Manchester Borough Council in 1880, and in 1884 again elected for three years, and has been secretary of the council for ten years. Being elected justice of the peace of Manchester Township in 1863, he has held that office nearly twenty-two years. Since 1857 he has also been engaged in butchering, and with the exception of ten years has followed it ever since. He attends also to surveying and conveyancing. August 23, 1864, he enlisted in Company D, Two Hundredth Regiment Pennsylvania Volunteers, and served until the end of the war. When the regiment was properly organized, he was elected first lieutenant, while his son was elected captain. His company served in the Army of the Potomac, and participated in the battles in front of Petersburg. At Fort Steadman he was wounded by a piece of shell striking him in the left leg; he lay in the hospital about eight days, but could not do any duty for fifteen days. The company was raised by him and his son, and it was his express wish that his son should be its captain. It left Harrisburg with 104 men, and returned with only seventy. In politics Mr. Duhling is a Republican. In 1870 he took the census for Manchester Township and Borough, and from 1860 to 1866 he was postmaster at Manchester. His children, with the exception of the youngest, have all been teachers in the public schools.

W. H. EISENHART, son of Adam and Leah (Forry) Eisenhart, was born in Manchester Township, York Co., Penn., April 6, 1840. His ancestors, the Eisenharts, were among the earliest settlers in this county. He was married, November, 1860, to Helena Schriver, daughter of Daniel and Catherine (Schriver) Schriver, of this township. By this union they have been blessed with two children: Flora K. and Emma J. Mr. Eisenhart is a member of the Lutheran Church.

DR. HERMAN ANDREW EISENHART, of Manchester Township, was born January 25, 1843, and is a son of Dr. Adam and Leah (Forry) Eisenhart, natives of the same township, who had a family of eleven sons and three daughters, of whom our subject is the second son and fourth child. His grandfather, Dr. George Eisenhart, emigrated from Germany in the early history of our county, and ocated in the present limits of West Manchester. From him descended the numerous families of Eisenharts, most of whom reside in York County. The subject of this sketch was brought up on his father's farm, at the same time attended the public schools. At the age of nineteen he began the study of medicine in the office of his father, and at the age of twenty-nine, upon the death of his father, succeeded to the practice, which he still retains. August 19, 1864, he enlisted at York, in Company H, Two Hundredth Regiment Pennsylvania Volunteers, and was honorably discharged with his regiment, May 30, 1865, at Alexandria, Va. He participated in the battle in front of Petersburg and the first and second attack on Fort Steadman. After the war he returned home and resumed his medical practice at his present home, three and a half miles north of York. He married Rebecca Hamme, a native of York County, October 14, 1866. They have eight children: Lillie Cora, William McCall, Harvey G., Adam, Kurvin C., Annie Kate, Herman A. and Howard Filmore. Dr. Eisenhart is a member of the Lutheran Church, is a Republican in politics, and served one term as school director. In addition to his medical practice the Doctor pursues farming, a part of his time, as a healthy recreation. His father died in 1872, aged sixty-two years, and his mother in 1882 at the same age.

SOLOMON EISENHUR was born in Conewago Township, August 15, 1834. His parents were George and Magdalena (Wire) Eisenhur, of Pennsylvania, but of German descent, who reared a family of nine sons and eight daughters, of whom Solomon was the thirteenth child. He remained on the farm up to his manhood, and has followed farming ever since. His education he received at public schools. At the age of twenty-three he was married, in Minnesota, to Sarah Wilhelm, of Manchester Township, and a daughter of John Wilhelm. She bore him eleven children, one died in infancy: Frances, wife of Jacob Lautz; Ida Belle, wife of Jacob Bair; James, a farmer; Della, Laura, Wesley, Charles, Minnie, Eli and William H. Mr. Eisenhur is one of the deacons of the United Brethren Church, and also vice-president of the Sabbath-school. He is also a member of the Easton Building Association at York. In politics he is a Republican. While in Shakopee, Minn., he enlisted, in 1862, in Company A, Fourth Minnesota Volunteer Infantry, and served one year's term of enlistment. With his command he was in the campaign along the Mississippi River, in the battle of Iuka, Miss., and at Corinth. In 1863 he returned to Pennsylvania, and lived three years at Williamsport, where he was engaged in the planing-mill. From there he moved to Manchester Township, and now lives on his fine farm of eighty-five acres.

JOHN EMIG, JR, was born April 4, 1812, in Manchester Township, and died December 24, 1882. His parents were John and Anna Mary (Smyser) Emig, natives of West Manchester Township, and of German ancestry. They had four sons and one daughter, of whom John, Jr., was the third son. He grew up on the farm of his father, which had come into the hands of his grandfather in 1802, and into his father's hands in 1806, and became his property in 1840, but in 1876 passed into the hands of William H. Emig, eldest son of John, Jr. The subject of this sketch was educated at the subscription schools of his neighborhood. He was married, October 2, 1838, near Prospect, in Lower Windsor, to Ellen S. Knisely, daughter of John Knisely, of German descent. They had eleven children, one of whom, Amanda, died, aged about three years. The others are Louisa; William, a farmer; Ellen, wife of M. W. Bahn, at New Freedom; Mary Jane, a teacher in select schools; J. Albert, Emma, Alice, Flora A., Belle L. and Edward K., farmer and manufacturer. They belong to the Reformed Church. In 1840 he began the lime burning business, and was the first to engage in that business in his vicinity. In 1849 the Northern Central Railroad was run through his farm, and at once established a station there, which is known as Emigsville. The farm contained about 200 acres, and came into his hands from his father by his paying $500 in installments. He built about eleven houses in Manchester Township, had owned seven farms, and at his death owned three fine farms. The largest portion of his property was acquired by his own industry. In 1850 he engaged in a building scheme at Baltimore, and erected about ten fine dwelling houses and two warehouses, and at his death owned six of these dwellings. He was one of the few men in his neighborhood favoring public schools. So bitter was the opposition that he, with a few others, was compelled to guard the schoolhouse of his neighborhood from destruction. He was a school director for six years, and always took an active part in education. He was a leading man in the erection of the first chapel, and gave the ground upon which it was built. He laid out the town of New Freedom in 1868, and gave the ground on which two churches were erected (Methodist Episcopal and Reformed). The latter was first given to the Baptists, who sold it to the Reformers. He began the mercantile business about the time the railroad passed through, and, with the exception of a few years, was interested in the house as a partner or sole owner up to 1874, when his son, John Albert, became owner. He was agent for the railroad company up to one year before his death, also postmaster from the establishment of the office until 1880. J. Albert Emig, born August 9, 1849, was reared on the farm at Emigsville. He received his education in the public schools, and at York County Academy, and at Millersville Normal School. He entered his father's store at Emigsville, and assisted as clerk until 1874, when he bought the store. He was married in Windsor Township, March 19, 1874, to Ella S. Detwiller, daughter of John Detwiller. They had two children: Carrie D. and John W. He is head of the firm of Emig & Gable, Manchester, and E. K. Emig & Co., manufacturers of wagons and agricultural implements, at Emigsville, and flour and feed store and wagon depot at York. He owns 165 acres of land, and superintends it himself. In 1880 he was appointed railroad agent at Emigsville, as also Adams Express agent and postmaster.

HENRY M. EVERHART, undertaker and cabinet-maker, is a son of Daniel and Sallie (Mohr) Everhart, of York, Penn., who were parents of ten children: William (deceased), Elizabeth, Mary, Henry M., Daniel, John, Leah, Sarah, William and Ellen. After learning his trade he began business for himself in 1859, and continued until the war broke out, when he enlisted in Company A, Eighty-seventh Pennsylvania Volunteers, and took part with his regiment in the battles of Winchester, Monocacy, Petersburg and second Bull's Run, besides a number of skirmishes. Mr. Everhart's first marriage was to Maria Duhling, daughter of M. L. and Eliza (Pentz) Duhling, of this township, and to this union were born three children: Annie K., Henry M. (deceased) and Ellen. Mrs. Everhart died and Mr. Everhart married Lizzie Stahle, daughter of Col. J. A. Stahle, of this township. This union has been blessed with one child—Flossie Mary. Mr. Everhart is a first-class mechanic and does an extensive trade in his line. He is a member of the United Brethren Church of Manchester.

DAVID G. FOOSE, son of Isaiah and Margaret (Fagan) Foose, was born in Perry County, Penn., February 4, 1845, and after attending several terms at public school in his native township, began to learn the trade of blacksmith (with his father), and after working ten years, began on his own account, in 1873, at his present stand on Harrisburg Pike, near York. Our subject was married, September 16, 1869, to Margaret A. Harley, daughter of Rudolf and Rebecca (Cramer) Harley, of Chambersburg, Franklin County. Two children were born to them—Mary Carrie and Martha Rebecca. Our subject's paternal ancestors came from Germany and his maternal ancestors from England. Isaiah Foose, the father of our subject, was a gallant soldier in the late war; he enlisted in the Two Hundred and Eighth Regiment, Pennsylvania Volunteers, Gen. Hartranft's Division, and after participating in all the battles in which his regiment was engaged, and being present at the surrender of Gen. Lee, April 9, 1865, he was honorably discharged from the service. He married Margaret Fagan, and their marriage was blessed with seven children: Rachael J. (deceased), David G., Sarah Ann, Enoch T., Martin M., James M. and John Wesley. Isaiah Foose, our subject's father, died January 6, 1879, from heart disease, aged fifty-six years five months and one day. Margaret (Fagan) Foose, his wife, died April 9, 1870, aged about fifty years.

HENRY S. FORRY, born in Spring Garden Township, January 16, 1853, is the eldest son and second child of Rudolph and Angeline (Strickler) Forry, of Hellam and Spring Garden Townships, and of German descent. He grew to manhood on the farm and received a good common school education. He was married in York, October 18, 1877, to Amelia E. Flory, daughter of John Flory, of Spring Garden Township, farmer, and of German descent, and has had two children: Daisy E. and Howard Ralph. In the spring following his marriage he removed to the farm of 180 acres in Manchester Township, since successfully managed by him. He devotes his entire attention to farming and stock raising.

HENRY FREE was born in Manchester Township, August 25, 1831. His parents were Adam and Mary (Hake) Free, natives, respectively, of Maryland and Pennsylvania, and of Scotch and German descent. They reared six sons and five daughters. Henry is the fourth son and child. He was brought up on a farm and educated in the common schools. At the age of twenty-four or twenty-five he began life for himself. He traded for some time in stock, but in 1856 he commenced distilling at Goldsborough, Penn., and in partnership with his brother, Augustus, has followed it since. They began with a capacity of 100 bushels per day, but at the beginning of taxation reduced the capacity. He was married in Manchester Township, March 1, 1857, to Leah Rutter, daughter of John Rutter (deceased). She died in November, 1881, leaving four children: George B. M., M. D., at Philadelphia; Kate, at home; Samuel, a student at York Collegiate Institute, and Harry, also a student at York. Mr. Free belongs, as did also his wife, to the Lutheran Church; in politics he is a Republican, and has been elected township auditor several times, and is the present incumbent. He was one of the organizers of the State Capital Oil Company, and for many years one of its directors. He left Manchester Township for Newberry Township in 1858, and in 1869 he came to where he has since lived upon a small farm one mile north of York. He is partner in three fine farms near Goldsborough, aggregating about 400 acres. Mr. Free made all his property by his own industry. His daughter is keeping house for him. His father, who died in 1854, came to Pennsylvania in 1818, and worked some as a carpenter, then commenced farming and distilling near Emigsville; here he died at the age of fifty-eight years, possessed of property worth upward of $75,000, and yet, at the age of thirty, he had nothing and had done nothing. He was once elected county commissioner.

SAMUEL GLATFELTER was born near Hanover, York County, Penn., August 4, 1819. His parents were John and Margaret E. (Keyser) Glatfelter, of York County. They had three sons and one daughter. Being the eldest of the children, Samuel remained on the farm, and like his father, has followed farming ever since. In his youth he attended subscription schools, and at the age of nineteen years, went to Indiana, with his parents, but stayed there only a few months, and then returned to Pennsylvania, stopping in Indiana County about four years. Coming back to his native county, he followed distilling for a few years. July 25, 1844, he married Susan Heindel, daughter of Jacob Heindel, a farmer. Mr. and Mrs. Glatfelter were of German descent. Mrs. G. died January 28, 1879, leaving six children. Two children were buried before her: Catharine, in her twenty-second year, and Isabel, in her twenty-seventh year. Since his mother's death, Samuel L. died in his twenty-sixth year, and Amanda Jane April 13, 1883, aged thirty-four years, leaving the following: Susan, Julian, Margaret E. and Emma L. The family belong to the Lutheran Church. Mr. Glatfelter has for some time been school director. In politics he is Democratic. In the spring of 1859 he removed to the place he now owns and occupies, a fine thrifty farm of about 155 acres.

LUTHER S. GLATFELTER, merchant at Starview, was born in New Salem, North Codorus Township, December 23, 1860, and is a son of Franklin and Rebecca (Smith) Glatfelter, of German and Swiss descent, respectively. He remained with his father on the farm until the age of fourteen, when he entered the employ of Eli Goodling as clerk in his store. He next attended school one winter, and then became a clerk for Mr. Whitman and others, of York, in the store business. In 1881 he began business for himself as a merchant in Dover Township, and in 1884 moved to Starview, where he is now conducting a store of general merchandise, and since locating there has been postmaster of the village. Mr. Glatfelter was married, August 14, 1881, to Jennie E. Hake, daughter of Frederick Hake. They had two children. One, named William Jacob, died in infancy. The name of the second child is Charles Walter. Mr. Glatfelter is a member of the Lutheran Church.

ELIAS GOOD (formerly spelled Guth), the third of five children of Rudolph and Elizabeth (Engle) Good, of Manchester Township, was born November 8, 1828, in Manchester Township, at the old homestead. He was reared to farming and has always followed that occupation. September 16, 1852, he married Louisa Baer, daugher of George and Sarah (Smyser) Baer, of Spring Garden Township. Three children were born to this marriage: Adeline, Amanda, deceased; and Annie. On the 21st of January, 1875, Mr. Good married Susan Musser, daughter of Benjamin H., and Elizabeth (Rupley) Musser, of Fairview Township. Our subject's grandfather, Peter Good, was born November 11, 1755, in Martick Township, Lancaster County, Penn.; his first wife was Susan Stehman, of Lancaster County; eleven children were born to them: John, Henry, Barbara, Elizabeth, Susanna, Anna, Jacob, Peter, Rudolph, Catherine and Abraham. His second wife was Barbara Treigber, of Spring Garden Township; to this union were born two children: Maria and Daniel. Rudolph Good, the father of the subject of this sketch, was born August 23, 1794, on the homestead where David Good now resides. He died December 22, 1869, aged seventy-five years three months and twenty-nine days. Elizabeth (Engle) Good, our subject's mother, was born October 27, 1801, was married to Rudolph Good, March 11, 1824, and died March 4, 1853, aged fifty-one years, four months and five days. Their children were Jacob, deceased; Magdaline, deceased; Elias, Susanna and David. Mr. Good, our subject, is a member of the German Baptist Church (usually known as Dunkards), and is one of Manchester Township's best citizens.

DAVID E. GOOD (formerly spelled Guth), is the youngest of five children of Rudolph and Elizabeth (Engle) Good, of Manchester Township, and was born at the homestead where he now resides, August 30, 1832. He was reared to and has always followed farming. In December, 1856, he married Susan R. Ginter, daughter of Jacob and Ann (Rodes) Ginter, of Manchester Township. Ten children have been born to them: Harvey G., William, Elizabeth (deceased), Rudy, David, Jacob, Martha (deceased), Edward, Fannie (deceased), and Harry. Harvey Good, son of the subject of this sketch, was born November 6, 1858. December 4, 1881, he married Catherine Melhorn, daughter of George and Louisa (Lory) Melhorn, of Manchester Township; one child has blessed their union—Roy Edwin. Harvey Good is engaged in the cigar business and has a factory in Manchester Township. William and Jacob, second and sixth sons of David E. Good, have charge of the telegraph office at the Summit, between Emigsville and Mount Wolf; William is the day and Jacob the night operator for the Pennsylvania Railroad, at the Northern Central Railroad, at this point; they are steady, trustworthy young men, and conscientious in the discharge of their duties. Rudy and David, the fourth and fifth children, respectively, are working at cigar-making.

HENRY V. GRESS, M. D., was born in Lancaster County, November 3, 1846. His parents were John and Elizabeth (Von-Nieda) Gress, both of whom are dead, the father dying when Henry V. was but a year old. They were natives of Lancaster County and of German descent. They had two sons, of whom Henry V. was the youngest. Until his seventeenth year he remained on the farm, attending also the common schools, where at the age of sixteen years he first learned English. At the age of twenty years he entered the office of Dr. Hoffman at Sinking Springs, Berks Co., Penn., and read medicine one year; then entered Jefferson College and took a course of lectures. After reading another year with his old preceptor he returned to his *alma mater*, and graduated in March, 1871, as M. D., not getting his diploma, however, until some months after passing the examination, on account of a "commencement." He had really practiced his profession nine months before he received his diploma. At Brickerville, Lancaster County, he began practice in September, 1870, and stayed some time over a year. He then removed to Bachmansville, Dauphin County, where he practiced nearly three years. From there he moved to Manchester, where he has since practiced with success. September 20, 1870, he was married, at York, to Ella Boyd, of Columbia, Penn., a daughter of John Boyd, of Scotch-Irish descent. Four children were born to them: Ray, Guy, Grace and Elizabeth B. Both parents belong to the United Brethren Church. Dr. Gress was elected school director in 1882. He was also one of the organizers of the Provident Life Association of Baltimore, Md., and has been one of the directors since its organization in 1882.

SAMUEL GROSS, the second of six children of John and Barbara (Melhorn) Gross, was born May 25, 1813, in Manchester Township, on the old homestead farm where he was reared. His first wife was Susan Wolf. Six children were born to them: Mary, Amanda, John, George, Emma and Susan (deceased). His second wife was Lena Gotwalt, daughter of John and Catherine (Wilt) Gotwalt of Dover Township. One child was born to this marriage—Alice S. Mr. Gross and family are members of the Lutheran Church. of Manchester. Mr. Gross' ancestors were among the first settlers of Manchester Township. They came to the neighborhood of Manchester 110 years ago, and their descendants in Manchester Township have always been upright. honorable men and good citizens.

MICHAEL GROSS, the third of six children of John and Barbara (Melhorn) Gross, of Manchester Township, was born January 15, 18—, in Manchester Township; he was reared on his father's farm and followed farming for thirty years, when he retired. He married Leah Hake, daughter of Jacob and Lydia (Miller) Hake, of Conewago Township; to this union were born Eliza, John W., Eli, Lydia, Sarah A., Louis and Leah. The grandfather of the subject of this sketch was born in Germany, and located in Manchester Township, on the farm, where Jacob Free now resides, near Emigsville; after a short stay there he bought the farm where Benjamin Gross now lives, about one mile from the village of Manchester. He bought this farm, February 8, 1777, from Frekerick Zorger, of Newberry Township. Samuel Gross, our subject's grandfather, had two brothers, one settled in Lancaster County, the other near Hagerstown, Md. Samuel settled in York County and had seven children: George, Samuel, John, Daniel. Eve, wife of Michael Beltzhover, of Cumberland County, and one daughter, the wife of Rev. Schucker (deceased). of York; the other daughter was the wife of John Strayer, of Dover Township. Our subject's ancestors were among the earliest settlers of Manchester Township. Mr. Gross is a prominent member of the Lutheran Church.

GEORGE GROSS, son of John and Barbara (Melhorn) Gross, was born February 16, 1817, in Manchester Township. Mr. Gross was reared to farming and followed the occupation all his life. February 17, 1848, Mr. Gross married Eliza Rutter, daughter of John and Catharine Brillinger Rutter, of Manchester Township. Fourteen children were born to this union: Ellen, deceased; Albert, deceased; Emma, deceased; George, deceased; Andrew, deceased; Adam, deceased; Zacharias, William, Sarah, Kate, Edward, Charles, Eliza and Jennie. Mr. Gross and family are members of the Lutheran Church, of Manchester. (For Mr. Gross' ancestral history, see his brother's sketch.)

BENJAMIN GROSS, the third of six children of Daniel and Elizabeth (Myers) Gross, of Manchester Township, was born August 20, 1819, in Manchester Township. He was reared to farming and followed that occupation until 1860, when he retired. In April, 1843, Mr. Gross married Sarah Shettel, daughter of George and Elizabeth (Bentz) Shettel, of Conewago Township. Two children have blessed this marriage: Eli and Alfred S. (now a resident of Goshen, Ind.) Our subject's grandfather bought and located on the farm where Benjamin now lives, in 1777, having purchased the same from Fred Zorger on the 8th of February, 1777. The Gross family has been among the pioneer settlers of Manchester Township. Benjamin Gross, the subject of this sketch, is well and favorably known as one of Manchester Township's influential men. He is a member of the Lutheran Church.

FREDERICK G. HAKE was born in Manchester Township, York County, May 29, 1837. His parents were Andrew F. and Eliza (Gross) Hake, of York County, and of German descent. They reared a family of four sons (of whom Frederick was the eldest) and three daughters. Frederick G. remained on the farm until grown, receiving his education in the public schools. At the age of twenty-one he began life for himself. When twenty-three years old he was married to Sarah Moore, daughter of Jacob Moore, of Manchester Borough. Ten children were born to them: Edward M., a railroad official at St. Louis; Mary Ellen, wife of Joseph Eisenhart; William Albert, grocer; Jennie, wife of Luther Glatfelter; Elizabeth, Annie, Augustus, Maggie, Carrie and Hattie—the last six being at home. Brought up in the Lutheran Church, they, for convenience, joined the United Brethren Church in 1874. Having a fine farm of 163 acres of well cultivated land, about four miles west of York, Mr. Hake left Manchester Borough in 1874, and located on this farm. His parents left Manchester, in 1872, for Harrisburg, where they have since resided, leading the easy life of retired farmers. Mr. Hake owns very valuable property in Harrisburg, as also valuable farm lands in Kansas.

ALBERT HAKE, son of Daniel and Mary (Boose) Hake, of Manchester Township (now York), was born April 24, 1851, and is the second of eight children. He attended the public schools of his native township, and went two sessions to the York County Academy (Prof. Ruby). December 12, 1872, Mr. Hake married Adeline Good, daughter of Elias and Louisa (Baer) Good, of Manchester Township. Four children have been born to them: Carrie, Estella, Nora Louisa and Elias. Mr. Hake is a successful florist and apiarist, and sells largely to the York market, and lives near the village of Manchester, on the Harrisburg pike.

WILLIAM J. HAKE, son of Jacob and Cassandria (Neiman) Hake, was born December 14, 1852, in Manchester Township. He was the ninth of ten children: George, Leah, Emanuel, Ellen, Mary, Louisa, Jacob (deceased), Henry (deceased), William J., and Albert (deceased). The mother of our subject was Cassandria Neiman, daughter of George and Mary (Rupert) Neiman, of Conewago Township. His father. Jacob Hake, was born February 20, 1809, and died May 25, 1875. Our subject's grandfather was Jacob Hake; he married Mary Copenhafer, of Heidelberg Township; he was a farmer and owned the farm now occupied by Daniel Hake, one mile and a half from Manchester, on the Harrisburg pike (see history of the Hake or Hock family, page 137).

JACOB HARTMAN, son of Christian and Mary (Moore) Hartman, was born March 8, 1820, in this township, the sixth of the following family: John (deceased), Catherine (deceased), Christian, Peter (deceased), Henry (deceased), Jacob, Samuel (deceased), Isaac, Elizabeth (deceased), Susanna, Daniel, Abraham (deceased), Leah and William (deceased). The father, Christian Hartman, was a soldier in the war of 1812. Our subject was married, November 14, 1844, to Leah, daughter of John and Christiana (Lichtenberger) Schroll, and by her became the father of eleven children: Justice (deceased), Mary Ann, Samuel (deceased), William H., Sarah J., Annie (deceased), John, Leah, Emanuel F., Daniel B. and Catherine (deceased). Mr. Hartman is the owner of several excellent farms, and in the spring of 1865 retired to his new mansion to pass in quietude his remaining years.

ANSON C. HARTMAN, born in Manchester Township, March 29, 1862, is the sixth son of Peter and Mary (Hartzler) Hartman, of York and Dauphin Counties. He was brought up in Manchester Borough, received a good education in the public schools, and at the age of seventeen years began the trade of stone-cutter with his brother in Manchester Borough, and in September, 1883, he went into business for himself. He is a skilled workman, and the only stone-cutter in the place. He is financial secretary of the P. O. S. of A. at Manchester, and has filled all the official chairs of the order. He is leader of Mt. Wolf Cornet Band, and instructor of the Starview Cornet Band. He is an accomplished cornetist, and plays any and all of

BIOGRAPHICAL SKETCHES.

the brass instruments. His musical education is self-acquired.

HENRY HOFF, son of Henry and Mary (Moul) Hoff, was born in Manchester Township, York Co., Penn., March 16, 1830, and was reared on his father's farm. The father was born in this township, and the mother in Heidelberg Township, near Hanover, Penn. They had six children: John, Rebecca, Mary, Henry, Samuel and Susan. Our subject was married, November, 1859, to Sarah, daughter of Jacob and Elizabeth Baer, of Conewago Township, this county. By this union they have been blessed with four children: Albert, Henry B., Eli W. and an infant, deceased. Mr. Hoff is the owner of a valuable farm, well cultivated and improved. The village of Mt. Wolf, where Mr. Hoff resides, is built on land owned by his father, Henry Hoff.

SAMUEL M. HOFF, the founder of Mt. Wolf village, and the son of Henry and Mary (Moul) Hoff, of this township, was born February 16, 1833, and was reared on his father's farm. December 5. 1851, he married Sarah, daughter of George and Leah (Shindle) Lichtenberger, of Fairview Township, the result of the marriage being three children: Carlton L., George L. and an infant (deceased). The father of our subject, Henry Hoff, died in October, 1884, at the advanced age of eighty-nine years, a sincere member of the United Brethren Church of Mt. Wolf, of which he has always been a liberal supporter.

THE HÖCK (HAKE) FAMILY. An old family bible which has come down to the present, states: Jacob Höck (always written thus in the German) was born June 10, 1724, in Hanau Land, Holzhausen, Germany; his father was John Frederick Höck, and his mother was Anna Catharine Foobach ; she was born at Rothine, a small half hour from Holzhausen. The Provincial Council of Pennsylvania adopted a resolution September 14, 1727, that the Masters of Vessels transporting Germans and others from the Continent of Europe, take a list of emigrants "from whence they came." Those who could write were obliged to subscribe their names in their own hand. These lists are still preserved at Harrisburg. Some old deeds and writings, containing the signatures of our forefathers, have been preserved to the present, and comparing these with the ones on the lists at Harrisburg, we find they correspond to signatures on lists in the years of 1748 and 1749. "September 15, 1748, Foreigners imported in the Two Brothers, Thomas Arnott, Master, from Rotterdam, last from Portsmouth;" Jacob Höck. "September 26, 1749, Foreigners from Hanau, Wirtenberg, Darmstadt and Eisenberg, Ship Ranier, Henry Browning, Master, from Rotterdam last from England. 277 passengers;" John Frederick Höck, John Conrad Höck. The above facts show that our family immigrated to America in the years 1748 and 1749; Jacob Höck in 1748, and we have a number of reasons to believe he was the elder son; September 26, 1749, the father, John Frederick Höck, the founder of the family, and John Conrad, a son, probably the younger son. We have not been able to discover if they settled in York County immediately or not. We are inclined to believe they did. As early as April, 1752, we find a record, the baptism of a child of said Jacob Höck—Maria Barbra—born January 24, 1752, baptized April 26, 1752, at Christ Evangelical Lutheran Church, York. March 25, 1753, John Frederick Höck and wife, Anna Catharine, stood god-father and god-mother to the child of John Adam Schedle, a son, John Frederick, at same church. Among old papers still in possession of the family we find a draft of a tract of land No. 3048. This tract was formerly owned by Gottfried W. Noedel, of York, owned at present by Louis Zurn, of Philadelphia. From a deed we extract; "Michael Houck, by his deed poll of 5 August, 1755, for the consideration therein mentioned, did grant and convey all his right, title and interest of in and to a certain Improvement and tract of Land situate in Codorus Township unto a certain Frederick Heck. And the said Frederick Oblad Heck, an order to survey and lay out the same by his Application No. 3048 for 200 acres, bearing date at Philadelphia, 3 March, 1767. And whereas the said Frederick Heck afterward died intestate, being so seized of said Improvement, and Tract of Land and Order of Survey, together with other Land in said County of York, leaving lawful issue to survive him to witz: Conrad Heck, Jacob Heck and Phillipina, the wife of Phillip Wintermeyer. And whereas in pursuance of Application and Order of Survey aforesaid there was surveyed and laid out after the death of the said Frederick Heck, for the use of his issue (7 May, 1771,) aforesaid, the above recited Improvement and Tract of Land." The time of death of Frederick Höck, the father, we have not been able to determine definitely. He stood god-father to a child of his son-in-law, Phillip Wintermyer, on January 1, 1768. Letters of administration in common form were granted to Jacob Hake of the estate of Frederick Hake, late of York County, yeoman, deceased on September 9, 1770. Of the daughter Phillipina, wife of Phillip Wintermeyer, we have not been able to get much information. We have knowledge of two children: Anna Catharine, born December 8, 1767, and Susanna, born August 6, 1776, both baptized at Christ Evangelical Lutheran Church, York. The said Phillip Wintermeyer came to America October 25, 1748. He received tract No. 3048, by deed of release of Conrad Hake and Jacob Hake November 2, 1771. Sold the same to Peter Miller July 20, 1773. A tract of 164 acres was surveyed to him in Manchester Township April 9, 1778, in pursuance of a warrant dated the 24th day of March, 1767. Present owner of this tract, Samuel Glatfelter. The last assessment we can find of him in Manchester Township is 1801. Conrad Höck, one of the two sons and probably the younger son, arrived with his father, John Frederick, in America, as previously given, September 26, 1749. A warrant was taken out by said Conrad on February 24, 1767, for "about 200 acres situate in Dover (now Conewago) Township, including his improvement about four or five miles from York." This tract passed to his "eldest son," Christian, from him to his younger brother, Frederick, and by public sale after decease of Frederick to George Loucks, of West Manchester Township, on March 31, 1882, whose son, Israel Loucks of York, is present owner. Said Conrad was assessed to 150 acres in Dover (now Conewago Township) in 1780. In 1781 he was assessed to one lot in Carlisle, Cumberland County. In 1783 to one house and lot in same place. Made his will at Carlisle, February 7, 1785. Letters testamentary were issued in common form March 7, 1785, to Elizabeth (wife) and Jacob Greason. We extract from above will: "My eldest son, Christian Hick, shall have the profit of my plantation in Dover (now Conewago) Township, as long as his Mother lives " "My son, Frederick possess the House that I have in Carlisle during the life of his mother." "My son, Christian, shall have it in his choice to take either the plantation or house in Carlisle to possess." "My eldest daughter, Anna Maria Greaves." "Second daughter, Catharine Ottenberger." "Third daughter, Phillipina Hoofman." "Fourth daughter, Susanna Fisher." "Second" daughter Catharine, wife of Jacob Ottenberger, second husband Jacob Wiser, of Carlisle; "Third" daughter, wife of Nicholas Hoofman, lived in York County, Quickel's Church. Their children,

MANCHESTER TOWNSHIP.

were: John Jacob (eldest, born January,1780), John Phillip, Anna Maria, Susanna, Henry and Nicholas. Of Anna Maria Greaves, Catharine Ottenberger, afterward Wiser, and Susanna Fisher I have not learned anything. Christian, the "eldest son," was assessed to a farm in Dover Township in 1782-83; 1785-87 to a house and lot in Carlisle; 1788-89 to a farm in North Middletown Township, Cumberland County. He settled in Trumbull County, Ohio, but at what time I have not discovered. His children were Christian, who came from Ohio and married Elizabeth Hake, of the branch of Jacob Höck, and lived near Quickel's Church; their children living and dead are Susanna, wife of Benjamin Deardoff; Sarah, wife of Andrew Beuhler; Elizabeth, wife of Henry Loucks, and Samuel. The other children of Christian Hake, Sr., were Frederick, one of whose sons is Jesse S. Hake, superintendent of public instructions of Wayne County, Neb. The remaining children of Christian Hake, Sr., were George, Samuel, Elizabeth, Maria Barbra, wife of Samuel Wanemaker, and Catharine. The younger son of Conrad Höck, Frederick, who lived on the homestead, the farm now owned by Israel Loucks, of York, died April 12, 1830. The farm was sold March 31, 1832, and the family shortly after moved to Trumbull County, Ohio. The children were Elizabeth, John Phillip, Daniel, Frederick, John George; Catharine, wife of Michael Wire, Conrad, Samuel, David, Mary, wife of Jacob Holabush, and Jacob. John Phillip, Daniel, Frederick, John George and David or some of the descendants of each—live in Jefferson County, Wis. The children of Jacob were: Emanuel, Elizabeth, wife of Jacob Core, now living at Highspire, Dauphine County; John A. Hake, Pittsburgh, and Daniel J. Hake, of Middletown, Dauphin County. Jacob Höck, the other son who arrived in America, September 15, 1748, was born June 10, 1724—wife Susanna Dorothea. He received his naturalization papers of the supreme court held at Philadelphia, September 24, 1762, under King George III, king of England. "Before William Allen and William Coleman, Esqs., judges of the said court, between the Hours of 9 and 12 of the Clock in the Forenoon of the same Day, Jacob Heek, of Manchester, in the county of York, being a Foreigner, and having inhabited and resided for the Space of Seven Years in His Majesty's Colonies in America, and not having been absent out of some of the said Colonies for a longer Time than Two Months at any one Time during the said seven Years; and the said Jacob Heek having produced to the said Court a Certificate of his having taken the Sacrament of the Lord's Supper within Three Months before the said Court," etc. This interesting document was found among a number of old papers, which have passed down directly through the several generations, and are still in the possession of the family. The earliest record of said Jacob Höck, in York County, is the baptism of his daughter, Maria Barbra, April 26, 1752, at Christ Evangelical Lutheran Church, York. April 9, 1761, he bought of Sebastian Fink, of Dover Township, twenty acres of land "by little Conewago." February 23, 1762, he sold to George Stevenson, of York Town, Esq., " The plantation and tract of land whereon I lately dwelt, situate on branch of Codorus Creek, in Codorus Township." The same was surveyed to Tobias Amspoker in pursuance of warrant, dated at Philadelphia, March 9, 1753. He must have moved to Manchester Township from Codorus Township between April 9, 1761, and February 23, 1762. He made his will October 6, 1802. He signed a receipt December 10, 1802. This son, Andrew, received letters of administration November 2, 1803. His children were Maria Barbra, born January 24, 1752. Probably died without issue as she is not mentioned in the will. The other children, as given in the will, are Andrew, Frederick, "my daughter Lousia intermarried to Jacob Barr," "my daughter, Mary Elizabeth, intermarried with George Neyman." Of Lousia Hake, born September 9, 1761, the wife of Jacob Barr, I have not been able to learn anything. Mary Elizabeth Hake, born July 22, 1756, wife of George Neiman, who was born September 1, 1750. Their children were: Susanna, wife of Daniel Jacoby, moved to Somerset County, Penn., and from there to Ohio; Maria Elizabeth, wife of George Benedict; George, born January 30, 1782. His children living and dead are Catharine, wife of Jacob Hake, Manchester Township; Sarah, wife of David Maish; Levi Maish, ex-congressman, a son; Eliza, wife of Jacob Shettle; Elizabeth, wife of Samuel Shettle; John Neiman, York; George, Samuel R. and Adam R. Neiman, of Conewago Township; Mary, wife of Solomon Shettle; Rebecca, wife of Peter Atland; Lavina, wife of Henry Hoofman; Susanna, wife of Jacob Rudy,and Leah, wife of William Metzger. Michael, born February 16, 1785, no information. Jacob's descendants were living in and by Indianopolis. Maria Catharine was born December 9, 1786, wife of John Jacoby; descendants are: Rebecca, wife of John Ginter; Catharine, wife of Henry Fink; Leah, wife of Jacob Miller; Eli Miller, of York, a son; Eliza, wife of Christian Miller; Lydia, wife of John Charleston, and John Jacoby. Andrew Neiman was born November 5, 1790; his children were: Jacob; Mary Ann, wife of Daniel Gross; Andrew, Leah; William, husband of Susanna Hake, and Levi. Margret was born August 25, 1794, wife of Peter Boose; children living and dead are Elizabeth, wife of John Zimmerman; John, Peter, Mrs. Daniel Hake, York, a daughter; Jacob and Catharine, wife of Jacob Christine. Mary was the wife of Jacob Meisenhelder; their children were Elizabeth, widow of John Spar; Mary Ann, wife of Peter Boyer; Catharine, wife of ———— Wynkoop; Emanuel, Samuel, one of whose sons is Dr. Meisenhelder, of York; Lavinia, wife of John Shellabarger. Jacob Höck, a brother to Conrad Höck, who died at Carlisle 1785, had two sons: Andrew and John Frederick. Andrew was the elder; born March 13, 1754; baptized at Christ Evangelical Lutheran Church, York; his children were in the order of their age: Anna Mary, Jacob, Andrew, Frederick, Susanna Catharine; Simon, John, Elizabeth, Salome and Sarah. The children of Anna Mary, the wife of Sebastian Fink, were Allen, Sarah, the wife of Jacob Zest, and Anna Maria, the wife of David Cocklin. Jacob Hake; wife, Anna Mary Copenhafer, their children in order of age: John; Mary, the wife of Adam Free; Jacob; Leah, the wife of Jacob Fahs; Sarah, the wife of Frederick Schindle; Frederick; Elizabeth, wife of John Reeser; Catharine, wife of Peter Good; Daniel; Susanna, the wife of William Neiman; Elias and Lousia Anna, who died single. They reside, or some of the descendants—John, Jacob. Henry, Mrs. Frederick Schindle, Mrs. Peter Good, Mrs. William Neiman—in Manchester Township; Mrs. Adam Free, Mrs. Jacob Fahs, Frederick and Daniel Hake, in York; Mrs. John Reeser, Conewago; Andrew and Elias Hake, in Fairview Township. Next in age to Jacob was Andrew, who moved to Baltimore a good many years ago. His descendants write their name Hack. Their children were Augustus A.; William A.; Frederick A.; Elizabeth, wife of David Ruthraff; Mary A., wife of Morris J. Jones. Next in age, Frederick, who lived in Conewago Township. His children, living and dead, are: Sallie, wife of John Schindle; Andrew; Elizabeth, wife of Deweese Beck; Julia, wife of Abraham McNeal; John, Henry and William Hake. Next in order of age

Susanna, wife of Jacob Wilt, had two daughters. Leah, the wife of William Tyler, one of whose daughters—Margaret, the widow of John B. Eversole—lives at Middletown, Dauphin County. The other daughter of Jacob Wilt was Julia, the wife of George W. Geiselman. Next in age, Catharine, wife of Henry Grove; they had two children: Henry Hake Grove, one of whose sons is Dr. Eugene Grove, of Carlisle, and Susanna C., the wife of Rev. John Ulrich. Simon was the next in age, who probably died without issue. Next in order of age was John, who moved to Baltimore at an early day, and his descendants write their name Hack. His children, living and dead, are: Susanna; Mary Anna, wife of James H. Warner; John W.; Orlando V.; Oliver F. Hack, attorney, Baltimore; Elizabeth, Andrew C. and George W. Hack. Next in order of age was Elizabeth, wife of Christian Hake, grandson of Conrad Höck; their children, living and dead, are Susanna, wife of Benjamin Deardoff; Sarah, wife of Andrew Beuhler; Elizabeth, wife of Henry Loucks; Samuel and Andrew. Salome, next in age, probably died without issue. Sarah, the youngest, wife of Joseph Kroft; their children, living and dead, are Mary Ann, wife of Eli Free; Washington, Hack, Oliver, John Andrew, Frederick Augustus, Sarah and Amanda. The younger of the two sons of Jacob Höck, John Frederick and brother to Andrew, whose descendants we have enumerated, was born June 5, 1759. We give his descendants as far as we have been able to learn. Jacob is probably the eldest; two children: Leah, wife of Michael Gross, and Daniel Hake, Manchester Borough. Henry, who lived at McKnightstown, Adams County, had two children: Peter and Harriet, both died without issue. Anna Maria, wife of George Gross; their children, living and dead, are Adam, George, John, Anna Mary and Elizabeth. John, one child—Leah, widow of Jacob Eppley, Manchester Borough. Next in age two daughters: Susanna and Sarah, no knowledge of any descendants. Frederick, known as "Captain," moved to Lynchburg, Va., about 1825 or 1830. His children were, as far as we have been able to learn, Helen Mary, wife of Mr. Thomas; Susanna, wife of Mr. Oaks; Frederick and Annie. Elizabeth, wife of George Smith, a daughter of said John Frederick; their descendants, living and dead, are: Sarah, wife of Thomas Bennett; Samuel, Daniel and Elizabeth. Peter, the last we have to enumerate of the children of John Frederick Hake, lived at McKnightstown, where the most of his descendants still live. His children, living and dead, are: Henry, Peter, James, Matilda, William A. Abraham and Anna Mary, wife of Aaron Loher.

E. G. HAKE, M. D.

FRANKLIN L. JACOBS, born in Lower Windsor Township, June 11, 1851. is the eldest son of William and Mary (Landes) Jacobs, natives of York County, and of English and German descent. He lived with his parents, working some at farming, but before he was twenty-one he learned the trades of cigar-maker and plasterer, and has followed both trades since. He began business for himself in his native township, when about twenty-one years of age. He was married, September 24, 1874, to Annie E. Paff, daughter of Amos Paff of Hellam Township, and has had four children, one—Horace C., died in infancy; the living are Mary Estella, William Garfield and Ivy Rebecca. He removed to Manchester Borough in the spring of 1875, and has since been engaged in the manufacturing of cigars, employing a few hands, and making 150,000 cigars per annum. His plastering work is done under contract, and he does most of the first class work in his neighborhood. He has held the offices of inspector of elections and auditor of Manchester Borough; was elected chief burgess of Manchester Borough in the spring of 1884, and is an active Republican. He belongs to the Evangelical Association.

JOHN JACOBY was born October 22, 1819, on the place now owned and occupied by him, and where he has spent his life. His parents were David and Elizabeth (Miller) Jacoby, of York County, Penn., who reared three sons and one daughter. John was the youngest child and lost his father, when he was only fifteen years old. He grew up on the farm and attended the public schools. October 15, 1844, he was married in Manchester Township to Catharine, daughter of John E. Frantz, and has had fifteen children, four of whom have died: two unnamed infants; Catharine, a baby, and John at the age of twenty years. The living are Lewis, a carpenter; Henry, a butcher; Elizabeth; Sarah, married to Daniel Shettle; William, a butcher; Adam, a carpenter; Amanda, married to Alfred Shoop; Anna; Samuel, a butcher; Augustus, and Alfred, a merchant at York. Mr. Jacoby and wife belong to the Lutheran Church. For about thirty years he was engaged in butchering, but gave it up in 1878. He owns a fine farm of forty-eight acres, where he now lives, and some woodland in Conewago Township. What he has he has earned by the sweat of his brow.

LEWIS JACOBY, carpenter and builder, was born in Manchester Township. York Co., Penn., August 19, 1844, eldest son of John and Catherine (Frantz) Jacoby, who were parents of fifteen children, eleven of whom are now living: Lewis, Henry, Elizabeth, Sarah, William, Adam, Amanda, Anna, Samuel, Augustus and Alfred. Our subject was reared on his father's farm and has always lived in this township. He began learning his trade in York, Penn., in 1862, and started business for himself in 1880. Since he began contracting for the erection of buildings he has all the work he can attend to, and has built nearly every house in the village of New Prospect, on Cemetery Hill, near York, Penn. December 25, 1868, he married Adeline Myers, daughter of Peter and Sallie (Hummer) Myers, of Dover Township, and this union has been blessed with five children: Mary Alice, Adelia E., James Latimer. Laura E. (deceased) and Margaret Lucretia. Mr. Jacoby is a member of the Lutheran Church.

H. C. KAUFFMAN is a son of Henry and Rebecca (Heininger) Kauffman of Manchester Township, where our subject was born October 3, 1858. He received a common school education, and began the business of manufacturing cigars in September, 1881, in Manchester Borough. He gives constant employment to eighteen hands. February 19, 1880, Mr. Kauffman married Annie Schroll, daughter of Samuel and Anna (Snyder) Schroll, of Manchester Township. Two children have been born to them, Harry A. and Marcus L. His parents still live in this township, where they were born; his grandfather was also a native of York County—so that his ancestors were among the pioneer settlers of Manchester Township. Mr. Kauffman, although a young man, has been very successful in his business.

ALEXANDER KLINDINST, son of Daniel and Leah (Shindle) Klindinst, was born June 28, 1862, in York, Penn. He was reared on his father's farm, and attended the public schools of his native township, also three terms at the Emigsville Academy; began teaching school at Eisenhart's schoolhouse, Manchester Township; after teaching two terms removed to York to accept a responsible business position in the firm of E. K. Emig & Co. November 27, 1884, Mr. Klindinst married Katie A. Smyser, daughter of Augustus and Catherine (Schriver) Smyser, of Manchester Township. Mr. Klindinst is a young man of pleasing address, conscientious in the discharge of his duty, steady in his habits, trustworthy and esteemed by all who know him. He is a member of Christ Evangelical Lutheran Church of York, Penn., the E. M. R. A. and E. L. and R. C., of Emigsville.

HENRY KOHR, is the second son of Henry and Lydia (Stauffer) Kohr, of York, and was born in Manchester Township, October 29, 1833. He was reared a farmer and married Mary, daughter of George and Eve (Fink) Bower. This lady died October 9, 1880, the mother of four children: George, Augustus, Emma and Stephen. Our subject next married Isabella, daughter of Emanuel and Sarah (Zorger) Good, of Manchester Township. Our subject resides at Mount Wolf, where he is highly esteemed by his neighbors.

ADAM KOHR, born in Emigsville, November 14, 1834, is the eldest son of Lewis and Rebecca (Westhafer) Kohr, natives of York and Dauphin Counties, and of German descent. His father was a miller, farmer, distiller, tavern-keeper, etc., in his time, and died in 1861, aged sixty-four years. Adam Kohr was educated in the public schools of Emigsville, and has always followed farming. He was married at York, January 18, 1859, to Mary Fink, a native of York County, and daughter of John Fink, of German descent. They have had two children: Eli, died in 1875, aged sixteen years; and Hyman F., a school teacher and student at Newark, N. J., Commercial School. Mr. Kohr is a member of the church of the United Brethren in Christ, and has been trustee of Bethany Chapel, Emigsville, since 1871. He was director of the poor of York County from 1877 to 1880, and is an active Democrat. He removed to his present place of abode, an eighteen-acre farm, from an 118-acre farm, which he still owns near Emigsville. He also owns a small farm in Newberry Township. He has one brother in Illinois, and one in Michigan.

ZACHARIAH KOHR, born near Emigsville, August 18, 1851, is the youngest of ten children of Lewis and Rebecca (Westhafer) Kohr. He was reared on a farm near Emigsville, and educated at the common schools, until twenty years of age, when he began work at the trade of shoe-making, which he has followed since in connection with the cultivation of a farm of seventy-seven acres. His mother resides with him. He was married in York County, November 14, 1876, to Dollie Smith, daughter of Jacob Smith. They have two children: Allen Jacob and Edward Lewis. He is a member of the church of the United Brethren in Christ, and is treasurer of the church at Emigsville. In politics he is a Democrat.

WILLIAM S. KUNKLE, auditor of York County, was born April 7, 1843, in Manchester Borough. His parents were George and Mary (Bull) Kunkle, natives of York County, who had seven children, of whom three are dead—William S. being next to the eldest living. He lived mostly on the farm, was educated at the public schools, and learned something of the carpenter's trade, before he became of age. In 1862 he enlisted at York in a nine months' regiment. From 1865 to 1868 he kept a livery stable at York. In 1867, he was married at York to Miss Owens, of Adams County, Penn. He belongs to the order of I. S. of A., and holds the office of Master of Forms, and has at different times held all the chairs. In 1875 he was elected constable, and held the office five years; he was elected county auditor in 1881, and served one term. In 1882 he was elected school director. At present he is engaged in raising Havana tobacco, and works also at carpentering. He is an active Democrat

JABOB LICHTY was born in Manchester Township December 4, 1828. His parents, Michael Lichty and Hannah Forringer, natives of Lancaster County, and of German descent, married and brought up their children in York County. Michael Lichty died when subject was but three years old, leaving the widow and three children, subject being the youngest. The latter worked for different farmers until he was nineteen years old, when he began work at the trade of cooper. This he abandoned in 1858, and farmed until 1863, when he embarked in the mercantile business in New Holland, where he has since lived. He was educated in the public schools, and one term in York County Academy. He was married to Mary Wolf, a daughter of Adam Wolf, of New Holland, and had nine children, two of whom are dead. He is an active Republican, and has been a member of the Republican county committee. He farms a small place of twenty-five acres, and carries a stock of general merchandise.

GEORGE LICHTENBERGER, retired farmer, is the son of George and Mary (Laucks) Lichtenberger, and was born in Manchester Township September 8, 1829. He was reared on the home farm and attended the public schools. He married Phebe M., daughter of Samuel and Ann (McGary) Prowell, of Fairview Township, the result of the union being six children: Carrie (deceased), Edward, William, Maggie, Annie and George (deceased). Our subject's paternal grandfather, Casper Lichtenberger, married Catherine Nieman, who bore him the following children: George, Rudolph, Benjamin, Henry, Samuel and Eva. Our subject's mother is still living at the ripe age of eighty-five, and is the mother of the following children: Henry, Sarah (deceased), Margaret (deceased), Elizabeth (deceased), Samuel, Mary (deceased), Leah, Jesse (deceased) and George.

SAMUEL LIGHTNER was born in Manchester Township April 18, 1828, and died April 3, 1881. His parents were Charles and Sarah (Myers) Lightner, of York County, and of German descent. They were married in Lancaster, Penn., August 9, 1821, and had six children—three sons and three daughters—of whom Samuel was the fourth child and second son. He was brought up on the farm and educated at the York Academy. Nathaniel Lightner purchased the tract of land lying about a mile and a half north from Harrisburg road, from Penn; it descended to Nathaniel second, then came to his son George, then to his son Charles, then to the subject of this sketch. Samuel Lightner was married, in Manchester, November 12, 1863, to Barbara M. Herman, of the same township, daughter of Emanuel Herman, of English descent. They had one son, Harry G., who is a farmer and at home. They were all brought up in the Lutheran Church. Samuel entered the army November, 1862, as second lieutenant of Company A, One Hundred and Sixty-sixth Pennsylvania Volunteer Infantry, and served nine months. He participated in the defense of Suffolk, at Somerton Road, and in the expedition up the peninsula. While in service he contracted disease, which resulted in his death.

ALBERT C. LIGHTNER was born in Manchester Township, January 24, 1855. His parents, George and Anna Mary (Ebert) Lightner, were natives of York County, and of German descent, and had two sons and one daughter. Albert C. is the second and only one of the three now living. He grew to manhood on the farm, was educated in the common schools of West Manchester Township, supplemented by a thorough course in York Academy. He was married in West Manchester Township, December 24, 1878, to Isabel E. Sprenkle, a native of that township, and daughter of George W. Sprenkle, farmer, and of German descent. February 28, 1879, he removed from West Manchester to his farm where he now resides. His farm is situated in Manchester Township, about one mile north of York, and was bought from Penn by one

BIOGRAPHICAL SKETCHES.

of Mr. Lightner's great ancestors, and has remained in the Lightner family ever since. He was brought up in the Lutheran Church, and belongs to that denomination in York, Penn. He is a Republican in politics, devotes his entire time to the farming interest, and is one of the educated farmers of York County.

ALEXANDER W. LOUCKS was born June 1, 1845, and is the eldest son of Zachariah K. Loucks. His early life was spent principally at the schools. His primary education he received at the York County Academy, supplemented by a thorough course at Eastman's National Business College at Poughkeepsie, N. Y., from which he returned in 1864. From that time he assisted his father in business until 1867, when he took charge of his father's mill and farm, about one mile north of York on the Codorus Creek, to which he has given his entire attention ever since. February 5, 1867, he was married, in York, to Catherine Wanbaugh, a native of York, and a daughter of John and Mary Ann Wanbaugh. Four children were born to them: Annie Mary Kate, Henry John, William Ebert and Isabella Lydia. Mr. Loucks and his wife are members of Zion Lutheran Church, of York. Mr. Loucks has held different offices to which he was elected, such as inspector and school director. In politics he is an active Republican, and has served as member of the central county committee, and as a delegate to the county convention.

JAMES C. MAY, M. D., was born in Dover Township, York County, January 14, 1858. His parents were John B. and Caroline (Leatheny) May, of York County, and of German descent. They reared a family of four sons and three daughters, of whom James C. is the second. He remained on the farm until his fifteenth year, and attended the common schools and the York County Academy; at the age of seventeen he began teaching in the public schools. After teaching four terms he entered the office of Dr. Kain, at Manchester, and at the end of two years went to Jefferson Medical College, at Philadelphia, where he graduated in March, 1881. Returning to Manchester he formed a partnership with his preceptor, and began practicing at once. In the spring of 1884, he bought the interest of his partner, and has since been practicing for himself. All his time is devoted to his profession. In October, 1882, he was married, in Columbia, Penn., to Ellen M. Yinger, a native of Manchester. They have one child—a boy. Both are members of the Lutheran Church. Dr. May has served as school director for Manchester Borough.

ZACHARIAS METZGER, eldest of eight children of John and Elizabeth (Wilt) Metzger, was born March 21, 1823, on the old Metzger homestead, in Manchester Township. He was reared to farming and November 30, 1848, married Maria Feiser, daughter of Jacob and Catharine (Bupp) Feiser. Three children blessed this marriage: Mary E. (wife of Abraham Hartman), Louisa C. (deceased) and Rev. John A. Metzger. Our subject's great-grandfather, George Metzger, was the first of this name that settled in Manchester Township, on the Altland farm, near the village of Manchester. He was among the first settlers in this township.

SAMUEL R. MILLER was born in Conewago Township, September 13, 1834. His parents were Samuel and Lydia Ann (Rudy) Miller, of York County and of English and German descent. They had seven children—four sons and three daughters—of whom Samuel R. is the third child and second son. He was brought up on a farm, but also worked at milling and carpentering. His education he received at the common schools. At the outbreak of the late war, he enlisted in Company E, Sixteenth Pennsylvania Volunteers, a three-months' regiment. On his return home from the service he re-enlisted on the twenty-fourth of August, 1861, in Company E, Eighty-seventh Pennsylvania Volunteer infantry for three years. He was in the battles of Winchester, Locust Grove, Mine Run, Wilderness, Spottsylvania, Cold Harbor and front of Petersburg. In June, 1863, he was captured at Winchester, and for twenty-one days he was a prisoner at Belle Isle, and Libby prison; he jumped his parole, and after a French furlough, returned to his regiment. June 23, 1864, he was captured again in front of Petersburg, held in different prisons, including Andersonville, where he was kept until Sherman's army appeared. From there he was taken to other prisons: Blackshear, Thomasville, Albany (Ga.), and on Christmas, 1864, back to Andersonville again. April 8, 1865, he left Andersonville for Albany again, marched seventy-two miles to Thomasville, then to Baldwin, where he was finally released, and at the end of two weeks started for home, where he arrived June 15, 1865, after an absence of nearly four years. In 1866 he started for Ohio, but stopped a few months at Goshen, Ind., where he remained peddling pumps until the following spring, when he went to Ohio, where he farmed a few months, and then returned home. He was married in December, 1872, at York, to Rebecca Siffert. They have three children: Laura Jane, Edward and an infant. They settled at Round Town, about three and one-half miles northwest of York, in 1880. Mr. Miller is a Republican, was constable in 1875 and 1876, and was also tax collector for township and school at the same time.

SAMUEL MYERS, son of Samuel and Elizabeth (Shelley) Myers, was the fourth of eight children, born on the 25th of December, 1802, at the old Myers' homestead, near where he now lives. He was reared on his father's farm and always followed farming. In 1829 Mr. Myers was married to Mary Ann Blausser, daughter of Matthias and Elizabeth (Bahn) Blausser, of Spring Garden Township. Ten children were born of this marriage: Samuel, Elizabeth (wife of Christian Brubaker), Mary (wife of Tobias Engle), Henry (deceased), Zacharias, Susan (deceased), wife of Jeremiah Shelley), Cassia (deceased), Ellen (wife of Amos Hively), Charles, and Eli (deceased). Mr. Myers is one of the oldest citizens of Manchester Township. He is held in high esteem by his neighbors; was director of the poor for York County in 1830-31-32.

EDMUND B. MYERS was born in this township, October 3, 1829. His parents, Benjamin and Louisa (Smyser) Myers (the latter, a daughter of Jacob and Elizabeth Smyser, of West Manchester Township), were married February 28, 1828, and had a family of seven children: Edmund B., Alexander A. (deceased), Andrew J., Albert S. (deceased), Eli S. (deceased), Ellen E. and Louisa S. (deceased). His mother's ancestors, the Smysers, were among the very first settlers in West Manchester Township. Margaret Smyser (wife of Christian Eyster), was probably the first white woman that settled in West Manchester Township. She and her husband located in the vicinity of Wolf's Church, where they took up 600 acres of land, October 30, 1736, as shown by the records in the surveyor-general's office, at Harrisburgh, Penn., The treaty of session was made October 11, 1736. Edmund B. Myers has traveled extensively; has made an extended trip through Europe, and two trips to California. He has recently become widely known throughout the entire country in connection with the wonderful cures effected by him, by what is known as electro-vital nervaura, or laying on of hands (without medicine). Many in-

MANCHESTER TOWNSHIP.

valids who failed to get relief from the best physicians of New York, Philadelphia and other cities, came to him, and in many instances have gone away in perfect health.

ANDREW J. MYERS was born February 6, 1833, in Manchester Township, near Emigsville, upon the same place now occupied by him, and which was occupied by his father and grandfather. His parents were Benjamin and Louisa (Smyser) Myers, of York County, and of German descent. They reared four sons and one daughter, and buried two children. Andrew J. is the third son. He grew up on his father's farm, but after he became twenty-three years of age learned the miller's trade, which he followed for six years. He attended the common schools, and had one term at the York Academy. After giving up milling, he re-

Edmund B. Myers

sumed farming. January 24, 1860, he was married, at Jackson Township, to Mary Ann, daughter of Daniel Smyser. They had six children, of whom one, Lillie, died in her second year. The living are Allen, Jane (wife of Caleb Wogan), Lucy, Kurvin and Minnie. They are Lutherans. Mr. Myers has repeatedly held positions of trust, such as inspector, school director, and appraiser of merchandise. He is an active Democrat, and one of the organizers of the Drovers & Mechanics National Bank, and is yet a prominent stockholder. He also served five years as director and treasurer of the Paradise Mutual Fire Insurance Company. He is one of the firm of Emig, Ruby & Co., manufacturers of cigars and dealers in leaf tobacco at Emigsville, employing about twenty-five hands. He owns and works a farm of 150 acres, and also owns eight dwelling houses at Emigsville. His father died in 1880, aged seventy-one years.

JOHN B. PFALTZGRAFF is the second child of George and Eleanora (Braumer) Pfaltzgraff, and was born in Conewago Township, October 14, 1835. He was reared on the home farm, was educated at the public schools, and in 1856 married Susan, daughter of Henry Keeney, of Shrewsbury Township. Nine children have been born to this union, viz.: Elizabeth, Henry (deceased), John, Ellen, Leah, George, Annie, Joseph (deceased) and Susan (deceased). In 1865 Mr. Pfaltzgraff was elected county auditor, and served one full term, giving entire satisfaction to the people, who, in 1875, called him to the responsible office of county commissioner, which he filled for one term equally to the satisfaction of both parties. The parents of Mr. Pfaltzgraff were members of the German Baptist Church, while Mr. Pfaltzgraff is a member of the I. O. of R. M. and of the K. of P.

HENRY B. PFALTZGRAFF was born in Manchester Township May 10, 1854. His parents were George B. and Eleanora (Braumer) Pfaltzgraff, of Germany, who came to America soon after being married. They lived in Baltimore one year, and then removed to Conewago Township, where they remained only a few years, and then removed to York Borough, where they lived several years, and then removed to Manchester Township, about three miles west of York, where the father died in 1873. They had a family of six sons and five daughters, Henry B. was next to the youngest. As he grew old enough he began the pottery trade with his father, but in 1869 he commenced to manufacture pottery on his own account. For six years he manufactured red ware, and then removed his works to where they are now located, near the old homestead of his father. He employs four hands in manufacturing stone ware, to the amount of from 50,000 to 100,000 gallons annually. He receives the clay for his wares from New Jersey, and makes none but the best of goods. He also runs a small farm of forty acres. In 1878 he was married, at York, to Elizabeth Bentzel, who died September 25, 1881, leaving two children: Lucy and Elizabeth. October 2, 1882, he married, at Mount Wolf, Arabella Kohr, from which union two children issued: Henry and Isaac. Mr. Pfaltzgraff belongs to the Dunkard Church, is a Democrat in politics, and was a delegate to the county convention in 1883.

REV. WILLIAM S. PORR was born in Pottsville, Penn., February 19, 1830. His parents were Lewis and Lydia (Zeigler) Porr, who had four sons and four daughters, of whom subject was the eldest son. His father was a tailor, and William S. worked some at the same trade. When quite a small boy his father moved to Bernville, Berks Co., Penn. In his boyhood he spent much of his time with his grandfather at Reading, where he attended the common schools, and at the age of sixteen went to Stouchesburg Academy, where he remained two years, and thence went to Gettysburgh College, where he spent two years. On account of ill health he left, however, and prosecuted the study of theology privately, at Pottsville, under Rev. D. Steck, D. D. In 1854 he was admitted to the synod and licensed to preach. His first charge was Ashland, Penn., where he remained three years, then Harrisburgh three years; Palmyra, four years; Centre Hall, Centre County, nine years; Lancaster, six years; Steelton, two years; in 1882 he came to Manchester, Penn.; has charge of three churches, and preaches in English and German. His father was German, but his mother was born in Pennsylvania. He was married, July 21, 1855, at Shaefferstown, Penn., to Henrietta, daughter of Tobias Fernsler, of German descent. They had six children, three of whom are now living: Theodore N., William H. and John Luther. Rev. Porr is an indefatigable worker in the church, and has organized a number of congregations, built and remodeled and beautified a number of churches, and was instrumental in bringing a number of able men into the Gospel ministry, among whom are Revs. J. Harpster, now in Ohio; M. Fernsler and S. G. Shanon.

DAVID S QUICKEL was born in Manchester Township April 6, 1837. His parents were Henry and Magdalene (Strickler) Quickel, of York County, and of Dutch descent. The Quickel family in York County, descend from Michael Quickel, the founder of Quickel's Church, in Conewago Township, about the middle of the eighteenth century. David S. had two brothers and three sisters, of whom he is the eldest. He grew up on a farm and enjoyed the advantages of the common schools. While yet young he commenced to read medicine, but abandoned it and took up dentistry, which he followed up to 1869. He was married at Manchester, in 1860, to Leah Ginter, and in 1864 moved to Ohio, where he remained only one year, and then returned to Manchester, where he engaged at once in dentistry. He was appointed postmaster in 1869, and has held the office fourteen years. In 1872 he engaged in mercantile business, which he has followed since, gradually retiring from business, however, since 1880. In 1873 he took up dentistry again, which he intends to follow in the future. He had four children, of whom three are living: Annie M., Daniel S., and Harry David. Being a Republican he has held the position of township clerk for twenty years. He was also one of the incorporators of Manchester Borough. In 1869 his little boy was burned to death, and in his efforts to save him, the father was severely burned, disabling him for four years.

HENRY H. QUICKEL was born in Manchester Township May 2, 1846. His parents were Henry and Magdalene Quickel. Henry H. was the second son and the fourth of the children. He was reared on the farm and educated at the public schools. He lived with his parents until he was twenty-eight years of age. On the 1st of November, 1874, he was married in Hellam Township to Annie S. Stoner, and has three children: Edgar Stoner, Elmer David, and Cora Ellen. From the spring of 1881 to 1883 he was engaged in milling; also in dealing in grain, coal, lime, phosphates, etc., at Hellam Station, in partnership with L. S. Stoner. In the spring of 1888, he removed to his farm, about one and three-quarter miles north of York, containing about fifty-four acres. He is an active Republican.

WILLIAM REESER was born in Manchester Township September 2, 1814. His parents were William and Elizabeth (Shelley) Reeser, of Pennsylvania, and of German descent. They reared a family of six sons and one daughter, of whom William Jr. was the third child, and second son. He grew to manhood on the farm, and engaged in distilling. In Newberry Township he learned the milling trade, and worked at it about six years. In 1840 he was married, in Manchester Township, to Elizabeth Good, daughter of Henry Good, a German. They had eleven children, one, Mary, the wife of Tobias Quickel, died at the age of twenty-eight years; Louisa, Mary, Henry, John, Eli, Amanda, William, Benjamin, Amos, Augustus and Edward. Mr. Reeser was county commissioner from 1864 to 1867; is a very active Democrat, a very industrious man. and has besides his farm of 134 acres, considerable property.

HENRY REESER, a retired farmer, is the son of William and Elizabeth (Shelley) Reeser, was born in this township in February, 1829, and is the sixth of the following family: John, Mary, William, Elizabeth (deceased), Alexander, Henry and George. Our subject's first marriage was to Eliza Burger, daughter of Samuel and Elizabeth (Fortenbaugh) Burger. and to this union were born six children: William (deceased), Joseph, Susan, John (deceased), David and Henry. His second marriage was to Mary, daughter of Daniel and Mary (Nicholas) Hoppes, and this union has been blessed with three children: Hiram, Morris and Bertha. The second Mrs. Reeser was the widow of Jacob Test, to whom she had born three children: Ida J., William H. and Mary A. Mr. Reeser, through his own industry, has become the owner of two superior farms in his native township, and for some years has led a retired life in the borough of Manchester.

ZEBULON P. RODES, eldest child of Daniel and Susanna (Palmer) Rodes, was born February 28, 1834, and still resides in the house built by his grandfather, Christian Rodes, son of John Rodes, the pioneer of Manchester Township. In March, 1856, our subject married Sarah Zorger, daughter of Samuel Zorger, of Newberry Township, and by this marriage have been born to him five children: John M., Samuel (deceased), Christian, Rufus R. and Jesse J. Mr. Rodes is a warm friend of educational projects, and is a worshiper at the United Brethren Church.

CHARLES J. ROLAND, artist, is the son of Daniel and Ellen (Busey) Roland, of Manchester Township, and was born in York, February 16, 1857. He divided his earlier years between attending the public schools, working on the farm, and assisting his father in quarrying stone, and finished his literary education at the Emigsville Academy. He then turned his attention to house painting, which occupation he followed for seven years, although his inclinations led him toward art. for which he seemed especially gifted. He went under instruction to a Mr. H. Barrett, of York, and then took two courses at the Academy of the Fine Arts, Philadelphia, painting in oil and modeling in clay from life. He is one of the best crayon artists in the interior of the State, and is constantly and lucratively employed at his chosen profession. He has been a member of the P. O. and S. of A. and of the E. M. R. A., of Emigsville, his present post-office address.

GEORGE RUTTER, son of John and Elizabeth (Brillinger) Rutter, was born in Manchester Township, June 16, 1827. His boyhood days were spent on the farm and in attending the subscription schools. At the age of twenty-four years he began farming his father's farm, containing 167 acres, which he now owns. It is in a high state of cultivation, and produces all the cereals in abundant crops. Mr. Rutter devotes a great deal of attention to stock raising and fattening cattle for the markets. During Gen. Early's occupancy of York a squad of Confederates took his horses during harvest time; he was thus compelled to hitch a pair of green mules together with a horse to the reaper; they became unmanageable, and ran away; the reaper passed over Mr. Rutter and crippled him for life. Mr. Rutter was married in York, November 30, 1851, to Anna Mary, daughter of Charles Diehl. There were born to them eight children, three of whom are deceased. The living are George D., Jacob Charles, Edwin S., Albert C., Leah E., the only daughter living, is married to Philip Burg, of Hellam Township. Mr. Rutter and his family are members of the Lutheran Church. His father died March 13, 1868, aged seventy-two years four months and twenty-six days, and his mother died on the same day of the same month, 1879, aged seventy-nine years and eleven months.

SAMUEL RUTTER, the eighth child of John and Elizabeth (Brillinger) Rutter, was born June 15, 1835, and was reared on the farm which he still occupies. The homestead comprising 232 acres, is the joint property of our subject and his brother, is highly cultivated and is improved with a fine residence, barns and all the modern improvements. Mr. Rutter was one of the first to introduce blooded stock into the county and is a pioneer in the breeding of short-horn cattle. November 17, 1867, he married Emma J. daughter of Herman and Elizabeth (Free) Hoke, and has had born to him the following children: John H., Lizzie Ellen, James E. (deceased), Thomas B. (deceased, April 8, 1885) and Jennie May.

JOHN S. SCHISLER, son of John and Liddie (Shenberger) Schisler, was born December 20, 1828, in Windsor Township, and was reared to farming. The mother of our subject was the daughter of George and Mary (Zeigler) Shenberger, of Lower Windsor Township. In 1856 Mr. Schisler married Harriet, daughter of Daniel Brunaw of Conewago Township. Mr. Schisler has had born to him by this marriage four children, viz.: Henry (deceased), an infant (deceased), John and Sarah Ann. The Schisler schoolhouse, in Springfield Township, stands on the farm once owned by our subject's grandfather. Mr. Schisler is a consistent member of the Brethren Church. Grandfather Schisler emigrated from Europe and was well known as a teamster from York Haven to Baltimore; probably in the hottest contest of the Revolution, while on his way to Baltimore with a load of produce he was pressed to do service for the army. Subject's father, John Schisler, was born in 1800, and was married four times; first to Lydia Shenberger, of Lower Windsor; second to Magdelena Myers, of Springfield Township; third to Ester Sipe, of Newberry Township; fourth to Teeny Hildebrand, of Springfield Township; he had fourteen children born to him by the four marriages.

JOHN SHEPP, son of John and Elizabeth (Slagle) Shepp, of German descent, was born in West Manchester Township, Christmas day, 1834, and is the eighth child of a family of sixteen children—eight sons and eight daughters—six of whom are yet living. He remained at home until eighteen years of age, when he began to learn the trade of a miller with G. W. Lightner, at Brillinger's Mill, continuing three years as an apprentice and afterward worked there for a period of nine years as chief miller. For a number of years he worked in the Codorus Mills and in 1871 took charge of Myers' Mill on the Codorus Creek for P. A. & S. Small, and has shown great skill and ability in managing its interests ever since. He was married at the age of twenty-one, in Manchester Township, to Leah, daughter of Anthony Dessenberg. Their children are as follows: Henry C., cigar-maker; Susanna, wife of Franklin Dillinger, a miller; Mary Ellen, wife of Henry Strickler; Elizabeth Jane; John Wesley, a miller; Henry C., a teacher in the public schools. Mr. Shepp and family are members of the United Brethren Church, of which he has been a class leader for twenty years, and served one term as a school director of his township. He was one of the organizers and is a director of the Pleasureville Building and Loan Association and owns a fine property in that village. John Shepp, father of our subject, was born in West Manchester Township in 1798; was a farmer, and died in 1856; subject's mother was born in 1801 and died in 1872.

DANIEL SMYSER (deceased) was born in Manchester Township, about 1807, and was married, November 25, 1841, to Sarah Ann Herman, daughter of Jacob and Sarah Herman, of West Manchester Township. Five children were born to this marriage: Amanda M., Albert, Emma J., Sarah E. and Jacob H. Mrs. Smyser was the second child of Jacob and Sarah Herman. Her elder brother, Adam, and a younger sister, Catherine, compose the family (see sketch of the Smyser family, for Daniel Smyser's ancestral history).

EDWARD SMYSER was born in December, 1837, in Manchester Township. His parents were George and Susanna (Brillinger) Smyser (of German descent),who had three sons and six daughters, of whom Edward is the eldest. He was brought up on a farm and educated at the public schools. At the age of twenty he began farming for himself; from 1860 to 1878 he was also engaged in the lime business, and made more lime in that time than any other one man. In 1878 he engaged in the lumber business in York and Lancaster Counties, and in 1882, also in Baltimore County, Md., in partnership with M. Schall. Their business has become very extensive. In 1883 they made 1,500,-000 feet of lumber. At present he is also trading extensively in mules, horses and cattle; he farms also in Manchester Township. He removed to his present place of residence, about one mile north of York, in 1882. He was also an organizer of the Drovers and Mechanics Bank at York, and was for many years a director. Now he is a director in the Dover and Manchester Townships Mutual Fire Insurance Company.

MICHAEL SMYSER was born in Spring Garden Township, July 8, 1846. His parents were Henry and Mary (Emig) Smyser, of York County and of German descent. They had three sons and one daughter, of whom Michael is the eldest. One of the sons, Alexander, resides in Kansas; Horace in Spring Garden Township, and the daughter, who is married to Abraham Flory, in Lancaster County. Michael is a descendant of the elder Mathias Smyser, who came from Germany in 1738, and settled in Kreutz Creek Valley,in York County, where he carried on weaving in a small way. He took a large tract of land, much of which he afterward gave away in order to induce settlers to locate. He afterward removed to a place three miles west of York, where, in 1778, he died. He had three sons: Michael (probably grandfather of the subject of this sketch),Jacob and Mathias. Michael wa- captain of a company in Col. M. Swope's regiment, in the Revolutionary war, and was captured at Fort Washington, November 16,1776. He was several times a member of the Pennsylvania legislature, and from 1794 to 1798, a member of the State senate. The subject of this sketch was brought up on this farm in Spring Garden Township, and received his education in public schools and in the York Academy. He began for himself at the age of twenty-seven, when he was married, at York, to Sarah Kauffman, daughter of Joseph Kauffman (deceased farmer of Spring Garden Township). They had two children: Henry K. and Susan M. In 1874 he removed to his present residence, known as the "Old John Brillinger Farm," of about 200 acres, to the cultivation of which and stock raising he devotes his entire attention. He belongs to the Lutheran Church, is a man that attends entirely to his own business, and is considered one of the most enterprising and successful farmers in York County.

JOHN C. SUNDAY was born in Dover Township, November 21, 1855. His parents were Jacob and Louvina (Cochenauer) Sunday, who were na-

BIOGRAPHICAL SKETCHES. 145

tives of Dover and of German descent. They had eight children, of whom two sons and two daughters are living, John C., being the eldest. Until his seventeenth year he lived on the farm and enjoyed a common school education, and began learning the trade of carriage-making and smithing with Mr. Gross, in Dover Borough. He learned the trade and worked at it, together with dealing in merchandise, for about five years. In the fall of 1877 he came to Manchester, and began manufacturing carriages, wagons, phaetons and buggies, and is doing good and solid work. He employs six first class mechanics. In February, 1877, he married in Berlin, Adams County, Alice E. Hantz, daughter of Joseph Hantz, and a native of York County. Two children have been born to them: Carlton P. and Harvey James. Mrs. Sunday belongs to the Reformed Church. Mr. S. has retired from farming.

AMOS G. THRONE was born in Spring Garden Township, May 16, 1844. His parents were Samuel and Harriet (Green) Throne, natives, respectively, of Adams and York Counties, Penn., and reared six children—four sons and two daughters—of whom Amos G. is the eldest son and second child. Until he became of age he lived on his father's farm, and attended the common schools in his township. At the age of twenty-five he began for himself. His father having died in 1862, he remained with his mother in charge of the farm until 1869. May 5, 1868, he was married at Harrisburg, Penn., to Amanda M. Smyser, of Spring Garden, daughter of Daniel Smyser. The Smyser and Throne families came originally from Germany, but the Green family came from England. This marriage was blessed with two children: Wilmer Clayton and Nettie Augusta. Both he and wife belong to the Lutheran Church. Mr. Throne is an active Republican, was inspector of election in Spring Garden Township, and one term school director, elected in 1882, in Manchester Township. He takes an active part in the cause of education. In 1876 he removed from his home to Manchester Township, but in 1882 removed again to his home about one mile north from York. He also owns a very fine farm of upward of 150 acres, in the township, which he rents out. In September, 1884, he was elected a director of the Farmers Mutual Fire Insurance Company of Dover, Conewago, Newberry, East and West Manchester Townships, in the county of York and the State of Pennsylvania, and elected secretary of the company by the board of directors.

HENRY S. TYSON, son of Henry and Susanna (Shultz) Tyson, was born October 8, 1829. His father, of English descent, a native of Ohio, died in this county in 1879, aged eighty-one years. His mother, a descendant of a German family, who were among the first settlers of York County, died in 1881, aged eighty-seven years. By this marriage six sons and four daughters were born. The subject of this sketch was the fourth son and eighth child, and grew to manhood on his father's farm, afterward learned the carpenter's trade, and pursued it in York from 1849 to 1853. He practiced veterinary surgery for a few years; from 1863 to 1873, he followed mining at Smyser Iron Ore Bank, and for two years was an engineer on the York Water Works. In the spring of 1882, he took charge of "Sinking Spring Farm," of 335 acres, owned by P. A. S. Small. Mr. Tyson was married to Leah E., daughter of Herman Hoke. They had two children: Herman (deceased), and Mary Jane. Mr. Tyson and his family are members of the Lutheran Church.

DANIEL H. WIER was born in Conewago Township, York County, September 28, 1848, and is the eldest of three sons of Moses and Catherine (Hake) Wier, natives of York County, and of German descent. He was brought up on a farm and worked some at the trade of carpenter. He was educated at York County Academy and Normal School, and at Gentzler's Practical Schools. He taught five terms in the public schools of York County, from 1868 to 1873, two in Conewago, and three in Manchester Township. He was married at York, May 8, 1873, to Leah Shindel, a native of Manchester Township. They have one child, Katie Ellen. He removed to the farm now occupied by him about two miles north of York, where he is engaged in farming and stock raising. He is a member of the Reformed Church, and his wife of the Lutheran Church. He was clerk of Manchester Township in 1874–75–76, and auditor of Conewago Township in 1879–80–81. In politics he is a Republican.

JOHN H. WOGAN was born in Manchester Township, December 16, 1837, upon the farm purchased by John Wogan from the sons of William Penn. From John it descended to his son, John, Jr., then to George, then to another John H. Subject was the only son, with one sister. He was educated at different academies in Pennsylvania. On his becoming of age he went into business for himself, such as farming, raising and dealing in leaf tobacco, handling as many as 1,600 cases at 400 pounds per case in a single year. At the age of twenty-one he was married at Lancaster, Penn., to Sarah Wolf. They had six children: Caleb L., Annie W., George, William W., Edmond and Ira Park. Mr. Wogan is an active Republican, was school director two terms, is a director in the Dover Fire Insurance Company, and is a member and manager of the York Agricultural Society. He owns and manages 800 acres of land in York County, employing from ten to thirty-four hands, all the year around. He is also a member of the firm of Wolf & Co., at Mount Wolf. His father died aged eighty years, but his mother is still living, now seventy-five years old. The Wogans are of Scotch-Irish descent. His mother was Margaret Hay, daughter of John Hay, and sister of Cols. George and Alexander Hay, who served in the late war. Mr. Wogan's grandfather, John, was a fifer in the Revolutionary war. The Wogans first settled in Maryland, but afterward came to York County, and settled a large tract of limestone land, on the west bank of the Susquehanna River, then in Lancaster County, and in New Holland, then an important lumber point. They had then five farms and owned a number of fox hounds, and the same breed of hounds are still on the place, and are used by the Wogans in fox chases. The present owner is an expert fox hunter.

CHARLES H. YINGER is the fifth of twelve children of Paul and Christine Yinger, of Manchester Township. Early in life, Mr. Yinger worked as a blacksmith in his father's shop, with whom he learned the trade. He carried on this business for twelve years—ten years in York Township, and two years in Manchester Township. March 15, 1849, Mr. Yinger married Mary Hoover, daughter of William and Rebecca (Matthias) Hoover, of Manchester Township. Three children have blessed this marriage: Margaret (deceased), Albert (deceased) and Ellen. Mr. Yinger has been school director two terms, also member of the council of Manchester Borough, and enjoys the confidence and esteem of his neighbors and all who know him. His ancestors were early settlers in Manchester Township.

GEORGE S. YINGER was born in this township, August 8, 1838, son of Paul and Christine (Snyder) Yinger. He began learning the carpenter's trade in his sixteenth year and commenced contracting on his own account at the early age of twenty years. He has been very successful in his

10

business, and has erected some of the finest private residences in York and York County. In October, 1859, he married Cassandria Weigle, daughter of Martin and Mary (Schriver) Weigle, and six children have blessed this union: Annie, Brize, Alice, Aquila, and two infants (deceased). Mr. Yinger was a sergeant in the Two Hundreth Regiment Pennsylvania Volunteers during the late war, and participated in all the battles of his regiment, including Bermuda Hundred, Fort Steadman and the final charge on Petersburg. At the latter place his regiment was engaged immediately in front of the famous "Fort Hell."

JOHN S. YINGER is a son of Paul and Christine (Snyder) Yinger. His grandfather, Martin Yinger, lived and died near Lewisberry, York County. Subject's grandmother, Catherine (Grove) Yinger, was a daughter of Sam Grove, the gunsmith, well known in Lewisberry, where he resided. Paul Yinger, father of John S., was born September 17, 1793, was a blacksmith, was reared and lived on the homestead now occupied by our subject, and died May 7, 1876. Christine Yinger, his wife, was born July 24, 1794, and died June 17, 1870. They had twelve children: Jacob, born September 10, 1818; Samuel, born January 15, 1820, died September 11, same year; Elizabeth, born August 6, 1821; John S., born December 27, 1822; Daniel, born November 23, 1824; Charles Henry, born November 10, 1826; William, born September 10, 1828; Paul S., born April 30, 1830; Abraham, born February 9, 1832, killed in battle at Cold Harbor, Va., June 1, 1864; Ann Maria, born November 29, 1833; Samuel (second), born October 6, 1836, and George S. born August 8, 1838. John S. Yinger learned the blacksmith's trade with his father, with whom he afterward worked two years. In 1847, he married Anna Good, daughter of Henry and Elizabeth (Strickler) Good, of Hellam Township. To this union have been born seven children: Franklin G., born December 6, 1849; Absalom G., born March 15, 1851; Emma G., October 12, 1852; Charles G., January 1, 1855; Henry G., July 17, 1856; Benjamin G.; September 20, 1858, and Amanda G., June 8, 1861. Mr. Yinger, though advanced in years, still carries on blacksmithing in the old shop where he learned his trade and where his father worked for many years.

JACOB YOST was born in York Township, July 7, 1820, and is the sixth of a family of fourteen children born to Abraham and Mary (Feiser) Yost, as follows: Elizabeth (deceased), Mary (deceased), Rachel (deceased), Rebecca, Charles, Jacob, Leah, Caroline, Abraham, Elizabeth Ann, Peter, Isaac, Jesse and Sarah. February 5, 1845, our subject married Leah, daughter of David and Mary Magdalene (Feigley) Brillhart, of Springfield Township, and this union has been blessed with two children: Sarah, wife of Charles Herbst, and Mary, wife of Peter Burgard, of Manchester Township. Mr. Yost's ancestry were among the pioneers of York Township, and his wife's forefathers, paternal and maternal, were among the earliest settlers of Springfield Township. Mr. Yost is a gentleman of industry and perseverance, and has secured for himself and family a handsome competence. He is a member of the Baptist Church.

MONAGHAN TOWNSHIP.

HENRY BEELMAN was born April 26, 1840, and is the son of Adam Beelman, German Baptist minister of Carroll Township. His boyhood was passed on the farm until the age of eighteen, when he began to learn carpentering with his father. He afterward became a teacher, and while thus engaged was drafted in 1862, but was exempted on account of his profession. In 1863 he went to Washington, D. C., was secured by the government as a carpenter, and was employed a year at Alexandria, Va. In 1866 he married Maggie E., daughter of David Williams, of Monaghan, went to housekeeping on the old homestead, where he farmed six years, and then moved to Dillsburg, and followed carpentering ten years. In the fall of 1882 he bought the Williams homestead, took possession in the spring of 1883, and still resides there, engaged in farming. From 1881 to 1884 he was also engaged in the dairy business at Dillsburg. Mr. and Mrs. Beelman have been members of the German Baptist Church since 1869, and are the parents of six children—two boys and four girls. Mr. Beelman has served his township as school director and auditor.

JACOB COCKLIN was born January 30, 1797, in Upper Allen Township, Cumberland Co., Penn., and was reared a farmer. At the age of twenty-four he began farming on his own account in his native township, continued for several years, and then came to this township, and, until 1827, followed the same vocation; he then engaged in pomology and arbor culture for about thirty years. About 1855 he made a trip to Iowa, purchased 3,000 acres of land, returned to York County, and subsequently made twenty trips to Iowa, covering a traveled distance of over 40,000 miles; he also had dealings with over 1,500 persons; built seven houses, dug ten wells (four of which were over fifty feet deep), cut timber off 100 acres of land, burnt over 1,000 bushels of lime, built several hundred rods of stone fence, and planted three miles of hedging. He commenced business with $10,000 and increased his capital to $60,000, employing a host of laborers, who participated in his gains. He was a pioneer in the nursery business in the upper part of this county, and the country is filled with fruit trees of his introduction. He has never had a law suit, never been ill for any length of time, and never belonged to any secret order. He has assisted over fifty families to homes by advancing funds payable in from one to ten years, and in many other respects has proved himself a philanthropist. January 29, 1828, he married Catherine, daughter of Michael Hoover, of Lancaster County, and of German descent. This lady died March 13, 1872, the mother of six children, of whom two are living and have families: Sarah C. and Eli H. Mr. Cocklin's father was born in Lancaster County, and was the son of a native of France. On the maternal side Mr. Cocklin is of Welsh descent. He has served as school director, constable, supervisor, collector, clerk, auditor, and in other positions of public trust, but has always been a "poor customer" to saloons, preachers, doctors and lawyers. Mr. Cocklin says of himself: "I never was drunk, never used tobacco or opium, never was in a house of ill fame, nor gambled; have not eaten more than two meals a day—in the morning and noon. From 1877 to this date, June 8, 1885, the following work has been done: 500 rod stone fence, four feet wide and four feet high; planted 1,500 locust trees along the fence, 3,200 locust trees in a grove of five acres, 6,800 fruit trees in orchard; ten acres of raspberries and strawberries; digging and hauling stones for fence; planted 400 grape vines, etc. My great-grandfather wrote his name Jacob Caquelin (French), my father wrote his in German, Gacklin. Some write it Cockley, Gockley, Conklin, etc."

ELI H. COCKLIN is the son of Jacob and Catherine (Hoover) Cocklin, and was born in this township, March 8, 1835. He was reared as a farmer and nurseryman until the age of eighteen, when he went to Waterloo, Black Hawk Co., Iowa, and for two years engaged in the propagation of evergreen and deciduous trees; he then returned to his native township, and has since followed farming and fruit growing. He has originated several varieties of fruit, including the Ida strawberry and Ida cherry, a description of which is given in Downing's "Fruits and Fruit Trees of America," third appendix. In 1861 he was elected school director, served six years, and in 1883 was re-elected for three years. He married Miss Sarah E., daughter of Chambers and Docey Caley, of Blackhawk County, Iowa. Mr. and Mrs. Caley are of English descent, and came from England, with four small children, in the ship "Victory," in 1840, having been fifty-eight days on the ocean. To Mr. and Mrs. Cocklin have been born six children, as follows: Ida May, April 9, 1861; Charles Chambers, June 29, 1862; Russell Trall, October 1, 1864; B. Franklin, July 9, 1867; Alice Dunn, January 31, 1871, and John Ault, April 26, 1873. Mr. and Mrs. Cocklin are members of the St. Paul's Reformed Church, of Mechanicsburg, Penn.

JOHN K. COCKLIN, son of David Cocklin, of this township, was born June 21, 1844, and was reared on the farm until sixteen years of age; he then served two years at carpentering. In 1863 he enlisted in Company A, Eleventh Pennsylvania Cavalry, under Col. Spear, took part in Big Bethel and other battles, and was present at the surrender of Gen. Lee; he served until August 20, 1865, when his regiment was discharged, after which he followed butchering two years. He next attended school at Dillsburg, under Prof. G. W. Hedges, with a view of becoming a teacher, and since 1867 has taught every year in York County, with the exception of one year in Upper Allen Township, Cumberland County, his terms in York consisting of sixteen in Monaghan Township and twelve at Filey's. July 13, 1867, he married Amanda J., daughter of James Collins, of Monaghan. Four sons and three daughters have blessed this union. Mr. and Mrs. Cocklin and two of the children are members of the Lutheran Church at Filey's, of which Mr. Cocklin is a deacon; he has also been superintendent of the Filey's Union Sunday-school for a number of years. He has been a K. of P. about eight years, and has served his township in the capacities of auditor, assessor, inspector and clerk.

HENRY DIETZ, son of Eli Dietz, of Lower Allen Township, Cumberland County, was born January 16, 1848, and was reared on the home farm. His first work on his own account was driving a mill team for Henry McCormick for two years and a half. In 1877 he commenced farming on the old homestead, but in 1879 moved to Andersontown, and started a blacksmith shop; never having learned the trade, however, he employed John Miller, an excellent workman and a finished coachsmith, to superintend; together they made a success, and through Mr. Miller's advice, coach-making in a small way was added and the business so flourished that Mr. Dietz was compelled to erect a one-story blacksmith shop and a two-story carriage shop, and he is now conducting the leading industry of the village. Mr. Dietz and wife became members of the Bethel Church, at Andersontown, in 1882, and they have had born to them two children; Jacob Eby, August 21, 1877, died September 22, 1877, and John L. Ru, born in 1879.

JOHN EICHELBERGER, Esq., was born April 6, 1816, and is the son of John Eichelberger, Sr., a captain in the war of 1812, and Barbara. He was born February 20, 1787, was of German descent and died July 15, 1833, at the age of forty-six years four months and twenty-five days. Our subject was sent to school two years at Lititz, in Lancaster County, and afterward was about ten months in a store at Baltimore, Md.; then for two years served as clerk in the store of Alexander Cathcart, in Shepherdstown, Cumberland Co., Penn., and was there married. He then moved to and farmed on the old homestead, near Dillsburg, for two years, and then settled on his present place near Andersontown, York County. He was elected justice of the peace for thirty-three years, and in 1880 was appointed to the same position by Gov. Hoyt; he has also been a very successful pension solicitor. November 2, 1837, he married Jane Eckels, of Upper Allen Township, Cumberland County, Penn., and to this union children were born as follows: James, born December 8, 1838, died August 30, 1861; William Henry, born March 25, 1841, died April 1, 1844; John J., September 13, 1843; Adaline, October 18, 1845; Jacob Trego, February 17, 1848; Alfred, April 5, 1850; Mary Jane, September 3, 1853; Alice, July 6, 1856, and George Washington, April 17, 1859.

HENRY S. FORRY, son of Henry Forry, Sr., of Upper Allen Township, Cumberland County, was born April 23, 1846. Reared a farmer, he commenced on his own account in 1869; in 1875 he bought a dwelling and sixteen acres of land in Andersontown, and engaged in growing small fruits and garden truck; he now ships about 5,000 boxes of strawberries each season, together with raspberries, blackberries, grapes, etc. Mr. Forry served during the late war, until August, 1865, in Company F, One Hundred and Ninety-second Pennsylvania Volunteer Infantry, under Col. Stewart, and received an honorable discharge. He was married June 21, 1868, to Lydia A., daughter of Henry Kimmel, of Monaghan Township, and the result of this union is Laura Ellen, born February 18, 1874. Mr. and Mrs. Forry are members of the Bethel Church.

ZACHARY TAYLOR FORTNEY, son of David W. Fortney, was born in this township March 20, 1847, and was reared a farmer. He began life for himself in 1868, and then, from 1876 to 1878, was engaged in saw milling; in the latter year he opened a small store in connection with the saw-mill, etc., near Mount Pleasant; then in the spring of 1880 moved to Mount Airy, Warrington Township, where he spared no means but made every effort to build up and establish a permanent trade, and also established the postoffice at that place; remained about three years, but by that great effort sunk $2,000 in cash; and then returned to Monaghan again; where he has built a new store and is establishing a flourishing trade. He was the first postmaster of Fortney, and held the office about two years. January 2, 1868, he married Sarah A., daughter of George Wilson, of Upper Allen Township, Cumberland County, and to this union have been born George W., October 18, 1868; Francis G., April 4, 1870; Clara Melissa, October 2, 1871; Harvey Shopp, December 12, 1874, and Josephine Bertha, April 15, 1879. Mr. and Mrs. Fortney are members of the Chestnut Grove United Brethren Church.

JOHN HYDE was born in this township, June 10, 1810, to John and Barbara (Wolf) Hyde. His grandfather, Michael, came from Germany. John Hyde (father of subject) was born in Cumberland County, was a shoe-maker and farmer, served in the war of 1812, and died in this township in 1850, aged eighty-three, the possessor of sixty acres of land, and the father of eight children, viz.: Michael, Barbara, Jennie, Elizabeth, Kate, Mary, Fannie and John (subject). Our subject is the owner of forty-five acres of land in this township, where, with the exception of one year in Fairview Township, he has passed his whole life, and is its oldest living citizen. His land he has gained through his own industry, and he still cultivates it. In 1853 he married Susan, daughter of Henry K. Kohlar, a native of York County, and this union has been

MONAGHAN TOWNSHIP.

blessed with the birth of ten children, of whom nine are living, viz.: Barbara, Elizabeth, Mary, Angeline, Sarah, Margaret, George, Andrew and William. Mr. Hyde is a Democrat, has filled the office of commissioner, and has been for many years school director.

HENRY KIMMEL was born September 1, 1826, to John and Susannah (Wonders) Kimmel, in Washington Township, and is the second of three children: Leah, Henry and John. The grandfathers of subject, David Kimmel and Henry Wonders, were natives of York County and both farmers. John Kimmel, subject's father, was born in Washington Township in 1793, was the owner of two farms, and died in 1853. Our subject, at the age of twenty-five, began farming on his own account in Monaghan Township and at the death of his father fell heir to a fine piece of property of eighty-three acres, well improved with buildings, etc. In 1850 he married Mary M., daughter of Peter and Lydia (Crone) Ference, of York County. The six children born to this union were named as follows: Lydia A. (Ferry), Susan (Sutton), Sarah J. (Frysinger), John (deceased), Leah C. (deceased), and Alice (Myers). Mr. Kimmel has held a number of local offices, and with his wife is a member of the Church of God.

WILLIAM KIMMEL was born in Monaghan Township, October 14, 1854, and spent his early life on a farm, and in attending school. September 30, 1880, he married Miss Minnie, daughter of Warren Whipp, of Frederick County, Md. He has had born to him two children: Gertie May, August 6, 1881, and Norma Blanche, September 29, 1882. Mr. Kimmel began teaching school in 1877, filling six terms at Myers' school and one term at Andersontown. In the spring of 1881 he commenced farming on his own account. He has served his township as assessor and clerk, and is the present auditor. He is a deacon in the Bethel Church, at Mount Pleasant, of which Mrs. Kimmel is also a member.

DANIEL LANDIS, son of Jacob Landis, of Upper Allen Township, Cumberland County, was born January 4, 1829. He was married, October 14, 1851, to Barbara Ann, daughter of Joseph Solenberger, of Dickinson Township, Cumberland County. This lady died March 22, 1853, the mother of one son, who died at the age of twenty-one years and nineteen days. Our subject began for himself by doing days' work for about six years, and then farmed on shares for Jacob D. Mohler, near Mechanicsburgh, for twelve years, then moved to that village and worked in the warehouse of T. B. Bryson; from the spring of 1872 until the fall of 1873 he farmed for C. B. Hertzler, near Shepherdstown, Cumberland County, and then bought, from the executors of Mrs. Mary Kinsley, a farm that had been deeded, in 1746, to Roger Cook by Thomas and Richard Penn. April 10, 1874, he took possession of and still resides on this farm. He also leases to H. O. Shelly a magnetic ore mine of about eight acres. Mr. Landis' second marriage took place February 6, 1855, to Mary Ann, daughter of Henry Miller, of Mechanicsburgh, and to this union have been born one son (who died at the age of five years five months and seven days), and two daughters: Ellen and Nora. Mr. and Mrs. Landis are members of the German Baptist Church, of which Mr. Landis is a deacon, and which he joined at the age of fifty years. The maternal great-grandfather of Mr. Landis came from Switzerland; he landed in America August 29, 1730, from the ship Thistle, which sailed from Glasgow, Scotland. His paternal ancestors came from Holland.

PETER A. MYERS, son of Jacob Myers, Sr., was born in Monaghan Township, April 12, 1838. He was reared a farmer, and was educated in the public school and select schools of Wellsville and at Dillsburg; subsequently he became a teacher and taught thirteen terms—two while single. May 1, 1872, he married Elmira J., daughter of Daniel S. Hammacher, and to this marriage children were born as follows: Catherine L., June 19, 1863; Ulysses A., May 28, 1865; Will Penrose, February 24, 1867, died December 16, 1869; Clara E., December 31, 1869; John A., September 28, 1872; Anna M., February 18, 1876; Ira Calvin, March 23, 1879; Russel Melvin, October 1, 1884. Mr. and Mrs. Myers started housekeeping in Henry Kimmell's springhouse, at an annual rental of $4; the next spring he rented a tenement from Samuel Myers, and for two years engaged in cultivating tobacco, in butchering and teaching. In April, 1865, he rented Daniel Frysinger's farm, and for a year engaged in cultivating tobacco, butchering and dealing in stock. In the spring of 1866 he purchased a house and thirteen acres of land half a mile south of Mount Pleasant, and turned his attention to fruit culture, planting 555 apple trees, 1,800 peach trees of twenty-five varieties, 100 pear trees, 50 apricot and 25 varieties of cherry trees, and two acres of small fruits. Twelve years later he purchased his present homestead of 150 acres. Here he has three acres planted in strawberries, and in one season has shipped as high as 16,000 boxes, besides 10,000 boxes of raspberries, together with grapes, plums, peaches, apples, cherries, apricots, etc. Mr. Myers has held several offices of public trust, including those of supervisor, assessor and auditor.

ELI D. MYERS, son of Jacob and Sarah (Miller) Myers, of this township, was born October 17, 1843, and grew to manhood on the farm, receiving his education in the public schools during the winter months. He began business for himself in the spring of 1869 on the farm of William B. Miller, in this township, remained one year, and then moved to his father's place near Siddonsburgh, where he still resides. He married Rebecca, daughter of Peter Huntzberger, of Newville, Cumberland County, and was born October 11, 1844. To this union have been born five children: Alvin G., September 21, 1870; Harry E., March 23, 1873, died May 7, 1879; Willie Clarence, April 17, 1875; Mervin Hayes, July 1, 1878, and Laura May, May 28, 1888. Mr. and Mrs. Myers are members of the Reformed Church, at Filey's, of which Mr. Myers has been a deacon for six years; he has also served his township as inspector and collector, one year in each capacity.

JACOB MYERS, son of Jacob Myers, Sr., of Warrington Township, was born December 20, 1850, and is of German descent. At the age of five years he lost his mother, when he went to live with his grandfather; at the age of nine he returned to his father, and at fourteen hired out to an uncle; two years later he returned to his grandfather, and remained with him until twenty-two years old, when, December 24, 1872, he married Anna, daughter of John B. Grove, of Warrington Township. He was employed in trucking with Mr. Cocklin a year, and then bought a tract of land near Mount Pleasant, where he is still engaged in trucking and raising berries. He has had born to him a family of five children—three boys and two girls—of whom one boy and two girls are living.

SAMUEL MYERS was born in Monaghan Township, July 3, 1820, and is of German and English descent. He was reared a farmer and, in 1843, began on his own account. January 2, 1845, he married Leah, daughter of John Kimmel, of Monaghan Township, and of German descent. The children born to this union were John A., November 6, 1845; Elmira Jane, May 14, 1847, died March 2, 1851; Susan, May 28, 1849; Samuel W., November 16, 1851; Henry W., March 15, 1853; Solomon B., December 3, 1854; George E., October 22, 1856;

BIOGRAPHICAL SKETCHES.

David M., February 15, 1858; Elizabeth E., December 22, 1859; Daniel E., June 24, 1862, died March 14, 1863; Charles L., November 6, 1864. Our subject has been a member of the Bethel Church at Mt. Pleasant since 1844, and for over thirty years an elder; for twenty-five or thirty years he has been superintendent of the Union Sunday-school, and for about twelve years was superintendent of the Myers' Sunday-school; he organized the first Sunday-school convention in the upper end of the township and for a year acted as president; he served as supervisor for several years, and for seven years was a member of the Warrington Rangers, as orderly, having been honorably discharged in 1843. He assisted at the revival meeting at the Marshall farm near Wellsville in 1844, and was the first young man to make a public prayer in that neighborhood.

WILLIAM A. MYERS, justice of the peace, was born in this township, October 8, 1842, was reared a farmer, and at the age of twenty went to New York City, then to Lycoming County, this State, where he engaged in the lumber business, and in the fall of 1863 returned to his native county, and taught school in Washington Township six terms, and fourteen terms in Monaghan Township, doing farm work during the summers. He now owns two small farms devoted to fruit culture. He married Mary, daughter of Daniel S. Hammacher, of Monaghan Township. To this union have been born four children, viz.: Anna L., August 30, 1871, died September 17, 1876; Levi Milton, January 22, 1873; Elizabeth Ida, October 7, 1874, died September 15, 1876; and Harry Calvin, June 22, 1876. Mr. Myers has served as assessor one year, auditor three years, tax collector one year, and was elected justice of the peace in the spring of 1884. He is a member of the Church of God, at Mt. Pleasant, of which church he has been a deacon three years and an elder three years.

JOHN ANDREW MYERS, postmaster, was born November 6, 1845, and is a son of Samuel and Leah Myers, of this township. He was reared a farmer, engaged in agricultural pursuits on his own account in 1866, and so continued until 1869, when he entered the mercantile trade at Siddonsburg; in 1873 he was appointed postmaster. June 3, 1884, he started on an extensive tour of the South and visited the southern part of Florida, and all points of interest in the Gulf States. He was married, December 26, 1865, to Sarah A., daughter of Peter Brenneman, of this township, and to this union were born Rosetta E., January 13, 1867, died October 8, 1870; Sarah Alice, November 13, 1868, died January 1, 1879; Clarence B., January 29, 1871, died March 29, 1871; Agnes, September 14, 1873; Jenny May, September 7, 1875. Mr. and Mrs. Myers are members of the Church of God, Siddonsburg, of which Mr. Myers has been deacon for a number of years, as well as superintendent of the Sunday-school. Mr. Myers is a stockholder in the Harrisburg & Potomac Railroad, and a stockholder in and director and secretary of the Mt. Pleasant Hall Association.

DAVID D. MYERS, son of John and Eliza Myers, of this township, was born February 1, 1847, and is of German descent. He was reared on the home farm, of which he assumed charge in 1868. In 1871 he made an extensive tour of the West; in 1874 he commenced dealing in agricultural implements at Dillsburg, and in 1881 he bought the home farm of eighty-seven acres, of which fifteen acres are in woodland. Mr. Myers has taken great interest in politics; has served his township as inspector; was a delegate to the Republican county conventions from 1868 to 1884 twelve times; and to the State conventions of 1881 and 1883, and he is also a prominent member of the P. of H. In December, 1867, he married Eliza Jane, daughter of Joseph Elcock, of Mechanicsburg, and this union has been blessed with six children: Minnie Florence, Elizabeth Lillian, Walter Loudon, Mary Ellen, Eliza Edith and Lura (deceased). Mrs. Myers is a member of the Bethel Mt. Pleasant Church.

WILLIAM R. PROWELL, M. D., was born in Fairview Township, this county, March 20, 1854, and was reared on the home farm. He was educated in the public schools, and at the normal school, Millersville, Lancaster County. During the winter of 1872-73 he was engaged in teaching, and in the spring of 1873 began the study of medicine under Dr. Swiler, of Yocumtown. From 1874 to 1876, inclusive, he attended Jefferson Medical College, Philadelphia, graduating March 10, 1876. He began practice April 11, 1876, at Siddonsburg, and now has a very large practice—has visited as high as thirty-five patients in twenty-four hours. October 5, 1876, he married Miss Jennie, daughter of the late John Elcock, Sr., of Siddonsburg, and this union has resulted in the birth of four children: Viola May, October 17, 1878, died September 13, 1882; Tolbert, born April 4, 1882, Ella and Nellie, born August 15, 1884. Ella died March 26. 1885. The doctor is a member of the Cumberland County Medical Society.

GEORGE D. SHAFFER, son of James Shaffer, was born in this township, November 15, 1822. At the age of eighteen he began stone-masonry, but disliking the trade, after three or four years, undertook farming. April 16, 1846, he married Margaret, daughter of John Myers, of Monaghan Township, and went to housekeeping on the farm of Judge Dare, near Siddonsburg, for whom he was manager for nineteen years. After the Judge's death, Mr. Shaffer removed to his present farm of 130 acres near Bryson Stone Bridge, which farm he had purchased from Jacob Cocklin. In addition to this place, Mr. Shaffer is now the owner of two other farms, on which there are good buildings. In 1876 Mr. Shaffer embarked in the lumber and coal trade at Bowmandale, Cumberland County, ten miles from Harrisburg, on the Harrisburg & Potomac Railroad, in which road he is a stockholder; he has also traveled through the West and the Canadas, and was once a delegate to the Eldership of the Church of God at Findlay, Ohio. Mr. and Mrs. Shaffer joined this church in 1843, and Mr. Shaffer has been either deacon or elder ever since. He has also served his township as school director, treasurer and auditor. He is the father of eleven children: Dare G., in Kansas; Samuel M., mining in Colorado; James W., at home, assisting on the farm, and in the coal and lumber business, and eight daughters, of whom the eldest four are married, and two are dead.

JAMES WILLIAM SHAFFER was born March 16, 1852, in Monaghan Township, York Co., Penn. His father, G. D. Shaffer, being a farmer, his early life was spent upon the farm, and attending the district school. At the age of fifteen he entered the Cumberland Valley Institute at Mechanicsburg, remaining for several sessions, and then took a special course of instruction at the Chambersburg Academy. Wishing to learn a trade he engaged in the saddle and harness manufacturing business, and carried it on successfully from 1871 to 1874, when he sold out and engaged in farming. During the summer of 1875 he traveled extensively through New York State and the Canadas. Visited Maryland, Virginia, North Carolina, New Jersey and Delaware, during the winter of 1880. Engaged in the lumber and coal business with his father in Bowmansdale, Cumberland Co., Penn., in 1876, and has continued it until the present. He also traveled through Florida and some of the Southern States in the summer of 1884. He was appointed enumerator of the tenth census, and held other offices of trust and honor.

DANIEL W. WENGART, M. D., was born in Monroe Township, Cumberland Co., Penn., May 1, 1830. He was reared a farmer until the age of seventeen, when he entered the Mechanicsburg Institute, and a year later took up the study of medicine under Dr. Eckert, near Shippensburgh. He first engaged in practice three miles west of Mechanicsburg, but, owing to ill-health, relinquished the profession until 1854, when he resumed at Mt. Pleasant, and in a short time established a remunerative business, which he held until his removal to Mechanicsburg to engage in the drug trade, in connection with practice. One year later he returned to Mt. Pleasant and resecured his old patronage, which he has also increased to a flattering degree, having been remarkably successful in obstetrics and the treatment of typhoid fever. He married, April 6, 1853, Miss Elizabeth, daughter of John Cooper, of New Kingston. To this union have been born three children: Mary E., September 26, 1857; John C., February 24, 1859; Daniel Webster, August 31, 1861.

JONATHAN WILLIAMS was born December 7, 1821, and is a son of Jonathan Williams, Sr. He assisted his father on the home farm until his marriage, February 18, 1847, to Margaret, daughter of Elihu Park, of this township. In 1849 he settled on his present farm of 140 acres, all under cultivation, and erected his dwelling and barn. There were born to him ten children, of whom four are living: Elspy J., at home; Mary Elizabeth, wife of Amos Fortney; Elverda Frances, wife of David Brougher, and Maggie C. The parents are members of the Presbyterian Church at Dillsburg, having joined in 1860. Mr. Williams has served as school director, two terms; assessor, one year; assistant-assessor, three terms, and auditor, three years.

NEWBERRY TOWNSHIP.

CHARLES E. BAIR was born May 7, 1852, in Newberry Township, York Co., Penn., and is a son of Benjamin and Anna (Rudy) Bair, natives of Lehigh and York Counties, Penn., respectively, and of German descent. Charles E. is the eighth of a family of fifteen children. He is a cigar-maker by trade, and owns and controls a cigar factory near Newberrytown, Penn. Until his eighteenth year, he remained with his parents, and received a common school education. At the age of eleven years he began learning his trade, which he has since followed. In 1877 he opened a factory one mile from Newberrytown, but in 1883 removed to Newberrytown, where he is at present located, manufacturing about 400,000 cigars annually, and employing from six to ten men. In 1871 he was married to Ellen B. Beshore. They have had seven children: William, Fillmore, Annie, Harvey, Daniel, Vernon (deceased) and Ross. Mrs. Bair is a daughter of Daniel and Mary (Fink) Beshore, native of York County, Penn. She is a member of the Church of God. Mr. Bair started in life as a poor boy, and by his own industry and economy, has accumulated some property. He owns good property in town, and, eighteen acres of land. He is a Democrat, has been elected to various offices, and at present holds the office of justice of the peace of the township.

PROF. SAMUEL J. BAKER was born in Paradise Township, York Co., Penn., January 21, 1856. His parents were Samuel and Catharine (Jacobs) Baker, of the same township, and of English descent. They had eleven children—three sons and eight daughters, of whom Samuel J. is the third one in the family. At an early age he assisted his father at shoe-making and attended the public schools. At the age of eighteen years he commenced studying brass band music at Big Mound, and became so proficient in a short time, that he became leader of a band at Big Mound, in 1875; and, since 1878, has given his whole attention to music and band teaching. He is also a teacher of classes on the organ and violin. In 1880 he removed to Goldsboro, where he has since made his home. He has instructed nine bands in York County and one in Lancaster County, and is at present teaching four bands: Independent Band (Goldsboro), Manchester Cornet Band, Strinestown Band and New Salem Band. He is also leader of Baker's Orchestra at Goldsboro, and arranges and composes music for bands, etc. December 23, 1880, he married Susan Ziegler, of Wellsville, York County, Penn. They have one child, Lottie May. Prof. Baker is a member of the Reformed Church, also of the S. of A.

ELIAS D. BRECKINRIDGE was born in Lancaster County, Penn., April 22, 1834. His parents were William and Elizabeth (Duck) Breckinridge, natives of Chester and Lancaster Counties, Penn., and of Scotch-Irish and German descent, respectively. They were married in Lancaster County, Penn., and reared a family of three sons and five daughters, one infant deceased. Elias D. is the eldest son, and he remained on the farm until sixteen years of age, when he began learning the business of woolen manufacturing, which he followed for twenty-six years. In 1879 he was appointed storekeeper and gauger, and assigned to Reynold's distillery, Ninth District, Penn., but was transferred at the end of a few months to Kauffman's distillery, in the same district, where he remained a little over a year. In July, 1880, he took charge at Free's distillery, in York County, Penn., where he remained till June, 1882. In January, 1883, he came to Goldsboro, where he has since been keeping the Railroad Hotel. He was married, in Salisbury Township, Lancaster Co., Penn., May 21, 1857, to Susanna Nixon, of the same county, and of Irish descent. They have had nine children: Florence E., Cora A., U. S. G., Charles S., Oscar L. (deceased), Eugene O., Imogene M., William Robert and Roscoe G. (deceased). Mr. Breckinridge is P. G. of the I. O. O. F., and also a member of the K. of P. He is a Republican.

AMBROSE BRINTON was born in November, 1851, in York County, Penn., and is the third of nine children born to John and Sarah (Sunday) Brinton, natives of York County, Penn., and of English descent. The father followed farming until his death in 1876. The mother is still residing at the old homestead. Ambrose received a common school education, and remained with his parents until his twenty-second year, when he began business for himself. He followed farming until the fall of 1883, when he came to Lewisberry, Penn., where he opened a first-class hotel. His brother, John, has since torn down the old structure, and erected a fine frame building, which is an ornament to the borough. The hotel has seventeen rooms, elegantly furnished, and Mr. Brinton is prepared to furnish first-class accomodations to the traveling public. He was married, July 26, 1874, to Margaret Shank. They have had four children: Emma J., Herman (deceased), Samuel H. and Annie B. In politics he is a Democrat.

ABRAM COBLE was born July 25,1843,in York County,Penn., and is the fifth of eight children of Peter and Mary (Christ) Coble, deceased, of York County, Penn., and of Dutch descent. The father was a shoe-maker by trade, but quitted that occupation and began farming, which he followed till his death. Abram Coble was brought up a farmer, and followed that occupation until the fall of 1861, when he enlisted in Company H, Eighty-seventh Regiment Pennsylvania Volunteer Infantry, for three years, and participated in the engagements of Mine Run, Wilderness, Cold Harbor, Petersburg, Winchester and numerous others. He was discharged as corporal at York in 1864. In the fall of 1865 he began learning the blacksmith's trade, and moved to York, Penn., where he worked nine years. Thence he went to Fairview Township, where he remained three years, and then located in Yocumtown, Penn., where he is now doing a good business. In 1867 he married Susan Hartman, daughter of Cornelius and Mary A. (Danner) Hartman, of German descent. By this union they have three children: John W., Mary A. and Carrie E. Mr. and Mrs. Coble are members of the United Brethren Church.

MARTIN S. CRULL was born in Newberry Township, York Co., Penn., July 6, 1841, and is the eldest of the two children born to John and Lydia (Shelley) Crull, natives of York County, Penn., and of English and German descent. The father followed farming until 1856, then engaged in the mercantile business until 1861, when he enlisted in the United States army for two years. The hardships and exposure undermined his health, which he never recovered. He died July 17, 1876. Martin S. remained on the farm until he was seventeen years of age, when he assisted his father in the mercantile business until 1862, when he purchased his father's stock of goods and continued the business until 1876. He enlisted in the army; was mustered in Company B, Two Hundredth Regiment Pennsylvania Volunteers, in the fall of 1864, and served till the close of the war in the Third Division, Ninth Corps. He took part in the battles of Spring Hill, Fort Steadman, Petersburg, was mustered out at Fort Ellsworth, Va., May 29, 1865, and discharged June 5, 1865. He was married to Mary Sipe in 1861. They have eight children: Henrietta, Grant, Clara J., Abraham S., Cecelia, Josephine, Daisy and Ada. In 1875 Mr. Crull removed to his present fine farm of 130 acres. For sixteen years he held the office of postmaster in Newberrytown.

DUGAN & FUNK, manufacturers and dealers in cigars, Goldsboro, Penn. This firm is composed of Ross W. Dugan and John C. Funk, of Newberry Township, York Co., Penn. They both learned the trade of cigar-making with Jesse Funk, father of one of the firm, and worked at it as journeymen for a number of years. They formed a partnership in 1878, and for some time did all the work themselves, but as the business increased they employed other labor until they had about eleven hands, manufacturing nearly half a million cigars in a year. In addition to their own cigars they handle and sell a great many made by other manufacturers. The senior member of the firm is a step-son of Jesse Funk, the father of the junior, under whom they learned their trade. They are both married. Mr. Dugan married Susan Berger, of Goldsboro, and has one child living, one having died. Mr. Funk married Lillie K. Reider, of Steelton, and has one child. Both gentlemen are members of the Church of God. Neither of them takes any active part in politics. Mr. Dugan is the only child of Levi and Catharine (Wolf) Dugan, natives of York County, Penn., of Irish and German descent, respectively. His father dying when he was but two years old, his mother was married to Jesse Funk, who had nine children.

WILLIAM EPPLEY was born February 3, 1852, in Newberry Township, York Co., Penn., and is the youngest of a family of three sons and three daughters of William and Sidney (Hays) Eppley, natives of York County, and of English and Welsh descent, respectively. The father kept hotel in Newberrytown for thirty-five years, but a few years before his death retired from business. The grandfather, Mills Hays, was once associate judge of York County. William Eppley was brought up in the village of Newberrytown, where he received a good public school education. At the age of twenty-one he went to Harrisburg, Penn., where he engaged as salesman in a cigar store; remained about one year. He then returned to his native town and engaged in the hotel business and the manufacture of cigars, which he has since followed with great success. He manufactures about 200,000 cigars a year. He was married, October 7, 1875, to Maggie Bower, a daughter of Henry and Mary J. (Kister) Bower, of York County, Penn., and of Dutch and English descent, respectively. By this union they have two children: William B. and Maude B. Eppley.

DANIEL F. FISHEL was born in Manor Township, Lancaster Co., Penn., October 13, 1838, and is a son of Henry and Mary (Frey) Fishel, of York and Lancaster Counties, Penn., and of German and English descent, respectively. Daniel F. is the eldest son in a family of four sons and seven daughters: two of the daughters died at the ages of six and seven; all the other children, with the exception of Daniel F. and another, still reside in Lancaster County with their father, their mother being dead: One sister resides in Indiana. At the age of eighteen, Daniel F. began learning the painting trade at Washington Borough, Penn., and worked at it five years. In August, 1864, he engaged in the saw-mill business at Washington Borough, and has since followed it. For three years he was a partner of Mr. Stamen, of that place. In 1880 he removed to Goldsboro, York Co., Penn., and took charge of Isaac Frazer's saw-mill, as superintendent. In addition to his duties as superintendent, he, in 1883, also took charge of a farm of 162 acres, which belonged to Mr. Frazer. In all, he has charge of thirteen men on the farm and in the mill. In the winter of 1862 he enlisted, at Harrisburg, Penn., in Company E, One Hundred and Seventy-eighth Regiment Pennsylvania Volunteers, a nine months' regiment connected with the Army of the Potomac. He was in the engagements at Bottom Ridge and Baltimore Cross Roads, and a number of skirmishes. Returning to his native county, he was married, December 31, 1871, to Mary E. Stamen, a daughter of his late employer. They have six children: Eugenia, Josephine, Mary, Stamen, Myra and Anna. Mr. Fishel is a member of the I. O. O. F. He was school director of Washington Borough three terms, councilman one term, and chief burgess one term.

ELI H. FREE was born in 1825, in York Co., Penn., and is the eldest of eleven children of Adam and Mary (Hake) Free, natives of York County, and of German descent, respectively, and both deceased. The father was a carpenter, but at the age of twenty-five years, began farming and running a distillery, which he followed until his death in 1854. Eli H. was brought up a farmer, received a good education, and taught school for two terms, when the free school system was first introduced. In 1847 he married Mary Krafft, who died in 1865. They had six children: Oliver, Mary, Emma, Amanda, Sarah and Ida. In 1863, when the rebels came to York, Penn., they passed his residence, then in Manchester Township, and took one of his best horses. In the spring of 1863 he moved to York, Penn., and established a hotel, now known as the Pennsylvania House. He remained there six years, when he sold the hotel, and moved to his present farm, located in Newberry Township, which contains 112 acres of land in a high state of cultivation, and finely situated. Mr. Free's second marriage was, in 1868, to Catherine Cassel. They have had three children: Clara E., Louisa and Daniel H. (deceased). Mr. and Mrs. Free belong to the Lutheran Church. He is a member of the I. O. R. M. Lodge [37, of York, Penn. In politics he is a Republican. He was a member of the school board in Manchester Township, and is a member of the board where he now resides. He served as justice of the peace in Manchester for five years, receiving his commission from Gov. William F. Johnson. He also enrolled Manchester Township in the fall of 1861, for the draft.

JACOB GARRETSON was born in 1826, in Warrington Township, York Co., Penn.; his parents were Israel and Ruth (Walker) Garretson, natives of York County, and of English descent. They had eight children, of whom Jacob is the eldest. His father was a son of Jacob Garretson, who was a son of William Garretson, one of the first settlers of Newberry Township, who left a farm, which was given by him to Jacob and by him to Israel, and by him given to the subject of this sketch. At his father's death subject was appointed administrator of his father's estate, and sold the old homestead, which had been in the family for over 100 years, and on which he had been reared. In 1877 he married Eliza Betz. In religion, the Garretsons have all been Friends, and in politics they had always been Whigs and Republicans. Mr. Garretson and family at present reside on the old Hoops property, in sight of the old homestead. He owns over 250 acres of choice land and is a prosperous farmer. Previous ancestry of Jacob Garretson were: Great-great-grandparents John and Content Garretson. John Garretson was born 1715, his children were William Garretson, born in 1738-39; John, 1741; Ann, 1745; Samuel, 1750; Sarah, 1752; Content, 1754; Cornelius, 1756; Joseph,1759. Great-grandfather, William Garretson, was born 1738-89; Lydia his wife was born 1744. Their children were William, born in 1762; Elizabeth, 1763; John, 1765; Jacob, 1767; Martha, 1769. Grandfather, Jacob Garretson, and Mary, his wife, were born in 1763; their children were Lydia, born in 1796; Israel, 1798; Jacob, 1800; Daniel, 1802; James 1809. Parents. Israel and Ruth (Walker) Garretson, and their children: Jacob Garretson, was born in 1826; Lydia, 1828; Ruthanna, 1833; Mary, 1836; Martha, 1839; Robert, 1842; and Marie, 1845. Jacob Garretson's wife's paternal ancestry: Great-great-grandfather Betz died at the age of one hundred and five years; he had six sons, who were all stonemasons, the grandfather of George Betz being one. The father of George Betz died about 1822; he was about fifty years of age. George had one brother, Michael, who died about 1832, aged about thirty years; he had four sisters, all dead except one. George Betz's mother was born February 1, 1775; died about December 9, 1844, aged seventy years. She was, before marriage, ◆ Elizabeth Sheaffer. George Betz was born 1812, died March 28, 1885, aged seventy-two years ten months and four days. Her maternal ancestry: Jacob Hummer, grandfather, born 1748; died, 1854, aged ninety-six years. Mrs. Jacob Hummer, born 1773, and died February, 1811, aged thirty-eight years; her maiden name was Treimyer, a family of very high standing; she had a brother, Jacob. Jacob Hummer moved from New Holland, Lancaster County; he had a sister, Rachel, who reached ninety years of age; he had a son, John, born in 1794, died 1855, aged sixty-one years; he was a man of culture. Jacob Hummer had four sons and four daughters. Rebecca Hummer, wife of George Betz, was born in 1811, died in 1871, aged fifty-nine years eight months and two days.

DAVID H. GOOD was born September 21, 1839, in Dauphin County, Penn., and is the fifth son and seventh child of a family of nineteen children born to Peter and Catharine (Zorger) Good, natives of York County, Penn. He was brought up a farmer and remained with his parents until his twenty-second year, when he enlisted in Company A, Second District of Columbia Volunteer Infantry, January 17, 1862, and participated in the battles of Antietam, Fort Washington and second Bull Run. At the expiration of his term of service, three years, he was discharged, January 18, 1865, when he came home and resumed farming, and after two years engaged in the mercantile business, which he has followed since. He began business at Eberly Mills, Cumberland Co., Penn., but came to his present place in 1870. In 1871 he was commissioned postmaster of Yocumtown. In 1868 he married Mrs. Carrie (King) Tate, widow of Martin Tate, and daughter of Henry and Susan (Raffensberger) King, of York County, and of English and German descent. They have two children: Maggie and Catharine.

REV. WILLIAM JOHN GRISSINGER, resident pastor of the Bethel Church of God at Goldsboro, York Co., Penn., was born in Huntingdon County, Penn., January 16, 1844, son of Samuel and Mary (McNeal) Grissinger, natives of York and Huntingdon Counties, and of German and Irish descent respectively. They had three sons and six daughters. William was the eldest of the family. He remained on his father's farm till he was fifteen years old, attending the public schools, and also for one term the Millersville Normal School. He acquired a thorough English education, and at thirty years of age began studying for the ministry. In October, 1876, he was licensed and ordained to preach, and at once went to Newport, Perry Co., Penn., where he preached two years. His subsequent charges were Clearfield Mission at Clearfield, Penn., one year; Newville and Plainfield, Cumberland County, two years. He then returned to Newport and thence to Goldsboro, in October, 1882. Before studying for the ministry, he taught school for five terms. He was married at Mt. Carrol, Ill., in 1865, to Catharine Chitty, of Illinois. They have five children: Samuel C., Benjamin F., Clarence Rudolph, Carrie A., Juanita and Oliver L. Mr. Grissinger was brought up in the church of God, and became a member at the age of eighteen years. At present he has charge of four congregations: Goldsboro, Newberrytown, Yocumtown and Smoketown. From 1869 to 1876 he was engaged in mercantile business at New Grenada, Penn. His great-grandfather, John Grissinger, who came from Germany, located near Lewisburg, where he died in 1853, aged nearly ninety-eight years. He had 382 descendants: 123 grandchildren, 242 great-grandchildren, 3 great-great-grandchildren and 14 children.

HERVEY HAMMOND. About the year 1634, William Hammond, son of Admiral Hammond, of the English navy, embarked in the ship Francis, from Ipswich, England, and immigrating to America, joined the Boston colony, and settled at Watertown, Mass. He descended from a prominent family of his native country, and from him and his brother, Thomas, also an immigrant to Massachusetts, most of the Hammonds in this country descended. Like many other people of the thrifty and intelligent classes of Englnad, these brothers determined to seek a new home in the Western world, where civil liberty and religious freedom would be honored and respected. It was contemporaneous with this emigration, that the tyranny of Charles I. was greater than the liberty-loving people could endure, consequently most of the members of the Boston colony were generally enterprising and intelligent Puritan stock, and some of their descendants have become prominent and influential in the history of America. Among them were the ancestors of President Gar

BIOGRAPHICAL SKETCHES. 153

field and Gen. Sherman, who also settled in Watertown and intermarried with the Hammonds. Jabez (or Jason) Hammond, grandfather of the subject, located in Canterbury Township, Windham Co., Conn., about 1760; when the Revolutionary war opened, he entered the military service and participated in several hard-fought battles in that prolonged struggle for American freedom. Elisha Hammond, his son, was born in Connecticut, February 7, 1769. He received an excellent education in the schools of his native State. He was acquainted with I. M. Singer before he invented the sewing machine; met him in Pittsburgh and examined his rough model, approved, suggested some improvements and loaned him $10 to go ahead with his invention, but the money was never returned. Elisha afterward became a skillful and successful teacher; understood the higher mathematics and theoretical surveying. While yet a young man he removed to Marbletown, New York, and taught there in 1791, and later followed the same profession at Owego in the same State. His endorsements of qualifications and success in his work are still kept by his grandson as family relics. Leaving Owego, he entered the Wyoming Settlement in Luzerne County, Penn., and from thence came down the Susquehanna River on an ark, then a common craft for floating lumber and produce down the stream to market. He located in Fairview Township, in the vicinity of Lewisberry, about 1797. He brought with him many books of science and literature, and soon afterward engaged to teach the youths of the intelligent Quaker settlement. He was a man of undoubted integrity. He married Rebecca Frankelberger, of a prominent family in the Redland Valley. They had ten children, viz.: Hervey, Maria, Mary, David, William, Hannah, John, Thomas, Philip and Sarah. Elisha Hammond died March 28, 1824, at the age of fifty-five years. He was highly respected in the village in which he lived. His widow survived him until January 31, 1863, and died at the advanced age of eighty-two years. Hervey Hammond was born December 23, 1800; grew to manhood in his native town; attended his father's school and that of Isaac Kirk, the distinguished surveyor. The youth soon became the most active pupil of the school, and early in life followed the same profession as his father. From his ancestors he inherited a thirst for study, and soon became proficient in the ordinary branches of learning, and under his father's private instruction, pursued advanced studies. As early as 1825, he introduced the study of scientific English grammar in his neighborhood. The book used was Greenleaf's Practical Grammar. He was also of a mathematical turn of mind, which endowment he turned to practical account by his invention of the famous Hammond Window Sash Spring, which has since had an immense sale. It was patented in 1837, and during the following year he placed his springs in the windows of the White House at Washington; received a recommendation for them from the noted orator, Henry Clay, and from other distinguished persons. Mr. Hammond traveled extensively wholesaling goods and merchandise and introducing his window springs and appointing agents for the sale of them. In those times there were very few appliances for window sashes, in general use, and Mr. Hammond had to first teach the people the necessity of ventilating their dwellings in order to create a market or demand for his springs. In the year 1840, the annual sales of springs numbered 85,000. He introduced many improvements into the village of Lewisberry; was a supporter of the cause of free education; became one of the first school directors under the new school law, and was an active director, present at the election of his friend and neighbor, the Hon. Jacob Kirk, as the first superintendent of the schools of York County. He was married at Carlisle, Penn., September 15, 1825 to Katherine Ann Harman. They had nine children, viz.: Andrew (deceased); Bennett, died of cholera at Aurora, Ind., in 1849; Caroline E., in Wichita, Kas.; Delilah A., in Missouri; Edward W., in Oregon; Rebecca R., in Cantrall, Ill.; Mary (deceased); Winfield Scott, and Ida C., in Waynesburgh, Green Co., Penn. Mrs. Hammond was born August 31, 1807, in Warrington Township; was a daughter of Adam and Rachel (Diceman) Harman, members of the Methodist Church, and representatives of intelligent families. She, herself, was possessed of a well-trained mind. She died July 31, 1863; Hervey H. died August 27, 1855.

WINFIELD SCOTT HAMMOND, the youngest son of Hervey Hammond, was born in Lewisberry September 11, 1847. He attended the public schools and studied the higher branches at home. When quite young he acquired a fondness for reading, and hence made good use of his father's library, and such other libraries as the town afforded. In the spring of 1865 he enlisted in Company I, One Hundred and Ninety-second Regiment of the Pennsylvania Volunteers, and remained in the service until the fall of the same year. Shortly after the war he went to southeast Missouri, and remained in that section about eighteen months, spending a part of the time in a printing office as compositor and local editor, and assisting in the United States land office, which was under the charge of one of the proprietors of the paper. While there Mr. Hammond became intimate with the leading business men and politicians of the county; one was State senator, and afterward land agent for a leading railroad in the West; another, a prominent lawyer, pleading before the Supreme Court of the United States; another, State treasurer of Missouri; another, delegate from the State-at-large to the National Democratic Convention; another, district attorney, etc. This was under the "carpet bag" *regime*, and Mr. Hammond being a "Radical" (in Missouri politics) was offered the office of county clerk in one of the southeastern counties, which he refused and returned home to take charge of the window-spring business, and became owner and controller of the popular springs, which he has manufactured and sold with great success. He introduced some new improvements in the construction of them, and entirely changed the process of manufacture, doing by machinery what was formerly done by hand. He has recently invented some new styles of springs, and is engaged in their manufacture, and has a number of workmen in his employ. Large quantities of the springs are sold annually to wholesale dealers. Early in life Mr. Hammond developed a taste for painting, and now spends his leisure hours in sketching places interesting to the scenes of his childhood, and the picturesque ravines and hills of the upper end of the county. Mr. Hammond is the artist who furnished the sketch, from which we have engraved the cut of the "Old Friends Meeting House," two miles east of Lewisberry; which engraving will be found in this work. Mr. H. is at present secretary of the school board, and was a member of the committee on resolutions in the late Republican State convention. Mr. Hammond was married, in 1873, to Miss Jeannette Starr, daughter of Reuben T. Starr, and Elizabeth (Lloyd) Starr, of Lewisberry. They have two children, viz.: Edward and Grace. Mrs. Hammond is a descendant of the Friends of Chester County, her ancestors being of the celebrated Taylor, Sharpless, Lloyd and Starr families, and is an active member of the Methodist Episcopal Church. Mr. Hammond keeps himself abreast of the times in literature, science and art, being a constant reader of various periodicals, literary and art

154   NEWBERRY TOWNSHIP.

magazines, mechanical, scientific and architectural journals, etc., etc., and is a book buyer.

MORRIS M. HAYS is a lineal descendant in the fourth generation of Jesse Hays, who in 1770 immigrated to York County from Chester County, Penn., and purchased land one mile north of the village of Yocumtown. Jesse Hays was of Welsh descent. His ancestors were among the first immigrants to America from Wales, who located in the northern and western parts of Chester, and most of whom became prosperous citizens in this country. Being a member of the Society of Friends, who, in principle, were non-resistants, when Jesse Hays was drafted during the Revolutionary war, his land was sold to furnish a substitute in the army. His occupation was that of a tailor. In 1780 he married Margery, daughter of James Mills, who built the historic stone house, one-half mile east of Yocumtown, known later as the "Brubaker property." Their children were Susan, Hannah and Mills, who in 1851 was elected associate judge of York County. A sketch of him will be found in the chapter on the Bench and the Bar, in this work. Mills Hays was married to Eve Crull. They had children as follows: John; Sidney married to William Eppley; Mary, married to George W. Hall; Jesse, born July 24, 1818, and now living in Mechanicsburg, married to Mary Miller; and Jane, married to Samuel P. Herman. John Hays, the eldest son of Judge Mills Hays, was born October 11, 1810, in Newberry Township, where he spent his entire life, a highly respected citizen. He served for many years as a director in the Dover Fire Insurance Company, and filled many local positions of trust and responsibility. He was married to Jane Morris, daughter of Charles Morris, of Warrington Township, of Scotch-Irish descent. In 1814 he marched with a company of soldiers to the defense of Baltimore. Jane (Glass) Morris, his mother, died in Warrington at the age of ninety-six years. The children of John Hays are Sidney, married to David Ort; Adacinda, married to A. B. Kurtz; Morris Mills; Granville, married to Kate Reiff; Crull, a soldier of the One Hundred and Sixty-sixth Regiment, Pennsylvania Volunteers during the Civil war, and Ninth Pennsylvania Cavalry; Ellen; Lucetta; Servatus, married to Kate Feiser, and now a merchant in Newberrytown, and John Pierce, a graduate of Shippensburg State Normal School, married to Maggie Flora of Franklin County. Morris M. Hays, the eldest son and third child, was born September 13, 1841. He spent his early days on the farm and attending the public schools; afterward was a student in the Normal and Classical School, at York, and in the Millersville State Normal School. He taught school three successive terms. In 1867 he was married to Emma Fisher who died August 23, 1872. On the 20th of February, 1876, he was married to Sara M. Krone. They have three children: Ira, Kent and Boyd. In November, 1882, Mr. Hays was elected a member of the legislature of Pennsylvania, and while a representative in that body, served with great acceptance on the committees on labor and industry, insurance, military and geological survey. He now owns a farm on which he resides, located one mile east of Newberrytown, and is engaged in cultivating it. He is a practical surveyor, and has served in various township offices. Mr. Hays, in the midst of his farm and professional labors, finds time for reading and general literary culture, and has accumulated a library of well selected books.

LAFAYETTE M. HERMAN was born in Newberrytown, York County, September 13, 1853, and is the second son of William P. Herman, of German descent, who was born in Fishing Creek Valley, York County, and was the father of eight children—two sons and six daughters—and of Jane, daughter of Joseph McCreary, who was of Irish ancestry, though native born, and who, during his life time, held the offices of supervisor, overseer of the poor, justice of the peace, and commissioner of the County of York, and under whose supervision the present county alms house was built. William P. Herman, after the death of his father, Samuel Herman, resided in Fishing Creek Valley, among the friends of his mother (whose maiden name was Mary Prowell), until becoming of age, when he married and removed to Newberrytown, where he remained engaged in the manufacture of cigars, until the time of his death, which occurred September 25, 1868, in the forty-eighth year of his age, leaving to survive him a wife, two sons, Clayton and L. M., and two daughters, Sadie E. and Eva. L. M. Herman, at the time of his father's death, was fifteen years of age, and had to support the remaining family, consisting of a mother and two sisters. At the age of fifteen years he left the public schools and continued to work among the cigar factories for two years, at the end of which time, by his own exertions, and through the kindness of others, he attended a select school at Goldsboro, Penn., and was enabled to procure from W. H. Kain, county superintendent, a provisional certificate to teach in the common schools of the county for one year. He applied to the directors of his township and they granted him a school, which he taught three successive terms. During the summer vacations he attended the Cumberland Valley State Normal School until enabled to procure a professional certificate, granted by county superintendent, D. G. Williams, and up to the present writing he has taught twelve successive years in his native township. June 10, 1882, he received from Prof. E. E. Higbee, superintendent of public instruction, a permanent certificate. In politics he is a Republican, and has held the office of township clerk for seven successive terms. At the expiration of his seventh term he was elected to the office of justice of the peace of Newberry Township for the term of five years, beginning on the first Monday in May, 1882. At various times he has been committeeman, and represented the district as delegate to county conventions. January 1, 1883, he engaged in manufacturing cigars. He is unmarried, and still remains at the old homestead, with the family, which consists of his mother and one sister, Eva—Sadie E. having died April 14, 1884, in Urbana, Ohio. The family are members of the Bethel, or Church of God.

ALFRED HUMMEL, was born at Hummelstown, Dauphin Co., Penn., July 12, 1833, and is a son of David and Barbara (Shirer) Hummel, natives of Dauphin County, Penn., and of German descent. His great-grandfather, Hummel, came to this country some time in the eighteenth century, and located the village of Hummelstown, and laid out the lots and sold them (60x198 feet) at an annual rent of $2.22. David and Barbara (Shirer) Hummel reared a family of nine children—eight sons and one daughter—of whom Alfred is the eldest. Two of the sons are dead, and four of the sons and the daughter still reside in Dauphin County, Penn. Alfred moved to Goldsboro in 1879, where his family followed him the following spring. In his youth he learned the carpenter's trade with his father, but at the age of seventeen years went to Harrisburgh, where he worked as journeyman for three years. He then returned to his native place and engaged as a builder and contractor until 1869. He was married at Harrisburgh, Penn., January 1, 1854, to Harriet W. Kennedy, a native of Pennsylvania, and of German and Irish descent. They had nine children: William D., died July 4, 1877; Emma L., Arthur L., Lizzie B., Winfield Scott, Calvin F., Estella H. and two who died in infancy. Mr. Hummel is a Lutheran, and his wife belongs to the Methodist Episcopal Church. He is also a member of

BIOGRAPHICAL SKETCHES. 155

the Masonic fraternity. He has held various public offices: Assessor of Derry Township, Dauphin County, in 1862; collector of taxes for the same township; school director nine years; treasurer of Dauphin County in 1868, and since coming to York County, as school director. He is in the employ of Isaac Frazer, as manager of the large planing-mill at Goldsboro, and has from twenty-five to thirty men under him.

ISAAC KISTER was born in December, 1823, in Newberry Township, York County, and is the fourth of nine children of Henry E. and Tacey (Hart) Kister, natives of York County, and of German descent, both deceased. The father was a farmer, and acted as justice of the peace several times during his life. Isaac Kister was brought up as a farmer, and remained with his mother until he was sixteen years of age, when he hired out to work on a farm, performing any kind of labor until he was thirty-three years of age, when he purchased some land, where he finally made his home. He built large and commodious buildings, adding acre after acre to his farm, and has now a fine farm of seventy acres, as the result of his industry. In 1856 he married Letitia H. Shelley, who died in 1874. They had nine children, four now living: Crull S., Ulysses G., Annie E. and Harry. Those who died were Viola, Flora E., Ida and two infants. In 1876 he married Mrs. Sarah Gross, widow of Daniel Gross; they have one child: Charley. Mr. Kister enlisted in February, 1865, in Company K, One Hundred and Ninety-second Regiment Pennsylvania Volunteer Infantry, and served until the close of the war. Although in no engagement, he received a severe injury in the right knee in crossing a fence, the top rail giving way and throwing him to the ground. In politics he is very liberal, always voting for the man rather than the party.

DAVID H. KISTER was born in Newberrytown, York County, Penn., September 2, 1830, and is a son of Jacob E. and Catherine (Hart) Kister, of York County. At the age of nineteen years he began to learn the cigar-maker's trade, which he has continued to the present day. He manufactures from 100,000 to 800,000 cigars per annum. He enlisted, in Harrisburgh, Penn., February 20, 1865, in Company K, One Hundred and Ninety-second Regiment, Pennsylvania Volunteer Infantry, to serve for one year, or during the war, and was honorably discharged at the end of his term. On his return home he purchased several tracts of land, which he also cultivates. July 16, 1854, he was married to Mary J. Mills, of the same county, and daughter of James and Elizabeth (Miller) Mills, who was born July 2, 1835. To this union have been born eleven children: Elizabeth M., born July 1, 1855; Jane M., born March 7, 1857; Inza M., born March 11, 1859; Ellsworth M., born May 4, 1861; Catherine M., born June 29, 1863; John M., born October 6, 1865; Mary M., born March 1, 1868; Annetta M.; born September 8, 1870; Charles M., born January 11, 1873; Gertrude M., born March 20, 1875; Lulu M., born March 21, 1878—all living.

JOHN KISTER was born in Newberry Township, York Co., Penn., June 24, 1833, on the place where now stands a part of Goldsboro. His parents were Jacob G. and Nancy (Bowen) Kister, natives of York County, of German descent, who had eleven children, of whom four sons and three daughters grew up, and of whom John was the sixth child. At the age of nineteen years John left the farm, and followed saw-milling, running a stationary engine in York County, until he was twenty-six years old, when he engaged in farming, which he followed eight years. June 27, 1863, he enlisted at Harrisburgh, Penn., in Company B, First Regiment Pennsylvania Volunteer Infantry—six months' men—and served until October 3, 1863. August 17, 1864, he re-enlisted at Harrisburgh as second sergeant of Company B, Two Hundredth Regiment Pennsylvania Volunteers, and served until the close of the war. His regiment was connected with the First Brigade, Third Division, Ninth Corps, and fought at Fort Steadman, Petersburg, and until Lee's surrender. At the close of the war he returned to Goldsboro In 1867 he quit farming, and again ran a stationary engine. In 1869 he was appointed postmaster at Etters, Penn., and has held that office since. In 1855 he was married, at Shiremanstown, Penn., to Hannah Willis, who died January 8, 1867, leaving two children: Frazer and Nora. The son Frazer is engineer for Mr. Isaac Frazer, occupying his father's old position. The daughter, Nora, died a short time after her mother. March 10, 1868, Mr. Kister was married, at Goldsborough, to Mrs. Catherine A. Wise, daughter of G. C. Wentz, and widow of W. Wise, who was killed in the late war. They had one child: Robert, who died in infancy. Mr. Kister belongs to the I. O. O. F., and is also a member of the Junior Mechanics; he was chief burgess four terms, councilman two terms, and school director two terms. He is a Republican. He owns a farm, is a stockholder in the Star Building & Loan Association of York, and keeps a confectionary store in the postoffice building. In 1883 he organized the Independent Cornet Band, of Goldsboro, and equipped it with uniforms and instruments at his own expense. He has traveled a great deal, but lives now within 300 yards of his birthplace.

JACOB S. KOCH was born March 26, 1823, in Newberry Township, York Co., Penn., and is the ninth of the eleven children of Daniel and Mary (Stair) Koch, natives of York County, Penn., and of German descent. He remained on the home farm until he was twenty-six years of age, when he began for himself, first working on a farm, and then farming for himself, which occupation he followed until 1868, when he engaged in milling, and followed that for three years. He next engaged as foreman in the manufacture of cigars, employing from four to eight hands, and making about 335,000 cigars annually. In 1849 he married Ann Fry, a daughter of Conrad and Nancy (Burger) Fry, natives of York County, Penn They have had eleven children: Henry (deceased), Daniel (deceased), Benjamin. Samuel (deceased), Silas, Rosetta, Paul, George, Mary, Kate and Reuben. Mrs. Koch is a member of the Church of God. Mr. Koch is a strong advocate of temperance, and was a member of the S. of T. until the order went down.

LUTHER M. LANDES was born in Baltimore County, Md., April 26, 1856. His parents were John and Elizabeth (Fair) Landes, of Pennsylvania and Maryland, respectively, and of English descent. They had seven children—four sons and three daughters—of whom Luther is the fifth child and third son. At the age of fourteen years, he entered John Bahn's mill in Carroll County, Md., where he remained two years. He then came to York County, Penn., where he worked two years in A. Miller's mill, in Lower Windsor Township. He afterward worked for P. A. & S. Small five years, at Loucks' mills; then went to Selin's Grove, Snyder Co., Penn., where he worked in Schoch's mills two years, and in the spring of 1880, came to Goldsboro, where he took charge of P. A. & S. Small's mill, and where he has been since; he is a thorough miller, and gives entire satisfaction to his employers and patrons. May 26, 1880, he was married at Selin's Grove, to Ada Ott, daughter of Daniel Ott, a farmer of Snyder County, Penn.; they have one child—George Erskine. Mrs. Landes belongs to the Lutheran Church.

I. LEO MINGLE, M. D., was born September 15, 1839, in Berks County, Penn., and is the third of four sons in the family of ten children of Jacob and Hannah (Leoscher) Mingle (both deceased), of Berks County, Penn. The father was a mason by trade, but spent the last thirty-six years of his life in farming. Our subject was brought up to farming, attending the public schools until he was eighteen years of age, and then attended two years at Freeland Seminary, now Ursinus College, in Montgomery County, Penn. He then taught school in Berks County for four terms. In the fall of 1861 he began studying medicine under Dr. F. B. Nice, and in July, 1862, joined the State militia; after leaving it he resumed the study of medicine with his former preceptor, and remained with him until the fall of the same year, when he entered the Jefferson Medical College at Philadelphia, where he remained until the following spring. March 8, he entered Long Island College, Brooklyn, N. Y., and remained until midsummer, when he returned home, opened an office and practiced one year. In the fall of 1865, he again went to Jefferson College, graduated in 1866, and returning home resumed his practice again. He practiced six years in Lebanon County, and eight years in Northumberland County, Penn. In the fall of 1878, he came to Newberrytown, where he has a lucrative practice. He was married, August 20, 1864, to Lydia A. (Loose), who died, leaving one child—Lu Annie L., May 29, 1865. Dr. Mingle next married, November 5, 1868, Mary M. Herr; they have had three children: Otis W. (deceased), Lillia G., and Almeda C. Dr. Mingle and wife, belong to the German Reformed Church.

HIRAM PAUP was born August 3, 1829, in Warrington Township, York Co., Penn., and is the eldest of the eight children of Valentine and Catharine (Raffensberger) Paup, natives of York County, Penn., and of English and German descent respectively, both deceased. Valentine Paup was a weaver by trade, but gave it up and went farming, which he followed until his death. Hiram, at the age of eighteen years, began learning the trade of blacksmithing, which he has followed, with the exception of a few years, until the present time. He came to Newberry Township in 1851, first locating in the country, and then in 1872, removed to Lewisberry where he has since carried on business. In February, 1865, he enlisted in Company K, One Hundred and Ninety-second Regiment Pennsylvania Volunteers, and served as blacksmith until August 16, 1865. In 1853, he married Phœbe A. Hoopes. They have had six children, of whom four are living: Emma J., Mary E., James M. (deceased), Catharine (deceased), Amanda A. and Marlette C. Mrs. Paup is a daughter of Daniel and Mary (Nicholas) Hoopes, of York County. Mr. and Mrs. Paup are members of the Evangelical Church. He is a Republican, and has been elected chief burgess of Lewisberry, and school director. He is a class leader in the church.

JOHN A. RYNARD M. D., was born in Cumberland County, Penn., September 19, 1839, and is a son of Cyrus A. and Susan (Landis) Rynard, natives of Cumberland County, Penn., and of German descent, who had eight children—six daughters and two sons—of whom John A., is the eldest. The pioneer of the Rynard family was Christian Reiner, born in Wurtemburg, Germany, who came to this country about the year 1750, and settled in Northampton County, Penn., where he spent the rest of his life. His eldest son, John, who was born in Northhampton County, Penn., and died in Cumberland County, Penn., aged ninety-five years, was the great-grandfather of John A., and wrote his name Reinert. His son John, who spent his life in Cumberland County, Penn., was the first to write his name Rynard. The whole family has been more or less interested in agriculture. Our subject spent his younger days on his father's farm; for one year he worked at cabinet-making, but in 1858 he attended the normal school at Newville, Penn. The year following he attended a select school at the same place, and in 1860 he attended the Big Spring Academy. In the same year he was licensed to teach in the public schools, and taught eight years, and at the same time followed surveying. In 1869 he began the study of medicine with Dr. S. H. Brehm at Newville, Penn., and in the fall of 1870 entered Jefferson Medical College in Philadelphia, from which he graduated as M. D. in the class of 1872. He first located at Bloserville, Penn., but after a short time removed to Greasonville, Penn., where he practiced medicine until 1875, when he located at Goldsboro, York County, Penn., where he has since practiced medicine and surgery. In 1880 he was appointed railroad surgeon at Goldsboro by the Northern Central Railway Company, which position he still holds. He was married, in 1863, to Sarah A. Daelhousen, of Cumberland County, Penn., daughter of Daniel Daelhousen. They have four children: Mary E., teacher; Mina B., wife of George W. Wise, of Goldsboro, Penn.; Charles W. and Norman B. Dr. Rynard was a member of the I. O. O. F. Encampment at Newville, while he resided in Cumberland County. He was at one time justice of the peace, which office he resigned when he began the study of medicine. He and his wife are Lutherans.

JACOB F. SCOTT was born October 31, 1848, in Baltimore County, Md., and is the eldest of seven children born to Frederick T. and Elizabeth A. (Cook) Scott, natives of Maryland, and of Irish and German descent, respectively. He remained with his parents until he was eighteen years of age, when he began business for himself. He served an apprenticeship in a machine-shop in Baltimore, and came to York, Penn., about 1868, and worked at his trade. He was married, in the fall of 1872, to Ellen T. Ihnen, daughter of Henry S. and Eliza (Sigersmith) Ihnen, of German descent. They have had five children: Frederick I., Jeanetta C., Oscar C., Emma H. and an infant, deceased. Mr. and Mrs. Scott belong to the Episcopal Church. He is a member of the Masonic Lodge No. 240, at Whistler, Ala.; and of Division 93, Jackson, Tenn., of the brotherhood of Locomotive Engineers. He is an engineer and has run the engine on the Peach Bottom Railroad for seven years. He is also working his father's farm and saw-mill.

ABRAHAM SHELLEY was born in Dauphin County, Penn., October 3, 1809, and is the seventh of eight children of Daniel and Elizabeth (Shuman) Shelley, of Dauphin and York Counties, Penn., respectively, and of German descent, now deceased. Abraham Shelley, at eighteen years of age, began serving an apprenticeship at shoe-making, but followed his trade only one year, when he began farming, and has since followed that occupation. At one time he operated two saw-mills in connection with the farm. For more than sixteen years he ran timber on the river. At one time he was said to be worth $18,-000, but lost most of it by giving securities. For about eight seasons he followed shad-fishing. June 14, 1832, he married Henrietta Crull, who died in 1855. They had twelve children, four living: Bartram, Henry, Walter and Abraham. Those deceased are: Martin, Oliver, Daniel, Elizabeth, Catharine, Albert, Jane and Mary E. He married Annie M. Hess, February 2, 1862. They have had eleven children: Edward, Mary, Clymer, Latimer, Lewis, Ida (deceased), Lydia (deceased), Swiler, Ella, Russell S. (deceased) and Mina. Mr. Shelley is still hale and hearty. He and his wife belong to the United Brethren Church. He cast his first vote for Gen. Jackson. Although formerly a Whig he has, since Taylor's time, cast his lot with the Democrats.

HENRY C. SHELLEY was born March 3, 1844, in York County, Penn., and is the eighth of eleven

BIOGRAPHICAL SKETCHES.

children of Abraham and Henrietta (Crull) Shelley, the former a native of Dauphin County, Penn., and the latter of York County, and of German descent. The mother died in 1856. The father is living in Newberry and is overseeing his farm. Henry C. remained on the farm until 1864, when he enlisted in Company B, Two Hundreth Regiment Pennsylvania Volunteer Infantry, under Col. Divens and Capt. Hoover. He was in two engagements—Fort Steadman, March 25, 1865, and at the capture of Petersburg. At one time he suffered from a severe attack of typhoid fever. He was discharged at Washington, D. C., May 31, 1865. October 11, 1863, he married Prudence B. Prowell, by whom he has had nine children: Ella K. (deceased), John P., Fannie E., George (deceased), Myrtie, Ettie R., Lloyd (deceased), Harry E. (deceased) and Edith. In politics he is a Democrat. Mrs. Shelley was born September 30, 1846, daughter of John M. and Barbara Prowell, of York County, Penn., now of New Cumberland, Penn., and of English and Irish descent. After his return from the army Mr. Shelley engaged in hucksteringfor five years. In the winter of 1872 he engaged in his present business—groceries and confectionery.

LYMAN L. SHETTEL was born in Lewisberry, Penn., June 7, 1851, and is the youngest of the four children of John and Caroline (Harman) Shettel, natives of York County, and of German descent. Lyman L., at the age of fifteen years, began to manufacture matches, and prospered so well that now he owns and controls the factory at Lewisberry, Penn., where he manufactures block or percussion matches, which have a rapid sale. July 6, 1873, he was married to Laura A. Stonesifer, daughter of Henry and Eliza (King) Stonesifer, of Maryland. They have one child—John H. Mr. Shettel manufactures about 1,200 gross of matches in his factory.

JOHN A. SMITH was born in 1857, in Maytown, York Co., Penn., and is the fourth of eleven children of William and Harriet (Jacobs) Smith, natives of York County, Penn., and of English descent. His father is a carpenter by trade, and is a resident of Lewisberry. John A. was brought up in a small village, and received a common school education. In the fall of 1873, he, in company with his parents, came to Lewisberry, Penn., where he assisted his father at his trade, until he was seventeen years of age. He then took up the trade of silversmith, and, though having no instructor, made such rapid progress, that at present he has a good paying business. In politics, he is a Republican.

DR. W. H. SPANGLER was born in York County, Penn., in 1856, and is the third of seven children of David and Louisa (Melsheimer) Spangler, of York County, and of Dutch descent. Until he was twelve years of age he remained on the farm, but after that he commenced looking out for himself. He began the study of veterinary surgery, when he was twenty-one years of age, under a German graduate—Dr. Joseph Keiser, of York, and remained under his instruction for four years. He then went to Urbana, Ohio, where he opened an office, and remained there one year and a half. He then went to Minnesota, and located in St. Paul, where he remained for a short time and then came to Lewisberry, where he has since been doing a good business, and has been very successful. With the help of his father he is now very comfortably situated. In politics he is a Republican.

J. C. STEM, M. D., was born July 26, 1855, in Cashtown, Adams Co., Penn., and is the son of William and Eliza (Watson) Stem, natives of Adams County, and of German and Irish descent, who had two children (twins), J. C. and Annie. The father is a retired physician in Cashtown, and his father, Reuben, now eighty years of age, is a retired merchant and resident of Adams County, Penn. Our subject's grandfather, on the mother's side, James Watson, died at the advanced age of one hundred and two years. Dr. J. C. Stem spent his younger days in Cashtown, where he attended the public and select schools, and afterward attended a select school at Gettysburg for five terms, and taught school at Buchanan Valley, Adams County, three winters. At the age of seventeen years he began the study of medicine with his father; then attended the Cincinnati College of Medicine and Surgery, and graduated in the class of 1878. He then took a tour through the West, after which he settled in Lewisberry, Penn., in the fall of 1878, where he has built up a lucrative practice. He was married, in 1880, to Mary Paup, daughter of Hiram and Phœbe A. (Hoopes) Paup, of York County.

ROBERT N. STONESIFER, justice of the peace, was born in Carroll County, Md., in March, 1852, and is the eldest of a family of eleven boys and two girls born to Jacob H. and Eliza (King) Stonesifer, natives of Pennsylvania, and of German and English descent, respectively. His father is a resident of Harrisburg and a dealer in produce. Robert N. at the age of sixteen began learning the tinner's trade, which he has followed ever since. He learned his trade at York, Penn.; went from there to Mechanicsburgh, and soon after settled in Lewisberry, where he is at present doing a good business. June 9, 1878, he married Alice M. Griest, daughter of Jonathan and Harriet (Prowell) Griest, of York County, and of English descent. They have two children: Vernie M. and Anna A. Mrs. Stonesifer is a member of the Methodist Episcopal Church. He is a Democrat, and was elected justice of the peace in 1888. In 1871 he started business at Lewisberry, as dealer in stoves and tin-ware, and established a good business.

REUBEN P. STROMINGER, ESQ., was born in Newberry Township, York Co., Penn., October 8, 1888, son of Michael and Catharine (Eternan) Strominger, of York County, Penn., and of German descent, who had a family of four sons and four daughters, of whom Reuben P. was the youngest son. April 21, 1861, he left the farm to enlist, at York, in Company F, Sixteenth Regiment Pennsylvania Volunteer Infantry, and served three months. August 12, 1863, he re-enlisted as a private in Company K, One Hundred and Forty-third Regiment Pennsylvania Volunteers, and served till the close of the war, when he was mustered out at Hart's Island. His regiment was connected with the Army of the Potomac, and took part in the battles of Mine Run, Weldon Railroad, Hatcher's Run and Wilderness, besides numerous skirmishes. After his return home he worked for about four years at carpentering and bridge building, and in 1869 removed to Goldsboro, where he has lived since. He was married at Goldsboro, in 1866, to Elizabeth Millard. They had two children, one of whom died in infancy, the other, Jennie, is married to Charles Breckinridge, of Goldsboro. Mr. Strominger was elected constable in 1870, and has held that office six terms. He was again elected in 1878, and held the office three terms. In 1882 he was appointed justice of the peace, to serve the unexpired term of F. R. Prowell, and in the ensuing election was elected for five years. He engaged in the fire insurance business in 1878, and is now the agent of the Farmers', of Dover; Manheim, of Lancaster; Valley Mutual, of Lebanon, of which latter he is also a director; Farmers', of York; Sun, of England; Pacific, of New York, and the Pennsylvania Mutual, of Columbia. He is also a dealer in tobacco.

J. M. SWEIGART was born in Lancaster County, Penn., in 1829, and is the second son in a family of four children born to Adam and Ann (Hartley) Sweigart, natives of Lancaster County, Penn., and of French and German descent, respectively, both deceased. The father was a school teacher and wagon-maker, and died in his eighty-fifth year. Subject's grandfathers, Sweigart and Hartley, were in the Revolutionary war, in which the latter received a serious wound, from which he never fully recovered. J. M. Sweigart was brought up a farmer, and remained with his parents until he was nineteen years of age, when he began the trade of milling, which he has followed through life. He came to York County, Penn., in 1840, with his parents, who resided there until they died. He purchased several old farms, improved them, and sold them again, and finally, in 1838, purchased what was known as Oil-Mill, a dilapidated structure, which he rebuilt, and which is now one of the best flour-mills in the county. Its capacity is twenty barrels per day. In 1850 he was married to Jane Stetler. Having no children they adopted one—Jennie R. Stetler.

WILLIAM E. SWILER, M. D., was born in Cumberland County, Penn., October 23, 1833, and is the second child in a family of three boys and two girls of John and Isabella (Eckels) Swiler, natives of Cumberland County, and of Scotch-Irish and English descent. The father followed farming and teaching for a livelihood, and died in 1839. The mother died in 1858. At the age of six years William E. was taken by his grandfather, who owned a farm, where he grew up, attending school until he was sixteen years old, when he went to Mechanicsburg, Penn., where he engaged in the mercantile business with his uncle. Here he remained two years, and then attended the academy at Mechanicsburg for two years. His health becoming impaired he quit the academy and went to Harrisburg, where he engaged in the mercantile business. He next came to Yocumtown, where he engaged in the mercantile business for a year, after which he went to Shiremanstown and commenced the study of medicine under Drs. Robert G. Young and Jacob C. Black. Under their instructions he remained one year, and then entered Jefferson Medical College, at Philadelphia, in 1855, and graduated in 1857. In the following spring he located at Yocumtown, Penn., where he still resides, and has acquired a large and lucrative practice. He was married, November 26, 1859, to Kate E. Pretz, who died December 9, 1878. They had five children: Minnie I., Lizzie L., Robert D., Carrie E. and Annie (deceased). November 9, 1880, he married Mrs. Matilda Groom, widow of William Groom, and daughter of Hiram and Susan (Reeser) Prowell.

JOHN H. TROUP was born in Lewisberry, Penn., in 1861, and is the second of eight children born to Abraham and Mary (Fox) Troup, the former a native of Adams County, Penn., the latter of Prussia. The parents are residents of Lewisberry, where the father carries on the trade of blacksmithing. John H. was brought up in the borough of Lewisberry, where he attended the public schools until he was twenty years old, when he went to Lockhaven, Penn., where he studied one term. He began the study of music at twelve years of age, and made such rapid progress that, at the age of seventeen, he began teaching music, and has since made it his profession. He also sells pianos and organs. He attended the Musical Normal School, held at Kittanning, Penn., with Dr. Maas and Eugene Thayer, as instructors, for one term. He was married, May 14, 1882, to Lizzie Swiler. They have one child—Vernie. In politics he is a Republican. At present he has a class of 100 scholars, and never has less than sixty.

JOHN A. WILLIS, Esq., was born in Newberry Township, York Co., Penn., March 1, 1835. His parents were George and Emma (Kister) Willis, of Newberry Township, and of English and German descent, respectively. They had six sons and six daughters, of whom John A. was the second son. He remained on the farm until fourteen years of age, when he went into the lumber business. At the age of nineteen he began working for Small, Stair & Co., and continued with them twenty-six years, spending seven years of that time in Clearfield County, Penn. Since 1871 he has been in the employ of Isaac Frazer, at Goldsboro. In 1856 he was married, in Cumberland County, Penn., to Caroline Crome, daughter of George Crome. She died April 3, 1884. They had eleven children, five of whom are living: Ida, Charles, Edwin, Latimore and John Guy. Mrs. Willis was a member of the Church of God. Mr. Willis has held various offices of trust, as borough councilman, school director, inspector, secretary of I. O. O. F., and at present he holds the office of justice of the peace, having been elected in the spring of 1884. He was one of the organizers of the Goldsboro Building and Loan Association.

GEORGE S. WOLF was born in York County, Penn., near the Maryland line, August 5, 1831. His parents were John and Elizabeth (Souders) Wolf, of York County, and of German descent, who had seven sons and five daughters—five children deceased. George S. was next to the eldest child. He remained on the farm until he was nineteen years old, when he commenced to learn blacksmithing, which he carried on for himself at the age of twenty-five, and which he has since followed. In his youth he attended the common schools at Goldsboro, walking in from the country a distance of nearly three miles. He was married, November 16, 1856, on Hill Island, Dauphin Co., Penn., to Lydia Groom, daughter of William Groom, a mason by trade, and of English descent. They had five children, all of whom are dead: Carrie, Cecilia, David, Laura and Maggie. Mr. Wolf belongs to the Church of God, and is sexton of that church. He is a member of the I. O. O. F. lodge, at Goldsboro, and of the American Mechanics. He has held the office of borough councilman for two terms, that of treasurer for three years, and chief burgess since 1879. He was one of the organizers of the Goldsboro Loan Associations, Nos. 1 and 2.

GEORGE D. ZEIGLER was born January 22, 1840, in Wrightsville, York Co., Penn., and is the eldest of eleven children born to George and Susan (Delingler) Zeigler, natives of York County, and of German descent. When fifteen years of age he began learning the tailoring trade, and followed it for eighteen months; after that he worked in a saw-mill until August 22, 1861, when he enlisted at Wrightsville, Penn., Company I, Seventy-sixth Regiment Pennsylvania Volunteer Infantry, under Col. J. M. Powers, and was at Fort Wagner, and also in the second attack on the same fort, where he was wounded in the left shoulder by a piece of shell. He was then taken to New York; thence to Pittsburgh, Penn., where he remained until fit for duty. He next engaged in the campaign against Hilton Head, at Butler's Front, S. C., and Petersburgh, and was wounded May 7, 1864, in the left arm. He was discharged July 28, 1864, and on account of wounds received in the army, is receiving a pension of $10 per month. April 7, 1864, he married Elizabeth Thompson. They had thirteen children, of whom six are living: Mary, Flora, George, Robert, Charley and Alide. Mrs. Zeigler is a daughter of Samuel and Sarah Thompson. Mr. Zeigler is a Republican. He owns considerable property in Goldsboro, Penn., and is at present a street commissioner.

NORTH CODORUS.

DR. W. F. BRINKMAN, a son of Henry N. and Catherine Brinkman, of Carroll County, Md., where our subject was born, in the village of Manchester, May 20, 1822. After attending the public school and the Manchester Academy he began to read medicine with Dr. Beltz, of Manchester, and after attending three full terms at Washington University, of Maryland, graduated at this institution, and began the practice of medicine in Manchester. After three years he removed (1849) to Jefferson, Codorus Township. In October, 1849, Dr. Brinkman married Sarah Ann Motter, daughter of Michael and Elizabeth (Roat) Motter. Eight children have been born to them: Rosetta, Virginia, Sarah, Emma, Josephine, Adolf, Harman and Horatio. Dr. Brinkman's ancestors came from Germany. The Doctor is a member of Mount Zion Lodge, I. O. O. F., also of the Grand Lodge of Pennsylvania, and attends the Lutheran Church. He is one of the leading physicians of York County; has a large practice in Codorus and adjoining Townships, and is one of the most influential citizens of that section.

M. T. CRIST, son of John and Sarah (Thoman) Crist, was born April 25, 1845, in Jefferson Borough. He was the fourth in a family of twelve children; received a common school education in his native town, and began life as a clerk in Brodbeck's store, in Jefferson. He began business for himself at the early age of twenty years at Glenville, then removed to North Codorus Township, near Spring Grove, having embarked in the saddlery and harness business; he then removed to his present location, New Salem, North Codorus Township. January 13, 1867, he married Susan Rohrbach, daughter of Joseph and Catherine (Runkle) Rohrbach, of Codorus Township. Seven children have blessed this union: Aggie S., William C., Alice C., Lizzie, Joseph (deceased), Mollie and John. Mr. Crist was a mercantile appraiser for York County in 1875; has been justice of the peace for his township, and taught school three terms. He attends the German Reformed Church.

WESLEY GLATFELTER, recorder of deeds for York County, is the second son of George and Christiana Glatfelter, and was born December 7, 1848, in North Codorus Township. Mr. Glatfelter received only a common school education, but took advantage of every chance that was afforded him to improve his mind by study, and he is to-day one of the best informed men in North Codorus Township, and has taught school seven terms in his native township. March 12, 1874, he married Melinda C. Rohrbach, daughter of Peter and Elizabeth Rohrbach, and five children blessed their marriage: Warren A., Laura I., Jennie L., Elizabeth A., and Annetta W. Mr. Glatfelter has held various township offices at various times, and is a member of the order of K. of P., also a member of the Jeffersonian Democratic Association of York.

JOHN M. HENRY was born in York County, September 10, 1856, to George Henry and Susanna (Martin) Henry, also natives of York County. The father was a carpenter, then a farmer, and about 1860, became a merchant at Stoverstown. John M. was reared a farmer, and was educated in the district school, and at York County Academy. In the fall of 1877 he began teaching in North Codorus, and has taught each consecutive term since, with the exception of that of 1880, when he was the secretary of the, Seven Valley Mutual Aid Association. December 4, 1881, he married Barbara Alice, daughter of Samuel G. Hildebrand. Mr. Hildebrand was also a school teacher, then a farmer, afterward a merchant, and is now a cigar box manufacturer. Mr. and Mrs. Henry are members of St. Paul's Lutheran Church, and are the parents of one child, Robert Pattison. They own ninety acres of land at Stoverstown and the lot on which the church edifice stands was sold to the congregation by Mr. Henry. Daniel M. Henry, brother of the above, was born in Stoverstown, November 2, 1860. He was reared a farmer and was educated in the district and select schools of his native place, and has been teaching since 1882. He is a member of St. Paul's Lutheran Church.

DR. H. KEHM, son of Henry and Anna M. (Swope) Kehm, was the seventh of nine children, and was born October 10, 1848, in Oxford, Adams Co., Penn., and was educated at Dr. M. D. G. Pfeiffer's Æthenia et Hygea, of Oxford. Our subject read medicine under Dr. G. H. Jordy, and after two courses at Jefferson Medical College, of Philadelphia, was graduated from this institution, March 13, 1871, and immediately began the practice of medicine at Kralltown, York County; after four years there he removed to Hagersville, Bucks County, remained six years, then returned and located at Dover, York County; after four years at Dover he came to his present location. The Doctor's ancestors came from Darmstadt, Germany.

JOHN S. KLINE, youngest of three children of John and Eve (Schultz) Kline, was born November 23, 1813, in Hellam Township, where he was reared and sent to his trade (miller) in his nineteenth year at Weist's Mill. He rented this mill and began business on his own account in 1838; taught school in North Codorus Township, two terms. In 1834 Mr. Kline married Lydia Glatfelter, daughter of Jacob and Lydia (Folkomer) Glatfelter, of North Codorus Township. Four children were born to this union: Franklin, Henrietta, Sarah and Julia Ann. Mrs. Kline died in 1850. Mr. Kline next married Melvina M. Raber, daughter of Abraham and Julia Ann (Bletcher) Raber. Six children were born to this marriage: M. Alice, Fannie, Clementine, Ellen, John H. and Emma. John H. is the only child yet living, born to the last marriage. Mr. Kline was constable four years, ten years justice of the peace, and postmaster thirteen years, school director and secretary of the school board. In 1880 he was appointed enumerator for North Codorus Township and New Salem Borough, and at the present time, secretary of the school board of New Salem Borough. He learned surveying in 1829 and followed it ever since. Mr. Kline is the oldest surveyor of York County, with possible exception of Daniel Ettinger, of York.

DR. WILSON A. LONG, son of Jonathan and Sue (Boyer) Long, of Rabersburg, Centre County, was born January 31, 1860. Dr. Long attended school there until his tenth year, he then came to Glen Rock to attend normal school under Prof. Gray; he taught school three terms in Codorus Township; then began to read medicine with Dr. Stick, in Codorus Township, attended two courses at College of Physicians and Surgeons in Baltimore, and was graduated from this institution in 1882; began the practice of medicine at New Salem, North Codorus Township, where he is at present located. On the 25th of March, 1883, Dr. Long married Annie Grothey, daughter of Charles and Annie E. (Marker) Grothey, of York, Penn. One child has blessed their union—Blanche Edith. The Doctor took a special course on diseases of the chest and throat and operative surgery.

DR. EDWARD STERNER, son of Jesse and Leah (Dagen) Sterner, was born June 15, 1855, in Codorus Township. The Doctor is the eldest child in a family of eight children. In 1875 Dr. Sterner married Lydia Spangler, daughter of Bernard and Susan (Asper) Spangler, of Jackson Township. Five children have been born of this marriage: Maggie G., Flora (deceased), Joseph F., Edward M. and Charles Austin. Dr. Sterner was reared on a farm. After receiving a common school education he began to read medicine with Drs. Jones and Evans. The Doctor began the practice of medicine in Jefferson, in 1880; and, although a young physician, has met with flattering success.

DR. J. J. STEWART, second of six children of James W. and Martha L. (Campbell) Stewart, was born March 1, 1862, in Lower Chanceford Township. The Doctor read medicine with Dr. W. F. Smith, of Lower Chanceford Township, and after attending three terms at Jefferson Medical College, of Philadelphia, was graduated from this institution April 2, 1885, and began the practice of his profession at the village of New Salem, about five miles from York. Dr. Stewart's ancestors settled early in York County, his grandparents being natives of the county. Dr. Stewart is a hard student, loves his profession and will make his mark in his chosen profession.

PETER STRICKHOUSER, son of Peter and Polly (Rennoll) Strickhouser, was born January 26, 1827, in North Codorus Township. Our subject was the youngest of two children, James Kelly and Peter. December 25, 1848, Mr. Strickhouser married Mary Hetrick, daughter of John and Wilhelmina (Wolfrom) Hetrick; eight children were born of this marriage; Wilhelmina; infant, deceased; Amanda; Fannie; Calvin; Howard; Clayton; and Edward, deceased. Mr. Strickhouser was reared on his father's farm. He held the responsible office of commissioner of York County from 1869 to 1872, with credit to himself and entire satisfaction to the people of York County. At present Mr. Strickhouser is keeping hotel at Hanover Junction. He has been school director in his native township at various times.

ISRAEL K. ZIEGLER was born in North Codorus Township, October 11, 1840, and is the son of John E. and Barbara (Coller) Ziegler, the former born in North Codorus, April 14, 1806, and the latter in Shrewsbury Township, January 20, 1804. They died, respectively, November 19, 1874, and March 25, 1883. They were the parents of five children. Subject's grandfather, John Ziegler, was born December 18, 1767, was married November 23, 1790, to Catherine Epley, and died July 9, 1845. He donated the land on which Ziegler's Church now stands, and, with his son John E., helped to build the edifice. Our subject was married, April 27, 1865, to Ann Maria Stick, daughter of Henry Stick. To this union have been born the following children: William H., February 16, 1866, died August 3, 1867; John C., born July 13, 1868; Janny M., December 16, 1869, and Edwin, May 17, 1878. Immediately after his marriage, Mr. Ziegler settled down to farming on the old homestead, which comprises 300 acres, which he now owns, and which is renowned for its dairy and grain products. Mr. Ziegler is also owner of 300 acres more at different places, and other valuable real estate in York, Seven Valleys and in Gettysburg. Both the Ziegler and Stick families are among the oldest and most respected of York County, and have always been firm adherents of the Evangelical Lutheran Church. Mr. Ziegler is now a resident of York Borough, to which point he removed in 1882, to obtain better educational facilities for his children.

JOHN K. ZIEGLER, farmer, son of John E. and Barbara Ziegler, was born in North Codorus Township, on the farm where he now lives. Mr. Ziegler married Elizabeth, daughter of Jesse and Elizabeth Shaffer, of Codorus Township. This marriage was blessed with five children: Emma J., John C., William (deceased), Paul and Allen. Mr. Ziegler has been for many years a director in the York National Bank. He is widely and favorably known in York County, and has always been a prominent and influential man in his section of the county.

PARADISE TOWNSHIP.

P. S. ALWINE, son of Samuel and Mary Shaeffer, was born November 4, 1831, in North Codorus Township, and removed in 1840 to Paradise Township. When seventeen years of age he began to make brick, and frequently made the trip to Peach Bottom Township where he was engaged to make brick. When he attained his majority he began the brick business for himself and has followed this occupation ever since. September 20, 1860, Mr. Alwine married Catharine Dahlhammer, daughter of William and Sarah (Sour) Dahlhammer. Eleven children were born to them: Emma J., Sarah E., Ida, Harvey, Samuel, William, Lewis H., Cora A., Edward R., Percy and Emery S. Mr. Alwine is widely known in York and Adams Counties. He taught school twelve terms in Jackson and Paradise Townships, and is one of the best informed men in Paradise Township. His father was a native of Lebanon County.

A. Z. LEIB, son of Abraham and Matilda (Zeigler) Leib, was born February 3, 1853, in Jackson Township; was reared to farming; began to learn his trade (saddle and harness-maker), at Davidsburg. In 1876 he began business for himself at Baughmansville, Paradise Township. December 30, 1879, Mr. Leib married Sallie Baughman, daughter of J. B. and Lydia (Schwartz) Baughman, of Paradise Township. Three children have blessed this marriage: J. B., Lydia R. and Matilda G. Mr. Leib's ancestors were early settlers in Paradise Township. Abraham Leib died when our subject was only six years of age. Matilda (Zeigler) Leib, the mother of our subject, is still living. Mr. Leib is held in high esteem by his friends and neighbors in Paradise Township. There were eight children in Abraham Leib's family, viz.: Emanuel, deceased; Elizabeth, deceased; Agnes; Jesse, deceased; John, now in Illinois; Jonas, in Adams County; A. Z. and Alice. Mr. Leib is a member of the Paradise (Lutheran) Church.

E. C. MASEMER, son of Jesse and Catharine (Joseph) Masemer, was born January 18, 1854, in Hellam Township, and for the past twenty-two years has been a resident of Paradise Township (his father having purchased the mill property, where our subject now resides, in 1876). Our subject began to learn his trade with Peter Kimkel, 1873, in Warrington Township, York County, and began business for himself in the spring of 1884. February 10, 1883, he married Ida Ramer, daughter of Henry and Annie (Myers) Ramer, of Paradise Township. One child was born to them—Ira.

JOHN S. TRIMMER, son of Barnet and Catharine (Schriver) Trimmer, was born January 13, 1812, in Paradise Township, where he now resides. He was reared to farming, and when eighteen years of age learned the carpenter trade, and followed it about seven years. He then began the mercantile business, which he followed for twenty-two years, then retired from active business. He began business at Big Mount forty-eight years ago (1837).

PEACH BOTTOM TOWNSHIP.

WILLIAM E. AILES, son of William and Elizabeth (Black) Ailes, was born in Lancaster County, Penn., December 8, 1840, and was married, December 11, 1867, to Martha Jane Carrick, daughter of Alexander Carrick, of Philadelphia, and has had born to him nine children: Alexander C., William B., Robert E., George M., Elizabeth H., Joseph H., Charles M., Franklin A. and Edwin H. In the fall of 1869 Mr. Ailes came to York County and purchased the "Gordon property," a farm of 172 acres, and since that time he has been engaged in agricultural pursuits. He served with the Twelfth Pennsylvania Regiment, "Emergency" men, and participated in the battle of Antietam, and was drafted afterward in the One Hundred and Sixty-sixth Pennsylvania, and served one year, mostly at Suffolk, Va. He is a member of Corporal Baer Post 277, G. A. R., and also a Master Mason.

EPHRAIM ARNOLD was born in Lancaster County, Penn., November 3, 1834. His parents, William and Julia A. (Barnett) Arnold, were natives of that county, and of Irish extraction. They reared a family of eight sons and two daughters, and lost four by death in infancy. William Arnold was for many years a slate operator, but late in life his attention was given to mercantile pursuits. Our subject is the fifth of the children reared to maturity, and his early life was passed on a farm. After receiving a liberal education at Chestnut Level Academy and Millersville State Normal School he taught several terms in the public schools. When grown to manhood he passed several years as a canal boatman in summer, and continued to teach in winter. From 1862 to 1866 he was engaged as clerk with McConkey Brothers at Peach Bottom; later with Rufus Wiley, same place; then with Lewis C. Wiley, Slate Hill, and again with Rufus Wiley. In the spring of 1873 he formed a partnership with Hugh N. McConkey, and bought out L. C. Wiley, general merchant at Slate Hill. About one year afterward he bought out his partner's interest and admitted James A. Towson, of Harrisburg. In 1878 Mr. Towson sold out to his son, who continued in the firm until 1882, having in the meantime removed their store to Delta. Mr. Arnold married Eliza A. Patton, in Philadelphia, November 28, 1867. Mrs. Arnold is a native of York County, and is a sister of John F. Patton, druggist, of York. The family are of Irish origin. Mr. and Mrs. Arnold have five children: John P., William E., Mary L., T., Frederick and Edith R. Mr. Arnold was a member of the first council of Delta, was active in securing its incorporation, and has held and acceptably filled a number of other offices under the corporation. He was a charter member of Esdraelon Lodge, A. F. & A. M., and has been its secretary since its organization. He is also secretary of Mount Hebron Lodge, I. O. O. F., and is vice-president of the Delta Building and Loan Association.

SAMUEL JOHN BARNETT was born in Peach Bottom Township, York County, Penn., January 5, 1846, the son of John and Catharine A. Barnett, who came from Lancaster County in 1838. His mother was a woman of great vigor and business activity. She was of German descent, with an admixture of Irish blood. His paternal grandfather was John K. Barnett, who lived near Fairfield, Lancaster County; his great-grandfather was Mark Barnett, who moved from Upper Hartford County, Md., to Ohio when that State was the "far West," and who is said to have lived to the age of one hundred and ten years. The nationality of the Barnett ancestry is involved in some obscurity, though the original members in this country probably emigrated at an early period from the north of Ireland. The name appears to be derived from the Roman title "baronettus," Norman French "baronette," English "baronet," from which comes the English-Irish name Barnet, Barnett or Barnette. Samuel J. Barnett was the fourth son of his parents, his elder brothers being Martin Sylvester, now a book publisher in St. Louis, Mo.; Sergt. David Alva, who lost his life in defense of his country in the war of the Rebellion while color-sergeant of his regiment, and William James, now a prominent farmer in Peach Bottom Township. Besides these there were two younger sisters, both now dead. The subject of this sketch was reared on a farm and trained to agriculture. When he was six years old he lost his father, and his education was entrusted to his mother, who struggled hard to give all her children as good an education as the public and private schools of the community would afford. Samuel J. was fond of reading and an apt student. He early developed a talent for mathematics, and soon distanced most of his teachers in that line. Later, however, his tastes led him more into philosophical and metaphysical subjects. Early in the year 1866 he spent a few weeks at the Millersville State Normal School, where he almost immediately gained recognition as an original thinker and strong debater. His attendance at this school was broken by terms of teaching to raise funds. In 1869 he graduated in the elementary course. After further teaching and study he finished the scientific course in 1874, his only fellow-graduate being Frank Ibach, since a teacher in Pierce's Business College, Philadelphia. With the exception of a few intervals he followed the vocation of teacher from 1864 to 1884, most of the time in the public and private schools of his native township. In 1869, after finishing the elementary course at Millersville, he became principal of the public schools at Shamokin, Penn., and organized the high school of that town. In 1874-75 he filled a similar position in Lehighton, Penn. As a teacher he was enthusiastic and thorough, and as a disciplinarian very successful. During the years of his teaching he usually gave a few months each year to farming. In 1865 he went to Cincinnati, where he was engaged for a time clerking for the National Publishing Company. In 1872 also he served as clerk to the Presbyterian Board of Education, Philadelphia. In 1880 he purchased the *Delta Herald*, after the paper had had a precarious existence of eighteen months. Under his care it has become not only a success as a business venture, but a power for good which is widely felt, the paper taking high rank with the older papers of York County. In 1884 he quit teaching and devoted himself to the editorial and business management of his paper. September 14, 1869, he was married to Miss Martha McCurdy, daughter of W. J. McCurdy, of Peach Bottom Township, and sister of J. C. McCurdy, publisher, Philadelphia. She was a most lovely woman in heart, life and person, and proved a valuable helpmeet; but after three years of happy wedded life death removed her to a brighter world. After trying the world alone for eleven years, September 27, 1883, he married Miss Fannie K. Vogt, daughter of Herman Vogt, of York. Miss Vogt had for several years been a successful teacher in the public schools of York, and is a lady whose culture, vivacity and personal attractions win her friends wherever she goes. Her attainments render her an efficient help to her husband in his literary labors. Following this marriage a son was born November 6, 1884. In life, character and business, Samuel J. Barnett is upright and very conscientious. He has been a warm advocate of temperance, and an active worker in church and Sunday-school. In youth he united with the Slateville Presbyterian Church, with which he is still connected, and has for several years filled the position of Sunday-school superintendent. In politics he has been a Republican. Three times he ran as candidate for county superintendent in York County; but though acknowledged to stand head and shoulders above any other candidate, the strong political sentiment which was brought to bear against him caused his defeat. Mr. Barnett now lives in Delta, where he has built for himself a commodious dwelling and printing office.

WILLIAM BARTON was born in Peach Bottom Township, York County, May 23, 1832, on the farm of 180 acres now owned and occupied by him. His parents, William and Elizabeth (Heaps) Barton, were both natives of Harford County, Md. The subject of this sketch has passed his entire life on a farm, and by his industry and skill has acquired a competence. He has held the offices of assessor, inspector and school director. He married Miss Sarah M. Fulks, daughter of Benjamin Fulks, May 23, 1860, and has two sons: John A. and Harry A. Mrs. Barton is a member of the Slateville Presbyterian Church.

WALTER BEATTIE was born February 13, 1810, in Dumfriesshire, Scotland. His parents, Simon and Nancy Beattie, came to America in 1817, and settled in Peach Bottom Township. The family consisted of the parents and fourteen children—six sons and eight daughters—one daughter having died on the passage over. Walter, like his brothers and sisters, was brought up on the farm, and from his earliest boyhood was accustomed to hard and incessant labor, receiving his education during winters in the indifferent county schools of that day. He purchased in 1838 a tract of land known as the "Warm Spring Farm," and at present owns four farms in addition to a fine mill property known as Wiley's Mill. The family are members of the Presbyterian Church, and Walter has been active in works of charity in the community where he resides. His too confiding disposition has occasioned him frequent pecuniary losses, notwithstanding which he has, by his industry, become one of the solid men of the county. In politics Mr. Beattie has never aspired to office, though his fellow-citizens have conferred on him various local positions, among others those of supervisor, assessor and collector.

EMANUEL J. BLAIN was born in Fawn Township, York County, July 16, 1840. His parents, Moses and Sarah (Bulett) Blain, were natives of the same place, and of Scotch-Irish extraction. He is the second of fourteen children, being the eldest son. His early life was passed on a farm and as a clerk in his father's store. Having received a good education at Bryansville High School and York County Academy, he devoted about four years to teaching a public school. He married, November 21, 1861, Mary S. Webb, daughter of William Webb, a prominent citizen of Fawn Township. About 1863 Mr. Blain embarked in the mercantile business at Bryansville, and continued in the same at that place and at Delta until the opening of the York & Peach Bottom Railroad in 1876, when he entered the employ of that company as baggage master, which position he acceptably filled until February, 1884. He then resigned and resumed his old business as a member of the firm of Lloyd & Blain at Delta. While a merchant in 1875, Mr. Blain invested a large part of his capital in slate-mining, which proved a failure, and forced him to make an assignment for the benefit of his creditors. On settlement of his affairs, however, every claim was fully paid, which is a conclusive proof of his business integrity. He has held the office of councilman of the borough of Delta, and is a Past Master of Esdraelon Lodge A. F. & A. M. He and wife are members of the Slate Ridge Presbyterian Church.

CAPT. ASAPH M. CLARKE was born in Jefferson County, Penn., February 11, 1844. His parents, Dr. Asaph M. and Rebecca M. (Nichola) Clarke, were of English extraction. The subject of this sketch is the eldest of six children—four daughters and two sons. At the beginning of the war he enlisted in Company K, Eighth Pennsylvania Infantry (three months' men), and served chiefly in Virginia, taking part in the battle of Falling Water and others. He was honorably discharged July 9, 1861, and in November following entered Company F, Sixty-seventh Pennsylvania Volunteer Infantry as orderly-sergeant, and was promoted to second lieutenant July 27, 1863. December 13, 1864, he was made first lieutenant of Company K, and commissioned as captain of the same company May 1, 1865. During his latter term of service he took part in the battles of Berryville, Opequan, Winchester, Mine Run, both engagements at Weldon Railroad, both at Hatch's Run, Brandy Station, Petersburg. Cedar Creek, Middletown, Wilderness, Cold Harbor, White House, Fisher's Hill and a number of others of minor importance. At Winchester, June 15, 1863, he received a wound in his left ankle, breaking the bone, which caused his capture and subsequent confinement in Libby and Belle Isle until August, 1863. The promotions he received were for meritorious conduct and distinguished services, and since the close of the war he receives a pension on account of his wound. After his discharge he spent some time in the study of medicine, and afterward registered as a law student, but did not complete a course in either. He was married, June 13, 1869, to Clara F. Butler, of Brookville, and has one son, Milton B., living, having lost a daughter, Nora, in infancy. Capt. Clarke is a member of the Masonic fraternity, Grand Army, Odd Fellows, I. O. K. M., K. of P. and other societies; is at this writing a justice of the peace, and was a candidate for the legislature in 1884. He is engaged in the jewelry business at Delta. The father of our subject, Dr. A. M. Clarke, was born in Hartford, Conn., March 22, 1808, was taken by his parents in infancy to St. Lawrence County, N. Y., and in 1819 brought to what is now Elk County, this State. He was married, March 6, 1831, and celebrated his golden wedding in 1881, and died suddenly in the spring of 1884.

JESSE T. CRAWFORD, second son of Joseph and Frances (Taylor) Crawford, was born in the extreme southeastern part of York County, March 25, 1831. His father was of Scotch-Irish origin, and his mother of the English Taylor family, well known in the southern part of Harford County, Md. Soon after their marriage they located on a small farm in Peach Bottom Township, where they reared a family of four sons and four daughters—two sons and two daughters are still living. The subject of this sketch received a fair education at Chestnut Level Academy, and adopted the profession of teaching, a pursuit which he followed almost continuously for thirty years, in Pennsylvania, Maryland and Kentucky. He taught one year in York, three years in Hanover, Penn., and for eight years had charge of the high school at Delta, where a large number of young persons of both sexes were prepared for teaching. He served five years as justice of the peace in Peach Bottom Township, and after the incorporation of Delta, was elected to the same office in the borough, which office he still holds. He took an active part in this incorporation, made the survey, and has been town clerk ever since. He, in addition to his official duties, does an extensive business as a surveyor and conveyancer.

BIOGRAPHICAL SKETCHES.

He was one of the charter members of Esdraelon Lodge No. 176, A. F. & A. M., as well as of the Delta Building and Loan Association, of which he is the secretary. He was, in 1884, a candidate for county commissioner, but failed to secure the nomination. He married, September 5, 1860, Sarah A. Healey, of Harford County, Md., a descendant of the Ellicott family, of Ellicott's Mills, Md., and has had five children, four of whom, Elizabeth F., Agnes I., James C. and Joseph R., are living, and one Minnie J., dead. The eldest daughter is a teacher. His mother died in 1861, and his father in 1872.

RUDOLPHUS D. DODSON, born in Peach Bottom Township, February 27, 1856, is the youngest of four sons of Henry and Elizabeth (McCurdy) Dodson, the former a native of Ireland, and the latter of York County, and also of Irish parentage. The subject of this notice was reared on a farm, attending school in the winter until, at the age of sixteen, he entered a drug store in York, where he remained a year and a half. Some time after this he began the study of dentistry with Dr. W. C. McCurdy, in Baltimore County, Md., with whom he remained two years. Returning to York County he practiced about two years, and then entered the Baltimore College of Dental Surgery, where he remained one term. In the fall of 1882 he entered the University of Maryland, from the dental department of which he graduated in March, 1883. Since that time he has pursued his profession with success at Delta. He married Miss Rose A. Poist, of Peach Bottom Township, April 17, 1876, and has two children: Henry M. and Elizabeth O. He is the owner of a fine house in Delta, lately erected, and though a young man, has a lucrative practice.

CONSTANTINE F. DOUGHERTY, a native of Donegal, Ireland, was born October 10, 1839. He, with his parents, Henry and Mary Dougherty, came to America and settled at Delta in 1852. Constantine is the eldest of eight children—four sons and four daughters. He received a fair education in the public schools, and was for some time employed in a slate quarry. At the age of eighteen he began the trade of blacksmith, and has successfully carried it on ever since. During the war he spent about two years in the government employ in Washington, D. C., and Baltimore. He married Miss Kate Barr, daughter of Hugh and Fannie Barr, of Donegal, Ireland, at Philadelphia, June 6, 1866, and has ten children: James H., Mary E., Fannie, Michael H., Charles, Francis, Joseph, Kate, Susan T. and Sarah A. (living), and John F. (who died at the age of five years). In politics Mr. Dougherty is a Democrat. In 1884 he was elected chief burgess of Delta, though two-thirds of the voters of the place are Republicans. This fact is an evidence of the esteem in which he is held by his neighbors. His father died in 1879, at the age of seventy-three; his mother is still living. The family are members of St. Mary's Catholic Church, of Harford County, Md.

EDWARD W. EVANS was born in the slate district of north Wales, December 7, 1838, and came to America in 1860. He located in Peach Bottom Township, where he began work for John Humphrey in his slate quarry. In the spring of 1861 he went to California, where he, for several years, engaged in gold mining with varied success. He afterward traveled extensively through New Mexico, Arizona and Colorado, meeting with numerous adventures in those almost unexplored regions. In 1865 he came East, and was employed about two years in Utica and in Washington County, N. Y. On his return to Pennsylvania in 1868, he engaged in mercantile business at West Bangor, as a member of the firm of William E. Williams & Co., where he remained four years. He then resumed work as a quarryman, and has been so engaged ever since. In December, 1881, he leased about ten acres of slate land, and reopened a quarry. After working a year and a half to remove the accumulated rubbish, he has succeeded in developing a paying quarry. He married Miss Mary F. Roberts, at West Bangor, in 1869. She is of Welsh parents, and was born on the ocean, while her parents were on their way to America. They have one child—Hugh. Mr. Evans is one of the trustees of Esdraelon Lodge, A. F. & A. M., and is a Republican.

ROBERT T. FRY, son of Elias and Martha (Groff) Fry, was born at York Furnace, January 20, 1855. His parents are natives of Lancaster County, but came to York Furnace in 1854, where they still reside. Robert was married, May 18, 1880, to Ella E., daughter of R. K. Boyd, of Lower Chanceford, and has one child—Elias K. He has held the offices of clerk of Lower Chanceford and assessor of Peach Bottom Township. His present occupation is that of general merchant at Coal Cabin, on the Tide Water Canal.

DAVID FULTON was born in Peach Bottom Township, May 12, 1816. His parents, John and Elizabeth (Creswell) Fulton, were like most of the early settlers of this township, of Scotch-Irish descent. John Fulton was, for many years, a prominent school teacher, as well as farmer. He acquired a large tract of land by his industry and economy, and was the father of five sons and two daughters. David, the eldest of the family, was educated as a farmer, and was married June 29, 1839, to Sarah Jane, daughter of Allen and Margaret (Regan) Miller. They have had six children: John H., Robert A., Martha A., Margaret A., Elizabeth J. and Agnes M., all of whom reside in Peach Bottom Township, except Margaret, wife of Thomas Gregg, of Lancaster County. Mr. Fulton has filled with credit the offices of supervisor and school director in his native township, and by his own industry has acquired a competency, while enjoying the respect and confidence of his neighbors. The family are connected with the Slate Ridge Presbyterian Church.

CUNNINGHAM R. GLASGOW, son of Hon. Hugh Glasgow, was born June 29, 1806, on the old homestead, near Slate Hill, York County. His father was a native of Chester County, and removed when a young man, to York County, where he resided on the above mentioned farm until his death, in 1818. He was chosen to represent the district in the national congress and was associate judge of this county. While in congress, he secured the establishment of Peach Bottom Postoffice, the first, and for many years the only one in the township. Prior to that time, the nearest office was Bel Air, Md. His mother Maria (Ramsay) Glasgow, was a native of York County, a member of a family, which for many years has been prominent in this township. They were married in 1804, and she died in 1820, leaving four sons, of whom the subject of this sketch is the only survivor. He remained on the farm until the age of thirteen, when he entered a store in Wrightsville, Penn., where he remained about six years, and then went to Baltimore, Md., where he remained six years; returning to York County, he engaged in farming a vocation which he has since followed. In 1841 he purchased the farm of 125 acres, on which he now resides. This farm is mostly in York County, though the dwelling house is in Harford County, Md. In 1837 Mr. Glasgow married Mary A. Beven, a native of York County. He has held the office of commissioner of Harford County, and has always enjoyed the confidence and esteem of his neighbors.

J. WILLIAM HICKMAN, M. D., is the eldest son of William C. and Victorine E. (Gibbons) Hickman. His father was a native of Chester County, and his mother of Fayette County, Penn. They are of English descent, and reared two sons and four daughters. The Doctor was born in Chester County, September 23, 1856, and passed the first sixteen years of his life on the farm and in the public schools. Later he spent two years in the State Normal School, at Westchester, and then entered the Washington and Jefferson College, where he began the study of medicine. In 1873 the family moved to Michigan, where the father died in the fall of the same year, aged fifty-eight. The remainder of the family resided there two years, our subject teaching in the public schools. In 1876 he entered the office of Dr. G. A. Dougherty, at Washington, Penn., where he pursued his medical studies, attending one year's lectures at Baltimore, and then entering Jefferson Medical College, Philadelphia, where he graduated in March, 1879. Shortly afterward he came to Delta, where he enjoys a remunerative practice, in addition to which he conducts a drug store. He was married to Miss Hannah J. Hickman, at York, October 3, 1879, and has one child—Carrie R. He is a member of the borough council, a Master Mason, and a member of the York County Medical Society, and of the Slateville Presbyterian Church. The Hickman family own and occupy the same land in Chester County which was taken up by their ancestors on their arrival in America.

SAMUEL P. JOHNSON, son of James W. and Sarah (Wilson) Johnson, was born July 20, 1845, on the homestead in Peach Bottom Township. His father was a native of Peach Bottom, and a son of James Johnson, who came from Dublin, Ireland, and purchased about 500 acres of land, a part of which still remains in possession of the family. James W. Johnson, father of Samuel P., was for several years justice of the peace. He was noted for his charity and benevolence, and suffered many pecuniary losses, in consequence of designing persons taking advantage of his too confiding nature. He died September 16, 1884, at the age of seventy-four. The subject of this s.etch was reared on the farm, and for many years had its management. In 1882 he purchased about 300 acres of it, and has since continued a successful farmer. He married Martha A. Fulton, December 7, 1869, and has four children: Sally W., James, Grace A. and Samuel P. In 1862 he enlisted in Independent Battery I, of Pennsylvania, and served nine months. Like his father, Mr. Johnson is respected by his neighbors and regarded by all as a good citizen.

ROBERT L. JONES, a prominent slate manufacturer of Peach Bottom Township, is a native of Carnaervonshire, in north Wales, was born March 15, 1841; came to Peach Bottom Township in 1860, engaged in slate quarrying, in the employ of a Philadelphia company, and afterward for John Humphrey. August 22, 1862, he enlisted in Company A, Third Pennsylvania Heavy Artillery, and served until June 14, 1865. During the last eighteen months his company was on the gun-boat "Shrapnel." He was never on the sick list nor lost a day from duty. He was discharged with the rank of first sergeant at Camp Hamilton, Va., and returned to West Bangor, where he resumed work at his old place, and continued so employed until 1871, when he became associated with four partners in operating a quarry. Selling out in 1879, he, in company with P. B. Shank, leased about twenty-five acres of slate land, and opened a new quarry about one-fourth mile from West Bangor, which has proved one of the most productive on the ridge. He manufactured, in 1883, with about twenty hands, 2,800 squares of roofing slate. Since 1882 Mr. Jones has been sole owner, and his entire time is given to the management of the business. Though he attended school in Wales only two years (between seven and nine), and about two months in America, yet he keeps his own books, and directs his large business unassisted. He married, in Philadelphia, in 1870, Miss Isabella Roberts, a native of Wales, and has four children: Emma, William J., Arthur and Isabella. Both Mr. Jones and wife are members of the Calvinistic Methodist Church, and he is treasurer in the Esdraelon Lodge, A. F. & A. M., and also treasurer of the Building and Loan Association of Delta.

FOULK JONES was born in Carnaervon County, Wales, December 25, 1822, and came to America in 1848. He settled in Peach Bottom Township, and engaged in slate quarrying for about eighteen months, and then crossed to Lancaster County, where he operated a quarry for about nine years, after which he returned to Peach Bottom, and bought a tract of slate land at Slate Hill, on which he, with a partner, opened a quarry, and worked it with varied success until 1873, when it was abandoned. He was active in building the York & Peach Bottom Railroad, and was a member of its first board of directors, and he also contributed largely to the construction of the Maryland & Central Railroad, being, for a time, a director and president of the Pennsylvania Division. Mr. Jones owns three fine farms in Peach Bottom Township, besides one in Harford County, Md. On one of his York County farms he has conducted a successful dairy. He has a fair English education, received in Wales and after he came to America. He married, in Lancaster, Penn., November 5, 1885, Miss Rebecca Marshall, a native of that county, and has had born to him six children, three of whom are living: Maggie J., Dienal Wyn and Marshall F. Mr. Jones has held the office of township auditor and school director. The family are connected with the Presbyterian Church.

WILLIAM HOLLINGSWORTH KILGORE, M. D., of Delta, Peach Bottom Township, was born in Lower Chanceford Township October 31, 1815. His parents, John and Margaret (Nelson) Kilgore, natives of the same township, were of Scotch descent, and had eight children, of whom Dr. K. is now the only one living. His father was a farmer, and subject remained with him until he was fifteen years of age, attending the common schools. In 1830 he attended a Latin and Greek school in his township for one year and nine months, when he entered the office of Dr. Levingston, of Chanceford Township, and continued the study of Latin and Greek. In 1833 he went to Newark, Delaware Academy for one year, then to York Academy for two years, first as a student and then as assistant teacher. From there he went to Franklin College, New Athens, Ohio, for two years, and graduated in 1836 as A. B.; then he taught at the Academy at Wheeling, Va., until the spring of 1837. At the office of Dr. McIlvain he next began the study of medicine, and in the fall of 1837 he entered the Jefferson College at Philadelphia, graduating in 1839. He first began to practice at Liverpool, where he resided four years, then removed to York, and remained until 1848; then to Peach Bottom Township. In 1851 he removed to Delta Borough, where he has since resided, and is very successful in his practice. November 24, 1840, he married Maria Louisa Haller, daughter of George Haller, Esq., and is the father of ten children: Edwin Haller, William Nelson, Frances Louisa, Florence Susan, Ida Augusta, Clara (deceased), Thomas P., Lucy J., John G. (deceased) and an infant unnamed. The Doctor has held a number of township offices, such as school director and judge of elections.

THE McCONKEY FAMILY. About the middle of the last century Hugh and James McConkey, two brothers of pure Scotch-Irish origin, emigrated from north Ireland to America. Hugh purchased land, and located in Lancaster County, Penn., and James

BIOGRAPHICAL SKETCHES.

went to Baltimore. John McConkey, probably a brother, came to America soon afterward, and during the Revolutionary war enlisted in Capt. Matthew Smith's company of Lancaster County Volunteers, in 1775, and endured all the perils and hardships of the famous march to Canada and the attack on Quêbec. Judge John Joseph Henry, of the Lancaster and York courts, in his personal reminiscences of this battle, speaks in glowing terms of the endurance and bravery of his comrade in arms, John McConkey. Hugh McConkey, the ancestor of the family in this county, was born March 14, 1757, and on May 13, 1783, was married to Jane Neeper, of Lancaster County, who was born September 5, 1760. Their children were Jesse, James, Anne, Andrew, Margaret, Janetta and Hugh J. The father, Hugh McConkey, who was a Revolutionary soldier, died at Peach Bottom, August 11, 1839.

JAMES MCCONKEY, the second son, was born in Lancaster County, May 27, 1787. In the year 1808 he removed to Peach Bottom, and was in the employ of John Kirk, who then owned the ferry at this place, and conducted a general merchandise business. He soon became a partner with Kirk on a capital of $500, borrowed from his father, which he soon returned with interest. Subsequently he purchased the entire business interest of the place and a tract of 300 acres of land on Cooper's Upper Rock Run. At the time of the invasion of the British toward Baltimore, in 1814, he enlisted and marched with his regiment to the defense of that city. He subsequently procured the bounty land on the western frontier for the members of his company. In the militia service afterward he attained the rank of major, by which title he was familiarly known. Early in his business career his father joined him in the management of the grist-mill at Peach Bottom. On account of the scarcity of wheat in the vicinity, caused by the sterility of the soil, in that vicinity, they floated wheat, corn and potatoes down the Susquehanna River in arks and keel-bottom boats. Here he ground the wheat into flour, corn into meal, and supplied the inhabitants over a large extent of country. In the year 18— he was elected by the Whig party to represent York County in the State senate at Harrisburg. He took a prominent part in urging the construction of the Susquehanna Canal from Columbia to join the Tide Water Canal in Maryland, which, when completed, in 1839, greatly increased the business interests of Peach Bottom. It was then that the farmers of this section began to use lime so extensively as a fertilizer, and he brought immense quantities of the stone down the river and burned it here. In every respect he was a prudent, exact and prosperous business man, and at the time of his death, in 1861, had accumulated a handsome competence as the result of his assiduous labors. In every respect he was a prominent and influential citizen of his township, and intimately connected with the affairs of the county and State. In 1815 Maj. McConkey was married to Julia Ann Wiley, by whom he had eleven children. Of these two are now living: Stephen D., of Baltimore, and John Q. A., of Peach Bottom. Henry F., the eldest, died at home, while in business with his father, in 1859. William moved to Wrightsville, and became a very influential citizen of that town, and was largely interested in the business affairs of that place. He was elected a member of the legislature from York County, which he represented with acknowledged ability and credit. He died in 1880. The first wife of Maj. McConkey died in 1833. His second marriage was with Rachel Ramsay, who lived but a short time afterward. In 1838 he was married to Mary A. Ramsay. Their children were Charles R. McConkey and Mrs. Julia A. Ross, widow of the late William G. Ross, Esq., of Lower Chanceford.

JOHN QUINCY ADAMS MCCONKEY, son of James McConkey, by his first marriage, was born February 20, 1828. He received his mental training in the schools of the township, and also grew up as a clerk in his father's store. At the age of thirty-three years, upon his father's death, he and his brother, Charles R., succeeded the father in the mercantile business at Peach Bottom. In 1866 he purchased the interest of Charles R. in the store, grain and boating business, in which he is at present engaged. He has served the township in various local offices. In 1874 he was nominated for county treasurer by the Republican party; in 1880 he was the party nominee for State senate. In both instances he received a large vote, but not sufficient to overcome the large majority of the opposition. In 1882 he declined the nomination of his party for congress. He was appointed postmaster in 1878, and has since held the position. As partners, he and his brother Charles own all the business interests of the village of Peach Bottom and a tract of 350 acres of valuable farming land. Mr. McConkey is an active Mason, a member of the K. T., Columbia Commandery, at Lancaster. In 1860 he was married, in Harford County, Md., to Sarah S. Whiteford, daughter of Hugh Whiteford, a descendant of Col. Whiteford, who commanded at Havre de Grace during the British invasion of Baltimore in 1814. They had two children, one who died young and Edward Everett McConkey, now in business with his father.

CHARLES R. MCCONKEY, son of James McConkey, by his last marriage, was born in 1839; attended the public and private schools of the vicinity, and afterward, for a time, was a pupil in an academy in the city of Philadelphia, then taught by Gen. Joshua T. Owens. Returning home he assisted his father in business until at the age of twenty-two, when his father died. Then with his brother, John Q. A., engaged in the lumber, lime, coal, grain and store business. Disposing of his interests at Peach Bottom, in 1870, he removed to Philadelphia, and was engaged there in the wholesale boot and shoe business. At the expiration of two years he returned to his old home, and embarked in the lumber trade and the selling of fertilizers, which he still continues, and also assists in the management of a tract of 350 acres of farming land, of which he and his brother are joint partners. In 1872 he was elected a director in the York & Peach Bottom Railroad, and was subsequently elected to the office of president of the railroad. For a time he was appointed receiver of the corporation. He then assisted in reorganizing the road, and was again elected its president. He has served his township very satisfactorily as school director, and in various ways has been a public spirited and enterprising citizen. Mr. McConkey was married, December 27, 1866, to Rachel S. Alexander, a native of Belmont County, Ohio, daughter of James and Elizabeth (McGregor) Alexander. Her mother was a native of Peach Bottom. They have three children: Henry Alexander, Charles Reynolds and Mary E. Mr. McConkey and family are members of the Presbyterian Church, to which nearly all of his relatives and ancestors belonged.

WILLIAM J. MCCURDY, son of James and Martha (Hepburn) McCurdy, both natives of County Derry, Ireland, who immigrated to America in 1808, was born March 16, 1813, in Lancaster County, Penn. His parents soon afterward removed to Peach Bottom Township, in York County. February 25, 1840, he married Alice J. Fulton, daughter of John Fulton, and has five children living: James C., in Philadelphia; John F., in Chicago,

Ill.; William H., a physician of Delta, and two daughters, Alice and Guianna, residing with their parents. He purchased the farm, on which he lives, in 1844, and by a judicious system of tillage has brought it into a high state of cultivation. In 1880 he became engaged in the business of canning fruit and vegetables, which he has since then successfully carried on in connection with farming. Mr. McCurdy has held the offices of supervisor, auditor and school director, is a Mason, an Odd Fellow, and a deacon in the Baptist Church.

WILLIAM H. McCURDY, M. D., was born in Peach Bottom Township, October 26, 1854. His parents were William J. and Alice J. (Fulton) McCurdy; the former a native of Lancaster County, the latter of York County, and were respectively of Irish and Scotch-Irish origin. They were parents of nine children, of whom three sons and two daughters are living, and one son and three daughters dead. William H. McCurdy left home at the age of fourteen to attend Lewisburg University, Penn., and at the age of seventeen entered Lafayette College, where, in 1876, he graduated. After teaching in the common schools two years, meantime reading medicine under Dr. Scarborough, of Dublin, Hartford Co., Md., he entered Jefferson College, at Philadelphia, in 1878. After graduating in 1881 he began to practice near State Hill, and in May, 1884, removed to Delta, where he is now in practice. He married Miss Laura J. Jenness, a native of Maryland, February 8, 1883, and has one child—Russell W. In 1879 he began the canning business in Peach Bottom Township. In 1881 took his father into partnership, and in 1883 consolidated thirty-one canning firms into the Northern Harford Packing Association, an incorporated company, with a capital stock of $200,000, of which he is the secretary. He was among the organizers of the Delta Building and Loan Association, is a member of the York County Medical Society and chaplain of Esdraelon Lodge, A. F. & A. M., at South Delta. His wife is a member of Slateville Presbyterian Church, while he is connected with the Delta Baptist Church.

WATSON A. McLAUGHLIN, proprietor of the Railroad Hotel in Delta, was born to John and Mary (Miller) McLaughlin, in Mifflin County, Penn., February 14, 1842, is of Irish descent, and is the eldest of six children. The family immigrated to Dayton, Ohio, when the children were young, and there the parents died. Watson returned to Pennsylvania soon after this event, and for some years lived in Lancaster, attending school and clerking in his uncle's store. He began the miller's trade at the age of eighteen, and followed the business about ten years in Conestoga Township. During the war he enlisted in 1862, as teamster, served a year and then passed about one year in government employ at Washington, D. C., and next worked eighteen months at milling, after which he worked at milling and on a tobacco farm at Lancaster County. In 1864 he married Miss Elizabeth Moore, a native of Lancaster County. They have had seven children, five of whom are dead. Those living are Daniel and Nora O. In 1874 he removed to Fawn Township in York County, and kept hotel for one year, and afterward came to Peach Bottom. The following year he moved to Centreville, in Lower Chanceford Township, and then to Delta, where he still resides, having conducted a hotel ever since leaving Lancaster County. In 1879 he embarked in slate quarrying, and spent a large sum of money in prospecting, having since then opened five different quarries, without finding a profitable vein. He is at this writing engaged in a new quarry in Harford County, Md., which promises to be remunerative. Since June, 1884, he has acted as superintendent of a slate quarry in Peach Bottom Township for a Lancaster firm.

WILLIAM T. McLAUGHLIN, second son of Theodore and Sarah (Eckman) McLaughlin, was born in Harford County, Md., May 19, 1847. The family are widely known as millwrights. James McLaughlin, grandfather of the subject of this sketch, with his sons Theodore, Parke, Daniel and Joshua, having for a great number of years worked at this trade in York and the adjoining counties of Lancaster, Cecil and Harford. The grandfather was a man of immense physical strength and endurance, and was highly respected for his integrity of character. He died in Harford County, in 1876, at the age of ninety-nine. He was in Chester County, Penn., and it is reported that his infant slumbers in the cradle were broken on the morning of September 11, 1777, by the cannonading at the battle of Chad's Ford. The family are of Scotch-Irish origin. William T. McLaughlin's boyhood was passed on a farm, and his education obtained in a public school. At the age of twenty-six he formed a partnership with Foulk Jones, and for five years carried on farming and butchering at Slate Hill. With the same partner he then engaged in the hardware business at Delta. In 1883 he became sole proprietor, and has since successfully conducted it. He married Annie M. White, January 31, 1873, and has three children living: Howard L., Jarett B. and Theodore, besides one who died in infancy. He has served one term as borough auditor, and is a member of Mount Hebron Lodge, I. O. O. F. His parents are both living.

WILLIAM McSPARRAN, a native of Lancaster County, Penn., was born November 20, 1820. His parents, James and Eleanor (Neal) McSparran, were of Irish extraction, the paternal great-grandfather having come from Ireland and settled on land purchased from the Indians, in the southern part of Lancaster County. This tract has ever since been owned and occupied by the family, which is a large and influential one. The subject of this sketch, after having received a training in farm life and a fair education, entered the mercantile business at the age of twenty-one at Liberty Square, and after two years removed to Chestnut Level, where he remained two years more. He then removed to Peach Bottom in York County, where for five years he was engaged in the lumber and lime trade and in boating. In 1850 he removed to West Bangor and formed a partnership with James A. McConkey, which continued one year. At about the age of thirty-three he commenced farming, which business he continues to pursue with eminent success. When about twenty-five years of age he married Miss Alice Caldwell, who lived only three months after marriage. He next married when about thirty, Miss Masaline Williamson, daughter, of Maj. Thomas S. Williamson, who was the pioneer of the Peach Bottom Slate business. She died in May, 1883, leaving one daughter, Henrietta, who now resides with her father. On the land occupied and managed by Mr. McSparran, all the slate quarries now operated in York County are located. This tract comprises about 700 acres, fifty of which are leased as slate quarries. These pay a royalty on all slate taken out, which yield an income of about $3,000 per year. Three schoolhouses and three churches are located on the property, which in addition to the slate leases, is divided into three fine farms, two of which are rented out. Mr. McSparran's second wife was a near relative of Gov. Kirkwood, of Iowa. The family are members of the Slateville Presbyterian Church.

ROBERT W. MORRIS, a member of the Peach Bottom Slate Manufacturing Company, is a native of Dinorwig, Carnaervonshire, north Wales.

He was born January 27, 1847. His parents, William and Catherine (Roberts) Morris, had three sons and five daughters, all of whom, except one brother and two sisters, came to America. Robert came to Slatington, in Lehigh County, and for eighteen months worked there in a slate quarry, then came to West Bangor, in York County, where he has pursued the same vocation ever since, having obtained an interest in the quarries of the above mentioned company in 1884. He was married, September 5, 1870, to Anne Jane, daughter of Hugh and Margaret Roberts, and has two sons and four daughters: Hugh R., Catharine, Annie, Bertha, Maggie and Willie. They removed from West Bangor to Delta in 1884 after the death of his father-in-law, and Mrs. Roberts, his mother-in-law, resides with him. Mr. Morris is a member of the Calvinistic Methodist Church at West Bangor. His parents died in Wales.

WILLIAM ORR, son of Mordecai and Mary (McNutt) Orr, both natives of Harford County, Md., was born June 3, 1820, near Darlington, Harford County. He came with his parents to York County, Penn., when about fifteen years of age, and settled in Lower Chanceford Township. He married September 11, 1842, Dorcas Jones, daughter of Theophilus Jones, of York County, and has five children: Mary A., Blain, Mordecai J., William B., Rachel W. and Alverda. Since his removal to Peach Bottom, twenty-seven years ago, Mr. Orr has been engaged in farming and shoe-making. He has been collector of taxes for the township, and is held in high esteem by his neighbors. He is a member of Mount Hebron Lodge, I. O. O. F.

JAMES M. PARKER was born in New York City, February 19, 1838. His parents, Isaac and Margaret (Mill) Parker, came to York County in 1857, and here the father purchased a lease, in Peach Bottom Township, of what was then called the "old quarry." After carrying on the business here successfully for some years he purchased another lease of a quarry in Harford County, Md., and operated the two for a number of years. They reared two sons and three daughters, of whom James M. is the eldest. He is a graduate of the University of the City of New York, and while his father was engaged in slate mining in Pennsylvania, he was general manager of the business. In 1871 he went to Philadelphia as book-keeper in a shoe house, but after one year returned to York County, and became the principal of Pleasant Grove Academy, near High Rock. He next accepted the position of book-keeper in a wholesale house in Baltimore, and remained one year. He then resumed the profession of teaching, which he still follows, having for several terms had charge of the Delta High School. While the York & Peach Bottom Railroad was being built, he was for a time connected with the engineer corps. He was also the first postmaster appointed at Slate Hill, and served two years. In 1881 he was elected justice of the peace in Peach Bottom Township. He married Elizabeth R. Beattie, June 30, 1859, and has three children: John M., James D. and Margaret A. He is a skillful accountant and is frequently employed in settling estates as well as in conveyancing. The family are Presbyterians and of Scotch-Irish descent.

ROBERT RAMSAY, son of John Ramsay, was born in October, 1795, in York County. His father died in 1797, and the son passed the days of his boyhood on a farm, receiving such an education as could be had in the common schools of that time. When the militia were called out in 1814 for the defense of Baltimore, Mr. Ramsay was enrolled as a substitute, joined the company of Capt. F. T. Amos, of Harford County, and with it marched to the defense of the threatened city. They did not, however, reach there in time to participate in the engagement. For his services he has for several years received a pension from the Government. He married in April, 1821, Jane Whiteford, daughter of Hugh Whiteford, of Harford County, Md., and niece of James Ross, of Pittsburgh, a gentleman distinguished in the political history of the State. Mrs. Ramsay died in 1876. To her and husband were born the following-named children: J. Ross, Hugh W., William, Robert, Joseph G., Sarah E. and T. Cooper. Mr. Ramsay is a farmer owning 220 acres. A large part of the borough of Delta stands on what was once his land, he having sold it in lots. He has held the office of supervisor in the township, and was one of the first council of Delta. Notwithstanding his age, nearly ninety years, he is active and intelligent, manages his own affairs and attends Slateville Presbyterian Church, of which he is a member, regularly. He called upon the writer of this sketch to-day (December 22, 1884), having traveled on foot through snow half a mile to transact a matter of business relating to his real estate.

HUGH W. RAMSAY, third son of Robert and Jane (Whiteford) Ramsay, was born in Harford County, Md., February 11, 1827, his parents were of Irish and English extraction, and their children were reared on a farm, now a part of the borough of Delta. The subject of this sketch was educated at the common schools and at the age of twenty-three began the trade of a carpenter, at which he worked four years. He then embarked in the mercantile business at West Bangor, and with the exception of two years on a farm, has remained in business at Delta, Philadelphia and (since 1876) at Delta Station, of the York & Peach Bottom Railway. At about twenty-eight years of age he married Priscilla Hatton, a native of Lancaster County, and has two children living: Edgar L. and Eliza P. He is an Odd Fellow, and has held several offices in the township and borough, as judge of elections, councilman and supervisor. He is not connected with any church. His father is still living and is one of the few surviving "Old Defenders."

T. COOPER RAMSAY, youngest son of Robert and Jane (Whiteford) Ramsay, was born in Peach Bottom Township, July 31, 1839, on the homestead near Delta, where he resided until the age of seventeen, when he became a teacher, which profession he abandoned after two years, and with his brother, Joseph G., purchased a farm of 181 acres near Muddy Creek, on which he still resides, having bought his brother's interest. In 1871 he purchased a property at Coal Cabin on the canal and embarked in the mercantile business, which he conducted until 1877, when he returned to the farm. Since then, he has to some extent, been connected with the canning business. He married, December 16, 1865, Miss Ritchie, of Peach Bottom Township, and has five children: Luella, Jane O., Robert R., Howard I. and Eva E. Mr. Ramsay is at present a school director, and is superintendent and secretary of the packing firm of Eby, Barnett & Co. The family are members of the Slateville Presbyterian Church.

JOHN C. RAMSAY was born on the farm now owned and occupied by him near Slate Hill, September 17, 1825. His parents, William and Matilda (Cooper) Ramsay, were both natives of York County, and acquired by purchase, a farm of 130 acres, where they resided until their death. William Ramsay was one of the "Old Defenders," having been at Baltimore with the militia in 1814; he died in 1841, his widow surviving him until 1882. They left two sons and one daughter: James D., John C. and Mary A. James went to Nebraska about the time of its admission as a State, and was a member of its legislature; he died a few years after his return to York County; he was prominent here in local politics, and was one of the leading citizens of the township. John C. has never taken an active interest in politics, but has for many years been noted as among the most intelligent and successful farmers in the township. He is unmarried.

JAMES H. RAMSAY, deceased, was born in 1844 in Peach Bottom. He began teaching at fourteen years and at seventeen years entered Princeton College. He did not graduate on account of losing his eyesight. He was a very remarkable young man and possessed a wonderfully vigorous mind. He died February 22, 1884.

HUGH WHITEFORD RAMSAY, son of Robert S. and Isabella R. Ramsay, was born in Peach Bottom Township, March 5, 1850. He remained on the farm until 1883, having, most of the time, been engaged in teaching in the common schools. He began teaching school in the district in which he resided, in 1867. From that time on until 1883 he spent much of his time teaching and in attending the State Normal School at Millersville, Lancaster Co., Penn. During the period spent as teacher he was engaged three years at Lititz, Lancaster Co., Penn., and two years in the schools of Harford County, Md. He has given some attention to the study of law, and has acted as an attorney in securing pensions for disabled soldiers; was a member of Company A, Pennsylvania National Guards, and was stationed with a part of the regiment at Shenandoah, Schuylkill Co., Penn., June 13, 1875, at which place he remained until the suspension of the trouble, ten days later. Since 1883 he has been engaged with the Equitable Life Insurance Company, of New York. He is unmarried.

WILLIAM J. RITCHIE, son of Joseph A. and Nancy J. (Barnett) Ritchie, was born in Lancaster County, December 31, 1844, and, in 1846, came with his parents to Peach Bottom, where they located on a farm of forty-six acres. Here they continued to reside until the father's death in 1866. Our subject having purchased the homestead and added to it about forty-five acres, has carried on farming successfully, and for the past few years has also been concerned in fruit canning. December 31, 1867, Mr. Richie married Annie E. Hickman, who died June 4, 1881, leaving four daughters: Dora L., Marian C., Nannie and Mary A. His second marriage, December 17, 1884, was with Miss Sallie E. McConkey, daughter of S. D. McConkey, of Baltimore, Md. Mr. Ritchie is a member of the Slateville Presbyterian Church.

WILLIAM R. ROBINSON, deceased, son of James and Rachel (Kerr) Robinson, natives of Ireland, was born in Peach Bottom Township, on the farm now occupied by his family. He married, in 1861, Margaret Ailes, daughter of William Ailes, of Lancaster County, Penn., and had born to him three children: Lizzie B., Rachel K. and Mary B. The homestead contains about 220 acres, on which Mr. Robinson successfully pursued farming until his death, which took place March 23, 1876. Mrs. Robinson remarried in November, 1879, with John T. Smith, a native of Baltimore, Md., who came to Peachbottom in 1872. The family are members of the Slateville Presbyterian Church.

BENJAMIN F. RUFF, a native of Harford County, Md., was born April 29, 1820. His parents, Richard and Lovina (Montgomery) Ruff, were of English descent. His father was one of the "Old Defenders," having been with his company at Baltimore in 1814. He died in 1823. The subject of this sketch spent his early life on a farm, and received his education in a subscription school, and at Abington Academy. After leaving school he served an apprenticeship at blacksmithing at Bush Furnace, and afterward worked at Patterson's Iron Works, in Baltimore County. In 1842 he came to Peach Bottom Township, rented a shop one year from James Ramsay, after which he built a shop at Slate Hill, where he now resides. He was married in 1845, to Elizabeth, daughter of James and Elizabeth (Bankhead) Alexander, of Harford County, Md., and had born to him five children, all of whom died soon after they were grown up. His wife died in 1862, and in a few years he entered into a second marriage with Virginia, daughter of John L. and Mary Ann (Gibbons) Sterns, by whom he has two sons: Purlee and James Ross. His second wife died February 22, 1884, and she as well as the first, was interred at Slateville Presbyterian Church, of which the family are members. Mr. Ruff enjoys a reputation among his neighbors for strict integrity of character and upright dealing. By his industry he has acquired a fair competence.

REV. JOSEPH D. SMITH was born May 30, 1828, in Londonderry, Ireland, and accompanied his parents to America in 1847, landing at Philadelphia, where the family resided until 1860, when the father died at the age of sixty-five. In 1872 the mother came to reside with the subject of this sketch until the time of her death in June, 1882. Her age was ninety years. Joseph was the eldest of the family, which consisted of three sons and one daughter. William resides at Philadelphia; David at Edgewater Park, N. J., and the sister resides with our subject at Slate Ridge. Joseph was partly educated in Ireland, and after coming to America attended the preparatory department of the freshman class in Danville, Ky. In 1853 he entered Jefferson College, at Cannonsburg, Penn., and after graduating there passed a theological course in Princeton, N. J. He was licensed to preach in 1859 by the Presbytery of Philadelphia, and a few months later came to York County, and assumed the pastorate of Slate Ridge Presbyterian Church. As a minister Mr. Smith has endeared himself to his people by his eloquence and earnestness in the pulpit, and his zealous advocacy of everything tending to the benefit of the community and the elevation of morality. During the past ten years he has prepared several young men for college, in addition to his ministerial duties. He has also purchased about thirty acres of land, which he cultivates principally with his own hands. Mr. Smith is unmarried.

ASAHEL STEWARD, M. D., the eldest son and sixth child of the ten children of Nehemiah and Amelia (Cooper) Steward, was born in Peach Bottom Township, March 10, 1841. His parents were natives of York County, his father of Irish and his mother of English extraction. His boyhood was passed on his father's farm, and his early education received in the common schools, and at York County Academy. At the age of twenty-two he began the study of medicine with Dr. James Y. Bryan, and graduated at the Bellevue Hospital Medical College, New York City, in the class of 1868–69. His first practice as a physician was in Fulton Township, Lancaster Co., Penn., where he remained about eight years. In 1877 he returned to Peach Bottom Township, where he still pursues his profession, enjoying a large and lucrative practice. He was married, December 9, 1875, to Miss Cassandra I. McCullough, daughter of Robert K. McCullough, of Lancaster County. Their children are William J., Amelia F., Montgomery L., Asahel, who died in August, 1884, and Robert King, who died in infancy. Mr. Steward is a member of Mount Hebron Lodge No. 516, I. O. O. F., and also of Esdraelon Lodge No. 176, A. F. & A. M. His parents are both living at the age of seventy-five years.

REV. ALFRED WELLS, pastor of the Baptist Church, of Delta, is a native of Wales, and came with his parents to Minersville, Penn., in 1859. He is the sixth of eight children, and was born August

BIOGRAPHICAL SKETCHES.

8, 1846. At the age of seventeen he began the trade of carriage smith at Tamaqua, and worked about a year and a half, when he went to coal mining, which business he continued to follow for several years. His education was acquired at common schools, and by making use of the hours that could be spared from his labor. At the age of twenty-nine he was ordained a minister of the Baptist Church, though he had been for ten years before a licentiate. His first charge was at Mahanoy, Schuylkill County, from which he went to Coleraine, Lancaster County, next to Green Valley, Chester County, and in 1879 came to Peach Bottom Township, York, where he took charge of a small congregation at Glenwood School House. On the completion of the new church in Dela in 1884, he removed there. From the age of nineteen until 1873 he was a member of the Methodist Episcopal Church. He married in 1870, Martha Boughey, a native of Pennsylvania, and has four children living: Adeline, William A., Josiah B. and Joseph T. Mr. Wells, by his earnest devotion to his chosen work, has been largely instrumental, in building up a flourishing congregation in Delta. He also has charge of the Drumore Baptist Church, Lancaster County.

CHARLES H. A. WHITEFORD, the eldest son of Hugh C. and Cassandra (Silver) Whiteford, was born in Harford County, Md., March 27, 1839. His parents were of Scotch-Irish and Welsh descent, both families being prominent in the politics and business of Harford County. He remained on his father's farm until the age of twenty years, having, in the meantime, obtained a fair education. In 1865 he entered the mercantile business at Delta, in which he continued until 1872. He then opened, at the same place, a photograph gallery, and gave his attention to that business for some years. He married Miss Cassandra Findley, a native of Lancaster County, December 4, 1866. They have one child living—Lizzie Grace—and have buried one in infancy. He has held the office of borough auditor for two terms, and is now principally engaged in the business of slate roofing. The Railroad House, one of the principal hotels of the place, is owned by Mr. Whiteford.

E. HOWARD WILEY was born in Peach Bottom Township, September 13, 1859. His parents, David E. and Margaretta (McConkey) Wiley, were both natives of this township, the former the son of Joseph D. Wiley, for many years the leading business man in the community, and the latter is a daughter of the late Andrew McConkey. The subject of this sketch is an enterprising farmer, occupying a farm of 140 acres of fine land, near Slate Hill. He married, April 14, 1881, Miss Anna M. Jenness, a native of Cecil County, Md., who has borne two children: Paul C. and Margetaretta. The family are members of the Slateville Presbyterian Church.

WILLIAM E. WILLIAMS is the third son of Evan and Elizabeth Williams, and was born in north Wales August 5, 1830. His parents died in Wales, and he, with two brothers and a sister, came to America in 1852, and settled near the slate quarries of York County, Penn., where he worked for John Humphrey for several years. He afterward entered the mercantile business, first with E. D. Humphrey, and later with E. E. Williams and H. Evans, under the firm name of William E. Williams & Co. Besides the store at West Bangor, the firm now own several tracts of slate land, both in York County and Harford County, Md. They have a large and productive quarry in the latter place, purchased in 1874 from Isaac Parker, from which, in 1888, they took out more than 3,000 squares of roofing slate. Mr. Williams was married, at Manchester, Wis., in 1863, to Elizabeth Roberts, and has five children: John R., William, William R., Elizabeth Maritte and Maggie. He has held the office of judge of elections, and has been a school director two terms. He has also been assistant postmaster at West Bangor for about twenty-eight years. The family are connected with the Calvinistic Methodist Church.

SHREWSBURY TOWNSHIP.

REV. EDWARD EVANS ALLEN was born in Accomack County, Va., August 15, 1805, of very pious parents, members of the Methodist Episcopal Church. His father, who was a planter of means, died while Edward was yet an infant, leaving three sons. Their mother removed to Baltimore shortly after the death of the father, where she had the boys educated. When seventeen years old, Edward attended Light Street Church at Baltimore, and there, influenced by a powerful sermon of Rev. Val. Cook, he embraced religion. Choosing the ministry for his profession, he entered it in 1827, and was first assigned to the Bellefonte Circuit, Penn. As he was a member of the Baltimore conference, he was, by request, transferred to Baltimore, where he was stationed many years, the members petitioning the conference to have him remain. He was a zealous worker, and beloved by all who knew him. He was of a kind, genial disposition, full of humor and wit. Ex-President Buchanan and ex-Gov. Packer, of Pennsylvania, were warm friends of his, the former saying that he was one of the finest speakers he knew. He was a member of No. 45, A. Y. M. of Baltimore. While in Bellefonte he was married to Senator Wilson's daughter, of Williamsport, Penn., and had three children, the eldest died in infancy: Thomas Edward and Mrs. Mary R. Campbell, of Baltimore. His second wife, Lizzie Wiley, of Baltimore, left five children. He died in Shrewsbury, May 28, 1872, to which place he came to recruit his health. As one of the old ministers remarked: "He died in the harness, and did not rust out." He was buried in the Baltimore Cemetery.

MILTON W. BAHN was born June 26, 1839, in Hellam Township. His parents, David and Rachel (Witman) Bahn, natives of York County, had six children, two died in childhood, and Milton W. is the only son and the youngest of the family living. He was brought up on a farm and educated at the York County Academy, and State Normal School, at Millersville, Penn. From the age of eighteen to twenty-four, he taught in York County public schools. In January, 1865, he engaged in the mercantile business in partnership with W. H. Emig, at New Freedom, which he has since followed. Mr. Emig retired from the firm in 1880. Mr. Bahn was married November 4, 1864, at Emigsville, to Miss Ella S. Emig, of that place, daughter of John Emig (deceased), and has had four children—two have died: Lillie Alice, aged eleven years, and Corrinne Ella, aged eight years. The living are Arthur W. and Walter D. Mr. Bahn was appointed postmaster of New Freedom, in 1865, and with the exception of one year (1881–82) has held the office since. He is also agent of the Northern Central Railroad Company, and of the Adams Express Company. He is interested in a new railroad enterprise between Stewartstown and New Freedom; was one of the organizers and president ten years out of twelve of the "New Freedom Building and Loan Association," and was a member of the borough school board, three years, ending in 1879, and a member of the borough council one year (1880). He is an active Republican; also an elder in the Reformed Church, in which he and wife have been brought up. His father died in 1863, aged sixty years.

JEREMIAH BAILEY, farmer, was born in Springfield Township, June 2, 1825. His parents, John C. and Barbara (Allison) Bailey, were natives of York County, and of German and English descent, respectively. They reared a family of twelve children—seven daughters and five sons—of whom Jeremiah is the eldest. He was brought up on a farm and educated at the common schools. At the age of nineteen he went to New Market, Md., and learned the trade of wheelwright. He worked at Logansville, Wrightsville, and West Manchester, at which latter place he remained five years; then returned to Wrightsville; there he worked three years, then went back to West Manchester, at which latter place he remained for four or five years. He then went to Maryland, where he worked at his trade, and farming nineteen years. He also worked about four years at New Freedom. In the spring of 1880, he removed to his farm in Shrewsbury Township, near the Maryland line, where he has since been farming and working at his trade. In 1848 he was married at Wrightsville, to Elizabeth Jane Detweiler, of Wrightsville, who died October 24, 1874, leaving ten children—three of whom died also. The living are William G., Charles G., Emma J., John M., Webster O., Jeremiah D. and Ida L. He was next married, March 11, 1877, at York, to Barbara Bahn, widow of Samuel N. Bahn, who was mother of ten children, by her first husband—seven girls and three boys: Alice, Agnes Ammeda, Sylvester, Ida, Anna, Barbara, Ellen and Samuel Howard; Walter and Rosetta are deceased. The family were members of the Evangelical Church. Mr. Bailey belongs to the P. of H.. was a director of schools three years; a trustee in Maryland twelve years, and is a director of New Freedom Cemetery Association.

D. A. BECKER, son of Peter and Sarah (Henry) Becker, was born in North Codorus Township, September 9, 1849, was reared on his father's farm until the age of sixteen, when he rented Bott's store at Smyer's Station, Northern Central Railroad. He then began the business of manufacturing cigars. March 5, 1869, Mr. Becker married Matilda Krebs, daughter of Jere and Rachael (Schwartz) Krebs, of North Codorus Township. Three children were born to this marriage: Annie M., Leona M. and Jeremiah E. T. Mr. Becker is a member of the firm of Bortner & Becker, wholesale ice cream manufacturers and ships largely in this line through Pennsylvania and Maryland.

FRANCIS R. BLASSER, D. V. S., was born in Shrewsbury Township, March 2, 1845, and is the youngest of the twelve children born to John and Esther (Ritchey) Blasser, natives of Pennsylvania, but of German and Scotch-Irish descent. He was reared a farmer, but subsequently followed pumpmaking for twenty years, both in Pennsylvania and Maryland. In 1872 he began the study of veterinary surgery, and since 1874, has been in active practice, having met with the most flattering success, as is instanced by the fact that for the past four years he has lost but four animals in a list of 450. He has care of some of the finest trotting horses in the land, is the regular professional of the Ashland Iron Company, and also surgeon of Post 342, G. A. R. In 1866 he married Mary J. Miller, of Maryland, and has had born to him ten children —of these are living only four: Harry G., Lulu May, Della G. and William H. In 1862 he enlisted in Company K, One Hundred and Sixty-sixth Pennsylvania Volunteer Infantry; was promoted to drum-major and served a term of nine months.

EMANUEL K. BOLLINGER, born in York County, October, 1825, is the son of Peter and Catherine (Klinefelter)Bollinger, of Swiss and German descent. Joseph and Henry Bollinger, with their mother, came to America about the year 1754, and from Joseph has descended the subject of this sketch, who began life on a farm, and entered the milling business under his uncle, N. Seitz, at the age of fourteen years, and at the age of twenty-two, having saved $750 from his earnings, he began business for himself at Seitzland, where he has since resided, engaged in connection with milling, in mercantile business, as a member of the firm of Klinefelter & Co., sixteen years, and in the milling and grain business exclusively, eight years; bought the real estate now occupied by him, in his business in 1866; in 1874, began the manufacture of Bollinger's Ammoniated Phosphates, and is now doing business as miller, grain dealer, and manufacturer and dealer in phosphates; has been agent of the Northern Central Railway Company, at Seitzland, since 1872,and postmaster since 1875; is president of the Glen Rock Manufacturing Company,and a director of the First National Bank, of Glen Rock, and was a charter member of both organizations; is a member of the Masonic fraternity, and of the I. O. O. F. Lodge and Encampment. In Gettysburg, Adams Co Penn., in 1849, he was married to Barbara Roser and they have had eight children: Stephen R.. Abtil, Aaron, Amanda (wife of E. Dickson, Esq.), George W., Uriah G., Angelina (deceased), and Eva Jane, wife of T. B. Seitz, Esq. Mr. Bollinger is an elder and the whole family are members of the Lutheran Church.

JACOB G. BORTNER is a son of Jacob and Catherine (Garbeck) Bortner,of Codorus Township, where our subject was born November 23, 1826. He was reared on his father's farm, and after learning his trade, at Krouse tannery, Maryland, married March 10, 1852, Matilda Messomer, daughter of Daniel and Christine (Reitz) Messomer, of Manheim Township; this marriage has been blessed with seven children: Castila A.; Syrian P.; Josephine A.; Levina H., deceased; Catherine A.; Alvan D., deceased; and Matilda H. He built his tannery in 1851, and has kept it running at its full capacity ever since, employing on an average ten to twelve hands. Mr. Bortner manufactures (in connection with his tanning) flavine and extract of black oak bark. He built his present residence in 1852. Mr. Bortner is one of the leading business men of Shrewsbury Township.

JOHN L. BOYER was born in York County, Penn., November 7, 1820. His parents, Samuel S. and Sarah (Le Fevre) Boyer, were natives of Pennsylvania. Samuel Boyer, the great-grandfather, came from Switzerland. John L. spent the first twenty-one years of his life on the farm, in York County, getting his education at the local schools. At the age of twenty-one, his parents removed to Carroll County, Md., where they lived twenty years and then removed to Frederick County, where they died. John L. was married in Carroll County, to Nancy La Mott, daughter of Joshua and Elizabeth (Hershey) La Mott, Maryland and Pennsylvania, and of French and German descent. Joshua La Mott was a general in the war of 1812. To this union were born four children: Sarah Jane, deceased; Elizabeth W.; Joshua H. La Mott; and BelindaW., deceased. In 1870 Mr. Boyer removed to New Freedom, where the family has since resided. Mr. Boyer is a member of the German Reformed Church and his wife a member of the Mennonites. Joshua Henry La Mott Boyer was born in Carroll County, Md., November 22, 1857, was educated at the common schools, and taught singing when but sixteen years of age. He is organist and choir leader and quite a speaker.

WILLIAM H. BRENISE, superintendent of

BIOGRAPHICAL SKETCHES.   171

Young & Co's. flavine and extract works, at Shrewsbury Station, was born in Shrewsbury, December 29, 1856. His parents, were Samuel and Mary (Klinefelter) Brenise, of York County, who had six children, of whom he was the youngest. He was educated at the public schools, and at the age of sixteen years he began working in the above works, and April 1, 1883, became superintendent. He has under him fifteen men, and under his supervision 2,000 tons of bark are annually converted into flavine and extract. His father, who was a carpenter, died at Shrewsbury, May, 1883, aged sixty-seven years. Mr. Brenise belongs to the K. of P., of Glen Rock.

FRANKLIN W. BROWN, merchant, was born in West Manchester Township, October 10, 1850. His parents, Jeremiah and Christiana (Geise) Brown, were natives of Adams and York Counties, respectively, and of German descent. They had four children, of whom Franklin W. is the third son. He was brought up on a farm and attended the public schools. Until 1882 he was clerking in different places. From 1869 to 1870, he worked at cigar-making at Loganville. In April, 1874, he came to Glen Rock, and clerked for Miller & Glatfelter for seven or eight years. In 1882 he began business for himself by engaging in the merchandising business. November 5, 1878, he was married at Loganville, to Elenora Goodling, daughter of Daniel Goodling. They have one child—Thomas Morris. Mr. Brown is a member of the German Reformed Church, and his wife a member of the Evangelical Association. He is also trustee of the K. of P., and held the office of district deputy from 1883 to 1884; he was auditor of Glen Rock from 1876 to 1878.

HENRY G. BUSSEY, M. D., was born at Green Spring Plantation, Harford Co., Md., in 1816, and is the third son of Henry G. and Elizabeth (Harris) Bussey, of French and Scotch descent, respectively. The paternal grandfather was a colonel during the Revolutionary war, and the maternal grandfather a captain. Henry G. Bussey was a captain in the war of 1812. Our subject received his elementary education at the Green Spring Academy, on his father's premises; he then read medicine for two years with Dr. W. J. McElheney, of Bel Air, Md.; then, in 1834, entered the University of Maryland, from which he graduated in 1837; he practiced in Peach Bottom Township, this county, a few months, then in Maryland until 1840, when he settled in Shrewsbury Borough, where he has ever since enjoyed a lucrative practice. In 1837 he married Miss Catharine Boarman, who bore him two children (Mary Elizabeth and Henry G.), and died in January, 1884. The Doctor has held a number of offices, among them those of inspector and judge of elections, school director, physician to the county prison, physician to alms house in his native county, prothonotary, 1857 to 1863, and in 1874–76 State senator. In 1848 he was nominated for congress, but declined in favor of J. B. Dana.

ALEXANDER DAVID COLLINS was born in Hopewell Township, York County, February 14, 1853, and was the third son and child in a family of four sons and two daughters. His parents, Cornelius and Elizabeth (Gordon) Collins, were natives of York County, and of Scotch-Irish descent. He grew up on the farm; was educated at home and in Stewartstown Academy. He entered the Shrewsbury Savings Institution, in 1876, as assistant cashier. In 1879 he went to Cheyenne, Wyoming Territory, where he clerked in a bank two years. He returned to Shrewsbury in the spring in 1882, when he was elected cashier of the old bank, which position he has since held. He is a member of the United Presbyterian Church.

REV. FREDERICK EMANUEL CREVER was born in Carlisle, Penn., April 9, 1826. His parents, James and Mary (Cart) Crever, were natives of Carlisle, and of German descent. His father was one of the founders, and for many years the editor and proprietor of the *Carlisle Republican*, now the *Carlisle Herald*. Frederick K. was educated in the public schools of Carlisle, and beginning at the age of nineteen, served an apprenticeship of three years at the carpenter's trade, and worked three years more as journeyman; was baptized in infancy, and brought up in the Lutheran Church; united with the Methodist Episcopal Church; early felt called to the ministry, but learned his trade to satisfy his father; joined the conference as a candidate in 1853, and was appointed to Sinnamahoning Circuit; at once applied himself to the course of study required by the rules of his church, and, at the end of two years, was ordained deacon, and two years later elder, and was appointed to Newport Circuit, Perry County, Penn., remaining one year; continued in the regular work of the ministry until 1876, holding some of the most important charges in Pennsylvania and Maryland the full time; was placed on the supernumerary list in 1878; a year and a half later, on the superannuated list. His last regular charge was Castle Fin. He removed to his farm of ninety-five acres, two miles south of Shrewsbury, where he now resides, and is still a member of the conference, preaching where he may be called, averaging about twice a month, often in York and vicinity. In 1861 he made a war speech in McConnellsburg, in connection with the raising of troops, and during the war acted as volunteer chaplain, visiting hospitals and battle fields. He has always been an active temperance worker. He was married, February 26, 1857, to Rachel Ann Hendrix, of Shrewsbury Township, and daughter of Isaac Hendrix, and they had seven children, of whom five are dead: Katie, aged eighteen months; Charles A., aged four years; Susan, aged two years; James F., aged eighteen months, and Benjamin A., aged fourteen years. The two living are Annie Rozilla and James Willis, student. Mrs. Crever is a member of the Methodist Episcopal Church, although brought up in the Lutheran.

REV. EDWARD CRUMBLING, resident pastor of the Evangelical Association at Glen Rock, was born in Hellam Township, January 27, 1856, and is the eldest of two sons of Tobias and Sarah (Bupp) Crumbling, of Scotch and Swiss extraction. His early life was spent in the country, and from the age of twelve to seventeen he was engaged, when out of school, as clerk in the mercantile business. From the age of seventeen to twenty-two he taught in the public schools during the winter months. Having been educated in the public schools he began studying with a view to the ministry at about the age of twenty, and at once entered the local service. At twenty-two he entered the active work of the ministry, uniting with the Central Pennsylvania Conference of the Evangelical Association, as preacher on trial. After traveling Baltimore Circuit, Md., two years he was ordained deacon, and returned to Alberton Station, a part of the same circuit, where he was retained two years more. After an experience of four years he was ordained elder, which is the highest order in his denomination. He was appointed to Glen Rock in 1882, and Yorkana Circuit in 1885. He was married, March 15, 1881, at East Prospect, to Miss Arvilla Kise, a native of York County, and has two children: Mary Edith and Annie Elva. His only brother is also in the ministry. His parents reside in Lower Windsor Township, aged fifty-eight and forty-five years, respectively. He is an honorary member of the society of Rechabites.

JOHN L. DAY, born in Shrewsbury Township, August 4, 1817, was the eldest of a family of three sons and two daughters of David and Rebecca (Low) Day, natives of York and of English descent.

SHREWSBURY TOWNSHIP.

His grandfather, Matthew Day, was born in Chester County, Penn., and came to York County in the latter part of the eighteenth century. John L. grew to manhood on the farm, was educated in the schools of his neighborhood, and has never followed anything else but farming. At the age of eighteen he began farming on his own account. He was married, in September, 1847, in Shrewsbury Township, to Susan L. Taylor, daughter of John Taylor. He has had six children: John Millard, died, aged two and a half years; Sherman E., died, aged eight months; Rebecca C., wife of Henry Nonemaker; Otis C., Emma A. and Wilbert S. He went to Ohio before marriage, remained one year, returned to Pennsylvania, and after marriage removed to Maryland, where he farmed twelve years; removed to where he now lives in 1864, and owns forty acres of land. He is a trustee of the Methodist Episcopal Church at New Freedom, of which church himself and wife are members, and he also is a member of the I. O. O. F., at Shrewsbury. He has one brother in Maryland and one in Ohio, and two sisters in York County. His father died January 7, 1871, aged eighty years; his mother in 1839, aged fifty years. His wife's father, John Taylor, died November 27, 1861, aged seventy-three years, and her mother, January 24, 1873, aged seventy-eight years. Mrs. Day is a sister of Dr. John A. Taylor, of Shrewsbury Township.

ADAM DIEHL, a farmer, and son of Adam and Catherine (Shafer) Diehl, of York County, and of German descent, was born near Hametown, February 25, 1821, and is the third son and sixth child in a family of eight children—four boys and four girls. He was brought up on a farm, and attended the public schools. Early he learned the blacksmith's trade, and to do repairing of farming implements. At the age of twenty-one he began working for his father, and worked for him until twenty-seven years of age. His father died in 1848, aged sixty-two years, and his mother died aged eighty-two years. November 26, 1846, he was married at York, to Annie Tyson, of York County, and of English descent, who died in 1882, leaving eight children, one of whom died. The living are Isabel, Agnes, Harrison, Emma, Adam, Alexander and Ezra. Mr. Diehl is a member of the Lutheran Church, and has donated a good deal of money to all churches. He is a director of the Shrewsbury Bank, and has been for eight or nine years. The farm on which he resides contains about 155 acres, and has been brought to the highest point of cultivation by his untiring energy.

SAMUEL K. DIEHL, son of Isaac and Rose Ann (Klinefelter) Diehl, of York County, was born in Shrewsbury, December 24, 1848, and was the second of ten children. He remained on the farm until twenty-one years of age, attending in the meantime the public schools, and in his twentieth year he taught school two terms. At the age of twenty-one years he entered the mercantile house of J. S. Seitz, at Hametown and Seitzland, as clerk, and until 1875 he clerked for different firms at Hametown and Seitzland. In 1875 he went into business at Seitzland with Henry A. Young, having purchased the interest of Mr. Seitz. In 1878 Mr. Young retired, selling out to an elder brother of our subject, of Nebraska, the business being then conducted by S. K. Diehl & Bro., dealers in general merchandise, phosphates, etc. He was married in Shrewsbury in 1872, to Rosa Hildebrand, of Hopewell Township, Penn., of German descent, and has six children: Charles Schuyler, Isaac Palmer, Mabel Ella, Mary Naomi, Minnie Estella and an infant. The family are members of the Evangelical Lutheran Church. Mr. Diehl was inspector of elections in 1880. In 1882-83 he engaged in the manufacture of cigars with Seitz & Co., Seitzland.

REV. ALFRED FRANKLIN DREISBACH, A. B., resident pastor of the Reformed Church, at Shrewsbury, was born in Northampton County, Penn., September 8, 1851. His parents were Jacob and Matilda (Gormanton) Dreisbach, of Pennsylvania, and of German and French descent. They had a family of eight children—three sons and one daughter (of whom Rev. Alfred is the youngest) now living. Of the parents, the mother died in 1861, at the age of forty-nine years, while his father is still residing at his native place. The primary education of our subject was received at the public schools, but at the age of sixteen years he went to Easton Collegiate Institute, where he remained nine or ten terms. He studied the languages under Rev. Dr. E. W. Reinecke, of Nazareth, Penn., for two years, and also taught school for six terms. At the age of twenty-one he entered Franklin & Marshall College at Lancaster, Penn., and graduated in 1877 as A. B. He at once entered the theological seminary at Lancaster, from which he graduated in May, 1880, and in August he was called to his present charge, and was ordained as soon as called. June 29, 1880, he was married at Lancaster, Penn., to Mary E. Hoffmeier, daughter of William M. Hoffmeier, of Lancaster, and of German and Scotch-Irish descent. He reorganized a neglected congregation at New Freedom, and built a church and parsonage at Shrewsbury. At present he preaches at Shrewsbury; at St. Peter's, in Springfield Township; at Jerusalem, in Shrewsbury Township; and at Bethlehem in Codorus Township, and at New Freedom.

DAVID C. EBERHART, D. D. S., was born in Mercer County, Penn., November 19, 1826. His parents, Abraham and Esther (Ammond) Eberhart, were natives of Pennsylvania and of German descent. Paulus Eberhart, the progenitor of the Eberhart family in America, came from Wurtemburg, Germany, in 1744, the original seat of the Eberharts (who were reigning dukes for over 300 years), and settled in Baltimore County, Md. It appears from tradition his eldest son Paul was born on the ocean. He settled the manor in Westmoreland, Penn., where the grandfather and father of the subject of this sketch were born, and where a number of the old members of the family are buried. Sergeant Lawrence Eberhart, of Frederick County, Md , one of the family, distinguished himself in one of the engagements with the British, in South Carolina, during the Revolutionary war, by rushing to the rescue of Col. Washington, who was beset by a British officer and some dozen dragoons, and handing the colonel his sword, thus enabling that officer to cut his way out [see Romances of the Revolution. by Bunce]. He died in Frederick in 1840, aged ninety-five years. Abraham, the father, died at Chicago Lawn, Ill., in 1880, aged eighty-four years, where the mother is living at this writing (1884) aged eighty-four years. David C. is the third son of a family of seven sons and three daughters; grew to manhood on a farm in Mercer and Venango Counties; received an academic education, and at the age of twenty-one began the study of dental surgery; also studied medicine awhile at Middlesex, Penn., and at Warren, Ohio, and practiced that profession at New Bedford, Penn., a few months. In 1850 he went to Baltimore, Md., where he practiced dentistry for two years, studying theology in the meantime, and was licensed to preach in the Methodist Episcopal Church, and assigned to Shrewsbury Circuit. His health failing, he abandoned the itinerant ministry, and resumed the practice of dental surgery, preaching only occasionally. He was appointed chaplain of the Eighty-seventh Regiment Pennsylvania Volunteers, in February, 1863; was captured at Winchester, Va., June 15, 1863; taken to Castle Thunder, transferred to Libby

BIOGRAPHICAL SKETCHES. 173

Prison, released and rejoined his regiment October 7, 1863, and was mustered out in October, 1864, and resumed the practice of dental surgery at Shrewsbury. He was married, in 1854, at Shrewsbury, to Mary E. daughter of Dr. James Gerry, and had born to him five children, two of whom are now living: James Gerry, a distinguished minister in the Methodist Episcopal Church, in Illinois, and Zelia C. His wife died in 1867, aged thirty-two years. He was next married, in 1872, at Shrewsbury, to Wanetta I, daughter of William D. Benton, of Maryland, and they have had two children: Winona S. and David Cleon. Dr. Eberhart is Past Master, and now secretary, of the Masonic Lodge at Shrewsbury; is chaplain of Post No. 342, G. A. R.; was justice of the peace from 1874 to May, 1884; school director four terms; chief burgess in 1876. He is an active Sunday-school worker, having been superintendent of a Sunday-school for twenty years.

SAMUEL D. EHRHART, son of Henry and Julia A. (Diehl) Ehrhart, of York County, was born March 20, 1858, and is the fifth of seven children. His ancestors came to America before the Revolution. He was brought up in Shrewsbury Township, and educated at the district schools, and was two sessions at Glen Rock, teaching one year in Shrewsbury Township. When seventeen years of age he began huckstering in York, and continued it two years, and then engaged in the butchering business in Shrewsbury, which he carried on for two years; he also engaged in the horse business (sale and exchange), in which latter business he is still engaged, selling about one car-load per week. In February, 1879, he was married to Tillie Blosser, daughter of George Blosser, of Shrewsbury, and has three children: Erastus, Lester and Hannon. Mr. Ehrhart is a member of the I. O. O. F. Mount Vernon Lodge, No. 143, K. of P., and Friendly Circle No. 287 of Glen Rock. The family are members of the Lutheran Church.

GEORGE P. EVERHART, merchant, and a native of Manchester, Md., was born March 11, 1840. His parents, George and Catherine (Shower) Everhart, were natives of Maryland, and of German descent. Their ancestor, Paulus Everhart, came to America in 1744, and settled in Germantown, going to Maryland in 1752, to what was then Baltimore County, Bachman's Valley. His son George, a farmer, remained in that portion which was converted into Carroll County. He had four sons: George, Jacob, John and David, and five daughters. George, the father of the subject of this sketch, was born in 1800, and is still living at Manchester, Md. He had a family of five sons and six daughters, of whom George P. is the third son. He was educated at the Manchester Academy, and trained for the mercantile business by his father. In 1864 he began business at New Oxford, Penn., but soon returned to Manchester, where he clerked in his father's store until 1866, when he removed to Shrewsbury and engaged in the mercantile business until March, 1872, when he removed to Shrewsbury Station, in the same county, where he formed a partnership with Messrs. Kolter & Young, under the firm name of G. P. Everhart & Co. In October, 1878, Kolter & Young retired, and from that time Mr. Everhart has conducted the business alone. He is also engaged in the forwarding business, owning a line of cars, handles produce, railroad ties, lumber, coal, phosphates, etc. In 1866 he was married at Abbottstown, Penn., to Mary E. Hauer, daughter of Rev. D. J. Hauer, and had three children, only one of whom is now living. He was one of the organizers of the Shrewsbury Station, and Shrewsbury Turnpike Company; has been president of the Shrewsbury Savings Institution since 1876; is express agent, railroad agent and postmaster at Rail Road; he was also postmaster at Manchester from 1861 to 1864. In 1873 he was elected auditor of Rail Road Borough; in 1874, chief burgess; in 1876, one of the borough council, and again in 1883. Mr. E. is a member of the Reformed Church of Shrewsbury. He is a Master Mason, and Past Master of Shrewsbury Lodge No. 423, of which he was one of the charter members.

ISAAC K. FOLCKEMMER, stone-cutter, was born in Shrewsbury, February 9, 1847. His father, Jacob, died in 1871, and his mother, Susan (Boyer), in 1864. Both were of German descent. They had a family of nine children, four sons and five daughters. Isaac K. was educated at the public schools, and from fourteen to seventeen years of age carried the United States mail between Shrewsbury and Rail Road. When seventeen years of age he began to learn the trade of stone-cutter at London, Ohio, where he remained three years, and then returned to Pennsylvania. He then worked one year at Philadelphia, and about three months at York. In 1869 he went to Harrisburgh, where he worked five years at his trade. He then came back to Shrewsbury, and in 1875 bought out his employer, and has since then managed the business for himself. In 1872 he was married, at Shrewsbury, to Mary S. Klinefelter, daughter of Joseph Klinefelter, and has two children: Joseph and Clarence. Mr. Folckemmer is a member of the lodge of I. O. O. F. and Encampment; was in the council, and is a school director.

JOSEPH S. FREELAND, farmer, was born in Baltimore County, Md., August 15, 1851. His parents were Caleb and Sarah A. (Hendrix) Freeland, of Maryland and Pennsylvania, respectively, and of Scotch and German descent. They had two children, a son and a daughter. Like his ancestors, Joseph S. was brought up a farmer. He was educated at Mechanicsburgh, Penn., and taught school for a while. In 1867 he and his parents left Baltimore County for York County, and since that time he has lived upon a farm, which, for generations back, belonged to his ancestors. In 1872 he was married, in Baltimore County, to Edith Mackay, daughter of R. G. Mackay, of Pennsylvania, and of Irish-Scotch descent. They have four children: Helen, Clarence, Maud and Agnes. The family belong to the Methodist Protestant Church, although Mrs. Freeland was brought up in the Presbyterian Church. Mr. Freeland was school director two terms, was a director for three years of the Shrewsbury Savings Institution, and is treasurer and one of the organizers of the New Freedom Cemetery Association.

PROF. WILLIAM J. FULTON was born near Delta, York County, November 5, 1860. His parents, John J. and Sarah Ann (Heaps) Fulton, were natives of Pennsylvania and Maryland, and of Scotch-Irish descent, respectively. He was brought up on a farm, but spent most of his time at school. From the public schools he went to York Collegiate Institute, from which he graduated in 1880. He then entered Lafayette College, at Easton, Penn., and graduated in 1882, receiving the degree of A. B. He then commenced the study of law under ex-Judge Robert J. Fisher, of York. He was appointed principal of Shrewsbury English and Classical Academy March 5, 1883. He was married, June 28, 1883, at Easton, Penn., to Margaret Neigh, daughter of George P. Neigh, Esq., of Easton. He was admitted to the York, Penn., bar August 25, 1884, and while retaining the principalship of the academy, is, at the same time, actively engaged in the practice of law.

MARTIN GABLE was born June 9, 1824, in Darmstadt, Germany, and came to America in 1844. Landing at New York, he soon removed to Baltimore, where he learned shoe-making, at which he worked twelve years. He was educated in Germany, and followed farming. Two brothers followed him to America. His parents, Jost and Elizabeth (Brodrecht) Gable, died before he left Germany. He was married, in Baltimore, in 1849, to Miss Catharine Ketterling, a native of that city. She died in 1870, leaving one daughter, Fannie, now the wife of Joseph A. Klinefelter. Another child, Catharine, died in infancy. He removed to York County, and has lived about Shrewsbury ever since 1856; came to Rail Road in 1877. He followed shoemaking five years in York County, and huckstering about ten years; was collector for several years, and since 1877 has kept the toll-gate at Rail Road. He is a member of the Lutheran Church, as was also his wife. He earned his property by his own industry.

JOHN H. GANTZ, born in York County, March 29, 1820, is the fourth child and eldest son in a family of three sons and five daughters of John and Barbara (Hosler) Gantz. He was reared on a farm, and acquired a fair German and English education. He was married in 1841, in Shrewsbury Township, to Miss Lydia, a daughter of John Miller, and a native of York County. His wife died in 1850, having had three children; one, Margaret Ann, died at the age of five years, the two living are John W. and Susanna, wife of Adam Eighner. He was next married, October 5, 1851, to Mrs. Lucinda (Kerlinger) Ziegler. They have had five children—two have died: Ellen, aged three years, and Balinda, aged thirteen years. The three living are Eliza Ann, wife of L. R. Lentz; Alice, wife of George Bollinger, and Amelia, wife of Henry Allison. Mr. Gantz served his country in the nine months' service, entering the army in 1862, and participated in numerous skirmishes. He is a member of Post No. 342, G. A. R., at Shrewsbury. He is connected with the Lutheran Church, and his wife with the Reformed Church. He is a Republican and a hard working farmer, having acquired his property by his own labor.

ELBRIDGE HOFFMAN GERRY, A. B., M. D., was born in Shrewsbury, October 18, 1836, and is the eldest son of Dr. James Gerry, of Scotch-Irish and German descent. He was brought up in his father's drug store, and educated at the public and private schools, and at the academy at Shrewsbury. In the winter of 1858 he entered Dickinson College, at Carlisle, Penn., and graduated in 1861, as A. B. Returning to Shrewsbury he taught school for two years, public school in winter and select school in summer. In the fall of 1865 he attended the University of Maryland, at Baltimore, and graduated in the spring of 1867, as M.D. Until 1870 he practiced medicine with his father, but in that year he formed a partnership with his brother James, and they bought their father's drug store; since then he has followed his profession in connection with the drug business. In September, 1868, he was married, at Baltimore, Md., to Miss Scarborough, daughter of Ezekiel Scarborough. This lady died in February, 1871. Their only child, Sarah Salome, died also, aged twenty months. November 10, 1874, he was married, at Shrewsbury, to Miss Arabella, daughter of William McAbee, and had born to him four children, three of whom are yet living: Elbridge Beck, James John and David McA. The family are members of the Methodist Episcopal Church, to which also his first wife belonged. He is a very prominent member of the church and Sabbath-school—steward in the former and superintendent in the latter. In 1880 he was lay representative at Altoona, and in 1884 at Williamsport. He is a prominent Mason and K. T. and P. M. of Blue Lodge. In the borough he has held various offices of trust; being an active Democrat, he has been sent as delegate to State and county conventions. In 1878 he was appointed surgeon of the Northern Central Railroad.

JAMES GERRY, M. D., a physician of Shrewsbury, York County, was born February 4, 1839, and is the second son of James and Salome (Hoffman) Gerry, natives of Maryland, and of Scotch-Irish and German descent. James Gerry, the grandfather, came from Scotland in the eighteenth century, and located in Maryland, where at one time he was a member of the Maryland General Assembly from Cecil County. He followed farming, and was also a kind of a local lawyer. The subject of this sketch was brought up in Shrewsbury, where he learned the drug business with his father. His earlier education he received at the public schools, and at the Shrewsbury Academy. Being induced by his father to study the practice of medicine, he entered Dickenson College, at Carlisle, Penn., when twenty years old, but at the breaking out of the late war he left that college as a junior, and entered Jefferson Medical College, at Philadelphia, graduating in the spring of 1863 as M. D. He also took a course of operative surgery under Dr. Agnew. After finishing his studies he came to Shrewsbury, where he at once commenced to practice medicine in connection with the drug business. In January, 1876, he was married, at Weisburg, Md., to Miss Hunter, daughter of Pleasant Hunter, of Maryland; they have one child—Carroll. Dr. Gerry is a prominent Mason of the Knight Templar degree, and is also a member of Consistory S. P. R. S., Thirty-second degree, as well as a Past Master of Shrewsbury Lodge. For six years he has held the position of president of the school board. He is quite a successful physician, especially in the treatment of Bright's Disease, and is surgeon for the Northern Central Railroad Company.

CHRISTIAN GORE, born in Baltimore County, Md., October 23, 1818, and died at New Freedom, June 5, 1878, was the eldest of three sons of Charles and Mary (Price) Gore, of German and English descent, respectively. He was educated at Middletown, Md., and up to about thirty years of age, he taught school. He was married, April 4, 1850, at Baltimore, to Hester Ann Shamberger, daughter of Jacob and Hester (Souder) Shamberger, natives of Pennsylvania and of German descent. They had eight children, Millard S. (deceased), Mary, Jane, Edwin (deceased), Upton H., Harvey (deceased), George W. and Alverta. Mr. Gore has held the positions of commissioner, treasurer and assessor of Baltimore County. In the spring of 1871, he removed to York County, where he located in York Borough, but after a year removed to Glen Rock Borough, where, in company with Hashour & Fallen, he engaged in the planing-mill and lumber business, which was burned in 1876, causing a great loss. The mill was rebuilt, and Mr. Gore retired from business in 1878, and removed to New Freedom, where he died soon after. In 1850 he was engaged for six years at Hoffmansville, in the mercantile business and the manufacture of paper one year, and farmed about twelve years in Baltimore County. The family are leading members of the Methodist Episcopal Church, of which Mr. Gore was a class leader. Since the death of Mr. G., Mrs. Gore and her two sons have successfully conducted a mercantile establishment at New Freedom.

JAMES N. GROVE, youngest son of John and Elizabeth (Moore) Grove, of York County, Penn., was born in Shrewsbury, March 26, 1837. His parents were of German and Irish descent respectively, and had a family of six sons and five daughters Until his fifteenth year he remained on his father's farm, but at that age he began learning the trade of millwright with Robert Koller, near Shrewsbury, which trade he has followed since. He built the Spring Grove Paper-mill and two for Hoffman & Sons, in Maryland. During his life he has built five

BIOGRAPHICAL SKETCHES. 175

or six paper-mills, and from fifteen to twenty saw-mills. In 1861 he enlisted at York in Company D, Eighty-seventh Regiment Pennsylvania Volunteers, was ranked as corporal and was discharged in 1864 as sergeant. During his service he participated in many a hard fought battle; at Winchester, Va., he was captured and for twenty-four days was confined at Libby Prison and Belle Island. He also took part in the battles of the Wilderness, Spottsylvania, Cold Harbor, near Winchester, and many other battles and skirmishes. After leaving the service he returned to Shrewsbury, where he engaged at his trade. In 1865 he was married, at New Freedom, to Annie Singer, daughter of Charles Singer, and has six children: Luella, Charles Henry, William Emery, James F., Edward and Gertrude. Mr. Grove is a member of the Reformed Church and his wife of the Evangelical Church. He is a Mason, a prominent citizen, and holds and has held various offices of the borough. At present he is repairing a paper-mill at Woodbine, Md., for Capt. Tollun, who was Confederate officer of the day at Winchester on the day Mr. G. was captured.

JOHN L. HAILER was born in Wittenberg, Germany, March 30, 1822, and came to America February 9, 1852, landing at Baltimore, Md. His parents, John and Annie Mary (Stahle) Hailer had three children, of whom John was the second, and the only one that came to America. He went at once to York, began work shoe-making, continuing for one year, and then removed to Shrewsbury, where he remained three years. Returning to York again, he remained there one year. In 1856 he returned to Shrewsbury, where he resided until 1865, working at shoe-making. He then purchased a farm near the Maryland line, on which he built a residence, where he has since resided, carrying on his trade. September 29, 1854, he was married, at Shrewsbury, to Elizabeth Reuter, widow of John Reuter, and has had eight children born to him: Mary Ann, John H., Catharine, Lizzie, Annie, Mary (deceased), Charles (deceased) and George (deceased). The family are members of the Evangelical Lutheran Church. Mr. Hailer is a Granger, was inspector of elections at New Freedom, member of the council, and, in 1882, assessor for the borough; he was also deacon and elder of the Evangelical Lutheran Church at New Freedom, and has several times been elected delegate to the York County convention.

WILLIAM HEATHCOTE was born in Cheshire, England, January 31, 1806, was the eighth in a family of ten children—seven sons and three daughters—of John and Alice (Neill) Heathcote; his brother John, who died in 1884, aged ninety-three years, resided in Knox County, Ohio. William is the only member of the family now living. He grew up in a cotton factory and received the rudiments of an education principally in the Sunday-schools; came to America in 1826, stopped in Chester, Penn., about a year; removed to Brandywine, Chester County, and with his brother John operated a woolen factory six years, when his brother moved West; in 1837 he went to Ohio with a view to settlement; returning on horseback his road led him to the hills where he first saw the site now occupied by Glen Rock, where Simon Koller had erected a dwelling and saw-mill. Mr. Heathcote bought the whole plan and, in 1840, when the Baltimore and Susquehanna Railroad was opened through, laid out Heathcote Station, which, in after years, when a postoffice was established, he named Glen Rock, a name suggested to him by reading Walter Scott's works. He erected a woolen factory and operated it until 1855, then sold it to Philip Shaeffer, who converted it into a grist-mill, now known as Glen Rock Mills, and owned by G. F. Seitz since 1881; then built another factory, higher up the Codorus,

which has been operated by his sons since; in 1861 erected the building now occupied by the Centreville Rope & Cordage Company, and operated it as a mill seven or eight years; in 1881 he began the boot and shoe manufactory now managed by his sons; retired from active business about 1870; was a charter member and some years a director of the First National Bank of Glen Rock, and also of the Glen Rock Foundry and Machine Shops. He was married, in 1839, to Sarah Koller, a native of Glen Rock, and they had five children, only one of whom, Lewin K, is now living, two died in childhood, one daughter died after marriage, and one son died at manhood. In 1848 he was married at Lancaster, Penn., to Catharine Allison, a native of Glen Rock, and they have four children: Lewis, Granville, Alice, wife of Rev. J. C. Koller, of Hanover, and Willie T.; all members of the Evangelical Lutheran Church. Mr. Heathcote was brought up in the Church of England.

GEORGE W. HEINDEL, farmer and stock raiser, was born in York Township, York County, March 1, 1834. His parents, George and Leah (Winehold) Heindel, were natives of York County, and of German descent. They had a family of ten children, of whom nine are living. George W. was brought up on the farm, in which he retained an interest, attending the common schools. At the age of twenty-two he began business as a stock dealer. He removed to Ohio, and in Mahoning County he lived nineteen years, farming, stock dealing and coal mining. In 1858 he was married, at Lima, Ohio, to Lucy Anna Warner, of Mahoning County, and had six children: William A., Erasius E. (deceased), Cornelius M., Alice, Sidney (deceased) and Charles H. Both he and wife are members of the German Reformed Church. In 1875 he returned to Glen Rock, and for five years owned and ran the Cold Spring Hotel; he then turned his attention to farming and stock raising. He owns a farm of ninety-five acres, adjoining the town. Mr. Heindel was one of the organizers and is now a director of the Glen Rock Manufacturing Company, and was one term in the council. His father still lives at the age of seventy-seven.

FREDERICK HELB, a native of Wittenberg, Germany, and only son of Ulrich and Mary (Keim) Helb, was born March 9, 1825, and immigrated to America in 1847, landing at Baltimore, where, for two years, he was engaged at tanning, which trade he had learned in his native country. His German education was good, and he soon mastered the English language. In 1849 he came to Shrewsbury, where he established a small tannery, on a very primitive style, using hogsheads for vats, but increasing the capacity until he was able to handle 7,000 hides a year. In 1867 he built a beer brewery at Shrewsbury Station, with a capacity of 800 barrels per year, and three years later started a fruit distillery, manufacturing 500 barrels of apple brandy in a season. He also owns an extensive flour-mill (steam and water), the Jackson House (the only hotel in the borough), and a number of first-class tenement houses. He also owns about 450 acres of fine farming land in York County, and about 1,300 acres of valuable timber and farming land in Maryland, with saw and stave-mills. He is president of the Rail Road and Shrewsbury Turnpike Company, and a director in the Shrewsbury Savings Bank; was one of the incorporators of Rail Road Borough, and its first chief burgess. In 1849 he was married to Miss Rebecca Henry, of York County, who has been a true and faithful helpmate to him. They have six children: Theodore R. (brewer), Edward, J. P., Julius, Frederick, Lydia and Mary, all of them highly educated and accomplished. The family belong to the Lutheran Church.

EDWARD HELB was born at Rail Road, Shrewsbury Township, April 29, 1854, and is a son of Frederick Helb. He was educated in the district schools of his neighborhood and in the Shrewsbury Academy, and graduated from Knapp's Institute, Baltimore, in June, 1871. In the fall of the same year he began learning his trade in the tannery of his father, at Rail Road, and is at present following the business there. In 1875 he united with Shrewsbury Lodge No. 423, A. F. & A. M.; has passed all the chairs in Mount Vernon Lodge No. 143, I. O. O. F., at Shrewsbury; is a member of Mount Vernon Encampment No. 14, I. O. O. F., of York, and of Friendly Lodge No. 287, K. of P., of Glen Rock. He was married, July 8, 1879, to Jennie I., sixth daughter of Daniel and Sarah Rishel, respected residents of Troutville, Clearfield Co., Penn. They are both active members of the Lutheran Church at Shrewsbury. He has been secretary of the church council since 1881, and is also secretary of the Shrewsbury District Sunday-school Institute, and has been superintendent of the Lutheran Sabbath-school at Shrewsbury. He served as town auditor for several years; was secretary of the town council, and is at present secretary of the school board of Rail Road Borough. In the spring of 1882 he was elected justice of the peace on the Democratic ticket, and has several times represented the town in the Democratic county convention.

JAMES H. HENDRIX was born in Shrewsbury Township, October 31, 1838. His parents were Joshua H. and Susan (Klinefelter) Hendrix, of York County. His great-grandfather Hendrix, settled in Beaver County, Penn. There were but two children in the family, one sister having died while quite young. James H. was reared in Shrewsbury Village and attended the common schools. He learned the plasterer's trade while yet young, and followed it for five years. In August, 1861, he enlisted at Shrewsbury, and was appointed duty sergeant of Company D, Eighty-seventh Regiment, Pennsylvania Volunteers, and served three years, participating in the following battles: Cold Harbor, Wilderness and with Grant's army at Petersburg. He was with Sheridan at Winchester and Strasburgh; for three months was in the hospital. Returning from the war, he engaged in railroading; first with the Northern Central Railroad one year, then clerking in McDowell's store for three years. In 1868 he went to Illinois for four months, but returned to Shrewsbury; in 1869, he was appointed postmaster at Shrewsbury, which position he held up to January 22, 1874; was re-appointed postmaster December 3, 1874, and still holds the position (June 20, 1885). In 1869 he had engaged in mercantile business, which he is running in conjunction with the postoffice, and to this he has devoted his entire attention. In 1860 he was married to Angeline Sechrist, daughter of Abraham Sechrist, of Shrewsbury. They have one child—Eudora. His wife dying in 1865, he married, in 1873, in Fawn Township, Priscilla Davis, daughter of John W. Davis. Their only child died in infancy. Mr. and Mrs. Hendrix are members of the Methodist Episcopal Church, of which he is trustee and recording steward; he is also an Odd Fellow, member of the Encampment, and commander of Post 342, G. A. R., at Shrewsbury.

WILLIAM HERBST was born in Hopewell Township, August 15, 1817. His parents, David and Mary (Miller) Herbst, were natives of Amsterdam, Holland, and York County, respectively. They had three sons and two daughters. William, who was the eldest, helped his father on the farm until twenty years of age, attending the county schools about six months. He then spent four years at milling in Glen Rock Valley. In 1842 he began business for himself at Glen Rock, engaged in merchandising, which he continued for nine years, and then engaged in farming for ten years, Returning to Glen Rock, he again engaged in the merchandise business. In 1841 he was married to Mary Shafer, daughter of Philip Shafer, of Shrewsbury Township. They have three children: Eliza, Jacob and William H. Mrs. Herbst died in 1844, and in 1850, Mr. Herbst was married (again at Glen Rock) to Alice Heathcote (daughter of Mark Heathcote), a native of England, by whom he has three children: Mary Alice, Emma Jane, and Millie. Both parents are members of the Evangelical Church. Mr. Herbst is a director and one of the organizers of the Glen Rock Manufacturing Company, was treasurer and president of the First National Bank of Glen Rock, and for twelve years a school director.

LEVI W. HERSHEY, born in Shrewsbury Township August 31, 1845, is the eldest son of Christian and Margaret (Wehrley) Hershey, of German descent, being about the sixth generation in America. He has always lived on a farm, began teaching at the age of twenty-two, and has taught every winter except four up to 1884. Has served as inspector of elections, township clerk, assessor and judge of elections; has been secretary of the new Freedom Building and Loan Association for two years, and secretary of the Codorus and Manheim Fire Insurance Company since January 1, 1884; was Master of the P. of H. one year, and secretary five or six years, and is a member of Mt. Vernon Lodge No 143, I. O. O. F., of Shrewsbury. At the last election he was elected justice of the peace and school director, and is now secretary of the school board. He is also chancellor commander of Freedom Lodge No. 85, K. of P., of New Freedom. He was married, December 3, 1868, to Mary Jane Sheffer, and they have six children: Allie Jane, Lillie Virginia, Bertie Agnes, Nettie May, Arthur Lee and Iva Grace. He belongs to the Reformed, and his wife to the Lutheran Church. He owns a farm of thirty-eight acres, and has been engaged in the dairy business since 1883.

JEREMIAH S. HETRICK, M. D., son of Samuel and Louisa (Smith Hetrick, of York County, was born in Codorus Township, December 28, 1849, and was the second of a family of five children—two sons and three daughters. The parents were of German and English descent, and first settled in Codorus Township. The Doctor was brought up in a woolen factory, and educated at the common schools, and a course at the State Normal School at Millersville. In 1869 he taught school one year, and in 1871 he began reading medicine in the office of Dr. E. W. Free at New Freedom, and in 1872 he entered Washington University, now College of Physicians and Surgeons at Baltimore, and graduated in 1873 as M. D. He then spent one year as assistant resident physician in Washington University Hospital, and in the spring of 1874 he removed to New Freedom, where he became associated with his old preceptor until 1877, when he began the practice alone. His father was killed by a railroad train at Glen Rock in 1879, at the age of sixty-five years, and his mother still lives at New Freedom. May 13, 1875, the Doctor was married to Charlotte Wilson, of Maryland, and has four children: Gertrude F., Walter H., Fannie and Lorilla. He is a member of the Evangelical Association; was chief burgess in 1880–81–82, and a member of the council three years; is also a school director, president of the Cemetery Association, and one of the organizers of it; also one of the organizers of the New Freedom Literary Association; is a stockholder in the Stewartstown Railroad; was class-leader in his church a number of years, and a very prominent, influential citizen and popular physician.

BARTHABAS E. HINES, born in Hanover, October 20, 1842, is the only son of John and Sarah (Bart) Hines, natives of Maryland and Pennsylvania, and of French and German descent. He attended the public schools of Hanover, and at the age of sixteen began cigar-making, which he has since followed, with the exception of about one year as clerk in a store in Cincinnati, and one year at Westminster, Md.; went to Glen Rock in 1867; was married in May, 1868, to Agnes A. Decker, of Shrewsbury Township, and of German descent; has been deputy postmaster at Glen Rock since 1869; was borough councilman three terms, and chief burgess one term; was one of the original stockholders of the Glen Rock Manufacturing Company, and since 1877 has been engaged in the manufacture and sale, at wholesale and retail, of cigars; enlisted at Hanover in Company I, Twenty-sixth Pennsylvania Militia, for the emergency during Lee's invasion, his regiment really opening the battle of Gettysburg (see Batcheldor's History).

JOSIAH V. HOSHOUR, a prominent manufacturer, was born in Heidelberg Township, August 21, 1814. His parents, John and Elizabeth (Klinepeter) Hoshour, were natives of York County, and of German descent. When only three years old his father died, leaving six children, and his mother died in 1854, aged seventy-five years. His early days were spent on a farm, and when sixteen years old, he went to Gettysburg school for three years, and then taught school in the neighborhood for seven years. In 1842 he became engaged in the forwarding business at Glen Rock, and followed it until 1854. From that time until 1878 he was engaged in farming. In 1882 he took charge of the Glen Rock Works, manufacturing machinery, etc., as superintendent, and has held that position since. In 1883 the name was changed to "Glen Rock Manufacturing Company." June 18, 1838, he was married at Shrewsbury to Magdalena Koller, daughter of Jacob Koller, and had eight children, four of whom are living : Samuel K., Elnora, wife of N. Z. Seitz, Esq.; Maggie and John H. The family belong to the Evangelical Lutheran Church. Mr. Hoshour was once chief burgess of Glen Rock; school director for fifteen years, and justice of the peace from 1849 to 1864. He was also one of the organizers of the "Frey Herbst & Co. Works."

DANIEL R. KLINEFELTER, son of Abraham and Eliza (Ruhl) Klinefelter, of York County, and of German descent, was born in Shrewsbury Township, April 10, 1852, and was next to the youngest of ten children. He was brought up on a farm and received a common school education. At the age of nineteen years, he began the plastering trade, which he followed two years. In 1873 he commenced the manufacture of ice-cream, as an apprentice, and in 1874 he went into partnership with his employer, at Shrewsbury Station, but at the end of one year the firm dissolved, and with another partner, J. H. Hendrix, he carried on the business for two years. Later he bought out his partner, and has since been alone in the business. In 1882 he tried steam power, but it proved a failure, and returned to hand power. He manufactures about 5,000 gallons per year, and supplies the Baltimore and Washington markets. In 1883 he, in connection with J. B. Davis, of Maryland, engaged also in the buggy and carriage business. He was married, August 15, 1873, at Shrewsbury, to Lucretia Heathcote, daughter of John Heathcote, of York, and has had four children, one of whom died in infancy; Olin R., Gilbert A. and Irma R. He is a member of the Methodist Episcopal Church, while his wife belongs to the Evangelical Association. He is also a prominent Odd Fellow, Mount Vernon Lodge, No. 143, a member of the Encampment, and was assessor of Newbury Borough in 1881 and 1882.

ROBERT F. KOLLER, farmer, was born in Shrewsbury Township, December 24, 1828. His parents, Peter and Eve (Klinefelter) Koller, were natives of York County. They had thirteen children—eight daughters and five sons—of whom Robert F. is the youngest. He lived on the farm until nineteen years of age, receiving his education at school and from the newspapers. At the age of nineteen he went to Lancaster County, and served an apprenticeship of two years as millwright, which trade he followed fifteen years, but gave it up on account of his health. He returned to Shrewsbury Township, and farmed eight years. In 1866 he went into the lumber business, in which he lost $35,000, following it for ten years; then returned to New Freedom, where he bought a fine farm of seventy-four acres, upon which he has since resided. February 22, 1854, he was married at Seitzland, to Adeline Deviney, of York County, and of Irish descent; and has seven children: Charles W., Maria, John D., Edward G., Harry E., Ida Bell and Robert F. (deceased.) Since 1875 Mr. Koller has been engaged in the lumber business at New Freedom. He was a commissioner of Clinton County three years, and director of the poor three years. His wife died in 1879.

BENJAMIN F. KOLLER, an eminent civil engineer, surveyor, conveyancer, insurance and law agent, and justice of the peace of Southward, Shrewsbury Borough, was born here August 26, 1830. His father, Isaac Koller, a native of Shrewsbury Township, was born February 5, 1800, and was married May 1, 1825, at Peter Smyser's hotel (then the Blue Ball Tavern, on the York and Baltimore Pike), two miles south of Shrewsbury, to Sarah Shank, who was born near York, July 16, 1802. To this union were born the following named children: Margaret, Mary E., Benjamin F., George W., Andrew J., John W. and James B.—all still living. The ancestors of Isaac Koller came from Germany, and those of his wife were also German. During his life he was first a blacksmith, then a merchant, next a hotel-keeper, and finally associate judge of the court of common pleas, York County. He reared all his children in his hotel, and of the five boys not one is addicted to the use of intoxicating liquors. He died October 21, 1854, sincerely mourned by his family and a widely extended circle of acquaintances. Benjamin F. Koller has served as justice of the peace for thirty years, was elected State revenue commissioner in 1860; clerk of the several courts of York County in 1875, and is commissioner for the States of Maryland and New York. He was married, March 7, 1852, to Mary Magdalene Young, youngest daughter of the late Dr. Young, and has had born to him children as follows: Isaac D., Cyrus C., and Beulah, living, and Fannie V. and Cora Clotilde, deceased. Mr. Koller stands high in the order of F. & A. M., having attained the thirty-second degree, Scottish rite, than which there is but one degree higher. He is a member of the Evangelical Lutheran Church. His wife and son, Isaac, are members of the Methodist Episcopal Church; his son, Cyrus, is a member of the Evangelical Church. B. F. Koller was one of the principal men who secured and organized Summit Grove Camp-meeting Association in 1874, and has been identified with its management ever since.

JOHN L. KREBS was born in Codorus Township, June 19, 1859; he remained in the township until thirteen years of age, being taught in the district schools. He was the second of four sons of Adam and Mary (Warren) Krebs. When eighteen years old he began farming for himself, which he is still engaged in. September 18, 1881, he was married to Lucy Shaffer, daughter of Daniel Shaffer, a prominent farmer in Shrewsbury Township, and has two children: Harry C. and Allen. Mr. Krebs is a member of the Lutheran Church.

SHREWSBURY TOWNSHIP.

JACOB H. LAMOTTE, son of Joseph and Elizabeth (Hershey) Lamotte, of Maryland and Pennsylvania, and of French and German descent, was born in Baltimore County, Md., May 8, 1819, and was the eldest of seven children. He was brought up on the farm and educated in the common schools in Maryland. He was married in Carroll County, Md., to Elizabeth Zimmerman, of German descent, and had seven children: Joanna (deceased), Eli (deceased), Jeremiah (deceased), Joshua (deceased), Calvin, Cornelius and Ella. He brought his family to York County, in 1840, and settled in Manheim Township, where he lived until 1884, when he rented his farm and removed to New Freedom. He was one of the organizers, and is a director of Codorus & Manheim Insurance Company. He has held various township offices, and in 1879 he was elected county commissioner for three years. The family are members of the German Reformed Church. His parents died in 1865 and in 1847, respectively, aged seventy-six and fifty-four years. The farm which he owns in Manheim Township contains 170 acres of finely cultivated land.

JACOB LANIUS, born June 22, 1837, in Hopewell Township, is the eldest of a family of four sons and three daughters of John H. and Sarah M. (Hersey) Lanius. His mother was a native of Delaware. His great-grandfather, Lanius, came to America from Germany, in 1731, and settled in Kreutz Creek Valley, and all his descendants, with the exception of Jacob Lanius, a brother of subject's father, have resided in York County. The subject of this sketch attended the schools in his neighborhood and worked on his father's farm until he was seventeen years old. He engaged in the lumber business, in Hopewell Township, with his father, and followed it fifteen years. In 1872 he removed to Fawn Township, and engaged in the mercantile business in New Park, until 1879, when he removed to York, having been elected recorder of deeds for York County, which office he held for one term, and then engaged in the lumber business in Maryland (leaving his family in York), which business he is still carrying on. He was married, October 2, 1873, at Stewartstown, to Agnes E. Duncan, a native of Hopewell and daughter of John Duncan, of Irish descent. He has three children living: Walter M. V., Inez Loretta and Iona Veronica. Two daughters—Irena and Lelia—are dead. His father died in 1882, aged eighty-three years. In the spring of 1884, our subject purchased the farm now occupied by him near Shrewsbury Borough. He is an active Democrat and held the office of assessor of Hopewell Township and was postmaster at New Park five years. He and his wife are both members of the Presbyterian Church.

GEORGE C. LEE, a farmer in Shrewsbury Township, was born in Baltimore City, in 1851. His parents, John and Elizabeth (Carty) Lee, natives of England and Maryland, had four children, of whom two died very young. Of the remaining two George C. is the youngest. His education he received partly in Baltimore, where he remained until seventeen years of age, and in Shrewsbury Township. In 1868 he came to York County, where he has since resided, following farming. His parents are both dead; the father died in 1851, before subject was born, and the mother died in 1872, in Shrewsbury Township. March 1, 1877, he was married in New Freedom, to Isabel Hedrick, daughter of George W. Hedrick, of Baltimore County, and of German descent. They have three children: Annie Elsie, Maude Elizabeth and Lawrence Ray. In 1881 he removed to his present farm in Shrewsbury Township, containing 170 acres, to the cultivation of which he devotes his whole time. Mr. and Mrs. Lee are members of the Methodist Episcopal Church.

JOHN E. LOWE, a farmer in Shrewsbury Township, was born on the farm now owned by him, March 26, 1846. His parents, Isaac and Elizabeth (Stabler) Lowe, were natives of Pennsylvania and Maryland, and of English and German descent respectively. They had six children, of whom John E. was the youngest son. He was brought up on the farm, and learned the carpenter trade before he was twenty-one years of age. His education he received at the public schools. In 1875 he began the butchering trade and followed it about five years, and then returned to farming, which he has since followed. He was married in 1872, at York, to Elizabeth Singer, daughter of Charles Singer, and a native of Germany. They had five children, one of whom died when but three years of age. The living are Willie H., Ada M., Annie E. and Charles. Mr. and Mrs. Lowe are members of the Methodist Episcopal Church, although Mrs. Lowe was brought up in the Lutheran Church. He is a member and Master of the P. of H. No. 446, of New Freedom. Jacob Lowe, a brother of John E., was a soldier in the United States army and served about two years. The father died in 1875, aged seventy-two years, but the mother is still living, and about seventy-two years of age. Mr. Lowe was one of the organizers of the New Freedom Building Association; and is a director in the same.

ELI McDONELL was born in Shrewsbury, February, 18, 1835. He is the second son of twelve children of Hamilton and Sarah (Beck) McDonell. At the age of twelve years he entered the employment of Myers & Small, merchants, of Shrewsbury, and continued until : February 1, 1859, when he entered the establishment of Lewis Wagner, hardware merchant at Baltimore, remaining until July of the same year, when he returned to Shrewsbury, and, September 8, 1859, embarked in the general merchandise business which he has continued to the present. He carries a stock of $6,000, doing a business of $18,000 in dry goods, notions, groceries, boots and shoes, hats and caps, glass, queensware, etc. He was married, May 2, 1872, to Justie E. Berg, daughter of Rev. Andrew Berg, a citizen of Shrewsbury. They have four children: Emory C., Annie, Elsie and Mabel. Mr. McDonell and wife are members of the Lutheran Church. He has been treasurer of the Sunday-school since 1859; treasurer of the church since 1865; treasurer of the Shrewsbury & Rail Road Turnpike Company, since 1878, and is a director in the Shrewsbury Savings Institution; was postmaster during Lincoln's administration, and served one term as town councilman and one term as school director. He is a member of Shrewsbury Lodge No. 423, A. F. & A. M., and of Mount Vernon Lodge, No. 143, I. O. O. F.; has passed all the chairs in the latter, and is treasurer of same.

WILLIAM H. MANIFOLD, M. D., was born in Hopewell Township, September 5, 1830. His parents, John and Marenda (Meads) Manifold, were natives of Pennsylvania and Maryland, and of English and French descent. They had eleven children, of whom William H. was the eldest. His early life was spent on the farm, and he received his education at the public schools, and at the Tuscarora Academy. For six years he taught school. From Tuscarora Academy he entered the Allegheny College at Meadville, of the junior class, but abandoned it on account of ill-health. In 1858 he entered Dr. Gerry's office at Shrewsbury, and read medicine for six months. He then went to the University of Maryland at Baltimore, and graduated as M. D., in the spring of 1861. He first located at New Market, Md. In the summer of 1864 he went with the army as assistant army surgeon, and remained until the close of the war. At one time he was ordered to take charge of the field

BIOGRAPHICAL SKETCHES.

hospital of the Thirteenth New York and Ninth New Jersey Cavalry, who were then fighting Mosby. In May, 1865, he returned to Washington, and remained at the United States General Hospital. He then returned to New Market, where he remained till 1866. From there he removed to Loganville, where he practiced six years, and in 1872, he came to New Freedom, where he has since resided. In 1859 he was married in Baltimore, to Margaret Ann Sheffer, a native of Shrewsbury, York County. They had eight children: John H. C. (now a student of Pennsylvania College, Gettysburg), Sarah E., Aaron B. N., Luther C., William J., Mary M., Joseph (deceased) and LeRoy W. Mr. and Mrs. Manifold are members of the Lutheran Church, and Dr. M. is now serving his third term as school director.

EPHRAIM MILLER, D. D., resident pastor in charge of the Lutheran Church at Shrewsbury, was born December 8, 1818, in Cumberland County. His parents, Daniel and Elizabeth (Frankenberger) Miller were natives of Pennsylvania and of German descent. They had four sons and five daughters, of whom Rev. E. is the eldest. In his early life he assisted his father at his trade, and attended the public schools. At the age of fourteen he began clerking in a store in which he remained three and a half years. In his eighteenth year he entered Pennsylvania College at Gettysburg, and graduated in 1841, as A. B., and later received the degree of A. M. Up to 1844 he taught school in Illinois. In 1845 he was licensed at Shelbyville, Ill., and in 1846 was ordained and preached at Shelbyville until 1847. From there he went to Springfield, Ill., where he had charge of a Lutheran Church for four years; then to Oregon, Ill., for one year and a half; then to Cedarville, Ill., for seven years; then to Peru, Ill., two years; next to Mount Morris, three years; back to Springfield for six years and a half; then went to Dixon, four years; Cincinnati four years and a half; Smicksburg, Penn., two years. In 1881 he came to Shrewsbury, and has charge of New Freedom and Fissel's Churches. October 13, 1846, he was married at Hillsboro, Ill., to Mary J. Boone, of Kentucky, descended from a brother of the famous Daniel Boone. They have had eight children, of whom two died in infancy. The living are William E., Mary E., John Henry, Alice E., Walter Boone and Charles A. Rev. Miller was one of the organizers of the Hillsboro College, in 1846, and of Carthage College in 1870, and of Mendota College in 1856. In 1849 he established a classical school at Springfield, Ill., and continued it until 1851. He also helped to organize the synod of northern Illinois in 1851. He was twice elected to a professorship in the college at Springfield, Ill., but both times felt it his duty to decline.

JOHN E. MILLER was born in what is now New Freedom Borough, November 19, 1836. His parents, Meinrad and Anastasia (Dienst) Miller, were natives of Baden, Germany, near Freiburg, and came to America in 1833. They landed in New York, and went from there to Chillicothe, Ohio, returning, in a short time, to Baltimore, where they lived one year, and in 1834 settled in Strasburg, now Shrewsbury Township, where three of the children were born. One had been born in Ohio, and seven in Germany. Of the eleven children six were sons. The ancestors being farmers, the boys were brought up for the same purpose. Our subject received his education in the public schools. About 1850 he learned the cigar-making trade at Baltimore. At the age of twenty-one he began life for himself. In 1861 he went to Europe, and spent one year there visiting the birthplace of his parents, and many other places of interest. He also visited England, France and Holland. Returning, he located at Baltimore, Md., where he followed the cigar business until 1881, when he removed to New Freedom, where he began the manufacture of cigars exclusively. In 1879 he was married, in Baltimore, to Mary Wissel, of Maryland, of German descent, and had three children: Rita Mary, John E. and Joseph Vincent. Mr. and Mrs. Miller were brought up to the Catholic faith, and are active members of the church. His only brother, Albert A. Miller, carries on manufacturing, canning and farming at Upper Falls, Baltimore Co., Md., and his only sister resides in Hopewell Township, and is the wife of Andrew Bisker. The father died in 1856, aged sixty years; the mother died in 1839, aged thirty-nine years. The father of Mr. Miller was one of the principal men to build St. John the Baptist Catholic Church at New Freedom, in 1842; the only members were Meinrad Miller, Caspar Druschler, Anthony Dienst and John Dotterman.

GEORGE F. MILLER, son of Samuel and Mary (Fishel) Miller, of Pennsylvania and Maryland, respectively, was born in Shrewsbury Township December 19, 1843. He was the second son and fifth child in a family of eight children, and was reared on the farm, receiving a common school education. He taught school one winter, and then engaged in droving and butchering, which he followed up to 1883. January 10, 1867, he was married, at Shrewsbury, to Leah Koller, daughter, of J. P. Koller, of that place, and had eight children: Ida, Clinton, Elsie, Harvey, John, Lulu, Samuel and Mary. In 1871 he removed to Maryland, where he carried on the butchering and droving. In 1882 he purchased a tract of land, heavily timbered, near New Freedom, on which he erected a steam sawmill, and converted the timber into lumber, employing from eight to fifteen men. Mr. Miller belongs to the Evangelical Association, is a Granger, and for ten years was a school trustee in Maryland. His father still lives in Shrewsbury Township, aged seventy years, and his mother sixty-five years. He is a trustee of the church, an active worker and exhorter, and has been superintendent of Ruhl's Sabbath-school for eight years. He is still living in Baltimore County, Md., but keeps part of his family in York County, at the saw-mill, where he keeps a boarding house for the hands. His eldest daughter, now sixteen, attends to the work here.

MARK RADCLIFFE is a native of Yorkshire, England, was born August 3, 1827, and came to America in March, 1848. His parents, Joseph and Anna (Heathcote) Radcliffe, had six children, of whom he was next to the youngest. His brother, Abel, came to America in 1840, and died in Delaware County, Penn., in 1873. When fourteen years of age he was apprenticed to rope-making, which trade he has always followed. His mother died when he was but three years old, and his father when he was sixteen years old. He landed in Philadelphia, and came direct to Glen Rock, where he engaged in rope-making in company with George Shaw, a comrade who came with him to America. For two years he ran a walk out doors. In 1853 his establishment burnt out, but was rebuilt, and in 1873 they bought a large grist-mill at Centreville, and at once commenced the business of rope-making in an extensive way, working about 900 to 1,000 pounds of material a day. For three years he also ran a livery stable at Glen Rock. In 1847 he was married, in Lancashire, England, to Mary Ann Shaw, who died eight years after coming to America, leaving two children: Iveson H. and Joseph. In 1859 he was married, at York, to a younger sister of his first wife. They have had six children, four of whom are living: John S., Millie, Minerva and Edward B. Mr. Radcliffe was constable in Glen Rock about four years, also deputy United States marshal of the Fifteenth Pennsylvania District from

1861 till the close of the war; assistant assessor of the Fifteenth District in 1865; borough councilman and chief burgess for two years, ending in the spring of 1884.

JOSEPH RAFFENSPERGER, eldest son of Christian and Rachel (Wagner) Raffensperger, of German descent, was born in Paradise Township, August 18, 1838. Leaving home at the age of thirteen he went to live with Rev. Mr. Berg, in Shrewsbury, and at the age of seventeen entered the store of Myers & Small; remained with them and their successors eleven years. In the spring of 1868, in partnership with C. F. Ruling, he engaged in the mercantile business at Goldsboro, and after one year sold out to his partner, returned to Shrewsbury, and clerked with Mr. Hartman until 1872; then embarked in the hotel business, continuing with the exception of one year until 1880, then removed to York; clerked in a mercantile establishment there one year; returned and resumed the hotel business in Shrewsbury in 1881, and in the spring of 1882 purchased the Shrewsbury hotel, which he has since conducted. He was married June 12, 1859, to Arabel Hartman, daughter of Joseph Hartman, and they have had four children: Fannie Eliza, died at the age of four years; Effie D.; Claudie M., wife of Jacob Banner, of Baltimore, and Henrietta L. He is a member of both Lodge and Encampment of I. O. O. F., is now (1884) serving his third term as borough councilman, and has been delegate to Democratic county convention several times.

REV. JOSEPH A. RAMSAY was born in Baltimore, April 5, 1815. His father, Joseph Ramsay, came from Ireland to America in 1796, and stopped in York County, where he married Agnes Andrews, a native of York County. He was a shipsmith, and worked in 1812 under George Stiles, mayor of Baltimore, on the gun-carriages of Fort McHenry. Joseph A. was educated in St. Mary's College, and lived in Baltimore fifty years. Having learned the trade of shipsmith he formed a partnership, at the age of twenty-one, with Charles Hergisheimer, and continued four years; then engaged in the book business twenty-five years; bought a farm in 1865, on the Pennsylvania and Maryland line, on the Baltimore & York Turnpike; moved to it in 1866, and has resided there ever since. He was a member of the Baltimore city council in 1840-41; was one of ten "Maine Law Delegates" to the house of delegates in the Maryland legislature in 1853-54; was brought up in the Presbyterian Church, but united with the Methodist Episcopal Church in 1841; was licensed to preach in 1878, and has preached occasionally since that time; assisted by a liberal donation in building "Asbury Chapel," at New Market, and preaches there. He is an honorary member of the P. of H. and a member of the I. O. O. F. He was married October 29, 1840, at Pimlico, Md., to Mary Agnes Shaw, a daughter of Daniel Shaw, and a member of the Presbyterian Church.

CHESTER C. RICHEY, born in Shrewsbury, April 12, 1848, is the youngest of the family of five sons and two daughters of Robert and Margaret S. (Dinkle) Richey. At the age of eight he began cigar-making, and since 1865, when he began business for himself, he has been engaged in the manufacture of cigars, either on his own account or as a journeyman. In 1880 he went to Cincinnati, Ohio, where he worked a year, then returned to his native borough, and in 1881 started a factory, which he has since conducted, manufacturing 350,000 cigars annually. He was married in 1870, at Shrewsbury, to Elizabeth Hofacker, who died in October, 1879, leaving two children: Claudie and Harry. He was next married at Hametown, October 23, 1881, to Millie Anstine, daughter of Emanuel Anstine, and they have had two children; Elsie E. and Beulah Jane. Mr. Richey was educated in his native town. He is a Mason.

PETER RUHL, born in Baltimore County, Md., June 30, 1834, is the eldest son of William and Elizabeth (Crim) Ruhl, who had four sons and eight daughters. He was brought up on the farm, and attended the district school. At the age of twenty-six he began farming. He was married, in October, 1855, to Sarah Rogers, a native of England, and has had six children: Clara Virginia, died at the age of one year and a half; the five living are Robert J., mining in Virginia; John W., school teacher; George E., a farmer; Charles E., a farmer at home, and Sarah Lizzie Jane, at home. He removed to York County in 1867, and located where he has since resided; owns a fine farm of 167 acres. He has served one year as judge of elections; as school director since 1876; he was one of the organizers and for two terms a director of the New Freedom Building & Loan Association, and is a member of the Evangelical Association.

EDWARD K. SEITZ, born at Hametown, January 20, 1836, is the eldest son of a family of thirteen children of Samuel and Christiana (Klinefelter) Seitz. He lived on a farm, attended the common schools and Shrewsbury Academy. Beginning at the age of twenty-one, he taught school eight terms in the public schools of York County; has practiced surveying since 1865; has been keeper of the tollgate of York & Maryland Line Turnpike since 1867; has manufactured hames since 1869, besides managing his farm where he lives, about one mile and a half north of Shrewsbury. He was elected justice of the peace in 1883, by a large majority, although an active Republican in a Democratic township; was a candidate for recorder on the reform ticket in 1872, and was defeated by a small majority; is a member of the Republican county committee, and has been a delegate to the county convention at different times. He was married, in 1864, at Glen Rock, to Miranda Miller, daughter of Samuel Miller, and they have eight children: James Elmer, Lizzie Mary, Allen Harvey, Samuel Clayton, Henry Clinton, Charles Edward, Carrie Christiana and Alverta Miranda. He is a member of the Evangelical Association; is superintendent of the Union Sunday-school at Hametown, and has been Sunday-school superintendent or assistant for thirteen years.

ADAM D. SEITZ, son of Levi and Magdalena (Dice) Seitz, natives of York County, and of German descent, was born May 7, 1837. Of five children, he is the eldest. He remained on a farm until sixteen years of age, receiving his education at the public schools. He also attended Union Seminary at New Berlin, and the York Normal School. At the age of seventeen, he began teaching, and followed it for sixteen years. He was married at Loganville, November 3, 1859, to Anna Maria Hildebrand, daughter of Casper Hildebrand, of German descent. They have four children: Maggie, Susan E., Frederick C., and Martha Daisy. Mr. Seitz is a member of the Reformed Church, and was an elder for several years. In 1873, he was elected justice of the peace and served five years. He was also a school director for a number of years. In 1866 he removed from Loganville to Hametown, where he has since resided. In addition to farming, he has run a huckster route for eight years. In company with R. Seitz, he built the Hametown public schoolhouse. He is agent for the Southern Mutual Fire Insurance Company of York County, and was president of the building committee of Shrewsbury Reformed Church.

BENJAMIN SEITZ, son of John and Sarah (Schnell) Seitz, of York County, was born March 10, 1843. His father was born in Pennsylvania. Benjamin is the third of seven children, and the

BIOGRAPHICAL SKETCHES. 181

second son. His father being a hame-maker, he had to learn that trade early in life, also working on the farm and attending the common schools, attending, also, for one term, the State Normal School, at Millersville. At the age of twenty-one his father took him into partnership in manufacturing hames and merchandising in Hametown. The hame manufacturing he has since continued, manufacturing about 15,000 pairs per annum. He was married, at Hametown, November 24, 1864, to Barbara A. Stermer, daughter of Joseph Stermer, of York County, and has had ten children: Clara Matilda (deceased), William W., Emma L., John H., Sarah S., L. Amelia, Barbara Ella, Benjamin F., Joseph E. and Annie M. Mr. Seitz belongs to the Reformed Church and his wife to the Lutheran Church. He is the treasurer of the church, was inspector of elections, and is a director of the Shrewsbury & Railroad Station Turnpike Company.

N. Z. SEITZ was born in Shrewsbury Township near Glen Rock, York Co., Penn., January 20, 1843, and is one of a family of ten children—seven sons and three daughters. His father, Michael Seitz, and his mother, Anna Mary Zeigler, are natives of the same township, while the great-great-grandfathers of both were natives of Germany, but came to this country when quite young, and were sold as slaves to pay for their steerage. The subject of this sketch lived on the farm with his father near Glen Rock, Penn., until seventeen years of age, in the meantime attending public and select schools at intervals. At the beginning of the late civil war, not yet eighteen years of age, he entered the Union army, enlisting in Company D, Eighty-seventh Regiment Pennsylvania Volunteers, in which he served for three years, and was promoted to a non-commissioned officer. He subsequently re-entered the service as first lieutenant of Company B, Sixty-seventh Regiment Pennsylvania Volunteers, and was soon promoted to captain, in which capacity he held various important positions, and served until after the close of the war. On his return home he entered the profession of teaching, having charge of public and select schools to 1871, during which time he was also special contributor to various newspapers. In January, 1871, he became one of the editors and publishers of the Glen Rock *Item*, shortly thereafter taking editorial control of the paper, and continuing so up to the present time. During this period he has also edited a temperance paper, a musical journal and an educational monthly. He was three times commissioned as justice of the peace, served on the York County commission to reaudit the war claims for the county; was one of the deputy marshals in taking the census of 1870; has been school director in his town, and has held other important local positions of trust. He has been active in most of the public movements in his section, having served a number of years as president of the Shrewsbury District Sunday-school Institute; two years as the president of the York County Sunday-school Union, and two years as the president of the York County Educational Society, which latter position he is holding at this time. He has delivered a number of lectures and addresses on educational and scientific subjects; is an active member of the Masonic fraternity, K. of P. and G. A. R., and has held important positions in these organizations. He was one of the conferrees that nominated the Hon. William A. Duncan the second time for congress in the Nineteenth Congressional District.

LEWIS W. SHAFER was born in Manheim Township, December 16, 1843, is the eldest son of Nicholas and Elizabeth (Weigandt) Shafer, natives of Maryland and Germany, respectively. He lived on a farm until seventeen, attended York County Academy one term, taught school one term, then entered the service of the Northern Central Railroad Company at York, as clerk in motive power department, remained two years and a half; attended commercial college at Poughkeepsie, N. Y.; graduated in 1864; entered the office of Northern Central Railroad Company at Glen Rock as clerk and book-keeper, remained four years; engaged in business at Glen Rock two years; sold out, and returned to his clerkship in the railroad office, and four months afterward was appointed agent of the company, and at this writing (1884), is also telegraph operator, express agent, general insurance agent, and secretary of the Glen Rock Manufacturing Company, of which he was a charter member. He was married, September 27, 1868, to Addie C. Foust, of Glen Rock, and they have seven children: Ida A., Elizabeth, Addie, Charles F., Jennie, Lewis W. and an infant unnamed. He and wife are members of the Lutheran Church. He is a Master Mason, and has served one term as school director, and one term as councilman.

GEORGE R. SHAFFER, farmer and dairyman, in Shrewsbury Township, was born in Codorus Township March 21, 1841. His parents, Adam and Susanna (Ruhle) Shaffer, were natives of York County, and of German descent, and had eleven children—seven boys and four girls. George R. was brought up on the farm, and educated at the common schools. At twenty-one years of age he began the butcher business, and followed it four years. January 10, 1867, he was married, in Shrewsbury Township, to Rebecca Nonamaker, of York County, and had six children, one of whom died young; Henry Clinton, Jennie Florence, Arthur Ervin and Zura Alverta are living. Mr. Shaffer moved to his present farm of 100 acres, at the time he was married, working it until 1880; when he also commenced the dairy business. He is a member of the Reformed Church, while his wife belongs to the Lutheran Church. His father died in 1875, aged seventy-five years, and his mother in 1872, aged sixty-five years.

ANDREW SHAW was born in Hyde, Cheshire, England, July 22, 1838. His father came to America in 1848, and his mother and the entire family followed in 1850. They located at Glen Rock, where Andrew went to work in the woolen factory of William Heathcote, and where he has since lived, with the exception of one year spent in Delaware County, and four years in the United States army. He received his education in the public schools of Glen Rock. He enlisted in Chester, Penn., May 14, 1861, in Company C, First Regiment Pennsylvania Reserves; served three years, and before re turning home re-enlisted in Company G, One Hundred and Ninetieth Pennsylvania Volunteers, and served to the close of the war. He participated in all the battles of the Peninsular campaign, and in front of Richmond under McClellan, and at the second battle of Bull Run, Fredericksburg, Gettysburg, Grant's campaigns, clear through to the surrender of Lee's army, the first flag of truce on that occasion entering the Union lines through his company. He was mustered out July 3, 1865, and returned at once to Glen Rock, where he has since been engaged as manager in the woolen manufactory of Heathcote & Co. He was married, in 1866, at Glen Rock, to Lucinda, daughter of John Maddux, of Loganville, and has had nine children; three died when small. The living are: Mary Ellen, Lydia Ann, John Ridgeway, Ethel Amelia, Joseph Ernest and Flora Mildred. Both Mr. and Mrs. Shaw are members of the Evangelical Lutheran Church. He was the first presiding officer of the lodge of Red Men at Glen Rock, and has held all the offices in the lodge. He is treasurer of the lodge of K. of P., and has held the offices of councilman

SHREWSBURY TOWNSHIP.

and chief burgess, and is at present a member of the school board of Glen Rock Borough. In politics he is a Republican.

ISAAC SHEFFER, a miller of Shrewsbury Township, was born in Hopewell Township, April 12, 1844, and is the son of John and Hannah (Bahn) Sheffer. John Sheffer was born in Shrewsbury Township in 1800; followed milling for a business, and in 1822, married Hannah Bahn, a native of Springfield Township, born in 1804. He had born to him eight children, and departed this life about the year 1876. Isaac Sheffer was married, in 1868, to M. M. Moffett, and to this union have been born five children. The parents are members of the Lutheran Church and stand high in the estimation of the community.

E. H. SHIREY, born in Springfield Township, November 4, 1842, is the second son and third child in a family of seven children of Isaac and Sarah (Haines) Shirey. At the age of eighteen he began to learn the trade of miller, at which he continued until the age of twenty-one, when he worked about a year at cigar-making. At twenty-four he entered the employ of Jacob Winemiller, a merchant of Stewartstown, remaining one year, after which he drove a huckster wagon one year for Albert Miller, and about two years and a half for himself, and then engaged in farming two years. He next moved to Lebanon, Penn., remained there four years, then engaged in a general merchandise business at Felton two years. April 1, 1879, he came to Hametown, and embarked in the mercantile business, continuing until January 1, 1884. He is at present engaged in the manufacture of cigars. He was married, January 23, 1870, to Louisa, daughter of Ambrose McGuigan, of Hopewell Township, and has five children: Bernard W., Oscar C., Annie V., Mabel A. and Helen B.

LEWIS N. SCHRIVER, liveryman, was born in Hanover, Penn., December 22, 1848. His parents, Henry C. and Maria (Felty) Schriver, were of German descent, and reared four children, of whom Lewis N., is the youngest. Up to his fifteenth year he remained in Hanover attending the public schools. At fifteen years of age he left home without the consent of his parents, and enlisted at Baltimore, in Company K, First Maryland Cavalry, and served sixteen months, and at the close of the war was corporal of the company. Nearly all the time he was in the Shenandoah Valley. Returning to Hanover he began learning the cigar-making trade. He then went to Pine Grove, where he clerked in his brother's store for a year and a half. In 1868 he came to Glen Rock, and engaged in manufacturing cigars, but after two years engaged in the livery business, which he has followed since, also dealing in horses and mules. January 17, 1871, he married, in Glen Rock, Sarah J. Miller, daughter of E. R. Miller, of Goldsboro, Penn. They had two children, one of whom died, aged seven or eight years. The other is Bertha. Mr. Schriver was constable for three years, is a member of the K. of P., and was an original stockholder in the Glen Rock Manufacturing Company.

CONRAD SHUPPERT, farmer, was born in Baden, Germany, March 8, 1838, and came to this country with his parents, George and Mary (Braun) Shuppert, in 1848, and landed at Baltimore. His parents, who brought four children with them (four having died before leaving home), remained in Maryland until their death, the father dying in 1865, aged sixty-eight years, and the mother in 1869, aged fifty-eight years. Conrad had attended the schools in Germany, and, after arriving in this country, he attended the English schools for several months. In April, 1861, he was married at York, Penn., to Sophia Bush, also a German, and has eight children: Margaret, Mary, Rosa, Katie, Annie, Joseph, Dora

and Augusta. The family all belong to the Catholic Church, in which he had been brought up. In 1868 he removed from Baltimore County to his farm in Shrewsbury Township, containing about 140 acres, where he now resides.

CHARLES SINGER, farmer, was born in Hesse Darmstadt, Germany, May 10, 1838, and came to America in 1851, landing in New York. He came directly to Shrewsbury Township, where he engaged at farming. His parents, Charles F. and Margaret (Stark) Singer, had a family of five children, when they landed here, and one was born in this country. They remained in Shrewsbury Township, where the father died in 1875, aged sixty-seven years. The mother is still living, being sixty-eight years old. Charles Singer received his early education in Germany, and has acquired a good English education in this county. At the age of twenty-eight years he commenced business for himself by purchasing a farm of seventy-two acres near the Maryland line, in Shrewsbury Township, from his father. February 1, 1866, he was married, in Shrewsbury Township, to Magdalena Ziegler, daughter of Michael Ziegler, distiller and miller, of Shrewsbury Township. They had six children, of whom three are dead: Lillie Alice, Elizabeth M. and John P. The living are James F., Annie Jane and Eli M. The family are members of the Evangelical Lutheran Church, of which Mr. Singer is a deacon. He is also chaplain of the order of the P. of H. one of the organizers, and a director of the New Freedom Building Association, a director in the New Freedom Cemetery Association; was a school director and councilman for three years, and borough assessor for several terms.

HENRY SMITH, farmer, was born in Shrewsbury Township, May 9, 1836. His parents, Henry and Catharine (Hill) Smith, came from Germany to America, bringing five children with them, and having born to them four more in York County. The family consisted of four sons and five daughters, of whom Henry, Jr., was next to the youngest. At the age of fifteen years he began working for himself, and October 13, 1864, he was married, in Shrewsbury, to Leah Heindel, daughter of George Heindel, and had four children, one of whom, William Monroe, was born April 12, 1867, and died at the age of eight months. The living are: Leander James, born January 27, 1865; Emanuel Edwin, born March 19, 1868; and Emma May, born May 5, 1877. Mr. Smith is a deacon in the Lutheran Church, and Mrs. Smith is a member of the Reformed Church. He owns and resides on the homestead of his parents, a nice farm of eighty-five acres of well-cultivated land. In 1883, he purchased the grist-mill, known as the Shafer Mill, but rents it out. He is also engaged in running a steam thrasher. In 1873-74, he was supervisor of his township, and was one of the organizers of the New Freedom Building Association, and was twice elected to the board of managers, but refused to serve. The Smith family all follow farming, one brother in Baltimore, one in Illinois and one in York County. His father died at the age of eighty years and his mother at the age of seventy-four years.

ADAM H. SMITH, D. D. S., was born in Hopewell Township, York County, August 14, 1842. His parents, Frederick and Martha (James) Smith, natives of York County, and of German and English extraction, had thirteen children; three died in childhood, and one, Daniel L., a teacher, was killed by the cars at or near Coatesville, Penn., in 1879. Adam H. was the third son and child in a family of four sons and six daughters that grew to manhood and womanhood. He was brought up on a farm and educated at Stewartstown Academy, and at the age of twenty-one, taught in the public schools. In 1865 he began the study of dentistry

BIOGRAPHICAL SKETCHES.

with Dr. Burke, at Stewartstown, and remained with him about eighteen months. He then took a course at the Baltimore School of Dental Surgery, after which he located permanently at Glen Rock, and has now (1884) been in the practice of his profession about eighteen years. He enlisted in August, 1864, at Harrisburg, in Company C, Two Hundred and Tenth Pennsylvania Volunteers, and served in the Army of the Potomac to the close of the war, participating in the battles of Hatcher's Run, etc., and was promoted to be commissary sergeant of his regiment. He was married, in 1867, at Glen Rock, to Elmira W. Lamison, a native of York County, and has four children: Ernest Montville, Alta Cynthia, Howard Roy and Martha Maud. He is one of the trustees of the Methodist Episcopal Church, at Glen Rock, of which he and his wife are members. He has served one term as borough councilman (1868) and is auditor of Glen Rock Borough at this writing.

W. A. SPATE, a son of Joseph Spate, and a resident of Loganville, York County, was born in Springfield Township, near Glen Rock, York County, June 19, 1851. He is on his mother's side of English and Scotch ancestry, and of German on his father's. His father's parents immigrated to this country about sixty or seventy ago from Wittemburg, Germany. They were very unfortunate on the first vessel, having lost all their money through the captain of the vessel, who, instead of landing them on the coast of the United States, landed them somewhere on the coast of Europe. They took passage for America on another vessel bound for the United States. At that time the practice prevailed of selling the service of such passengers who could not pay their passage-money, to such persons in this country who would pay their expenses for them. The grandparents of Mr. Spate were among this number, and their services were secured by a Mr. Patterson, of Hopewell Township, for whom they worked for some time. Afterward they began farming for themselves. Their son Joseph received but a limited education, and made a livelihood by day laboring and carpentering. He served in the army about a year during the late civil war and died at home after the close of the war, in the winter of 1867, when his son was nearly sixteen years of age. W. A. Spate was then obliged to not only support himself, but had also a widowed mother and an invalid sister depending upon him. In the fall of 1867 he began teaching. After the close of the term he worked in the Feigley Ore Banks, where he was engaged as a cart driver for nearly three years, and then taught school again. After the close of the second term he again began work in the ore banks and was soon promoted to the position of clerk and weighmaster, which position he occupied until the fall of 1873, when the panic began. He again entered the schoolroom and taught successfully each year until the fall of 1884, when he entered the newspaper office of *The Item*, in Glen Rock, Penn., and in December of the same year he became a partner with Capt. N. Z. Seitz, in the publication of *The Item* and *The Monitor*, the first a weekly newspaper, and the second a literary and educational monthly, of which Mr. Spate is assistant editor. Mr. Spate had few educational advantages, being obliged to leave the common school soon after the death of his father, and before he was sixteen. He studied and read during his spare time, and often worked out problems in arithmetic while driving cart in the ore banks. After some years of study he secured a professional certificate and afterward a permanent certificate. December 25, 1879, he married Miss Sarah C. Fry, daughter of David Fry, of Loganville.

ELI STORMS, artist and teacher, is a native of Shrewsbury, where he was born June 16, 1855. He is a son of George W. and Margaret (Orwig) Storms; the former born in Baltimore County, Md., February 28, 1824, the latter a native of Hopewell Township. They were united in marriage September 8, 1850, and were parents of three children, two now living and one deceased. The subject of this sketch was educated in the Shrewsbury English and Classical Academy, and early in years gave evidence of artistic ability, which was greatly developed through persistent effort and constant practice. Previous to 1875 his sketches had been confined mostly to water colors and pencil etchings, but his later efforts have been in the field of portrait and landscape painting. Mr. Storms is also an excellent draughtsman, and in 1881 was selected to furnish draughts for the several government departments which were highly commended for accuracy, neatness and merit. He is a successful teacher, and since 1877 has taught seven terms in the public schools of the county. In the spring of 1880 he was appointed an instructor in drawing and penmanship at Cedar Hill Seminary, Mt. Joy, Penn. Mr. Storms is an active politician and has held various political offices in the borough of Shrewsbury since 1877, and is the present secretary of various organizations. He has been a member of the council several terms and clerk of that body for the past five years. In 1879 he became a member of Mt. Vernon Lodge, I. O. O. F., Shrewsbury; Shrewsbury Lodge 423, F. & A. M., in 1880, and Mt. Vernon Encampment of York, in 1880.

JOHN ASBURY TAYLOR, M. D., born in York County, April 30, 1888, is a son of John and Rachel (Gilbert) Taylor, of German, English and Irish extraction. The Taylor family came from Maryland to York County, about the year 1814. John Taylor (the father of John A.), served through the war of 1812, in a Maryland regiment, and died in 1861, at the age of seventy-one years. His wife, Rachel, died in 1873, aged seventy-nine years. They had four sons and five daughters, who are all living in York County, except one son and one daughter who are buried in Hancock County, Ohio. The subject of our sketch is the youngest of the family and received an academic education in Hopewell and Shrewsbury Academies; taught in the public schools six years; read medicine in the office of Dr. J. R. Bardwell, in Stewartstown, two years, then at the age of twenty-six entered Maryland University, at Baltimore, and while attending lectures, read in the office of Dr. John Starr; graduated March 3, 1866, with the degree of M. D.; returned to York County, and began the practice of medicine, where he has since lived, on his farm of 132 acres about one mile and a half south by east of Shrewsbury, where he devotes his whole time to his profession and to farming. He has served as clerk, as school director and as auditor of Shrewsbury Township; was a delegate to the State Democratic Convention in 1883, and to county convention at different times. He was married, in Fawn Township in 1876, to Augustina R. Barton, daughter of Thomas Barton, of English descent. She died March 8, 1883; a member of the Presbyterian Church. Dr. Taylor was brought up in the Methodist Episcopal Church, but is now of the Lutheran faith, though not a member.

JAMES S. VENUS, cigar manufacturer, was born in Shrewsbury Township, near Mount Zion, May 30, 1851, and was the third son of the six children of Henry and Ann (Sykes) Venus, of York County and England, respectively. Until fifteen years of age he remained in Shrewsbury Township, then went with his parents to Carroll County, Md. He received a good English education in both districts, and in 1870 he removed again to York County. In 1873 he began to learn photography at Shrewsbury, and followed it six years. In 1878 he learned cigar-making, and in 1879 began manufacturing, and at present makes about 200,000 a year. September 17, 1876, he was married to Sallie E. Eaton, daughter of John Eaton, of York County. He and wife are members of the Methodist Episcopal Church. Mr. Venus is a prominent Odd Fellow, and has held all the chairs in Mount Vernon Lodge No. 143.

AUGUST WEIHMILLER, cigar manufacturer, was born in Wurtemberg, Germany, January 28, 1858, and is the second son of the three children of M. and Margaret (Kimmel) Weihmiller. He came to America when twenty-three years of age. In Germany he received a first-class education. On his arrival here he learned the cigar-making business, in Seven Valleys with his brother, remaining two years following his trade until January, 1884, when he removed to Shrewsbury, and engaged in manufacturing cigars for himself. Mr. Weihmiller is a member of the F.& A. M., of Shrewsbury Lodge, and of Zion's Lodge K. of P., of Seven Valleys, York County. He employs seven hands and manufactures about 300,000 high priced cigars yearly.

GEORGE E. WERTZ was born in Manheim Township, September 18, 1829. His parents, Daniel and Margaret (Miller) Wertz, were born in York County, and were of German and Swiss descent. He lived on a farm until eighteen years of age; learned the trade of bricklayer, which he followed in connection with teaching, and the management of a small farm in Codorus Township; taught twenty-four terms in the public schools of York County up to 1879; was inspector of elections in Codorus Township, 1853; school director, 1872-75; auditor, 1876-79; took the enumeration of the United States census of 1880, of Codorus Township and Jefferson Borough; was appointed steward of the York County Alms House, and removed to York in 1883; removed to Glen Rock in 1884, where, at this writing, he is keeping a hotel. He was married, October 9, 1851, to Frances Ann Weaver, born in Maryland, and moved to Pennsylvania at an early age. They have had ten children: William, Jacob, Franklin (teaching in Kansas, was educated for the ministry); Eliza Jane, died at the age of ten years; James, died at the age of two years; Annie, wife of Joseph Small; Ammon, Agnes, Alice and Francis. Mr. and Mrs. Wertz are members of the Reformed Church, and he is a member of Friendly Lodge No. 287, K. of P., of Glen Rock.

REV. JOSEPH BITTINGER WOLFF, resident pastor of Zion's Evangelical Lutheran Church at Glen Rock, and St. Paul's at Hametown, was born January 9, 1848. His parents, John George and Eleanor (Bittinger) Wolff, were natives of Adams County, Penn., and of German descent. They reared a family of seven sons and one daughter. Rev. Joseph, who was the second of the family, was brought up on the farm, and educated at the public and private schools of his native county. In the spring of 1869 he entered Pennsylvania College at Gettysburg, and graduated in June, 1874, as A. B. In the fall of 1874 he entered the Theological Seminary at Gettysburg, and graduated from there in June, 1877. A few days after graduating he recived a call from Glen Rock, to take charge of Zion's Evangelical Lutheran Church, which he accepted, and has held since. In 1877 he was married, at Gettysburg, to Miss Priscilla E. daughter of Daniel Cashman, of Adams County. They have one daughter, Anna Eleanor, and one son, Joseph Harold.

GEORGE P. YOST, M. D., was born in Carroll County, Md., May 8, 1848. His father, Philip, was a native of Hesse Darmstadt, Germany, and when a small youth came with his parents to America, arriving at Baltimore in 1825, having been over five months in passage. His parents settled near the Mason and Dixon line in Carroll County, Md., where he was reared. He subsequently purchased a farm near his parents, and has followed farming up to the present time. The paternal grandmother of Dr. Yost was a French lady. The mother of our subject, whose maiden name was Lydia Utz, was a native of Carroll County, Md., of Welsh descent. Our subject was reared on a farm, and at the age of sixteen began teaching, subsequently attending Irving Institute at Manchester, Md., two years. After teaching another year he entered the office of Dr. William A. Albaugh, of Sticks, located in North Codorus Township, and commenced the study of medicine. He graduated from the Washington University, Baltimore, Md., in February, 1871, and began the practice with his old preceptor, with whom he was associated eighteen months. In 1872 he removed to Loganville, where he continued his practice for nearly thirteen years. In 1885 Dr. Yost located in Glen Rock, where he is now well established. In 1881 Dr. Yost was elected lecturer on Dermatology in the Baltimore Medical College, and for the past four years he has delivered weekly lectures at that institution. Dr. Yost is ardent in the practice of his profession, and an active worker in educational affairs. The Doctor is entirely a self-made man, never having had pecuniary assistance from any one, and having worked his way through schools and college by his own individual efforts.

SEBASTIAN ZELLER, farmer, was born in Bavaria, November 12, 1822, and came to America in 1847. Landing at Baltimore he stopped there about six months, and then came to York County, where, at Emigsville, he was engaged in burning lime for five years. From there he removed to Shrewsbury (1857), where he purchased a farm of seventy-five acres, on which he has resided since. He was educated in Germany, and was the elder of two sons of John and Barbara (Zuizor) Zeller. In 1848 he was married, at York, to Catharine Koch, a native of Bavaria. They had seven children, of whom two are dead: Sarah E. and John T. The living are Mary Ann, John A., Barbara, Franklin and Sophia. The family are Catholics. Mr. Zeller is a Democrat, and was one of the organizers of the New Freedom Building Association.

JOHN D. ZIEGLER, born in Shrewsbury Township, January 31, 1820, is a son of Michael and Magdalena (Dosch) Ziegler, being the third son and fifth child of a family of four sons and five daughters; was brought up on a farm, and educated in the subscription schools; began learning milling in Maryland at the age of twenty-one, and continued it for five years; was married January 31, 1847, in Manheim Township, to Mary A. Nace, daughter of John Nace. They had nine children—two, George Luther and Julia A. are dead; Belinda, at home; Oliver C., miller and farmer in York County; Cecelia, wife of Chester B. Wentz, a merchant in Carroll County, Md.; Agnes, at home; Virginia, at home: John S., M. D., practicing at Melrose, Md., and Upton A., at home. Mr. Ziegler and wife are members of the Lutheran Church. His father died in 1857, aged sixty-eight, and his mother in 1847, aged fifty-nine years. He served six years as school director in Shrewsbury Township; is a director in the Codorus & Manheim Fire Insurance Company, and was one of the charter members of the Shrewsbury Savings Institution. He purchased his present farm of 126 acres about 1855, to which he has added forty-nine acres.

SPRINGFIELD TOWNSHIP.

JOHN F. BECK (Commissioner of York County) was born August 16, 1829, in York, Penn. He attended the York schools one winter, and at the age of nine years, went to Loganville, where he received two winters' schooling. He worked three years at the carpenter trade. January 15, 1852, Mr. Beck married Matilda Leader, of York Township. This marriage was blessed with the following children: Mary Catharine, Charles F., Milton G., Franklin J., Paul J., Emma A., Harry C., Martha J. and Harvey G. Mr. Beck has at various times held township offices—school director, auditor, etc. In 1884 he was elected one of the commissioners of York County, and it is not too much to say that the office was never held by a more worthy and upright citizen than John F. Beck. He comes from good German ancestry, who were among the early settlers of York County.

JOHN F. BOPP, farmer, son of John Bopp, Jr. and Barbara (Folkenstein) Bopp, was born August 8, 1827. Our subject was the eldest of eight children: John F., Leah, Sarah, Catharine, Henry (deceased), Israel (deceased), Peter and Jesse. August, 1850, Mr. Bopp married Maria Allison, of Springfield Township. There were born to them by this marriage: Uriah, Jacob (deceased), George (deceased), Emanuel, Amos, Malinda (deceased), Emma, Jesse, William, Elizabeth and Barbara. May 2, 1865, Mr. Bopp married Priscilla Allison, daughter of John and Elizabeth (Reichard) Allison, of Springfield Township; to this union were born John (deceased), Peter (deceased), Ella M. (deceased), Levina, Taby and Eli. Mr. Bopp is a member of the Reformed Church, has been school director three terms, and is one of the most successful farmers of Springfield Township. For the past fifteen years he has been a director of the First National Bank of Glen Rock, and is also a director in the Codorus & Manheim Fire Insurance Company, of York County, having been elected for a term of three years.

HENRY BOTT, son of Peter and Elizabeth (Zeigler) Bott, was born in West Manchester Township, in September, 1818. He was reared on his father's farm. Mr. Bott married Sarah A. Zeigler, daughter of John E. and Barbara (Kohler) Zeigler (see Israel Zeigler's sketch for history of the Zeigler family). Five children blessed their marriage: W. W., Martin L., Henry C., John (deceased) and Rose E. (deceased). Mr. Bott's ancestors came very early to York; his great-grandfather came to York from Germany, long before the Revolutionary war. The subject of this sketch came to Springfield Township in 1855, and engaged in the mercantile business at Smyser's Station; has also been the agent for the Northern Central Railroad, at this point, for twenty years, having turned over the agency to his son, W. W. Bott, about ten years ago. Mr. Bott is a prominent member of the Lutheran Church, of Seven Valleys.

DAVID Y. BRILLHART, one of the successful farmers of Springfield Township, was born in that township, March 3, 1855. His ancestors were among the earliest settlers of York County. His parents were Jacob and Rebecca (Yost) Brillhart, residents of Springfield Township. Mr. Brillhart has been a resident of Springfield Township all his life, and engaged in agricultural pursuits, in which occupation he has been exceedingly prosperous. His farm, which contains over 200 acres of superior land, is well improved. He is also the owner of a valuable ore mine, which bears his name. Mr. Brillhart was united in marriage, January 26, 1879, with Miss Mary Alice Herbst, a daughter of Jacob and Julia (Diehl) Herbst, of Hopewell Township. Four children have been born to them—Jacob, Rebecca (deceased), David and Charles.

REV. CHARLES M. EYSTER, pastor in charge of the Lutheran Church, Seven Valleys, is the son of John and Susan (Eisenhart) Eyster, and was born December 21, 1857, in Jackson Township. Rev. Eyster attended the normal school at East Berlin, Penn., also Eastman's Business College at Poughkeepsie, N. Y., and took a full course at the Pennsylvania College and Theological Seminary, at Gettysburg, Penn. Although quite a young man in the ministry, his first charge was a very important one. The Eyster family were among the very earliest settlers of York County. It is claimed by this family, that their ancestors were the first white people that settled in West Manchester Township, in the vicinity of Wolf's Church, about five miles from York.

MARTIN FEIGLEY (deceased), was born in Springfield Township, December 4, 1881. His grandfather, Peter Feigley, was also a native of this township, and his great-grandfather settled in this township when a young man, thus making the Feigley family one of the pioneer families of York County. Mr. Feigley married Ellen Reichard, daughter of George and Liddie Reichard, of York Township. This marriage was blessed with nine children: Lucy R., Levi R., Katie R., Ellen R., Lizzie R., Martin R. John R., Sarah R. and Peter R. The large ore bank, known as Feigley Ore Bank (see mining interests of York County), was purchased by Mr. Feigley, in 1867; over 30,000 tons of hematite ore have already been taken from this mine. Mr. F. has been a successful farmer, in connection with his mining business; was school director for a number of years. The Feigleys are members of the Brethren or German Baptist denomination.

WILLIAM FOUST, son of John S. and Rebecca (Erhman) Foust, was born April 25, 1836, in Shrewsbury Township. He was reared on his father's farm, and followed farming and distilling until 1860, when he began distilling for himself at Foust's distillery, which he rebuilt after taking possession himself. March, 1859, Mr. Foust married Henrietta Bricker, daughter of John and Christina (Zeller) Bricker, of York County. Eight children were born to this marriage: John Q. A., Luther, William, Robert, Frederick, Maggie Jane, Estella May and an infant deceased. Mr. Foust is a member of the Lutheran Church. Few men are better known throughout York and adjoining counties than "Billy Foust."

PHILIP GLATFELTER (deceased), son of Philip and Anna M. (Emig) Glatfelter, was born in 1820, in Springfield Township. September 19, 1841, Mr. Glatfelter married Catherine Geiselman, of Springfield Township, daughter of George and Catherine (Erhart) Geiselman. This union was blessed with twelve children: Edward (deceased), George (deceased), William (deceased), Robert, Elenora (deceased), Emma, Jestie, Sarah, Mollie, Rosa, Lillie and Mahala. Mr. Glatfelter was a member of the Lutheran Church.

DEITRICK HILDEBRAND, second of four children of Casper and Susanna (Ness) Hildebrand, was born November 10, 1831, in Loganville, Springfield Township. He was reared on his father's farm, and went to his trade (shoe-making) when fifteen years old, and has always followed this occupation; has been justice of the peace seventeen years. April 8, 1858, Mr. Hildebrand married Anna Maria Leader, daughter of Charles and Sarah (Hildebrand) Leader, of Springfield Township. Three children have blessed this union: Charles G., Annie and Robert. Our subject's grandfather was Casper Hildebrand. His grandmother's maiden name was Cranmer, and it is worthy of mention about this family that the seven boys and the two girls all attained the ripe old age of eighty years. The father of our subject died in his eighty-sixth year. The subject of this sketch is a well known and highly respected citizen, and always active in any movement that has for its object the welfare of his township and fellow-citizens.

EMANUEL HILDEBRAND, the fourth of ten children of Adam and Rebecca (Combs) Hildebrand, was born February 11, 1834, in Springfield Township. In his father's family were: Liddie (deceased), Sarah (deceased), Mary, Emanuel, Jonathan, Adam (deceased), Rebecca, Leah, Levi (deceased), and Annie (deceased). Our subject was reared on his father's farm. September 12, 1858, he married Annie Hain, daughter of George and Annie (Hupp) Hain, of Saxe Weimar, Germany. Seven children were born to them: Agnes, Caroline, George (deceased), Catharine, Alice Ann, Nathaniel (deceased) and Emanuel (deceased). Mr. Hildebrand is a member of the Lutheran Church of Glen Rock, and one of the leading farmers of his township.

WILLIAM N. HILDEBRAND, son of Casper and Susanna (Ness) Hildebrand, was born in Loganville, Springfield Township, January 8, 1838. He was the youngest of four children: Aaron (deceased), Deitrick, Maria and William N. He was reared on the farm, and taught school ten terms in his native township. He was appointed storekeeper at Foust's Distillery by the United States Government, and in 1879 was appointed guager and storekeeper. March 26, 1864, Mr. Hildebrand married Susan Howard, daughter of Edward and Catharine (Strayer) Howard, of Springfield Township. Four children were born to them: Frederick, Harry, Minnie and Maggie. Mr. Hildebrand is a member of the Reformed Church, and a well-informed, progressive citizen.

L. F. HILDEBRAND, merchant and postmaster, Loganville, was born in Springfield Township in 1848, and is the son of Isaac and Elizabeth (Feigley) Hildebrand. The father was a farmer as well as merchant, and died in September, 1880; the mother is still living, and of the three children born to those parents our subject alone survives. He assisted his father on the farm until sixteen years old, and then in the store until he succeeded him in business. About 1870 he was appointed postmaster, and he has also served as school director. In 1875 he married Miss Lizzie Gontner, of Lancaster County, and to this union have been born three children: Jennie May, Daniel W. and Mary D.

GEORGE E. HOLTZAPPLE, M. D., son of Israel E. and Christiana (Leckrone) Holtzapple, was born May 22, 1862, in West Manchester Township, York Co., Penn. On his father's side his great-great-grandfather came from Germany. George E. spent the days of youth at home, engaged in work there and out on farms as a laborer. At the age of fourteen he was engaged a short time in the City Drug Store, York, Penn, after which he spent most of his time in study, giving instruction in instrumental music. At the age of sixteen he commenced teaching public school at Bott's, in West Manchester, where he taught four terms in succession. During the spring previous to the last term he taught a select school in Seven Valleys. His school days in public school were spent at Neiman's, in West Manchester. In the spring of 1876 he went ten weeks to the York Collegiate Institute; in the spring of 1877 ten weeks to the York County Normal. The teachers were Kand and Gardner. In the spring of 1878 he attended ten weeks, and in the spring of 1879 eight weeks at Normal School, in Hartman's Building. He commenced reading medicine in the fall of 1880, under the preceptorship of Dr. George P. Yost, Loganville. He continued his medical studies till March 13, 1884, when he graduated at the Bellevue Hospital Medical College, New York City. After graduating he went in practice with his preceptor at Loganville a few months, then located a few months at York, after which he bought out his preceptor's practice, the latter going to Glen Rock, and Dr. Holtzapple taking his place at Loganville December 11, 1884, where he is practicing at present. The Doctor is a member of the York County Medical Society, a member of the West York Eye, Ear and Throat Dispensary, and also a member of Christ's Lutheran Church, York, Penn.

HENRY KREIDLER is the eldest of the five children of Michael and Catharine (Wackarman) Kreidler, and was born in York Township February 29, 1832. At the age of seventeen he began to learn milling, and has followed that business ever since. In 1878 he purchased his present farm of 100 acres, and erected his mill, carrying on extensively both milling and farming. In 1855 he married Miss Elizabeth, daughter of Jacob Gable, of Windsor Township, and is now the father of twelve living children: Annie M., John C., Priscilla J., Mary J., Malinda A., Ida A., Jacob E., Sarah A., George E., Samuel E., Martha A. and Henry E. Mr. Kreidler has served as inspector of elections, school director and township auditor, and was once elected justice of the peace, but declined to serve. He is a Mason of the Royal Arch degree, and with his wife is a member of the Evangelical Lutheran Church of Paradise.

D. M. LOUCKS was born in Windsor Township May 14, 1844, and is the son of Levi and Elizabeth (Myers) Loucks, now living in retirement at York. Our subject received a good education in youth, and for fourteen years, from 1859, was a school teacher. In 1867 he was elected justice of the peace, and served five years. In 1867 he began the manufacture of cigars, which he followed until the spring of 1873. In 1872 he was elected to the legislature and served one term. In 1873 he removed to New Paradise in Springfield Township, and the same year was re-elected to the legislature. In 1880 he was elected justice of the peace of his township; his term expired May 6, 1885, but he refused to again accept a re-election. He was married, in 1862, to Miss Emeline Peeling, a native of York Township and a daughter of John Peeling, and to this union have been born five children: Joshua P., Joseph E., Addison P., Media L. and Ada E. Mr. Loucks has been very successful as a business man, and in his cigar manufactory employs at times as many as twenty hands.

GEORGE W. RENNOLL, son of Sam and Mary (Sheffer) Rennoll, was born April 23, 1847, in Shrewsbury Township. His parents were natives of this township. His grandmother, on his mother's side, was the daughter of Jacob Sheffer and Mary Gerbrick, of Shrewsbury Township. Our subject was the eldest son in a family of four: George W., Charles S., Nathaniel and Franklin (deceased). Mr. R. was reared on the farm, and began his occupation as miller in 1865 at Sheffer's Mill, Glen Rock. After having learned the trade and working a year here he went to Louck's Mill, operated by P. A. & S. Small; after three years at this mill he went to Small's Goldsboro mill; ten and a half years were spent here, when he was called to Small's warehouse in York for one year, then to his present mill, which he purchased in 1880, and after operating successfully for three and a half years he introduced in his mill the celebrated roller process mode of making flour, and it may be proper to mention here, as an evidence of Mr. Rennoll's push and energy in the prosecution of his business, that he was the second man in York County to adopt this popular method of manufacturing flour. He finds

BIOGRAPHICAL SKETCHES.   187

ready sale with merchants in York for all the flour he can furnish. January 9, 1870, he married Rebecca Laucks, daughter of Benjamin and Elizabeth (Beaverson) Laucks, of Spring Garden Township. Two children have been born to this union: Annie E. and Charles Latimer. Mr. R. was a member of the American Mechanics until it dissolved. He is a member of the Lutheran Church.

E. P. ROHRBAUGH, M. D., a native of Codorus Township, was born in 1858, is a son of Peter L. and Elizabeth (Bortner) Rohrbaugh, and is the youngest of their ten children. The father died in 1882, but the mother still survives. Our subject received a good common school and academic education in youth, and for three years was a student of medicine under Dr. J. A. Glatfelter, of Seven Valleys, attending college in the meanwhile. He graduated from the University of Maryland in 1881, and also took a course at Johns Hopkins University of Baltimore. For two years he practiced at Glen Rock, and then located at New Paradise, where he has an extensive patronage. In 1881 he married Miss Ellen Hengst, who has borne him two children: Charles H. and Annie C. The Doctor is a member of the York County Medical Society, also of the Yosemite Lodge of Red Men, of Glen Rock, and with his wife of the Reformed Church.

SPRING GARDEN TOWNSHIP.

JOHN L. ARNOLD, son of Jacob and Sarah (Leib) Arnold, of West Manchester Township, was born August 5, 1849, at East Berlin, Adams Co., Penn. Mr. Arnold received a common school education. He learned his trade (miller) with his father and has always followed that occupation; he thoroughly understands his business, and at present has charge of one of the best equipped mills in York County—Matthew Tyler's mill. Mr. Arnold married Amanda Allison, daughter of John and Elizabeth (Musser) Allison, of York, Penn. This marriage has been blessed with five children: Arthur E., Nettie K., Howard E. (deceased), Claude A. and Mammie B. (deceased).

D. H. G. BEECHER, son of Samuel and Sarah A. M. (Wagner) Beecher, was born September 16, 1848, in Beecherville, Adams County, where, after attending the public schools, he began his first work in his father's paper-mill, remaining until his twenty-second year, when he came to Spring Garden Township, and for three years worked in the Erhart paper-mill; he then learned cigar-making and carried on the manufacture in York Township six years, when he returned to Green Hill, this township, his present home. December 8, 1872, Mr. Beecher married Miss Catherine, daughter of George and Catherine (Shell) Druck, and has had born to him six children: George H. (deceased), Samuel A. (deceased), Annie L., Charles E. (deceased), Willie C. (deceased) and Harry D. Our subject comes from a good German family and is the third of nine as follows: Annie May, George C., D. H. G., Charles F. (deceased), Samuel (deceased), Clara J., Emma (deceased) Sally A. M. and Annie. The great-grandmother of our subject was Elizabeth, wife of John Beecher, died August 14, 1845, aged ninety years. His grandparents were David Beecher, born September 8, 1793, died April 13, 1880, aged eighty-six years, seven months and five days. Anna Mary Gilbert Beecher, born April 26, 1797; and their children were: Elizabeth, born December 25, 1815; died November 8, 1827, aged eleven years, ten months and thirteen days; Ann Margaretta, born November 16, 1817, died June 21, 1822, aged four years, seven months and five days; Samuel, born March 5, 1820; Sophia Susanna, born September 27, 1822; Bernhard John, born August 23, 1824, died June 5, 1831, aged six years, nine months and twelve days; Catharine, born December 13, 1826; Lucy Ann, born December 17, 1828; David Henry Gilbert, born July 1, 1831, died November 16, 1839, aged eight years, three months and fifteen days; George, born September 11, 1833, died October 24, 1846, aged thirteen years, one month and thirteen days.

GEORGE BENDER is a son of George Bender, a native of Germany, and a brick-maker by trade, who immigrated to America, settling in York County, Penn., and establishing the business now carried on by subject. George, Jr., was an assistant of his father from his youth up, and upon the death of his father was fully competent to succeed as manager and proprietor. This business he has successfully carried on in this vicinity up to the present time. His establishment adjoins the limits of York. Mr. Bender was married, January 21, 1863, to Miss Emma J. Kiser, of York, Penn. They have five children: Annie K., Lydia M., Imilda A., George F. and Jeremiah. Mr. Bender is a member of the Spring Garden Relief Association, also of the order of R. M. of York, and of the Ridge Avenue Methodist Episcopal Church of Frystown.

EDWARD BLAUSER was born in Spring Garden Township, October 5, 1836, and is the third of ten children in the family of Jacob and Ann (Myers) Blauser, natives of York Township. He passed his time in attending school and assisting on the home farm until his seventeenth year; when he began his trade as carpenter. January 30, 1859, he married Miss Mary, daughter of John and Liddie (Sowers) Runk, and to this union have been born: Allen, Elizabeth, Ida, Lillie, Henry and Fernando. In 1875, Mr. Blauser began contracting and building, and, being a master of his profession, has been very successful, averaging twenty-five to thirty-five houses per year. Among the specimens of his contract work may be mentioned the remodeling of the old German Reformed Church edifice, and the building of Bethany Chapel on King Street; the Methodist Chapel on East Philadelphia Street; the three story brick business house of A. C. Fahn; the dwelling of W. A. Tomes; Daniel Moore's residence; Capt. William Fry's elegant cottage, etc., etc. Mr. Blauser has served as school director and is an esteemed citizen.

WILLIAM BLESSING, second of eleven children of Henry and Elizabeth (Crone) Blessing, was born March 24, 1824, in Hellam Township; he was reared on a farm and always followed that occupation. June 1849, Mr. Blessing married Leah Paules, (daughter of Adam and Elizabeth Hartzler) Paules, of Lower Windsor Township. Four children were born of this marriage: Henry A., J. Milton, Sylvester C. and Elizabeth C. Our subject's grandfather's name was Henry Blessing. Our subject's ancestors on his father's and mother's side settled very early in York County.

DR. GEORGE CONN, seventh of eleven children, of Henry and Mary (Shrum) Conn, was born August 25, 1819, in Manchester Township. He was reared on a farm and educated in Spring Garden Township. November 8, 1849, Dr. Conn married Maria Shepp, daughter of John and Elizabeth (Slagle) Shepp, of Manchester Township. Three children blessed this union: Annie Mary, wife of John Sipe; Susanna, wife of Albert J. Bower, and Alexander (deceased). When our subject was twenty-eight years of age he began the successful treatment of cancer; his success in the treatment of this

SPRING GARDEN TOWNSHIP.

loathsome disease was so marked and exceptional that he made it his life work. Many persons in York and adjoining counties in the enjoyment of health to-day can testify to Dr. Conn's success in their cases after having failed to get relief from eminent physicians in the large cities. Dr. Conn resides in the village of Pleasureville, about three miles from York, in Spring Garden Township. His postoffice address is Box 509, York, Penn.

DANIEL DIEHL was born September 11, 1807. His great-grandfather, John Adam Diehl, emigrated from Germany and took up 360 acres of land in York County, Penn., in what is now Spring Garden Township, paying an English agent £12 ($60) for the whole tract. At that time the nearest mill was at Downington, Chester County. He had four sons: Peter, Daniel, George and Nicholas. Daniel settled in Seven Valleys, York County; George in Virginia; Peter and Nicholas in Hellam Township, York County, having purchased the original tract of land from the heirs, after the death of their father. The grandfather of our subject, Peter Diehl, was born in Hellam Township, York County, and had six children: Jacob, Nicholas, Daniel, Peter, Catherine (married to John Brillinger) and Elizabeth, who married Henry King. The father of our subject, Jacob Diehl, married Polly Pflieger, both being natives of Hellam Township. Our subject, Daniel Diehl, was married May 15, 1836, to Miss Louisa Loucks, a daughter of Casper Loucks, of Spring Garden Township. Six children have been born to them: Malinda Kauffman, Cecelia Witmer, Adaline, Milton (deceased), Marcellus and Nicholas. Mr. Diehl was actively engaged in farming all his life, but is now passing the evening of his life retired from active labors. He is now seventy-seven years of age, and residing in Frystown. His wife died several years ago. Mr. Diehl owns a mill property in Spring Garden, situated upon an old site, the second mill being built there in 1775, and the third built by himself in 1860. He also owns a well-improved farm of 110 acres, which is operated by his son, Nicholas. The family are members of the Lutheran Church.

BENJAMIN S. DIETZ, son of George and Catherine (Hammer) Dietz, of Spring Garden Township, was born September 21, 1831. He is the fourth of a family of five children, was reared on a farm and has always followed farming. In December, 1853, Mr. Dietz married Lydia Kauffman, daughter of Samuel and Mary (Wagner) Kauffman, of Windsor Township. Six children (all deceased) were born to this marriage: Uriah K., David K., Mary K., Samuel K., George K. and Benjamin K. Mr. Dietz is a prominent farmer, having managed one of the largest farms in Windsor Township. Hattie D. Kauffman, daughter of Moses and Sarah Kauffman, of Spring Garden Township, was taken to rear by Mr. and Mrs. Dietz, when she was two weeks old, and lived with them until her death in 1880, being in her seventh year; she was treated as kindly and tenderly by Mr. and Mrs. Dietz as if she were their own child. Mr D. has been school director and assessor in Windsor Township, and was always a leading citizen of that township during his residence there.

JOSEPH S. DIETZ was born in Spring Garden Township in 1843. His parents, Joseph and Elizabeth (Strickler) Dietz, were natives of Hellam Township, and represent old families of York County. The father is a farmer, and a resident of Spring Garden Township. The mother died in 1864. Joseph S. was reared a farmer, and is still following that vocation. He resides upon the farm owned by his father, which he is cultivating, and also owns a farm in Hopewell Township, consisting of 108 acres. He was married in November, 1866, to Miss Sarah Weigle, daughter of John Weigle, of Manchester Township. This union has been blessed with eleven children: Augustus H., Ida A. (deceased), Joseph M. (deceased), Winfield H., Curtis A., Lilly M., Daniel M. (deceased), Mary E. (deceased), Agnes A. (deceased), Herman W. (deceased), and Erney A. Mr. and Mrs. Dietz are members of the Lutheran denomination.

ELIAS EBERT, a prominent citizen of Spring Garden Township, was born in York County, October 25, 1829, and is the second son of Michael and Lydia (Diehl) Ebert, natives of York County. His great-grandfather came from Germany and settled in West Manchester, where his grandfather was born. His father was a farmer in West Manchester, and a colonel in the war of 1812, which title he always retained. He came to Spring Garden in 1829, and located on the farm now owned and occupied by Elias Ebert, and resided on it until his death in 1863. The mother died in 1858, leaving five children: William (deceased), Sarah, George D., Annie M. and Elias, our subject. Elias was born on the homestead, and has resided on it all his life, following farming and also keeping a dairy. The farm contains 210 acres, and sixty-three acres are owned by his son. In 1853 he was married to Susan Butt, daughter of Jacob Butt, of Jackson Township, an old settler of York County, who died in 1884, aged eighty-four years. Mr. and Mrs. Ebert have three children: Albert M., Annie F. and Ida V. Mr. Ebert is president of the Spring Garden Mutual Fire Insurance Company, and has been connected with it for twenty years. He is a prominent agriculturist, and was one of the managers of the York County Agricultural Society for five years. Himself and wife are members of Mt. Zion Lutheran Church. Mr. Ebert is one of the representative and progressive citizens of York County. As a business man he has attained an honorable reputation, and as a citizen and neighbor he is highly respected and esteemed.

JOHN EMIG was born in 1831, in York County, Penn., and is a son of Valentine and Rebecca (Loucks) Emig, both natives of York County, and descendants of old families. His father was a farmer and our subject was reared a farmer and has devoted his entire time and energy to farming. Mr. Emig came to Spring Garden Township in 1854, and purchased the farm upon which he has ever since resided. It consists of 126 acres of land situated in the Codorus Valley. This tract of land he has greatly improved, raising all the cereals, and a large crop of fine tobacco each year. He was married, in 1853, to Miss Sarah Eyster, a native of West Manchester Township, and a descendant of an old family of the county. She died in 1857. Two children were born to them: Horace E., a farmer in York County; and Frank, deceased. In 1858 Mr. Emig married Miss Susan Roth. They have had nine children: Margaret R., Emma R., Edward R., Augustus R., Henry R., Valentine R., William R., George R. and Amanda (deceased). Mr. and Mrs. Emig are members of Mt. Zion German Reformed Church.

HENRY ERB is a native of York County, born in 1831, and resides on the same farm upon which his grandfather, John Erb, settled in the early history of York County. John Erb was a native of Lancaster County, Penn., and a prominent farmer of York County, from his first settlement here until his death upon the same farm, which descended to his son Jacob, the father of our subject. Jacob Erb married Miss Elizabeth Wambaugh, and followed farming on the homestead farm until his death. His wife, a descendant of one of the old settlers of the county, still survives and resides upon the old place. Three of their children are living: Henry, Mrs. Mary Wise and Mrs. Leah Gable, of York Township. Henry Erb has always been engaged in agricultural pursuits; he became the owner of the old homestead, which comprises over 170 acres of superior land, in 1879. This farm is one of the most productive and finely improved tracts of land in the county, with as fine a residence and bank barns as any in the township. Mr. Erb was married October 5, 1857, to Miss Mary Driver, a native of Spring Garden Township, and daughter of Jacob Driver. They have four children: Granville, Jacob, Clara A. and Mary A.

JOHN FLORY, one of the old settlers of Spring Garden Township, was born August 18, 1818, a son of Abraham and Magdalena (Strickler) Flory. He has been one of the leading farmers of York County and has resided the principal portion of his life in Spring Garden Township, where he has followed milling and farming. He owns a fine farm of 178 acres in Manchester Township, and thirty acres in Spring Garden Township, where he resides, and which is cultivated for market produce. Mr. Flory served as assessor and supervisor several years, has acted as guardian for twenty-one children, and has settled up four estates, real and personal. In 1841 he married Miss Leah Diehl, a daughter of Jacob Diehl, of Spring Garden. They are the parents of six children: Thaddeus E., married Mary Kauffman; Abraham, married Amanda Smyser; Sarah, married Frederick Dietz; Killam J.; William A. and Amelia (married to Henry Forry). Mr. and Mrs. Flory are members of the Lutheran Church.

RUDOLPH FORRY was born in Hellam Township, York Co., Penn., October 18, 1827. His parents, Henry and Magdalena (Newcomer) Forry, were also natives of York County. His father died in 1836. Mr. Forry has been a resident of Spring Garden Township for forty-seven years. He owns 110 acres of land finely improved, and all under cultivation. He has always taken a leading position in public affairs, and has served as school director and supervisor. Mr. Forry was married, in 1849, to Miss Angelina Strickler, daughter of Ulrich Strickler, a prominent citizen of Spring Garden Township, who died in 1882, aged fifty-two years. Mr. and Mrs. F. have had six children, five now living: Lavina S., married to Nicholas Diehl; Henry S., married to Amelia Flory; Rudolph L., Angelina S.; Mary S., married to John Throne (all residents of the township), and Ulrich S., deceased.

WILLIAM FREY was born February 7, 1834, a son of George and Mary (Spangler) Frey. His grandfather, George Frey, a native of Spring Garden Township, died of apoplexy in 1849, aged sixty-eight years. He was a veteran of the war of 1812; served in Capt. Spangler's company; marched from York to Baltimore, and engaged in the battle of North Point, his wife becoming a pensioner until her death in 1872, at the age of ninety-two years. They had seven children: Charles, George, Frederick, Enos, Catherine, Mary and Leah. Subject's father, George Frey, was a captain of militia some years, and private in a company of Independent Blues, under Col. Alex Hay, at the Catholic and Native American riots, in Philadelphia, in 1844; also a private in the Second Maryland Regiment in the civil war of 1862-65; he died in 1882 of apoplexy, aged seventy-two years. He had five children: William, John, Charles, Lewis, and Eliza. William Frey was married, December 24, 1854, to Elizabeth Boekel, daughter of Michael and Anna Maria Boekel. By this union they have had the following children: William B., Flora M. Rouse, Ferdinand C., Emma E. Christine, George T., Katie, Anna M., Robert E., Mollie E., Hattie M. and Harry S. Mr. Frey is the pioneer of the Spring Garden Band, starting in 1855, and held the leadership over twenty-three years. He took the band into the United States service, and it served one year as regimental band of the Eighty-seventh Pennsylvania Volunteers. He also held the office of treasurer of York County, having been elected in 1876, and having served three years. He is the owner of forty-nine acres of finely improved land, and raises vegetables, fruit, etc., for market. He makes a specialty of bee culture. The family are members of the German Reformed Church.

JOHN FRITZ, deceased, was born in 1805, and was a son of John and Elizabeth (Kurtz) Fritz, both natives of York County, Penn. He was reared a farmer, and passed his life engaged in farming. He died in 1863, aged fifty-eight years. He married Miss Susanna Billit, September 25, 1834. Mrs. Fritz is a daughter of Jacob Billit, of Spring Garden Township, and was born January 29, 1818; she is still living on her farm in Spring Garden, which consists of 111 acres of valuable land, from which iron ore has been extracted since 1866, but which has been lately closed. The farm is now operated by her sons. Mrs. Fritz has eight children: Sarah (Kauffman), born April 16, 1836; Henry, March 2, 1839; Catherine (Coldrider), September 28, 1841; Samuel, October 8, 1844; John, November 15, 1847; George, February 13, 1851; Susan (Shenberger), April 18, 1853; and Elizabeth, born April 13, 1861, all natives of York County, Penn. The family are members of Mt. Zion Lutheran Church.

CHARLES H. FRY, justice of the peace, is one of a family of thirteen children, and was born on a farm near what is now known as Frysville, then Fry's Church, in Windsor Township, York Co., Penn., September 20, 1833. The father, John Fry, was born near the place where all his children were born. The mother's name was Juliann (Haines) Fry, who was of English descent, and was born in Philadelphia. Charles H. worked on the farm in summer, and had about three or four months to go to school in winter. When old enough he learned the carpenter's trade, but not liking it, worked at his trade in summer and attended school in winter, until he was able to teach a primary school. The money he made teaching in winter, he took to pay his tuition in summer, at a select school at Wrightsville, Penn., for one term. The following winter he taught school again, and in the spring, entered the York County Academy, taught by the late Prof. George W. Ruby, and D. M. Ettinger, for one term. This completed his schooling, except lessons in surveying, by D. M. Ettinger, civil engineer. Mr. Fry was appointed postmaster, at Margaretta Furnace, in 1861, which office he held during the greater part of the late war. The office was removed from Margaretta Furnace to East Prospect, where it is at present. Mr. Fry resigned the office, and some time afterward moved to Spring Garden, where he accepted the secretaryship of the Spring Garden Mutual Fire Insurance Company, which he has held up to the present time—about twenty years. He was elected a justice of the peace of Spring Garden Township in 1866, and re-elected three times, holding the office at the present time. He was elected county surveyor of York County last fall. Mr. Fry was instrumental in getting up one of the first building associations (now one of the largest in the county), about eighteen years ago, and has been secretary of the same ever since. He was married at York, Penn., January 5, 1858, to Catherine Fitzkee. They have had eleven children, three of whom are dead, four boys and four girls living. Mr. and Mrs. Fry are members of the Ridge Avenue Church (Methodist Episcopal). Their residence is corner of East Market Street and Ridge Avenue, East York.

JOHN S. GEIST, was born October 13, 1834. His parents, Baltzer and Anna M. (More) Geist, were natives of Germany, and immigrated to America over fifty years ago. They located in Lower Windsor Township, where the father was employed

SPRING GARDEN TOWNSHIP.

as a teamster at the Slaymaker Furnaces for six years, and then had charge of a furnace until the failure of the Slaymaker firm, in which he lost heavily. The mother of our subject died in 1837, leaving three children: Mary M., Elizabeth and John S. His father subsequently married Miss Maria Hains, a native of York County, Penn. John S. has a fine farm of sixty-five acres, located in Spring Garden Township, which is well cultivated and improved. He was married, February 5, 1856, to Miss Harriet Wolf, a daughter of Peter and Catherine Wolf, of Hellam Township. By this union they have had six children: Henry, married to Mary J. Smith; Aaron A., married to Sarah Bender; Sarah A., wife of Granville Forry; Anna M.; William H. and George W. (deceased). The family are members of the Evangelical Lutheran and Mennonite denominations.

CHARLES GLATFELTER is a retired farmer of Spring Garden Township, and a descendant of two old families of York County. His great-grandfather was a native of Switzerland. Subject's grandparents, Phelix Glatfelter and wife, were natives of York County, and parents of nine children—Jacob, Casper, John, Daniel, Frederick, Philip, Elizabeth, Margaret and Barbara—all natives of North Codorus Township. The father of our subject, Philip Glatfelter, married Mary Emig, daughter of Charles Emig, and also a native of North Codorus Township. Eleven children blessed this union: Jonas, Charles, Jacob, Philip, Jesse, Lydia, Catherine, Margaret, Leah, Elizabeth and Mary. Our subject was married, in January, 1833, to Miss Louisa Fishel, a daughter of Jacob Fishel, of Spring Garden Township. This union has been blessed with eight children: Jacob, Philip H., Edward, Clementine Shunk, Jane Peeters, Anna M. Myers, Louisa Eyster and Emma E. Forry. Mr. Glatfelter has been a resident of the township about forty-five years. He still owns ninety-five acres of well-improved land. His wife is deceased. Mr. Glatfelter is a member of the Lutheran Church.

DANIEL GOTWALT, a representative of two old families of York County, Penn., is a son of Felix and Christiana (Wilt) Gotwalt, natives of York County. He was born in Manchester Township, September 24, 1796, and at the age of eighteen began learning the carpenter's trade, with Peter Small, of York. This occupation he followed until he was thirty-five years of age, when he began farming in Spring Garden Township, which business he continued until old age compelled him to cease hard labor, and he is now living in retirement upon his land in that township. Mr. Gotwalt has a fine property, well improved. He was married in December, 1819, to Miss Susanna Rupp, of York County. By this union thirteen children were born, of whom the following are living: George F., Samuel, Daniel, David R., Benjamin, John J., Mary and Susanna, all married. Mr. Gotwalt has been a member of the Lutheran Church, of York (Rev. Dr. Lockman's), over sixty-eight years, and has been elder for six years.

HENRY F. W. GROTHE is a native of Germany, born April 27, 1829. His parents were also natives of Germany, where his father followed the tailor trade all his life. At the age of twenty-five years our subject immigrated to America, landing in the fall of 1855, and immediately locating in York County, Penn. In 1858 he began the business of lime-burning, and in 1859 added to it brick-making. In this business Mr. Grothe has continued up to the present time, and has established an extensive trade. His brick-yard, kilns and residence are located on the plank road, upon the limits of York Borough. In February, 1855, he was married to Miss Willmana Hitecomp, a native of Germany. They have nine children, six living: Charles H., Anna M., Louisa W., Henry F. W., Frank H. and Anna M. L. Mr. and Mrs. Grothe are members of the St. John's Lutheran Church of York, Penn. Mr. Grothe has served for nine years as trustee of his church.

HENRY S. HEINDLE was born in Spring Garden Township, April 2, 1849. His parents, Peter and Leah (Spangler) Heindle, are also natives of York County, Penn., and descendants of an old family. Henry learned the blacksmith's trade with his brother, Edward, and has since followed that occupation. He began business for himself at Stoney Brook, Penn., subsequently purchasing the shop there, where he has remained and established a good business. He has devoted his entire time and attention to his trade, and is a skillful and efficient mechanic. Mr. Heindle was married in 1879 to Miss Susan, daughter of George and Susan Miller, of York County, Penn. They have five children: Emma J., Harvey H., Verley V., Gertie S. and Leah R. Mrs. Heindle is a member of the Lutheran Church.

JOHN S. HIESTAND was born in Spring Garden Township, in May, 1837. His parents, John and Elizabeth (Sultzbaugh) Hiestand, were also natives of York County, Penn. Subject was reared on the farm, attended the common schools and supplemented his education by a regular course at the York Academy. Mr. Hiestand has always followed farming, and is the owner of part of the old homestead farm in Spring Garden Township, two and a half miles from York on the pike. This farm is in a high state of cultivation, with an elegant residence, and fine barns and out-buildings. He has served in various offices of public trust; he was register of wills three years, and director upon the school board fifteen years. He is a member of the order of Heptasophs. Mr. Hiestand, in November, 1857, was married to Miss Annie M., daughter of Philip and Mary (Gish) Oldweiler. This union has been blessed with two children: Thomas B. G. and Katie. The grandfather of the subject of this sketch, Abraham Hiestand, came to York County in the year 1792, and first settled where Spring Grove now is. Then moved to the old homestead, the place now known as Hiestand's, in Spring Garden Township. He had married Miss Fitz, from near Wrightsville, when he first came to this county. They had eight children. He lived to the age of eighty-eight years, seeing many great-grandchildren before he died, in the year 1859. The Hiestands are of Swiss extraction, the ancestor here having come over in 1727. [See II Col. Rec. or Rupp's History of Lancaster County.]

SAMUEL HIVELY was born August 12, 1817, a son of George and Anna M. (Roth) Hively, both natives of Spring Garden Township. The grandfather of our subject, Christopher Hively, emigrated from York County, Penn., to Ohio, where he settled. He had seven children. George Hively returned from Ohio in 1813, and located in Spring Garden Township. He had three children: Samuel, John and Susanna (deceased). Samuel Hively, our subject, has now retired from active labors, but still retains two valuable farms, one consisting of 125 acres, operated by his son William, and one of 123 acres, farmed by his son Enos. His land is well tilled and supplied with all modern improvements. Mr. Hively has served his township and county in public offices of trust. He was director of the poor three years, and assessor and collector of taxes. He was married, in January, 1839, to Miss Sarah Miller, daughter of Christian and Elizabeth Miller, of Spring Garden Township. This union has been blessed with four children: George S., William C., Enos F. and Sarah J. Miller (deceased). The family are members of the Lutheran Church.

GEORGE HYDE was born January 15, 1838,

and is a son of Joshua and Lucinda (Weyer) Hyde, natives of Spring Garden Township. His grandfather, George Hyde, was a native of Lancaster County, Penn., and had seven children: Henry, Samuel, Jacob, Joshua, George, Nancy and John. Joshua Hyde, subject's father, had born to him the following children: Margaret, Lizzie, Sarah, Matilda, George and Daniel. George Hyde, our subject, was married in November, 1862, to Sarah A. Dorsch, daughter of George Dorsch, of West Manchester Township. They have had three children: Sallie A., George J. and Lucy (deceased). He has a farm of 162 acres, well improved, with two fine dwellings and two bank barns. He was drafted in 1863, and paid commutation. He was formerly a member of the Grangers. His family are members of the Reformed Church.

WILLIAM ILGENFRITZ, son of Martin and Margaret (Stauffer) Ilgenfritz, of Manchester Township, was born in Conewago Township, November 14, 1842. He is the fourth in a family of seven children. September 11, 1861, Mr. Ilgenfritz enlisted in Company E, Eighty-seventh Pennsylvania Volunteers, and was engaged in the battles that his regiment was in: the skirmishes at Fisher's Hill, April 28, 1863; Newtown, Va., June 12, 1863; Winchester, June 13; Carter's Woods, June 15; Locust Grove, November 27; also at Coal Harbor, Petersburgh and Bermuda Hundred; on the 6th of July, 1864, he came to the Shenandoah Valley; 9th of July, was in the battle of Monocacy; at the battle of Opequan, September 19, 1864; battle of Fisher's Hill, and at Cedar Creek, October 19, and was honorably discharged at Chester Hospital, Penn. February 11, 1869, Mr. Ilgenfritz married Eliza Boyer, daughter of Jonas and Huldah (Kline) Boyer, of Newberry Township. Seven children have blessed this marriage: Annie, Katie (deceased), Ellen, Martha, Elmer, Nettie and Harry. Mr. Ilgenfritz is a member of Post 37, G. A. R. of York, Penn. He has charge of the first toll gate on the Baltimore pike.

BENJAMIN KISSINGER is engaged extensively in brick-making in Spring Garden Township, adjoining the limits of York Borough. He is a descendant of two old families of the county. The Kissingers began the manufacture of brick in York County, over 100 years ago, the business being started by the grandfather and subsequently continued by the father of our subject. They were among the first to engage in this business in the county, and were residents of Spring Garden Township, where Benjamin was born in 1832. He is a son of William and Rosanna (Swartz) Kissinger, who were natives of this township. At the age of fourteen, Benjamin began learning the brick-making business, and has devoted his time and energies to that occupation up to the present time. He operates from ten to fifteen men during the season, has superior resources and produces goods second to none. Mr. Kissinger is also successfully engaged in the coal business under the firm name of Kissinger & Keller. April 15, 1853, he married Miss Caroline Adams. By this union eight children have been born: Louisa, Belle, Emma J., John F., Savilla, Howard A., Stewart H. and Carrie S. Mr. and Mrs. Kissinger are members of Christs' Lutheran Church, of which he is an elder. Mr. Kissinger is a member of the order of Red Men, No. 37 of York County.

FREDERICK KLEFFMAN is a native of Germany, born March 29, 1833. His parents, Christian and Mary Kleffman, were also natives of Germany. His father followed the trade of carpenter. When nineteen years of age, Frederick immigrated to America in 1852, and for four years was variously employed. By industry and economy he saved $300, with which he embarked in his present business—brick-making and lime-burning. By close application to business he has succeeded in building up an independent trade. His works are situated in East York. In the fall of 1856 he was married to Miss Charlotte, daughter of William H. Hitecomp. This marriage has been blessed with eight children—five now living: Frederick, Mary, Emma, Lizzie and Nettie. Mr. and Mr. Kleffman are members of St. John's Reformed Church. He served as one of the trustees of that denomination over two years.

GOTTLIEB KLEFMANN is a native of Germany, born December 12, 1835, and is the son of Christian and Mary (Stallman) Klefmann. He worked upon a farm in his native country until he was eighteen years of age, when he immigrated to America and came to York County, where he engaged in lime-burning, farming, etc., until 1870, when he began the brick-making business. Mr Klefmann has succeeded in establishing a large and lucrative business. His brick-yard is situated just outside of York Borough. April 7, 1859, he was married to Miss Louisa Spangler, daughter of Harmon Spangler. Her parents were natives of Germany. Mr. and Mrs. K. have had nine children—two now living: John E. and Edward H. They are members of the United Brethren Church.

JOHN LEFEVER was born in November, 1819, upon the old homestead farm, in Spring Garden Township. This farm was purchased by his grandfather Jacob. Upon this farm our subject has resided since his birth, with the exception of fourteen years that he spent upon the old Daniel Loucks' farm, in Spring Garden Township. The house upon the old homestead farm, where he now resides, is about one hundred and seven years old. Mr. Lefever was married, in 1843, to Miss Catherine Rhinehart, daughter of John Rhinehart, of York County, Penn. Nine children have blessed this union: Phares, Lizzie, Susan, John, William, George, Daniel, Agnes and Kate. Mr. Lefever has been for many years an active member of the German Reformed Church.

PETER LINT is a representative of two old families, who were among the earliest settlers of York County. His grandfather, Peter Lint, came from one of the Carolinas to York County, Penn., at an early day, and settled in West Manchester Township, where the father of our subject, Peter Lint, was a farmer, and resided until his death. Our subject is the eldest of a family of three children, and was born in 1826. He was reared a farmer, and to farming together with fruit culture he has devoted the energies of his life. In 1850 he became a resident of Spring Garden Township, where he has lived ever since. Mr. Lint is the possessor of 140 acres of finely improved land, and devotes much care and attention to fruit culture with gratifying results. In 1852 he married Miss Leah Eyster, of Paradise Township, whose parents were old settlers of the county. She died in 1864. Five children were born to them: Peter F., George E. and Christopher C. (now in the West). Jennie E. and Christianna E. Mr. Lint is a member of Mt. Zion Lutheran Church.

ALBERT LOUCKS was born October 31, 1850, in Frystown, Penn. His father, Daniel Loucks, deceased) was born in Berks County, Penn., and came with his parents to York County when nine years old, where he became a successful farmer and resided until he died. He was twice married; first in 1824, to Miss Margaret Diehl, daughter of Nicholas Diehl, of York County. Four children blessed this union: Elizabeth, Anna M., Susan and Rebecca. His second marriage was, October 20, 1837, to Miss Elizabeth Diehl, a daughter of Jacob Diehl. By this union, seven children were born: Sarah, George, Amanda, William H., Alexander N., Eliza

SPRING GARDEN TOWNSHIP.

A. and Albert. Our subject has retired from farming and is a resident of Frystown. He owns a good farm of 105 acres, in the township, which is tilled by a tenant. Mr. Loucks was married, October 16, 1877, to Miss Anna J. Miller, a daughter of Jacob Miller, of Shrewsbury. They have had four children: Arthur C., Albert D., Edwin M. and Clair M. Mr. Loucks' religious faith is the Trinity Reformed.

REUBEN F. MINNICH, youngest son of Simon and Lena (Geiskman) Minnich, was born in April, 1824, at the homestead in Spring Garden Township, which homestead has been in the possession of the Minnich family over 135 years. The children born to the parents of our subject were: George (deceased), Henrietta (deceased), Simon (deceased), Lena, Susan and Reuben F. Our subject was reared to farm life on the home farm, which was purchased by his grandfather about 1750, from Michael Kurtz. The old stone house on the place was built in 1722, by Michael Kurtz. November 25, 1851, Mr. Minnich married Elizabeth, daughter of Zacharias Spangler, of Jackson Township, and to this union were born the following children: Edwin, Emma J., Agnes (deceased), Leander, Ezra, Priscilla (deceased), Simon (deceased), and Flora B. and Rosella (twins). Mr. Minnich is owner of three good farms, and is a prosperous agriculturist.

JOHN MYERS was born March 18, 1807, a son of Jacob and Elizabeth (Cookes) Myers, the former a native of Lancaster County, the latter of York County, Penn. Jacob Myers died at the age of sixty-six years. He had two children, Rebecca and John. Our subject has always followed farming, but now has retired from active life. The homestead where he resides comprises 125 acres of land, well improved. He also owns a farm of eighty-five acres in York Township, and one of 105 acres in Spring Garden Township, both well improved. His farms are worked by tenants. Mr. Myers was married, September 6, 1826, to Miss Leah Laucks, daughter of Casper Laucks, and by this union they had seven children. Mr. Myers lost his wife and four children within three months, his wife dying in 1862. He is a member of the Lutheran Church.

JAMES PEELING was born in this county, May 1, 1820. His grandfather emigrated from Ireland to America before the Revolutionary war, in which he served seven years, during which time he was once taken prisoner by the Hessians, but soon after exchanged. He died, aged eighty-six years, leaving seven children: James, John, Robert, Mary, Betsey, Isaac and Thomas. The parents of our subject were James and Ellen (Parker) Peeling, both natives of Lancaster County, Penn. They had thirteen children, nine of whom are living, and all natives of York County, Penn.: John, Eliza, James, Mary, Harriet, Josiah, Rebecca, Lucinda and Joshua. James Peeling, our subject, who owns a farm of 188 acres located in West Manchester and Conewago Townships, which is under good cultivation and finely improved with buildings, also a well-improved farm of eighty-five acres in York Township, and he resides upon the homestead in Spring Garden Township. He has his land tenanted, but exercises general supervision. He was elected sheriff of York in 1877, and served until 1880. While a resident of York Township he filled several minor offices. In 1840 Mr. Peeling was married to Miss Mary Inerst, of York Township. They have had eight children, seven of whom are now living: Sarah Krebs, Eliza McDowell, Ellen Cameron, Isabella Egie, Mary Garrity, James (married to Jane Dick) and Rebecca. Upon the death of his first wife, Mr. Peeling married Miss Dorcas A. Leib, in 1863. Of their children, seven are now living: Lucinda, Joshua, Alpharetta, Ida, Martha, Horace and Henry L.

ABRAHAM PFEIFFER (deceased) was a native of Bavaria, Germany, and came to this country in 1853. After a year's residence in Baltimore he came to York, lived in Queen Street, and then removed to the home where his widow now resides on the Baltimore pike. Mr. Pfeiffer married Elizabeth, daughter of Michael and Sarah (Rost) Ruppecht, of Bavaria. Three children were born to them: Charles A., John F. and William H. Mr. Pfeiffer engaged in the brewing business, and built his brewery in 1860, selling to York and surrounding towns. He died about two years ago. His widow is still carrying on the business. John F. learned his trade of carpenter with Jacob Sechrist, of York. Having served his time he still works for Mr. Sechrist. Charles A. learned his trade, machinist, with George F. Baugher, and is still in the employ of Baugher, Kurtz & Stewart, successors to George F. Baugher. The youngest brother, William H., has divided his time between attending school in this township and assisting his mother in the business at home. Mrs. Pfeiffer has good reason to be proud of her sons, as they are steady, industrious young men.

ISAAC RUNK was born December 3, 1829, and is a son of John and Lydia Runk. He embarked in business at Frystown, in 1854, and has continued there up to the present time. He carries a well selected line of dry goods and groceries, and has established a good business. Mr. Runk is one of the prominent citizens of the township, and is the present auditor. He is a member of the Spring Garden Relief Association. In January, 1855, he married Miss Eliza Fry, daughter of George and Mary (Spangler) Fry. By this union there were born five children: Emma F., deceased, Adda L., Mary A., Irena A. and Cora A.

CHARLES G. SCHASZBERGER was born June 22, 1818, and is the son of John Frederick and Mary C. (Gross) Schaszberger. Mr. Schaszberger is by trade a wheelwright, and a resident of East York. He owns a tract of six acres of fine land in Spring Garden Township, and three fine dwelling houses at Frystown. He has served as school director several years. He was married, September 10, 1840, to Miss Ruth A. Armour, of Carlisle, Penn. They have been blessed with seven children, four of whom are living: Edward F., who married Amanda Myers; Louisa A., wife of Francis W. Armor; Levena S., and Katie S., wife of Russell Hollebaugh. The family are of the Lutheran Church.

GEORGE W. SCHEFFER is a native of Spring Garden Township, born at Frystown, March 4, 1843. He learned the milling business when young, and followed it in York County for fifteen years. He next engaged in the dry goods and grocery business at Frystown, where he is at present located. Mr. Sheffer was appointed postmaster at Frystown, July 1, 1882, which office is known at present as East York. He has always been prominent in religious and local affairs, and has been warden of the St. Mark's Lutheran Church, of which he is a member. He is at present president of the Spring Garden Relief Association, and a trustee of the Goodwill Fire Company, of East York. September 7, 1862, he married Miss Anna Wallick, of York County.

URIAH S. SHAEFFER, youngest of five children of John and Christianna (Leibenstein) Shaeffer, was born September 10, 1824, in York Township. He went to his trade (miller) in 1843, at the mill now owned by Frank Deitz, on the Baltimore pike, about four miles from York. August 29, 1852, he married Margaret C. Shank, daughter of John and Mary (Busser) Shank, of Spring Garden Township. This marriage was blessed with five children: Mary Ann, Barbara E., John C. (deceased), William Henry and George Latimer. Mr. Shaeffer was in the employ of P. A. & S. Small, for twenty-seven years,

BIOGRAPHICAL SKETCHES.

twenty-six years at the Spring Garden Mill. Mr. Shaeffer's grandfather, John Jacob Shaeffer, was born December 22, 1761. January 4, 1785, married Dorathy Walter. She was born September 20, 1761. Their son (subject's father) John Shaeffer, was born July 13, 1786, and died October 2, 1835, aged forty-nine years, two months, nine days. His wife, Christianna Shaeffer, was born in York Township, September 1, 1790, and died August 1, 1880, aged eighty-nine years and eleven months.

JACOB B. SHANK, son of John and Mary A. (Buser) Shank, was born in Spring Garden Township, June 3, 1832. He learned his trade (miller) at Philip Shaeffer's, Glen Rock. He then went to Loucks' in 1856, and has been at this mill ever since, having charge of it for P. A. & S. Small. December 4, 1859, Mr. Shank married Mary A. Landis, daughter of Benjamin and Elizabeth (Klincfelter) Landis. Two children were born to them: Agnes A. and Henry J. (deceased). Our subject's grandfather was George Shank. His grandmother was Margaret Brown. Mr. Shank says his great-grandmother cooked for the soldiers in the war of the Revolution during their stay in York, and that his great-grandfather was a soldier in that war. Mr. Shank is a member of the Moravian Church.

WILLIAM H. SHEFFER, is a son of Uriah S. Sheffer, of York County, Penn., and was born April 5, 1858, in Spring Garden Township. His father was a miller by trade, and our subject learned the business under his instruction. William H. assisted his father in conducting the Spring Garden Mills for several years, and assumed the management of P. A. & S. Small's mill in Spring Garden Township, in 1884. He thoroughly understands his business, and is doing a large amount of work. Mr. Sheffer was married, March 4, 1884, to Miss Mary Stacks, daughter of Abraham Stacks, of York County. March 29, 1885, Mr. Sheffer's name was entered on the record of the Moravian Church of York, Rev. E. W. Shields, pastor.

SAMUEL D. SHELLENBERGER, was born March 30, 1832, a son of Michael and Lydia (Strickler) Shellenberger. His great-grandfather emigrated from Germany and settled in Berks County, Penn. There the grandfather of our subject was born. He subsequently settled in Hellam Township, and was the father of sixteen children. Samuel D. is the seventh of a family of eleven children: John (deceased), Michael, Elizabeth, John, Jacob, Lydia S., Samuel D., Ulrich, Benjamin S., David and Sarah. He was married to Miss Sarah J. Gallatin, January 18, 1857; she is the daughter of Albert Gallatin, of York Township. This union has been blessed with eight children: Laura J. Snyder, Samuel D. Jr., Robert L., Jacob M., John A., James B., Joseph and Sarah L. (deceased). Mr Shellenberger first followed the tinner's trade, but is now manufacturing cigars. He has a fine residence, located in the village of Green Hill, where he has ten acres of land, upon which he has erected fifteen fine dwellings. The family are members of the Evangelical Church.

HENRY SLEEGER was born in York, Penn., December, 6, 1824. In 1844 he was apprenticed to the cabinet-maker's trade, with Samuel Fahs, and after serving three years, and becoming a skilled mechanic, engaged in business for himself, establishing a cabinet shop at Frystown, in 1848. This, together with, the undertaking business, Mr. Sleeger has continued up to the present time, having succeeded in establishing a successful business. Mr. Sleeger has taken an active part in all township affairs, has served as school director of Spring Garden, for six years, and is a member of the Township Relief Association. He is a member of the I. O. O. F., and of the Christ's Lutheran Church. Mr. Sleeger was married in December, 1852, to Miss Anna Myers, daughter of Jacob and Elizabeth Myers, of York. They have had ten children, two of whom are dead, and four boys and four girls are living.

JOSEPH SLENKER was born February 4, 1830, and is a son of Joseph and Catherine (Tschorp) Slenker, natives of York County, Penn. His grandparents, Martin and Franey (Leahmy) Slenker, were natives of Windsor Township, and parents of four children, the father of our subject being the only son. Joseph, our subject, is the second child in a family of six boys and two girls, all of whom are natives of Windsor Township; Lydia, Joseph, Martin, Henry, John, Rebecca, Jacob and Isaac. Joseph followed farming nineteen years, and worked at the carpenter trade about the same length of time. He is now engaged in the ice business. He has served in various township offices. Mr. Slenker was twice married; his first marriage was in October, 1853, to Miss Caroline Seachrist, a daughter of Henry Seachrist, of York Township. She died February 6, 1880. They have had fifteen children, of whom eleven are living: Emeline Keesey, Benjamin F., Reuben H., Rebecca J. Richcreek, Moses, Lydia A. Seitz, Anna M. Sweitzer, David, Ida E., John W., Charles A. October 9, 1882, Mr. Slenker was married to his second wife, Miss Carrie Erving, daughter of Henry Erving, of Conewago Township, York County, Penn.

HENRY SMYSER is a native of York County, Penn., born in 1812, and is a son of Michael and Mary (Wolf) Smyser, natives of York County, Penn. His father was a farmer and tavern-keeper. Henry was reared on a farm, and, in 1845, came to Spring Garden Township, locating on the farm where he now resides. The homestead contains 170 acres, finely located on the banks of the Codorus, and he also owns 200 acres in Manchester Township, and another farm of 100 acres in Spring Garden Township. Mr. Smyser has retired from active life, and his sons now manage his farms. An iron mine, which has produced a large amount of ore, was opened on the old farm, and is operated by P. A. & S. Small. Mr. Smyser was married, in 1844, to Miss Mary Emig, native of York County, Penn. By this union they have been blessed with five children: Michael, now working the farm in Manchester Township; Horace, now working the home farm; Alexander, in Kansas; Jacob, deceased, and Amanda Flora, living in Lancaster County, Penn. Mr. Smyser is a member of the Lutheran Church, and his wife is a member of the Presbyterian Church.

FREDERICK Z. STAUFFER was born April 24, 1857. His father, Rev. Frederick Stauffer, was a minister in the Mennonite Church, and bishop of the diocese of York County, Penn. He was a resident of Windsor Township at the time of his death. Our subject was a school teacher from 1876 to 1882, when he assumed the management of the Plank Road Mills, two miles east of York, which he is still successfully conducting. Mr. Stauffer was married to Miss Mollie M. Dosch, daughter of John C. and Charlotte Dosch, old settlers of York County. To this union have been born two children: Guy Carlton and Blanche Estella.

WILLIAM A. TOMES was born July 7, 1829, son of Peter and Sarah (Keesey) Tomes, who were the parents of eight children: John, William A., Peter, Margaret, Mary, Sarah, Marcellus and Arabella. His grandfather emigrated from Germany and settled at Cornwall Furnace, afterward moving to Colebrook Furnace, Penn. He had six children: Peter, William, John, Elizabeth, Charlotte and Henrietta. Mr. Tomes is superintendent of the York Variety Iron Works. This establishment is the most widely known of its kind in this country, and sends its productions to many foreign countries, as well as throughout America. This house supplied the ornamental work for the great New York and

Brooklyn Bridge, and the Market Street Bridge, Philadelphia, besides many other important structures throughout the country. They make a specialty of statuary. Mr. Tomes was married, November 20, 1851, to Miss Mary A. Cook, daughter of Frederick B. and Harriet C. Cook. By this union they have been blessed with ten children: Charles C., Henry A., Francis, Camelia, Edward, Peter, Albert, William, Clara and Mary E. He was drafted in 1863, but procured a substitute for $300. He has a fine three-story brick house and a lot in East York, Penn.

JACOB WEIDMAN was born September 2, 1830. The ancestry of Mr. Weidman can be traced back to Martin Weidman, who emigrated from Germany to America in 1733. He received a patent from William Penn for 385 acres of land in Lancaster County, where he was one of the pioneer settlers. He had two sons, Christopher and Jacob, and one daughter. Jacob was married to Barbara Hoover, and bore him ten children: George, Christopher, Martin, John, Jacob, Samuel, Peter, Catherine Sees, Elizabeth Yundt, Susanna Elser, and Barbara Zeigler. His great-grandfather, Elias Myers, on mother's side, came from Lancaster County, Penn., about 1770, and purchased 400 acres of land, principally woodland, in what was then Hellam, now Spring Garden Township. Subject's grandfather, John Weidman, was born and died in Lancaster County, Penn. The father, Michael Weidman, was a native of Lancaster County. He married Miss Rebecca Myers, daughter of Jacob Myers, and settled in Spring Garden Township in 1829, upon the same tract of land now owned by subject. Their union was blessed by two children: Jacob and Mary E., now the wife of John F. Hiestand of Spring Garden. The father died in January, 1880, aged eighty years. The mother died in April, 1878, aged seventy-three years. Jacob Weidman has always resided in Spring Garden Township, following farming. He has a fine farm of 100 acres about three miles east of York, highly improved. He was married, February 18, 1858, to Miss Margaret Heilman, of West Manchester Township. They have nine children living: Mahala Gross, Isabella Kinard, Eva E., Emma M., Michael, Ida J., George, Harry A. and John J. The family are members of the Lutheran Church.

PHILIP WILLIAMS is a son of Philip and Elizabeth (Crone) Williams, natives respectively of Hellam and Manchester Townships, York County. His father was a cooper, shoe-maker, and farmer, and died in 1877, aged eighty-nine years. Our subject was born November 27, 1816, and for forty-four years has been following agricultural pursuits. He is the owner of two excellent farms, one situated in Hellam Township, consisting of 131 acres, and one of thirty-five acres in Spring Garden Township. He also owns a tract of land, consisting of ten acres in Pleasureville. He was married, January 9, 1840, to Miss Magdalen Smyser, daughter of Christian Smyser, of Manchester Township. Mrs. Williams was born August 1, 1814. The have had five children: Anna M. and Susan (deceased), George H., Clara A. and Leah A.

DAVID WITMER, pastor of the Witmer Church, of Spring Garden Township, is a native of Spring Garden, and was born December 16, 1811. He is the son of David and Magdalena Witmer, natives of Lancaster County, Penn. His father was for many years a minister of the Mennonite denomination. The Witmer Church, built in 1816, of which our subject is the present pastor, was named after him. Our subject followed farming on the old homestead until fifty years of age, when he entered the ministry. Mr. Witmer was married, January 29, 1837, to Miss Anna, daughter of John and Esther Koffman, of Lancaster County, Penn. This union has been blessed with two children: Magdalena and Susan. Mr. Witmer is an earnest and zealous pastor.

JESSE WORKINGER, sheriff of York County, was born October 15, 1820. His parents, Peter and Sarah (Schall) Workinger, of Manheim Township, had seven children: John, Margaret, David, Elizabeth, Jesse, William and Jacob. Mr. Workinger was reared upon a farm, and has been prominently engaged at this calling until his election as sheriff. He owns a farm of 135 acres of improved land in Chanceford Township, and sixteen acres, upon which there is a hotel and other extensive buildings, located in York Township. Mr. Workinger has always taken an active interest in all the interests of the county, and has been honored with positions of public trust. He was elected a commissioner of the county in 1856, and served three years. He was elected to the sheriffality in 1883, and is now serving a three years' term. Mr. Workinger was married, November 22, 1842, to Miss Mary E. Warner, a daughter of Samuel and Catharine Warner, of Chanceford Township. They are parents of four children: Samuel, Jacob G., Sarah C. Trout and Barbara A. Hovis. Mr. Workinger was united to his present wife March 9, 1872. Her maiden name was Miss Magdaline Glatfelter, daughter of Casper and Elizabeth Glatfelter, of Hellam Township. The family are members of the Lutheran Church.

WARRINGTON TOWNSHIP.

PHILIP ALTLAND was born in Dover Township, York County, Penn., May 22, 1807, and is a son of Jacob and Catherine (Trimmer) Altland, natives of York County. The Altlands are of German extraction, the great-grandfather of subject having emigrated from Germany and settled in Paradise Township, this county. The father of our subject was born May 3, 1785, and died in Dover Township February 15, 1830. When Philip was nineteen years of age, he commenced learning the miller's trade. His life as a farmer dates from 1832 until 1878, when he retired from active life. As a tiller of the soil he has been one of the most successful in the township. He was married, in 1830, to Miss Catherine Grove, daughter of Daniel Grove. They have been blessed with thirteen children. For thirty years Mr. Altland was justice of the peace. Mr. and Mrs. Altland are members of the United Brethren Church, and are among the pioneers of York County.

CALVIN C. ANTHONY, a native of Franklin Township, York Co., Penn.. was born March 25, 1849, and is a son of Michael and Rebecca (Smith) Anthony. The father was born in York County, and the mother in Adams County, Penn. Subject's grandfather Anthony, was a farmer, and a member of the German Reformed Church, and died in 1870. The father of subject was a farmer and merchant and for a time postmaster at Mount Top, Penn. Calvin C. spent his early life on the farm, and at sixteen years of age began clerking in his father's store. In 1870 he bought his father's stock and began business for himself, which he still continues. In 1875 he was commissioned postmaster at Mount Top, Penn. He was married in 1873 to Miss Jennie Wickey, daughter of Rev. Lewis Wickey. They have six children. Mr. Anthony is a Democrat. Mr. and Mrs. Anthony are members of the United Brethren Church.

BIOGRAPHICAL SKETCHES.

WILLIAM BEITZEL was born in Dover Township, York Co., Penn., November 11, 1822, and is a son of Daniel and Magdalena (Frantz) Beitzel, the latter a native of Manchester Township. His grandfather, William Beitzel, was a shoe-maker in Germany, and died in his native country. The father of subject was born in Prussia in 1792, came to America in 1817, settled in Dover Township, and there resided until 1842, when he removed to Warrington Township. He had five children: William, Elizabeth, Susanna, Daniel and Leah. He died in 1867. At eighteen years of age, our subject commenced learning the carpenter's trade, which he followed for ten years. He then began farming, and now owns nearly 500 acres. He was married in 1845 to Miss Leah Bentz, daughter of Jacob Bentz. They have had the following children: Leah, Daniel, Elizabeth, William B., Tillie, Rose, Nanny, Ellen, George W. and Charles. Mr. and Mrs. Beitzel are members of the United Brethren Church.

ANDREW BENTZ was born October 28, 1826, in Warrington Township, York Co., Penn., son of Jacob and Mary (Bushy) Bentz, natives of York County, Penn. His great-grandfather was a native of Germany. Subject's grandfather lived in Codorus Township, York Co., Penn., but about 1790 removed to Warrington Township. The father of subject was born in 1781. He was a farmer and died in 1888. He had thirteen children. Our subject remained on the farm until seventeen years of age, when he began serving an apprenticeship at carpentering, and worked at that trade for a number of years. He then began farming, which he has since followed successfully. He was married, in 1852, to Miss Lydia Bushy, a native of York County, and daughter of George Bushy. Mr. Bentz is a Democrat, and has held various political offices. In 1883 he was elected director of the poor of York County. He is a director of the Dillsburg National Bank. Mr. and Mrs. Bentz are members of the church, and are among the first citizens of Warrington Township.

SOLOMON BENTZ is a native of Warrington Township, York Co., Penn., and was born October 28, 1841. He is a son of George and Nancy (Grove) Bentz, natives of York County, Penn. His grandfather, Jacob Bentz, was born in 1781 and died in 1888. The father of subject was born in 1807, was a farmer, and is still living. He has had ten children: Elizabeth, Susanna, Daniel, George, Solomon, Mary, Andrew, Catherine, Moses S. and Mary A. Our subject was educated at the public schools, and during the winters of 1861, 1862 and 1863 taught school. He is a farmer, and in 1868 settled where he now lives. He also owns the Bentz homestead. He was married in 1867 to Miss Henrietta Hershey, a native of Washington Township. Six children have blessed this union: William, John, Monroe, Elizabeth, Mary and Nancy J. Mr. Bentz is a member of the Lutheran and his wife of the Reformed Church.

HON. MILLARD J. BLACKFORD is a native of Carroll Township, York Co., Penn., and was born May 5, 1832. He is a son of Aaron and Christiana (Miller) Blackford. His father was also born in York County, and his mother in Perry County, Penn. Subject's great-great-grandfather was a native of Scotland, and came to America about 1600, and settled in New Jersey. The grandfather of subject was Joseph Blackford; he was born in Warrington Township, this county, and died in 1884. The father of subject was born October 30, 1794. He followed the cooper's trade in the early years of his life, and afterward was a farmer. He was a soldier in the war of 1812, and took part in the battle of North Point, near Baltimore. In 1854 he was elected commissioner of York County, and held the office three years. He died in 1884. They had the following named children: Harriet, Catherine J., Millard J., Lewis, John and Alfred. Our subject was a school teacher in his earlier years. He learned the brick-maker's trade, and worked at that during the summer. In 1856 he began farming, and continued until 1876. In March, 1878, he was elected teller of the Dillsburg National Bank, and is at present a director of said bank. In 1880 he was elected to represent York County in the State legislature, and re-elected in 1882. He was married, in 1855, to Miss Louisa, daughter of Andrew Shearer, of Washington Township. They have had six children: Aaron, Lewis, Beckie, Ida, John and James. Mrs. Blackford died March 24, 1880, and the following year Mr. Blackford married Miss Sallie Altland, daughter of Philip Altland, Esq., and to them have been born one daughter—Viola. Mr. and Mrs. Blackford are members of the United Brethren Church.

JACOB BRENNEMAN was born in Washington Township, York Co., Penn., June 13, 1833, and is a son of Martin and Elizabeth (Asper) Brenneman, natives of York County, Penn. His grandfather, Joseph Brenneman, a native of Lancaster County, Penn., came to York County in 1806, and died in 1846. The father of subject was born in 1803, and is a weaver by trade. He had eight children: John A., Jessie P., Joseph, Jacob, Adam, Susan, Lewis and Mary A. Our subject learned the weaver's trade with his father. When twenty-three years old, he began the manufacture of woolen goods, and continued that occupation for seventeen years. In 1873 he moved to Warrington Township, and since that time he has been a farmer. Mr. Brenneman was married, in 1856, to Miss Elizabeth Berkheimer, a daughter of Henry Berkheimer, of Washington Township. They have three children: Henry C., Martin L. and Andrew J. Mr. and Mrs. Brenneman are members of the Lutheran Church. Mr. Brenneman is a Democrat.

SOLOMON BUSHEY, a native of Warrington Township, was born September 30, 1837, and is a son of George and Elizabeth (Bender) Bushey, natives of Adams County, Penn. His grandfather, Jacob Bushey, was also a native of Adams County. George Bushey, subject's father, was born in 1800. He had a family of six children: Catherine, Lewis, Elizabeth, Lydia, Mary and Solomon. The latter remained on the farm until nineteen years of age, when his father died; he then began brick-making, which he continued for three years, and then went to Canada, remaining there one year. In 1861 he began farming in Warrington Township, which he followed for ten years. In 1872 he engaged in the mercantile business in Wellsville, where he now resides. He continued merchandising for three years, and is now engaged in farming. He was married, in 1860, to Miss Rebecca Morthland, daughter of Hugh Morthland, of Warrington Township. Six children have blessed this union: Margaret A., George B. and Hugh M. (twins), Syvan G., Mary L. and Harry F. Bushey. Mr. and Mrs. Bushey are members of the Methodist Church, and old settlers of York County.

RICHARD F. ELCOCK was born in Warrington Township, March 1, 1832, and is a son of David and Rebecca (Frazer) Elcock, natives of York County, Penn. The Elcock family is of Irish origin, the grandfather of our subject having emigrated at an early day from the "Emerald Isle," and made a settlement in Warrington Township, York County. The father of subject was born June 9, 1807. He was a school teacher and farmer. Richard F. was reared on the farm, and had the advantages of early schools. In 1850 he went to Iowa, and engaged in farming, but after remaining two years returned to his native county. He served his country in the late war, being a lieutenant in Company G, One Hundred and Sixty-sixth Pennsylvania; he also served 100 days in an independent company, furnishing his own horse. He was married, in 1866, to Miss Adeline Jones, of Warrington Township. Mr. Elcock is one of the leading farmers of his township, and now owns nearly 300 acres of well-improved land.

DR. JOEL R. GARRETSON was born in Adams County, Penn., February 8, 1828, and is a son of Joel and Elizabeth (Everett) Garretson, natives of Adams County, Penn. His great-grandfather Garretson, was a native of New Castle, Del., and came to York County, Penn., and settled in Newberry Township. Subject's grandfather, John Garretson, was born in that township, February 23, 1741. The Garretsons were among the first settlers of Newberry Township. The father of Dr. Garretson was born October 8, 1782. In 1847-48 our subject attended the academy at Kennett Square, Penn. From 1849 to 1852 he was engaged in school teaching, and during these years he read medicine. In 1852 he attended lectures at Cincinnati, Ohio, and the following year began the regular practice of his profession at Rossville, Penn., and remained until 1858, when he removed to Salem, Iowa, and continued the practice. In January, 1862, he enlisted in the Fourth Iowa Cavalry. In 1863 he was captured and for some time was a prisoner of war, but was paroled in the autumn of 1863, when he went to St. Louis, and continued in the general hospital until January, 1865. In 1867 he returned from the West to York County, Penn., and, in 1881, graduated from the Eclectic Medical Institute at Cincinnati. He then located at Wellsville, Penn., where he has since resided. After his divorce, in 1867, he married Mrs. Sarah Hopson, daughter of William and Julia McMullin. Their children living are: Elizabeth, Clara, William and John.

JOSEPH K. HART was born in Fairview Township, October 11, 1824, the third of seven children born to Isaac and Elizabeth (Moore) Hart, as follows: Sarah J. Ross (deceased), John M., Joseph K., Jacob, Andrew, Robert (deceased) and Elizabeth Strominger. Subject's paternal grandfather was a native of York County, was a farmer of German descent, and died in 1848, at the age of eighty-six; his maternal grandfather, Moore, a native of Chester County, died in 1851, at the age of seventy-five years. Isaac Hart, subject's father, was born in 1788, and died in 1839, aged fifty-one years. Joseph K. Hart assisted on the home farm until 1848, when he started for himself, marrying the same year, Sarah A., daughter of Michael Wallet, of Warrington Township, and to this union have been born four children: Elwyn, Michael E., Mary E. (deceased) and Robert. In 1851, Mr. Hart came to Warrington Township and took possession of his present farm of 146 acres, all under good cultivation and well improved.

AUGUSTUS C. HETRICK, M. D., was born January 11, 1835, in Codorus Township, York Co., Penn., and is a son of Christian W. and Henrietta (Wolfran) Hetrick, natives of York County. His maternal grandfather was a native of Saxony, and came to York County, about 1800, was one of the leading men of his time in York County, and held various positions of trust, besides having represented York County in the legislature about 1820. His death occurred in 1834. The father of subject was born December 2, 1799, and was a farmer by occupation. He had ten children: Edmund, Hezekiah, Augustus, A. J., Chester E., Abraham, Tilmán F., Octavius, Elma and Wilhelmina. He died in 1878. Our subject grew to manhood on the farm. He attended the public schools and the York County Academy, and from 1852 to 1856, was a student at White Hall Academy, in Cumberland County, Penn. During a term of years, in which he was engaged in school teaching, he studied medicine with Dr. Mechem, of Pleasantville, Md. In the fall of 1856, he entered the Ohio College of Medicine at Cincinnati, and in the spring of 1858, located in Warrington Township, where he has since continued the practice of his profession. He was married, in 1860, to Miss Amanda Hayward, daughter of Dr. Hayward, of Warrington Township. They have five children: Gerney H., Russie, Bruce, Anna and Effie B.

JOHN IRRGANG was born in Philadelphia, December 25, 1841, to Benjamin and Julia (Doll) Irrgang, natives of Germany. Benjamin Irrgang began learning cabinet-making in Germany, and finished his trade in France. On coming to America he landed in Baltimore, whence he walked to Philadelphia, where, for a number of years, he followed his trade, and then opened a fancy goods store, which he conducted to within ten years of his death in 1881, at the age of eighty-two. The mother still lives in Philadelphia at the age of eighty. John Irrgang, our subject, at the age of sixteen, came to Wellsville, this county, and worked in a whip factory until the opening of the late war, when he enlisted in Company H, Seventh Pennsylvania Reserves, under Gen. Meade, and took part in the engagements at Gainesville, Mechanicsville and Ganes Hill, in the last of which he was wounded and captured, and imprisoned in Libby prison and at Belle Island for three months; on his release he was placed in parole camp at Annapolis, whence he was taken to Alexandria, Va., where he received his discharge, December 26, 1862. Returning to Philadelphia he learned the hatter's trade, which he followed until the invasion of this State by the Confederates, when he enlisted in the militia, from which he was discharged July 13, 1863, when he resumed his trade. In May, 1865, he settled in Wellsville, acting as postmaster, and was engaged in mercantile business four and a half years. In May, 1875, he married Miss Emma, a daughter of Thomas Medcalf, and a native of Maryland. To this union have been born four children: William F., Blanche, Julia and Lewis E.

JACOB B. KUNKEL, miller, was born March 12, 1862, in York County, Penn.; son of Elijah and Mary A. (Bennedict) Kunkel, natives of York County, Penn. His great-grandfather was a native of Germany, and came to America in its early history. The father of subject was born in 1838; he was a miller by occupation, but is now living a retired life in Warrington Township. Jacob B., like his paternal ancestors, follows the milling business, having served a regular apprenticeship at the miller's trade. In 1882 he took charge of his father's mill, and is doing a successful business. He was married, in 1881, to Miss Mary E. Spangler, daughter of Jacob Spangler. They have one son—Marl Elijah. Mr. Kunkel is a Democrat.

JACOB A. MOORE is a native of Fairview Township, York Co., Penn., was born October 20, 1847, and is a son of John and Mary (Stittle) Moore. The Moore family have been known in York County for more than 100 years. John Moore, subject's father, was born in 1805, and lived and died in this county. He was one of the leading early men of his township, and held the offices of commissioner and associate judge. He was elected to the latter office in 1867, and held it until his death in 1869. Our subject spent the first fifteen years of his life on the farm, and then went to Mechanicsburgh, Penn., and served a three years' apprenticeship at carpentering. After working at this trade and coach-making several years, he, in 1881, came to Warrington Township and engaged in farming, which occupation he still continues. He has 180 acres of well-improved land. He was married, in

1871, to Miss Mary Elcock, of Warrington Township. They have one child—Jennie May.

WILLIAM W. RAMSEY was born in Lewisberry, York Co., Penn., August 9, 1840, and is a son of William and Mary (Walker) Ramsey, both natives of York County. His paternal grandfather was also William Ramsey, and a farmer of Fairview Township. His maternal grandfather, John Walker, was a resident of Warrington and also a farmer. The father of our subject was born in 1799. He was a farmer, hotel-keeper and merchant, served as justice of the peace five years, and died in 1884. He had five children: William W., Anna L., John K. (deceased), Mary M. and James (deceased). The mother of these is still living, a member of the Evangelical Church, as was her husband. The early life of William W. was spent in attending school and clerking in his father's store. In 1869 he took charge of the mercantile business, which had been conducted for years by his father, and has since carried on general merchandising. In 1870 Mr. Ramsey was appointed postmaster at Alpine, Penn. He was married, in 1869, to Miss Lydia Spangler, daughter of John Spangler, a native of York County, a farmer, and of a very old York family. They have one child—John W. Mr. Ramsey is a Democrat, and is the owner of three tracts of land, one of which comprises eighty acres in Warrington Township.

LEVI REIVER was born in Washington Township in 1824, and is a son of Peter and Susanna Reiver, natives of Dover Township. Peter Reiver died in Warrington Township, August 27, 1866, at the age of seventy years, a member of the Reformed Church, and the father of three children: Levi, Samuel (deceased) and Mary A. Lenhart, of Ohio. Levi Reiver was reared a farmer, but at the age of twenty learned the cabinet-making trade under Lewis Shibe, in York, and for twelve years followed the business in Washington Township, and then conducted farming in Warrington Township until 1880, when he retired from active business. He is the owner of a tract of land of 135 acres, and also a tract of fifteen acres on which he resides. In 1849 he married Sarah, daughter of George Horn. To this union seven children have been born as follows: William, Alice Zeigler, Amos, Mary Urich, Oliver, Amanda Spangler and Arvilla Kapp. Mr. and Mrs. Reiver are members of the German Reformed Church, and in politics Mr. R. is a Democrat.

GEORGE W. SMITH was born in Washington Township, June 10, 1862, and is the second of the six children born to Jacob T. and Catherine (Hollinger) Smith, as follows: Anna, George W., Katie C., John C., Jacob H. and Jonas. Subject's grandfather, John W. Smith, was a native of York County, was a miller and farmer, and died in 1878 at the age of seventy-six; grandfather George Hollinger was also a native of York County and a farmer. Jacob T. Smith, subject's father, is a native of Washington Township, and is the owner of two farms of 120 acres each. George W. Smith was reared on the home farm until the age of twenty-one, when he went West for a while; he then returned and engaged in mercantile business at Rossville where he has a prosperous trade, and of which point he was appointed postmaster in February, 1884. June 5, 1884, he married Amanda J., daughter of Jacob H. Spangler, of Dover Township.

LEVI M. SPANGLER was born in Warrington Township May 19, 1825, and is one of the ten children born to John and Susanna (Maish) Spangler, as follows: Harriet Shelley (deceased), Mary Cammon, Levi M., David (deceased), Sarah (deceased) Daniel (late captain in the army and afterward in the navy, and now deceased), Lavinia Gochenauer, David, Susanna and Eliza A. Subject's grandfather, Joseph Spangler, was one of six brothers, who came from Germany, and from whom the Spanglers of this country sprang. John Spangler was born February 2, 1789; was the possessor of 130 acres of land on the Conewago; sixty acres in Cumberland County, and also twenty acres of additional woodland; he served in the war of 1812, and died in 1850, a member of the Lutheran Church. Our subject was reared a farmer, was educated at the public schools and at the York County Academy, and subsequently taught six terms of school. In 1848–49 he attended the Dickinson College at Carlisle, and the following winter again taught school. He took charge of the home farm at his father's death; subsequently he bought the place, and there he still resides. December 24, 1850, he married Margaret J., daughter of Samuel Smith, and to this union have been born four children: Emily J. Miller, Amanda E. (deceased), Emerson and Albert. Mr. and Mrs. Spangler are members of the Lutheran Church, and Mr. S. also takes an active part in Sunday-school work. He has served as school director of Warrington Township eight years, and once had the nomination by the Republicans for county auditor.

DR. W. H. SPANGLER, a native of Warrington Township, York Co., Penn., was born August 18, 1832, and is a son of Daniel and Mary C. (Hobaugh) Spangler, natives of York County, Penn. His grandfather, Spangler, also a native of York County, was a farmer, as was also the father of our subject, who had ten children: David, Samuel, Elijah, Daniel, William, Jacob, Henry, Mary, Lydia and Nathan. Our subject remained at home and worked on the farm until his twentieth year, when he attended the York County Academy for one year, and then for two years clerked in a store. He subsequently engaged in the mercantile business for himself, which he continued for seven years, and then took up the study of dentistry under Dr. Bricker. In 1867 Dr. Spangler settled where he now resides, and has since continued the practice of his profession. He was married, in 1865, to Miss Gulielma Vale. They have one child—Alberta May. Dr. Spangler is a member of the Reformed Church and Mrs. Spangler is a Methodist.

WASHINGTON TOWNSHIP.

J. H. DEARDORFF, second in the family of eight children of Joseph and Lucy (Hoover) Deardorff, was born in Adams County, June 20, 1831. His grandfather, Samuel Deardorff, a farmer, died in 1844, aged seventy years. His grandfather, Hoover, was a native of Germany, and an early settler in York County. Subject's father was born in 1806; followed farming in Washington Township until 1849, and then retired to his present residence in Adams County. Our subject was reared in Adams County until thirteen, when he removed with his father to Washington Township, this county, and here he remained on the farm until twenty-three years of age, when he began for himself. He now owns 149 acres, under fine cultivation, and a grist and saw-mill. In 1854 he married Barbara A. Pressel, daughter of Joseph Pressel, of Washington Township. Eleven children have blessed this union, viz.: Mary A. (deceased), Edward, Jacob, (deceased); Joseph, William, Henry, Elmira, Nancy, John, Milton and Rosa. Mr. Deardorff is a member of the Lutheran Church, and Mrs. D. of the Reformed Church.

JOHN GOCHNAUER, native of Washington Township, was born July 13, 1825, and is a son of

198 WASHINGTON TOWNSHIP.

Joseph and Sarah (Leathery) Gochnauer, natives of Dover Township. His paternal grandfather was a native of Germany, and died in Washington Township about 1839, aged about eighty years, the owner of five farms, two in Dover and three in Washington Township. He had served in the war of the Revolution. Subject's maternal grandfather was a farmer of Dover Township. Subject's father was a farmer and owner of 150 acres in Washington Township, and thirty-one acres in Adams County. He died in 1877, at seventy-five years of age, the father of five children. At the age of twenty-seven, subject left the home farm, and for three years managed a farm for his father. He then bought the homestead of 147 acres, and in 1867 bought his present homestead of 230 acres. He now owns three farms in this township, aggregating 527 acres, beside two tracts—ninety-six and thirty-one acres—in Adams County. In 1852 he married Elvina, daughter of John Spangler, of Warrington Township, and has had born to him seven children, viz.: Susan (Bosseman), Daniel, Elmira, Sarah J., Joseph, Charles and Jesse. Mr. and Mrs. Gochnauer are members of the Evangelical Church.

GEORGE B. KRALL was born in Washington Township, March 30, 1837, is the eldest of the six children of Jesse and Maria (Brubaker) Krall, and is of German descent through his great-grandfather. Subject's father was born in 1810, was a farmer, millwright and merchant at Kralltown for many years. He now resides on his farm of 100 acres in Washington Township, and owns, beside several smaller tracts of land, the saw and grist-mill, where our subject is engaged. At the age of fifteen, subject apprenticed himself for five years to learn the millwright's trade with his father; then followed the trade for himself until his enlistment, August 8, 1862, in the One Hundred and Thirtieth Pennsylvania Volunteers, Company B. He was in the engagements at South Mountain, Antietam and Chancellorsville, and returned home at the end of ten months. He followed his trade until September, 1863, when he enlisted for three years, or the war, in Company C, Seventy-ninth Volunteers, and took part in the battle of Raleigh, N. C. He was honorably discharged July 12, 1865. Thereafter he engaged in his trade in Maryland until 1879. In 1859 he married Sarah J., daughter of Henry B. Smith, of York County, and to this union were born four children: Ellis C., Jessie F. (both deceased), Gertrude and Grace. In 1872, Mrs. Krall died, and in 1877 Mr. Krall married Della B., daughter of George Ford, and a native of Delaware. In 1879 Mr. K. moved from Maryland to Carlisle, Penn., then to Loudon, Franklin County, and in the spring of 1884 settled down in this township.

SAMUEL McCREARY, a native of Franklin Township, York County, was born October 19, 1819, and is a son of John and Julia (Lease) McCreary. The great-great-grandfather, John McCreary, was a native of Scotland, a member of the high church of England, was married to Miss Edwards, of England, and a settler of Lancaster County, this State. The great-grandfather, Thomas McCreary, was born in Lancaster County, and married Miss Elizabeth Bowen, a native of Wales, and a member of the Society of Friends. He afterward joined the same church, and settled early in York County near Hanover, and was extensively engaged in farming, both in this and Adams Counties. The grandfather (Thomas also) was born in 1754, in this county, was a merchant and hotel keeper and captain of the State militia, and afterward major, and was married to Miss Mary Garretson, of this county. The father of our subject was born in Washington Township, this county, November 3, 1791, and died in December, 1822. Subject's mother died September 23, 1881, in her eighty-fifth year. Samuel McCreary left the home farm at the age of sixteen, worked in a brick yard; he next served an appenticeship of two years at tailoring; from 1842–48 carried on brick-making in the summer and taught school in the winter; in 1849 began farming in connection with brick-making. He is the owner of a farm in Washington Township, and two tracts of woodland, one situated in Franklin and the other in Warrington Township. In 1848 he married Harriet A. Blackford, daughter of Aaron G. Blackford, who was born November 24, 1827. To this union have been born seven children: Julian Ruhl, Aaron B. (deceased), John L., Elizabeth J. T. Baker, Samuel L. (deceased), Katie R. and S. U. G. McCreary. Our subject, his wife and sister, Julia A. (who was born December 22, 1821), together with two of his children, Katie R. and S. U. G., constitute the family at the homestead, and all but three belong to the United Brethren Church.

WILLIAM H. SCHWEITZER was born March 17, 1825, in Dover Township, and is the son of William and Catherine (Hoover) Schweitzer, also natives of Dover Township. His grandfather, George Schweitzer, came from Switzerland in 1784, and it was he who introduced the Swiss or bank barn into this country. He died in 1854, aged ninety-six years and six months. Our subject's father was born in 1800, and now resides in Ohio, to which State he removed many years ago. At the age of twenty-one our subject left the home farm, and engaged in carpentering, which he followed seven summers, teaching school in the winters. In 1864 he began farming in Franklin Township, remaining four years In 1872 he was elected county recorder on the Democratic ticket and served three years and one month. In 1878 he settled on his present farm of thirty acres in this township. In 1864 he married Miss Nancy, daughter of Jacob Arndt, of Codorus Township, and to this union have been born seven children: Mary, Emma C., Lydia A., William A., Lillie M., Ida (deceased) and Jacob O. (deceased).

LEWIS STRAYER, a native of Dover Township, and son of Andrew and Catherine (Sheffer) Strayer, was born August 5, 1827. His father was born in 1780, was a farmer and carpenter and died in 1875; the mother died in 1875, aged ninety-three. Our subject left the home farm at the age of sixteen, and served an apprenticeship of two years at shoe-making, which trade he followed in Dover and Warrington Townships fifteen years. In 1859 he began farming in Warrington, four years later moved to Dover Township, and after one year returned to Warrington. In 1873 he came to Washington Township, where he is engaged in farming and operating a chopping-mill, woolen and saw-mill. In 1870 he was elected county commissioner by the Democrats for three years. He was married, in 1847, to Miss Catherine, daughter of Peter Kapp, of Warrington Township. There have been born to this union eleven children, viz.: William, Emilia Kinter, George, Andrew, Peter, Henry, Martin, Sevilla, Katie, Mary and John C. Mr. and Mrs. Strayer are members of the Lutheran Church.

A. K. STRALEY was born in Dover Township, December 8, 1856, and is the younger of two children born to John and Mary A. (Kimmel) Straley. His grandfather, Philip Straley, was born in Dover Township, in 1793, and died in this township, October 15, 1878; he married Rebecca Bassen, who was born in York County in 1797, and who died November 25, 1863. Grandfather David Kimmel, was a native of Washington Township, and married Elizabeth Gentzler, a native of Codorus Township. Our subject's father was born in 1823, and was a farmer, a teacher, a hotel keeper and a merchant, and died in 1882, being at that time postmaster, a position he had held since 1870. Our subject, Andrew J. Straley, remained on the home farm until twelve years old, from which time until 1880

BIOGRAPHICAL SKETCHES.

he assisted his father in the store, then became his partner, and is now his successor in business, and is doing a prosperous trade. In 1882 he was appointed postmaster at Hall.

WEST MANCHESTER TOWNSHIP.

JACOB ALDINGER was born February 22, 1833, and is a son of Frederick and Elizabeth (Myers), late of Sprinfield Township, formerly of Heidelberg Township. Subject's great-grandfather, Matthias Aldinger, who died in Germany, was of royal descent. On account of the persecutions of the family by Napoleon, the grandfather of our subject, after being driven up and down the Rhine from 1814 to 1817, succeeded in making his escape to America. He was the father of seven children: Margaret, Barbara, Frederick, Frederica, Elizabeth, Christiana and Louisa, all natives of Germany. The father of our subject had born to him eight children: John, Emanuel, Jacob, William, Daniel (deceased), Barbara, Matthias and Abraham. Our subject, a minister of the Old German Baptist Church, commonly called the Dunkard, was married, October 29, 1854, to Elizabeth, daughter of John and Lydia Sprenkle, of West Manchester Township, and to this union have been born three children: Samuel, Annie and Lydia. Mr. Aldinger is the owner of a fine farm of 217 acres in West Manchester, improved with two fine dwellings, a large bank barn and other out-buildings, also a tract of thirty-one acres in North Codorus Township, and also five acres in building lots at Brillhart's Station, in York Township. Mr. Aldinger has served York Township several years as school director.

J. L. BAER, Baer's Station, is a son of John H. and Malinda (Lau) Baer, of West Manchester Township, and was born February 20, 1854, in West Manchester Township. He was reared on his father's farm, and his time was divided between farm work and attending the public schools of the township. He also went several terms to Prof. Ruby's York County Academy. November 10, 1878, he married Martha J. Sprenkle, daughter of Peter and Matilda Sprenkle, of West Manchester Township. Two children have been born to this marriage: Katie and Erwin. He began general merchandising at his present location (Baer's Station, of Frederick Division of Pennsylvania Railroad), March 1, 1879. He is thoroughly familiar with its details, and well calculated for the business in which he is engaged. Mr. Baer's great-grandfather, David Baer, was born April 11, 1780; died October 16, 1831. His great-grandmother, Maria Baer, was born June 20, 1772; died November 4, 1868. They lived on the same homestead on which his father now lives. His grandfather was born October 27, 1805; died June 10, 1845. He lived in the conjugal state seventeen years, and begat two sons and four daughters. His wife, Mary, was born February 14, 1800; died July 10, 1849. His father, John H. Baer, was born February 4, 1832; married O. Malinda Lau (born February 8, 1833) the 12th of May, 1853. He is the father of nine children— three sons and six daughters: J. L. Baer (born February 20, 1854), Ros Ellen (September 28, 1855), Kate (October 30, 1858), Clara Ann (September 26, 1860), George L. (May 19, 1862), Ida V. (April 17, 1864), Annie (September 2, 1865), Lillie May (January 15, 1867), Harvey L., (April 3, 1870). George L. died September 12, 1863; Lillie May, July 22, 1868; Annie, December 28, 1870.

PETER BOTT, Sr., was born August 31, 1801, and is the son of Peter and Elizabeth (Zeigler) Bott. The grandfather of our subject, John Bott, of Germany, was father of four children: Eve, Susanna, Elizabeth and Peter, all born in West Manchester Township. Our subject's father, Peter Bott, had born to him nine children: Jacob, Peter, John, Adam, William, Henry, Mary, Eliza and Mary. The father of Mrs. Peter (Zeigler) Bott was Killian Zeigler, a native of Germany, who came when young to West Manchester Township. Peter Bott, our subject, was married November 9, 1826, to Miss Elizabeth, daughter of Jacob and Elizabeth Smyser, of this township, and to him have been born ten children, viz.: Michael (married to Louisa, daughter of George Julius), Louisa (wife of Samuel Menough), Sarah (wife of Peter Yost), Eliza A. (wife of William Smyser); Caroline (wife of John Smyser), William H. (married to Lucy Hoke), Anna M. (wife of Joseph Martin), Peter J. (married to Sarah Hoke), Alice A. (wife of Dallas Julius) and Edward C. Our subject, at the age of eighty-four, is leading a retired life on his homestead of ten acres. The family are members of the Lutheran Church.

WILLIAM H. BOTT is the son of Peter and Elizabeth (Smyser) Bott, natives of West Manchester Township, and was born January 23, 1841. He was married, December 9, 1871, to Miss Lucy, daughter of Michael Hoke, of old Manchester Township, and has had born to him four children: Flora K., Harvey H. (deceased), Minnie M., Lucy E. and William E. Mr. Bott is an agriculturist, and the owner of three farms, to-wit: his homestead of 223 acres, improved with fine buildings and extra large bank barn; another of 126 acres, well improved and cultivated, and a third in North Codorus Township, also well improved with first class buildings and very productive. Mr. Bott was drafted in the first draft of the late war, but paid $350 for a substitute; he afterward enlisted in Company B, Seventy-eighth Pennsylvania Volunteers, and served to the end of the war. Mr. Bott is a member of the Lutheran Church, and his family of the German Reformed.

ABRAHAM GENTZLER, farmer, son of Jesse and Eliza (Zorbach) Gentzler, eldest of nine children, was born November, 1836, in North Codorus Township; he was reared on a farm and has always followed farming. October, 1859, he married Sarah Josephs, daughter of Henry Josephs, of Paradise Township. Seven children have blessed this union: Charles A., John H. (deceased), Katie (deceased), Henry F., Milton, infant (deceased) and Martin. Our subject's grandfather, Conrad Gentzler, was a native of York County and always lived in North Codorus Township, so that the Gentzler family is one of the oldest families in York County. The subject of this sketch is an industrious, progressive farmer; he has a thorough knowledge of farming and has farmed for the Hokes for the past eighteen years.

JACOB F. GLATFELTER, farmer, son of Charles and Louisa (Fishel) Glatfelter, of Spring Garden Township, was born August 23, 1835, in Spring Garden Township, where he was reared on his father's farm; he always followed farming. January 23, 1859, Mr. Glatfelter married Margaret Hyde, who bore him four children: infant (deceased), Charles H., Clara E. and Willie J. Margaret (Hyde) Glatfelter was the daughter of Joshin and Lydia (Wire) Hyde, of West Manchester Township. February 5, 1884, our subject married Maria Hamme, daughter of Frederick and Margaret (Gentzler) Hamme, of Manchester Township. Mr. Glatfelter is the owner of an excellent farm of 121 acres, about five miles from York, in Manchester Township. He has lived on this farm since 1859.

ADAM H. HAMME, son of Jonas and Catherine

WEST MANHEIM TOWNSHIP.

(Eisenhart) Hamme, of West Manchester Township, was born December 3, 1833, in Dover Township on the old homestead farm, where his brother, John H. Hamme, now lives; as a boy his time was divided between school and farm work. October 25, 1860, he married Mary Ann Ketterman, daughter of George and Anna Mary (Bush) Ketterman, of North Codorus Township. This union has been blessed with four children: Alice M., Catherine J., Mary E. and John H. Jonas Hamme, our subject's father, died in his seventy-third year; his widow is still living. Christian Hamme, our subject's grandfather, was one of the first settlers of Dover Township, having taken up the land and getting a patent deed for his farm. Our subject is a progressive, wide-awake farmer, and is the owner of one of the finest farms in the neighborhood.

HERMAN HOKE was born October 9, 1811, and is the son of John and Catherine (Harman) Hoke, natives respectively of Adams County and West Manchester Township, York County. Subject's paternal grandfather, Conrad Hoke, was a native of York County, was a farmer and the father of three children: Jacob, Conrad and John. The grandfather of Mrs. Hoke was a native of Germany. Herman Hoke, our subject, is the eldest of three children born to his parents, viz.: Herman, Emanuel and John. September 19, 1832, our subject married Elizabeth Free, daughter of Peter and Mary Free, of Hopewell Township, and has had born to him seven children, viz.: Leah E., wife of Henry S. Tyson; Adam H., married to Sarah Smyser; Sarah A., wife of Noah Ness; Catherine A.; Rebecca L.; Emma J., wife of Samuel Rutter, and Mary A., deceased.

NOAH NESS, son of Mathias and Elizabeth (Myers) Ness, is the fifth of eleven children and was born February 2, 1835, in Springfield Township; was reared on his father's farm and removed to West Manchester Township when nineteen years of age. In September, 1858, Mr. Ness married Sarah A. Hoke, daughter of Herman and Elizabeth (Free) Hoke, of West Manchester Township. Eleven children have been born to them: Catherine E. (deceased), Adam, Annie, John, Elizabeth, Sarah (deceased), Noah, Tillie, Emma, Thomas and Rebecca. Matthias Ness, the father of our subject, was born February 24, 1801, in Shrewsbury Township. He died aged seventy-eight years, five months and twenty-nine days. Our subject's grandfather's name was Jacob Ness; he was a native of York County. Our subject's mother was born August 27, 1804. She died April 23, 1873, aged sixty-eight years, seven months and twenty-seven days. Matthias Ness was a prominent and well known farmer, having with credit to himself filled the office of county auditor for two terms.

HENRY H. SMYSER, son of David and Rebecca (Eyster) Smyser, was born July 16, 1840. The subject of this sketch was the fifth of ten children: Eliza, Martin, Sarah, Louisa, Henry, Mary (deceased), Jacob, Amanda, Charles and Albert. David Smyser, the father of our subject, was born in 1806, he was a prominent and influential farmer, and was elected county commissioner in 1872. and served the full term with credit to himself and satisfaction to the people of the county. (For our subject's ancestral history, see sketch of the Smyser family, York Borough.)

J. MATTHIAS SMYSER, son of David and Rebecca (Eyster) Smyser, was born March 18, 1845, in West Manchester Township, where he was reared on his father's farm, and remained here until his twenty-sixth year. He married Amanda Smyser, daughter of Adam and Eliza (Brillinger) Smyser, Spring Garden Township. To this marriage were born seven children: Nettie E., Annie R., Howard D., Matthias, Mary, Adam and Lucy E. Mr. Smyser started in business as a member of the firm of Menges, Smyser & Co., of York, Penn. He next began the milling business in West Manchester Township, at Smyser's Mill; during this time he was one of the firm of Fahs, Smyser & Co., grain, coal and general commission merchants; he was in this firm for eight years. He then removed to his present home, East Berlin, Adams County, where he is engaged in the banking business and is one of the managers of the Keystone Manufacturing Company, of East Berlin. Our subject's ancestors, the Eysters and Smysers, were the first settlers in West Manchester Township.

ABRAHAM H. SPRENKLE, son of George Sprenkle, was born in West Manchester Township, October 9, 1844, at the homestead where he has always resided. December 3, 1867, he married Louisa Emig, daughter of Valentine and Rebecca (Loucks) Emig, of West Manchester Township. One child has been born to them, Harvey E. Sprenkle. Our subject's wife was born August 12, 1845; her people were among the first settlers of her native township. It is claimed by the Sprenkle family that their ancestors were the first white people who took up land and settled in West Manchester Township; 900 acres of land were taken up by their ancestor, Adam Sprenkle, and the name Sprenkle is one of the best and most respected in West Manchester Township.

N. B. SPRENKLE, son of Jacob and Barbara (Baer) Sprenkle, was born April 6, 1857, in West Manchester Township, where he was reared on his father's farm. He received his education in the schools of his native township, and two terms in the York County Academy. He taught school one term at Sprenkle's School house in 1867-68, in West Manchester Township; went into the grain and coal business in 1868 at Baer's Station, West Manchester Township; after three years there he moved to his present location, East Berlin, Adams County, where he is at present engaged in the grain, coal and lumber business. February 16, 1879, Mr. Sprenkle married Kate Masemer, daughter of Jesse and Catharine (Joseph) Masemer. Our subject's paternal ancestors, the Sprenkles, were among the pioneer settlers of West Manchester Township. (See history of Manchester Township.)

MARTIN B. SPRENKLE was born January 29, 1861, in West Manchester Township, and has been a resident of his native township all his life. He received a common school education and began business for himself at Baer's Station, on the Frederick division of the Pennsylvania Railroad when quite a young man, and is probably the largest buyer of wheat in West Manchester Township. January 16, 1880, Mr. Sprenkle married Sallie E. Martin, daughter of Solomon Martin, of Stoverstown, North Codorus Township. Two children have blessed this union: Sadie E. (deceased), and Charlee M. Mr. Sprenkle pays close attention to his business, and as a result of this his business is increasing every year.

WEST MANHEIM TOWNSHIP.

PHILIP J. BARNHART, collecting agent and farmer, was born in Heidelberg Township, June 8, 1846, is a son of Adam and Eliza A. (Jackson) Barnhart, is of a German-English origin and the eldest of a family of four living children. He was reared on the farm, and received his education at the public schools of Heidelberg Township. In 1864 he came to West Manheim Township, and settled near where he now lives. He worked by the day until 1869, when he engaged in general merchandising at Green Point. He continued this eight years, and since that time has been engaged in farming and as general collector. In 1865 he married Barbara Kehlbaugh, a native of West Manheim Township, and daughter of Jacob Kehlbaugh. Four children have been born to this union: Mollie A., Lyman A., Missouri J. and Philip C. He is a Democrat, and for many years has taken an active part in politics. Mr. and Mrs. B. are members of the Reformed Church.

HON. SIMON J. BARNHART, present member of legislature from York County, is a native of Heidelberg Township, York Co., Penn.; was born April 19, 1848; is a son of Adam and Eliza A. (Jackson) Barnhart, and is of Dutch-English descent. In a family of seven children, he is the second, and his parents are both natives of York County. At nineteen years, Mr. Barnhart began teaching school and this occupation he continued for twelve years. In 1879 he began farming in West Manheim Township, where he now resides. Politically he is an earnest supporter of the Democratic party, and after holding various offices of minor trust he was, in 1884, elected to represent York County in the State General Assembly, his majority in the county being more than 3,600. He was married March 4, 1877, to Miss Anna M. Houck, daughter of Henry P. and Angeline Houck, of Carroll County, Md. To this marriage have been born two children, viz.: Cora E. and Ellen J. Mr. and Mrs. B. are members of the Lutheran Church.

JESSE W. GARRETT, farmer, was born in what was formerly Manheim Township, York Co., Penn., October 4, 1836, is a son of Jacob and Elizabeth (Wildason) Garrett, of German descent, and is the seventh of thirteen children. His parents were both born in York County, and the Garrett family has been known in this county 100 years. Mr. Garrett, at nineteen years, began the labors of life for himself; when twenty-five years old he began huckstering, and that continued for fifteen years, and then began farming; he now has 120 acres of well improved land, and is a successful farmer of West Manheim Township. In 1860 he married Miss Eliza A. Nace, of West Manheim Township. Eight children have blessed their union: John F., Eliza E. A., Emma J., Missouri E., Marcellus J., Horace J., Amelia C. and Birda E. He is a Republican and has held the office of school director for seven years. He is a member of the Reformed Church and his wife of the Lutheran Church.

OLIVER W. GARRETT, farmer, was born in West Manheim Township, York County, November 21, 1845, is a son of Jacob and Elizabeth (Wildason) Garrett, and is of German descent. He was educated at the schools of West Manheim Township, and in 1859 was hired out to work on the farm by his mother. Then he began the huckstering business, which he has since continued, but in 1881 he added general merchandising. He keeps dry goods, boots, shoes, groceries and notions. He has also a small but well improved farm where he lives. He was married, in 1866, to Miss Eliza Utz, and had born to him two children: Lillie A. and Minerva A. Mrs. Garrett died in 1872, and the next year Mr. Garrett married Emily Jane Klinedinst, a native of Manheim Township. To this union have been born seven children, viz.: Clara M., Annie E., Harrison M., Mary V., Oliver C., Jacob V. and Macy J. Mr. Garrett enlisted in 1865 in Company G, Seventy-fourth Pennsylvania Volunteers for one year. He is now a Democrat but was formerly a Republican, and with his wife is a member of the Lutheran Church.

E. C. HOFFACKER was born in Manheim Township, York County, in 1842, is a son of John W. and Maria (Craunur) Hoffacker, and is of German extraction. His father was born in Carroll County, Md., and his mother, in York County, Penn. His father's death occurred in 1881, and his mother's in 1883. Our subject was reared on the farm, and at the age of twenty-one began life for himself. He is one of the leading and most successful farmers in the township. Mr. H., in 1864, married Miss Susanna Fridinger, a native of Maryland. They have five children: Ida A., Granville T., Oliver S., John G. W. and Alice S. M. He is a Democrat, and has been school director five years. Mr. and Mrs. H. are members of the Lutheran Church.

J. D. STERNER was born in Carroll County, Md., in 1832, is a son of Nathaniel and Anna Mary (Feeser) Sterner, is the youngest in a family of seven children, and is of German descent. His parents were also natives of Carroll County, Md. He received a common school education, and at eighteen years of age began teaching school and taught seven winters. In 1857 he began clerking in the store of David Bachman at Bachman's Mills, Carroll Co., Md.; in 1862 he came to York County, and settled in West Manheim Township, and began general merchandising, which he has since continued. He was married, in 1859, to Miss Sevilla Warehime, a native of Carroll County. They have five children living: Charles M., Ella M., George W., Emma J. and Martha S. He is a Democrat; in 1862 was elected justice of the peace of West Manheim Township, and held the office three terms, or fifteen years. Mr. and Mrs. S. are members of the German Reformed Church. He has made his own way in life, and is one of the leading citizens of West Manheim Township.

WINDSOR TOWNSHIP.

DANIEL ANSTINE, son of Simon and Elizabeth (Smith), was born in Windsor Township July 7, 1855. After leaving the public schools of his township our subject learned cigar-making, which he followed as a journeyman six years, when, in 1876, he commenced manufacturing on his own account at Frysville. In 1883 he married Miss Matilda, daughter of Adam Sechrist, of York Township.

JOHN W. BURGER is a prominent brick merchant of Windsor Township, and was born in Adams County, Penn., October 15, 1846. He has served as chief burgess of Red Lion Borough, York County, and is a member of the Lutheran Church. He was married, October 27, 1867, to Millie Myers.

WILLIAM BROOKS BIGLER, M. D., was born October 6, 1833, in Fairview Township, York County. His father's family was of Swiss origin; his mother's of Scotch-Irish, having immigrated to this country from County Antrim, Ireland, about 1752, and settled in Delaware; thence the great-grandfather, Brooks, went to Cumberland County, Penn., purchased a tract of land from William Penn, on Yellow Breeches, and built a mill, where he made flour for Braddock's army. This mill is now owned by Elias Hake. David Bigler was a farmer; was married in December, 1832, and had a family of three sons and five daughters. He died in August, 1872. William B. Bigler attended Jefferson Medical College, from which he graduated in 1865. He has been school director, and was a member of the legislature, 1883–84. October 12, 1865, he married Amelia M. A.

Boyer; to them have been born the following named children: William M., Edith M. and Mabel B. Dr. Bigler is a Mason.

JAMES CROSS was born in Windsor Township, York County, in 1826, and is the son of James and Elizabeth (Grove) Cross. The father was born in this township in 1787, was reared a farmer, filled the office of justice of the peace; in 1814 married Elizabeth Grove, who was born in Chanceford Township, in 1787; became the father of two boys and four girls, and died June 9, 1872; his wife died November 15, 1842. James Cross, the grandfather of our subject, was one of the earliest settlers of York County, having taken up from the government the farm on which his grandson now resides, at a time when the Indians were numerous in the township. He was a prosperous farmer, and served his country in the war of 1812. James Cross, our subject, still cultivates the farm entered by his grandfather. He was married, in 1859, to Jane Ann Wallace, who was born in Hopewell Township, in 1835, and who is the mother of one son—James Nelson Cross. The family attend the Guinston United Presbyterian Church, of which Mr. and Mrs. Cross are members.

DANIEL L. GEHLY, was born October 15, 1807. His father, a farmer, was born May 20, 1773. in Warwick Township, Lancaster Co., Penn. His mother, whose maiden name was Nancy Lehman, was born in the same township, February 28, 1779. They were married October 20, 1801. Their children were Lidia, born September 18, 1802; David, October 31, 1804; Daniel L. (as above) and Nancy, May 27, 1811; all deceased, except Daniel L. The father died in 1846; and the mother in 1858. Daniel L. commenced wool manufacturing in 1825, which business he still continues. In 1835 he was elected lieutenant-colonel of the Sixty-fourth Regiment, Pennsylvania Militia; in 1846 was elected member of the State House of Representatives and served one term. October 28, 1828, he married Margaret Ann Dosch. Of the eight children born to this union four are living, viz.: John C., D. W., T. H. and Mary M. Mr. Gehly's great-grandparents came from Germany; his grandfather, Frederick Lehman, was born in Lancaster County; his grandmother, Anna Habaker, was born in the same county, three miles north of Lititz. Mr. Gehly is a member of the Evangelical Church.

HARVEY WHEELER HAINES was born October 11, 1888, in Stark County, Ohio. His father, Charles H. was born in 1814, in Windsor, York Co., Penn.; and in Lancaster City, in 1834, he married Barbara Funk; she was born in Lancaster County in 1816. They had nine children—three boys and four girls now living: Charles H. was a carpenter by trade, but for many years engaged in farming. Harvey W. Haines taught school for many years in the city of Baltimore, but is now engaged in farming near Freysville Church, in this township. February 16, 1871, he married Mary E., daughter of David Leber; Florence Leber and Horace Becker are their children. Mr. Haines' grandfather came to Windsor Township, from Frankford, Philadelphia, after the war of 1812. When Harvey W. was a child his father and neighbors, owning large farms, would take sickle or cradle and go to the valley of Lancaster County to work six or eight weeks at harvesting to earn money to buy bread for the year; now the grain in Windsor is as good as in the limestone lands, and farmers can hardly get laborers to put away their crops. Land that was then $5 or $10 per acre is now worth $100 per acre. Mr. Haines is a F. & A. M., and is the present auditor of the township.

AMOS HENGST was born in Windsor Township, October 12, 1841, and is the son of Samuel and Barbara (Anstine) Hengst, also natives of Windsor Township, as were Michael Hengst and Simon Anstine, subject's grandfathers. Samuel Hengst was born, reared and lived all his life on the same farm. He held the office of school director, and was a lieutenant of militia. Samuel Hengst was the father of nine children, of whom eight are living, viz.: Henry, Benjamin, a member of the Evangelical Church for thirty-eight years; Samuel, a merchant; Reuben, in the grocery and commission business at Baltimore, Md.; Amos, Catherine, Julia and Magdalena. Leah died in infancy. The father died January 28, 1884, and his wife, November 25, 1871. Amos Hengst was reared a farmer, taught school thirteen terms, was engaged in mercantile business sixteen years, and then purchased one of his father's farms of about fifty acres, with improvements, and is still engaged in farming. He has served one term of five years as justice of the peace. November 24, 1874, he married Debbie S., daughter of George and Mary (Schnell) Fox, of Windsor Township. F. B. Fox, a brother of Mrs. Hengst, has been a professor in Knapp's Institute, Baltimore, for twenty-five years, and A. F. Fox, another brother, has for twenty-five years been in the real estate business at Washington.

JEREMIAH BIXLAR JONES, for thirty-one years a preacher of the Gospel in the church of the United Brethren in Christ, was born in Carroll County, Md., April 3, 1829. His father, John Jones, of Welsh descent, and mother, Elizabeth (Bixlar) Jones, of German descent, were also natives of Carroll County, Md., and were the parents of eleven children—eight boys and three girls. The father died in 1878, and the mother in 1864. Jeremiah B. Jones was married, February 4, 1868, to Miss Amanda Anstine, who has borne him the following children: Mary K., Claria A., Annie B., Maggie E. and Gracie W.

DAVID FRANKLIN MAISH was born January 5, 1845, in Windsor Township. He is a son of George and Lydia (Moser) Maish; the former a native of Fairview Township, and the latter of York Township, born February 15, 1816. They were married November 22, 1838, and are the parents of eight children—three sons and five daughters. George Maish has always followed farming. David F. Maish is also a farmer. March 15, 1877, he married Eliza J. Paules. Their union is blessed with one child. George P. Maish.

SETH MINNICH, of Windsor Township, was born in Hopewell Township, York County, September 13, 1849. His father, Daniel Minnich, was born in Hopewell Township also, January 9, 1828, is a house carpenter by trade, and in 1848 married Elizabeth Miller, a native of Shrewsbury Township, and born March 22, 1829. Of the five children born to this union there are still living. Seth Minnich by trade is a painter. In 1877 he married Annie Smith, who has borne him three children: Daniel B., Howard H. and Addie I. In 1880 Mr. Minnich was elected justice of the peace, which office he administered in so satisfactory a manner that he was re-elected in 1885. He is a member of the Masonic fraternity and also of the Reformed Church.

PHILIP MITZEL was born January 24, 1826, and is the son of Philip and Lydia (Saylor) Mitzel. The former was born in Windsor Township, November 30, 1800, and the latter in Chanceford Township, where they were married; they were the parents of three sons and two daughters, and the father died March 13, 1832. The mother is still living, aged eighty one years. Her daughter, Elizabeth Croley, died May 22, 1885, aged sixty-three years, three months and twenty-two days. Philip, our subject, is a merchant, and manufacturer of and dealer in cigars. He has served as school director and township assessor, and is a member of the Evangelical Association. March 9, 1848, he married Catherine Hengst.

JOHN SEITZ is the son of Jacob and Priscilla

(Tyson) Seitz, and was born in Hopewell Township, February 9, 1827. He was educated in the public schools, then learned milling, which he followed fifteen years, then learned blacksmithing, which he followed for six years. In 1878 he established a general merchandise business at Spring Vale, where he is now doing a good trade, and where he is also the agent for the York & Peach Bottom Railroad, and where also he has served as postmaster six years. Mr. Seitz, besides, owns a farm of seventy-five acres, which he conducts in conjunction with his other business. In 1857 our subject married Miss Matilda, daughter of Frederick Husal, of Chanceford Township, and to this marriage were born twelve children, as follows: Jacob, Susan, Emanuel, Eller, Carrie P., Lemuel L., Savill, Emma J., Tillie, John H., Janie and Alice. Mr. and Mrs. Seitz are members of the United Brethren Church of Zion, Windsor Township.

DANIEL STEIN is the third of the eight children of Daniel and Mary M. (Holtzapple) Stein, and was born in Windsor Township, December 8, 1826. After receiving an education in the public schools he left the homestead, engaged in farming, and in 1881 purchased two farms of 164 acres in all, which he now rents and lives in comfortable retirement at Spring Vale Station, in a fine dwelling erected in 1859, but remodeled in 1882. In 1854 Mr. Stein married Miss Susan, daughter of Henry Grove, of this township. To this union have been born six children, named Mary, Ellen, Susan, Daniel C., Sarah and Henry. During the late civil war Mr. Stein was drafted, but, unfortunately, owing to business and family matters, was compelled to hire a substitute. Mr. and Mrs. Stein are respectively members of the Lutheran and Presbyterian Churches of Frystown.

YORK TOWNSHIP.

WILLIAM H. CROLL, son of Joseph and Elizabeth (Reisinger) Croll, was born in Manchester Township, March 28, 1840. About 1850 the family removed to York Township, where our subject attended school until his sixteenth year. He learned the printing business at the York *Gazette* office, after which he worked in Philadelphia and Pittsburgh, after which he assumed full charge of the Hanover *Gazette*, this county. At the first call for troops by President Lincoln he promptly enlisted in Company A, Sixteenth Pennsylvania Volunteer Infantry, and at the expiration of his three months' term enlisted in Company I, Eleventh Pennsylvania Cavalry, in which he faithfully served for three years, eighteen months of which were served on the field. Having been thrown from a horse on a night charge and partially disabled, he was detailed by Gen. Butler to the charge of the Government printing office at Norfolk, Va. March 31, 1866, he married Laura V. Whitehurst, of Norfolk, Va., who has borne him the following children: Eugenia A., George (deceased), Minnie E., Wilson J. (deceased), Lucy and Alma. Mr. Croll in 1872 was elected county auditor, and was re-elected to the same office in 1884.

FRANK P. DIETZ, son of John and Susanna (Lutman) Dietz, was born in Hellam Township, January 18, 1847; was brought up on the home farm and began milling in 1868, learning his trade at Diehl's Mill, Spring Garden Township. He worked two years at this mill as a journeyman, after learning his trade, and ran it on his own account for eight years, when he removed to his present location, known at this time as Louck's Mill, on the Baltimore Pike, four miles south of York, near New Paradise, he having purchased this valuable mill property, which embraces ninety-six acres of good land in connection with a large saw and flour-mill. In December, 1870, Mr. D. married Clayanna Jane Dosch, daughter of J. C. and Charlotte (Leber) Dosch, of Windsor Township. Six children have been born to them: Mary M., John C., Dora S., Eddie (deceased), Harry S. and Charles L. (deceased). Mr. D. has a large custom trade in York, Paradise and Loganville for his flour, and is the fortunate possessor of the best water-power in York Township, which enables him to run his mill in dry seasons when the neighboring mills are forced to stop. Mr. D. is a member of the Reformed Church of New Paradise, and has been a member of Conewago Tribe I. O. of R. M. of York, Penn.

AMOS DRUCK, son of George and Catherine (Shell) Druck, was born November 10, 1851, in Hellam Township. and is the fifth of twelve children: Henry (deceased), Elizabeth (deceased), Susan (deceased), Amos, Aaron, George W., Moses F., John Wesley, Emma Jane, Annie (deceased), Elemina (deceased) and Catharine. November 25, 1872, Mr. Druck married Eliza Campbell, daughter of Henry and Lydia Campbell, of Windsor Township. Seven children were born to this marriage: Florence L., Edward H., Mary J., Emma J., Virgie May, Daisey May and Annie (deceased). Mr. Druck was reared on his father's farm, and began business (the manufacture of cigars) in 1879, and employs from ten to twelve hands at this business. The Druck family settled early in York County; our subject's grandfather, Gottleib Druck, was born in Hellam Township. Mr. Druck is a good citizen and highly esteemed by those who know him well. He is a member of the Evangelical Church.

GEORGE W. DRUCK, son of George and Catherine (Schell) Druck, was born April 18, 1857, in Hellam Township, was reared on a farm and went to his trade of cigar-maker in 1881, which occupation he still follows. July 12, 1881, he married Eliza A. Stump, daughter of Benjamin and Eliza Ann (Mitzel) Stump, of York Township. Two interesting children have been born to this union: Elenora and Martha Washington. Mr. and Mrs. Druck's ancestors were early settlers in York County, and Mrs. Druck's great-grandfather, Adam Stump, and great-grandmother are buried in the family burying ground in York Township, at the Stump homestead. The subject of this sketch, George W. Druck, is a steady, worthy young man, and held in high esteem in his neighborhood.

JOHN FLINCHBAUGH (farmer), son of Adam and Catherine (Dohm) Flinchbaugh, was born July 3, 1819, in the old homestead on the farm where Mr. Flinchbaugh now lives and which he owns. He was reared to farming, and has always followed that occupation. January 5, 1843, he married Julia Ann Flinchbaugh, daughter of Jacob and Denah (Diehl) Flinchbaugh, of Windsor Township. Thirteen children were born of this marriage: Charles, Adam, Amanda (deceased), Jacob, Ephraim, Eli, David (deceased), Samuel, John (deceased), Liddie Ann, Julia Ann, Mary and Annie. Adam Flinchbaugh, the father of our subject, died in his sixty-first year. Catherine Flinchbaugh, his mother, died in her sixty-eighth year. The Flinchbaugh family has always been very numerous in this section of York Township. The subject of this sketch has been for many years one of York Township's leading, influential farmers, and no man in the township enjoys a better reputation for sterling honesty than John Flinchbaugh.

AMOS GABLE, son of Valentine and Mary (Miller) Gable, is the second in a family of nine children, and was born in Windsor Township, York Co., Penn., June 10, 1838. At eighteen years of age he began learning the blacksmith's trade, which he followed for about twenty-five years. In 1878 he purchased his present residence and thirteen acres of land in Longstown, and here has since resided. Mr. Gable was married, in 1865, to Miss Leah Erb, daughter of Jacob Erb, of Spring Garden Township. They have two children: Levi E. and Solomon E.; another son, Jacob, died on June 17, 1868, aged two years, five months and eighteen days. Mr. and Mrs. Gable are members of the United Brethren Church at Longstown.

DR. JAMES. B. GLATFELTER, son of H. K. and Lucinda (Elhart) Glatfelter, was born in York Township, December 6, 1856. He was educated at the township schools, and after completing his school work took up the study of dentistry at Adamstown, and began the practice of his profession in Adams County, where he remained two years. In 1879 he located in Dallastown, where he has been very successful in his profession. Dr. Glatfelter was married, in 1876, to Lizzie McLean, daughter of Jacob McLean, of Adams County. They have two children: Melvin and Maud. The Doctor and wife are members of the Lutheran Church.

WILSON F. GLATFELTER, son of William and Catherine (Flinchbaugh) Glatfelter, was born December 19, 1860, in Hopewell Township, and reared on his father's farm. He received his education in the public schools of his native township. He went to his trade in 1878 and worked journey work until 1884, when he embarked in the furniture business in Dallastown. He carries a large stock of goods in his line, and manufactures all kinds of furniture to order. His store-room and building is the largest and most attractive house in Dallastown, located in the center of the town, and although he began business within the last year, he is doing a large trade in York and surrounding townships.

PIUS E. GEESEY is a son of Jonathan and Sarah (Flinchbaugh) Geesey, natives of York County, Penn. His father was one of the early day men of York County, and for half a century lived on the farm now owned by the subject of this sketch. Pius E. is the seventh child in a family of nine children, and was born July 5, 1845, on the Geesey homestead, which he purchased at the death of his father and where he now lives. By occupation he is a farmer. In 1873 he married Miss Malinda Miller, daughter of Jacob Miller, of Windsor Township. Three children have blessed their union: Jacob Jonathan, Adam M. and Mary Edith. Mr. and Mrs. Geesey are members of the Evangelical Lutheran Church.

ARCHIBALD P. T. GROVE, M. D., a native of Chanceford Township, and son of A. G. and Elizabeth (Thompson) Grove, was born March 21, 1854. Dr. Grove was educated at the public schools of Chanceford Township, Pleasant Grove and Stewart's Academies. For three years he taught school, during which time he also began the study of medicine, but subsequently he prosecuted further this study under the direction of Dr. Curran, of Cross Roads. With him he remained three years, and then entered the College of Physicians and Surgeons at Baltimore, and graduated from that institution March 6, 1878, and the same month located at Dallastown, York County, and began the practice of his profession. Here he has since resided. As a practitioner Dr. Grove is most successful, and he enjoys an enviable reputation. He was married in 1879 to Miss Cora E. Shaw, daughter of Z. S. Shaw, of Dallastown. They have one child, viz.: Austin M. Dr. and Mrs. Grove are members of the Harmony Presbyterian Church.

MICHAEL HOSE, SR., is a son of Deitrick and Receni (Frank) Hose, and was born September 26, 1822, in York Township, where he was reared, and has always resided. He learned the trade of blacksmithing early in life, and has followed it up to the present time. At the breaking out of the Rebellion he enlisted in Company C, Eighty-seventh Regiment Pennsylvania Volunteers, and served with this regiment eighteen months, two months being passed in the hospital at Fort McHenry. He subsequently re-enlisted in Company K, Two Hundredth Regiment, Pennsylvania Volunteers, and was in service until the close of the war. His regiment participated in the battles around Petersburg, Butler's Front, Hatcher's Run, and was a witness of the surrender of Gen. Lee to Gen. Grant at Appomattox Court House. He was mustered out of the service May 30, 1865, at Alexandria, Va. December 3, 1848, Mr. Hose was married to Miss Sarah, daughter of Jacob and Polly (Flinchbaugh) Geesey, of York Township. They have had born to them fifteen children. Three are now living in the county: Amanda, Louisa and Michael, Jr. Mr. Hose is a respected citizen of his township.

MICHAEL HOSE, JR., son of Michael Hose, of York Township, York Co., Penn., was born in that township, November 13, 1854. He first learned the shoe-maker's trade, which he followed about ten years, and then worked at carpentering for eight years. In 1882 he began the manufacture of cigars at Dallastown and is now doing a thriving business in that line. Mr. Hose was united in marriage in 1879, to Miss Mary Adelaide Keesey, daughter of Harrison Keesey, of York Township. They have one child, Emory Michael. Mr. and Mrs. Hose are members of the United Brethren Church.

SAMUEL PIUS ILYES, son of John and Elizabeth (Hess) Ilyes, was born in 1857, in York Township, on the homestead farm where he has always resided. There were eight children in his father's family: George (deceased), John, Jeremiah (deceased), Eliza (deceased), Louisa (deceased), Ellen, Aaron and Samuel. Aaron married Jane Day, daughter of Jesse Day, and John married Mary Hovis, daughter of Isaac Hovis. Our subject's parents are of German extraction, who, by hard labor and strict economy have been enabled to secure a competency. They own a farm of 200 acres of the best land in York Township, well stocked, cultivated and improved. The Ilyes family are members of the Lutheran Church.

HENRY INNERS is a son of George and Leah (Ebard) Inners. His father was a native of York County, Penn., and his mother was born in Adams County, Penn. Jacob Inners, the grandfather of our subject, was a native of Switzerland, came to America some time in the last century, and was a soldier in the Revolutionary war. He took up a large tract of land made a settlement in York County. He was twice married and had several children by each wife. George Inners, the father of our subject, was the third son by the second marriage, and was born in York Township in 1804, where he lived until his death in 1876. Our subject, the eldest in a family of eight children, was born December 18, 1840, in York Township, York Co., Penn. At nineteen years of age he began learning the miller's trade. In 1862 he enlisted in Company B, Second District Columbia Volunteers and served nine months. After returning home he resumed his trade at his present location. Mr. Inners was married in 1865 to Miss Casinda Conway, daughter of Rev. John Conway, formerly of Dallastown. Seven children have been born to their union: Clara E., Annie, Rebecca, Minnie, Cora, George H. and Chauncey P. Mr. Inners is a member of the Reformed Church and his wife of the Lutheran Church.

JOHN S. KEECH, second of eight children of

BIOGRAPHICAL SKETCHES.

David and Magdeline (Patton) Keech, was born March 25, 1824, in Lower Oxford Township, Chester Co., Penn. When seven years of age he removed with his parents to Lancaster County. He received a common school education. When he was nineteen years of age he came to York Township where he has always resided (except when in charge of the county almshouse). He taught school ten terms in York County and one term in Lancaster County. April, 1869, he was appointed steward of the county almshouse and hospital; he remained until 1874, then was appointed again in 1876 and filled the position until 1881, with credit to himself and entire satisfaction of the people of the county. Was elected county auditor in 1854, and has been justice of the peace for York Township for twenty-two years, filling that office at the present time. April 4, 1847, he married Mary Ann Weitkamp, daughter of Charles and Louisa (Bierman) Weitkamp, of Westphalia, Germany. Ten children were born to this union: Charles F., William H., Albert J., Edith M. (deceased), J. Edward, Jerome H., Arthur S., James J., D. Hays and Harry E. Our subject's grandfather, Nathaniel Keech, died in 1841, aged seventy years. His maternal grandfather, James Patton, saw hard service as a soldier in the Revolutionary war. Mrs. Keech's father, Carl Weitkamp, died in his seventy-first year. Her mother, Lousia Bierman Weitkamp, is still living with Mrs. Keech, at the advanced age of eighty-three years.

CHARLES H. KEESEY, son of Henry and Elizabeth (Glatfelter) Keesey, was born April 4, 1847, in Springfield Township, York Co., Penn. On attaining his majority he engaged in the nursery business with a Mr. Evans, of York, Penn., and in this business continued three years. In 1869 he engaged as gatekeeper on the York & Chanceford Pike, and followed that occupation five years. In 1876 he leased his present hotel at Dallastown, and engaged in the hotel business. In 1879 he established a general store in Dallastown, which he runs in connection with the hotel, and is doing a good business. Mr. Keesey was married, in 1869, to Miss Elizabeth C. Hovis, daughter of Jacob Hovis. They have two children: Percy E. and Minnie May. Mr. and Mrs. Keesey are members of the Lutheran Church.

JACOB C. KING, seventh of nine children of John and Magdelena (Conkley) King, was born December 21, 1854, in York Township, on the old King homestead. He went to his trade (carpenter) in his seventeenth year, followed his trade ten years, carrying on the business himself two years. August 29, 1882, Mr. King married Sarah A. Sakemiller, daughter of Frederick and Susan (Dretz) Sakemiller, of York Township. One child has been born to them, John Frederick. John King, our subject's father, was born at the King homestead and died in his sixty-eighth year. Our subject's grandfather, Peter King, first settled on the King farm. He bought the farm (at that time 180 acres) from John and William Penn.

ADAM KOHLER, son of Jacob and Mary (Sechrist) Kohler, was born in York Township, January 2, 1841. He was educated at the township schools and Cottage Hill College. The early life of Mr. Kohler was spent in school and at schoolteaching. He afterward began clerking in a store in Dallastown, where he remained one year, and then went to York and spent about the same length of time at the same vocation. In 1872 he engaged in general merchandising. In 1876 he established his present business, and, in connection, in 1882 began the manufacture of cigars. He is a successful merchant and now enjoys an extensive trade. Mr. Kohler was married, in 1370, to Sarah A. Geesey, daughter of Samuel Geesey, of York Township.

They have five children: Lillie M., Alverta B., Claudie E., Howard L. and Mabel G. Mr. and Mrs. Kohler are members of the Lutheran Church.

CHARLES KOHLER was born in York Township, September 5, 1846, son of Jacob and Mary (Sechrist) Kohler, and is of German descent. He engaged as clerk in a general store at Dallastown, and afterward at Windsor, where he remained about ten years. In 1870 he purchased a half interest in his brother's store and carriage business, and this partnership continued until 1881, when he bought his brother out, and is now doing a very extensive business. Mr. Kohler was married, in 1872, to Miss Emiline Geesey, daughter of Jonathan Geesey, of York Township. They had one child. Phineas L. Mr. and Mrs. Kohler are members of the Lutheran Church.

LEMUEL S. LAWSON, M. D., son of Thomas and Ellen Lawson (whose maiden name was Stansbury, a native of Carroll County, Md.). The father of Dr. Lawson was born in York County, Penn.; April 2, 1837, dates the birth of our subject in Manheim Township. He was educated at the public schools of Carroll Township, Md., and at Irving College. After completing his course he taught school for five years and then began the study of medicine in the office of Dr. Henry Beltz, of Carroll County, Md. Dr. Lawson graduated from the Maryland University in 1867, and then located at Klinefeltersville, and commenced the regular practice of his profession. Here he remained only a short time and then went to Dallastown, where he has ever since continued the practice. He was married, in 1870, to Miss Margaret A. McFagen, of Chanceford Township. Mrs. Lawson died in 1872, and five years later Dr. Lawson married Miss Sarah Neff, daughter of Charles Neff of Dallastown. They have one child. Dr. and Mrs. Lawson are members of the United Brethren Church.

SAMUEL H. LEADER, eldest of three children of Charles and Salona (Hildebrand) Leader, was born August 20, 1836, in York Township; he was reared on a farm and received a common school education; taught school three terms in York Township. December 26, 1861, Mr. Leader married Mary Ann Naly, daughter of Henry and Magdeline (Cornbau) Naly, of York Township. To this marriage were born Clara E., Henry A., Minnie M., Charles M., Sallie A. and Addie L. Mr. Leader's grandfather's name was Frederick Leader. The Leader family is one of the earliest that settled in York Township.

A. P. NEFF, son of Jonathan and Eliza (Peeling) Neff, was born in York Township, York Co., Penn., January 18, 1839, and is the eldest in a family of four children. He was educated at the public schools and at the York County Normal School, at York, Penn. For twenty-seven years he followed school teaching and taught in the townships of York, Spring Garden and Hellam. In 1882 he began the manufacture of cigars and the "Perfect Rest" bed spring at Relay, and is now doing an extensive business. He was married, in 1861, to Miss Susan McAllister, daughter of William McAllister, of Chanceford Township, and Mrs. Neff died in 1877, leaving four children, three of whom are living: Lucinda, Samuel J. and Laura E. Mr. Neff was married in 1879, to Miss Annie B. Snyder, daughter of John A. Snyder, of York Township. They have two children: Eliza and Minnie M. Mr. and Mrs. Neff are members of the United Brethren Church at Dallastown.

JAMES B. PEELING, a native of York Township, York Co., Penn., was born September 5, 1856, son of Josiah Peeling. In early life he learned the millwright's trade, which he followed for eleven years, and then engaged in the restaurant business in New York for one year. In 1888 he removed to what is known as the Fair Mount Home, on the York and Chanceford Road, where he now resides. He was married, in 1878, to Miss Eliza Goodling, of Manchester Township. They have one child, Kirben Cleveland.

JACOB SECHRIST was born in York Township, York Co., Penn., November 22, 1845, son of Jacob and Susan (Stabley) Sechrist. He learned the millwright's trade, which he followed for two years, and then engaged in the butchering business in Dallastown; then began the manufacture of cigars, and is now one of the most extensive manufacturers in the county. He has 193 acres of farming land, which he cultivates in connection with the cigar business. He was married, in 1869, to Miss Annie Green, daughter of Rev. John R. Green, of Dallastown. Mrs. Sechrist died in 1870, leaving two children: Clara J. (and John. Mr. Sechrist was married, in 1874, to Miss Sarah J. Stein, by whom he has had five children: Annie M., Emma K., Jacob S., Harry S. and Prudence M. Mr. Sechrist has held the office of inspector and constable of the borough for three years.

J. F. SPOTZ, son of Jacob Spotz, was born in York Township, York Co., Penn., April 28, 1836. He first followed farming and then learned the basketmaker's trade, at which he continued for nineteen years. In 1872 he purchased property in Dallastown and commenced the manufacture of cigars and leaf tobacco. He has since resided in Dallastown, and his business has grown to extensive proportions. He has a fine farm, which he manages in connection with his other business. Mr. Spotz was married, in 1861, to Miss Leah Miller, daughter of Henry Miller, of York Township. They have four children: Ida Agnes, Maggie May, Clara Bell and Henry L. Mr. and Mrs. Spotz are members of the United Brethren Church, of Dallastown.

MOSES SNYDER was born in Windsor Township, York Co., Penn., February 13, 1851, a son of Aaron and Catherine Snyder. He first learned the stone mason's trade, which he followed for five years, and then purchased a farm in Windsor Township, where he remained six years. In 1882 he established a general merchandising business at Snyderstown, in York Township, and is doing an extensive business. Mr. Snyder was married, in 1872, to Miss Catherine Sechrist, daughter of Henry Sechrist, of York Township. Mrs. Snyder died in 1874, leaving one child, Emeline. In 1875 Mr. Snyder was married to Miss Mary Ann Deitrich, of Chanceford. They have four children: Henry A., Annie M., Barbara and James. Mr. and Mrs. Snyder are members of the United Brethren Church, of Red Lion, Penn.

AARON STRICKLER, son of Henry and Cassandria (Bahn) Strickler, is the eldest of ten children, was born ·in 1887 in Spring Garden Township, reared to farming, and followed it all his life, except ten years that he ran a saw-mill. May, 1864, he married Sarah Hartman, daughter of John and Henrietta (Crone) Hartman. Six children have blessed their marriage: William H., Annie, Ida J., Sarah E., John A. (deceased) and Ezra (deceased). Mr. Strickler removed to York Township when seventeen years old. Our subject's ancestors were among the very earliest settlers in York Valley. His great-grandfather, Henry Strickler, was born in 1746, where Winfield Howser now lives, at Stony Brook. Christian Strickler, the grandfather of our subject, died in 1840. Our subject's great-grandmother's maiden name was Landis. His grandmother's maiden name was Keller.

WASHINGTON D. STRIEBIG, only child of John K. and Harriet (Day) Striebig, was born September 19, 1826, at his present home, where he has always lived. He always followed farming; received a common school education. December 24, 1857, Mr. Striebig married Delalah (Emmel), daughter of John and Mary (Mull) Emmel, of Spring Garden Township. Seven children were born to them: John, Elenora, George, Eliza, Mary, Edward and Josiah (deceased). The Striebig family is a very old one in York Township. Our subject's great-grandfather, George Striebig, purchased the farm on which our subject now resides, from the Penns, 111 years ago (1774).

SAMUEL WAGNER was born in Spring Garden Township, York Co., Penn., September 29, 1821, and is a son of John and Barbara Wagner. When a child he came with his parents to York Township, and here he has since resided. In 1853 he purchased his present farm, which is located near Longstown, and consists of 140 acres of well-improved land. Mr. Wagner was married, in 1845, to Miss Susanna Heidelbaugh. They have the following children: Sarah Ann, William, Lucinda, Samuel, John, Susanna, Annie C., Ella M. and Eli. Mr. Wagner has been assessor of York Township. John H. Wagner, a son of Samuel and Susanna (Heidelbaugh) Wagner, was born November 26, 1853, in York Township. He received a common school education, and has always followed farming. October 24, 1876, he married Anna Kauffman, daughter of Joseph and Susan (Flory) Kauffman, of Windsor Township. Mrs. Wagner's paternal and maternal ancestors were early settlers of York County.

JOHN C. WEISER, son of John K. and Elizabeth (Crosbey) Weiser, was born on the farm on which he still resides, June 25, 1831, and is the second in the family born to his parents as follows: Benjamin, John C., Alexander, Charles, William H. (deceased), two infants (deceased), Granville and Mary J. At the age of seventeen our subject left the home farm and went to York, and learned the carpenter's trade, which he followed for twenty-three years. He then returned to his home, and, in connection with farming, started the nursery and seed business. March 20, 1853, he married Leah J., daughter of Henry and Catharine (Kochenour) Myers, of York. To this marriage have been born William H., Charles F., Emanuel J., Emma C. E. and Carrie E.

SUPPLEMENTAL BIOGRAPHIES.

J. EDWIN SPRENKLE, A. M., M. D., is a native of Hanover, and is a son of Josiah S. and Margaret A. (Buchen) Sprenkle, natives of Pennsylvania and Maryland. He spent his boyhood at the public schools of Hanover and prepared for college by a four years' course under Prof. Baugher. He entered Franklin and Marshall College at Lancaster, Penn., in 1877, and graduated therefrom June, 1881, as A. B. He entered Jefferson Medical College, Philadelphia, in October, 1881, and graduated therefrom with honors, March 29, 1884. He received the prize for the best original research in *Materia Medica* Laboratory. Returning at once to Hanover he there began the practice of his chosen profession. He is a member of the Chi Phi fraternity of his *alma mater*.

DR. JOHN WIEST, the subject of this sketch, was born in Paradise, now Jackson Township, February 24, 1846, being a direct descendant from one of the oldest families in the county; his great-grandfather, Jacob Wiest, having emigrated from Switzerland, and having located about nine miles west of York previous to 1740. Dr. Wiest worked on his father's farm until he was fifteen years old, when he entered the York County Academy, and took a classical course at this institution. After teaching school for two successive terms in Jackson Township and one term at the York County Academy, he commenced the study of medicine at the Jefferson Medical College in Philadelphia and graduated at the University of Michigan on the 27th of March, 1867. When he was twenty-one years of age he commenced to practice medicine near Spring Grove, York County, and at once acquired a large and lucrative practice. In 1878 he went to Philadelphia and took a special course in the treatment of eye diseases at Will's Hospital. In 1879 Dr. Wiest moved to York and opened an office for the treatment of eye diseases and the adjustment of spectacles. His practice in this specialty rapidly increased, and at present his reputation as a successful eye doctor is known all over the county. His practice in the treatment of eye diseases and adjustment of spectacles now extends all over the county and into Adams and Lancaster Counties, and Carrol County, Md. Dr. Wiest was one of the first directors in the York Hospital and Dispensary Association, and was the originator of the West York Eye, Ear and Throat Dispensary. He is a regular attendant at the Eye, Ear and Throat Dispensary, and gives one hour every day of his time to the poor gratuitously. The Doctor is a member of the County Medical Society since its organization; a member of the State Medical Society since 1871, and a member of the National Medical Association since 1883. Dr. J. Wiest, at an early age, took an active interest in politics, and an active part since he is a voter. He has frequently been elected delegate and committeeman to the county conventions and State conventions. In 1878 he was nominated and elected by the Democrats to the legislature, and was re-elected in 1880. He took an active part in the legislature, served on all the important committees, and introduced and had passed a number of important measures; among them was a law to compel school directors to grant teachers the time to attend the county institute, and one to repeal an act allowing constables, justices of the peace and district attorneys to draw their fees out of the county in certain cases. The repeal of this law saves the tax payers of York County thousands of dollars annually. Dr. Wiest was a member of the revenue commission in 1881 and advocated the release of property covered by mortgages or judgment from taxation, and advocated the taxation of corporate property for local purposes in the towns and townships in which it is located. In 1885 Dr. Wiest was appointed one of the pension examiners of York County under President Cleveland's administration; subsequently he was elected president of York County pension board.

www.ingramcontent.com/pod-product-compliance
Lightning Source LLC
Chambersburg PA
CBHW051057230426
43667CB00013B/2343